A History of the Muslim World to 1750

A History of the Muslim World to 1750 traces the development of Islamic civilization from the career of the Prophet Muhammad to the mid-eighteenth century. Encompassing a wide range of significant events within the period, its coverage includes the creation of the Dar al-Islam (the territory ruled by Muslims), the fragmentation of society into various religious and political groups including the Shi'ites and Sunnis, the series of catastrophes in the twelfth and thirteenth centuries that threatened to destroy the civilization, and the rise of the Ottoman, Safavid, and Mughal empires.

Including the latest research from the last ten years, this second edition has been updated and expanded to cover the fifteenth to eighteenth centuries. Fully refreshed and containing over sixty images to highlight the key visual aspects, this book offers students a balanced coverage of the Muslim world from the Iberian Peninsula to South Asia and detailed accounts of all cultures. The use of maps, primary sources, timelines, and a glossary further illuminates the fascinating yet complex world of the pre-modern Middle East.

Covering art, architecture, religious institutions, theological beliefs, popular religious practice, political institutions, cuisine, and much more, *A History of the Muslim World to 1750* is the perfect introduction for all students of the history of Islamic civilization and the Middle East.

Vernon O. Egger is Professor Emeritus of Middle Eastern and Islamic History at Georgia Southern University. His other books include *The Muslim World Since 1260* and *A Fabian in Egypt: Salamah Musa and the Rise of the Professional Classes in Egypt, 1909–1939.*

A History
of the Muslim World
to 1750

The Making
of a Civilization

Second Edition

Vernon O. Egger

Routledge
Taylor & Francis Group

NEW YORK AND LONDON

Second edition published 2018
by Routledge
711 Third Avenue, New York, NY 10017

and by Routledge
2 Park Square, Milton Park, Abingdon, Oxon, OX14 4RN

Routledge is an imprint of the Taylor & Francis Group, an informa business

First edition published by Pearson Prentice Hall 2004

Library of Congress Cataloging-in-Publication Data
Names: Egger, Vernon, 1948- author.
Title: A history of the Muslim world to 1750 : the making of a
civilization / Vernon O. Egger.
Description: Second edition. | Milton Park, Abingdon, Oxon :
Routledge, 2017. | Includes bibliographical references and index.
Identifiers: LCCN 2017023445 | ISBN 9781138215924
(hardback : alk. paper) | ISBN 9781138215931 (pbk. : alk. paper) |
ISBN 9781315143309 (ebook)
Subjects: LCSH: Islamic civilization. | Islamic countries–History. |
Islam–History.
Classification: LCC DS36.85. E34 2017 | DDC 909/.09767—dc23
LC record available at https://lccn.loc.gov/2017023445

ISBN: 978-1-138-21592-4 (hbk)
ISBN: 978-1-138-21593-1 (pbk)
ISBN: 978-1-315-14330-9 (ebk)

Typeset in New Baskerville
by Keystroke, Neville Lodge, Tettenhall, Wolverhampton
Printed in Canada

Contents

List of Figures

List of Maps

List of Tables

Preface to the Second Edition

The first edition of this book examined Muslim history to 1405, but this second edition overlaps more with the second volume of the work, as it extends the coverage to 1750. The change makes it possible to show the transition of the Ottoman Sultanate into the Ottoman Empire, the transformation of the Delhi Sultanate into the Mughal Empire, the creation of the Safavid Empire, and the fate of the Muslims of Iberia after the completion of the Reconquista. It also allows the reader to gain a better sense of the global nature of the Islamic movement by discussing the Islamization of Southeast Asia and sub-Saharan Africa that took place during the sixteenth and seventeenth centuries. Every chapter in the book has been updated and extensively rewritten.

The first edition appeared not long after the horrific events of September 11, 2001, when members of al-Qaeda hijacked four airliners in an attack on American commercial and government targets, murdering 3000 people. Since then, other groups of Muslim extremists have engaged in murderous attacks on innocent people in a large number of countries. The Western news media provides extensive coverage of those killed in Europe and North America but fail to note that ninety percent of the victims of the extremist groups are Muslims. Even though the treatment of the development of modern Islamic currents is left to Volume 2, I hope that this book will also enable its readers to gain an appreciation of how aberrant the actions and goals of these violent groups are within the stream of Islamic history. Not only is their random killing of innocents not justified by the doctrine of jihad, but their goal of creating a universal caliphate betrays an ignorance of the history of the notion of the caliphate and blindness to the strength of regional and ethnic identities. The groups are extreme examples of the reactionary political movements that are rocking many countries in the world today. Unnerved by modernity's rapid social and technological change, they seek to "restore" a golden age of stability and traditional values that has never existed except in their imagination. Whereas some reactionaries attempt to stop history in its tracks by propaganda or the ballot box, others use senseless violence on the grounds that anyone who does not agree with them is enabling a descent into a new dark age. History has yet to cooperate with reactionaries, especially those that make mortal enemies of everyone else.

Preface to the First Edition

This book is an introduction to the history of the Muslim world for readers with little or no knowledge of the subject. I use the term *Muslim* rather than *Islamic* because this is a study of the history made by the Muslim peoples rather than a history of the religion of Islam. It is important to make a distinction between *Muslim* and *Islamic*— properly speaking, *Islamic* should refer to elements of the religion, while *Muslim* relates to the adherents of the religion. Thus, not all customs followed by Muslims are Islamic, and although a mosque is an example of Islamic architecture, a palace is not. A generation ago, the great scholar Marshall Hodgson wrestled with this problem and coined the term *Islamicate* to describe the cultural features of Muslim societies that were not strictly religious, such as secular architecture. The term has not gained widespread acceptance, and this book will avoid it.

If the distinction between *Islamic* and *Muslim* seems strained, suppose that someone said that the White House is an example of Christian architecture because a Christian designed it, or that Bastille Day is a Christian holiday, since it is celebrated in a country with a Christian majority. No one is tempted to make such assertions, and yet they are equivalent to speaking of *Islamic* palaces or *Islamic* medicine, as many historians do. Much of the history related in this book is not directly related to Islam, and so it is more appropriately called Muslim history.

The phrase *Muslim world*, as used in this book, refers to regions ruled by Muslim-dominated governments, as well as areas in which the Muslim population is a majority or an influential minority. For several decades in the seventh century, the Muslim world was coterminous with the region often referred to today as the Middle East, but it soon expanded far beyond that heartland. By the tenth century, many of the most important cultural developments in the Muslim world were taking place outside the Middle East. The size of the Muslim world has alternately expanded and contracted over time, and we will be concerned to see how and why that has happened.

The themes of the book are tradition and adaptation. The history of any society is one of the preservation of core values and practices but also one of adaptation to changing conditions. Muslims follow a religion that is strongly anchored in both scripture and authoritative codes of behavior and are conditioned to adhere closely to the canon of their religious tradition. On the other hand, from the very beginning of their history, Muslims have found ways to adapt elements of their faith to their culture, as well as to adapt their cultural values and practices to the core of their faith. Islam is no more of a homogeneous world religion than is Christianity or Judaism.

The themes of tradition and adaptation allow us to make sense of some important issues in Muslim history. By being aware of the premium placed on faithfulness to the scriptures, we can understand more clearly how Muslims were able to maintain a common sense of identity throughout the wide expanse of the world in which they settled. Further, we can more readily appreciate why Muslims have accepted certain features of alien cultures and rejected others. From the first century of the Islamic calendar, when Muslims were having to decide how to administer a huge majority of non-Muslims in the former Byzantine and Sasanian empires, until today, when many Muslims are concerned about the impact of a secular, global economy on their heritage, the tension between adherence to tradition on the one hand and adaptation to changing conditions on the other has been at the center of Muslim concerns.

This book treats economic, political, intellectual, and social developments over a wide area and across many centuries. Of these topics, the intellectual and political developments receive more attention than social and economic history. The study of the social history of the Muslim world is in its infancy. Therefore, it is not possible at this point to write the history of the daily lives of ordinary men and women in large areas of the Muslim world. Economic history tends to stress connections among areas of the world, which is why it is a popular theme in the field of world history. The motif of connections and of global integration that economic history can convey runs throughout this book as a powerful undercurrent. In the first decade of the twenty-first century, however, I am convinced that our awareness of connections in Muslim history needs to be balanced by an awareness of diversity and discontinuities. Troubling stereotypes of Islam and of Muslims loom large in our culture and can be modified only by our becoming aware of the diversity of religious and political expressions within the Muslim world.

A widely held assumption in our society is that Islam is a crystallized artifact from the seventh century—or, at best, from the tenth or eleventh century, when Islamic law is often said to have stopped developing. It is important to be aware of the important stages in the historical development of Islam and to realize that critical periods in history have encouraged Muslims to be either flexible or inflexible in their reception of new ideas. It is also important to be aware of the varieties of expression of Islam. Many generalizations about Islam are actually applicable only to Sunni Islam, and even then, to the Sunni Islam practiced in certain countries, not to regions in other parts of the world. The history of Shi'ite Islam is usually ignored—or recognized only in passing. Shi'ites have played a major role in history and should be recognized for having done so.

Another widely held stereotype is that Muslims form a monolithic, homogeneous mass that acts in concert on given issues. In recent years, this assumption has given rise to the notion that "Islam" and "the West" are on the eve of a "clash of civilizations." According to this theory, when Muslims in one area have a grievance against "the

West," other Muslim groups will come to their aid on the basis of their civilizational "kin." The impression of a monolithic Muslim world is reinforced by the fact that many world history books discuss the Abbasid caliphate (750–1258) as though it were an empire that united the great majority of the world's Muslims of that age, leaving the impression that Muslims have a history of political unity. Even the textbook discussions of the sixteenth- and seventeenth-century empires of the Ottomans, Safavids, and Mughals rarely note their great differences. The fact is that Muslim political unity was shattered in the third decade after the Prophet's death. There have been numerous Muslim political entities ever since then. Not only have conflicting interests divided them, but Muslim states have also frequently allied with Christian, Hindu, or other states against fellow Muslims.

Just as intellectuals prior to the seventeenth century thought that the universe possessed different physical properties from those on earth, so have historians and political theorists often treated Muslim history as different in kind from the history of the rest of the world. This book attempts to show through an examination of their history that Muslims are an integral part of the world community and have functioned as other human beings have under similar conditions.

Acknowledgements

This project has taken much longer than I anticipated when I began it with a naive expectation that it would require a couple of years to fill in the gaps in my lecture notes. Gaps, indeed. The book relies almost entirely on the work of other scholars. I have listed the sources that I have found most valuable—and that I recommend to other readers—at the end of the relevant chapters. I wish to express my appreciation to the members of the staff of the Interlibrary Loan office of the Henderson Library at Georgia Southern University for their consistently excellent help and to the Faculty Research Committee and the Faculty Development Committee for making it possible for me to devote several months to full-time research and writing on this project.

I am also grateful for the comments, insights, and corrections that I received on the manuscript from Herbert Bodman, Donald Reid, David Commins, Gladys Frantz-Murphy, Erik Gilbert, John Parcels, Kenneth Perkins, and two reviewers who wished to be anonymous. They saved me from several egregious errors, although I obstinately persisted in certain interpretations despite their best efforts (but never when they agreed on a criticism). I invite readers to send me their own suggestions on how to improve this book—I have been known to yield in the face of overwhelming odds.

Finally, anyone who works on a major project within the context of a family knows that an author's acknowledgment of a family's support and patience is not a perfunctory gesture: The writing of a book inevitably disrupts family life. I welcome the opportunity to thank Mary, Krista, and Rachel for their good-humored patience and encouragement throughout this endeavor.

Disclaimer

The publishers have made every effort to contact the copyright holders for images and extracts reprinted in *A History of the Muslim World to 1750* and to obtain permission to publish them. This has not been possible in every case; however, and we would welcome correspondence from those individuals/companies whom we have been unable to contact. Any omissions brought to our attention will be remedied in future editions.

Note on Transliteration and Dating

Any work that deals with the Muslim world faces the challenge of the transliteration of words from one alphabet to another. Scholars need a comprehensive system that represents in the Latin alphabet all the vowels and consonants of other alphabets, but nonspecialists can find such a system more confusing and alien than useful. The problem is a serious one when transliterating only one language; in this book, we have to deal with several. I have tried to compromise between accuracy and ease of use.

Geographic place names are spelled in this book as they appear on modern English-language atlas maps (Khorasan, Baghdad, Cairo). In some cases, no consensus exists among cartographers on the spelling of place names, and so this book occasionally provides alternate spellings (Zaragoza/Saragossa, Qayrawan/Kairouan). In a few cases, this book uses names that are more easily understood by English speakers than some that are more culturally authentic. An example is the Greek-based "Transoxiana" for the Arabic phrase *ma wara' al-nahr.*

In the interest of trying to make transliterated words less of an obstacle to the task of understanding the material, I have also used the more popular spellings for some words, even when doing so seems inconsistent with the practice of the book as a whole. Thus, I discuss "Sunnis and Shi'ites" rather than "Sunnis and Shi'is" or "Sunnites and Shi'ites."

For personal names and technical words in the Arabic, Persian, and Turkish languages, a simplified version of the Library of Congress system is used. No distinction is indicated in this book between long and short vowels, nor are diacritical marks provided for the vowels of words from any language. For the Arabic language, no attempt is made to indicate the so-called velarized consonants, and no distinction is made between the forms of the letter *h*, which should be sounded or aspirated.

The combination _dh_ represents the sound of the _th_ in the English word _then_; _kh_ is similar to the _ch_ in the Scottish _loch_; and _gh_ is best described as the sound made when gargling. The _q_ is pronounced farther back in the throat than the _k_. The symbol ' represents a glottal stop, the sound that begins each syllable of the English expression _uh-oh_. The symbol ' represents an Arabic consonant with no English equivalent, but it is important in words such as 'Ali or Shi'ite. Phonetically, it is a "voiced guttural stop" produced in the very back of the throat by constricting the larynx to stop the flow of air. An approximation may be achieved by making a glottal stop as far back in the throat as possible.

The prefix _al-_ is the definite article in Arabic, meaning _the_. Before most letters in the alphabet, the prefix sounds the way it is spelled, but it assumes the sound of certain letters when it precedes them (_t, th, d, dh, r, z, s, sh, n_). Thus, al-Rahman is pronounced ar-Rahman.

Notes regarding the significance of names containing 'Abd, Abu, and Ibn may be found in the glossary. Understanding these terms makes the learning of Arabic-based names easier and more meaningful.

This book uses the abbreviations B.C.E. (Before the Common Era) and C.E. (Common Era). The abbreviations refer to the same dates that are designated as B.C. (Before Christ) and A.D. (_anno Domini_), respectively, on the Gregorian calendar, but they are an attempt to use religiously neutral nomenclature. They have almost totally replaced the B.C./A.D. designations in books on world history because of the latter's Christian-specific nature. In a book on Muslim history, the most logical (and considerate) way of dating would be to use the A.H. (_anno hejirae_) system, which is based on the Islamic calendar. The first year of this system began in July 622 on the Gregorian calendar. Most readers of this book, however, are non-Muslim citizens of the United States, who, in my experience, are usually confused rather than helped by the use of the A.H. dating system. It is explained in the glossary.

AKA
non-religious

PART ONE

The Formative Period, 610–950

Islam arose in the early seventh century as a religious and social reform movement in the small, hot, and dusty town of Mecca in the western Arabian Peninsula. During its first decade, the movement appeared to be highly vulnerable, attracting only a few dozen followers. Many observers expected it to fail miserably. If those same skeptics could have used a time machine to travel one century into the future, they would have found Muslims ruling an empire from the Atlantic to the Indus River valley in modern Pakistan—a region that stretched across 5000 miles. Other groups before and after this period also conquered huge territories in a very short time, but their rule proved ephemeral. The Muslims, by contrast, created a new civilization in this vast area that played a significant role in the creation of our modern world.

The period of Muslim conquests was necessarily followed by an extended period of consolidation. Muslims shared a common set of beliefs and practices, but they lived in dramatically different cultures, had access to a wide range of resources, and were confronted with challenges specific to their region. As they worked out the implications of their faith, they found that their solutions differed from those of their fellow Muslims in other parts of the world. One of the most fascinating features of Muslim history is the continuity of Islamic identity in the absence of a central religious authority such as a pope, patriarch, or synod. The important developments in religious doctrine and practice were the products of pious individuals who communicated with each other across vast distances. As a result, differences arose among those who called themselves Muslims. In a few cases, such differences were irreconcilable and even deadly. In general, however, the story of Muslim history is that devotion to the Qur'an and emulation of the behavior of the Prophet have enabled Muslims across a wide spectrum of societies to recognize that they belong to the same community of faith.

Chapter 1 provides a broad overview of the areas in which Muslim societies first developed: the regions of what had been the eastern Byzantine Empire, the former Sasanian Empire, and the Arabian Peninsula. Muhammad's career was confined almost exclusively to the peninsula, but his immediate successors as leaders of the Muslim community were preoccupied with the areas they were conquering in the Byzantine and Sasanian empires. It was here that Islam in the post-prophetic period largely developed, and it is important to understand the pre-Islamic history of these territories. Chapter 2 discusses the conquests of the first century of Muslim history and the development of administrative structures in the newly conquered areas. It shows that this first Muslim state created after the death of the Prophet was an "Arab empire" that failed to live up to the ideals of Islamic equality and justice. Chapter 3 examines the first major divisions within the Muslim community. It traces the rise of a movement known as Kharijism and explores the early history of Shi'ism. It shows how the history of Shi'ism was linked to the revolutionary Abbasid movement that overthrew the Arab empire. Chapter 4 examines the political fragmentation of Muslim society after the eighth century and its organization into three caliphates. The apparent disunity of these political systems was balanced by the development of a highly integrated and sophisticated economic system that linked all of the regions under Muslim control. Chapter 5 surveys the religious and intellectual developments of the era. It is here that we can see more clearly the correlation between the cessation of the conquests on the one hand and the establishment of the foundations of religious institutions on the other.

The period from 600 to 950 is called "formative" not because Islam assumed its permanent form during this time, but because its possibilities for future development were narrowed into specific directions. For nearly three centuries after the conquest of the Pyrenees Mountains and the Indus valley, the frontiers of Muslim-ruled territory remained essentially stable. During this time, the methodology for determining Islamic law was developed, Islamic mysticism and theology developed their frameworks, science and philosophy were introduced as fields of study, and the distinctions between the terms *Sunni* and *Shi'ite* became well defined. As we shall see in Part Two, the subsequent three centuries saw further elaborations on Islamic traditions, but they were channeled by the developments of the period to 950.

CHRONOLOGY

570	Traditional date for the birth of Muhammad
602–628	Last Byzantine–Sasanian war
610	Traditional date for the first revelation to Muhammad
622	Hijra
632	Death of Muhammad; Abu Bakr becomes caliph
633	Muslim army crushes Ridda
634	Muslim conquests begin; 'Umar becomes caliph
637	Muslim armies conquer Syria
638	Muslim armies conquer Iraq
642	Muslim armies conquer Egypt
644	Slave murders 'Umar; 'Uthman becomes caliph
651	Muslim armies conquer Iran
656	Muslim soldiers murder 'Uthman; 'Ali becomes caliph
661	Kharijite murders 'Ali; Mu'awiya becomes caliph in Damascus; Umayyad dynasty begins
680	Battle of Karbala
685–705	Caliphate of 'Abd al-Malik, who makes Arabic the official language of the empire, mints coins with Islamic details and builds Dome of the Rock as symbol of Islamic supremacy
705–715	Muslim armies conquer Central Asia and Sind
711–720	Muslim armies conquer Iberian peninsula
740	Berber revolt in North Africa and Iberia
750	Abbasids overthrow Umayyads
756	'Abd al-Rahman establishes the Umayyad amirate of Cordoba
762	Al-Mansur founds Baghdad
765	Death of Ja'far al-Sadiq
768–814	Reign of Charlemagne in Western Europe
813–833	Caliphate of al-Ma'mun creates the Bayt al-Hikma and provokes a storm of criticism for his attempt to enforce Mu'tazilism
860s	Anarchy in Baghdad, provinces become autonomous; Isma'ilis become active in Iran, Iraq, and Syria
874	Imami twelfth Imam goes into Lesser Concealment
850–900	Feudalism emerges in Western Europe
909	Fatimids declare a caliphate in Ifriqiya
900–950	Acceptance of Shafi'i synthesis for jurisprudence
929	'Abd al-Rahman III declares a caliphate in Cordoba
936	Abbasid caliph cedes power to Turkish general
941	Imami twelfth Imam goes into Greater Concealment
945	Buyids seize power in Baghdad

CHAPTER 1

Origins

Islam arose in the Arabian Peninsula in the early seventh century. Arabia is surrounded on three sides by ocean and on the north by the Fertile Crescent, the arc formed by the life-giving rivers of Iraq and the green plains and mountains of western Syria. A remarkably arid region of almost one million square miles, the interior of Arabia attracted little interest from its neighbors. On the other hand, the era's superpowers—the Byzantine Empire and the Sasanian Empire—*were* keenly interested in Arabia's coastline and its frontiers with the Fertile Crescent. The traditional Byzantine–Sasanian rivalry entailed a competition for control both of those coasts and the desert frontiers. Thus, when a highly destructive conflict took place between the two imperial powers throughout the first quarter of the seventh century, the entire region was affected.

The inhabitants of Arabia followed the conflict closely, for they knew that its conclusion would determine which of the powers controlled their frontiers. What they—and the superpowers themselves—could not know was that during the war the balance of power in the region had completely changed. The two combatants were exhausted by 628, when the Byzantines appeared to have won the war. Meanwhile, however, a prophet named Muhammad was in the final stage of consolidating his political and religious authority in the peninsula and was creating a dynamic and seemingly irresistible force. Only a decade after the Byzantine triumph, Arab armies fighting in the name of the movement created by Muhammad would seize the greater part of the Byzantine Empire and utterly destroy the Sasanian Empire.

Southwest Asia in the Seventh Century

The Arabs would conquer their two imperial neighbors in the name of a monotheistic faith that bore striking similarities to Judaism and Christianity. Like these two other faiths, Islam would take centuries to develop many of the institutions and doctrines that are most characteristic of it today. Many of these developments would take place in territories formerly under Byzantine and Sasanian rule. Thus, before we examine the career of Muhammad, it will be useful to survey certain features of the Byzantine and Sasanian empires, as well as of the Arabian Peninsula.

The Byzantine Empire

The Byzantine Empire owed a large debt to Alexander the Great, whose bloody campaigns between the Mediterranean Sea and the Himalayas during the late fourth century B.C.E. introduced Greek culture into southwestern Asia and northeastern Africa. In the centuries after Alexander's death in 323 B.C.E., the Macedonians and Greeks who came into this area as soldiers, merchants, craftsmen, and rulers brought with them their language, architecture, and social institutions. The result was a synthesis of Greek and indigenous cultures that is called Hellenistic civilization. Urban life along the eastern Mediterranean seaboard experienced a cultural transformation. Newly established cities, such as Alexandria in Egypt and Antioch in Syria, became the dominant economic and cultural centers. The architecture of older cities received new inspiration with the advent of Greek styles for theaters, gymnasia, and temples. Greek became the language of learning and of politics. The era was remarkable for its scientific, artistic, philosophical, and economic achievements. This was the period when such philosophical schools as Stoicism, Epicureanism, Skepticism, and Cynicism flourished. Aristarchus devised his seemingly audacious theory that the sun, rather than the earth, occupied the center of the universe; Archimedes introduced the concept of *pi* and developed theories of the properties of the lever and of the specific gravity of water; and Eratosthenes became the first man known to have measured with remarkable accuracy the circumference of the earth.

The chief threat to the Hellenistic kingdoms was the Roman Republic, which began flexing its military muscle in the mid-third century B.C.E. by challenging Carthage for control of the western Mediterranean. Soon its ambitions extended to the eastern Mediterranean as well, and between 146 B.C.E. and 30 B.C.E. it absorbed its Hellenistic neighbors. The last of the Hellenistic rulers was Cleopatra of Egypt. She might have been as little known to most of us as the other Hellenistic rulers had it not been for her tragic affairs with the Roman leaders Julius Caesar and Mark Antony.

With the defeat of Mark Antony and Cleopatra, Octavian assumed the title of Augustus Caesar, and the Roman Republic became the Roman Empire. The empire's eastern half was in effect the Hellenized region. When Rome took over this area, the language of governmental administration changed to Latin, but the power of the Hellenistic legacy is revealed in the fact that Greek remained the most influential language of culture in the eastern Mediterranean until the Arabs came, six centuries later. The Romans themselves continued to look to Greek sources for the inspiration of much of their own cultural production.

Even during the famous *Pax Romana* of the two centuries during and after the reign of Augustus (the period 27 B.C.E.–180 C.E.), the former Hellenistic areas remained the most populous and wealthy sections of the empire. The emperor Constantine's decision to establish an eastern capital (Constantinople, or "Constantine's City") on the site of the ancient Greek colony of Byzantium, at the mouth of the Black Sea, reflected the importance that the East had for the Roman Empire. The dedication of the new capital in 330 C.E. is a convenient point to identify as the beginning of Byzantine history. It is important to remember, however, that the Byzantines always regarded themselves as "Romanoi" and that a distinctive Byzantine culture required at least two centuries to emerge.

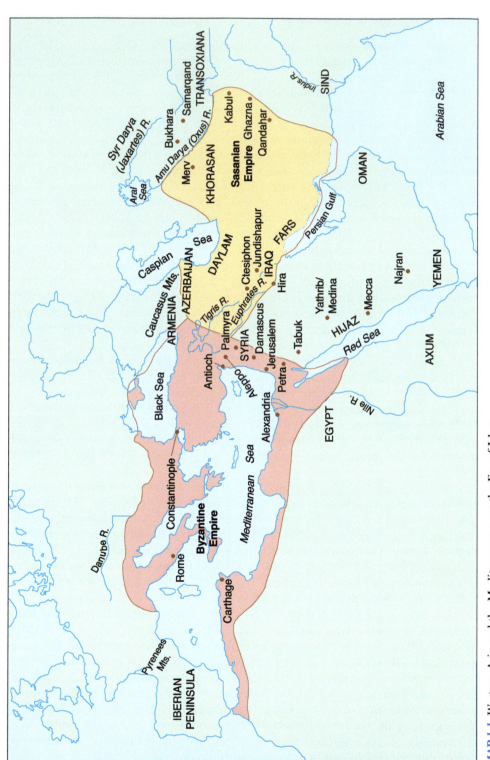

MAP 1.1 Western Asia and the Mediterranean on the Eve of Islam.

The eastern half of the Roman Empire remained stable and even flourished over the next two centuries, while the western half succumbed to the attacks of Germanic invaders in the fourth and fifth centuries. By 410, Germanic tribes controlled Europe west of the Adriatic Sea and North Africa west of modern Tunisia. Constantinople ruled over an area that extended across southeastern Europe to the Adriatic Sea, eastward into Asia to a frontier just west of the Euphrates River, and westward across North Africa as far as modern Tunisia.

The Mediterranean climate of the coastal areas produced long, hot, and dry summers and temperate, rainy winters. The agriculture of these regions usually specialized in the production of grapes, olives, and grain. Away from the coast, agriculture was much more limited. Topography was one factor. Rugged mountains and narrow valleys are the dominant feature of the Balkans (southeastern Europe) and characterize all but the narrow coastal plains and central plateau of Anatolia (the bulk of modern Turkey). Spotty rainfall was another factor. The Anatolian plateau typically receives just enough rainfall to make growing wheat worthwhile, but the interior regions of Syria, Egypt, and North Africa are arid, making agriculture impossible without irrigation. Irrigation had made Egypt one of the earliest centers of civilization, and the centrality of irrigation to the life of Egypt had prompted the ancient Greek historian Herodotus to call Egypt "the gift of the Nile." In Syria, the Euphrates and Orontes rivers and numerous oases provided water for irrigation. The river valleys and oases were the most densely populated regions of both Syria and Egypt. Because of their grain-producing potential, the two regions were invaluable "breadbaskets" for the empire, and they were more important than ever after the loss to the Germanic invaders of grain-growing areas in the western Mediterranean.

The inhabitants of the eastern Mediterranean and the Black Sea engaged in a flourishing commerce in order to exchange the cash crops of one area for those of another. The Byzantine Empire possessed a remarkably long coastline relative to its land area. This geographical fact was a great benefit to its economy and to its government's ability to remain in communication with outlying areas. Goods could be shipped much more rapidly and cheaply by ships and boats than by carts and pack animals. Since most of the empire's hinterlands were within a short overland trip from water routes, travel between the geographic extremities of the empire was remarkably efficient. The huge city of Constantinople could safely outgrow the ability of its own region to produce food and rely instead upon Syria and Egypt to ship much of the grain that fed its people.

The region's foodstuffs were also valued commodities in other parts of the world. Grain traveled well without further processing, and it was ground into flour by either the wholesale or retail customer. Olives and grapes, however, spoiled quickly in their natural state and needed to be processed prior to shipment. Olives were pressed for their oil, which was used as food, lamp oil, and a soap substitute; grapes were fermented into wine. The Byzantines traded these products for furs, timber, amber, spices, and other items that they needed. They had access to Russia by way of the great rivers that drain into the Black Sea, and they were able to trade for the gold of Nubia (in the northern part of the modern country of Sudan) by sailing up the Nile.

The middle half of the sixth century may well have been the period of the empire's greatest triumph and influence. By that time, the areas that had composed the western half of the Roman Empire were divided into feuding Germanic kingdoms, whereas the emperor Justinian (r. 527–565) ruled the Byzantine half. Justinian aspired to reunite the entire Mediterranean under "Roman" rule (he spoke Latin and regarded himself to be the Roman emperor) and led military campaigns that regained large areas of the Italian Peninsula, the southern Iberian Peninsula, and North Africa. He codified Roman law in the *Corpus Juris Civilis*, which influenced both canon and civil law in Europe over the next several centuries. Justinian also wanted his city to reflect imperial brilliance, so he embarked on a huge construction program that included the Church of Holy Wisdom, or Hagia Sophia. During his reign, Constantinople became the largest city west of China and was home to perhaps half a million people.

The empire remained a formidable presence for many centuries, but already by the sixth century it was clear that the state was having problems retaining the allegiance of all the various peoples of its complex society. Despite the brilliance of its culture and the achievements of Justinian, the Byzantine Empire experienced several devastating blows during the sixth century. The bubonic plague struck in 541 and recurred frequently over the next several decades; earthquakes caused great damage to several important cities in Lebanon; the Persian Sasanians sacked the great city of Antioch in 540 while Justinian's armies were engaged in campaigns in the western Mediterranean; the Avars and Slavs devastated the Balkans; and the Lombards seized large areas in Italy that Justinian had recently won at great cost.

FIGURE 1.1 Justinian's Hagia Sophia (537), the largest church ever built until St. Peter's Basilica in Rome surpassed it in the sixteenth century. After 900 years as a church, it was turned into a mosque by the Ottomans in 1453.

Artur Bogacki / Alamy Stock Photo.

Justinian's successors were forced to raise taxes to pay for the great emperor's ambitious projects and campaigns, and they revoked the financial and political autonomy of the empire's cities in order to expropriate their surpluses more effectively.

Egyptians and Syrians, in particular, resented these new measures. Egypt and Syria had been Hellenized since the time of Alexander, and the cities of Alexandria and Antioch were awe-inspiring centers of Greek culture centuries before Constantinople's foundations had been laid. It was precisely their increasingly secondary status that rankled the pride of the Hellenized provincial elites. They were acutely aware of their vulnerability to economic and political exploitation by Constantinople, and they were resentful of the loss of their religious leadership to the rising power of the patriarch in the capital city. Non-Greek-speaking inhabitants of these provinces had even less reason to be loyal to the capital.

Political opposition to the Byzantine government's policies often took the form of religious dissent. This is a phenomenon that we shall see replicated many times in the history of Muslim societies in which the government derives much of its legitimacy from its support of, and identification with, an official state religion. Advocating a different religious expression from that of the ruler in effect challenges the legitimacy of the ruler's religion and thereby indirectly challenges his political legitimacy. Religious dissent in the Byzantine Empire often took the form of arguments over the nature of Christ. From the beginning of the Christian movement, the followers of Jesus had wrestled with the issue of defining his nature as man *and* divine being. In the fifth and sixth centuries, the question had developed serious political repercussions, and the disputes over the issue later played a role in the spread of Islam into the area. It is useful, therefore, to note the distinctions among the terms *Orthodox*, *Nestorian*, and *Monophysite*.

The official interpretation of the state (Orthodox) church was defined at the Council of Chalcedon in 451, which stated that Christ had two "natures" (human and divine), perfect and perfectly distinct, which were united in one "person" (or being). Two major dissenting views existed, with special strength in Egypt and Syria. Their differences from the Orthodox position seem quite subtle and innocuous today, but in the fifth century, social and religious tensions were so great that any deviation from the official view was considered a threat to the civil order and to the integrity of Christianity itself. The group the Orthodox persecuted the most were the Nestorians, who derived their name from Nestorius, bishop of Antioch, the greatest city in Syria. Nestorians were accused of holding a heretical view of Christ's "person." It is not clear what Nestorius' actual position was, but his political enemies insisted that he taught that the presence of the divine and human in Christ was such that there were in him two distinct persons, as opposed to the Orthodox doctrine of two natures concurring in one person. To many of us today, that sounds like hairsplitting, but in those days, to hold the Nestorian position was to court imprisonment or even execution.

The other major dissenting group, the Monophysites, clashed with the Orthodox position over the subject of Christ's "nature" rather than over his "person." They rejected the Orthodox doctrine that Christ's divine and human natures were separate. In practice, they usually even went further and stated that Christ had a single, divine nature. Monophysitism became the doctrine of the Coptic Church, to which the vast majority of Egyptians belonged. Monophysitism was also widespread in Syria, where its adherents formed the Syrian Orthodox Church, whose members are commonly known as Jacobites. A third group, the Armenian Church, formally adopted Monophysitism in 506, and by doing so, planted Monophysitism strongly in eastern Anatolia.

Both Monophysites and Nestorians suffered persecution from the Orthodox Church, and Nestorians suffered persecution even from the Monophysite group in Syria. In the late fifth century, thousands of Nestorians migrated to the east, taking refuge in the Sasanian Empire. Although subject to periodic persecution from the Sasanian religious establishment, in general, Nestorians found a refuge among the Sasanians. Intensely evangelistic as well as involved in international commerce, they spread as far as India and China. Merchants and traders reported encountering them in considerable numbers along the Eurasian trade routes until the late fourteenth century.

Language was another factor that played a role in shaping social identities in the Byzantine Empire. Like any major society, it was multilingual. Latin remained the language of administration until the early seventh century, while Greek was the dominant spoken and written language in the basin of the Aegean Sea and was employed by elites in the large cities throughout the empire. The most widely used spoken languages in the Byzantine provinces of the eastern Mediterranean, however, belonged to the Afroasiatic language family: Coptic, Aramaic, and Arabic. Coptic was the primary spoken and written language in Egypt. Aramaic had been the lingua franca of southwestern Asia and the eastern Mediterranean since at least the fourth century B.C.E. By the dawn of the Christian era, it had displaced Hebrew as the language of the Jews other than for liturgical purposes. It was the language of Jesus and the apostles in the first century, and Jewish rabbis used it to write the Babylonian and Jerusalem Talmuds. Aramaic was the language of commerce between the Mediterranean and the Indus River and was the majority language in both Byzantine Syria and in Sasanian Iraq. One of its dialects, Syriac, became the most prestigious written form of Aramaic from the third through the seventh centuries. It was used for Christian liturgies as well as for philosophical and scientific treatises.

Substantial minorities in Syrian cities spoke Arabic, as did nomads and peasants in the frontier areas of eastern and southern Syria. Arabs had been a significant presence in the eastern Roman–Byzantine provinces for centuries, particularly in the semiarid central region and the desert region of the east and south. In northern Syria, the predominantly Arab city of Palmyra had arisen by the first century B.C.E. as a trading center between Rome and the Parthian kingdom that lay to the east. Over the years, it came under increasing Roman influence. A major caravan center, Palmyra reached its zenith of wealth and cultural development between 130 and 270 C.E., becoming the seat of Roman control over Asia Minor, Egypt, and Syria. It was during Palmyra's golden age that Philip the Arab became the Roman emperor (244–249). Important economically and politically, Palmyra was best remembered in the popular imagination for the "Arab queen" Zenobia, who rose in revolt against Rome when her husband, Odenathus, was assassinated in 266. Rome regained control only with great difficulty in 272.

As the sixth century came to a close, the population of Arabs was increasing in Damascus, Aleppo, and other cities in Syria. The reasons for this demographic surge are not clear, but much of the increase in numbers may have been the result of migration from the northern Arabian Peninsula, where a sustained drought had led to a palpable "desertification" of the area. Arabs were not regarded as aliens within Byzantine society. Like the majority of the population in the area, they spoke Aramaic as well as their native tongue, and many knew Greek. Most of the Arabs of the Byzantine Empire, even the nomads of eastern Syria, seem to have been Monophysite Christians.

The Ghassanids are the best-known Arab tribal confederation of the Byzantine Empire during the sixth and early seventh centuries. Based between Palmyra and Damascus, they served the Byzantines as a buffer against the nomads from the Arabian Peninsula and the Sasanians to the east. Their performance against the Sasanians in the sixth century was so valuable that Justinian rewarded their chief with the titles of patrician, phylarch, and king—the highest honors that he could bestow on anyone. Their service was important, since the regular Byzantine units were concentrated on the northern borders of the empire.

By the beginning of the seventh century, however, the Ghassanids and the Byzantine court had become suspicious of each other. Despite their service to the Orthodox emperor, the Ghassanids had been Monophysites since at least 540. By 584, they had become so ardent in their faith that the Byzantines stopped paying regular subsidies to them. Since the government did not send additional regular army units to the frontier in order to compensate for the loss of dependable service by its Arab clients, the security of the area was thereafter in jeopardy.

By the end of the sixth century, the Byzantine Empire was the preeminent power of the Mediterranean and the worthy heir of both Alexander and Augustus. As the seventh century dawned, its leaders could be sanguine about the future. There were, in fact, serious disputes within the royal family and sporadic attacks on its frontiers, but because feuds among the ruling elite and war with neighboring states were the norm rather than the exception in the empire's history, no leading figure saw reason for alarm.

The Sasanian Empire

The Byzantine Empire's only rival was the Sasanian Empire. The Sasanians were Iranians who seized power in 226 C.E. Iranians of various dynasties had dominated the Iranian plateau for most of the period after Cyrus the Great (ca. 550 B.C.E.). Their Persian culture and dialects had become the standard for a huge area whose eastern frontiers extended to the Syr Darya River in the northeast, the cities of Ghazna (modern Ghazni) and Qandahar in the east, and the Indus River in the southeast. After quickly conquering all of that area, the Sasanians soon lost the area between the Amu Darya River and the Syr Darya to outside invaders, but the region would remain culturally Persian for centuries. Because the Greek name for the Amu Darya was the Oxus River, Europeans have traditionally referred to the region between it and the Syr Darya as Transoxiana (or Transoxania), "that which lies beyond the Oxus." It was the area known later by the Arabs as *ma wara' al-nahr*, or "that which lies beyond the river."

By contrast with the Byzantine Empire, the Sasanian realm was a great interior land mass that relied more on transport by land than by water. The great majority of the region was in a desert setting. The Iranian plateau itself is ringed by mountains.

In the west, the Zagros range extends from modern Azerbaijan in the northwest to the Persian Gulf, and then eastward toward modern Pakistan. The Elburz chain runs along the south shore of the Caspian Sea to meet the border ranges of Khorasan to the east. The arid interior plateau is distinguished by the remarkable Dasht-e Kavir, an impenetrable, salt-encrusted, muddy waste covering 20,000 square miles. Even the inhabitable areas of the plateau average less than ten inches of rainfall annually (comparable to Phoenix, Arizona). Cities of any size on the plateau had to be located within a short distance of the mountains in order to benefit from the spring runoff from melting snow. Otherwise, only small settlements could survive, relying on springs or a remarkable system of underground irrigation canals. These canals, or *qanat*s, brought water to villages from highland water sources. They were usually one-half mile to three miles long, but could extend as far as thirty miles, and were often intermeshed in networks of astonishing complexity.

Transoxiana was also a desert region, but it was bounded by the rich agricultural valleys of the Amu Darya and Syr Darya and was dotted with many large and small oases. The cities of Samarqand and Bukhara were the largest and wealthiest in Transoxiana. Both were situated on the Zeravshan River, which rises in the mountains that border China and flows westward until it disappears in the desert west of Bukhara.

The region south of the Caspian Sea is little known outside Iran, but it plays an important role in our story. The southwestern coastal plain of the sea is known as Gilan, and to the east is Mazandaran. In the period covered by this book, the coastal plains and the mountains south of them were usually referred to as Daylam. Some areas of Gilan receive up to seventy-eight inches of rainfall per year, with Mazandaran receiving somewhat less than half of that amount. (By comparison, New Orleans, Louisiana, receives an average annual rainfall of sixty-two inches.) Unlike most of the arid regions of southwestern Asia, rainfall here falls throughout the year, rather than only during the short winter. Gilan and Mazandaran were, consequently, the most densely populated regions of Iran and grew a wide variety of crops. They were distinguished by a reliance on rice, rather than wheat or barley, for their principal grain.

While Gilan and Mazandaran were the most densely populated areas of the empire, the region with the largest total population was Iraq. Iraq contained the two largest rivers in the empire, the Euphrates and the Tigris. Like the Nile, they had given birth to civilization in a desert environment as early as the fourth millennium B.C.E., when local farmers began constructing ground-level canals to bring water to their parched fields. Both rivers were also navigable for hundreds of miles of their length and thus encouraged commerce. Iraq was the empire's wealthiest province, generating forty percent of the imperial revenues, but of all the regions of the empire, it was the most alien to the ruling elite. It lay west of the rugged Zagros range and was not culturally Iranian. Nevertheless, its wealth was essential to the imperial economy, and as a result, the Sasanians placed a priority on protecting it from Byzantine encroachment.

Thus, despite its extensive desert regions, the Sasanian Empire enjoyed an adequate supply of agricultural production, and it was strategically located for long-distance commerce. Its position allowed it to control both the land route to China and India and the approaches to Persian Gulf ports. Because of the activity of its merchants, Iranian culture became influential along the central Eurasian trade routes for centuries to come. Overland transport was slow: Large caravans or armies could expect to travel only fifteen miles per day. The government made great efforts to provide security for major routes, maintain roads and bridges, and provide hostels and caravanserais.

The wealth that was derived from agriculture and trade is reflected in the art of the Sasanian period. Enormous rock sculptures were carved into the limestone cliffs that are found in many parts of Iran. Architecturally, the most celebrated achievement of the period is the vast palace at Ctesiphon, near modern Baghdad. Archaeologists have not been able to agree on when the Sasanians built it, and only part of it still stands. What remains is impressive. Its open frontal arch is the largest brick vault ever known to have been constructed, and it was the inspiration for much later architecture in Iran during the Islamic period. Metalwork and gem engraving attained high levels of technique and artistry, with particularly striking examples in jewelry, body armor, and tableware. Iran's central geographic position enabled its artists and craftsmen to benefit from foreign ideas and techniques. These are particularly apparent in the pottery and silk sectors, in which Chinese styles and techniques were influential.

The dominant religion of the Iranian plateau since at least the sixth century B.C.E. had been Zoroastrianism. Its founder, Zoroaster, lived sometime between 1000 B.C.E. and 600 B.C.E. Although its presence in the world today is limited to the small group of Parsis, most of whom live in India, Zoroastrianism played a major role in history. It shaped many features of Iranian cultural identity, and it apparently bequeathed to Judaism (and, consequently, to Christianity) the concepts of a bodily resurrection, last judgment, heaven and hell, and Satan. Those ideas cannot be found in Judaism prior to the conquest of Babylon by the Iranian Cyrus the Great, who allowed the Jews to return to Jerusalem from Babylon and set up an autonomous province within the Iranian empire from the sixth to fourth centuries B.C.E. Zoroastrianism focused on the worship of Ahura Mazda (Ormazd), who was challenged by the evil principle Ahriman. Zoroaster was clearly opposed to polytheism, but by the Sasanian period many of the old gods whose worship he had attacked were members of the pantheon again. The Sasanian version of Zoroastrianism is usually referred to as Mazdaism.

In Iraq, the westernmost territory of the Sasanian Empire, Zoroastrianism was a minority religion and had to coexist, sometimes uneasily, with other faiths. The Sasanian policy of granting refuge to non-Orthodox Christians from Byzantine territories affected the demography of the empire. The evidence suggests that so many Syrian Christians emigrated to Iraq that, by the early seventh century, Christians may have formed the largest single religious community in Iraq. By the late sixth century, even some members of the Sasanian royal family were converting to Nestorianism.

Judaism also flourished in Iraq, and it was probably the second largest religious community there. Jews formed the majority of the population in central Iraq, where they had lived since the time of the Babylonian Captivity of the sixth century B.C.E. During the late fourth and early fifth centuries C.E., Jewish scholars in Iraq compiled the famous Babylonian Talmud. For the most part, Sasanian rulers did not interfere unduly with their subjects' religious lives, but periodically the Zoroastrian priesthood, the Magi, persuaded them to persecute Christians and Jews.

FIGURE 1.2 The Great Hall of the Sasanian royal palace in Ctesiphon was built sometime between the fourth and fifth centuries C.E.

Henry Arvidsson / Alamy Stock Photo.

The various Iranian peoples within the empire spoke different dialects of Persian, and those on opposite ends of the region found each other's language almost unintelligible. Nevertheless, the Sasanians found the culture of even distant fellow Iranians more congenial than that of Iraq, where the majority of the people spoke Aramaic. The Persian language is a member of the Indo-European family of languages and, as a result, is structurally more similar to Greek and Latin than to Semitic languages such as Aramaic, Arabic, and Hebrew. Little remains of Sasanian literature other than Zoroastrian religious texts or translations from other cultures, especially the Byzantine.

Iran had great centers of learning. One was Merv, which was also the primary military garrison in the east, and the most famous in the west was Jundishapur (Gondeshapur) in Iraq, some one hundred miles east of modern Baghdad. At Jundishapur, Nestorian scholars worked with pagan philosophers from Athens who, like the Nestorians, sought refuge from Byzantine persecution. The school became particularly famous for its medical instruction. At these cities and other, less important, intellectual centers, scholars translated many books from Greek, Sanskrit, and Syriac into Persian.

The empire struggled to maintain stability in a context of greater cultural diversity than the Byzantines faced. The Iranian peoples themselves, who inhabited the vast area between the Persian Gulf and the Syr Darya, were divided not only by a wide range of dialects but also by means of subsistence: They included nomads, peasants, and wealthy urban dwellers. The diverse nature of the empire's subjects became more pronounced in Iraq, where Semitic culture predominated. Iraq was an ancient urban society whose wealth the court needed, a fact that the dynasty acknowledged only late in its history by constructing Ctesiphon as the empire's chief administrative city. Most of the Persian-speaking ruling elite preferred the province of Fars, in the vicinity of modern Shiraz, and left Ctesiphon for vacations in Shiraz whenever they could.

Arabs were an important segment of the empire's population along and west of the lower Euphrates River in southern Iraq and between the Tigris and Euphrates in northern Iraq. Like their Byzantine counterparts, the Arabs of the Sasanian Empire included nomads, seminomads, peasants, and townsmen. Some Iraqi Arabs followed traditional polytheistic religions and a few adopted Judaism, but, as was the case among the Byzantine Arabs, most appear to have been Christian. Among the Christian Arabs, the nomads tended to follow Monophysitism and the urban dwellers tended to be Nestorian. The city of Hira, which was the largest Arab town in the empire, contained a sufficient number of Nestorians to qualify as the seat of a bishopric as early as 410.

The Lakhmid tribe ruled Hira, which was a sophisticated community in southern Iraq. The Arabs of that region developed an influential poetic tradition as well as the so-called Kufic script for their dialect of the Arabic language. Later, under Islam, the Kufic script would become important not only for writing but also for the decorative arts. The poetic vocabulary of this tradition, as well as its script, would contribute to the development of a common Arabic language in the early Islamic period. The Lakhmids were important enough for the Sasanians to rely on them for the same purpose that the Byzantines used the Ghassanids. They were responsible for warding off raids by nomads from the Arabian Peninsula and serving as auxiliaries against their imperial Byzantine enemy.

Perhaps in response to Justinian's own assertion of power, Khusrow I initiated a new, aggressive policy toward the Byzantines. Justinian's militarism posed a potential threat to Sasanian control of Iraq's valuable agriculture, and the Sasanian ruling elite felt a new urgency regarding competition with the Byzantines for control of international trade routes. In addition to establishing control of ports on the western coast of the Persian Gulf, the empire began diplomatic and military initiatives in the Red Sea in order to control the trade routes from the Indian Ocean to the Mediterranean. From 570 to 630, the Sasanians succeeded in controlling most of the coastline of the Arabian Peninsula. It is worth noting that not all of the interaction with the Byzantines was hostile. In the sixth century, Byzantine architects helped to build the palace at Ctesiphon, and Sasanians borrowed Aristotelian concepts to redefine points of Zoroastrian ethics. It was during this period, moreover, that much of the translation work of Byzantine medicine, philosophy, and courtier literature into Persian was commissioned at Jundishapur. Nevertheless, diplomatic and military conflicts with the Byzantines dominated the last century of Sasanian history.

In 540, major warfare broke out between the Sasanians and the Byzantines, and the former were able to control Aleppo temporarily. Fighting continued until 561 and then broke out again in 572, lasting for another twenty-year period, to 591. Only one decade of peace followed before the final war between the two powers began. Neither empire was prepared for the conflict. The Byzantines had lost the loyalty of the Ghassanids, and the Sasanians terminated their relationship with the Lakhmids in 602. In that same year, skirmishing began between the two great powers after a Byzantine emperor was overthrown in one of the many episodes of dynastic instability that characterized Byzantine history. Even the accession of a new emperor, Heraclius, in 610 did not end the plotting, and the Sasanians took advantage of the disunity in Constantinople. They inflicted a series of military disasters on the Byzantines, taking Antioch in 613, Jerusalem in 614, and the Nile delta in 619. By 620, Sasanian troops stood on the banks of the Bosporus Strait and taunted the watchmen atop the walls of Constantinople. Heraclius was finally able to begin a counterattack in 622, and with help from Khazar tribesmen from north of the Black Sea, he waged a major campaign from the Caucasus, penetrating behind Sasanian lines into the heart of Iraq. By 628, all the Sasanian troops had been expelled from Byzantine territory.

The two empires were exhausted. Byzantine agriculture and town life in Anatolia, Syria, and Iraq were devastated, and the assassination of the Iranian emperor in 628 left the Sasanians in confusion and fear. Monophysites in Syria and Egypt, having been under Sasanian rule for a decade, were anxiously waiting to see if Byzantine policy would be more sensitive to provincial needs than it had been before the war. Jews in both empires were desperate, having been punished during the war for suspicion of helping the enemy. Arab nomads in the desert south of the traditional frontiers were probing the imperial defenses and discovering that the Ghassanids and Lakhmids no longer provided a barrier to plunder. Had the political elite in both empires not been so preoccupied with rebuilding, they might have been able to realize their precarious position and to take steps to prevent disaster. Instead, in less than a decade, the Byzantines would lose their territories in Syria and Egypt forever, and the world of the Sasanians would utterly collapse.

The Arabian Peninsula

Despite the proximity of the Arabian Peninsula to the Byzantines and Sasanians, imperial officials in neither empire regarded it as major security threat. Militarily, the vast, northern plains normally represented only a nuisance, as small bands of tribesmen would occasionally raid border settlements in southern Syria and Iraq. Throughout the centuries, an occasional, temporary, tribal confederation would arise that each empire then confronted with a massive show of force, but the confederation would collapse after a few years due to internal conflicts. On the whole, however, the peninsula was of more importance to both empires for its strategic position. The Sasanians depended on the Persian Gulf for access to African and South Asian ports, and the Byzantines relied on the Red Sea basin for its southern trade routes. Both empires carefully monitored the security of those trade routes.

Arabia is almost a million square miles of largely arid to semiarid terrain, but both its climate and topography reveal surprising variety. In the west, a highlands area, the Hijaz, intersperses barren valleys and sheer crags with numerous lush oases. It slopes to the east, where pebbly plains can spring to life with seasonal grass and flowers after the winter rains. The famous Empty Quarter of the south-central region cannot support human or large-animal life. Its tens of thousands of square miles of sand dunes receive only a trace of rain, and temperatures can exceed 125 degrees Fahrenheit. In Yemen, however, peasants laboriously carved out terraces on the slopes of mountains that soar to over 12,000 feet above the narrow Red Sea coast. The terraces trapped the rainfall from monsoons and produced grains, vegetables, and fruits without irrigation. Some of the valleys made lush for a few months by the monsoons grew semitropical fruits and boasted of waterfalls. For at least three millennia, until the last quarter of the twentieth century, Yemen's agriculture sustained by far the largest population in the peninsula.

The wide variety of climate and topography in Arabia resulted in a corresponding variety of means of subsistence. In Yemen, the agricultural and commercial economy supported royal dynasties for much of the first millennium B.C.E. These governments had been able to mobilize their populations to construct impressive monuments, such as temples, palaces, and dams. International trade supplemented the agricultural wealth of Yemen and other South Arabian kingdoms. Several cities, some on the coast and some in the interior, thrived on the trade of luxury goods from the Indian Ocean basin to the Mediterranean. The most famous of the products from Yemen itself was frankincense, an aromatic tree sap. Frankincense was a luxury product, much in demand throughout the Mediterranean. All the major pre-Christian religions of southwestern Asia and northeastern Africa—as well as Christianity itself—required the incense in their rituals, and families used it as an air freshener in their homes during the centuries before soap, toilets, and garbage disposals came into use.

Outside Yemen, most farmers in the peninsula depended on irrigation from underground wells. Usually the water sources were artesian wells, whose natural pressure sent water to the surface without pumping. Numerous oases lay scattered about the peninsula except within the Empty Quarter. Some were tiny, but others could be surprisingly large. Yathrib (later known as Medina), for example, in the Hijaz, was a cluster of hamlets located in an oasis that was several miles across. An oasis located in the middle of a desert was a refreshing delight for a traveler. It would present the visual appearance of a thick forest of date palms, but would typically also support citrus trees, banana trees, and grains. Cool water was almost always flowing from one part of the oasis to another, and the combination of the water and the dense shade yielded a dramatic contrast in temperature with that of the surrounding desert.

Every town and city had to rest on an economy whose base was agriculture, but a few cities obtained the bulk of their surplus wealth from the profits derived from the transit trade. Some cities in southeastern Yemen appear to fit that model, and so did Petra. Petra was founded by an Arabic-speaking people known as the Nabateans, who migrated to the northwestern fringe of the peninsula as early as the sixth century B.C.E. By 200 B.C.E., they had established Petra as an entrepôt for the overland transit trade. A century before Jesus was born, Petra controlled the area as far north as Damascus, and Nabateans continued to exercise local authority even after the Romans annexed their domain: The apostle Paul escaped over the walls of Damascus in the first century C.E. under the rule of a Nabatean governor. Petra's rulers were sufficiently wealthy to hire Greek architects to design the facades of monumental structures carved into the sheer cliffs of the gorge into which Petra was fitted.

The appearance of Petra marks a watershed in the history of the area, for it was the first of the great caravan cities that were to play an important role in the history of southwestern Asia for the next millennium and more. The evidence suggests that, sometime between 500 B.C.E. and 100 B.C.E., the Arabs of the northern half of the peninsula developed a new saddle that provided two improvements over the old.

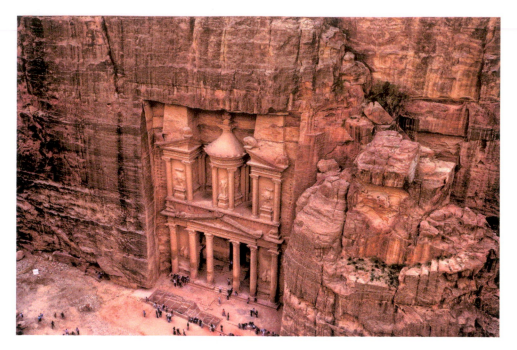

FIGURE 1.3 The Treasury at Petra (first century B.C.E.), one of the city's notable examples of rock-cut architecture.

Sam Oakes / Alamy Stock Photo.

For military purposes, the new saddle provided a secure perch from which to use a long sword and lance with devastating effect; when used as a pack saddle, it allowed a larger load to be mounted on the camel. In the wake of this new development, the camel herders of the northern part of the peninsula became prominent in regional trade and formidable as a military force. The camel was soon such an important means of transport that it displaced wheeled vehicles from the region. As one historian has written, "the North Arabian saddle made possible new weaponry, which made possible a shift in the balance of military power in the desert, which made possible the seizure of control of the caravan trade by the camel breeders, which made possible the social and economic integration of camel-breeding tribes into settled Middle Eastern society, which made possible the replacement of the wheel by the pack camel."[1] As the economic and military advantages of the camel became apparent, caravans and caravan cities became more numerous.

The merchants of Petra maintained relationships with the bedouin, or Arab nomads. The bedouin were of two basic types, the camel tenders and the seminomads. The most famous are the camel-tending bedouin, whose use of the camel provided them with remarkable mobility and independence from settled authority. In terms of material wealth, the camel-tending bedouin might appear to be very poor compared with those who dwelt in settled communities and with the seminomads. Because they grew no crops, their diet was restricted to camel milk and dates for most of the year, and they were also dependent on agricultural settlements and towns for tools, weapons, and food supplements. On the other hand, their martial skills, speed, and ability to escape into the wastelands enabled them to steal such items with near impunity from oases and towns, even within imperial territories. They were also able to extract "protection money" from settlements and caravans, contracting to protect their clients in return for tribute money (and attacking anyone who failed to agree to the offer). For this reason, the leaders of all caravan cities attempted to maintain peaceful relationships with the bedouin through whose grazing territory their caravans passed.

Contrary to a popular image, camel-herding bedouin appear never to have formed the majority of the population of Arabia. They have been present in almost all areas of the peninsula, but the agricultural settlements have always been able to support more families than has camel tending. Among the bedouin themselves, seminomads were more numerous than the camel tenders. As in other arid and semiarid regions of the world, most of the bedouin herded sheep and goats and kept a few camels on the side as pack animals. They spent the summers in the higher and cooler plateaus to allow their herds to graze and then moved to the lowlands during the winter in order to plant crops. Sheep herders occupied areas in which they had access to plentiful sources of water for their animals. Because of this dependence on reliable water sources, they were forced to maintain amicable relations with both agriculturalists and any state authorities in their area.

At their height, the agriculture-based South Arabian kingdoms of Yemen had the wealth to organize states that boasted institutions of commerce, law, and justice. Elsewhere in the peninsula, societies of oasis dwellers, camel tenders, and sheep herders were too small or too poor to organize states. Instead, they were organized by a set of relationships for which we use the inadequate term *tribe*. A tribe was a grouping of people who usually claimed to be descended from a common ancestor, but whose kinship ties might have been quite vague and uncertain. Nevertheless, they found it mutually advantageous to claim family ties, particularly for security. In the absence of a state, there were no written law codes, courts, or police. There appears not to have been even the concept of a law that transcended the limits of the tribe. In such circumstances, tribal ties protected individual life and property. Violence and theft were discouraged by the knowledge that a tribe would retaliate for the harm inflicted on one of its members. The more powerful the tribe, the less likely its members were to be violated. But weaker tribes felt compelled to retaliate against stronger tribes if only to preserve their honor. Retaliation itself demanded retaliation, spawning vendettas that could last for generations. Thus, tribalism did, in fact, deter individual violence, but it exacerbated conflict among tribes themselves.

Tribes were also important for economic reasons. Marriages took place within closely related families so that the two families' assets would not be dissipated, and when any family lost its assets due to drought or theft, the tribe would try to replace at least the animals. Generosity was a major virtue among tribesmen, symbolizing the dependence that each individual had on the group as a whole. Being part of a tribe was important for survival: One's identity was tribal, and one had nothing if he rejected the tribe. Not to have tribal protection was to be at the mercy of potentially hostile individuals and groups, as well as of nature. Because life outside the tribe was practically impossible, each individual felt an overwhelming pressure to conform to tribal norms.

The vast majority of the inhabitants of the peninsula spoke one or more dialects of the Arabic language. By the sixth century, the dialect of Hira had come into common use in the northern half of Arabia, primarily in the service of poetry—the primary artistic production of the Arabs at the time. Through this poetic language, Arabs were beginning to share a common vocabulary and legendary tradition, thus gaining a semblance of a common identity. Poetry was not written down, for it was valued in its oral form, but an alphabet was developing at the time, based on the Aramaic one. The earliest Arabic inscription found to date is from the first half of the fourth century. It evolved into the Kufic script that became dominant among the Lakhmids at Hira. It later came to be used for the text of the Qur'an and for official documents and monuments of the early Islamic state.

Arabs in the interior of the peninsula were overwhelmingly followers of traditional tribal gods and goddesses, but large numbers of Christians and Jews lived in settlements on the periphery. As we have seen, many Arabs on the Byzantine and Sasanian frontiers were Christian, and large numbers of Arab Christians lived in the southern part of the peninsula as well. Najran, a refuge for Syriac Monophysites, became the most important Christian settlement in Arabia. Christian communities existed in Oman, and the religion seems to have come into Yemen from the Kingdom of Axum, on the coast of what is today Ethiopia. South Arabia and Axum had much in common: They were similar in climate and terrain; both were centers of frankincense production; and they shared Red Sea routes to the Mediterranean world. Christianity had penetrated Axum by the fourth century, and it showed up on the southwestern coast of Arabia perhaps as early as the fifth century.

Judaism became well established in oases in the Hijaz and South Arabia after the fall of Jerusalem to the Romans in 70 C.E. Jews eventually made up a large minority at the oasis of Yathrib (later known as Medina), and the royal house of Yemen was Jewish perhaps as early as the fifth century. A Jewish ruler in Yemen, Dhu Nuwas, began persecuting Christians in his realm, apparently out of fear of a growing Byzantine influence in the Red Sea. In 523, his massacre of thousands of Christians at Najran provoked the Christians of Axum to intervene. With Byzantine help, Axum invaded Yemen and occupied much of the region. For the next fifty years, Yemen was under Axumite Christian occupation, until the Sasanians invaded in the 570s.

In the sixth century, Arabia was undergoing changes that would have profound implications for the future. Economically, Arabian agricultural societies in general were deteriorating. Yemen had experienced a slow decrease in wealth and power since the first century, and other areas of the peninsula offer evidence of a sustained drought. Many peasants were forced into a seminomadic life, and some former seminomads became pure nomads, harassing caravans and raiding settlements. Large numbers of Arabs were migrating to the north, settling on the frontiers of Iraq and Syria.

The northward migration of Arabs coincided with a new determination on the part of the Byzantines and Sasanians to intervene in the affairs of the peninsula. The invasion of Yemen both by the Byzantine–Axumite alliance and by the Sasanians within a span of half a century suggests that the fortunes of Arabia were becoming intertwined in an unprecedented way with those of its imperial neighbors to the north. Large areas of the eastern, southern, and western coasts of the peninsula were under direct or indirect Sasanian control after 575, and economic contacts were increasing between the peninsula and the Iranian empire.

In spite of these developments, the apparent disparity of power between the empires and the societies of the peninsula was deceiving. The migration of peninsular Arabs was increasing the demographic weight of Arabs in the area between the Euphrates and the Jordan. Moreover, the fact that the Ghassanids and the Lakhmids were no longer serving to restrain the aggression of nomads on imperial borders meant that the two great empires were more vulnerable to attack from the desert than they had been in two centuries. In their obsession with each other's ambitions, they neglected their desert frontiers.

The Rise of Islam

During the first decade of the seventh century, the Byzantines and Sasanians began their last, titanic struggle for dominance in western Asia. During the second decade, their armies fought in Syria and Egypt, and their navies clashed in the Red Sea. Meanwhile, the economic and demographic changes occurring in the Arabian Peninsula were beginning to have social consequences. It was in this context that the town of Mecca gave birth to a religiosocial movement that would transform large parts of the world for centuries to come.

The Meccan Environment

According to Muslim tradition, Muhammad was born about the year 570 in the Hijazi city of Mecca. Visitors to Mecca in the sixth century must have been surprised to find a town there at all. It lay in a dry gorge, surrounded by barren mountains, some of which thrust into the air more than a thousand feet above the town's mud-brick houses. Mecca was devoid of green plants, and its inhabitants had to import much of their food. The town possessed a spring that yielded slightly brackish water but otherwise had little to commend itself as a place of human habitation. Perhaps because of the unlikely presence of the spring in that stony, barren wilderness, the site had been a holy place, apparently for centuries. The town itself, however, was little more than a century old when Muhammad was born.

Mecca was built around the Ka'ba, the shrine that made the place a cultic center for local tribes. Although it has been restored several times, it seems always to have been in the shape of a cube, some fifty feet on each side. Its corners roughly correspond to the four points of the compass. Embedded in the eastern corner are two stones—one of which is the famous Black Stone—that serve ritual, rather than structural, purposes.

Two different traditions exist regarding the function of the shrine, but they may be complementary. According to one tradition, the Ka'ba was unusual among the shrines in Arabia in that it housed many (perhaps as many as 360) representations, or idols, of gods, instead of just one. On the other hand, Meccans are said to have considered the Ka'ba the house of Allah, a deity worshiped widely among the Arabs of Syria and the Hijaz as the creator god and supreme god. He did not have an idol to represent him, a feature that conforms to the experience of many other cultures in which the supreme creator- or sky-god becomes removed from the everyday concerns of the people but is still revered as the god with the highest status.

FIGURE 1.4 The Ka'ba in Mecca.

Bildarchiv Steffens / Bridgeman Images.

The content of the worship at the Ka'ba is not known, but evidence exists that some individuals had come together as a group and practiced what the Qur'an calls the "religion of Ibrahim (Abraham)." Apparently, an oral tradition already was strong that linked Abraham with the site of the Ka'ba, a tradition echoed in the Qur'an's assertion that he and his son Isma'il (Ishmael) constructed it.

Within several miles of Mecca were other sites considered holy by Arabs all over the Hijaz. Dedicated to various gods and goddesses, in pre-Islamic times they were much more important and better known than the Meccan shrine. During three holy months of the year, tribesmen came on pilgrimage from a wide area to these other sites to trade and then perform their rituals. The most important such ritual acts took place at Mina and Arafat and made up the bulk of the rituals later included within the Islamic pilgrimage.

The dominant tribe at Mecca, the Quraysh, made money from serving as custodians of the shrine in their town, but there is no evidence that any of the great trade fairs associated with the pre-Islamic pilgrimages took place there. Mecca's chief source of wealth was its regional trade, which had begun in the second half of the fifth century C.E. Meccan merchants bought Hijazi agricultural products (especially raisins), hides, skins, and leather goods, as well as Yemeni perfumes, and traded them in southern Syria for products that were prized in the Hijaz and Yemen, such as textiles, weapons, olive oil, and Syrian perfumes. Mecca was not the commercial heir to Petra or Palmyra. There is no evidence that it possessed the wealth that had produced the impressive architecture of those two centers of international trade, and Mecca seems to have been practically unknown outside the peninsula. The international trade in luxury goods did not pass through the town, and even the trade in Yemeni incense seems to have been negligible. Nevertheless, Mecca had become a bustling center of regional trade at the end of the sixth century, and its merchants were confident and knowledgeable about the world outside their narrow, rocky valley. Trade with the southern districts of the Byzantine Empire was regular and lucrative, and travelers were constantly coming in from Hira. The Meccans were well informed about developments in the two empires to the north and had become familiar with the dominant economic, political, and religious characteristics of both empires.

Muhammad

Muhammad was born into a family stricken with tragedy: His father had died by the time he was born, and his mother died when he was six years old. He found a home first in the household of his grandfather and then of an uncle. As a young man, he became involved in the caravan trade and made trips into Syria. To all appearances, Muhammad was a man with remarkable personality gifts. He became known for his empathy, mediating abilities, and patience. Having grown up an impoverished orphan, he was acutely aware of how precarious life can be and of the need for mutual support.

When Muhammad was about twenty-five years old, he attracted the attention of a wealthy widow and business woman by the name of Khadija, and they married. Suddenly his life changed, for he no longer had to worry about making ends meet. But rather than indulging in conspicuous consumption, he began a quest for a deeper religious experience. Muhammad began frequenting a local cave to meditate, and he made a habit of helping the poor. His increasing impatience with the dominant religious tradition in the Hijaz is mirrored in developments elsewhere in the region, suggesting that changing social conditions had begun to make the old religious traditions of the peninsula inadequate for many people.

hanifs – followers of monotheism

Muslim tradition remembers numerous other individuals in the Hijaz who were monotheistic in the era just before the coming of Islam. These *hanifs* are associated with the "religion of Abraham" in the Qur'an and in the Muslim traditions that arose later. In the interior of the peninsula as well, near present-day Riyadh, the tribe of the Banu Hanifa was led by a Christian who was a contemporary of Muhammad. When he died in 630, he was replaced by a prophet named Musaylima. Musaylima taught about a god named al-Rahman who demanded of his followers an ascetic lifestyle. Although there are legends about Muhammad's contacts with Syrian Christians in his work in the caravans, we do not know how familiar he was with the doctrines and rituals of Christianity or Judaism, nor the extent of his contacts with Christians and Jews in Arabia.

About the year 610, Muhammad began experiencing visions and trances in which he received messages that he understood to be the words of God. A figure, whom he later identified as the archangel Gabriel, was the channel through whom God provided His message to Muhammad. The experience was physical as well as spiritual, and Muhammad was afraid and even embarrassed, for his symptoms were similar to those of the *kahin*s, or pagan diviners and soothsayers of the region. With the support of Khadija and her cousin, however, he continued to be receptive to the visions and soon came to the conviction that he had been chosen for the role of prophet to deliver God's revelation to the Arabs. He identified it with the revelation originally sent through Abraham, the Hebrew prophets, and Jesus. Muhammad shared his revelations with his friends and family for about three years and then began preaching publicly. He gained a small band of followers, but most of them were of a distinctly common origin; his themes did not gain widespread acceptance among the Meccan elite.

The concepts and symbols of Muhammad's teaching bear a striking similarity to those of Judaism and Christianity. Muslims, in fact, have often pointed out that the expression, "the Judeo–Christian tradition," should be revised to "the Judeo–Christian–Islamic tradition." Muhammad taught that his message was the one that the Jewish prophets, including Jesus, had brought earlier, but that in the course of time, their teachings had been distorted. With Muhammad, God was once again bringing the pristine message, this time directly to the Arabs. Muslims believe that God's message came through Muhammad in two important ways. One was through the episodic revelations that Gabriel conveyed to Muhammad from God. The Prophet's followers wrote these down and eventually collected them together in the book known as the Qur'an (Koran). It would eventually be divided into 114 *sura*s, or chapters. Apart from the formal revelations, however, were the Prophet's commentary on daily issues and his own example of the upright life. His charismatic personality and his stature as the Prophet were both compelling reasons for people to look to him for guidance on a multitude of issues as they tried to live in conformity to the will of God. The recollections of his followers regarding his sayings and his behavior under certain circumstances were later recorded as *Hadith*, or traditions, a topic that is treated in detail in Chapter 3.

hadith – words & deeds of Muhammad

At the center of Muhammad's teaching was the majesty of Allah. The word *Allah* derives from the Arabic word for *deity* or *god*, which is *ilah*. Allah is simply *ilah* with the definite article *al*- in front of it, rendering the same effect as in English: the supreme or the only god, or God. *Allah* is not a word specific to Muslims. Because of the meaning of the word, Christian Arabs refer to the focus of their worship as Allah, just as Muslims do. Worshipers of Allah in pre-Islamic Mecca probably recognized Him as the supreme deity within a pantheon of many gods and goddesses, whereas Muslims understand the term to mean the only deity at all. What appear to be the earliest passages in the Qur'an stress God's majestic power, His compassion for His creatures, and His justice. Gradually, the theme of the unity or oneness of God became prominent, leading to a clash between Muhammad and the polytheism of his environment. Many verses in the Qur'an refer to Allah as *al-Rahman al-Rahim*, usually translated as "the Merciful and the Compassionate." God is a loving God who wants the best for those whom He has created and who is quick to forgive those who err.

God's mercy is required, however, because of His justice. He demands a high standard of behavior, which is predicated on obedience to His commands. The term most often associated with obedience to God in the Islamic tradition is the verb *aslama*, which means to submit or to surrender. The noun form, *islam*, thus means submission or surrender (to God). Submission entails acceptance of the legitimacy of the Prophet's mission and obedience to God's will as revealed through revelation. The Qur'an contains numerous specific injunctions that are elements of the path of obedience, but the righteous life is exemplified most clearly in two major categories of attitude and action. The first is recognition and affirmation of the unity of God. The Qur'an makes it clear that to associate any being or object with God is the greatest sin that a person can commit. *Shirk*, or the compromising of God's sole claim to worship, is the unforgivable sin.

The emphasis on God's oneness and on His sole claim to worship led quickly to the frequent use by Muslims of the phrase *allahu akbar*. This phrase is often translated into English as "God is Greatest," but more correctly it has the meaning, "God is Greater"—whatever one can think of or be tempted to worship or give ultimate allegiance to, God is greater and more worthy of worship, loyalty, and commitment than that.

The other primary indicator of obedience to God is the conscientious use of wealth. The insistence on generosity to the poor, the orphan, and the widow runs as a theme throughout the Qur'an in a manner strikingly similar to the words of Hosea, Amos, Jesus, and other figures in the Bible. The Prophet himself was reminded of his humble origins and of God's concern for him, obliging him to be generous in turn to those who were on the margins of society:

> Did He not find you an orphan, and shelter you?
> Did He not find you straying, and guide you?
> Did He not find you needy, and enrich you?
> As for the orphan, do not oppress him,
> And as for the beggar, do not drive him away,
> And as for the grace of your Lord, declare it. (93:6–11)

The Qur'an portrays the greedy and stingy individual as doomed to a miserable end:

> As for him who gives and is God-fearing
> And affirms goodness,

> We shall "ease him to the Easing."
> But as for the miser and the self-absorbed,
> Who declares the Good to be a lie,
> We shall "ease him to the Hardship,"
> And his wealth will be of no use to him when he perishes. (92:5–11)

The pious believers, by contrast, show a concern for a relationship with both God and with the poor:

> They would sleep but little at night,
> And as dawn broke, they would seek forgiveness,
> And they shared their belongings with the beggar and the dispossessed. (51:17–19)

Those who persist in disobedience by refusing to worship Allah and recognize His Prophet are subject to punishment in this world and the life to come. Muhammad asserted that at the Last Judgment the fate of the wicked will be a fiery torment. On the other hand, those who submit to God will enjoy His favor in this world and will be generously rewarded at the Last Judgment. The imagery used to describe the bliss of paradise is as vivid as that of hell. In both cases, it is calculated to resonate with populations acquainted with the desert. The hellish fire and blasts of wind are contrasted with the gardens, cool water, and pampered service by young men and women that await the righteous in paradise.

It is clear from the wording of the Qur'an that the doctrine of the physical resurrection of the dead was incomprehensible and even ludicrous to many of Muhammad's audience, who raised many of the same objections to it as skeptics in other religious traditions have throughout the ages. Many in Mecca also objected to Muhammad's insistence that the basis for one's eternal fate at the Last Judgment would be merit rather than status as a member of a particular tribe. That membership in a tribe with high status would not avail a person when it mattered most was inconceivable to members of the elite tribes. When skeptics challenged the doctrine of the Last Judgment and asked about the fate of revered ancestors of the current generation, Muhammad replied that, because of their polytheism, they were now in hell. Muhammad's teachings were thus particularly galling to the aristocrats of Mecca. On the one hand, he used the traditional value of generosity against them and exposed the fact that they had betrayed those values by becoming greedy and stingy. On the other hand, he turned upside down the traditional criterion for status, which was a prominent position in a powerful tribe. According to him, individuals from undistinguished backgrounds who submitted to God and His Prophet would fare better in eternity than would the most revered tribal leader who rejected the new teaching. Given the prevailing values of the period, it is clear why his message was welcomed by some groups, detested by others, and simply not comprehended by many.

The leaders of the dominant Quraysh tribe in Mecca were bitter critics of Muhammad's mission. Only the protection of Muhammad's uncle, Abu Talib, prevented him and his followers from being persecuted, rather than merely harassed. In 619, however, the Prophet's circumstances changed for the worse. In that year, both Khadija and Abu Talib died, leaving him without psychological support and social protection. The leaders of the Quraysh were free to impose an economic boycott on the small Muslim community, and individual Muslims became the target of physical beatings. With tensions growing between the leaders of the Quraysh and the Muslims, it became clear that Muhammad and his followers would have to find another setting in which to practice their faith. Muhammad investigated the possibilities at several nearby towns, but he was unable to elicit any interest.

Then, unexpectedly, in 620, a group from the oasis of Yathrib, some 240 miles to the north, converted to Islam when they heard him preaching in Mecca. The next year, another group from Yathrib came to Mecca and embraced Islam. Members of the second group invited Muhammad to come to their oasis in order to mediate quarrels among tribal factions there. In 622 c.e., Muhammad and his followers emigrated to Yathrib, which later in Islamic history became known as The City (*madina*) of the Prophet, or Medina. This trek of perhaps a few hundred individuals is known as the *hijra*. Years later, Muslims came to see that the Hijra was the decisive moment in Islamic history, and they accepted the year in which it occurred as the beginning of the new Islamic calendar. Year One of the Muslim era had begun.

Hijra has often been translated into English as "flight," but doing so misses an important element of Islamic history. It is true that the account of Muhammad's transfer to Medina points out the danger that he and his followers were exposed to, and that Muhammad left Mecca just in time to avoid an attempt on his life. On the other hand, Muslims have always seen the Hijra as a rejection of Meccan unbelief, rather than a flight to escape danger. Throughout history, many Muslims have been convinced that, should they come under non-Muslim rule, they should "perform hijra" by moving to an area ruled by pious Muslims.

In the early seventh century, Medina was not a city in the traditional sense of the term. Instead, it was a large oasis that contained several hamlets. It was the home of thousands of Jews, some of whom were descendants of refugees from the second great Jewish revolt against Rome, which occurred in the second century. They formed at least three tribes. Two Arab tribes had come into the oasis later than the Jews, but they had become the dominant forces there. The two Arab tribes engaged in continual warfare with each other and had thrown the oasis into turmoil. The delegation that invited Muhammad to the oasis had done so in the hope that he could bring stability to the various settlements. The delegation and Muhammad worked out an agreement that has come to be known as the Constitution of Medina. In it, the inhabitants of the oasis recognized Muhammad as the community's political leader. As such, he was able to influence more people than ever before. His undeniable talents as a negotiator and arbiter reinforced his prophetic claims, and the number of his followers began to grow rapidly.

For the next eight years, Muhammad sought to implement Islamic principles in Medina and build up the economic and military resources of his city. His responsibilities were vastly more extensive than they had been in Mecca, and the revelations that continued to come to him reflect the new circumstances. Whereas the Meccan revelations had focused on the majesty of God, those of Medina are more concerned with legislative matters, rules for communal living, and rebuttals to criticism of his message made by Jews and Christians.

Muhammad's first concern upon arriving in Medina was to provide a means of support for the Muslims who had accompanied him. Opportunities for the *why?*

employment of recent immigrants were limited in the oasis economy, so Muhammad resorted to raiding caravans that carried the Meccan trade. By 624, the raids had damaged the Meccan economy, provoking the Quraysh to attack Muhammad's forces at a caravan watering hole called Badr. The Battle of Badr was a shocking loss for the Meccans and a corresponding boost to the prestige of Muhammad throughout the Hijaz. The next year, the Meccans attacked Medina itself, and this time, the Quraysh won a decisive victory at the Battle of Uhud. Inexplicably, they failed to follow up on their victory, allowing the Muslim community an opportunity to recover.

The defeat at Uhud led to a period of self-doubt and reflection among the Muslims. This shock could have terminated in despair, skepticism, and the end of the Islamic experiment. What emerged instead was a maturity and seriousness of purpose that the Muslims had not possessed before then. The results were manifested when, in 627, Mecca launched the largest attack yet. Greatly outnumbering the Muslim forces, the Meccans and their allies were confident of victory, but Muhammad had anticipated the attack and inspired the Medinans to work hard to prepare their city's defenses. Hills and large boulders presented obstacles to any attack on three sides of the city. The northern approach was the only one that was level and unobstructed. There, the Medinans dug a large ditch, which rendered the Meccan cavalry useless. After several days of frustration, the attackers were forced to retreat. The "Battle of the Ditch" convinced Muhammad's followers that their cause was poised for imminent victory.

The battle was, in fact, a turning point in Muhammad's career. Throughout the five years of struggle with Mecca, Muhammad had already developed a reputation throughout the Hijaz as a leader who had to be taken seriously. He had sent out emissaries to oases and nomadic tribes in an effort to gain allies. Several communities agreed to help him in the event of clashes with Mecca, and some of them accepted his religious teachings—he did not force his allies to become Muslims. Other communities, however, feared his growing power and allied with Mecca instead.

How do you reconcile Muslim teaching and people of The Book?

In the year following the Battle of the Ditch, Muhammad felt strong enough to begin testing the military power of his new community. In 628, he captured at least two oases in the northern Hijaz, and then he led a group of followers toward Mecca, declaring that the Muslims wished to perform the rites of pilgrimage at the city. Although his group was deliberately *not* heavily armed, the Meccan leaders did not order an attack on them. Instead, they asked to negotiate. Muhammad, realizing that they had lost their nerve and would no longer be a serious threat to him, agreed to do so. The two groups signed a treaty that postponed the pilgrimage for one year. Although some of the Muslims thought the concession was a humiliation, Muhammad realized that the Meccans had recognized him as a legitimate and equal power and had conceded his right to enter their city. The pilgrimage occurred in 629, as the two parties had agreed.

During the two years following the agreement with Mecca, Muhammad's military forces captured several oases in the northern tier of the peninsula and made an unsuccessful raid into Byzantine territory in southern Syria. In 630, he forced the issue of supremacy with Mecca by leading an army against the city. The Quraysh capitulated with almost no resistance. Muhammad entered Mecca, cleansed the Ka'ba, and dedicated it solely to Allah. Most Meccans made their submission to

Muhammad's cause, and Muhammad immediately named several of the most talented of them to be high-level administrators and advisors. Some of his longtime followers, who had been persecuted by these same people, were bewildered and angered by the appointments, but Muhammad continued to reveal his keen political instincts and his astute assessment of personalities by co-opting the talent and ultimate loyalty of his former enemies.

The Prophet continued to base his operations in Medina. From there, he ordered a campaign to the far north of the peninsula that resulted in the capture of the oasis of Tabuk and three Byzantine towns near the Gulf of Aqaba. Numerous tribes in the peninsula now began sending delegations to Muhammad, seeking terms of understanding with this formidable new ruler. Muhammad was content to make alliances with some of the more powerful ones; with others, he secured agreements to submit to Islam and pay a tax. By 632, he dominated western Arabia, and Muslim communities could be found from the Persian Gulf to Yemen. In March of that year, Muhammad's health began to fail. His condition deteriorated rapidly into June, when he died.

Reasons for conquest?

A Framework for a New Community

Muhammad's sudden death in 632 was a shock to those who had been caught up in the dramatic developments of the previous decade. The course of events after the Battle of the Ditch had been particularly riveting and had seemed to be the prelude to a new order in the region. With the Prophet's death, however, what would become of his movement and the nascent state that he headed? Few were aware of it at the time, but Muhammad had transformed the Hijaz irrevocably, and his career has become one of the turning points of world history.

Confronting the Death of the Prophet

The Prophet died in the arms of his favorite wife, the young 'A'isha. The passage that follows, which comes from the earliest extant biography of Muhammad, captures the shock of the community in Medina when the news of his death spread. It also emphasizes the centrality of the tenet of strict monotheism in Islam. The two major figures mentioned here, Abu Bakr and 'Umar, were among the first converts to Islam, were fathers-in-law of the Prophet (Abu Bakr was 'A'isha's father), and became the first two leaders of the Muslim community after the Prophet's death.

When the apostle was dead 'Umar got up and said: "Some of the disaffected will allege that the apostle is dead, but by God he is not dead: he has gone to his Lord as Moses b. 'Imran went and was hidden from his people for forty days, returning to them after it was said that he had died. By God, the apostle will return as Moses returned and will cut off the hands and feet of men who allege that the apostle is dead." When Abu Bakr heard what was happening he came to the door of the mosque as 'Umar was speaking to the

(Continued)

people. He paid no attention but went in to 'A'isha's house to the apostle, who was lying covered by a mantle of Yamani cloth. He went and uncovered his face and kissed him, saying, "You are dearer than my father and mother. You have tasted the death which God had decreed: a second death will never overtake you." Then he replaced the mantle on the apostle's face and went out. 'Umar was still speaking and he said, "Gently, 'Umar, be quiet." But 'Umar went on talking, and when Abu Bakr saw that he would not be silent he went forward to the people who, when they heard his words, came to him and left 'Umar. Giving thanks and praise to God he said: "O men, if anyone worships Muhammad, Muhammad is dead: if anyone worships God, God is alive, immortal." Then he recited this verse (3:138): "Muhammad is nothing but an apostle. Apostles have passed away before him. Can it be that if he were to die or be killed you would turn back on your heels? He who turns back does no harm to God and God will reward the grateful." By God, it was as though the people did not know that this verse had come down until Abu Bakr recited it that day. The people took it from him and it was (constantly) in their mouths. 'Umar said, "By God, when I heard Abu Bakr recite these words I was dumbfounded so that my legs would not bear me and I fell to the ground knowing that the apostle was indeed dead."

SOURCE: Ibn Ishaq. *The Life of Muhammad. A Translation of Ibn Ishaq's Sirat Rasul Allah.* Translated with introduction and notes by A. Guillaume. Lahore and Karachi, Pakistan Branch: Oxford University Press, 1967, 682–683.

Muhammad lived in Arabia at a time when the inhabitants of the towns there seem to have been experiencing a crisis of faith. The situation was analogous to that of the Roman Empire in the second century, when millions of its inhabitants flocked to the so-called mystery religions that had begun to challenge the traditional state-sponsored pantheon of Roman gods and goddesses. For reasons not clear to us in either case, the old gods and goddesses began to lose their ability to hold the faith of the masses, prompting many individuals to embark on a quest for a more meaningful religion. We do know that Judaism and Christianity were the dominant religions of Syria and Iraq to the north of Arabia and were also well established in the northern and southern extremes of the peninsula. As religions of settled communities and of a literate, cultured tradition, they were respected by the polytheistic Arabs. At first, Muhammad seems to have thought of Jews and Christians as natural allies in the struggle against polytheism. As we have seen, he taught that his message was the same as that preached by the Jewish prophets, including Jesus. While still in Mecca, he followed the Jewish example and ordered his followers to face towards Jerusalem while performing their prayers. During that period, he seems to have followed the Jewish example in several other points of ritual and doctrine.

No later than the early period in Medina, however, it became clear that Islam would have to define itself apart from each of these other two religions. After the Hijra, Muhammad's relations with the Jews deteriorated rapidly. Indirect evidence in the Qur'an suggests that certain Jews in Medina challenged the Prophet's versions of several narratives because they did not conform to the Biblical renderings. Muhammad also apparently had reason to suspect certain Jews of complicity with the enemy during the three battles with Mecca. After each of the first two battles, he exiled a Jewish tribe from Medina. As harsh as those actions were, they were mild compared with the aftermath of the Battle of the Ditch, when he executed the adult males of the remaining Jewish tribe, a number that amounted to several hundred individuals. He then sold the women and children into slavery.

It also seems to be the Medinan period when criticisms of Christians became more commonplace. Christians claimed to follow the teachings of Jesus, but the Jesus of the Qur'an is quite different from the one whom the Christians worshiped. According to the Qur'an, Jesus was indeed born of a virgin named Mary (although the birth took place at the base of a palm tree instead of in a stable), performed miracles, and brought a message from God. Contrary to the account in the Bible, however, the Qur'an teaches that the plans to crucify Jesus were thwarted and that God delivered him from execution. More important, the Qur'an denies that Jesus is the incarnation of God, as the Christians claimed. In one passage (5:116–120) it portrays a conversation between God and Jesus in which God asks Jesus if he ever claimed that he and Mary were divinities worthy of worship. Jesus emphatically denies having done so, reinforcing a passage earlier in the sura that rejects the concept of the Trinity and emphasizes Jesus's status as a mortal prophet (5:72–75).

Because of the controversies between Muhammad on the one hand and Jews and Christians on the other, certain passages in the Qur'an are highly critical of those two religious groups. Sura 5 is particularly harsh, calling Christians "unbelievers" whose fate is the fire of hell because of their concept of the Trinity (5:72–73); Jews are linked with the polytheists in their hostility to Islam (5:82); and Muslims are warned not to take Jews or Christians as friends because of their mockery of Islam and their unfaithfulness (5:51, 57). On the other hand, the Qur'an more often refers to Jews and Christians as "People of the Book"—that is, as having a version (albeit distorted) of the revelation from God. In some passages (2:62, among others), the Qur'an seems to state explicitly that Jews and Christians should be recognized as spiritual kinsmen to Muslims. Many of them, it points out, are clearly God-fearing and righteous. Despite the political tensions and the doctrinal differences separating Jews and Christians from Muslims, the Qur'an's overall evaluation of the Jews and Christians was that, as People of the Book, they deserved to be allowed to practice their religion. As we shall see in subsequent chapters, the Muslims who conquered the vast areas from the Atlantic to the Indus River would regard the People of the Book as protected peoples.

The controversies that swirled between Muhammad and the established communities of Jews and Christians helped to establish the separate identity of Islam. Muslims understood Islam to be within the tradition of Judaism and Christianity, but it was God's original revelation, without the distortions that had accumulated in those two communities. The doctrine emerged that the Prophet had brought the original version of both Judaism and Christianity—the version held by Abraham, revered by both Jews and Christians—and this time the Arabs would be the first to hear it. The new faith was vehement in its rejection of polytheism, and its uncompromising monotheism would force even Christians, who considered themselves to be monotheists, to rethink their doctrines and practices in the face of Islamic criticism of the doctrine of the Trinity and the use of images and statuary. If differences existed between the Qur'an on the one hand and the Torah and the Gospel on the other, it was because Jews and Christians had distorted the revelation.

This sense of having completed the revelation and of having corrected the errors of previous generations was an inspirational force that generated a profound sense of self-confidence within the new Islamic community. Arab Muslims were no longer Arab polytheists who lived on the periphery of superior civilizations. They were bearers of the original and authentic revelation from the one true God, and their neighbors could only benefit from their counsel.

Conclusion

The sense of mission that the Arabs of the Hijaz gained from Islam would have dissipated rapidly without an institution to channel it. Muhammad's monumental political achievement was to create a polity in western Arabia that served in effect as a substitute for tribal membership. Just as the Monophysites and Nestorians of the Byzantine Empire had expressed their dissatisfaction with the economic, political, and theological developments within their society through the medium of divergent religious claims, so Muhammad's critique of his society took a religious form. When Muhammad donned the prophetic mantle in the streets of Mecca, criticizing the polytheism, greed, and selfishness of the people of his hometown, his opponents perceived an implicit claim for political and religious leadership of the community. Unlike the Monophysites and Nestorians, Muhammad was able to overthrow the old order and establish both a new religion and a new polity in Arabia.

As we have seen, no state had existed in northern Arabia before Muhammad's time, and yet his success seems to have filled a yearning felt by tribesmen scattered over a vast area. Over the centuries, northern Arabia had witnessed the rise of impressive, but ephemeral, tribal confederations. Only in Yemen had there existed a political and revenue system such as Muhammad created. In Medina, Muhammad had created an *umma*, or a community that agreed on certain standards of behavior and certain fundamentals of governance. In his original agreement with the inhabitants of Medina, Muhammad had meant by *umma* everyone in the city, not just the Muslims. By the end of his career, however, he had restricted the use of the term to Muslims only. Perhaps the most novel feature that the Umma entailed was the concept of a law to which all members of the polity were bound. As we shall see, Islamic law later developed into a complex science, but even during the early years of Islamic history, the standards of behavior and the obligatory acts that are detailed in the Qur'an constituted a concept of law that, at least in theory, transcended tribal custom and tribal competition. All who called themselves Muslims were expected to obey God's revealed standards. Tribal loyalties and customs were clearly secondary in this understanding. As subsequent history shows all too clearly, tribal identities and antagonisms did not fade away. But the idea that one's ultimate loyalty was to God, rather than to one's tribe, contained powerful latent possibilities. Oppression no longer had to be viewed as simply a fact of life in a cruel world; it was an affront to God and a violation of His law against which His community should take a stand. Tribal, regional, and ethnic obligations had now become, at least theoretically, subject to the greater claims of a divine and universal law. The foundations had been laid for a new human community. The superstructure would be built by subsequent generations of Muslims.

NOTES

1   Bulliet, Richard. *The Camel and the Wheel.* Cambridge, Massachusetts: Harvard University Press, 1975, 110.

FURTHER READING

Southwest Asia in the Seventh Century

Bulliet, Richard. *The Camel and the Wheel.* Cambridge, Massachusetts: Harvard University Press, 1975.

Cameron, Averil. *The Mediterranean World in Late Antiquity: A.D. 395–600.* London and New York: Routledge, 1993.

Crone, Patricia. *Meccan Trade and the Rise of Islam.* Princeton, New Jersey: Princeton University Press, 1987.

Frye, Richard N. *The Golden Age of Persia.* New York: Barnes & Noble, 1975.

Jenkins, Romilly James Heald. *Byzantium: The Imperial Centuries, AD 610–1071.* Toronto: Published by the University of Toronto Press in association with the Medieval Academy of America, 1987.

Hoyland, Robert G. *Arabia and the Arabs from the Bronze Age to the Coming of Islam.* New York and London: Routledge, 2001.

Morony, Michael G. *Iraq After the Muslim Conquest.* Princeton, New Jersey: Princeton University Press, 1984.

Shahid, Irfan. *Byzantium and the Arabs in the Sixth Century.* Washington, D.C.: Dumbarton Oaks Research Library and Collection, 1995.

Whittow, Mark. *The Making of Byzantium, 600–1025.* Berkeley, California: University of California Press, 1996.

Yarshater, Ehsan, ed. *The Cambridge History of Iran,* vol. 3, *The Seleucid, Parthian and Sasanian Periods.* Cambridge, New York: Cambridge University Press, 1983.

The Rise of Islam

Denny, Frederick Mathewson. *An Introduction to Islam,* 2d ed. New York: Macmillan Publishing Company, 1994.

Kennedy, Hugh. *The Prophet and the Age of the Caliphates.* London and New York: Longman, 1986.

Peters, F.E. *Muhammad and the Origins of Islam.* Albany, New York: State University of New York Press, 1994.

Ruthven, Malise. *Islam in the World,* 2d ed. New York: Oxford University Press, 2000.

Watt, W. Montgomery. *Muhammad at Mecca.* Oxford, U.K.: Oxford University Press, 1953.

Watt, W. Montgomery. *Muhammad at Medina.* Oxford, U.K.: Oxford University Press, 1956.

There are several good English translations of the Qur'an. It is important to understand that, unlike the Bible, the Qur'an in any language other than the original is not considered to be the Qur'an itself, but only a translated version: The Qur'an is to be found only in the Arabic language. As is the case with translations of the Bible, however, one can choose from a wide variety of prose styles. The following are two popular styles:

Ali, Ahmed, tr. *Al-Qur'an: A Contemporary Translation.* Princeton, New Jersey: Princeton University Press, 1984.

Dawood, N.J. tr. *The Koran*. London: Penguin Books, 2000.

Many features of the early history of Islam are controversial. This chapter is based on the work of scholars who try to discover the historical events behind the (often problematic) traditional Muslim accounts. Another, quite different, approach of the past twenty-five years has been to consider the traditional accounts to be of almost no historical value and to suggest new chronological and geographical frameworks within which to understand the origins of Islam. Some scholars suggest that Islam did not arise in Mecca and Medina, but that it arose within a dominant monotheistic—rather than polytheistic—society, and that the Qur'an was collected over the course of a century, rather than two decades. For an introduction into this line of historical revisionism, consult the following works:

Crone, Patricia, and Michael Cook. *Hagarism: The Making of the Islamic World.* Cambridge, New York: Cambridge University Press, 1977.

Hawting, G.R. *The Idea of Idolatry and the Emergence of Islam: From Polemic to History.* Cambridge, New York: Cambridge University Press, 1999.

Wansbrough, John. *Qur'anic Studies: Sources and Methods of Scriptural Interpretation.* Oxford, U.K.: Oxford University Press, 1977.

For a thoughtful critique of this revisionist approach, consult the following text:

Donner, Fred M. *Narratives of Islamic Origins: The Beginnings of Islamic Historical Writing.* Princeton, New Jersey: The Darwin Press, Inc., 1998.

CHAPTER 2

Arab Imperialism

Because of Islam, the Arabian Peninsula became the locus of a dynamic society at the very time that the two great civilizations to the north had exhausted each other. In less than a decade after Muhammad's death, the Arabs came into possession of the territories of what had been the Sasanian Empire and took over the wealthy Syrian and Egyptian provinces of the Byzantine Empire. Within the lifetime of some of the children who had met Muhammad and sat on the Prophet's knees, Arab armies controlled the land mass that extended from the Pyrenees Mountains in Europe to the Indus River valley in South Asia. In less than a century, Arabs had come to rule over an area that spanned 5000 miles.

The leaders of this unprecedented achievement included some men of remarkable ability, but, on the whole, their effectiveness was handicapped by their inability to transcend their provincial attitudes. Because their Arab identity was so strong, they could rarely see the conquered territories as the arena for the cultivation of a universal Islamic society; instead, they saw it as a cash cow to be exploited. When the pace of conquest slowed and the revenues from the pillaging began to dry up, they were unable to prevent tribal factionalism from developing as their followers began to compete for scarce resources. Perhaps an even greater failure was their refusal to receive into their society the non-Arabs who converted to Islam. The discrimination that the new Muslims experienced contrasted sharply with the ideals of justice and equality that had attracted the converts in the first place. It opened the Arabs to charges of hypocrisy and oppression. The inability of the leadership to resolve these problems led to a revolution that overthrew the Arab empire after a century of spectacular expansion.

Arab Conquests

During the last few years of his life, the Prophet gradually expanded his sphere of influence within the Arabian Peninsula by means of military campaigns and peaceful alliances. In the aftermath of his death, the Muslim leadership at Medina began a series of conquests that still have the power to amaze the observer. Taking place over a period of ninety years, these conquests swept away the imperial forces of the Arabs' proud neighbors to the north and resulted in a permanent cultural transformation of the societies that came under Muslim control.

Arabia and the Fertile Crescent

The Prophet's sudden death in 632 was a stunning and disorienting experience for his followers. Having become dependent on him to serve as both the channel of God's revelation and the political and military leader of the new state, the community was bereft of its religious and political leadership at a stroke. That the despair and confusion in the wake of his death did not cause the collapse of his nascent movement is a testimony to the strength of the institutions and the ideals that Muhammad had left behind and to the quality of the leadership that succeeded him.

Several factions emerged among the Muslims in the aftermath of the Prophet's funeral, each advocating a different candidate for leadership of the Umma. Among them were the original Muslims who participated in the Hijra, the converts from Medina, and the Meccans who converted only after the conquest of their city two years earlier. Some people felt the need for a continuing source of revelation; others stressed political or military abilities; and still others wanted a member of the Prophet's family to lead the Umma. Prominent among the latter was a group that was initially sidelined but increased in importance during the following decades. Its members became known in history as the *shi'a*, or Shi'ites, whom we will discuss in detail in Chapter 3.

In the days and weeks after the Prophet's death, two of the first converts to Islam, 'Umar ibn al-Khattab and Abu Bakr, filled leadership roles for the community. In the heat of the debate over the course of action to be taken, 'Umar made a passionate speech that convinced a majority of those present to accept Abu Bakr as the leader of the Umma. Abu Bakr was a pious, highly respected confidant of Muhammad who was famous for his knowledge of the genealogy of the region's tribes, a valuable asset for the politics of the day. He and the Prophet had solidified their relationship by Muhammad's marriage to Abu Bakr's nine-year-old daughter, 'A'isha, soon after the Hijra. The young wife became Muhammad's favorite, and he died in her arms. The title of the position that Abu Bakr now held came to be known as *caliph* (from *khalifa*, which can mean "successor" or "deputy"), although as we shall see later, it is not clear that Abu Bakr was addressed by this title during his lifetime. There is evidence, in fact, that 'Umar and Abu Bakr worked together closely during the latter's short administration.

With the loss of the Prophet, the new leader's most pressing challenge was that many of the tribes that had submitted to Muhammad no longer considered themselves under Medina's control. Interpreting the situation in traditional fashion, they felt that the terms that they had contracted with Muhammad had been of a personal nature and that it was incumbent on his successor to renegotiate the terms. They failed to pay their tax and waited for Medina to react. A reversion to paganism does not appear to have played a major role in this challenge to Medina's authority. There were, indeed, certain "false prophets" leading challenges to Islam's dominance among tribes in central and northeastern Arabia, but these were areas not yet within Medina's sphere of influence. In most cases, the revolt represented a residual tribal antipathy toward unfamiliar centralized control, and it is clear that in some cases the affected tribes were divided, with significant factions wishing not to break with the Umma. Abu Bakr's stature as a leader lay in his recognition that to allow tribes to secede from the union would doom the newly emerging society and allow a relapse into the polytheistic and violent tribalism of the recent past. He perceived that Muhammad's polity inextricably combined religious expression with political authority. Islam was not a religion that could recognize a difference between what belonged to God and what belonged to Caesar. In the Prophet's vision, any distinction between the "religious" and the "political" was fatuous. Political infidelity would result in religious infidelity.

The military campaign that Abu Bakr ordered to bring the recalcitrant tribes back under Medina's control is known in Islamic history as the Ridda Wars, or the Wars of Apostasy. The campaign is important historically because it marks the transition to the Arab wars of conquest outside the peninsula. The campaign to coerce rebel groups to resubmit to Medinan hegemony made two seamless shifts in policy. The first was a transition from pacification of the rebellious tribes to one of subduing Arabian communities that had never had a treaty with the Prophet. The subjugation of the rebels was a short affair, which may be explained in part by evidence that many of the secessionist tribes and settlements were experiencing internal divisions over the issue of rebellion and thus put up only a half-hearted resistance. In the process of coercing rebel groups back under Medinan hegemony, the Muslim army at some point began to subdue Arabian tribes that had not made submission. Despite fierce resistance from a handful of tribes, Medina won an overwhelming victory and was master of the peninsula by 634. Augmented by the manpower of the forces that it had conquered in the Ridda Wars, the Muslim army was large and confident, whereas its opponents could never unite against Medina. The decisive victory by the diverse coalition that made up the Islamic state made a deep impression on many Arabs regarding the inadequacy of a purely tribal identity.

Just as the Ridda Wars segued into a war for the conquest of the peninsula, so too the latter evolved imperceptibly into invasions of the Byzantine and Sasanian empires. The specific reasons for this evolution into major international military expeditions are lost to history, but scholars have suggested three factors that may have converged precisely when the two empires were at their weakest. The first was a geopolitical motivation on the part of the Muslim leadership. As Medina's campaign moved into the northern part of the peninsula, the objectives of the Muslim elite may well have expanded. Muhammad himself had already attempted to gain control of the Arabian tribes and settlements on the route from the Hijaz to Syria; now Abu Bakr seems to have been concerned about the threat posed to the Umma by nomads and rival settlements situated on important trade routes. He was concerned to bring under his control any potential security threat to the trade of the new state, and he used a combination of force, cajolery, and material incentives to do so.

The second factor was the inspiration of religion itself. Many of the soldiers who fought for Medina throughout the Arabian campaigns were genuinely motivated by religious concerns. The Qur'an repeatedly enjoins believers to engage in a struggle (*jihad*) against unbelievers until God's rule is established on this earth. Muslims who refuse to help, either by fighting or by helping the cause by contributing to it financially, are called hypocrites. On the other hand, those who fight are rewarded not only spiritually (in the afterlife), but also materially (the troops are to share four-fifths of the loot captured in fighting the infidels). The scriptures, the promise of material reward, and social pressure all combined to create a polity that offered powerful motivations for participation in warfare.

A third factor in the unexpected irruption of the Islamic movement into regions outside the peninsula was one that we shall see repeated many times during the next eight centuries when nomads were recruited into armies in the Afro-Asiatic land mass: Although the nomads were supposed to be instruments of the policy of political leaders, their own needs and expectations often dictated policy. The irony facing the Medinan and Meccan elites was that a majority of their troops were of necessity the very bedouin who historically had depended on raiding settlements for the acquisition of their surplus. In a sense, the Muslim leadership was riding a tiger by depending on armies made up of the social group that posed a perpetual threat to the personal, political, and economic security of town dwellers.

It would have been extremely difficult, if not impossible, for the Muslim leadership to have escaped the dilemma. Their followers expected raids and battles to yield plunder as well as strategic or religious gains. The Qur'an stipulated that the Prophet would retain one-fifth of the captured property from such battles for distribution among the community, and the remainder would be divided among the warriors who participated in the fighting. The wars under the first caliphs continued that policy, as the caliph received the portion that the Prophet had taken. Each Muslim victory yielded plunder as well as recruits from the ranks of the vanquished. The additional warriors made the next stage of conquest easier, but they also made the next stage imperative because the new recruits expected to share in the plunder. A cessation of the wars of conquest would raise the issue of providing the soldiers with a substitute for plunder, and so the caliphs took the route of least resistance by continuing territorial expansion. Controlling the forces that made their very success possible would be a continuing challenge for the Muslim leadership.

Topographically and climatically, the Arabian Peninsula merges imperceptibly with the land mass of Southwest Asia. Moreover, the overwhelming majority of the population of the peninsula, southern Iraq, and southern Syria spoke Arabic. From the Medinan perspective, the Syrian and Iraqi Arabs were obvious candidates for incorporation into the Umma. Syria was the main attraction. As we have seen, Muhammad had already sent more than one army in its direction. Its oases and green hills were known to those who plied the caravan trade, and it was the setting for many of the important religious figures mentioned in the Qur'an. Populated by numerous Arabs, it attracted Muslims for both religious and economic reasons.

In the autumn of 633, four Muslim armies entered southern Syria and were soon joined by a fifth army that Abu Bakr transferred to Syria from its location on the southern Euphrates in Iraq, where it had been engaged in raiding and reconnaissance. The total manpower of the Muslim forces probably amounted to about 24,000 troops, including both infantry and cavalry. Abu Bakr died a few months later and was succeeded by his friend 'Umar by the same process of deliberation that had brought Abu Bakr into the leadership role a mere two years earlier. Reflecting the common vision of the two men, the Syrian conquest proceeded without interruption.

Whereas the management of the Muslim conquest of Syria proceeded smoothly despite the death of the first caliph, the Byzantine defense of the region never became coherent. Plague and sustained warfare had reduced the population of the area by twenty to forty percent during the previous century, and adequate provision had not been made for the loss of the Ghassanid auxiliaries. Byzantine armies, forced to move at the rate of their infantry, usually marched only ten to

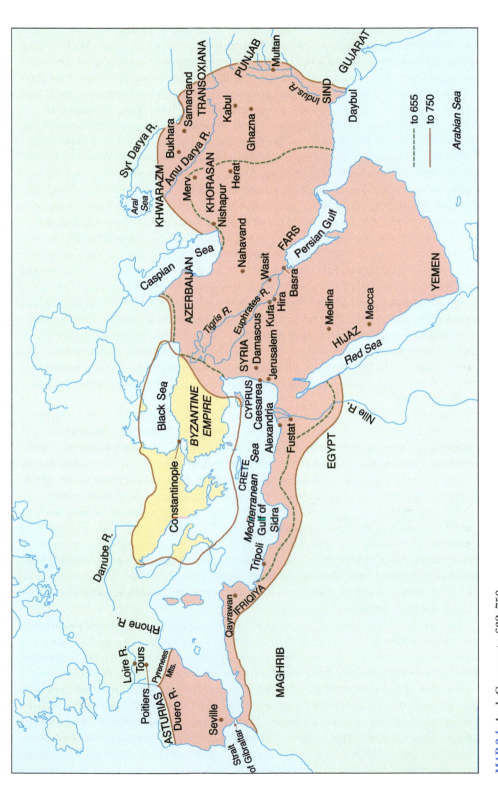

MAP 2.1 Arab Conquests, 632–750.

fifteen miles per day. Moreover, the war with the Sasanians had conditioned them to prefer a defensive, rather than an offensive, strategy. They had also lost much of their discipline and combat readiness. The best of the regular imperial troops were concentrated near Constantinople, and those in Syria were outnumbered by their own Arab troops by a ratio of at least two to one, and perhaps five to one. The populace was sullen. The numerous Monophysite Christians had no reason to feel loyalty to distant Constantinople, and the Jews were suffering severe persecution in retaliation for their active support of the Sasanian occupation that had just ended.

The first objective of the Muslims was to establish dominance over the Arabic-speaking areas of southern and eastern Syria. Many of these tribes put up stiff resistance against what they thought was another raid from desert dwellers, but many local Arabs, including Christians, joined the conquering armies. With these reinforcements, the invaders developed a numerical advantage over the local defenders. Syrian cities in the interior began to fall, and Damascus surrendered in 636. At that point, Heraclius realized that the invasion was a serious threat. He dispatched a huge Byzantine army that was reinforced by Arab and Armenian mercenaries. At the Yarmuk River, a tributary of the Jordan River just south of Lake Tiberias (the Sea of Galilee), the Muslims and their local allies decisively defeated the Byzantine coalition, effectively sealing the fate of Syria. The only question would be how long the sieges of the remaining cities would take. Over the next few months, Antioch and Aleppo fell, and Jerusalem capitulated in 637. The seaport of Caesarea was the last Byzantine city to fall, in 640. The Muslim Arabs now ruled the coastal plains and the interior, although they never gained effective control of the rugged Lebanese mountainous areas.

Although the chronology is not certain, it appears that after the Battle of Yarmuk, 'Umar felt that he could send troops into Iraq. When the Muslims began their attacks on Iraq, local Arab nomads and the Aramaic towns fought to protect themselves. Soon, however, the primary Muslim army devastated a much larger Sasanian force at Qadisiya, northwest of Hira. It then moved on to capture Ctesiphon. From that point, the largely Nestorian and Jewish population of central Iraq put up little resistance. Meanwhile, a second Muslim army captured southern Iraq, and, by 638, the Muslims had secured almost all of the Tigris and Euphrates valleys. The conquerors established military settlements to serve as garrison cities that could ensure security, serve as supply points, and keep the Arab troops from mixing with the local people. Kufa and Basra were the biggest of these new settlements, and within a short time, each of these new towns was thronged with tens of thousands of Arabs from the peninsula.

Meanwhile, in 639, one of 'Umar's military commanders requested permission to lead an army into the Nile valley. 'Umar, whose clearly stated focus had been the subjugation of Arab populations rather than conquest in general, initially refused. After further consideration, he gave his reluctant consent. Whether he changed policy because of the potential security threat posed by the Byzantine army and navy that were based in Alexandria or because of the need to keep his warriors engaged in fighting and plundering is unknown, but Muslim armies entered a new phase of their conquests. From that time on, they would spread the hegemony of Islam wherever their power enabled them to overcome local resistance. The Arab campaign in Egypt benefitted from the policies of the Orthodox patriarch, Cyrus. Eleven years earlier, after the Byzantines had retaken Egypt from the Sasanians in 628, Cyrus began a savage repression of Monophysitism. Now, with a conquering army in their midst, the Copts provided no support to their hated Byzantine overlords against the Muslims. The Arabs won control of Egypt by 641, and they created a military garrison and capital, calling it Fustat. Significantly, it was on the southern fringe of the Nile delta, rather than at the traditional seaside capital, Alexandria. Whereas Alexandria was Greek in culture and faced the Byzantine-dominated Mediterranean, Fustat— like Kufa and Basra—was for Arab troops, and it was oriented toward Medina. Although Fustat was unappealing to the sophisticates of Alexandria, its founding was a sound strategic decision. It was on the Nile, it was the site of an ancient Roman garrison, and in the tenth century it would become a suburb of a new and important city called Cairo.

Iran

Seven years of campaigning won the Fertile Crescent and Egypt for the Muslim armies. The flat terrain and the arid and semiarid climate were familiar and congenial to the victors; the poor organization and morale of the imperial armies had allowed the traditional superiority of nomadic attackers to prevail over settled life; and after the initial shock, the population had reacted to the new administration with a mixture of relief and resignation. The momentum of the victories carried the Muslim armies to the east and west simultaneously, and they were continuously augmented by migrants from Arabia, new converts in the conquered territories, and even by former Byzantine and Sasanian troops, who were not required to convert as a condition of service in the Muslim army. The next stage of the conquests would prove to be no less remarkable than the first but would be much more difficult.

The Sasanians had been defeated in Iraq, but their generals organized a large army on the Iranian plateau with the intention of driving out the invaders. 'Umar ordered a campaign to meet it that entailed having to advance through the Zagros Mountains. Prior to that campaign, the Arabs had not fought in mountainous territory, but the invasion route entailed a march of 125 miles across parallel, rugged ridges separated by deep gorges. The two armies met at Nahavand in 642 and fought the most difficult and costly of all the battles between the Arabs and Sasanians. The Arabs won, and the remnant of the Iranian army retreated to the east.

The Arab campaign to conquer Iran was well planned, but it faced formidable challenges. One was a change in leadership. In 644, Caliph 'Umar was stabbed to death by an Iranian who had been captured during the conquest. 'Umar's successor was 'Uthman ibn 'Affan, who had supported Muhammad from the beginning of his mission. Again reflecting the remarkable unity of the early leadership, the Iranian campaign continued without interruption under the new caliph.

The other challenges were the different terrain and a new level of resistance from the local inhabitants. Iraq, with its large non-Iranian population, was the only Sasanian province that put up merely perfunctory resistance. Other regions fought fiercely. The Muslim army encountered bitter and prolonged fighting in Azerbaijan from the independent mountain peoples there. As a result, the province suffered extensive destruction. On the northern Iranian plateau itself, the Arabs also faced stiff resistance. The Arabs secured the southern slopes of the Elburz Mountains while following the trade route east through Rayy en route to Khorasan. They took Nishapur (Neyshabur) and Merv (near modern Mary) in 651, but Khorasan was not under effective Arab control until 654. In southwestern Iran, the Sasanian royal family's favorite province of Fars produced the fiercest resistance of all. Five years (645–650) of sustained, brutal fighting were required to reduce the opposition, during which time the Sasanian aristocracy was exterminated. The surviving inhabitants of Fars resisted conversion to Islam longer than any other group in Iran. In 656, the conquests suddenly stopped for a decade, due to a civil war that rocked the young Islamic state. This bloody conflict was a shock to the many Muslims who had assumed that the principles of religious unity, equality, and justice would bring an end to factionalism. The civil war will be the subject of a detailed treatment in the next chapter. At this point, it is sufficient to summarize it as having begun when the third caliph, 'Uthman, was assassinated in 656 by disgruntled warriors from the garrison city of Fustat in Egypt. These men then secured the selection of 'Ali ibn Abu Talib as 'Uthman's successor. 'Ali was the Prophet's cousin and had been among the very earliest of the converts to Islam. He was widely admired, and a devoted group of followers had been demanding that he be selected caliph ever since the death of the Prophet. Now, however, because he took no steps to punish the murderers of his predecessor, 'Ali became the target of a vendetta by 'Uthman's kinsmen, who were members of the Umayyad clan.

The vendetta grew to such large proportions that it became a civil war. The leader of the Umayyad cause was 'Uthman's nephew, Mu'awiya, the talented governor of Syria. For five years, 656–661, he led a military force against 'Ali's army. In 661, 'Ali became the third caliph in a row to be murdered, stabbed to death while at prayers in a mosque. Mu'awiya now claimed the right to succeed 'Ali as caliph. Because Mu'awiya remained in Syria, Damascus became the center of Muslim political and economic power. Medina was thus relegated to the periphery of an expanding Arab empire. Mu'awiya (661–680) proved to be a skillful and honest administrator, but one of his decisions won him enduring enmity among many Muslims. Rather than relying on a council to select the next caliph, he named his own son to be his successor. His family, the Umayyads, thus became the dynastic rulers who claimed the leadership of the Arab empire from 661 until they were overthrown in 750.

Under the Umayyads, the conquests resumed. Using Coptic sailors who had been in the Byzantine naval squadron based in Alexandria, the Arabs led several fruitless naval raids against Constantinople between 667 and 680. Despite their failed objective of capturing the Byzantine capital city, the naval campaigns did capture Crete and Cyprus; the latter island became a base for attacking Byzantine shipping for the next three centuries. On land, Arab armies could not secure a lasting foothold in the densely settled areas north of the Taurus Mountains. The Byzantines had lost Syria and Egypt, but they still retained Anatolia and the Balkans. Anatolia's population was equal to that of Egypt and Syria combined, and by possessing it and the Balkans, Constantinople was sufficiently wealthy to remain the mighty capital of a powerful empire for centuries to come. The Sasanians had been destroyed, but the Byzantines would engage the Muslims in almost continuous warfare for centuries and present a difficult barrier against further Islamic expansion despite their notorious political instability.

North Africa and the Iberian Peninsula

North Africa did not lure the Arabs the way Syria and Iraq had. The Arab army based in Egypt did advance as far as Tripoli in order to eliminate any Byzantine threats to its position in Alexandria, but it attempted no conquests further west. For several decades thereafter, North Africa provided an opportunity for local warriors and adventurers to make raids, but the theater of conquest lay to the east.

North Africa west of central Libya (the Gulf of Sidra) is usually referred to as the *Maghrib*, an Arabic word meaning "land of the west" or "land of sunset." The Maghribi coastal plain is fertile for most of its length, and the area comprising modern Algeria and Tunisia was a major source of wheat, wine, and olive oil for the Romans and Byzantines. Peasant villages dotted the coast and were scattered throughout the valleys and passes of the mountain ranges, which become progressively more imposing from Tunisia into Morocco. Most of the towns were ports along the coast, although some were located in fertile wheat-growing areas dozens of miles inland. Roman Carthage had attained a population of at least 100,000 at its peak, but it never fully recovered after having been sacked by the Vandals in 439.

In the seventh century, Berbers were the dominant ethnic group throughout the 2000 miles from the Libyan plateau to the Atlantic coast. The Berber languages belong to the Afroasiatic language family, along with the Semitic, Chad, and ancient Egyptian languages. However, several of the major Berber dialects are almost mutually incomprehensible, and the result has been a long history of rivalry and conflict among the major groupings. Like the Arabs themselves, some Berbers were camel nomads, a greater number were seminomads, and the largest number were settled in villages and towns. The pastoral and village Berbers had always remained little touched by Roman and Byzantine culture, but urban Berbers had assimilated to it. This was especially the case in the beautiful and prosperous areas of northern Tunisia and eastern Algeria, the Roman province of Africa Proconsularis. Under the Arabs, this province would become known as Ifriqiya.

The coastal areas of the Maghrib were largely Christian. In an age when each town had its own bishop, the Maghrib boasted hundreds of bishops who had great influence in the Church-wide councils that created the doctrinal basis of Christianity. Luminaries such as Tertullian (c. 160–c. 220) and Augustine of Hippo (354–430) established Africa Proconsularis as a major center of Christian activity. Carthage was one of the major churches in the Christian world during the third and fourth centuries. During the fourth and fifth centuries, however, a major controversy broke out within the North African Church that opened ethnic and social cleavages, leaving the Christian community bitterly divided on the eve of Muslim expansion.

During the second half of the seventh century, the Maghrib became a venue for raids by Arabs stationed in Egypt. Under Mu'awiya, the Umayyads launched larger raids into Byzantine North Africa in the 660s and 670s, coordinated with their attacks on Constantinople. A notable accomplishment of these raids was the creation in 668 of a headquarters at Qayrawan (Kairouan), which eventually became one of the most important cities in North Africa. The raiders were not, however, able to capture Byzantine cities or subdue the Berber tribesmen during this period.

The first major invasion did not take place until 693. Although the army captured Carthage, it was soon expelled by tribal forces. A second invasion in 698 was more successful. In that year, the Muslim army destroyed Carthage, and during the period 705–714, the Maghribi governor, Musa ibn Nusayr, overran areas to the west all the way to the Atlantic. Musa owed much of his success to Berber tribesmen, many of whom converted to Islam during the 690s and joined his army. Unlike the sedentary Berbers, numerous nomadic Berbers from the coastal plains formally adopted Islam (albeit with a considerable admixture of folk religion) by the end of the seventh century. North Africa may well have been the most Islamized of the conquered areas by that time. Thousands of nomadic Berbers joined the conquering Muslim armies. Although they were not paid a stipend as the Arabs were, the Berber warriors were allowed to share in the distribution of the plunder of the conquests, unlike the non-Arabs in the Muslim armies of the east. Many Berbers became high-ranking civil and military officers in the new administrative system.

Before Musa had even consolidated his position in the Maghrib, he received an unexpected appeal from the Visigothic royal family of the Iberian Peninsula for support against a usurper named Roderick. The Visigoths had crossed the Pyrenees 300 years earlier as one of the Germanic tribes that harassed the western half of the Roman Empire. They managed to subdue the entire peninsula by the 630s, when Muhammad was consolidating his position at Medina. They had long been influenced by Roman culture, and they provided patronage to those who produced it. The great Latin scholar Isidore of Seville (c. 560–636) was a beneficiary of such cultural largesse. Initially maintaining a clear division between themselves and the much larger Hispano–Roman population, the Visigoths gradually adopted legal and religious policies during the seventh century that appeared to be creating a stable society. The economy, however, remained dangerously dependent on a weak agricultural sector that proved to be vulnerable to recurring droughts during the seventh and early eighth centuries. The famines and social unrest that resulted provoked the formation of factions within the military elite, causing great instability within the regime. The Jews, who had already been persecuted by the Visigoths, now became scapegoats for the growing unrest, and many were tortured, enslaved, and forced to convert to Christianity. The political crisis reached its peak in 710, when a military officer named Roderick seized the throne. A faction within the royal family appealed to Musa for aid to overthrow him.

In 711, Musa sent an army under the command of Tariq ibn Ziyad from Morocco to the Iberian Peninsula. Tariq ferried his army across the strait that connects the Mediterranean with the Atlantic. The strait is flanked by two promontories that the ancients called the Pillars of Hercules. The Muslims, however, renamed the one in Morocco *Jabal Musa* ("Mountain of Musa"), and they began calling the one in Iberia *Jabal Tariq* ("Mountain of Tariq"), which is the origin of the name by which we know it today: Gibraltar.

After organizing his troops in Iberia, Tariq devastated Roderick's forces. Whatever Musa's intentions for the expedition may have been, the campaign rapidly became one of conquest. The largely Berber force swept across the disorganized peninsula with surprising ease, subjugating the bulk of it within five years. The invaders met little resistance from the inhabitants of most areas; members of the substantial Jewish population actively aided them by serving in garrisons that were assigned the responsibility to preserve order in captured cities. By 720, the Iberian Peninsula had been pacified, except for a small area in the mountainous north called Asturias.

FIGURE 2.1   The view of Jabal Musa across the Strait of Gibraltar from the Iberian Peninsula.

Dmytro Surkov / Alamy Stock Photo.

Transoxiana and the Indus River Valley

Some towns in Khorasan took advantage of the civil war between 'Ali and Mu'awiya (656–661) to assert their independence, but they were almost immediately recaptured. In order to secure its position, the Arab army in the region captured Herat in 660, extending the empire's frontier considerably eastward. Khorasan was a wealthy province. As the Sasanians had known, it was the front line in the defense against Central Asian nomads, who typically invaded through the Transoxiana corridor. Control of distant Khorasan was a priority of the new Umayyad dynasty, which made the decision to settle the region with a reliable Arab population. In 671, Mu'awiya ordered a massive colonization effort that resulted in the settlement of 50,000 Arab warriors and their families in Merv. Merv thus reasserted the role that it had played under the Sasanians, serving as the primary garrison city in the east. For the next thirty years, Arabs simultaneously kept the peace in Khorasan while raiding across the Amu Darya for the purpose of looting and keeping the area disorganized, but not of annexing it.

Transoxiana, the target of the looting, had long been a cultural melting pot. Most of the area is desert or semidesert, but it was densely settled in its many oases and along the Amu Darya and Syr Darya river valleys that bordered it on the south and north, respectively. Because of the region's location, it was frequented by merchants from all over Asia, whose activities augmented the wealth derived from agriculture. The two most important cities were Samarqand and Bukhara, which became famous as cosmopolitan centers. Their inhabitants included Zoroastrians, Buddhists, shamanists, Nestorians, and Manichaeans, as well as adherents of other religious traditions. The two cities had a reputation as dynamic cultural centers because of the scholars and artists who were attracted to the stimulation of urban life, and rich merchants coveted the prestige of serving as their patrons.

In 705, the Umayyads began the destructive, ten-year conquest of Transoxiana. They captured Bukhara in 709 after a three-year siege. The ensuing sack of the city resulted in the deaths of thousands of people and the destruction of invaluable manuscripts. In 711–712, the Arabs annexed Khwarazm (the lower reaches of the Amu Darya) and Samarqand. A few years later, they subjugated Farghana (also spelled *Fergana*, the upper valley of the Syr Darya), which today lies in the eastern extremity of Uzbekistan.

The conquest of Sind began almost simultaneously with that of Transoxiana. Sind was the name Arabs gave to the valley of the Indus River and the territories lying to its east and west. It was one of the cradles of civilization, where Mohenjo-daro and other cities flourished about 2600–1900 B.C.E. Like Egypt and Iraq, Sind is a desert in which riverine irrigation produces a large surplus of foodstuffs. Because of the agricultural wealth to be derived from the area, it was contested by neighboring empires; even the Sasanians had extended their control this far east. By the early eighth century, the majority of the population was Buddhist, but newly arrived Hindus were engaged in an aggressive campaign to become the dominant community.

During the first decade of the eighth century, an Arab merchant ship was beached during a storm near the town of Daybul, approximately where modern Karachi is located. Pirates plundered the passengers' possessions and enslaved the women and children. Al-Hajjaj, the Umayyad governor of Iraq, demanded that the local ruler arrange for the release of the captives and the restoration of their property, but was rebuffed. Al-Hajjaj then sent two unsuccessful expeditions against the city, but a third one captured Daybul in 711 after a fierce siege. The army then moved north up the Indus. It captured the city of Multan in 713 after another arduous siege and overthrew the Hindu ruler there. Many of the local Buddhists, like those in other cities that were captured, welcomed the Arabs because they were anxious to be rid of their Hindu rulers, whom they viewed as usurpers. In fact, the bitter sieges of Daybul and Multan were the exceptions in a conquest that was characterized more by voluntary surrenders than by brutality. With the conquest of Multan, the Arabs ruled all of Sind and part of the Punjab, the name given to the area through which five rivers flow to form the headwaters of the Indus. As Muslims were approaching the Pyrenees in Europe, the Umayyads were also setting up a government over the Indus valley, 5000 miles to the east.

Umayyad Administration

Neither Islam nor the Islamic state was fully formed when the Arab armies burst into the Fertile Crescent. Both the religion and the political administration were little more than statements of ideals that would become institutionalized later within a variety of social contexts. The first three caliphs, based in Medina, were in office during a period (632–656) of rapid expansion out of the Arabian Peninsula. The civil war between Mu'awiya and 'Ali forced a temporary cessation of conquests, but Mu'awiya resumed them when he became the caliph in 661. He chose to remain in Damascus, where he had been governor and where his political and military support lay. Thus, Damascus served as the capital of the Umayyad Empire until the Abbasid revolution in 750. Because of the new conquests, immense amounts of treasure flowed into the new capital city, and much of it was invested in new palaces, mosques, fountains, and fortifications. Umayyad princes constructed palaces in the city and on the edge of the Syrian Desert. Although the caliphs and their officials in Damascus attempted to impose uniform policies throughout the empire, the frontiers had become so distant, and the cultures of the new territorial acquisitions were so different from that of the Arabs, that in many cases officials were forced to allow local practices to continue. During the first few centuries of Islamic history, Muslim administrators incorporated elements from Byzantine, Sasanian, and Qur'anic sources, as well as from local customs.

The Caliphate

As we have seen, the Prophet's death in 632 presented the Umma with a leadership crisis. Not only did his followers need a new leader, but they also had to confront the question of the nature of their future leadership. The Qur'an had made it clear that Muhammad was the last of the prophets. His teachings regarding any aspect of individual or collective behavior were accepted without question: His authority extended from the prayer mat to the battlefield. What, then, would be the scope of authority of his successor, since he would not serve in the prophetic role? Moreover, what would be the process of succession? That is, how would his successor be identified, and how would the Prophet's followers acknowledge his authority?

Given the importance of the issues surrounding the new leadership, it is surprising how little we know about them. The account accepted by most Muslims (those who would later be known as Sunnis) relates that Muhammad himself did not name a successor, his death brought about widespread confusion, and three major factions of Muslims were prepared to name their own leaders and go their separate ways. This account suggests that Muslim identity had not yet replaced more particularistic ones, even for Muhammad's earliest converts. Nevertheless, they knew and trusted each other well enough that 'Umar was able to arrange the acceptance of a candidate acceptable to all three groups. The description of how Abu Bakr was selected echoes the mode of succession familiar to tribal society. Upon the death of the chieftain, the most influential members of the tribe would swear allegiance to the most admired and influential member and signify their loyalty to him by clasping his hand. Similarly, 'Umar persuaded those present in the meeting in Medina to accept Abu Bakr by acclamation, and they offered him their handclasp (bay'a). This account is plausible, for it seems reasonable that the mode of selection in 632 would resemble the one with which Muslims were already familiar. As we will discuss in detail in the next chapter, however, the narrative omits mention of an important minority of Muslims—the Shi'ites— who insisted that Muhammad had, in fact, named his cousin 'Ali as his successor.

More baffling in the narratives of this crucial period is the silence regarding the nature of the authority that the Umma vested in the new leader. We do not even know for certain the title with which his followers addressed him. Abu Bakr is said to have been the first *caliph*, a word deriving from the Arabic word *khalifa*. The Arabic term, however, can connote both "deputy" and "successor," which are clearly distinct meanings. Many histories of this period assume that the title of the caliphs was *khalifat rasul Allah*, or "successor of the Prophet of God." Many writers have stressed the political and military responsibilities of the caliph and downplay the spiritual side. No existing document dating from before the mid-eighth century, however, contains the title in question; it first appears only during the caliphate of the Abbasids, the dynasty that overthrew the Umayyads in 750. On the other hand, it is certain that 'Uthman, the Umayyad caliphs, and the early Abbasid caliphs all used as their official title *khalifat Allah*. The latter term conveys the meaning "deputy of God," which suggests considerable spiritual authority. It is difficult to avoid the conclusion that, during the first century of Islamic history, the caliphate was universally believed to have the power to define religious obligations that related to ethics and the ritual of worship, and that caliphs adjudicated difficult religious cases that needed interpretation.

The confusion over the nature of the early caliphate appears to be the result of two important developments in the nature of the institution that we will explore in subsequent chapters. The first was the emergence of a schism within the Umma, clearly apparent by the mid-eighth century, over the nature of caliphal qualifications and authority that led to the distinction between Sunni Muslims and Shi'ite Muslims. The second was the fact that, by the late ninth century, caliphs in fact no longer participated in making religious law. Sunni scholars writing after that time, whose accounts are our primary sources for learning about early Islamic history, wrote from a perspective that has shaped our understanding of the period. They had no experience of a caliph with spiritual authority, and they were hostile to the Shi'ites, who insisted on the need for one.

What is clear is that, from an early time, caliphs were also addressed by the title *amir al-mu'minin*. This is variously translated as "Commander of the Faithful" or "Prince of the Believers." The title denotes no specific functions but can imply supreme military and political power, as well as responsibility for the preservation of the integrity of the religious community. The vast majority of Sunni Muslims have been willing to concede that the first four caliphs fulfilled these functions in admirable form. They generally refer to them as the "rightly guided" caliphs, whose integrity should be the model for all subsequent Muslim leaders. As we will see, the Umayyad caliphs gradually lost the support of important sectors of the Umma. Not only was their dynasty overthrown, but the role of the caliphate was altered as well.

The Administration of Non-Muslims

Within a remarkably short time after Abu Bakr became the caliph in 632, the complexities of the caliphal office multiplied exponentially. Initially responsible for the welfare of a small Arab society, the caliph was suddenly governing a huge, heterogeneous, and complex empire. It is not unrealistic to assume that when Abu Bakr was the caliph, he knew personally a large proportion of the people for whom he was responsible. Within a handful of years, however, any new caliph was confronted with the need to provide security and justice for millions of people scattered over thousands of miles of territory. The conquest was in many ways as unexpected for the Arabs as for the conquered peoples, and the new rulers had to improvise policy. It turned out to be quite simple: Leave the normal routines of life undisturbed for the conquered peoples, collect the taxes, keep the Arab soldiers at a social and religious distance from the natives, and implement the teachings of the Qur'an as fully as possible.

As Abu Bakr's military campaigns consolidated Medina's control over the northern section of the peninsula and entered the frontier zones of neighboring empires, Muslim armies increasingly confronted Christian Arabs. Deep in Syria and Iraq, the armies found that the majority of both the settled and nomadic populations were Christian or Jewish. The accounts of the surrender of Syrian cities were written years after the events in question, and they contain much confusing and contradictory information. In general, however, the impression we get from both the Christian and Muslim chronicles is that the initial phase of the campaign was violent, entailing the pillaging and destruction of property, indiscriminate killing, and the enslavement of considerable numbers of the local population. The visit of the caliph 'Umar ibn al-Khattab to Jerusalem in 638 seems to have marked a turning point in this regard. From that point on, a regularized administration and a more lenient policy characterized relations with the Christian and Jewish populations.

As the conquests became consolidated, Arab rulers found that the administrative policies of the Byzantines and Sasanians offered them contrasting models of governing a multireligious society. Whereas the Byzantine authorities sought to enforce religious uniformity within their realm, the religious pluralism within the Sasanian domain had forced the rulers to develop a practical compromise with their subjects' religious communities. Occasionally, Jews and Christians had even asked the Sasanian government to intervene in quarrels within their communities in order to determine policy regarding doctrine and leadership. By the end of the sixth century, the government had recognized the highest-ranking rabbi in Iraq as the legitimate ruler of the Jewish community. He was responsible for the collection of taxes and for the administration of justice (according to Jewish law) within the Jewish community. The Nestorians and Monophysites were also organized as religious communities, and the Nestorians were beginning to administer church law to the entire community. The Sasanian government thus granted a certain degree of autonomy to religious communities and guaranteed them military protection. The quid pro quo was that the non-Iranian, non-Zoroastrian subjects were required to pay a head tax in return for security.

The Arabs found the Sasanian religious policy to be more relevant to their needs than the Byzantine model. The Qur'an could be adduced as evidence that people with their own scriptures should not be persecuted; Muslims were a tiny minority within their own empire and could hardly expect to emulate the Byzantine persecution of other faiths; and Sasanian policy offered a welcome source of revenue from non-Muslims. The Arabs referred to Jews and Christians by the Prophet's term, "People of the Book." They were allowed, and expected, to continue practicing their religion. They and other non-Muslims who possessed their own scriptures and paid taxes to the Muslims for protection were called the *ahl al-dhimma*, meaning "protected peoples." A person who belonged to such a community was a *dhimmi*. Dhimmis were often retained as local officials in conquered areas, without regard to their religious

FIGURE 2.2 Relief figures within the stucco dome of the audience hall of Hisham's Palace (734) on the West Bank.

PRISMA ARCHIVO / Alamy Stock Photo.

affiliation. Even devotees of religions that might appear to be compromised by polytheism were often granted the status of protected peoples. The Zoroastrians of Iran, the Buddhists of Central Asia and Sind, and the Hindus of Sind were initially persecuted because of their polytheism, but most such communities became the beneficiaries of a laissez-faire religious policy.

The earliest treaties that the Muslims signed with cities in Syria and Iraq suggest that the entire city was responsible for paying a tribute to the central government. It was not long before these terms were revised so that <u>dh</u>immis were assessed an individual head tax (*jizya*). Also, because they were initially land owners and Muslims were not, <u>dh</u>immis paid taxes on their land and other property as well as the head tax. Policies toward <u>dh</u>immis varied according to period and place across the huge empire. For example, despite the concept that non-Muslims were paying taxes in return for protection, they could, and did, serve in the army during the period of conquest. Their services in some cases were so critical that certain governors refused to allow them to return to civilian life. In general, life for <u>dh</u>immis continued as before. Even on such issues as the drinking of wine or the eating of pork, both of which are forbidden to Muslims, the authorities rarely interfered with such practices as long as the <u>dh</u>immis did not try to sell those items to Muslims.

On the whole, non-Muslims received much better treatment than Jews did in Europe from the medieval period on, although we will see that circumstances arose that could make life difficult for them. Throughout history, the same factors have affected the relationship between Muslims and other religious groups as those affecting the relationship between religious and ethnic groups anywhere in the world: the health of the economy, the sense of personal security that people feel, the attitudes of the leading members of the regime, and the political and military relationship between the society in question and its neighbors. The large number of Christians and Jews living in Muslim-majority lands on the eve of the twentieth century was a testament to the modus vivendi that Muslims, Christians, and Jews were able to achieve (the twentieth century introduced unprecedented strains on the social cohesion of those countries).

The Administration of Muslims

From the beginning of the conquests, Muslim Arabs differentiated themselves from their subjects both ethnically and religiously. They sought to institutionalize those differences through the enactment of regulations that would keep Arabs and non-Arabs in separate social spheres. In many cases, those efforts conflicted with their attempts to implement the religious injunctions of the Qur'an into their own daily life.

Arab Warriors

One of the most pressing concerns for the Muslim leadership was controlling the movements of the Arabs who made up the bulk of the conquering army. On the one hand, it was essential to prevent them from assimilating into the conquered territories. If they became settled into the majority culture and economy, their military skills would be compromised and they would not be able to respond instantly to a mobilization order. On the other hand, their very unruliness needed to be controlled in order not to disturb the social order. It appears that 'Umar was the caliph who created the basic framework for dealing with Arab troops. First, he created garrison towns—Kufa and Basra in Iraq, and Fustat in Egypt were the best known—that were designed to house Arab soldiers and their families. The garrison cities were strategically located: They were easily accessible from Arabia in order to facilitate further Arab migration; they were in forward positions in order to facilitate future conquests; and they were on the margins of the settled areas of the newly conquered territories, which discouraged interaction between the Arabs and the local inhabitants.

Muhammad's practice in his military campaigns had been to award four-fifths of the plunder captured in raids to the troops and retain one-fifth for administrative purposes. The first caliphs continued this policy in the early conquests. But as the frontiers expanded, regular campaigning was more difficult to maintain, and the spoils of war could not be relied on to provide a steady income. Another method of subsistence had to be devised to supplement the plunder and keep the troops content. 'Umar seems to have been responsible for beginning the awarding of regular pay to the troops and promising them a share in the revenue of abandoned lands. The amount to be paid to an individual was determined by how long he had been involved in the campaigns. Those who fought for Medina in the Ridda Wars and initial conquests received more than those who began in the last stages of the Iraqi campaign. After the battle of Nahavand in 642, 'Umar equalized the stipends of the latecomers with those of the veterans. Reflecting Sasanian military policy, members of the cavalry were paid twice or even three times that of the infantry. The attraction of the share in the spoils of victory and the security of regular pay encouraged Arabs from the peninsula to migrate to the garrison cities.

Non-Arab Converts

The ruling elite of the Umayyad dynasty never fully came to terms with the fact that Islam might be attractive to non-Arabs. Islam had begun as a religion for the Arabs. It arose in Arabia, the revelation was delivered in the Arabic language, and it was Arabs who conquered in the cause of Islam. Many Arabs seemed surprised that non-Arabs began to convert to Islam, and they became annoyed when non-Arab Muslims insisted on being treated equally with the Arabs on the grounds of Islamic brotherhood. It was one thing to regard members of other Arab tribes as having a claim to equal treatment, but quite another for non-Arabs to claim such rights. The claims of the non-Arabs challenged not only the ethnic prejudice of the Arabs, but also the viability of the tax policy that had been devised for the new empire. To try to accommodate the non-Arab Muslims, the Arabs allowed them to become clients (*mawali*) of Arab tribes, much as the bedouin had long done for the practitioners of low-status, but essential, occupations, such as metalworking and the tanning of leather.

Most of the mawali during the early Umayyad period came from the huge number of prisoners of war captured during the conquests. Some of them became slaves of the conquerors, but most were freed. Some found that they could not return home, and others decided that the fastest route to social mobility was to assimilate into Arab culture and society. Despite the efforts of the mawali to assimilate, the majority of Arabs would not accept them as social equals. Normally, even if they fought in the armies, they were given neither pay nor a share in the spoils of war, because their adopted tribe was supposed to support them. When the military campaigns became as distant as Transoxiana and North Africa, military commanders felt compelled to share the plunder with their soldiers who were non-Arab converts. The unequal treatment regarding pay and the constant humiliation of taunts and discriminatory behavior, however, caused their resentments to build.

Over the years, more and more rural individuals and families converted to Islam. In village societies where religion is the primary identity marker, conversion to another religion can be inferred by others as a rejection of one's family or heritage. It is not uncommon for families to disown, and for neighbors to shun, someone who has converted to an outside religion. This pattern seems to have been the case with particular relevance to Iraq and Khorasan. The social isolation that converts to Islam experienced in their villages could often be intolerable, and as a result, many migrated to cities, where they could practice their religion in a Muslim-majority environment. Their departure from the village meant that the collective tax obligation fell more heavily on the remaining villagers, causing them considerable economic difficulty. In areas where a significant percentage of the population converted, a tax crisis occurred. The remaining villagers could not pay the collective sum, and many more peasants fled the land, leaving lands uncultivated. Arab chroniclers report that, by the last quarter of the seventh century, the large number of Iraqi peasants fleeing the villages and converting to Islam prompted the governor, al-Hajjaj, to send the new converts back to the land and to forbid further conversions.

Regulating Women's Roles

The development of Islamic norms for women has been a controversial issue. Little is known about the status of women in pre-Islamic Arabia or even in the Byzantine and Sasanian empires in the seventh century, making it difficult to assess the impact of Islam in any of those areas. Early Arabic chronicles provide little information regarding the roles and activities of women. Because the sources were written by literate men, the material that we do have focuses on the activities of women of the ruling class. At present, we have only tantalizing clues regarding the early norms for women's roles and status.

From the evidence available to us, it appears that women in early seventh-century Arabia participated quite freely in public life. Khadija, the Prophet's first wife, owned property, sought out Muhammad for marriage, and was sufficiently influential in Mecca to serve as a protector for his early career. On the other hand, when she died, Muhammad was reduced to poverty, suggesting that Khadija's property reverted by custom to relatives and was not hers to dispose of. Other women served as prophets and soothsayers, and in the battles between Mecca and Medina, women appeared on the battlefield to jeer the enemy, mutilate the bodies of wounded and dead enemy soldiers, and even use the sword and bow in combat. Female critics of the Prophet were not hesitant to belittle him publicly. Marriage and divorce practices varied considerably across the peninsula. Some tribes were matrilineal (descent was traced through the females) and others patrilineal; some tribes practiced polygyny (multiple wives), whereas others practiced polyandry (multiple husbands). Men often referred to their wives as their "property," and some scholars think that women had no right of divorce. Others point out that some women did divorce their husbands, and these scholars assume that women initiated divorce equally with men.[1]

The Qur'an contains some verses that appear to represent increased opportunities for women under Islam, whereas others seem to curb activity that had been possible earlier. One famous Qur'anic teaching is that Muslim men are allowed to have up to four wives if they treat them equitably (4:3). Some commentators infer that the limit on the number of wives that a man may have represents a gain for women, assuming that in the pre-Islamic era a man may have had an unlimited number of wives. Others argue that the verse is an exhortation to Muslim men after the battle of Uhud to marry more than one woman because the high battle losses had resulted in a surplus of women, who were economically vulnerable. The Qur'an specifies that a bridegroom must give his bride a dower (a negotiated amount of property for the bride), which she keeps with her, regardless of the fate of the marriage. The Qur'an also guarantees women a share of their family's inheritance equal to one-half that of their brothers. Again, many commentators think that both developments represent an advance in the rights of women. The dower served as an economic buffer in the event of divorce, and it compensated the woman for the smaller share of inheritance that she received compared to her brothers. The guarantee of a specified amount of inherited property gave women an economic security that women in most parts of Europe and the United States did not have until the late nineteenth century. Many of those European and American women not only had no legal property rights but also had to bring a dowry (the bride's contribution) to the marriage.

The Qur'an devotes considerable attention to the topic of relations between the sexes. It provides husbands with guidance on how to deal with recalcitrant wives (4:34–35) and how, if necessary, to divorce them. When the Qur'an treats the topic of divorce, it addresses men only (see 2:226–237, 241; 65:1–7). It goes into some detail on the fair—and even generous—way to treat a divorced wife, but it does not address the issue of a woman who wishes to divorce her husband.

The Qur'an also addresses the issue of modesty, and subsequent interpretations of those verses have had an important influence on Muslim life for centuries. The issue arose initially as a problem within the Prophet's own household. The Prophet's home in Medina became the gathering place of more and more people as the community grew. It had a large courtyard around which his wives' apartments were placed, and the courtyard itself served as Medina's first congregational mosque. Inevitably, some people began to treat the courtyard as public space, without consideration for the privacy of the family. Some would show up at the Prophet's door uninvited. Others, like guests throughout history, would fail to notice when it was time to go home after a dinner or wedding feast, with awkward consequences for the family. Still others would seek out the apartments of the Prophet's wives in order to deliver a petition, in the hope of having access to the Prophet himself. The revelation of 33:53–59 instructs the community to respect the privacy of the Prophet's house and to speak to his wives only from behind a curtain or screen. Another revelation (or perhaps a cluster of revelations) that seems to have been sent soon after this one is 24:27–32, which repeats the injunction to ask permission before entering a house. The passage adds that men and women alike must lower their eyes when encountering others and guard their private parts. Women were to cover their bosoms with veils and to refrain from showing off their beauty, except to close relatives.

The text of the Qur'an specifies that the Prophet's wives were to be veiled and secluded from the harassment that the celebrity status of their husband had brought upon them. On the other hand, the Prophet's favorite wife, 'A'isha, continued to play an active role in political life for several decades after his death. When and how veiling and seclusion became extended from the Prophet's wives to Muslim women in general is unknown, but it almost certainly required many decades to become normative.

Many historians suspect that the influence of Sasanian and Byzantine customs played an important role in the development of Islamic norms regarding women, but we know practically nothing about what was expected of Sasanian women. Byzantine women of the era were not secluded in their homes and were not subject to rigid dress codes. On the other hand, it was expected that women of the higher Byzantine social classes would wear a veil and not frequent the streets. Observers were shocked when they did happen to see a woman of high status without a veil. What is of importance in this regard is that such expectations were held of women among the elite social classes. It should be noted that the veiling and seclusion of women has never been universal among Muslims, either. Some (admittedly small) Muslim groups throughout history have rejected the practice outright, and it has always been more common among the wealthy urban social strata than among the poor and the rural population. Like the bound feet of aristocratic Chinese women, wearing a veil and seclusion within the home were declarations that a woman did not have to engage in manual labor. We shall see in later chapters how the development of Islamic law and the influx of new ethnic groups into the Umma affected the roles and status of women.

The Rationalization of Society

For the first half-century or more after the Arab conquests, subject peoples noticed very few changes in their lives. The ruling elites in the various territories were new, to be sure, but they did not have a social blueprint that they wished to impose on their subjects. This was due in part to the fact that Islamic institutions were still not fully formed and in part to the fact that continued military expansion remained the priority for the Arab leadership. In huge areas of the empire, the officials with whom the general public had to deal remained reassuringly familiar. The Iranian *dihqan*s, or lesser nobility, were the state's tax collectors in former Sasanian territories for the first half-century of Arab occupation. Christians and Jews continued to hold high administrative positions for many years in Iraq, and in Egypt the Coptic community maintained a monopoly on the accounting staff in the tax division until the late nineteenth century. In like manner, Persian continued to serve as the language of administration in former Sasanian territories, and Greek continued to be used in former Byzantine holdings.

FIGURE 2.3 The shrine of the Dome of the Rock in Jerusalem, built by the caliph 'Abd al-Malik (685–705). Its style was influenced by Byzantine architectural models.

Rafael Ben-Ari / Alamy Stock Photo.

A notable example of the appropriation of existing offices was that of the official that Muslims called the *muhtasib*. The first muhtasib appeared in Syria, but Muslim societies all the way to the Atlantic soon had one. The muhtasib clearly served the function of the Byzantine *agoranomos*, or market inspector, as well as the *astynomos*, a public health official whose primary function was to maintain streets in passable condition. The muhtasib's duties included the prohibition of the disposal of market and household refuse in the streets and the encroachment of buildings into public space. As the market inspector, he made sure that scales were accurate and that customers were not cheated by unscrupulous merchants. This official was so critical to the maintenance of a smoothly functioning urban society that the office remained active for over a thousand years.

Despite their own proud military tradition, the Arabs recognized advantages in the Sasanian military organization, supply, tactics, and arms, and they borrowed directly from them. Likewise, the organization of the civilian government borrowed heavily from the Sasanians, first at the provincial level and later (especially after the Umayyad period) in the imperial administration. Sasanian royal traditions of justice, court procedure, control, and enforcement were to prove highly influential in shaping Islamic institutions.

Sasanian and Byzantine legacies continued to shape Islamic history for many centuries to come. In some ways, Sasanian influence on the army and the central government became even more important in the eighth and ninth centuries. On the other hand, the last decade of the seventh century marks an important milestone in the Umayyad government's development of its Arabic and Islamic identity. Until that time, Muslim authorities had not bothered to mint new coins. Not only had they continued to use existing officials, policies, and official languages, but they also had allowed Byzantine and Sasanian coins to continue circulating. The caliph 'Abd al-Malik (685–705) valued many of the cultural appropriations from the Byzantines and Sasanians, but he was determined to establish an explicitly Islamic and Arab identity for his regime. First, he began constructing monumental buildings that symbolized the triumph of Islam over Judaism and Christianity. (The shrine called the Dome of the Rock in Jerusalem is the most famous of his buildings.) Second, he began minting gold coins that bore Arabic inscriptions to replace the Sasanian and Byzantine coins that had been used to that time. This innovation had great symbolic and ideological value, for the high-quality Umayyad coins would soon become prized all over the known world. Third, 'Abd al-Malik inaugurated a policy of converting the language of administration to Arabic.

'Abd al-Malik's process of Arabization took many years—it would be another fifty years before the chancelleries of Khorasan were transformed from the Persian language to the Arabic, and the Coptic accountants in the financial bureaus of Egypt maintained their arcane registry system for more than a millennium. But as a result of 'Abd al-Malik's policy, Arabic became the preeminent language of written communication in administration, literature, and religion over the vast region that the Arabs had conquered. It also became the majority language spoken west of the Iranian plateau. The Arabizing and Islamizing policies of 'Abd al-Malik's administration allow us to identify the 690s as a watershed in the cultural history of the area. From then on, visitors to the area knew that a new civilization was emerging.

Dissolution of the Arab Empire

In the early, heady days of conquest, the Arab leaders seemed to have found the formula for accomplishing their goals of extending the dominion of God's rule, the channeling of the martial culture of the peninsula toward external enemies rather than allowing it to disrupt Muslim society and the acquisition of a steady source of revenue. They could be forgiven for assuming that rapid expansion and the enormous inflow of plunder and taxes would continue indefinitely. This euphoria soon faded as the frontiers moved farther away and the issues of Muslim identity became more complicated.

As early as the battle of Nahavand (642), it became clear that further conquests would be less rewarding than the early ones. Syria, Iraq, and Egypt were wealthy, adjacent to Arabia, and relatively flat. As a result, their acquisition had provided a high return on the investment of troops and effort. Nahavand, however, was in the Zagros Mountains and, like the remaining conquests to the east, north, and west, it was hundreds of miles from the Muslim capital. It was beginning to dawn on Muslim administrators that further conquests would be in mountainous areas or across vast deserts, and usually against peoples who were not as wealthy as the victims of the first wave of conquests. Inhabitable North Africa was a thin strip two thousand miles in length but only a few miles wide; the Byzantines in Anatolia were Greek and much more loyal to the regime than the inhabitants of Syria and Egypt had been; and the Iranian highlands had wealth, but the area was conquered only after terrible fighting. The great wave of expansion in the second decade of the eighth century—the conquest of Iberia, Sind, and Transoxiana—was lucrative, but it came and went very quickly. No more conquests of significance were made, and yet spending was lavish in order to support irrigation projects, monumental building, a huge army, and extravagant palaces for Umayyad princes. As early as the caliphate of 'Umar II (717–720), the empire was facing major financial problems.

Another challenge facing the Umma by the early eighth century was social tension arising from the accelerated pace of assimilation within the empire. Much of the assimilation took place, ironically, in the garrison cities. As we have seen, the early Muslim leaders created these cities for Arab warriors during the first wave of conquest. Kufa, Basra, Fustat and other new military cities had several purposes. In them, army commanders could control the movements of their nomadic warriors, the presence of the army of occupation would intimidate subject populations, and the cities were convenient staging points for further military campaigns. Not the least of the goals was the shielding of Muslim soldiers from the corrupting influences of the non-Islamic environment. The policy of segregating the Muslim Arabs from their new environment proved to be unworkable. The clustering of thousands of troops in hastily constructed cities attracted large numbers of indigenous inhabitants who offered the troops highly desirable goods and services. These local immigrants came from a variety of ethnic and religious backgrounds, and they mixed socially with the Arabs. Inevitably, some Arabs intermarried with them despite the disapproval of many of their peers. A slowly growing number of Muslims in these cities were, therefore, the offspring of unions between Arab Muslim fathers and mothers who were Christian, Jewish, or Zoroastrian. Multilingual and multicultural, this group of second-generation Muslims felt at ease with elements from both the local and the Arab cultures.

Far from the garrison cities, on the distant frontier province of Khorasan, the assimilation of Arabs into local society was even more evident. The mass Arab colonization of Khorasan in 671 had entailed the relocation of 50,000 Arab troops and their families from Iraq. This enormous population transfer meant that, overnight, Khorasan had the third largest Arab population outside Arabia, after Iraq and Syria. Many of the settlers were already married, but many others now married Iranian women. Social assimilation progressed rapidly as Iranians converted to Islam and Arabs adopted local customs. The Arabs of Khorasan became landowners and merchants, began dressing like Iranians, and learned to speak Persian dialects. An Arab landowning class came into being whose members were reluctant to assume the military duties their fathers and grandfathers had welcomed.

By the end of the seventh century, many Muslim Arabs were "going native," while increasing numbers of non-Arabs were becoming Muslims. By serving in the military on crucial fronts, the mawali diluted the Arab nature of what had originally been an all-Arab force. In Khorasan, Iranians made up a large proportion of the military units that engaged in the conquest and defense of the Amu Darya frontier, and in North Africa and the Iberian Peninsula, Berbers constituted a majority of the military units. New converts were beginning to question the rationale for Arab social dominance as mixed communities containing Arabs and non-Arabs emerged in cities scattered all over the empire. With the passage of time, the ethnic slurs they received from some Arabs and the unequal distribution of revenue granted to non-Arabs became less tolerable.

The assimilation taking place in the garrison cities of Iraq and the Arab colonies in Khorasan was producing a new type of Muslim society that stood in stark relief to the Arab identity of the Muslims of Arabia and Syria. Arabia and Syria still lived by a tribal ethos, and the caliphs, with rare exceptions, were dependent on the loyalty of certain Arab tribes for their power. For the most part, the leadership seems to have failed to recognize the changes that were taking place, and only rarely did they make any attempt to address the new social realities. The first Arab civil war of 'Ali and Mu'awiya was followed by an even more destructive conflict from 685 to 692 that resulted from the development of tribal coalitions and the struggle for power that ensued upon the death of Mu'awiya in 680. The caliph 'Abd al-Malik, who had to fight that civil war from the time of his accession in 685, relied on Arab immigrants to Syria for his support. For that reason, the Umayyad army developed a well-deserved reputation as a "Syrian" army. Tensions between the Syrian-supported Umayyads and the garrison cities became so great that, in 701, 'Abd al-Malik created yet another garrison city, located between Kufa and Basra. Named Wasit, it was staffed by Syrian soldiers and was patently an effort to control and intimidate the Arabs of the two older garrison cities, whose multicultural ideas and actions were becoming irksome to the ruling elite. Later Umayyad caliphs tended to rely on one or another Syrian tribe for military support, with the result that even the Syrian Arabs became splintered into factions.

The caliph 'Umar II (717–720) attempted to address the resentments of both the mawali and the assimilated Arabs toward the Syrian elites, as well as the growing financial problems of the empire. He ended the practice of having mawali pay the head tax that was required of non-Muslims, and he ordered that all Muslims serving in the army be paid an equal stipend, regardless of ethnicity. He also removed the Syrian garrisons from Iraq. To the dismay of non-Muslims, he ordered all religious images, including Jewish and Christian ones, to be destroyed, and he forbade non-Muslims from wearing silk clothing and turbans. He seems to have been the first Muslim ruler to have instituted social distinctions between Muslims and non-Muslims based on the style of dress. He also ordered a halt to the wars of conquest, apparently with the objective of saving money, and he reorganized the caliphal finances in an effort both to economize and to eradicate corruption.

Those who benefited from the policies of 'Umar II had little time to rejoice. When he died in 720, all of his major policies were quickly reversed. Local governors resumed their raids and conquests, and some successes were recorded. From Sind, the Arabs invaded India and plundered the whole of Gujarat. These gains were rapidly lost, however, when Indian princes counterattacked. By 729, the Arab presence in Sind was threatened with extinction. In Europe, Muslims crossed the Pyrenees in the 720s and captured Narbonne, Carcassonne, and Nîmes, with the result that Muslims controlled the coast from the Pyrenees to the Rhône River in modern France. In Iberia, quarreling among Arab factions precluded further expansion into Europe for half a decade, but the Muslim successes north of the Pyrenees had alarmed Eudo, the Duke of Aquitaine. He joined forces with a Berber chieftain who was rebelling against the Arab governor of Iberia. The governor, however, defeated the duke and his Berber allies and began moving north, sacking churches and monasteries. Eudo called for aid from his former rival, the Frankish warrior Charles Martel, who met and defeated the Arab forces between Tours and Poitiers, probably in October 733[2].

The Arrival of al-Hajjaj in Kufa (694–695)

The Arab garrison cities were notorious for their unruliness, but none was more troublesome to the Umayyad authorities than Kufa. In 656, 'Ali had found his base of support there, and after his murder, it remained a center of opposition to Mu'awiya's dynasty. In 694, the Umayyad caliph 'Abd al-Malik appointed al-Hajjaj (661–714) to be the governor of Iraq. Al-Hajjaj had won a reputation for absolute loyalty to the Umayyads and for great brutality in suppressing revolts against the dynasty. As governor of Iraq, he proved to be an administrator of great ability, implementing many policies that promoted economic prosperity and sending out the expedition that conquered Sind in 711–713. The selection that follows is from his first speech as governor. It is one of the most famous speeches in early Muslim history, and several versions of it survive, with only slight variations.

Al-Hajjaj set out for Iraq as governor, with 1200 men mounted on thoroughbred camels. He arrived in Kufa unannounced, early in the day…. Al-Hajjaj went straight to the mosque, and with his face hidden by a red silk turban, he mounted the pulpit and said, "Here, people!" They thought that he and his companions were Kharijites and were

(Continued)

concerned about them. When the people were assembled in the mosque he rose, bared his face, and said:

I am the son of splendor, the scaler of high places.
When I take off my turban you know who I am.

By God, I shall make evil bear its own burden; I shall shoe it with its own sandal and recompense it with its own like. I see heads before me that are ripe and ready for plucking, and I am the one to pluck them, and I see blood glistening between the turbans and the beards.

By God, O people of Iraq, people of discord and dissembling and evil character! I cannot be squeezed like a fig or scared like a camel with old water skins. My powers have been tested and my experience proved, and I pursue my aim to the end. The Commander of the Faithful emptied his quiver and bit his arrows and found me the bitterest and hardest of them all. Therefore he aimed me at you. For a long time now you have been swift to sedition; you have lain in the lairs of error and have made a rule of transgression. By God, I shall strip you like bark, I shall truss you like a bundle of twigs, I shall beat you like stray camels. Indeed, you are like the people of "a village which was safe and calm, its sustenance coming in plenty from every side, and they denied the grace of God, and God let them taste the garment of hunger and of fear for what they had done" (Qur'an, xvi, 112). By God, what I promise, I fulfill; what I purpose, I accomplish; what I measure, I cut off. Enough of these gatherings and this gossip and "he said" and "it is said!" What do you say? You are far away from that! I swear by God that you will keep strictly to the true path, or I shall punish every man of you in his body.

And then he went to his house.

Source: *Islam from the Prophet Muhammad to the Capture of Constantinople. Vol 1: Politics and War* by Bernard Lewis (1974): 401 words from pp. 23–24. © 1974 by Bernard Lewis. By permission of Oxford University Press USA.

The Battle of Tours/Poitiers was an important achievement for Martel, but it was not, as many Europeans have claimed, the decisive blow that stopped Muslim expansion into Europe. Muslims continued to plunder the lower Rhône valley with impunity throughout the remainder of the decade. They captured Arles and other cities until Martel intervened in 739, taking the area for his kingdom. Muslim conquests had always been a matter first of reconnoitering and then of raids that, if successful, resulted in expeditions of conquest. In that sense, Martel's accomplishment can be seen as slamming the door shut on raiding the interior of Frankish territory. However, it had been clear for almost a decade before Tours that the Muslims' supply and communications lines were overextended whenever they crossed the Pyrenees on a raid.

The conquest of "Frankland" was the farthest object from any Muslim's mind. The halt to Muslim expansion into Europe owed much more to internal factors than to Martel's victory in 732. Factional fighting among the Arabs of Iberia in the

FIGURE 2.4 The Umayyad Mosque of Damascus (715), whose architecture influenced many other mosques over the following centuries.

imageBROKER / Alamy Stock Photo.

720s led to extended periods of anarchy there; officials in Qayrawan, the regional capital of both the Maghrib and Iberia, had no interest in dissipating their resources against the Franks; Berber revolts in Iberia and the Maghrib in the 740s ended Umayyad control in those areas; and the overthrow of the Umayyad dynasty itself in 750 led to a wholesale reordering of the administration of the western Muslim world. No one was surprised when Pepin the Short (son of Charles Martel and father of Charlemagne) recaptured Narbonne in 751, ending the Muslim presence in Provence. Muslims, however, continued to raid southern Europe for centuries to come, by land and by sea.

Court officials in Damascus paid little attention to developments in the west. The focus for the caliph's court was on a large number of military campaigns directed toward the north and east during the period 729–740. The frenetic pace of the expeditions suggests that the regime was trying to resolve the empire's financial crisis by means of acquiring plunder. Few gains were registered, and several catastrophic military failures occurred, particularly on the fronts in the Caucasus and Transoxiana. Tens of thousands of Arabs lost their lives in ill-planned battles, and Muslim rulers lost control over large areas on those frontiers. By 741, the Caucasus, Transoxiana, and Sind were again securely in Muslim hands, but for reasons due more to the weakness of the Umayyads' opponents than to Umayyad policy. Rather than producing revenue, the campaigning was extremely expensive and resulted in even graver economic problems. During the administration of the caliph Hisham (724–743), the Umayyad army numbered perhaps 400,000 troops,[3] and the plunder with which to reward them had largely dried up. Periodically, soldiers on most of the major fronts—in Sind, the Caucasus, and Transoxiana—expressed their displeasure at the relentless campaigning, sometimes in the form of ousting and killing their commanders.

In addition to the deepening financial crisis, another problem for the Umayyads was that the mawali showed their anger at having had their financial disabilities reimposed after the death of 'Umar II in 720. In Transoxiana and North Africa, they rose in revolt almost immediately upon the death of 'Umar II. The simmering resentment broke out again a decade later in a major rebellion in Khorasan, in which both Iranians and Arabs participated. Twenty thousand Syrian troops had to be brought in to quell the uprising. The biggest outburst, however, began in 740 in North Africa, with the outbreak of the Great Berber Revolt. Policies toward the Berbers had varied from governor to governor, but after 720 Berbers had more reasons to resent Arabs than appreciate them. They had never been paid military stipends, and now they were sometimes denied a share in the captured plunder; Muslim Berbers (especially females) were often taken as slave tribute to the East; and unprincipled Arab generals and governors frequently seized Berber property. The revolt of 740 took place simultaneously in several locations in North Africa, and it spread into Iberia. Thousands of Arab troops were sent to those two areas to try to suppress the rebellion, but the Umayyads lost the entire region west of Qayrawan. Qayrawan itself was retained by the Arab governor, but the rest of North Africa became a collection of quarreling Berber principalities.

When Hisham died in 743 after a caliphate of nineteen years, the empire entered a period of great instability. The expansionist policy was bankrupt both ideologically and financially. The majority non-Muslim population had no stake in it, and by now, many Muslims, as well, had no desire to make sacrifices for it. Many Arabs had lost confidence in expansionism as it had been practiced, and the mawali chafed under a discriminatory policy. The Syrian army on which the Umayyads had traditionally based their power was by now greatly reduced in size: Many of its members had been killed in futile expeditions, and most of the survivors were scattered to trouble spots all over the empire. Intertribal Arab conflicts broke out in Syria, Iraq, and Khorasan, and by the end of the 740s, the Umayyads were both weak and unpopular. The stage was set for the mobilization of a multiethnic revolutionary movement. When it overthrew the Umayyad dynasty in 750, a new era in Muslim history had begun, that of the Abbasid caliphate.

Conclusion

The Umayyads carved out a vast empire that extended from South Asia to Western Europe. This enormous area became the matrix within which the distinctive features of Islam would emerge over the next several centuries. The Arabs who created this empire were a proud and martial people. It may well be that Islam's survival in a new and hostile environment was due in large part to the Arabs' utter self-confidence and their assumption that Islam was exclusively an Arab religion. As the religion of the Arabs, Islam became a feature of their cultural identity that they jealously protected and did not allow to become submerged in the face of challenges from the long-established religions in the vast new empire. The Arabic language, as well, became a vehicle for Arab cultural hegemony. It was the language of the Qur'an; it soon became the language of administration and the lingua franca of commerce; during the next several centuries, it displaced most of the spoken languages between the Iranian plateau and the Atlantic Ocean; and its mesmerizing poetry, with its cadences and rich evocations of the independence and romance of the bedouin lifestyle, inspired subsequent literature, especially that of the Iranian peoples.

In this regard, the Umayyad achievement was monumental, but it was undermined by grave weaknesses that demanded radical solutions. The dynasty never developed a plan for administration other than constant conquest and the exploitation of non-Arabs for the benefit of Arabs. As a result, it failed to address the grievances that its subjects, Arabs and non-Arabs alike, were beginning to express. Tribal favoritism, the conscription of sedentary Arabs for campaigns of conquest, and a failure to develop policies that could accommodate non-Arab Muslims in the Umma became issues that eventually brought the dynasty to an end. Islamic principles of equality and justice became rallying cries against the Umayyad regime and demonstrated that the new religion was a powerful new force on the scene.

NOTES

1   For an indication of the ambiguity of the evidence, compare the differences in interpretation of the status of women in pre-Islamic Arabia found in the following works:

Ahmed, Leila. *Women and Gender in Islam.* New Haven and London: Yale University Press, 1992, 41–45.

Esposito, John L. *Women in Muslim Family Law.* Syracuse, New York: Syracuse University Press, 1982, 14–15, 28–30.

Hoyland, Robert G. *Arabia and the Arabs from the Bronze Age to the Coming of Islam.* New York and London: Routledge, 2001, 128–134.

Levy, Reuben. *The Social Structure of Islam.* Cambridge, U.K.: Cambridge University Press, 1971, 91–97.

2   The date is usually given as 732, but see the discussion in Roger Collins, *The Arab Conquest of Spain, 710–797* (Oxford, U.K.: Basil Blackwell, 1989), 89–91.

3   Blankinship, Khalid Yahya. *The End of the Jihad State: The Reign of Hisham 'Abd al-Malik and the Collapse of the Umayyads.* Albany: State University of New York Press, 1994, 82.

FURTHER READING

General

Hawting, G.R. *The First Dynasty of Islam: The Umayyad Caliphate, A.D. 661–750,* 2d ed. London and New York: Routledge, 2000.

Kennedy, Hugh. *The Prophet and the Age of the Caliphates: The Islamic Near East from the Sixth to the Eleventh Century.* London and New York: Longman, 1986.

Arab Conquests

Abun-Nasr, Jamil M. *A History of the Maghrib*, 2d ed. Cambridge, U.K.: Cambridge University Press, 1975.

Collins, Roger. *The Arab Conquest of Spain, 710–797*. Oxford, U.K.: Basil Blackwell, 1989.

Donner, Fred. *The Early Islamic Conquests*. Princeton, New Jersey: Princeton University Press, 1981.

Hoyland, Robert. *In God's Path: The Arab Conquests and the Creation of an Islamic Empire*. Oxford and New York: Oxford University Press, 2015.

Ikram, S.M. *Muslim Civilization in India*. Ainslie T. Embree, ed. New York and London: Columbia University Press, 1964.

Kaegi, Walter E. *Byzantium and the Early Islamic Conquests*. Cambridge, U.K.: Cambridge University Press, 1992.

Umayyad Administration

Crone, Patricia and Martin Hinds. *God's Caliph: Religious Authority in the First Centuries of Islam*. Cambridge, U.K.: Cambridge University Press, 1986.

Morony, Michael G. *Iraq after the Muslim Conquest*. Princeton, New Jersey: Princeton University Press, 1984.

Dissolution of the Arab Empire

Blankinship, Khalid Yahya. *The End of the Jihād State: The Reign of Hishām ʿAbd al-Malik and the Collapse of the Umayyads*. Albany: State University of New York Press, 1994.

CHAPTER 3

The Development of Sectarianism

The issue of legitimate leadership has been a central concern for Muslims since the death of Muhammad. The figure of the Prophet has cast a long shadow throughout history. Muslims have yearned to have a leader who embodied his qualities but have usually had to settle for men whose ambition and weaknesses only accentuated the contrast with the ideal. The issue of the caliphate was both a political question and one of maintaining the religious integrity of the community. Only fringe groups thought the caliph should have prophetic qualities, but most Muslims were convinced that in some sense he was responsible for continuing to provide religious guidance to the community in the absence of the Prophet.

Because no consensus existed regarding the nature of the caliphate, controversies swirled about the method of selecting the caliphs as well as about the adequacy of the men who were chosen. The quarrels ensured that the first century of Muslim history would be politically unstable. Three of the first four caliphs were murdered; a growing number of Muslims became convinced that the Prophet had chosen 'Ali as his successor and were angry that he was passed over in the selection process the first three times; and revolts began to break out more frequently against the Umayyad caliphs as their regimes became increasingly identified with injustice and corruption.

The debate over the nature of the caliphate had many repercussions. This chapter will revisit the Umayyad period to explore two of them. One was the emergence of divisions within the Umma that eventually crystallized into three major branches of Islam: Shi'ism, Kharijism, and Sunnism. The other was the Abbasid revolution, which resulted in the overthrow of the Umayyads and began a new chapter in Muslim history.

'Ali and the Politics of Division

One of the most recognizable figures in Islamic history is 'Ali, the cousin and son-in-law of the Prophet. His martial skills, dedication to the Prophet's cause, and concern for justice were widely admired. When the Prophet died, some Muslims claimed that Muhammad had formally named 'Ali to be his successor a few months before the former's death. As a result, they regarded the selection of the first three caliphs to be illegitimate. 'Ali finally became caliph in 656, but the circumstances of his coming to power cast the legitimacy of his own caliphate under a cloud of suspicion. His short and tragic career as caliph left a lasting mark on the Umma.

Political Dissension

The Arabs conquered Syria, Iraq, and Egypt during the caliphate of 'Umar. During the decade of his administration (634–644), the task of administering the Umma became vastly more complex than it had been when Abu Bakr was caliph. Many issues became controversial, such as the distribution of plunder, the allocation of revenues from seized land, the awarding of contracts and administrative offices to family members and friends of the ruling elite, and the legitimacy of local customs in the numerous new lands in which Muslims found themselves. The pace of the conquests was so rapid and the number of issues that everyone from the caliph on down had to deal with was so great, that none of the issues boiled to the surface during 'Umar's tenure. He was assassinated in 644, just as the more difficult and less remunerative phase of conquests was beginning. It was the ill fortune of his successor to confront the issues directly.

'Uthman, one of the Prophet's earliest converts, had been highly respected and was a popular choice for the caliphate at the time of 'Umar's murder. He served as caliph during the period 644–656. Overall, Muslims throughout history have held him in respect, particularly for his role in determining a standard version of the Qur'an. According to Islamic tradition, the Qur'an was not collected into its current form until after the Prophet's death. When it was completed, several versions existed. 'Uthman concurred with those Muslims who believed that, since the Qur'an is in fact the word of God, its various written expressions should not differ. He is credited with having named a commission that agreed on a standard text.

In general, 'Uthman's administration was similar to that of 'Umar. Like his predecessor, he awarded lands abandoned by the Sasanian elite to individuals and tribes despite the official policy that such properties should be held in trust for the Umma; he maintained the garrison cities as permanent settlements despite their growing irrelevance as forward outposts and purely Arab enclaves; and he attempted to bring local affairs within the far-flung administrative units increasingly under the supervision of Medina.

Where 'Uthman's administration diverged from previous practice was in its transparent favoritism of Meccan elites. Most of the soldiers in the Muslim armies that conquered Iraq and Egypt were from tribes of lesser status than the Quraysh, but they had been Muslims longer than the Quraysh elite, who had converted after the fall of Mecca. 'Umar had consistently given precedence to warriors who had entered the Muslim armies from the earliest period. They benefitted particularly in Iraq, where they were placed in charge of the revenues of many of the Sasanian royal lands and were named administrators of the province and cities. 'Uthman, by contrast, followed the time-honored tribal practice of appointing his close relatives to important positions. In this case, the offices were leadership positions in all the major provinces as well as the important garrison towns of Kufa and Basra. These

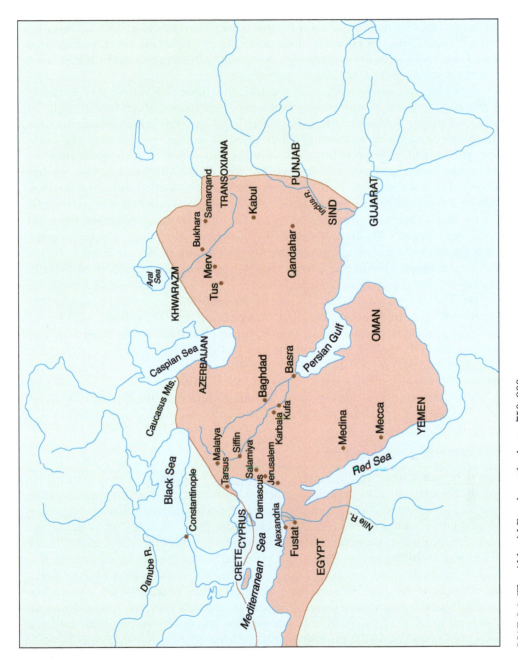

MAP 3.1 The Abbasid Empire at its Apex, 750–900.

leaders, in turn, enacted measures and made appointments that favored the Umayyad clan and the merchants in Mecca who were linked financially with them. As a result, those tribesmen whose status and wealth had risen due to their having been charter members of the Umma now saw their position threatened by the politics of "business as usual." The Umayyad clan and their allies, whose members on the whole had resisted the Prophet as long as possible, were now displacing those who had been the earliest supporters of the Islamic movement.

'Uthman was not intentionally hurting the "older" Muslims. He probably viewed his nepotism as not merely customary—and even obligatory in light of traditional tribal values—but also as necessary in his quest to bring some coherence to the administration of the growing empire. Only by naming people whom he knew and trusted could he hope to bring about uniformity to policy in the same manner that he had brought about uniformity to the text of the Qur'an. Likewise, he felt compelled to make changes in the process of revenue collection, now that the flow of plunder from the conquests had slowed. The traditional one-fifth of the captured treasure that had come to the caliphal coffers for administrative expenses, pensions for widows and early Muslims, and the like, had been shrinking. 'Uthman ended 'Umar's practice of allowing the provinces wide latitude in determining their tax policies and began channeling a larger fraction of the tax proceeds to Medina to make up for the lost revenue from plunder.

Despite 'Uthman's good intentions, by the early 650s important Arab families in Iraq and Egypt had become hostile to his policies, and Kufa, Basra, and Fustat had become centers of discontent. In 656, several hundred Arabs from Iraq and Egypt marched to Medina to protest the new policies before 'Uthman personally. The caliph made no secret of his impatience with the complaints, and some of the protesters interpreted his comments as an insult. With passions aroused, a few hotheads climbed the wall surrounding 'Uthman's home, broke through the door, and killed him in front of his wife while he was engaged in religious devotions.

'Ali's Caliphate: Shi'ites and Kharijites

Upon 'Uthman's death, the mutineers and others in Medina acclaimed 'Ali as their new caliph. Long critical of the policies that had benefitted the Quraysh at the expense of the common Muslim, 'Ali was popular among the insurgents as well as among many who had known and admired him all his life in the Hijaz. His lifelong loyalty to his cousin the Prophet, his courage and skill as a warrior, and his piety had caused many to hold him in high esteem. Over thirty years earlier, he had married Fatima, the daughter of the Prophet and Khadija, and the couple's two sons were Muhammad's only surviving grandsons. 'Ali's selection as caliph at this time, however, was controversial and bitterly resented by some. 'A'isha, Muhammad's youngest and favorite wife in his later years, held an old grudge against 'Ali, and others among Muhammad's closest friends resented 'Ali's popularity and his threat to the interests of the Quraysh. They seized on the fact that the mutineers had been responsible for 'Ali's elevation to the caliphate. They pointed out that 'Ali had not only failed to make any effort to bring 'Uthman's murderers to justice—he had not even condemned 'Uthman's murder.

Passions on both sides were high. 'Ali's supporters were euphoric that he had finally become caliph and would now bring justice to the Islamic community, whereas his opponents were possessed by a deadly rage stemming from their suspicion that his ambition had pushed him into becoming an accomplice in 'Uthman's murder. It was clear that a major clash was imminent, and both 'Ali's supporters and his opponents immediately set out for the garrison cities of Iraq in order to recruit troops for the struggle. 'Ali marched to Kufa, where 'Uthman's policies were especially resented, while his opponents tried to rally the garrison in Basra in their favor. 'A'isha and several of the Prophet's oldest and most loyal followers were unable to recruit as many soldiers in Basra as 'Ali was able to obtain in Kufa. The ensuing Battle of the Camel (so named because 'A'isha sat on one of the animals while she watched the conflict) resulted in a victory by 'Ali's forces.

Almost immediately, however, the legitimacy of his caliphate was challenged by Mu'awiya, whom we met in the previous chapter. For the next five years, 656–661, the attention of the Umma was focused on the grand struggle between these two men. The supporters of one side or the other were known as the partisans, or *shi'a*, of one or the other. Just as there had earlier been *shi'a 'Uthman* and *shi'a 'Ali* during the debate over 'Uthman's policies, so now the *shi'a Mu'awiya* were opposing the *shi'a 'Ali*. The term *shi'a* in this context had no specifically religious meaning; it simply connoted support for the legitimacy of the claim of one or the other man in the quarrel.

In 657, the two armies met at Siffin on the Euphrates River. After skirmishing for several months, it seemed that they were set for the decisive engagement. At that point, Mu'awiya's army asked for arbitration of the issues that divided the two men. 'Ali felt compelled to agree to the arbitration because of a widespread sentiment on

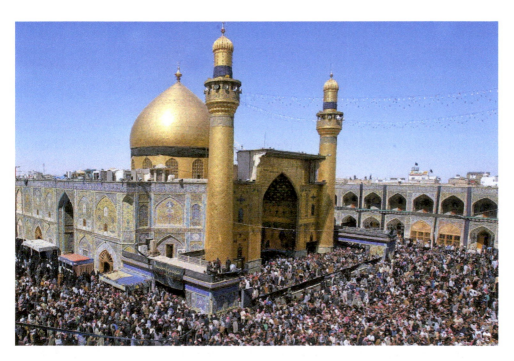

FIGURE 3.1   The shrine for 'Ali in Najaf, Iraq. The original portion dates from the tenth century.
Qassem Zein / Stringer.

both sides not to shed the blood of fellow Muslims. One group of his army, however, regarded his concession as an act of irresoluteness uncharacteristic of a true caliph. They defected and became known as Kharijites (*khawarij*, from *kharaja*, meaning "to depart or leave").

The term Kharijism appears frequently in Muslim history in the centuries after the Battle of Siffin. In the early years, it usually referred to the belief that a leader who violated a Qur'anic prescription was a grave sinner and should be excluded from the community of believers. The sinner had, by virtue of his error, become an unbeliever and should be killed. In practice, the groups who were called Kharijites were rarely in a position to exclude anyone from the Umma; rather, they themselves were a minority that withdrew from the larger community on the grounds that the majority had fallen into error. Kharijism was a feared and hated movement because most of its early adherents believed that they had the right—and even duty—to kill non-Kharijites. By making enemies of the vast majority of Muslims, the movement signed its own death warrant. Kharijites were hunted down and killed before they killed others.

One community of Kharijites in Basra, however, rejected the violence of the Kharijite tradition. It developed a theology and system of ethics that stressed coexistence with the larger Muslim community. It preferred to remain at arm's length from the corrupting influences of the majority culture rather than to provoke it. The Ibadis were one group within this moderate faction, deriving their name from one of their leaders, 'Abd Allah ibn Ibad. They sent missionaries as far afield as North Africa, Khorasan, Yemen, and Oman. We will meet them again in the Maghrib and Oman. By the late ninth century, it was the Ibadis' nonviolent policy of withdrawing from society that was more characteristic of Kharijism than the earlier tactic of violent attack. Unfortunately, non-Kharijite chroniclers during the next few centuries often labeled any group that rebelled against the government as Kharijite, lumping together a wide variety of movements and making it difficult to identify the actual beliefs of the groups.

Kharijite tendencies were particularly strong among nomads and peasants, who were suspicious of the motives and policies of urban leaders. The Great Berber Revolt of 740, discussed in the previous chapter, was raised under the banner of Kharijism, and the doctrine subsequently became highly popular among Berbers. Several Berber leaders established Kharijite states in the wake of the revolt, setting themselves apart from the Umayyad dynasty and its successor, the Abbasid dynasty. They set out to follow what they considered to be authentic Islam. Kharijism gave religious sanction to the inclination of these marginal groups to live separately from the rest of society, and it enabled them to feel spiritually superior to the majority, even if they were economically inferior.

The arbitration at Siffin dragged on for months without any resolution, and Mu'awiya's followers began proclaiming that their leader should replace 'Ali as caliph. 'Ali remained unaccountably inactive in Kufa after that, and in 661, a Kharijite assassinated him as an act of judgment on his failure to do God's bidding. Mu'awiya then claimed the caliphate but stayed in Damascus, where his political and military support lay. 'Ali's ineffective caliphate and his violent death were a profound shock to his followers. For the previous quarter of a century, a growing number of Muslims had come to regard him as an advocate for the principle of equality and for a government dedicated to justice. Many of his followers believed that he had spiritual gifts not accessible to other mortals. The triumph of the Umayyad clan exacerbated the sense of loss because its members were widely viewed as having become Muslims only as an opportunistic strategy.

'Ali and his family came to be regarded as symbols of protest against the growing power of the Umayyads and their Syrian supporters. 'Ali's fate was viewed by many as a tragedy. He became a symbol of a great man who was caught in the vortex of evil forces and destroyed. More important, however, was the growing sense among some of his admirers that he had been a virtuous man who gave his life in God's cause. In this sense, his death was a sacrifice to be emulated. Those who protested injustice or who sought a leader with great charisma, found him to be an attractive figure with which to identify. Many Muslims would come to agree that the Alids (members of 'Ali's family) had been blessed and chosen by God to lead the Umma.

Karbala

Despite the misgivings of many Muslims that 'Ali had failed to act with proper discretion in bringing the murderers of 'Uthman to justice, few could go so far as to believe that he had been involved in the plot. Thus, 'Ali's frustrated caliphate and his assassination were a loss felt by the Umma at large. Mu'awiya's hounding of 'Ali for the last five years of his life was viewed as unseemly, and although Mu'awiya ruled for almost twenty years with tact and propriety, he was never quite able to rehabilitate his image with a growing number of Muslims. No doubt his abandonment of Medina was a major source of hostility, at least from the Hijazis, for the city slid rapidly into the status of a backwater while Damascus became a glittering capital city by the end of the century. Pious Muslims who considered Medina and Mecca to be the center of the world became increasingly critical of the Umayyads over the years as it became clear that the new rulers were not as pious as their forebears had been. Tales of sumptuous palaces, wine drinking, and a generally dissolute lifestyle among the princes became the stock of anti-Umayyad sentiment.

Mu'awiya's critics grudgingly acknowledged that he was not the profligate that many of his relatives seemed to be, and he managed to maintain a simple style of ruling in which he made himself accessible to petitioners. In this regard, he was continuing the tradition of Arab tribalism and the early Muslim leadership alike. He also treated 'Ali's sons by Fatima with great courtesy. According to Shi'ite tradition, pro-Alid supporters in Kufa proclaimed the elder son Hasan to be caliph shortly after his father's murder. He abdicated, however, when Mu'awiya threatened violence against him. He returned to the Hijaz, where he lived comfortably on a generous financial settlement that Mu'awiya granted him, until his death in 669. His younger brother Husayn became the head of the family at that point, and it was in him that many pro-Alid individuals now invested their hopes. Since Mu'awiya had won his conflict with 'Ali, there was no longer reason for a group called the *shi'a Mu'awiya*, but those who continued to regard 'Ali's family to be the source for legitimate caliphal leadership were still partisans and continued to be called the *shi'a 'Ali*, or Shi'ites.

The Rightful Caliph: The Shi'ite Version

Shi'ites rejected the conciliar selection process for caliph that resulted in the choice of Abu Bakr, 'Umar, and 'Uthman. They were convinced that the Prophet had declared 'Ali to be his successor at a small pool (ghadir) called Khumm (hence, Ghadir Khumm, or Ghadir al-Khumm) while returning to Medina after having performed his last pilgrimage (the "Farewell Pilgrimage") shortly before his death. The following account is from Muhammad Baqir Majlisi's The Life of Hearts, *which dates from about the year 1700, but it reflects an early tradition (note the wry reference in the last sentence to 'Umar, the second caliph):*

When the ceremonies of the pilgrimage were completed, the Prophet, attended by 'Ali and the Muslims, left Mecca for Medina. On reaching Ghadir Khumm he halted. ... The reason for encampment in such a place was that illustrious verses of the Qur'an came powerfully upon him, enjoining him to establish 'Ali as his successor. He had previously received communications to the same effect, but not expressly appointing the time for 'Ali's inauguration, which, therefore, he had deferred lest opposition be excited and some forsake the faith. This was the message from the Most High in Sura 5:67: "O Messenger, publish that which has been sent down to you from your Lord, for if you do not, then you have not delivered His message. God will protect you from men; surely God guides not unbelieving people."

Being thus peremptorily commanded to appoint 'Ali his successor, and threatened with penalty if he delayed when God had become his surety, the Prophet therefore halted in this unusual place, and the Muslims dismounted around him.

... Having ordered all the camel-saddles to be piled up for a *minbar* [pulpit] or rostrum, he commanded his herald to summon the people around him. When all the people were assembled, the Prophet ascended the minbar of saddles, and calling unto him the Commander of the Believers ('Ali), he placed him on his right side. Muhammad now rendered thanksgiving to God, and then made an eloquent address to the people, in which he foretold his own death, and said, "I have been called to the gate of God, and the time is near when I shall depart to God, be concealed from you, and bid farewell to this vain world. I leave among you the Book of God, to which if you adhere, you shall never go astray. And I leave with you the members of my family who cannot be separated from the Book of God until both join me at the fountain of al-Kawthar."

He then demanded, "Am I not dearer to you than your own lives?" and was answered by the people in the affirmative. He then took the hands of 'Ali ... and said, "Whoever receives me as his [master or ally], then to him 'Ali is the same. O Lord, befriend every friend of 'Ali, and be the enemy of all his enemies; help those who aid him and abandon all that desert him."

It was now nearly noon, and the hottest part of the day. The Prophet and the Muslims made the noon prayers, after which he went to his tent, beside which he ordered a tent pitched for the Commander of the Believers. When 'Ali was rested Muhammad commanded the Muslims to wait upon 'Ali, congratulate him on his accession to the Imamate, and salute him as the *amir*, or commander. All this was done by both men and women, none appearing more joyful at the inauguration of 'Ali than did 'Umar.

SOURCE: Williams, John Alden, ed. *Themes of Islamic Civilization*. Berkeley, California: University of California Press, 1971, 63–64.

At the end of his life, Mu'awiya's tact and political judgment abandoned him. In 680, he made the shocking announcement that he had chosen his son Yazid to be his successor. The sudden imposition of the dynastic rule of an unpopular family provoked a severe reaction. The leaders of Medina refused to acknowledge Yazid, insisting that the new caliph be selected by consensus, as the first caliphs had been chosen. The deep-seated hostility in Iraq toward the family of 'Uthman now erupted anew, especially in Kufa, which had maintained a strong sympathy for the memory of 'Ali. Leaders of that city invited 'Ali's surviving son, Husayn, to lead them in armed resistance to Yazid. Husayn set out for Kufa from the Hijaz with several dozen armed followers and family members, but a military detachment sent by Yazid intercepted him on a plain called Karbala, not far from Kufa. There, on the tenth day of Muharram (the first month on the Islamic calendar), he and most of his followers were brutally killed.

Before 680, Shi'ism had been based on the conviction that 'Ali or his sons should exercise caliphal power. Before Karbala, this sentiment could be emotional and passionate, but we have no evidence that it had developed the characteristics of a religious movement. The negotiations between the Kufans and Husayn, for example, include no trace that support or lack of support for him was a matter of religious allegiance but rather was predicated on the implementation of justice.

Karbala marked a transition in this respect. Although religious ritual would not be worked out for several decades, there is an unquestionably different tone to Shi'ite sentiment after 680. Kufans felt a profound sense of guilt at not having come to the aid of Husayn's little band. A growing number of Alid supporters interpreted his death as a sacrifice made on behalf of God's people. The narrative account of his death became elaborated and embellished as time passed, and many Muslims, as they heard it, felt that they participated vicariously in his suffering during those agonizing last hours before Husayn and his followers, abandoned and suffering from thirst, were finally cut down without mercy.

The Abbasid Revolution

In the aftermath of Karbala, the idea that an Alid was more qualified than an Umayyad to be the caliph gained unprecedented strength and widespread support. The fervent supporters of an Alid caliphate, however, were frustrated in their hopes that one of the sons or grandsons of Hasan or Husayn would take up the cause. For the next six decades, their families were known for producing more religious scholars than political activists.

The accession of Yazid in 680 brought forward an opportunity for an Alid challenge to the Umayyads, but it came from an unexpected quarter. From 682 to 692, four successive Umayyad caliphs had to contend with a revolt by 'Abdullah ibn al-Zubayr, a son of one of Muhammad's closest companions. Ibn al-Zubayr claimed to be caliph, and he had a strong base of support in his home in the Hijaz as well as in Iraq, both of which broke loose from Umayyad control for several years.

Meanwhile, in Kufa, a man named Mukhtar took advantage of the Umayyads' loss of control over Iraq to raise a separate revolt. He claimed to be advancing the cause of Ibn al-Hanafiya, a son of 'Ali and his wife al-Hanafiya, whom 'Ali had married after Fatima's death. Ibn al-Hanafiya was thus a half-brother to Hasan and Husayn. Ibn al-Hanafiya lived in Mecca and was known as a gentle religious scholar. There is no evidence that he had any contact with Mukhtar, but the latter was able to take control of Kufa in 685–686.

Mukhtar claimed that Ibn al-Hanafiya was not merely the rightful caliph, but also the *mahdi*, a messiah figure who would bring justice in place of the oppression and wickedness that now prevailed in the world. *Mahdi* literally means "guided one," and in a religious context it implies "guided by God." Within the first few decades of Islamic history, informal traditions arose that claimed that the end of history would be heralded by a Muslim Mahdi and by Jesus. Some of the accounts predicted that Jesus would precede the Mahdi; others said the Mahdi would come first; and still others identified the Mahdi with Jesus himself. Some Muslims thought that the Mahdi was already present: The Umayyad caliph Sulayman (715–717) encouraged the belief that he was the Mahdi, and many pious scholars assumed that his sucessor 'Umar II (717–720) was the Mahdi during his short caliphate. As we shall see, the doctrine of the Mahdi became an integral feature of Shi'ism but remained only marginal to Sunni doctrine.

The Umayyads crushed Mukhtar's uprising in 687, but the magnitude of the religious evolution that was taking place in Shi'ite circles may be gauged by the speculations that began to appear when Ibn al-Hanafiya died in 700. Some of his admirers claimed that in fact he had not died but rather was in concealment on Mt. Radwa in the Arabian Peninsula, where he was nourished by springs of water and honey and protected by a lion and a leopard. In the fullness of time, he would return to put an end to the tyranny of the transgressors and bring about a reign of righteousness. Other followers of Ibn al-Hanafiya desired to have a leader in the flesh instead of on a remote mountain, and they turned to his son Abu Hashim for spiritual leadership. This disagreement among Ibn al-Hanafiya's followers prefigured the complexity of the early history of Shi'ism, which is replete with numerous groups claiming one or another charismatic figure as their spiritual leader and the rightful caliph.

The movement that centered on Ibn al-Hanafiya and his son is important for two reasons: the evidence it provides that certain Alid leaders were beginning to be viewed as messianic figures and its connection with the revolutionary movement that eventually overthrew the Umayyad dynasty in 750. The potential that Shi'ite sentiment held for challenging the Umayyads was becoming clear to the dynasty's opponents, and early in the eighth century, one group—the Abbasids—began cultivating that sentiment in a remarkably astute way. As we have seen, some Muslims felt that the leadership of the Umma should reside in the descendants of 'Ali and Fatima (and thus of the Prophet himself), while others were satisfied with leadership that lay in the hands of any of 'Ali's descendants (such as Ibn al-Hanafiya).

In addition to the relatively small group of people who held passionately to this "pro-Alid" sentiment was a much larger number of Muslims who were convinced that the ideal ruler should at least be a member of "the family of the Prophet." Defining the boundaries of "the family" was frequently a contentious enterprise, but all could agree that it was contained within the clan of Hashim and not of the clan of 'Abd Shams, from whom the Umayyads were descended. One of the families in the Hashimite clan was that of 'Abbas, an uncle of the Prophet. Its members are known as the Abbasids, and they became famous as the group that overthrew the Umayyads.

The Abbasids' success was due in no small part to the fact that they organized a sophisticated underground movement that eluded the best efforts of the Umayyads to ferret it out. The Abbasids patiently bided their time before challenging the might of the state. Because of the movement's secrecy, details about it are shrouded in obscurity, but the leaders exploited Alid sentiment by making two seemingly incompatible claims regarding their intentions. To the groups that had been attracted to the figures of Ibn al-Hanafiya and his son Abu Hashim, they claimed that the Abbasid family had inherited the mantle of spiritual leadership from them. The Abbasids claimed that when Abu Hashim died in Palestine in 716, he had designated Muhammad ibn 'Ali, a great-grandson of 'Abbas, to be his spiritual heir. By implication, Muhammad ibn 'Ali or his successor would be the caliph in the event of the overthrow of the Umayyads.

By the decade of the 740s, however, the leaders of the Abbasid movement were trying to make their cause attractive to an even wider spectrum of Muslims, and they broadened their propaganda by claiming that they would replace the Umayyads by "the accepted (agreed-upon) one from the family of Muhammad," the Prophet. The implication was that, once the Umayyads were overthrown, a consensus would determine the best-qualified member of the Prophet's clan to be the caliph. The ideal of having the leadership of the Umma once again in the hands of the family of the Prophet was one shared by a multitude of Muslims.

Muhammad ibn 'Ali lived in what is now southern Jordan, but the political activism that he directed was based in Iraq and Khorasan. Initially, Kufa was the actual base of operations. As a large urban center with a long history of antipathy toward the Umayyads, the city provided a warren of alleys in which Abbasid leaders and agents could operate for several years with relative security. On the other hand, the city's loyalty to 'Ali and Husayn was so pronounced that Umayyad police eventually placed the markets and public spaces under constant surveillance. Because of increasing pressure from the government, the Abbasids established another base 500 miles to the northeast, in Khorasan's capital of Merv.

Merv was a happy choice. It was remote from Damascus, it had numerous Arabs as well as a rapidly growing mawali population, and it was a center of discontent against the Umayyads. As we saw in the previous chapter, Arab settlers there had assimilated in many ways to Persian culture. Many of them bought land or became merchants in this entrepôt that opened onto Central Asia. They resented being conscripted into the massive military campaigns of 705–715 in Transoxiana, which forced them to abandon their farms or businesses for most of the year. Discontented with Umayyad policies, many Khorasani Arabs looked to the family of the Prophet for leadership. Merv's community of Persian-speaking Arabs and mawali produced many of the subsequent leaders of the Abbasid movement.

The decade of the 740s proved to be decisive for the crystallization of the Abbasid movement. The Great Berber Revolt shook the authority of the Umayyad government and forced it to shift thousands of troops into North Africa and the Iberian Peninsula. In 743, Muhammad ibn 'Ali died, and his son Ibrahim succeeded to his position as the spiritual leader of the Abbasids. In the same year, the caliph Hisham died. The Abbasid leadership soon moved to take advantage of Hisham's death by sending a representative to Khorasan to begin the revolution. Almost nothing is known of this man's background—whether Arab, Iranian, Kurd, or whatever—but that seems to have been an element of a masterstroke of propaganda by the Abbasid leadership. The other element was the name that they gave him: Abu Muslim 'Abd al-Rahman ibn Muslim al-Khorasani, which literally means "Father of a Muslim, servant of the Merciful, son of a Muslim, from Khorasan." The name avoided all clues by which his identity could be traced, and it suggested to all who heard it that the Abbasid movement was interested not in tribal or ethnic identities, but only in the welfare of the Muslim community as a whole.

Abu Muslim assumed the leadership of the anti-Umayyad movement in Khorasan, and in 747, he raised the black banners of revolt. He sent an army westward while he stayed in Khorasan to secure the movement's base. The campaign was a stunning success. The Umayyads, discovering Ibrahim's link to the movement, arrested and executed him, but the revolutionary army continued its inexorable march, taking Kufa in September 749. Because of Ibrahim's execution by the Umayyads, a period of uncertainty regarding the leadership of the movement followed. Abbasid agents sent correspondence to the leading Alid figures in the Hijaz, offering them the caliphate, but they could not negotiate an arrangement suitable to both sides. The Abbasid leaders in Kufa then selected a brother of Ibrahim named Abu al-'Abbas as caliph. During 750, the Abbasid army moved into Syria and Egypt and destroyed the last vestiges of Umayyad power. All but one of the members of the former royal family were murdered. The shedding of blood was so common an occurrence, in fact, that the new caliph's title, al-Saffah ("the Blood Shedder"), seemed apt. The only Umayyad prince who survived—'Abd al-Rahman—escaped to Iberia, where we will hear from him again in his capacity as founder of the independent state of Andalus. The Abbasids quickly consolidated power and remained in Kufa for the next decade before establishing their permanent capital in the new city of Baghdad.

Shi'ite Identities

The new regime proved to be a profound disappointment to the pro-Alids. The Abbasid campaign had raised the hope that an inspired Alid leader who combined both temporal and religious legitimacy would be installed as caliph. However, the leading Alids were not able to accept the leadership on the terms that the Abbasids offered. Moreover, the new Abbasid caliph, al-Saffah (750–754), was hardly known outside his family. Some Alids were fêted at court when the new dynasty established itself, but others rejected the new regime as illegitimate. Several of them revolted against the new regime. The most spectacular of the Alid uprisings took place in 762–763, carried out by two brothers who were descendants of 'Ali's son Hasan. They planned simultaneous revolts against the newly established Abbasid court from Basra and Medina, but they failed to coordinate their efforts and both were killed. Many pro-Alids decided against outright revolts and instead began creating organizations to cultivate piety in an otherwise corrupt world; others recruited members into groups that were prepared to take over the leadership of the Muslim world when conditions were favorable. Thus, rather than resolving the demand of the pro-Alids, the Abbasid movement and revolution seem to have intensified the speculation and activity within such circles.

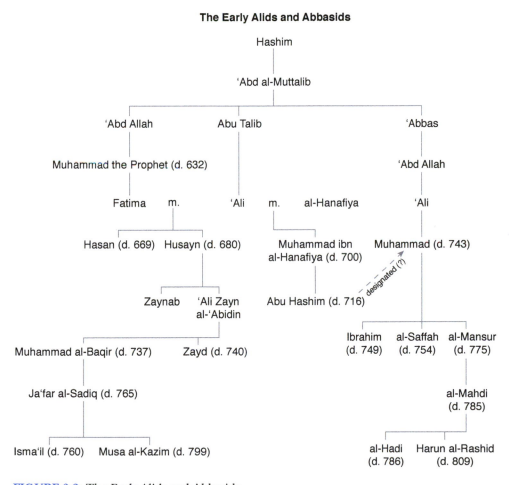

The Early Alids and Abbasids

FIGURE 3.2 The Early Alids and Abbasids.

The *Ghulat* and the Zaydis

The middle decades of the eighth century witnessed a remarkable range of activities among the pro-Alids. On the one hand were the so-called *ghulat*, "those who exaggerate" or "the extremists." This term did not refer to a particular group but rather to the members of numerous groups that championed the cause of individual Alids. They were lumped together under the label of "exaggerators" because of the claims for superhuman qualities that they made for their Alid leaders. Some of them denied that 'Ali had died, and some even claimed that he was divine. Typically, they claimed that in some sense God had become incarnate in their particular leader, and many asserted that, through him, God was continuing to bring revelatory truths. In order to provide legitimacy to the successors of such great leaders, some of the ghulat began developing sophisticated theories of the transmigration of the soul, asserting that the former leader's soul had taken residence in the new leader's body.

Often the term ghulat was applied to pro-Alids who substituted a reverence for their leader in the place of a concern for obeying the ritual requirements of Islam, such as the daily prayers. When it is recalled that the majority of Muslims believed that Muhammad himself was a mortal whom God had chosen to be the last prophet and that the early supporters of 'Ali had typically claimed only the qualities of piety and wisdom for their hero, we can understand why most Muslims were convinced that the ghulat had exceeded sensible, and even acceptable, bounds.

In contrast to the fervid speculations of the ghulat were the Zaydis. Zayd, a grandson of Husayn, led a failed revolt against the Umayyads in 740. Zayd asserted that the legitimate caliph was the man who combined descent from either Hasan or Husayn with learning, piety, and the political will to challenge the existing state authorities. This uncomplicated and activist program appealed to many Muslims, and several Zaydi ministates were set up in the highlands of Yemen and the Elburz Mountains of Iran in the decades after the Abbasid revolution. Zaydism rapidly became identified as an Alid challenge to Abbasid legitimacy. However, even though its Alid sympathies place it technically within the movement known as Shi'ism, its aversion to speculative thought kept it from developing a doctrine of the leader's unique spiritual role in the way that the majority of Shi'ites did. Zaydis differ little from the Muslims who have come to be known as Sunnis except for their insistence that their leader be descended from Hasan or Husayn.

The Husayni Alids

When the term *Shi'ite* is used today, it usually refers to a tradition that falls between the fervid speculations of the ghulat and the doctrinal simplicity of the Zaydis. To understand the origins of the major branches of modern Shi'ism, we must turn to early eighth-century Medina. There, the descendants of Husayn were quietly developing a reputation for piety and spiritual leadership. Several generations of Husayn's descendants lived in Medina, collecting the extra-Qur'anic sayings of Muhammad as well as anecdotes about his life that were transmitted by his companions. These scholars responded to questions from pious individuals who inquired about the best way to live a holy life, and they wrote commentaries on the Qur'an.

FIGURE 3.3 Interior of the shrine to Husayn in Karbala, Iraq.

Rasoul Ali / Alamy Stock Photo.

The Centrality of Muhammad al-Baqir and Ja'far al-Sadiq

The first of Husayn's descendants was his son 'Ali Zayn al-'Abidin, a survivor of Karbala. He in turn had two sons who became better known than he was. One was Zayd, for whom Zaydism was named. The other was Muhammad al-Baqir, one of the most highly respected religious scholars of the first third of the eighth century. He became the leader of the Husayni branch of the Alids about the year 713. Muhammad al-Baqir's son Ja'far al-Sadiq succeeded him as leader in 737 and became a major figure in the newly developing discipline of Islamic law. At the time of his death in 765, he was widely respected by Alids and non-Alids alike for his scholarship, wisdom, and generosity.

During the half century of leadership by Muhammad al-Baqir and Ja'far al-Sadiq, the self-conscious identity that we call Shi'ism can perhaps be seen for the first time. Both men won universal respect for their learning and wisdom, even among those who had no interest in the nascent Shi'ism of the day. A certain group of Alid supporters, however, regarded them to be more than mere scholars of erudition and piety: They were spokesmen for God. With them, one of the most distinctive doctrines of Shi'ism began to take shape, that of the Imam.

The word *imam* in Arabic is a preposition that means "in front of" or "before." It soon became widely used to designate the man who stands in front of the congregation in the mosque to lead the prayers, and this has been the typical meaning of *imam* among non-Shi'ites. In villages, he is probably the most pious man or otherwise a respected personage, while in urban areas he has scholarly credentials as well as spiritual responsibilities. The members of the congregation, however, do not regard him as having anything like the spiritual authority that Shi'ites invest in their supreme leader. In this book, *Imam* will be used to designate the man whom Shi'ites view as their legitimate leader, and *imam* will denote the Sunni prayer leader.

According to Shi'ites, the prophetic age came to an end with the Prophet Muhammad, but mankind was still in need of a divinely appointed and guided leader. The Prophet's heirs, the Imams, would continue the prophetic role in every respect except that they would explain the existing scripture, rather than introduce a new one. Each Imam was infallible and sinless and was the rightful leader of the entire Umma. The existing caliph, therefore, was illegitimate and a usurper. Shi'ites came to believe that to reject or disobey any of the Imams was an act of infidelity and was a sin on the same level as the rejection of the Prophet. Later Shi'ite hagiography portrayed 'Ali, Hasan, Husayn, and 'Ali Zayn al-'Abidin as having been recognized as Imams during their lifetimes. While there is no doubt that all of these individuals were regarded as leaders and sources of wisdom, the evidence suggests that it was the followers of Muhammad al-Baqir and Ja'far al-Sadiq who first constituted groups of disciples conscious of having an identity apart from other Muslims due to their allegiance to their Imam.

Even to be suspected of doubting the caliph's legitimacy, however, was clearly dangerous under either the Umayyads or the Abbasids. Muhammad al-Baqir and Ja'far managed to inspire a devoted following without appearing to threaten the political authorities. They developed three ideas that became characteristic of subsequent Shi'ite life and thought. First, they taught that an Imam acquired his status by virtue of having been chosen by the previous Imam. This doctrine stood in sharp contrast to the Zaydi position as well as to the belief that an Imam could be recognized simply by the quality of his teaching. Second, they confirmed that the Imam possessed spiritual knowledge that was different in kind, not just in degree, from other religious scholars. Learned and pious scholars were certainly useful in a community, but an Imam was indispensable. He had access to knowledge about God that was unavailable from any other source. Third, they convinced their followers to develop the discipline needed to refrain from trying to seize political power or acting in such a way as to bring scandal upon the community. They lived in dangerous times, and their followers had to act circumspectly.

The achievement of Muhammad al-Baqir and Ja'far al-Sadiq was to create a self-conscious identity for the Shi'ite community and make it possible for an individual to accept the authority of the Husayni Imams without engaging in a revolt against the government. Shi'ites were convinced that it was God's will that the Imam should also be caliph, but the majority recognized the political realities of the age. The Umayyads had been overthrown in 750 only to be replaced with another dynasty that did not represent the Alid line, but God would rectify that situation in His own good time. In the meantime, the Imam would be the channel that God would use to provide the spiritual guidance required for living the godly life.

In 760, Ja'far designated his son Isma'il to be his successor upon his death, which he believed was imminent. Soon thereafter, however, the one who died was Isma'il, not Ja'far. The community was stunned. No one within Ja'far's circle could believe that he had named the "wrong" successor, but they also could not fathom the mystery of Isma'il's untimely death. No evidence exists that Ja'far himself ever attempted another designation of a successor or sought to interpret the conundrum of his designated successor's having predeceased him.

At Ja'far's own death in 765, his followers had to decide on an Imam themselves. Dozens of different groups arose, distinguished from each other by their choice of Imam or by doctrinal differences. It would have been impossible at the time to know which sect would become the most influential, and many decades had to pass for two of them to become dominant. One denied that Isma'il had ever been the Imam and recognized his brother Musa al-Kazim as the rightful Imam after Ja'far. Its members came to be known as the *Imamiya*, or *Imamis*. We will see later why they are widely known today as the *ithna 'ashari* ("Twelver") Shi'ites. The other major group of Ja'far's disciples insisted that Isma'il had, in fact, been the seventh Imam and that his son Muhammad was the Imam upon Ja'far's death. Because of their belief that Isma'il was the seventh Imam, they have been known variously as *Isma'ilis* and as "Sevener" Shi'ites.

The Imamis

Our knowledge of the history of the Shi'ites during the two centuries after the death of Ja'far is remarkably limited. The paucity of information is testimony to the perilous and secretive life that Shi'ites usually had to follow as well as to the fact that many of the documents that we rely on from the period are hostile to Shi'ites. At some point in their history, in fact, they developed the doctrine of *taqiya*, or religious dissimulation: When threatened with the loss of life or property and when no danger to Islam itself is involved, Shi'ites are permitted to pretend to recant their faith. What is clear is that a bewildering variety of factions arose over the course of those 200 years and that no one in that period could have predicted with confidence that the Imamis and the Isma'ilis would eventually become the two dominant Shi'ite groupings.

As a rule, the Imamis followed Ja'far's dictum that a political challenge to the existing order would be counterproductive to their spiritual goals, and they were content to practice their faith in a world whose political order they despised. In spite of their caution, they could not escape the suspicions of some of the Abbasid caliphs. The caliph Harun al-Rashid (786–809) persecuted them and allegedly poisoned Ja'far's son Musa al-Kazim. During a civil war (809–813) between the sons of Harun al-Rashid, however, the central authority became so weak that several Shi'ite factions came out in open revolt in Iraq and the Arabian Peninsula. Harun's son al-Ma'mun won the civil war in 813 and seems to have been keenly aware of the need to appeal to Shi'ite sensibilities. When he claimed the caliphate in that year, he also claimed the title of Imam, a title all subsequent Abbasid caliphs would take.

What al-Ma'mun meant to convey by his new designation is unclear, particularly in light of a baffling announcement that he made in 817. He had fought the civil war of 809–813 against his brother from his base in Merv and had not returned to Baghdad even after he claimed the titles of caliph and Imam. Now, in late 817, he surprised the empire by naming Musa al-Kazim's son, the Imam 'Ali al-Rida, his heir-apparent and son-in-law. His motive for doing so is still widely debated. What is not debated is the fact that the rapidity of 'Ali al-Rida's rise to prominence was matched only by the suddenness of his decline. Soon after al-Ma'mun made his announcement, he began a march to Baghdad, which he had decided should be his capital after all.

FIGURE 3.4 Pilgrims in Mecca for the hajj. They are in the state of ihram, having exchanged their normal clothing for simple white cloths. Women who normally wear a face veil or gloves remove those during the state of ihram.

Art Directors & TRIP / Alamy Stock Photo.

En route to the city, ‘Ali al-Rida died suddenly in Tus (modern Mashhad). Shi‘ites believe that he was poisoned but cannot agree on who was responsible.

The Imamis enjoyed a respite from persecution under al-Ma’mun and his successor, but in 847, the new Abbasid caliph initiated a period of intense repression against them that lasted for the next twenty-five years. In 874, Hasan al-‘Askari, the Imamis’ eleventh Imam, died, apparently without a son. As had been the case when Ja‘far al-Sadiq had died, the community was thrown into confusion. Numerous sects formed (some traditions assert as few as fourteen, but others name as many as twenty), and for several decades the Imamis were severely splintered.

Under the leadership of a man named ‘Uthman al-‘Amri, however, a radically new doctrine provided the core for the unification of most of the Imami Shi‘ites. ‘Uthman claimed that Hasan al-‘Askari had been survived by a young son, who was now in hiding under God’s protection. That Hasan had a son was news to most of the faithful, but under the capable leadership of ‘Uthman and his three successors, this belief became standard doctrine. The young boy was named Muhammad and acquired the title Muhammad al-Muntazar (“the Looked-for” or “the Anticipated”). In practice, he was usually referred to as the Hidden Imam. ‘Uthman and his three successors claimed to be intermediaries between the Imam and his followers, bringing to the faithful the religious guidance granted by the Hidden Imam.

In 941, the Imam sent word that he would no longer have a spokesman or intermediary, and Imami Shi‘ism entered upon a new phase of history. The period from 874 to 941 soon came to be known as the Lesser Concealment (or Occultation), and the period after 941 came to be known as the Greater Concealment—"greater" in the sense that, without an intermediary, the Imam was even more concealed than before. The Hidden Imam was recognized as the twelfth in a line of Imams that began with 'Ali, and he was now designated as the Mahdi (as a result, he is sometimes referred to as Muhammad al-Mahdi as well as Muhammad al-Muntazar). From this time on, the Imamis have often been referred to as the Twelver Shi'ites.

The introduction of the doctrine of the Greater Concealment marked a surprising turn for a movement that had insisted on the need for constant spiritual guidance from an Imam. The Imami world view now became nostalgic and tragic, and Twelver Shi'ites longed for the time when they had had direct access to spiritual truth. Nevertheless, Twelvers had no reason to despair. Unlike previous Imams, the Hidden Imam did not die, and he is awaiting the command from God to intervene in history. Because of the new understanding of him as both the last Imam and the Mahdi, the task for the next period of their history was to understand how he continued to give guidance to his community and what his role in history was. We will explore this topic in more detail in Part Two.

The Isma'ilis

Both *Isma'ili* and *Sevener* seem to have originated as derogatory terms for the followers of Muhammad ibn Isma'il, but they have persisted because of their widespread use. The Isma'ilis themselves designated their movement simply as "the mission." We have no record of their activity between the death of Ja'far in the middle of the eighth century and the last third of the ninth century, when they emerged from obscurity. From evidence that exists from the time of their reemergence, it seems that they developed the doctrine that when Isma'il's son Muhammad appeared to die, he was, instead, hidden and protected by God. As the Mahdi/Imam, he was being prepared by God to return and bring justice and righteousness to the world at a time of God's choosing. In the meantime, the Imam communicated with his followers through designated spokesmen. Thus, from the late eighth to the late ninth centuries, the period when the Imamis relied upon a present, visible Imam, the Isma'ilis held a doctrine of a Hidden Imam.

The Isma'ilis also began to develop a theory of interpretation of the Qur'an that placed a premium on esoteric knowledge—that is, knowledge which, by virtue of its difficulty, was intended for a spiritual elite. We shall see that other Muslim groups also became preoccupied with esoterica during the same period, but the Isma'ilis became its outstanding practitioners. At the heart of the system was a distinction between the outer (*zahir*) and the inner (*batin*) meaning of the Qur'an, religious law, and ritual aspects of Islam. Religious laws and ritual prescriptions, it was asserted, change with every prophet that God has sent, but God's truths remain immutable and eternal. Thus, the revealed scriptures and the laws laid down in them must be understood as concealing a true, more spiritual, meaning that is superior to their literal appearance. Only individuals with superior insight are able to interpret the hidden meanings.

The zahir/batin polarity undergirds the exalted status of both the Imam and the religious hierarchy that came to characterize Isma'ilism. The divinely guided, infallible Imam interpreted the true meaning of revelation to individuals who had proven their ability and integrity as bearers of the truth. Such intermediaries between the Imam and the ordinary proselyte became designated as *hujja*s, or "proofs" of God's presence. These representatives of the Imam taught spiritual truths by means of allegorical interpretations to students who had committed themselves through a formal initiation into the serious work of the organization. The masses, meanwhile, continued to know only the zahir meaning of religious rules and rituals, and were therefore expected to concern themselves with correct behavior rather than with profound understanding. Isma'ilis expected that, at the end of time, when the Imam returns as the Mahdi, he will abrogate the law of the Prophet. At that time, there will be no need for laws, because spiritual truth will be directly accessible to everyone.

After a century of underground activity, the Isma'ili movement suddenly reappeared in southwestern Iran and southern Iraq in the second half of the ninth century, just as the period of the Lesser Concealment began for the Imamis. The Isma'ili movement emerged as a highly disciplined organization engaged in intensive missionary activity. Its members were uncompromising in their determination to create a new Islamic society characterized by justice and righteousness. They made impressive gains in Iraq and Syria and sent missionaries all the way to Khorasan, Sind, Yemen, and the Maghrib. By the last decade of the ninth century, the Isma'ilis had established their headquarters in Salamiya, Syria. They appeared to pose a formidable security threat to the Abbasids. In 902, however, 'Abd Allah, the leader of the headquarters at Salamiya, suddenly left his base of operations and headed to North Africa. In 910, he appeared in Ifriqiya, some 1600 miles from Salamiya. There he was welcomed by a Berber army that had recently seized power in Qayrawan. His supporters recognized him not merely as the spokesman for the Imam, but as the Imam-caliph and Mahdi himself, returning to take over the leadership of the entire Muslim world. This was a major challenge to the weakening Abbasid caliphate. 'Abd Allah's movement at this point becomes known to history as the Fatimid Empire. Because its subsequent narrative belongs as much to imperial history as it does to religious history, we will resume its story in the next chapter.

The Shi'ite Movement

By the middle of the tenth century, Shi'ism had spawned two major groups: the Twelvers and the Isma'ilis. Several small Zaydi states continued in existence for many centuries, but they were always in remote, mountainous areas, quite removed from developments in the rest of the Muslim world. Ghulat sects continued to appear, but they discovered that they had to shed their extreme views if they wished to have an influence in the wider Umma.

The label *Shi'ism* slowly accumulated connotations that set Shi'ites apart from the majority of Muslims. Some were subtle differences, whereas others were quite striking. As we will see later, the majority of Muslims agreed that religious truth was what the majority of pious scholars said that it was, whereas both Isma'ilis and Twelvers refused to admit that majority opinion is necessarily true or right. Because the two Shi'ite groups were, in fact, usually embattled minorities, both came to advocate the inherent virtue of belonging to a militant minority. Both of these groups of Shi'ites agreed that some truths can be known only by an elite and can be interpreted to the masses only by symbol and legend. Both groups tended to express emotion in their worship more than did the majority. They focused on the persecutions they had suffered and the martyrdom of the heroes of the faith.

Both Isma'ilis and Twelvers believed that their respective Imams should be ruling the entire Muslim community. A latent corollary of that conviction was that all temporal authority in the absence of the Imam is illegitimate. The biggest difference between the Isma'ilis and Twelvers was the identity of the Imam. An intriguing contrast between the two groups is the fact that, from the death of Ja'far al-Sadiq in 765 until the late ninth century, Imamis insisted on the need for a present, visible Imam but then accepted the doctrine of the Occultation after 874. Isma'ilis, on the other hand, had been comfortable with the idea of a concealed Imam until the beginning of the tenth century, when the loyal followers of 'Abd Allah converted from the idea that he was the *spokesman* for the Imam to the idea that he *was* the Imam. From the late ninth century until today, Twelvers have had a Hidden Imam, and Isma'ilis have usually had a visible Imam (although in particularly dangerous times they, too, would revert to a Hidden Imam).

The change in doctrine regarding the Imam had important political, as well as religious, consequences for both groups. As we shall see in subsequent chapters, various groups of Isma'ilis attempted to achieve political power for their Imam during the period from the ninth to the thirteenth centuries. Twelvers, on the other hand, were more ambivalent about the state during that period. There was no doubt that the Hidden Imam would soon be coming back to rule, but, in his absence, the practice of piety in this corrupt world was sufficient. God had His own plan for its purification, and any changes would be according to His timetable. As a result, Twelver Shi'ites were able to coexist with both the political and religious establishments much better than Isma'ilis or Zaydis did, and their persecution became a rare occurrence. The Isma'ilis, on the other hand, became the target of violent persecution.

The Sunni Consensus

As Shi'ites were developing their characteristic doctrines and practices based on the conviction that the caliph should be a member of 'Ali's family, the majority of Muslims were also engaged in the process of developing their doctrines and institutions. We will examine this achievement in some detail in Chapter 5. At this point, it is useful to note that Sunnis, who are about eighty-five percent of all Muslims, derive their name from their insistence on following the *sunna*, or "path," of the Prophet. Whereas Shi'ites are convinced that Muslims need the guidance of an Imam in order to follow God's will correctly, Sunnis are satisfied that conscientious and pious Muslims can determine God's will by means of a careful reading of the Qur'an and of authenticated accounts (the Hadith) of the Prophet's behavior and teachings. In the eighth and ninth centuries, scholars wrote biographies of the Prophet and collected thousands of anecdotes of the Prophet's actions and sayings, all for the purpose of using the Prophet's life as a model of upright behavior. As we will see, enormous efforts were expended in order to develop reliable methods for obtaining spiritual guidance.

These activities were part of a complex and arduous enterprise that only qualified scholars could adequately perform. For most Muslims, however, knowing the basic ritual obligations was sufficient. These rituals are known as the Five Pillars. The basis for all of them is in the Qur'an, although many of the details as they are practiced today were elaborated over the course of many years. Their repetition cultivated in Muslims a sense of identity and purpose that gave believers the assurance that their cause was in accord with God's will. Moreover, the rituals reinforced in the minds of Muslims the fact that Islam is a collective, rather than merely an individual, enterprise. They provided emotional support to individuals when their faith or physical strength faltered. The description of the rituals in the discussion that follows reflects Sunni practice; Kharijites and the various Shi'ite groups differ in some of the details.

Shahada, or proclamation of faith. To become a Muslim, one recites, "There is no god but God, and Muhammad is His prophet." Muhammad's central teaching was that there is only one God and that, therefore, the greatest sin is the denial of His singularity and unity and the placing of some other being to be equal to Him. God is all-powerful and created all life; it is the duty of His human creatures to give thanks to Him for life itself and to submit their will and their lives to Him through daily obedience. In the Arabic language, the word *Islam* denotes submission, and a *Muslim* is one who submits to God's will. Muslims believe that people are responsible for their actions; at the end of time, each person will account for all of her or his deeds at the Last Judgment and go to paradise or hell on the basis of the accounting.

Salat, or ritual prayer. One of the most powerful rituals that reinforce the collective nature of Islam is the *salat*, or ritual prayer. The sight of others—perhaps even thousands of others—performing the prayer in unison reminds the believer that untold millions of others are performing it all over the world at the appointed times. The frequent repetition of the prayer is a strong reinforcement of the conviction that one is participating in the most important enterprise in the world.

The salat is performed five times daily—dawn, noon, midafternoon, sunset, and evening—and the invocations and ritual movements are carefully prescribed. It can be performed at home, in a school or factory, or outdoors, but Muslims consider a mosque to be the most efficacious place for prayer. The mosque is explicitly designed for the salat. The English word *mosque* derives from the Arabic word *masjid*, which means "place of prostration," the name given to the pre-Islamic shrines. Mosques have always been constructed with the purpose of marking off space to consecrate for prayer. As a result, they do not have pews and they do not need to be tall or imposing, but simply large enough to serve the prayer needs of hundreds, or even thousands, of people.

The faithful know when it is time to perform the prayer when a functionary of the mosque known as the *mu'adhdhin* (frequently rendered *muezzin*) chants the call to prayer (*idhan*) from one of the minarets, or towers, that became a characteristic feature of mosque architecture. Before performing the prayer, the believer must enter a state of ritual purity by washing the face, feet and ankles, and the arms to the elbows. He or she then determines the *qibla*, or direction of the Ka'ba in Mecca, which is marked in a mosque by the *mihrab*, a niche in the wall. After declaring to God the intention of making the prayer, the ritual begins. Of the thirty-five prayer times in the week, the Friday noon service is the one that Muslims make the most

FIGURE 3.5 The mihrab in al-Azhar mosque (972), Cairo, indicating the qibla.

© Gerard Degeorge / Bridgeman Images.

determined effort to perform at a mosque. That is the occasion when the *khutba*, or sermon, is delivered. Because of the large number of worshipers, the Friday noon service is the one that most effectively reinforces the sense of community.

Zakat, **or almsgiving.** Concern for the poor, the widow, and the orphan is a constant refrain throughout the teachings of Muhammad. Since all humans are equally creatures of God, oppression of the poor and weak by the rich and powerful is therefore an affront to God Himself. It is incumbent on believers not merely to refrain from oppressing the poor but to be active in sharing their wealth with them as well. The zakat was the form of tax that Muhammad made mandatory on Muslims. In later centuries, Muslim jurists decided that the zakat should represent two percent of an individual's wealth. It came to be understood as a form of self-purification: By giving away part of one's property, one purifies the rest.

Sawm, **or fasting.** Ramadan, the ninth month on the Islamic calendar, is the month of fasting. From before dawn until sunset, Muslims do not drink, eat, engage in sexual relations, or, in modern times, smoke. Prepubescent children, the sick and infirm, and the pregnant are exempted from the obligation, and travelers can postpone it. Most Muslims continue their regular work schedule during the day, but some sleep during the day and sit up all night; others engage in around-the-clock reading of the Qur'an. The breaking of the fast in the evening is a festive occasion, and some families spend more on food during Ramadan than during the entire remainder of the year. Because Muhammad stipulated that Muslims use a lunar, non-intercalated calendar, each of the months begins eleven solar days earlier the next year. This causes the Islamic calendar to move through the solar calendar, completing a full circuit roughly every thirty-three years. Thus, Ramadan, like all the other months, will periodically fall in each of the four seasons. The impact of Ramadan on individual lives varies accordingly: The fast is shorter and less stressful during the short, cool periods of sunlight in winter than during the long, hot ones of summer.

Ramadan is a month that mingles hardship with joy. Muslims have come to associate the month with the revealing of the Qur'an to Muhammad, and therefore it celebrates the beginning of Islam. It encourages reflection on human frailty and the believer's dependence on God. Like the other rituals, it reinforces the collective, communal aspect of Islam as participants encourage each other through the experience and make a special effort throughout the month to help the poor and the hungry.

The *hajj,* or pilgrimage. According to the traditional account, Muhammad developed the rituals of the *hajj* after his conquest of Mecca. He combined elements of the pre-Islamic pilgrimage to the Ka'ba with others from surrounding shrines, such as Mina and Arafat, and he sanctified them as an Islamic practice dedicated to God. The new hajj became a complex event spread over an area twelve miles in extent that took several days to complete. Believers are expected to fulfill the pilgrimage at least once in their lifetime if at all possible. It is performed in the month of Dhu al-Hijja, the last month on the calendar. The event emphasizes the humility of the believer before God and the equality of all humanity. Upon entering the sacred precinct, male pilgrims don two simple pieces of white cloth and women dress in simple attire, as they dispense with all material goods that would establish ranks among them.

The pilgrimage has an awe-inspiring effect upon the participants. In part, this is due to being present where sacred history was made. Muhammad taught that Ibrahim (Abraham) and his son Isma'il (Ishmael) built the Ka'ba, which was also the center of Muhammad's career; thus, pilgrims can imaginatively reenact momentous episodes in Islamic history. Another feature of the pilgrims' experience is that, as Islam spread across the world, Muslims representing a wide variety of ethnic groups and geographical regions began coming on the hajj. The varieties of skin color and languages spoken were vivid statements of the powerful appeal of Islam and of its triumphal march across the world, reassuring the believer that he or she was participating in God's universal plan. Precisely because Mecca was the meeting place for Muslims from all over the world, it soon became the logical site for scholars and travelers to meet and to exchange ideas. Throughout history, it has served as a force for cosmopolitanism, the flow of ideas, and education.

Conclusion

The period between the Prophet's death in 632 and the Abbasid revolution in 750 witnessed momentous events that shaped the future direction of Muslim history. The frontiers of the Muslim world were established by the Umayyad conquests and would change very little for the next several centuries. The Abbasid revolution then transformed the Arab empire of the Umayyads into a cosmopolitan state that consciously attempted to incorporate a variety of ethnic groups not only into the community of believers but also into the ruling elite itself. These positive developments were countered by the emergence of profound differences among Muslims that proved impossible to breach. The different assumptions that would eventually crystallize into Sh'ism, Kharijism, and Sunnism began making their appearance during the first century of Muslim history.

Central to the emergence of both Shi'ism and Kharijism was the figure of 'Ali, the Prophet's cousin and the husband of the Prophet's daughter Fatima. 'Ali's role in history is unusual. He must be regarded as one of the most important figures in Muslim history, and yet he led no major military campaigns, left no corpus of writings, and was totally preoccupied during his five years as caliph with defending his office—so much so that he was unable to accomplish any notable objectives. His importance lay in the perceptions and expectations that people had of him. He had many opponents among the Quraysh because of his criticism of the administrative practices of the new empire. On the other hand, the Muslims who would eventually become known as Shi'ites saw in him the rightful successor to Muhammad as leader of the Umma, and they regarded the selection of Abu Bakr, 'Umar, and 'Uthman as the first three caliphs to have been a conspiracy against the implementation of God's will. Still other Muslims enthusiastically cheered the beginning of 'Ali's caliphate, even though they did not regard him as having been divinely ordained as Muhammad's successor: They were expecting him to reverse the policies of 'Uthman and to implement justice. When he faltered, they felt betrayed and initiated the Kharijite movement.

Most Muslims fell in between these two groups. They did not see evidence that 'Ali had been chosen as the Prophet's immediate successor, and they did not believe that he had committed a grave offense in being willing to negotiate with an enemy when the alternative would be a bloodbath of Muslim against Muslim. Members of this third group—the Sunnis—regard 'Ali to have been one of the four "rightly guided" caliphs—that is, the four caliphs who preceded the Umayyad dynasty.

FURTHER READING

'Ali and the Politics of Division

Kennedy, Hugh. *The Prophet and the Age of the Caliphates: The Islamic Near East from the Sixth to the Eleventh Century.* London and New York: Longman, 1986.

Watt, W. Montgomery. *The Formative Period of Islamic Thought.* Edinburgh, U.K.: Edinburgh University Press, 1973.

The Abbasid Revolution

Lassner, Jacob. *The Shaping of Abbasid Rule.* Princeton, New Jersey: Princeton University Press, 1980.

Sharon, Moshe. *Black Banners from the East: The Establishment of the 'Abbāsid State—Incubation of a Revolt.* Jerusalem: Magnes Press, and Leiden: E. J. Brill, 1983.

Sourdel, Dominique. "The Abbasid Caliphate." In *The Cambridge History of Islam*, I, 104–139. Cambridge, U.K.: Cambridge University Press, 1970.

Shi'ite Identities

Brett, Michael. *The Rise of the Fatimids: the World of the Mediterranean and the Middle East in the Fourth Century Hijra, Tenth Century C.E.* Leiden: E. J. Brill, 2001.

Brett, Michael. "The Mīm, the 'Ayn, and the Making of Ismā'īlism." *Bulletin of the School of Oriental and African Studies* 57, 1994, 25–39. Reprinted in Brett, Michael, *Ibn Khaldun and the Medieval Maghreb.* Aldershot, Hampshire, U.K., and Brookfield, Vermont, 1999.

Daftary, Farhad. *The Isma'ilis: Their History and Doctrines.* Cambridge, U.K.: Cambridge University Press, 1990.

Ibn al-Haytham, Ja'far ibn Ahmad. *The Advent of the Fatimids: A Contemporary Shi'i Witness.* Translated and edited by Wilferd Madelung and Paul E. Walker. London and New York: I. B. Tauris, 2000.

Jafri, S. Husain M. *Origins and Early Development of Shi'a Islam.* London: Longman Group Ltd., 1979.

Momen, Moojan. *An Introduction to Shi'ism: The History and Doctrines of Twelver Shi'ism.* New Haven and London: Yale University Press, 1985.

Moosa, Matti. *Extremist Shiites: The Ghulāt Sects.* Syracuse, New York: Syracuse University Press, 1988.

The Sunni Consensus

Denny, Frederick Mathewson. *An Introduction to Islam*, 2d ed. New York: Macmillan Publishing Company, 1994.

Esposito, John L. *Islam: The Straight Path*, 3d ed. New York and Oxford, U.K.: Oxford University Press, 1998.

CHAPTER 4

The Center Cannot Hold: Three Caliphates

The Abbasid victory over the Umayyads in 750 ushered in a genuine revolution, not a mere change in dynasties. The old Sasanian cosmopolitan and imperial tradition had triumphed over Arab particularism, and the revolution signaled a shift from the Umayyad focus on conquest to one of institutional consolidation. The Abbasid period was the era during which the major Islamic institutions and doctrines began assuming the forms that we know today. Abbasid patronage of the arts and sciences also contributed to a cultural efflorescence that would have a profound impact on Europe and, ultimately, other regions of the world.

On the other hand, the splendor of the Abbasid court, coupled with the 500-year history of the dynasty, has sometimes left the impression that the state it headed was as powerful as its cultural impact. The state actually flourished for only a century before losing control over its provinces. Even more significant, two competing caliphates arose in the first half of the tenth century to challenge the Abbasid caliph. The dream of a unified Muslim community, in which God's law would be implemented uniformly and impartially, seemed farther from fulfillment than ever, 300 years after the career of the Prophet.

These political and religious divisions are the flashy, centrifugal forces of this period that tend to capture the attention of the observer. Just as important for the history of the area, however, are centripetal economic developments that were working to bind together the far-flung regions of the Muslim world despite religious and political differences. Agricultural and manufacturing technologies, new crops, paper, precious metals, stylistic innovations for luxury goods such as ceramics and porcelains, and numerous other ideas and commodities were exchanged across thousands of miles, forever changing the means of production and the assumptions about everyday culture for Muslims and for the peoples who in turn borrowed from them.

The Abbasid Caliphate

The Abbasid revolt began a new age for the Umma. During the new dynasty's first several decades, it emitted occasional flashes of brilliance, and its subjects could feel justly proud of it. By the middle of the ninth century, however, it began to falter. It never attempted to regain the areas of the Maghrib and the Iberian Peninsula that the Umayyads had lost during the Great Berber Revolt, and in the ninth century it began losing effective control of its remaining provinces. By the middle of the tenth century, the Abbasid caliph was a figurehead for military officers who wielded effective power over a limited area.

The Early Period

As we have seen, the first Abbasid caliph, Abu al-'Abbas, assumed the title al-Saffah, or the Blood Shedder. It was an apt title for two reasons. First, it was a name that had been associated with the idea of the Mahdi in the literature of the previous decades, and therefore the new ruler was asserting his divinely sanctioned status in accordance with the propaganda of the Abbasid movement. (All subsequent Abbasid caliphs would follow his example in assuming titles with a religious implication; the third Abbasid caliph even adopted the title al-Mahdi.) Second, as in any revolution, the stakes were high, and much blood would have to be shed. The new regime executed several long-time leaders of the Abbasid movement itself for objecting to the selection of al-Saffah as caliph. Abu Muslim was perhaps the most prominent victim. The regime also killed or persecuted numerous Shi'ites who were suspected to be potential threats to its authority.

When al-Saffah died in 754, his brother Abu Ja'far succeeded him and assumed the title al-Mansur (the Victor). Al-Mansur (754–775) laid the foundations for the Abbasid Empire. He began by choosing a site on the west bank of the Tigris River for the new capital city. Officially named *madinat al-salam*, or "City of Peace," it came to be known by the name of the village that lay next to it, Baghdad. The choice of the site was particularly astute: The Tigris and Euphrates rivers came close together at this point and were connected by a navigable canal. Construction on the new capital began in 762, with 100,000 workers employed in the gargantuan project. It was a circular city some one and one-half miles in diameter that was designed for palaces, public buildings, and military barracks. Over the next few decades, the city grew into a large metropolis, and the original design was submerged in the welter of development. Extensive suburbs began springing up outside the circular walls to house those who flocked to the city to seek favors at the court or to participate in the city's flourishing international commerce. The wealthier neighborhoods boasted of sewers, courtyards, and pools lined with tiles. By the ninth century, the city was six miles long and four miles wide, a geographical area five times greater than that of Constantinople. With its population of close to half a million, it was certainly one of the two or three greatest cities in the world.[1]

The Abbasid revolution seems to have been a genuine attempt to make Islamic society more inclusive. The particularistic concerns of the Arab tribes that dominated the Umayyad government had led to policies that alienated other Arabs and non-Arabs alike. In North Africa and the Iberian Peninsula, the anger against such

FIGURE 4.1 The Abbasid fortress-palace of al-Ukhaidir (775) near Karbala, Iraq.

Jukka Palm / Alamy Stock Photo.

policies had expressed itself in the ferocity of the Berber Revolt of the 740s, which so shattered the edifice of central authority that the Abbasids themselves were not able to reassert effective control west of Ifriqiya. Even in Ifriqiya itself, they found it advantageous in 800 to concede autonomy to the province's governor, Ibrahim ibn al-Aghlab, a native of Khorasan. The Aghlabid state developed into a regional power that extended its sway to Sicily.

In the rest of the former Umayyad territories, however, the Abbasid cause successfully appealed to a powerful current of piety by virtue of its demand for the abolition of the Umayyad dynasty and the installation of the Prophet's family as the leader of the Umma. As we have seen, the Abbasid era disappointed the pro-Alids, and it was also a bitter pill for the Arab elites who had benefitted from Umayyad policies. The latter immediately lost their privileged position at court and their centrality in the army, where the Khorasani guard replaced them. Over the next few years, they also lost their tax exemptions for their property. Many Arabs, however, as well as most mawali, welcomed the new government because it did not favor any particular ethnic group. Its ideology was based on the spiritual and legal equality of all Muslims.

The Abbasid regime's more cosmopolitan and less parochial character was countered by its increasing remoteness from the ordinary citizen. It is easy to overdraw the contrast between the court ceremony of the early Abbasids and the late Umayyads, for Mu'awiya (d. 680) may have been the last caliph who actually welcomed the common people to his presence with their petitions and appeals. But despite the increasing pomp of the later Umayyads, the Abbasid caliphs soon became much more removed from their subjects than even their immediate predecessors were. In Baghdad, the legacy of Sasanian ceremonial was revived, and the caliph became shielded from his public not only by monumental palaces but also by a remarkably differentiated set of chamberlains and servants. Only the most important officials and foreign guests were allowed in the presence of the caliph. The new government quickly developed a complex bureaucracy, the members of which were recruited from throughout the empire. At the apex of the administration was the *wazir*, who served as the caliph's prime minister or chief executive officer. Reporting to him were ministries of the army, finance, posts and intelligence, and the chancery, among others.

The urbanity of the era is reflected in the poetry and prose that it produced. Poetry had been the greatest cultural expression of the Arabs. Although the Umayyad period had seen some development of poetic themes and styles, nostalgia for hunting parties and desert encampments remained dominant. Under the patronage of the Abbasid caliphs, new themes emerged. The most famous of the poets of the age was Abu Nuwas (d. ca. 813), who was of mixed Arab and Iranian origin. He spent time with bedouin in order to learn the venerated traditions of Arabic poetry and then sought patronage in Baghdad. He was unsuccessful for several years, which was a mixed blessing. Although he desired the financial support of a wealthy patron, not having one left him free to develop new themes instead of being bound to a patron's taste. His work came to reflect the worldly sophistication of the great metropolis. He gradually became famous for his wit, cynicism, and glorification of wine drinking and pederasty. He finally gained a coveted position at court during the last few years of the reign of the famous caliph Harun al-Rashid (r. 786–809).

Court poets such as Abu Nuwas were expected to demonstrate their command of one or more of the major genres of poetry popular at the time. Others rejected such conventions as being artificial and even dissolute. A stark contrast to the career of the social climber Abu Nuwas was Abu al-'Atahiya (d. 826), whose goal was to convey religious values and morality to the common people on the street. To do so, he discarded all the formal poetic conventions of his time and used only the simplest language that would be comprehensible to anyone.

Arabic literature broadened its scope during this period. A prose style emerged that was employed to convey the traditions of courtly behavior (primarily Sasanian in origin) to bureaucrats and courtiers and to record the historical exploits of the Muslim community. Many outstanding prose writers made contributions in the period that spanned the eighth, ninth, and tenth centuries, but some must be mentioned. Sibawayh (d. ca. 793) was an Iranian, but he composed the single most influential exposition of Arabic grammar. Ibn Ishaq (d. 768) was born in Medina but moved to Baghdad. He compiled the first major biography of the Prophet. Some of his fellow scholars criticized his use of sources, and his work was revised by the Egyptian Ibn Hisham (d. ca. 833). The latter version has remained the major source for details of the Prophet's life. Al-Jahiz (d. 869), who was descended from an African slave, lived in Iraq. His mastery of style and his combination of intellect, erudition, and wit made him a highly influential author. Al-Tabari (d. 923) wrote books on a wide variety of subjects but is most famous for his huge *History of Prophets and Kings*, a compendium of history from creation until his own time. It is one of our most important sources for the first three centuries of Muslim history.

The labeling of certain historical periods as "golden ages" is often misleading because economic, political, and cultural developments do not always coincide. In the Abbasid case, this caution is certainly justified. Culturally, its most productive period falls after the middle of the ninth century, but its political and economic high point was during the first few decades of the dynasty. The caliphate of Harun al-Rashid (786–809) is celebrated in the famous *One Thousand and One Nights* as the period of glory for the dynasty, even though to his contemporaries the caliph could boast of no special achievements. In retrospect, however, his reign of a quarter of a century was a halcyon period. The caliph was the unquestioned ruler of the realm, Baghdad had developed into a world capital, and a *pax Islamica* brought a sense of optimism and confidence that Southwest Asia has only rarely known.

Harun himself contributed to the undoing of that optimism. In 802, he designated his eldest son al-Amin to be his successor as caliph, but he also stipulated that a younger son, al-Ma'mun, should rule over an enlarged and autonomous Khorasan and succeed al-Amin as caliph at the latter's death. Soon after Harun died in 809, however, al-Amin demanded that al-Ma'mun cede the western parts of Khorasan to him and that the taxes from the remainder of the province be forwarded to Baghdad. Al-Ma'mun refused, and a long and destructive war between the brothers ensued. During 812–813, al-Ma'mun's army besieged Baghdad itself for a year, and al-Amin was killed. Al-Ma'mun named himself caliph in 813, but he elected to set up his court in Merv, where his base of support lay. Near-anarchy reigned in Baghdad, and the city was heavily damaged in internecine fighting over the next six years. We saw in the previous chapter that al-Ma'mun finally decided in 817–818 to relocate to Baghdad (with fatal consequences for the Shi'ite Imam 'Ali al-Rida). Moving slowly, he arrived only in 819. Exhausted, the factions in the city surrendered with hardly a struggle.

Military and Economic Problems

The heart of the empire had suffered a decade of warfare from 809 to 819. Not only did Baghdad and other cities incur major damage, but ambitious local leaders in every province had tried to take advantage of the confusion in order to bolster their own power. When al-Ma'mun took up residence in Baghdad in 819, he began trying to restore the unity of the empire. He had remained in control of Iran during the war, and he was successful in regaining the areas as far west as Benghazi in eastern Libya and as far south as the holy cities of Mecca and Medina. The area west of Benghazi, however, was permanently lost. The Aghlabids continued to rule in Ifriqiya for another century, technically as Abbasid vassals, but in reality as an independent principality. As a result, the Maghrib and the Iberian Peninsula remained outside the Abbasid orbit.

In the field of culture, al-Ma'mun was more successful, and in that context he became one of the most influential caliphs in history, as we shall see in the next chapter. With the coming to power of al-Ma'mun's younger brother, al-Mu'tasim (833–842), however, the Abbasid dynasty entered a new and tragic era. On the one hand, the middle third of the ninth century probably represents the zenith of Abbasid political power if measured in terms of the control that the central government was able to exert over the provinces. On the other hand, certain developments set the stage for a precipitous decline in the prestige and power of the central government in general and of the caliph in particular.

Changes in the army played a major role in this process. Throughout the ninth century, the army became increasingly multiethnic in its composition. This was not a unique development for the time, as the Byzantine army itself became dependent on Slavs, Turks, Armenians, and eventually Normans. But just as the Arab forces that had achieved the spectacular conquests of the first decades of Islamic history were replaced by Khorasanis early in the Abbasid era, the Khorasanis became supplanted in the ninth century by Daylamis (from Daylam, the region south of the Caspian Sea), Armenians, Berbers, Sudanese, Turks from Central Asia, and other ethnic groups. What is striking is that the vast majority of the Abbasid troops were beginning to come from the border areas of the empire or from outside it altogether—few Iraqis, west Iranians, Syrians, Egyptians, or peninsular Arabs served in the army.

The new pattern of composition of the army had advantages for the caliph. By not having to rely on the local populace for troops, a ruler was freer to use troops against either external or internal enemies without having to negotiate with chieftains or notables for the use of their subjects. In addition, his troops did not hesitate to attack civilians on the streets, since they had no local families at risk. Furthermore, the army of the ninth century was becoming more professional in general and was intent on employing a variety of weaponry on the battlefield in an effort to gain the tactical edge over its opponents. The different ethnic groups represented a military division of labor that, when used well, made an army a formidable force against a less diversified force. Turks specialized in mounted archery, Berbers and Armenians were lance-bearing cavalry, Daylamis were predominantly light infantry employing bows and javelins, and Sudanese served as heavy infantry.

The most notable ethnic group in the new army was that of the Turks. As early as the civil war between his older brothers, al-Mu'tasim had begun building a private army composed of slaves, and he continued to do so after he became the caliph. He eventually owned several thousand such soldiers, mostly Turks of Central Asian origin. These military slaves came to be referred to as *mamluk*s, from an Arabic term meaning "owned" or "belonging to." After a training regimen, they were usually manumitted and became clients of their former masters. As free clients, they gained limited legal rights to property and marriage. Mamluks, then, were not servile and abject victims of a brutal system; instead, they formed a proud and intimidating force that preferred the company of their own kind and regarded the civilian populace with contempt. They were answerable only to the caliph, and they could attain the rank of general or minister of state, controlling the destinies of hundreds of thousands of people and owning vast estates. Thus, rather than being a subservient part of the army, they actually enjoyed important privileges.

The value to caliphs of an army composed of foreign ethnic groups lay in the soldiers' undivided loyalty. Free, indigenous soldiers could be torn between allegiance to the court they served and the local interests of the region from which they came. The irony is that the new pattern developed instabilities of its own and caused even greater difficulties for the administration than the earlier system had. Two factors were prominent in the developing crisis. One was that the military was evolving into a de facto caste, separated by a wide cultural gulf from the rest of society. The martial values of the professional military had always set such a force apart from the rest of society, but now those differences were made all the greater by differences in language and customs. The other problem was that the economy upon which the caliphal government was based was growing weaker, making it more difficult to sustain the military at any acceptable standard of living. The rich province of Iraq was beginning to suffer a double blow to its agriculture. In some parts of the region, river channels were shifting, leaving irrigation works and fields without access to water. In the region close to the Persian Gulf, many fields were suffering from salinization due to repeated irrigation by river water containing high levels of salts. In an attempt to solve the latter problem, the central government brought in tens of thousands of slaves from East Africa to drain swamps and remove the salinated soil.

Because of the economic strains, the government had difficulty paying its troops regularly. The soldiers became restive, and the various ethnic groups suspected each other of benefitting from favoritism. The mutual suspicions led to frequent clashes among the various units, and the Turks gained a reputation for initiating many of the fights. More disturbing still, the civilian population of Baghdad frequently fell victim to slights or outright injury from the arrogant soldiers, most of whom did not bother to learn Arabic. As early as 836, al-Mu'tasim felt compelled to separate the Turks from the other troops and from the general populace by moving his capital some eighty miles to the north, where he built the city of Samarra. The move was intended to be permanent: Samarra entailed a massive investment on a scale not less than the founding of Baghdad itself. The palace and mosque complexes were imperial monuments, and within a few decades the city extended along the Tigris for twenty-four miles. Baghdad continued to function as a commercial and intellectual center, but it was no longer of political importance.

The Assertion of Regional Autonomy

The move to Samarra only postponed the resolution of the crisis, which could hardly be solved by creating yet another imperial capital, especially as the economy was heading into a slow decline. The problem of the rebellious Turkish mamluks became only more serious. These military slaves, totally dependent on the caliph for their subsistence, could be loyal to the death to him when his support for them was unquestioned; on the other hand, they could pose a threat to him when doubts arose regarding their own security. In 861, the caliph al-Mutawakkil (847–861) punished a corrupt Turkish officer by seizing his property. In retaliation, a group of Turkish soldiers murdered the caliph. The relationship between the soldiers and the court had become so poor that no caliph was able to repair it. The remainder of the decade was a period of anarchy during which three of the four caliphs who came to power were assassinated.

The chaos in the capital ended strong central control over the provinces, and local leaders were quick to seize the opportunity to enhance their own power at the expense of Samarra. A Turkish general by the name of Ahmad ibn Tulun was appointed governor of Egypt in 868, but he took advantage of the confusion in Samarra to establish an autonomous regime. He did not formally reject the authority of the caliph, but he stopped sending Egypt's critically needed revenue to Iraq. Under Ibn Tulun and his descendants, Egypt remained autonomous for almost four decades. Between 867 and 873, a coppersmith, al-Saffar, led a rebellion in Khorasan

FIGURE 4.2 The Ibn Tulun mosque in Cairo, completed in 877 by the Abbasid-appointed governor to Egypt after whom it is named. It was influenced by Iraqi architectural models; note the ziggurat-shaped minaret.

and Afghanistan and established the Saffarid dynasty. Although the Saffarids did not sever relations with the caliph, they openly expressed their contempt for him, and they sent the revenue from their area to Samarra only at their pleasure, rather than on demand. By the beginning of the tenth century, the Saffarids were in turn ousted by the Samanid regime, which became truly independent of Baghdad. The Samanids, who had begun as governors for the Abbasids in Bukhara in 819, continued to have the prayers in the mosques said in the name of the caliph but did not send revenue to his treasury at all by the late ninth century. Having taken Khorasan from the Saffarids and continuing to rule over Transoxiana, the Samanids were wealthier and probably more militarily powerful than the Abbasid central government.

Whereas the Tulunids, Saffarids, and Samanids took a passive-aggressive approach toward the Abbasid government, a violent uprising took place much closer to the capital. The tens of thousands of African slaves who had been brought into southern Iraq in order to try to remove salt from the soil were treated brutally, and in 869 they rose in revolt. They overwhelmed the local garrison, and for the next fourteen years the rebels, known as the Zanj, posed a continuous threat to Baghdad and Samarra. Their revolt deprived the caliphate of the revenue from its most productive province. The magnitude of the rebellion can be gauged by the fact that the rebels captured the military city of Wasit and the major city of Basra. Throughout the period, the rage that the ex-slaves felt about their treatment was expressed in the ferocity of their fighting. They massacred the inhabitants of the cities they captured and destroyed mosques and other public buildings. Because of the danger, commerce over the important Persian Gulf trade route was diverted away from Basra to Iranian ports and to the Red Sea. The army finally quelled the revolt in 883, but its damage was enormous: Basra had been severely damaged, large-scale land reclamation projects were never resumed, and the major trade routes had shifted permanently.

In 892, in an attempt to revive the fortunes of the empire, the Abbasid government began the formidable project of moving the government apparatus back to Baghdad. Abandoned, Samarra's vast and magnificent mud-brick structures began to melt into the desert, becoming a metaphor for the fortunes of the dynasty as the economic crisis of the caliphate accelerated. The political disintegration of the empire played a major role in this regard. The Samanid seizure of power ended the prospects of revenue coming from Khorasan, and the drying up of the Persian Gulf trade route starved both the customs revenue and the local retail trade. The land revenues from southern Iraq, which had already been declining before the Zanj revolt, continued to plummet. By the early tenth century, the revenues from the once-wealthiest province were one-third what they had been during the time of Harun al-Rashid. Egypt became increasingly autonomous throughout the tenth century and was able to reduce the amount of revenue sent to Baghdad. The reduction of the flow of revenue from the Nile valley was a catastrophic blow to the Abbasid court, for it meant that insufficient revenue was available to pay the army. The result was a state of perpetual mutiny.

In a desperate effort to bring order to the capital, the caliph in 936 agreed to give a Turkish general responsibility for both civil and military administration. The caliphal office, which had been weak for several decades to that point, now became ineffectual for the next two centuries. But even this fateful step did not bring stability. The devolution of power from the caliph to a general triggered a jealous struggle among the local military elite, leading to a decade of turmoil in Baghdad. The stage was set for a well-organized outside force to march in and take control. In 945, the Buyid clan did just that.

The Buyids were from Daylam, in the Elburz Mountains. Because it was a wild and remote area, it served as a refuge to people throughout history who wanted to keep imperial governments at arm's length. During the late eighth century, Alids began to seek refuge in the area, and over the next hundred years, this remote area became a stronghold of both Zaydi and Imami Shi'ism. In 932, a Daylami named 'Ali ibn Buya, along with two of his brothers and a few hundred infantrymen, ventured south into Fars. This province, the heartland of the old Sasanian Empire, had remained prosperous throughout the previous century, even as Baghdad suffered blow after blow. One of the few revenue-producing provinces left to the Abbasids, Fars had only recently fallen victim to the depredations of some renegade soldiers from Baghdad and was ripe for the plucking. In a single battle, 'Ali won control of the area, and from his base in the provincial capital of Shiraz, he and his brothers sought to expand their area of control. In 945 one brother, Ahmad, negotiated a takeover of Baghdad, and the following year the third brother, al-Hasan, conquered the Iranian plateau from Rayy to Esfahan.

The Buyid brothers and their immediate descendants ruled their provinces as a confederation. Utterly pragmatic, they acknowledged the spiritual authority of the caliph and asserted that he had appointed them to their posts. Ahmad assumed the title of Commander of Commanders, while 'Ali and al-Hasan took the title of governor of their respective provinces. Despite the connotation of the titles, 'Ali remained the most influential of the three rulers, and he sealed the issue by adopting the Sasanian title of *Shahanshah*, meaning "King of Kings." The first generation of Buyid rulers seems to have been Zaydi Shi'ites, but later they provided generous support to Twelver Shi'ism. Although the Buyids did not try to force their subjects to adopt Shi'ism, the Sunni Abbasid caliph was humiliated to be under Shi'ite control. After eighty years of splendor in Baghdad and a century of decline, the Abbasid caliphs had been reduced to figurehead status.

The Fatimid Caliphate

In the preceding chapter, we saw that the Isma'ilis were Shi'ites who recognized Isma'il's son Muhammad as the Imam when Ja'far al-Sadiq died in 765. After a century of underground activity, they reemerged as militant social and religious activists. One faction of Isma'ilis even set up a rival caliphate, challenging the Abbasid caliphate in Baghdad. This was a development of major importance for Muslim history. Shi'ites had verbally expressed their disdain of the Sunni caliphate, but never before had a competing caliphate actually been created. For over two and one-half centuries, the Fatimid caliphate would pose a threat to Sunni political and religious dominance.

Isma'ili Activism

The first two centuries of Muslim rule had brought about a dramatic urbanization of Southwest Asia, transforming the economic and social relationships of the area. By the middle of the ninth century, the Arab tribal aristocracy that had been dominant during Umayyad times was a secondary influence, having been shouldered aside by a ruling class composed of merchants, military leaders, administrators, religious leaders, and landowners. Many of the new elite were the offspring of marriages between Arabs and local women, and some had no Arab lineage at all. The striking wealth of the cities, and the relative impoverishment of the peasants and the bedouin, became a focal point of grievances that led to rural unrest. As we have seen, the Abbasid caliph had become more remote than before, causing some Muslims to mumble about their "Sasanian prince."

It was in this period of growing social cleavage, widespread perception of injustice, near anarchy in some regions, and the erosion of the legitimacy of the Abbasid regime that Isma'ilism burst onto the scene. From the outset, the movement served as a vehicle of social protest and promised that the existing order would be overthrown in favor of a just and egalitarian society. Isma'ilis preached that Muhammad ibn Isma'il never died; rather, he was very much alive under God's protection. His return as the Mahdi was imminent, at which time he would eliminate the corruption, favoritism, and oppression inherent in the materialist society that had been built on the trade of luxury goods and the exploitation of the poor. He would inaugurate a new age of justice and abrogate the old law. In the meantime, his intermediaries provided spiritual leadership to his followers. Initially, the peasants and bedouin were the most responsive to the appeal, but over time a small group of the intelligentsia became involved in the movement, as well as substantial numbers of artisans and day laborers.

Much about the reemergence of Isma'ilism is obscure, and the evidence is partial when it is not contradictory. Some of the confusion is due to the obsession for secrecy characteristic of an opposition movement; some is the result of genuine confusion on the part of observers, who could not distinguish among the many Shi'ite groups competing for followers; and some is due to the fact that the Isma'ilis' enemies slandered them when they were not confused by them. It is clear that more than one group of Isma'ilis arose toward the end of the third quarter of the ninth century.

One of these groups came to be known as the Carmathians (*al-qaramita*). They had their demographic support in Syria, Iraq, and the Persian Gulf coast. Because of their proximity to Baghdad, they were a serious threat to the Abbasid regime, which they vowed to destroy. They attacked several Abbasid installations during the 890s and developed a fearsome reputation. They captured Bahrain from the Abbasid governor in 900 and maintained a prosperous state there for almost two centuries. The Carmathians of Bahrain gained favorable publicity among the poor as a result of their policy of sharing material goods equally, whereas notorious rumors (such as the sharing of wives) gained it equal disrepute among its detractors. Bahrain became the base for numerous raids against the Abbasids.

The Carmathians became infamous for their massacres of pilgrims en route to Mecca. Making the pilgrimage was arduous and dangerous under the best of circumstances, but for extended periods of time, particularly during the years 902–906 and 923–939, Carmathian raids caused pilgrims to realize that performing the hajj could be an act of martyrdom. An episode in 930 won everlasting opprobrium for the sect when a group of Carmathian raiders attacked Mecca and carried away the Black Stone from the Ka'ba. It was kept in Bahrain until 951, when they returned it in exchange for a large ransom. On the one hand, this act of theft and desecration caused most Muslims to loathe the Carmathians; on the other, it helped to show how irrelevant the Abbasid caliph had become. Combined with regular Carmathian attacks on pilgrims, the theft demonstrated that the Abbasid caliphate had no power outside the metropolis of Baghdad. Bahrain remained a regional power until the second half of the eleventh century, when it began to experience political and economic problems. In 1077, a bedouin army defeated and destroyed it.

Another Isma'ili group appeared in Iran and Iraq in the 860s that resulted in the Fatimid movement. Its leaders, based in the lower Tigris River valley, established networks of agents throughout southern Iraq. Soon the Isma'ili headquarters was transferred to Salamiya, north of Damascus. Because of its implicit—and often explicit—criticism of the existing social and political order, the organization came under increasing repression by the Abbasid government. Already having developed a complex underground system of secret cells that communicated with each other across vast distances, the Isma'ilis accelerated their efforts to spread their message of an alternative to the Abbasids. By the end of the ninth century, Isma'ili missionaries were organizing cells in villages and cities from North Africa to India.

As noted in Chapter 3, the Isma'ili leader at Salamiya, 'Abd Allah, left Syria in 902 and made his way westward. The traditional account of the reason for this move attributes it to a schism within the Isma'ili leadership. There is evidence that, in 899,

'Abd Allah began suggesting to the leadership of the group that he would soon publicly announce that he was the Imam himself, rather than merely a spokesman for him. He also claimed that he was descended from Ja'far al-Sadiq's son 'Abd Allah rather than from Isma'il. These were shocking revisions of accepted doctrine. Isma'ilis had been accustomed to denigrating the followers of any claimant to the Imamate of Ja'far al-Sadiq other than Isma'il and his son Muhammad. For 'Abd Allah to claim that a rival of Isma'il's line was the true Imam required a greater shift in loyalties and identity than many Isma'ilis could muster. Many of them revolted, and in 902, 'Abd Allah was forced to flee.

After spending three years hiding in Egypt, in 905 'Abd Allah trekked all the way to Sijilmasa, a Kharijite oasis trading town on the fringe of the Sahara in modern Morocco. He took up residence there in the guise of a merchant. He then made contact with Isma'ili missionaries in Ifriqiya, where large numbers of Berbers from the Kutama tribe had joined the movement. They began making plans for his arrival, and in 909 their army overthrew the Aghlabids in 'Abd Allah's name. The following year, they escorted him from Sijilmasa to Qayrawan, where he took power in the royal suburbs of the city.

A Second Caliphate

As the self-proclaimed Imam, 'Abd Allah also adopted the title of Mahdi and was known thereafter as 'Abd Allah al-Mahdi. Since he claimed descent from Ja'far's son 'Abd Allah, in a technical sense his mission was not Isma'ili at all: It traced its origins to Isma'il's brother, rather than to Isma'il himself. As we shall see in Chapter 6, one of his descendants reclaimed the Isma'ili mantle several decades later. The followers of al-Mahdi's organization eventually came to be known as the *fatimiya*, or the Fatimids, which suggested descent from 'Ali and Fatima. This claim, of course, was not unique to his group, but it is the name that became permanently associated with it. The Fatimids themselves apparently did not use the label *fatimiya*. They simply called themselves *dawlat al-haqq*, which means "the legitimate governmental authority."

The ruling elite realized the importance of the Aghlabid navy that they inherited, and they enlarged it for military and commercial purposes. Their orientation toward the sea took graphic form when 'Abd Allah created a new capital on the coast and named it Mahdiya, "(The City) of the Mahdi." The Fatimid navy captured Sicily, raided the coasts of France and Italy, and plundered Genoa. The fleet dominated the central Mediterranean and threatened the trade of Iberia. The Fatimids also made great efforts to increase the existing trans-Sahara trade and were able to enhance Ifriqiya's importance as a commercial center for goods from both the Mediterranean basin and the sub-Saharan region.

The Fatimids did not try to convert the Sunnis of Ifriqiya by force, but they did gain a reputation for harshly suppressing some of the Sunni leaders. They may have been provoked: Sunni religious leaders in Ifriqiya had often deliberately antagonized the Aghlabids, as well, even though the regime was Sunni. The Fatimids did force all the mosques to institute the slightly different Shi'ite version of the call to prayer and to proclaim the Friday sermon in the name of the Fatimid caliph-Imam.

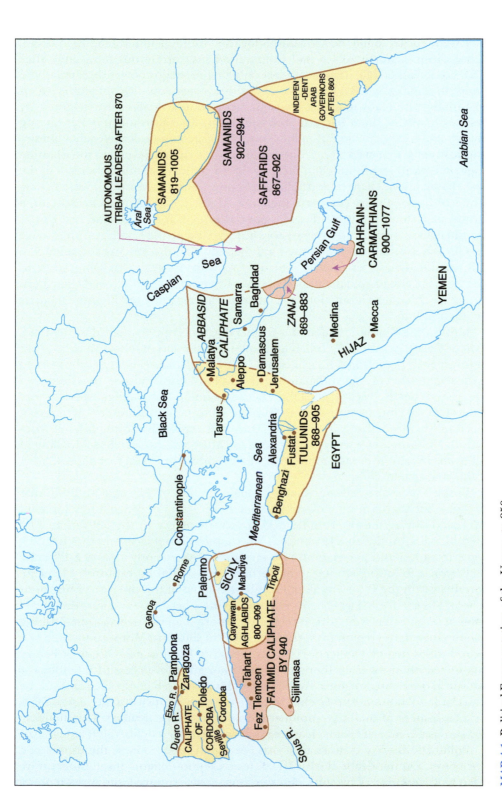

MAP 4.1 Political Fragmentation of the Umma, to 950.

Ifriqiya turned out to be a fortuitous location for the Fatimid Empire to begin, because most of North Africa had fragmented into numerous ministates after the Berber Revolt of 740. This meant not only that no major power threatened the Fatimids in their early days, but also that the ministates would be vulnerable when the Fatimids were ready to attack them. Berbers led almost all of the neighboring states, and many of them had adopted Kharijism. Kharijism was popular among Berbers because of its sanctioning of the overthrow of an unjust ruler, its egalitarianism, and its insistence that even a non-Arab could become caliph. Several of the Kharijite Berber states that were founded in the mid-eighth century became important in the trans-Saharan trade. Tlemcen and Sijilmasa (modern Rissani, Morocco) were among the first of these. Tahart (modern Tagdemt, Algeria) was founded by Rustam, a Kharijite of Iranian origin. It deserves special notice. It became the seat of the Rustamid dynasty, which had a remarkable history. Despite the Kharijites' preference for political decentralization and their antidynastic bias, the sanctity and dignity of the Rustamid dynasty enabled it not only to hold power from generation to generation, but also to hold the respect of other Kharijite oases all across the northern fringe of the Sahara. Its reputation as a center of learning attracted Kharijite scholars from as far as Iran.

Most of the Kharijite settlements from Tahart to Tripoli adhered to the Ibadi variant of Kharijism, and their inhabitants tolerated the sins of fellow Muslims more generously than the original Kharijites did. The original Kharijites typically insisted that the commission of a sin automatically made a Muslim an apostate, thus deserving the penalty of death. By contrast, Tahart became famous for its religious toleration, and it welcomed Christians, Jews, non-Kharijite Muslims, and adherents of different subsects of Kharijism. Ibadism even at this early date was hardly distinguishable from Sunnism. Nevertheless, it was attractive to many Muslims—usually those dwelling in small towns in remote areas—to whom it was important as a badge of dignity, piety, and spiritual egalitarianism.

Berbers were also the overwhelming majority west of Tlemcen and the Atlas Mountains, but Kharijism was not as prominent there. The most dynamic development in Morocco during the pre-Fatimid period was the arrival in the 780s of an Alid named Idris ibn 'Abdullah. He was from Mecca, but it is not clear whether he was a refugee from Abbasid persecution or a missionary. Apparently a Zaydi Shi'ite, he quickly won a following among local Berbers, and in 790 he captured Tlemcen. Before his death the following year, he subdued most of the interior of northern Morocco. His son Idris II was born a few months after his death and was recognized as ruler at the age of eleven. Idris II reigned for more than two decades, establishing his dominance in the region from the Sous River in southern Morocco to some one hundred miles east of Tlemcen. He welcomed into his new capital city of Fez an influx of Shi'ite Arabs from Iberia and Qayrawan after unsuccessful rebellions in those Sunni-dominated regions. By the time of his death in 828, the area around the city was largely Arabized, and Fez had become the dominant city in the region. With the establishment of two large mosques at midcentury, the city began challenging Qayrawan as a center of Islamic learning in North Africa.

Politically, there was no chance that Fez would soon become the capital of a major power. On the death of Idris II, the towns acknowledging his authority were divided among several of his sons. Morocco remained splintered into many feuding principalities. It remained largely Berber for many centuries, although considerable numbers of Arab adventurers and entrepreneurs came into the area over the next 200 years. The Atlas Mountains present a formidable obstacle to travel into the interior of Morocco, and so these immigrants tended to be funneled along the Mediterranean coastal plain to the Atlantic plain and then south, or into the oases on the eastern slope of the Atlas Mountains, and thence to the Sous River. Both of these areas had access to trade (maritime commerce for the former and the trans-Saharan trade in gold and slaves for the latter), whereas the interior of Morocco did not offer many economic opportunities. As a result of this pattern of settlement, the Arabization and Islamization of Morocco took place on the periphery of the country.

The Fatimids soon discovered that the Muslim rulers of Iberia were seeking favorable trade agreements with the commercial towns of the Maghrib. The Fatimid task was to subdue as many of these small principalities as possible before the Iberians gained a strong foothold in the region. The Fatimid targets were weak but numerous, requiring many battles and sieges. At the core of al-Mahdi's army was the cavalry of the Kutama Berbers of western Ifriqiya. They were rivals of the largely Zanata Berbers of the southern oases, and control of those commercial oases was critical for Fatimid prosperity. The political and economic rivalry of the Kutama and Zanata Berber groups was overlain by religious differences. The Fatimids and the Kharijites hated each other. The Kharijites placed a premium on piety and strict observance of ritual, and their egalitarian ideals included the conviction that truth was accessible to all. The Fatimids, by contrast, viewed ritual as the outer truth that was not as important as the inner, spiritual truth; their organizational hierarchy of religious officials was the absolute opposite of religious egalitarianism; and they taught that individuals have access to different levels of truth.

Al-Mahdi had spent four years (905–909) of his life as a fugitive in the Kharijite stronghold of Sijilmasa, but he did so inconspicuously. When his identity was discovered, he was placed under house arrest. Once his Fatimid supporters began their campaign to place him in power in Qayrawan, they turned on the Kharijites with a fury. One of the Fatimid army's earliest conquests in 909 was Tahart, where the Rustamids were massacred. Other Kharijite oases from Tripoli to Tlemcen fell and were also treated with brutality. By 917, al-Mahdi's army had captured Fez, and the Fatimids were well on their way to domination of the entire Maghrib.

Securing the Maghrib was important for security and commercial purposes, but al-Mahdi's most important goal was to conquer Egypt. The fertile Nile valley would be an ideal location from which to coordinate the plan to dominate the Muslim world. Although the Abbasids had ousted the independent-minded Tulunids in 905, Egypt remained turbulent and seemingly vulnerable. It proved to be more secure than it appeared: Al-Mahdi launched campaigns against Egypt as early as 913–915, and again in 919–921, but he was thwarted when the Abbasid army intervened both times. Al-Mahdi died in 934, and his son launched a third campaign against Egypt, once again without success. The Fatimid regime planned a fourth campaign, but it was aborted when a rebellion broke out among the Berbers of the Maghrib in 943. The Fatimids lost the entire Maghrib temporarily, and the capital city of Mahdiya was even besieged. For the next two decades, the Fatimid government was forced to concentrate its efforts on consolidating its power in the Maghrib. It relied increasingly upon the Kutama Berbers and the empire's urban population, who feared the unruly mountain and desert tribes. Not until the last third of the century would Muslims in other regions know how powerful this new Fatimid state could be.

The Umayyad Caliphate of Cordoba

The Iberian Peninsula witnessed the rise of yet a third caliphate during the first half of the tenth century. Its emergence was not inspired by a challenge to Baghdad, for the Abbasids never controlled the peninsula. The area's links even with the Umayyad central government in Damascus had been tenuous from the first, due to the great distance of the province from the capital and the preoccupation of Damascus with the northern and eastern frontiers of the empire. Commercial and cultural links with the Arab east remained close, but the Muslims of Iberia developed a distinctive identity that facilitated the declaration of a separate caliphate.

The Consolidation of Umayyad Power

Muslim raiders rapidly and easily subdued Iberia between 711 and 720, except for the north where prolonged, vicious fighting took place. Historically, the mountain people of the north had always resisted domination by the government of the south, whether Roman or Visigothic, and that pattern continued under the Muslims. The peoples of the north were, themselves, separated from each other by high mountain ridges. Although most of them spoke variations of Latin (the Basques were the notable exception), they formed distinct, rival communities. The Muslims were primarily interested in the northern section simply to protect their own lines of communication, for they quickly realized that the area had little wealth to offer. Indeed, when the small principality of Asturias revolted about 720, the Muslims made little effort to quell the rebellion. They chose, instead, to begin a series of raids north of the Pyrenees into southern Aquitaine and Provence that lasted for several decades. The Muslims would eventually regret not having stamped out the revolt in Asturias. For the moment, however, Asturias was merely an arid and stony hill country, offering little for the effort that securing it would require. The wealth of the cities, monasteries, and churches in southern France, on the other hand, proved to be irresistible raiding targets.

Despite the ease of the Muslim conquest of Iberia, the area was not politically stable under the Umayyads of Damascus. The primary threat to the dynasty was not that of the native population, but rather factional rivalry among Arab tribes. As a result, governors found that they were often opposed simply because of their tribal identity, and their authority was constantly challenged. The rivalry among the Arabs made the society vulnerable to the Great Berber Revolt of the 740s, which spread into the peninsula from North Africa. Several thousand Syrian troops, arriving from Damascus, suppressed the rebellion in Iberia. The uprising, however, had so shattered the administrative structure in North Africa that Damascus could not reestablish control over the peninsula, and it became autonomous. Moreover, in 750, a famine spawned by a sustained drought forced thousands of Berbers who had settled in the northwestern and north-central parts of the peninsula to migrate to the south, allowing Asturias to annex much of the vacated territory. For the next three centuries, the valley of the Duero River formed a permeable and elastic frontier between Christian and Muslim regions. Increasingly, Arab writers referred to the Muslim-held territories—as opposed to the Christian-dominated areas of the peninsula—as *al-Andalus* (hereafter, Andalus).

The Abbasid revolution was an epochal event for most Muslims, but its impact on Andalus was unexpected. As we have seen, the Abbasids attempted to eradicate the Umayyad family, but one of the princes, 'Abd al-Rahman, escaped to Egypt and then to North Africa. There his heritage served him well, for he was able to find refuge among the Berber tribe from which his mother had come. From the Maghrib, he made contact with Umayyad partisans who had sought refuge in Andalus, and he learned that his family had support among powerful units of the Syrian troops there. With their help, he resurrected the Umayyad dynasty, establishing a power base in Cordoba. The family would rule from there for almost three centuries, until 1031. 'Abd al-Rahman, not surprisingly, refused to recognize the Abbasid caliph, and he assumed the title of *amir*, which suggests "commander" or "leader." The Muslims of Andalus thereafter maintained close cultural contacts with the eastern regions of the Muslim world, but they acknowledged no religious or political authority outside the peninsula.

In spite of the fact that 'Abd al-Rahman was supported by the Syrian army units, he discovered that the Umayyad name held no mystique for the bulk of the Arab and Berber tribes in the peninsula. He had to lead military campaigns almost until his death in 788 in order to gain the submission of the Muslim warlords. One episode in 'Abd al-Rahman's campaigns made its way into the literature of the Franks. In 777,

FIGURE 4.3 The interior of the Great Mosque at Cordoba, constructed between 784 and 987.
Robert Harding / Alamy Stock Photo.

Arab and Berber chieftains in the foothills of the Pyrenees asked Charlemagne for help in resisting the encroachments of the Umayyad ruler. The Frankish king, who was in the early stages of his own conquests, recognized an unexpected opportunity to limit the power of a rival and simultaneously to secure territory on his southwestern frontier. When his army arrived at Zaragoza (Saragossa) in 778, however, the city's ruler changed his mind, revoked the alliance, and closed the city's gates to him. After an unsuccessful siege, Charlemagne was forced to withdraw through the western Pyrenees. At Roncesvalles, his rear guard, commanded by Roland, was attacked and massacred, inspiring the Frankish epic *The Song of Roland*. The actual identity of the attackers—Basques, Arabs, or Berbers—has not been conclusively determined, but Muslims received the blame in the poem. 'Abd al-Rahman captured Zaragoza and Pamplona the following year.

The Umayyads reigned over Andalus from their capital of Cordoba, but they never managed to rule the region as a centralized state. Even after 'Abd al-Rahman II (822–852) introduced Abbasid-style administrative offices and practices in an effort to centralize control, Berber and Arab tribes remained powerful down to the end of the dynasty in 1031. The central government was dominant, but the tribes tested its strength through frequent revolts. The native Hispano–Romans, both Christians and new converts to Islam, also engaged in periodic revolts against the government. The new converts seem to have been rankled by the same irritant that had bothered new converts in Umayyad Damascus: the privileges of the Arab elite.

Andalus was ethnically and religiously the most diverse polity in Western Europe during the period from the ninth to the thirteenth centuries. It embraced the Hispano–Roman Christian population, the Basques, a large Jewish minority, and the Muslims, among whom were Arabs, Berbers, and a growing number of Hispano–Romans. The Arabs and Berbers, as conquering and garrisoned soldiers, served in the army all over the country, but a difference emerged in the pattern of settlement of the civilians of the two groups. The Berbers lived in all parts of Andalus, but in the mountains that form the perimeter of the central plateau (the Meseta) they greatly outnumbered the Arabs and became identified as a troublesome mountain people. The Arabs, by contrast, tended to settle in the fertile lowlands. Prominent among these were the Ebro River valley that runs parallel to the Pyrenees Mountains, the Guadalquivir River valley in south-central Iberia, and the Valencian coast. The Jews, as in Christian Europe, lived primarily in urban areas.

The Muslims had conquered a land whose agriculture was typical of the Mediterranean region: sheep herding in the mountains and winter crops of wheat and barley, olives, and grapes in the valleys. Vegetables were grown on small irrigated fields in the Ebro valley and in Valencia. The Muslim settlement had a profound effect on the agriculture of Andalus and, subsequently, of Europe. The Arabs found that the old Roman irrigation systems, which were used to pump water from rivers into fields, had fallen into disuse. They repaired them and introduced into Andalus the *noria*, or water wheel, and irrigation from wells. The result was both an increase in the area of cultivable land and the ability to grow crops during the hot, dry summer.

The impact of the Muslim invasion on the variety of crops grown in Andalus was even greater. Due to the enormous extent of the conquests by the Arab armies in the seventh and eighth centuries, an extraordinary diffusion of edible plants occurred. Arabs in Andalus brought in plants from Syria, Berbers introduced crops from North Africa, and both groups experimented with new crops from as far away as Iran and the Indian Ocean basin. As a result, Andalus was soon home to the date palm, sugar cane, oranges (the Valencian orange and the tangerine—named after Tangier, across the Strait of Gibraltar—attest to the popularity of the oranges grown in the western Mediterranean), lemons, grapefruits, apricots, almonds, artichokes, rice, saffron, eggplants, and parsnips. Cotton, the mulberry tree, and the silkworm also made their first appearance in Iberia at this time. Elaborate gardens patterned after the Persian style became commonplace, and in the literature of the day, Andalus—particularly the rich agricultural province of Valencia—became a model for paradise. Because of the new crops and the improved irrigation systems, as many as four harvests per year were now possible, greatly increasing the productivity of the land and the density of the population.

The newly productive agriculture stimulated the economy of Andalus. Little commerce took place with the underdeveloped Christian areas to the north of the Pyrenees, but a lively trade developed between Andalus and the eastern Mediterranean, with both Byzantines and Abbasids overlooking political differences in order to benefit economically. The most important goods exported from the west were silk cloth, timber, agricultural products, and gold from West Africa. Toledan steel had been famous since Roman times; in the form of cutlery and swords, it was in high demand, as were Andalusi copper utensils. The Andalusian breed of horses became one of the most prized in European history. Although its origin is disputed, most equine specialists think that it was the result of local mares having been bred with the North African Barb horse, which was brought in during the eighth-century invasion.

As had been the case in Southwest Asia, the international economy stimulated urbanization. The cities of Andalus blossomed, in startling contrast to the absolute dearth of urban life in Western Europe before the eleventh century. Toledo, the old Visigothic capital, continued to flourish, but new cities to the south and east supplanted it in importance. The heart of Andalus was the Guadalquivir valley, and Cordoba was the center of Umayyad power. 'Abd al-Rahman I had revived the city when he made it his capital, and he is responsible for having begun construction of the Great Mosque, now famous throughout the world for its architectural splendor. 'Abd al-Rahman II enhanced the cultural life of the city with his patronage of music, poetry, and religious works, and he authorized a major expansion of the mosque. 'Abd al-Rahman III (912–961) founded a new complex of palace and official buildings at Madinat al-Zahra, some four miles outside the city walls. A veritable palace city, its size can be gauged by the 4100 marble columns that lined it. During the tenth century, the grandeur of Cordoba, with its libraries and creature comforts, awed visitors from Western Europe. It may well have had a population approaching 100,000 at a time when Paris and London were muddy villages. Seville, the second city in size and influence, may have been home to over 80,000 inhabitants by the eleventh century.[2]

A Third Caliphate

The Umayyad dynasty in Andalus experienced the pinnacle of its power in the tenth century. The late ninth century, ironically, provided little hope for that possibility, as the administrative reforms of which 'Abd al-Rahman II was so proud did little more than provoke uprisings against the attempts to centralize power. As a result, in 912, ʻAbd al-Rahman III inherited an amirate whose authority had shrunk to little more than the environs of Cordoba. By then, regional power was in the hands of many different strongmen, some of the most powerful of whom were Hispano-Roman converts to Islam, or *muwallad*s. ʻAbd al-Rahman III was determined to enhance his power, and throughout his long reign he fought almost constantly. During the first half of his career, he concentrated on subduing the rebels in Andalus and challenging the Fatimids in the Maghrib; then, during the second half, he concentrated on the struggle with the Christian kingdoms to the north. By the last decade of his reign, he had forced several of the Christian kingdoms to pay him an annual tribute.

In the year 929, ʻAbd al-Rahman III announced that he was not merely an amir, but rather was the true caliph of the Islamic world. He may have claimed the caliphate as a result of Fatimid activity. As we saw before, the Fatimids had seized power in Ifriqiya twenty years earlier and had immediately laid claim to the caliphate. Furthermore, the Fatimids expanded what had been the Aghlabid navy and soon dominated the western Mediterranean. The implicit Fatimid threat to Andalus from the sea was compounded in 922 with the Fatimid capture of Fez. Whereas previous Umayyads might have been restrained from claiming the caliphate for fear of appearing presumptuous, now ʻAbd al-Rahman III could claim it as the true champion of Sunnism, in opposition to the Shiʻite Fatimids and the remote and weak Abbasids.

The declaration of the Umayyad caliphate in Andalus raises the intriguing question of how many Muslims were in the peninsula by the mid-tenth century. What proportion of the society, after all, would be affected by the new claim? Some historians think that rapid conversion to Islam took place in the country during the first half of the tenth century and that by midcentury a Muslim majority existed. According to this view, conversion continued to the end of the eleventh century, by which time eighty percent of the population was Muslim. Other historians assume that Christians always remained the majority.[3] The evidence is inconclusive for either position, but most historians agree that tenth-century Andalus had at least a near-majority Muslim population whose numbers, wealth, and power made their cultural hegemony incontestable. Arabic was the lingua franca, both formally and informally; the manners and tastes of the Umayyad court were the arbiters of the social graces; and the transformation of the economy gave the Muslims great legitimacy and prestige.

It is worth noting in this regard that the substantial number of Jews in Andalus became Arabized, as most Jews throughout the Muslim world did. Little is known of them before the tenth century, but from the early tenth to the mid-twelfth centuries, Andalusi Jews experienced a revival of literature, science, and philosophy, and they wrote in Arabic, using Hebrew script. Many of them served as important court figures, the most famous being Hasday ibn Shaprut, the physician to ʻAbd al-Rahman III. His diplomatic services and patronage of the arts made him an important figure. Prior to the twelfth century, Jews throughout the world could hardly hope to live under more favorable circumstances than in Andalus. A pogrom did take place in Granada in the eleventh century, but it was the exception that proved the rule: It was a reaction by the common people against the great influence that Jews exerted at the court.

The extent of Arabization among Christians is unclear. Arabized Christians were called Mozarabs (from the Arabic *mustaʻrib*, meaning "Arabized"). Historians once thought that they were the most dynamic element within the Christian community. However, no Christian literature in Arabic has survived, in contrast to a large corpus of Latin literature that still exists. The evidence suggests that most Christians could speak Arabic and, in cities such as Toledo, may have used it exclusively. Moreover, many of the Christians who fled as refugees to the north in order to live in Christian societies had Arabic names. On the other hand, the frequent, small-scale riots of Christians in the cities of central and southern Andalus and the absence in the Christian literature of references to cultural developments outside the Christian community itself, suggest a religious community that sealed itself off from Islamic influences. The term *Mozarab* appears to have been an epithet hurled at Arabized Christians by other Christians who considered them to have betrayed their heritage. The Mozarabs were a small community and did not leave a cultural legacy, unlike the Arabized Jews.

At midcentury, the caliphate of Andalus was in an enviable position. Its two caliphal competitors were on the defensive. The Abbasid caliph had become a puppet, first to his own Turkish guard and then to the Daylami Buyids, and the Fatimid caliph was fighting for his life against the Berber revolt in North Africa. 'Abd al-Rahman III even contributed to the discomfiture of the Fatimid ruler by supplying several of the Berber chiefs with supplies and arms. His family's honor had been reclaimed with the establishment of a second Umayyad caliphate at the very time that the Abbasid usurpers had apparently faded into insignificance. His society was becoming Arabized and Islamized to such a degree that he could reasonably expect it to become the dominant region of the Muslim world within a matter of decades.

Economic Networks

The political and religious fragmentation of the ninth and tenth centuries contrasted sharply with developments in the economy of the Muslim world that were tying the regions together more closely than ever before in history. The Arab conquests of the seventh and eighth centuries had consolidated into one empire many previously hostile states and regions. Under the central administration of the Umayyads of Damascus, these far-flung regions enjoyed rapid communication and participation in a single huge market. The new garrison cities required food, building materials, and other everyday necessities that often had to be brought in from a considerable distance away. These demands stimulated migration, manufacturing, and commerce. Craftsmen, merchants, scholars, soldiers, and adventurers traveled to distant regions of the empire and encountered new foods, tools, implements, and styles of architecture and fashion. They brought home with them new tastes and demands, further stimulating trade. The vast area from the Indus to Andalus became a single economic unit, stimulating agricultural diversification, industrial production, international trade, and urban population growth. Despite the loss of central political control that took place after the overthrow of the Umayyads of Damascus, the economic and communication channels remained remarkably open.

A Single Economy

Agriculture formed the base of the economy almost everywhere. In most parts of the Muslim world, agriculture was dependent on irrigation. In the Iranian areas, the

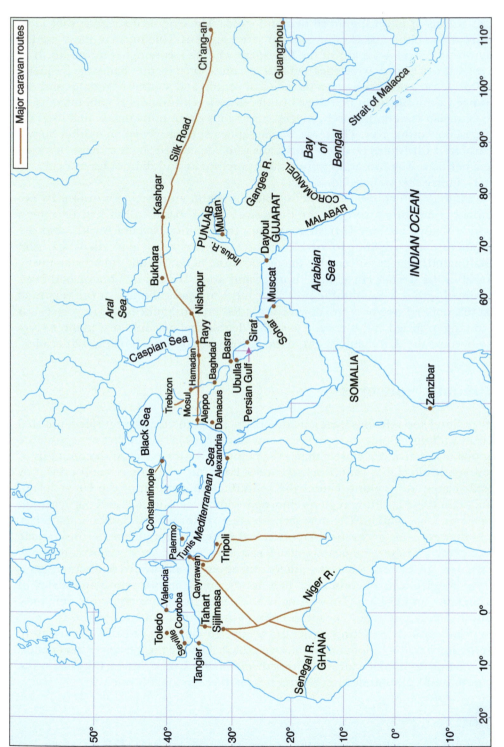

MAP 4.2 The Tenth-Century Muslim Trading Zone.

dominant irrigation system had long been based on *qanats*, the underground canals that the Arabs found in widespread use throughout the Sasanian Empire. Along the Indus, Tigris, Euphrates, and Nile rivers, elaborate networks of basins, canals, and dikes had been in place for thousands of years, employing water wheels, the Archimedes screw, and other lifting devices to move water to where it was needed. As these areas were incorporated into a single economic system, the techniques and the crops that were grown as a result of their use became available to other, distant regions. The most striking illustration of the process was the adoption of the *noria*, or Egyptian water wheel, in Andalus and the subsequent cultivation in that peninsula of citrus fruits, sugar cane, and other vegetables and fruits from Egypt and Iraq.

The cities depended on the surplus produced by local farmers so that their inhabitants, in turn, could produce manufactured goods. Like most advanced societies of the period, the Muslim world's primary manufactured product was textiles. Fars, in southwestern Iran, was probably the most important center of textile production, but others became famous, as well: Egyptian cottons and linens were in high demand, and Mosul and Damascus became immortalized in the fabrics known as muslin and damask, respectively. Damascus and Toledo were famous for their metallurgy. The carbon steel that they developed enabled them to manufacture sword blades of remarkable hardness, sharpness, and beauty.

Despite the excellent quality of the textile and metal industries, however, the glass industry may have achieved the highest level of artistic and technical sophistication. Glass was first manufactured in Southwest Asia in ancient times, and Muslims continued the tradition of innovation. Glassmakers in Baghdad developed spectacular new styles of relief cutting and decorated their products with the forms of running animals and plant scrolls. Glass makers in Egypt invented luster painting and gilding, in which gold leaf was applied to an object that was then fired to fix the glass.

The most noteworthy feature of the economy of the Muslim world was international trade. Commerce, of course, had taken place among the various regions of Eurasia and Africa for centuries. Rome had traded with Han China and East Africa, and even the hostile Byzantines and Sasanians had traded with each other. But the fact that Muslims now ruled the huge area from the Indus to the Atlantic resulted in profound changes. Whereas Sasanian–Byzantine commerce had been largely an exchange of luxury goods, the same trade routes by the early Abbasid period carried an astounding variety of goods destined for mass consumption, including textiles, foodstuffs, and utensils. As a result, new crops and new craft techniques spread rapidly across the vast trading network, transforming diets and material culture.

Muslim merchants between the Nile and Amu Darya had regular contacts with Andalus and the Maghrib. In fact, the extent of the travels undertaken by merchants in this period is quite impressive. Documents from this period reveal that merchants from Khorasan accompanied their goods to Andalus, and Andalusi merchants personally sold their goods in the Iranian highlands. Except in winter, ships made regular voyages between the eastern Mediterranean and the Maghrib, both individually and in convoys. Caravans made the route from Egypt to the Maghrib year-round. As a result, the eastern Mediterranean was in contact not only with North Africa and Andalus, but also with West Africa.

Overland Trade

International trade was conducted overland and by sea. Before the advent of the railroad in the nineteenth century, most of the world's long-distance trade went by sea if possible, due to the much lower costs and shorter times offered by sea travel. In the Muslim world, however, overland caravans played a more important role than in many other developed societies. One reason for that was its geographical setting. North Africa sought the goods of West and Central Africa, from which it was separated by the Sahara, and the great land mass of Southwest Asia made it impossible to ship goods by water from, say, Syria to Khorasan. This motive for long-distance overland trade was matched by the means to accomplish it: the domestication of the camel in the first millennium B.C.E. Camels offered a rugged, low-maintenance, "off-road" means of transportation with a quarter-ton cargo capability and an "all-terrain" ability that carts and wagons simply could not match.

International trade was valued most for filling the region's chronic need for timber and most metals. The purchase of timber and basic metals in the central Islamic lands was made possible by the abundant supplies of gold and silver that became a feature of the first three centuries of Muslim history. The Iranian plateau had ample supplies of silver, but the new Muslim regimes made special efforts to obtain control of trade routes with access to sources of gold. The main gold mines that supplied the Muslim world were in West Africa, accessible by caravan routes across the Sahara. The trade with West Africa was immensely profitable, for the North Africans were able to exchange cheap products such as beads and metal pans for gold.

The Sahara is so large (the size of the United States), hot, and dry that it is easy to assume that it is a trackless waste. In fact, however, several caravan routes wound their way for a thousand miles through the desert, following water holes and funneling a lucrative trade in gold and slaves from the south. North African states had long competed for control of these routes. The most westerly route linked the gold mines of Ghana with Sijilmasa, which quickly became the largest North African market for gold and slaves. Tahart, Qayrawan, and Tripoli were other major distribution points for the trans-Saharan trade. The commodities arriving at these points might be destined for ships or for other caravans that followed well-established routes along the North African coast. (Qayrawan gets its name, in fact, from *qayrawan*, the Arabic word from which we derive *caravan*.)

From these and other caravan cities, Muslim merchants embarked on trading ventures that might take them away from home for months, or even years, at a time. Other merchants sent agents to be permanent representatives in sub-Saharan towns. These merchants were emissaries of a flourishing urban civilization and received favored treatment at the hands of West African rulers. Their literacy in the Arabic language—the diplomatic and commercial language of North Africa—made them doubly valuable to the rulers, and they and their families increasingly served the royal courts as secretaries and interpreters. Because many of them were Ibadis during the early centuries of Islam, it is probable that the earliest converts in West Africa were also adherents of Ibadi Islam. By the tenth century, Muslim merchants and officials occupied separate quarters of several West African towns along the upper Niger River and the Senegal River, and several rulers of the area had become Muslim. Rarely did West African rulers attempt to impose Islam on their subjects. On the contrary, almost all of them were sufficiently astute politically to make a point of displaying the rituals of the traditional religion at court while patronizing Muslim scholars and merchants. As a result, Islam had little impact on the countryside until several centuries later.

Because the large cities of the Muslim world were confident of obtaining regular supplies of gold, the gold *dinar* (derived from *dinarius*, the standard unit of Byzantine currency) became the standard unit of Muslim coinage, usually worth ten silver *dirhams* (a term derived from the Greek *drachma*). The high-quality gold and silver coins minted by Muslims meant that the cities of the region could obtain the goods they needed from anywhere in the known world. A particularly dramatic demonstration of the utility of the coins is revealed in the caches of thousands of silver dirhams (struck in tenth-century Bukhara, under the Samanids) that have been discovered in northern Europe, attesting to the large volume of trade between the far north and the Muslim world. Russians and Scandinavians were too primitive to be able to use the scientific instruments, fine fabrics, paper, and ceramics that Muslims had to offer. Thus, when Muslims purchased timber, amber, honey, wax, furs, and white slaves from northern Europeans, they paid in gold and silver.

A Commercial City in the Mediterranean

The expanding networks of trade facilitated the flow both of goods and people. Scholars, merchants, and missionaries traveled extensively. During the tenth and eleventh centuries, several Muslim geographers became immortalized by virtue of their trenchant descriptions and analyses of what they saw during their long journeys. Ibn Hawqal (ca. 920–ca. 980), a native of northern Iraq, explored the enormous region from Khorasan to Andalus. His Surat al-Ard is a particularly good source for comparing the means of production in both agriculture and manufacturing across the Muslim world. In the excerpt that follows, he describes the market layout in Palermo, Sicily, which served as a conduit of goods between Europe and North Africa. He admired the landscape and architecture of Sicily, but he was quite critical of its inhabitants, whose character he believed to suffer from overconsumption of onions!

Among the countries in the hands of the Muslims, Sicily, by virtue of its fine situation, may be put in the same class as [Andalus]. It is an island in the form of an isosceles triangle, with its apex to the west. Its length is seven days' journey; its width, four… Sicily consists mainly of mountains, castles, and fortresses. Most of its soil is inhabited and cultivated. The only famous city is Palermo, the capital …, which is on the seashore. It consists of five quarters, adjoining and not separated by any distance but with their boundaries clearly marked.

… Palermo is surrounded by a huge stone wall, high and strong. It is inhabited by merchants. There is a great cathedral mosque, which was built as a Christian church shortly before the Conquest. … Facing Palermo there is a town called Khalisa, with a stone wall inferior to that of Palermo. Here live the Sultan and his entourage. There are two public

(Continued)

baths but neither markets nor inns. There is a small cathedral mosque, the Sultan's garrison, a naval arsenal, and the administrative offices. It has four gates in the north, south, and west, but in the east there is the sea and a wall without a gate. ... The quarter known as the Quarter of the Slavs is bigger and more populous than the two cities I have mentioned. In it is the seaport. There are springs which flow between this place and [Palermo], and the water serves as a boundary between them.

There is a quarter known by the name of the mosque of Ibn Saqlab. It is also big but has no streams, and its inhabitants drink from wells. By its edge flows the river called Wadi 'Abbas, a broad and swift stream on which they have many mills, but their gardens and orchards do not make use of it.

The New Quarter is large and adjoins the quarter of the mosque. There is no division or demarcation between them, and both are unwalled, as is also the Quarter of the Slavs. Most of the markets are between the mosque of Ibn Saqlab and the New Quarter. They are as follows: the olive oil sellers in their entirety; the millers, the money changers, the apothecaries, the smiths, the sword cutlers [polishers?], the flour markets, the brocade makers, the fishmongers, the spice merchants, the greengrocers, ... the fruiterers, the sellers of aromatic plants, the jar merchants, the bakers, the rope makers, a group of perfumers, the butchers, the shoemakers, the tanners, the carpenters, and the potters. The wood merchants are outside the city. In Palermo proper there are groups of butchers, jar merchants, and shoemakers. The butchers have nearly 200 shops for the sale of meat, and there are a few of them inside the city at the beginning of the main road. Near them are the cotton merchants, the ginners, and the cobblers. There also is another useful market in the city.

SOURCE: *Islam from the Prophet Muhammad to the Capture of Constantinople. Vol. II: Religion and Society.* by Bernard Lewis (1974):495 words from pp. 23–24. © 1974 by Bernard Lewis. By permission of Oxford University Press USA.

In the east, the famous Silk Road through Central Asia was an important link between Iran and China. Actually, there was no single Silk Road, but several roughly parallel routes that had been conduits of commerce and ideas since 500 B.C.E. or earlier. Under the Han dynasty (206 B.C.E.–220 C.E.), the links between Iran and China became a matter of Chinese state policy, and trade became regular and important. Transoxiana became the central link in a great network of roads that connected the Mediterranean with Ch'ang-an, the capital of several Chinese dynasties, including those of the Han and T'ang (618–907). Merchants from the Syrian coast followed a path through Rayy to Bukhara and Samarqand; merchants from the Aegean Sea would cross Anatolia and arrive at the Transoxiana oases either by crossing the Caspian Sea by ship or by following a road to Rayy.

From Samarqand, the routes to China were all daunting. The road due east scaled formidable mountain ranges so high they caused altitude sickness; the more indirect route to the north was less exhausting because it crossed the steppes of southern Russia, but it was often contested by competing tribes or states, making the journey risky at best. Regardless of the difficulties and dangers, the profits to be

FIGURE 4.4 A sambuk, the largest type of dhow. Dhows were the traditional seaworthy vessels of the western Indian Ocean for more than a millennium, and they are still in wide use today.

Dorling Kindersley ltd / Alamy Stock Photo.

made by engaging in long-distance trade encouraged numerous merchants to engage in the enterprise. The Silk Road encouraged a thriving trade in luxury goods and provided a route for the introduction of Chinese technologies and techniques into the Muslim world that craftsmen readily adopted.

Maritime Commerce

Overland trade was a long, dangerous, and expensive undertaking. Travel by sea had its own perils, but it was much faster and less expensive. It did not require the feeding and care of pack animals or the lodging of humans, and, because it was faster, it entailed fewer meals. That is why the bulk of the trade between the Muslim world on the one hand, and India and China on the other, took place by sea, utilizing the Indian Ocean. Until the beginning of the tenth century, the center of Muslim commerce in the Indian Ocean was the Persian Gulf. The metropolis of Baghdad served as an enormous siphon that attracted staples and luxuries of every kind. Even as it imported timber and metals overland from the north and west, it served as a magnet for luxuries coming by sea. Large ships bearing goods from China and South Asia tied up at the wharves of Ubulla, the port for Basra, where stevedores transferred their cargoes to river boats bound for Baghdad. There the boats unloaded their cargoes from all around the Indian Ocean basin: porcelain, silk, spices, precious stones, perfumes, incense and scented wood, and slaves.

Other ports in the Gulf—Siraf on the Iranian coast, and Sohar and Muscat in Oman—also became flourishing entrepôts of world trade during this time. Goods from China were highly valued, and even in the pre-Islamic era Arabs had established a colony in Canton (Guangzhou) in order to have direct access to Chinese silks, porcelain, lacquerware, and other goods. The Muslim community in Canton was temporarily expelled in 879 by the T'ang dynasty, and many of the merchants resettled in Southeast Asia, where they reestablished trading connections with the Gulf.

Direct trade with China, however, was rare. The long distances and the need to synchronize one's schedule with the monsoons meant that a round trip to China required a year and a half. As a result, the Muslim carrying trade was focused on the western half of the Indian Ocean basin. Merchants who wished to trade with the residents of East Africa could send vessels on winter's northerly monsoon to reach most of the east coast of Africa, and the southeasterly monsoon brought them back in summer. As a result of this trade, Muslim communities began to appear along the Ethiopian coast of the Red Sea during the eighth and ninth centuries. By the tenth century, several communities containing Muslim Arab traders were established along the Somali coast, and a few could be found as far south as Zanzibar.

East of the Gulf, Sind was an important stop. Although the region had long been famous for its agricultural potential, pre-Islamic Arabs valued it largely as a conduit for trade from India. Conquered by the Umayyads in 711, Sind gradually became autonomous in the second half of the ninth century. Daybul was a flourishing port of call for merchants crossing the Indian Ocean, and it was open to influences from many regions. Four hundred miles up the Indus River, Multan became the major Muslim city in the Punjab (the region that is defined by the five large tributaries of the Indus). Sind was predominantly Buddhist at the time of the Arab conquest, although Hindus were in the process of persecuting them and forcing them out of the region. Hinduism itself was only just beginning to be established in the region, and Sind was almost unique in being a region in which Islam gradually replaced it. Multan became notorious in the Sunni imagination when it fell to Fatimid-supported Isma'ilis in 977. Despite the efforts of certain Sunni rulers to crush the Isma'ilis, they maintained a significant presence in Sind for over two centuries and even expanded into Gujarat.

Muslims also established trading communities on India's Malabar Coast, south of Gujarat. Jews and Nestorian Christians, along with Arabs from Yemen, had established settlements there in pre-Islamic times, and the Arabs in the area rapidly Islamized after 650. Malabar had traditionally supplied spices and luxury goods to the Mediterranean region, and its merchant community served as middlemen for the commerce of the Indian Ocean. The coastal plain is separated from the rest of India by the Western Ghats, a steep escarpment that extends parallel to the Arabian Sea for more than 700 miles, insulating the coast from political and cultural developments inland. As a result, Malabar's contacts with the rest of the world were by sea, and hence with Southeast Asia, Arabia, and East Africa even more than with the rest of India. This orientation allowed the Muslims of the region to develop a quite different identity from those who subsequently settled the interior.

In contrast to the thriving trade of the Indian Ocean basin, the maritime commerce of the Mediterranean was in a depressed state for several centuries until the end of the ninth century. Although merchants from Muslim territories (both Muslims and Jews) and from the Byzantine Empire continued to trade throughout the intermittent warfare that erupted between the two sides, most of their commerce was conducted overland with the Black Sea entrepôt of Trebizon rather than through Mediterranean seaports. Maritime commerce in the eastern Mediterranean was jeopardized by Byzantine naval attacks on Muslim ports, and even great ports such as Alexandria and Antioch gradually lost population to interior cities located on caravan routes. In the western Mediterranean, the collapse of the Roman economy and administration in Western Europe after the fourth century had resulted in an impoverished society that could not afford to import many goods. Trade thus declined in that area. Contacts even between Andalus and Western Europe were few. The merchants of Andalus were much more interested in trade with the wealthier Byzantines and Muslims to the east.

The late ninth century witnessed an important shift in the movement of Indian Ocean trade into Southwest Asia, with important consequences for Mediterranean trade. The mamluk revolt in Samarra, coupled with the Zanj revolt in southern Iraq, contributed to political disruption and economic instability in the central lands of the Muslim world. As Baghdad declined, the Red Sea began to supplant the Persian Gulf as the main trade route from India to the Mediterranean. In the tenth century, Egypt began to enjoy a prosperity that it had not experienced for hundreds of years, making it all the more attractive to the Fatimids of Ifriqiya. Merchants from several European cities, primarily Italian, began establishing regular contacts with Muslim ports in the eastern Mediterranean. The new European demand for Asian goods revived the economies of ports such as Alexandria and Antioch, setting the stage for a vibrant international trade in the eleventh and twelfth centuries.

Conclusion

The first half of the tenth century witnessed a development that must have distressed many Muslims. In 910, the Fatimids announced the establishment of a second caliphate in the Muslim world. They claimed that theirs was not merely a second caliphate but the only legitimate one. Less than two decades later, in 929, the Umayyad dynasty in Andalus also claimed the caliphate. Sixteen years after that, the Buyids became the real power behind the Abbasid caliphate, raising the question of what meaning and function the caliphate served for Sunnis. Prior to the tenth century, the caliphate had been a symbol of (Sunni) Muslim unity, but now it represented differences within the Umma. For the most religiously sensitive believers, the competing claims of three caliphs must have raised religious anxieties. While more cynical or detached individuals could dismiss the fact of three caliphs as political posturing, at least some Muslims, who had been taught that the caliph represented God's authority on earth, had to wonder if they were recognizing God's actual representative. For them, the situation was not unlike the schism that developed within the papacy in the fourteenth and fifteenth centuries, when two, and then three, popes challenged each other, causing great anxiety among the Christians of Western Europe. As more and more political leaders claimed the title of caliph over the coming years, fewer Muslims could have felt that way.

But the growing religious and regional identities within the Umma were transcended by a sophisticated and efficient economic network that tied all the regions together. Caravans and ships brought goods from locations half a world away. Not only were manufactured goods exchanged in this manner, but crops as well, resulting in a foreshadowing of the so-called Columbian exchange 600 years later. Just as the voyages of Columbus opened up an era in which the flora and fauna of the western and eastern hemispheres would be exchanged, so was the ecology of the Mediterranean transformed by Muslim commerce.

In addition, as more and more Arab and Iranian merchants converted to Islam, the port cities and desert oases to which they moved or in which they established agencies became outposts of Islamic civilization. A Muslim diaspora began to extend around the Indian Ocean basin and in China. A similar development took place across the "sea" of the Sahara, as the "ships" of caravans brought Muslims into the oases of the desert and the cities of the sub-Saharan savanna, introducing Islam to those areas for the first time. These communities became centers of Islamic culture, and they would eventually radiate monotheism and Islamic law into their hinterlands.

NOTES

1   Population estimates for Baghdad vary widely, with some estimates ranging up to one million. The most carefully reasoned seems to be Jacob Lassner's study, *The Topography of Baghdad in the Early Middle Ages*. Detroit: Wayne State University Press, 1970, p. 160. For the land area comparison with Constantinople, see the same source, p. 158.

2   Tenth-century Cordoba is frequently said to have had a population of half a million people, but Thomas Glick makes a good case for a considerably smaller population of 100,000. The city would still have dwarfed any urban center in contemporary Western Europe, and its wealth and hygiene would have stood in even sharper contrast. See Thomas F. Glick, *Islamic and Christian Spain in the Early Middle Ages*. Princeton, New Jersey: Princeton University Press, 1979 113. By contrast, Andrew M. Watson, a specialist in medieval agriculture, says that the city attained a population of one million. (See "A Medieval Green Revolution: New Crops and Farming Techniques in the Early Islamic World," in *The Islamic Middle East, 700–1900: Studies in Economic and Social History*, A. L. Udovitch, ed. (Princeton, New Jersey: The Darwin Press, Inc., 1981, 57, n. 45.)

3   See Glick, *Islamic and Christian Spain*, pp. 33–35, and Roger Collins, *The Arab Conquest of Spain, 710–797*. Oxford, U.K.: Basil Blackwell, 1989, 217, for contrasting evaluations.

FURTHER READING

General

Kennedy, Hugh. *The Prophet and the Age of the Caliphates*. London and New York: Longman, 1986.

The Abbasid Caliphate

al-Hibri, Tayeb. *Reinterpreting Islamic Historiography: Harun al-Rashid and the Narrative of the 'Abbasid Caliphate*. Cambridge, U.K.: Cambridge University Press, 1999.

Lassner, Jacob. *The Shaping of Abbasid Rule*. Princeton, New Jersey: Princeton University Press, 1980.

Lassner, Jacob. *The Topography of Baghdad in the Early Middle Ages*. Detroit: Wayne State University Press, 1970.

Sourdel, Dominique. "The Abbasid Caliphate." In P. M. Holt, Ann K. S. Lambton, and Bernard Lewis, eds., *The Cambridge History of Islam*, vol. I. Cambridge, U.K.: Cambridge University Press, 1970.

The Fatimid Caliphate

Brett, Michael. *The Rise of the Fatimids: The World of the Mediterranean and the Middle East in the Fourth Century of the Hijrah, Tenth Century c.e.* Leiden, Boston: Brill, 2001.

Daftary, Farhad. *The Ismailis: Their History and Doctrines.* Cambridge, U.K.: Cambridge University Press, 1990.

Halm, Heinz. *Empire of the Mahdi: The Rise of the Fatimids.* Leiden: E. J. Brill, 1997.

Madelung, Wilferd and Paul Walker. *Advent of the Fatimids: A Contemporary Witness.* London and New York: I. B. Tauris, 2000.

The Umayyad Caliphate of Cordoba

Collins, Roger. *The Arab Conquest of Spain, 710–797.* Oxford, U.K.: Basil Blackwell, 1989.

Glick, Thomas F. *Islamic and Christian Spain in the Early Middle Ages.* Princeton, New Jersey: Princeton University Press, 1979.

Jayyusi, Salma Khadra, ed. *The Legacy of Muslim Spain.* Leiden, New York, Koln: E. J. Brill, 1992.

Economic Networks

Ashtor, E. *A Social and Economic History of the Near East in the Middle Ages.* Berkeley, California: University of California Press, 1976.

Bulliet, Richard. *The Camel and the Wheel.* Cambridge, Massachusetts: Harvard U Press, 1975.

Goitein, S.D. *A Mediterranean Society*, 5 vols. Berkeley, California: University of California Press, 1967–1988.

Hourani, George F. *Arab Seafaring in the Indian Ocean in Ancient and Early Medieval Times.* Revised and expanded by John Carswell. Princeton, New Jersey: Princeton University Press, 1995.

McNeill, William H. "The Eccentricity of Wheels, or Eurasian Transportation in Historical Perspective." In *American Historical Review*, 92, 5, December 5, 1987, 1111–1126.

Risso, Patricia. *Merchants & Faith: Muslim Commerce and Culture in the Indian Ocean.* Boulder, Colorado: Westview Press, 1995.

Watson, Andrew. *Agricultural Innovation in the Early Islamic World: The Diffusion of Crops and Farming Techniques, 700–1100.* Cambridge, U.K.: Cambridge University Press, 1983.

CHAPTER 5

Synthesis and Creativity

When the Arabs began their conquests in the 630s, their practice of Islam was rudimentary and simple. They possessed a body of scriptures, a few simple rituals, and the memory of specific teachings and acts of the Prophet that served as guides for behavior. It would be several decades before a class of Muslim religious specialists emerged whose careers were devoted to the elaboration of the deeper meaning of the principles of the faith and to the production of devotional literature, guidelines for ethical living, and theology. The vast majority of Arab Muslims, in fact, were removed from polytheism by only a handful of years, or even months.

The development of Islam as a major institutional religion began during the eighth century. After decades of expansion into new territories, it was becoming clear to some pious believers that guidelines for doctrine and correct behavior needed to be drawn up in order to stop the proliferation of quarreling sects and to obtain a consensus regarding doctrine, ritual, and ethics. Simultaneously, the Arabs now found themselves in the midst of millions of adherents of other major religions, whose institutions, doctrines, and rituals they found to be commendable or repugnant in varying degrees. They encountered bureaucratic organizations, civil and religious laws, social structures, foods, and types of entertainment that were entirely new to them. Which of these were compatible with the faith that the Prophet had brought to his people? What distinguished his community from those of Christians, Jews, and Zoroastrians, many of whose adherents were engaging in a polemical attack on the doctrines and rituals of Islam? In response to these questions, scholars began the process of articulating the implications of the faith and marking off the boundaries between Islam and the other monotheistic religions. By the middle of the tenth century, the foundations had been laid for Islamic law and devotional life, and subsequent discussions would refer back to this period as the touchstone for debate.

During this period, it became commonplace to refer to the area under the control of Muslims as the *dar al-islam*, or the "realm of Islam." Obviously, this region did not have a predominantly Muslim population in the early centuries, but it was one in which Islamic values were upheld and protected. The area of the world not under Muslim control was referred to as the *dar al-harb* (the "realm of war") or the *dar al-kufr* (the "realm of unbelief"). It was the realm of war precisely because the Qur'an enjoins believers to struggle, and even fight, against *kufr*, or unbelief.

The Origins of Islamic Law

The history of Christianity is replete with doctrinal disputes, and as a result, theology became the chief intellectual discipline of that religious tradition. Islam, by contrast, is more similar to Judaism in that correct behavior takes precedence over doctrine, and law has been the major intellectual pursuit within both religions. In the absence of the Prophet, Muslims sought guidance regarding how to live in accordance with God's will. Shi'ites looked to their Imams for that guidance. Sunnis found it in the Shari'a, or Islamic law.

Assimilation and Adaptation

During the earliest period of Islamic history, the Prophet served as the source of correct doctrine, the guide to the correct way to perform religious rituals, the judge for criminal acts, and the adjudicator of civil disputes. When he died, his followers were forced to make radical adjustments in their lives. Not only did they lose their source of divine revelation, but they soon lost the intimate and compact community of which Medina and Mecca were the largest population centers. The caliph was now the ultimate authority on religious and civil matters within the community, but his capacity for remaining the central figure in this regard was limited. He was expected to make judgments within the framework established by the Qur'an, but it has only some eighty verses that deal with matters that can properly be called legal. In addition, the Ridda Wars and the rapid conquests of Syria, Egypt, and Iraq greatly expanded the area under the caliph's jurisdiction. As a consequence, he became an increasingly remote figure to most Muslims, many of whom were moving to the newly conquered areas as soldiers, administrators, merchants, or other specialists. It was unavoidable that many important decisions regarding ritual behavior, property rights, commercial issues, criminal acts, and other pressing issues would be decided without immediate recourse to the caliph.

An organized Muslim judiciary became established only after Mu'awiya seized the caliphate in 661. Under the Umayyads, each garrison city was staffed with an agent to implement the body of administrative and fiscal regulations and laws that the rapidly growing military empire needed in order to function. This agent or judge, called a *qadi*, had wide discretionary powers. Whenever possible, qadis would rule according to the principles of the Qur'an, but often they had no choice but to utilize local legal traditions in order to make a ruling. In the absence of a comprehensive Islamic legal system, qadis relied on Sasanian, Byzantine, Jewish, and Orthodox canon law for many of their decisions. As a result, the legal administrative apparatus in different areas of the empire began revealing significant differences.

By the end of the seventh century, pious scholars began debating among themselves whether Umayyad legal practice adequately reflected the ethical values of the

Qur'an. The motives of some may have included hostility towards the Umayyads, but in general these scholars were acting on the profound conviction that each human has a responsibility to obey the commands of God. Not only should a believer live uprightly and desist from evil acts himself, but he should also "command the right and forbid the wrong," an injunction that implied a universal responsibility for maintaining the public order. During the eighth century, several of the influential urban areas had clusters of scholars (sing. *'alim*, pl. *'ulama'*; hereafter *ulama*, the most common English transliteration) who sought to Islamize the law by using Qur'anic principles as the standard by which to evaluate the adequacy of Umayyad legal practices.

The unusual feature of this movement of "legal review" was that it was conducted by pious scholars who did not hold positions of political authority. It was begun entirely at their initiative, and the Umayyad government played no part in its development. The ulama of Damascus, Kufa, Basra, Medina, and Mecca took the lead in this nascent jurisprudence. It soon became clear that, despite the intention of the scholars to use Qur'anic principles, differences began to develop among them.

FIGURE 5.1 Islamic religious art is famous for its depiction of patterns by using calligraphy, arabesque, and geometric designs. The Arabs relied almost exclusively on these designs for their religious art, fearing that the representation of human or animal forms would encourage idolatry (they sometimes represented humans and animals in nonreligious art). Non-Arab Muslims also used these designs, but they did not share the scruples against human forms; those in Persian cultural areas became famous for their paintings of humans and animals even in religious art. Pictured here is an example of calligraphic art, as a verse from the Qur'an encircles the otherwise bare dome of a religious school in Cairo.

Wael Hamdan / Alamy Stock Photo.

The social environments of Syria, Iraq, and the Hijaz differed significantly because of their Byzantine, Sasanian, and Arab legacies, respectively. These differences were reflected in the legal thought that emerged from the cities within each region. For decades, Muslims had adopted many local customs in each city, and even the pious naturally assumed that their local practice was identical with that of the first Muslim generation in Medina. The Qur'an, like any other revealed scripture, provides specific guidance on only a few of the issues that individuals in a complex society face. Unless a local custom conflicted with a Qur'anic directive or ethical principle, it was assumed to be legitimate. Religious scholars felt free to exercise their discretion when ruling on cases that presented original problems.

Groping Toward an Islamic Jurisprudence

With the advent of the Abbasids, the central government took an active role in encouraging the development of a legal system based explicitly on Islamic values. The new regime hoped to gain legitimacy by supporting the popular demand for an Islamic law, and it saw that the empire's legal system would benefit from uniformity in the determination and application of law. The caliphs and wazirs encouraged the office of the qadi to rely on the principles being articulated by the ulama. The new impetus for the development of an Islamic law led to the emergence of a generation of reformers who were critical of the approach of their elders. Whereas the first generation of jurists tended to accept current legal practice unless it violated some Qur'anic principle, the younger generation, working during the last third of the eighth century, insisted that all jurisprudence should be based only on the Qur'an and the example of the Prophet. The earlier jurists had sought guidance from the *sunna* (meaning "way," "custom," or "practice") of the first generation of Muslims, assuming that it ultimately derived from the example of the Prophet; now their successors explicitly sought only the Prophet's words and deeds. Those who sought guidance from the Sunna of the Prophet called themselves *ahl al-sunna wa al-jama'a*, or the "People of the (Prophet's) Sunna and of the Community." They collected reports or traditions (sing. *hadith*; the singular form is usually used in transliterations as a collective noun) of the Prophet's declarations and his behavior in certain circumstances and urged that Hadith and the Qur'an be the sole standards for legal practice. They had a powerful argument on their side, for if the law were not in fact derived directly from the Prophet's words and example, what guarantee would the believer have that it was God's will?

The new emphasis on the Sunna of the Prophet resulted in great efforts being exerted to discover it, and during the eighth and ninth centuries C.E., an enormous number of Hadith appeared. Several scholars organized the traditions into collections, the most famous and authoritative being those of al-Bukhari (d. 870) and Muslim (d. 875). The rapid appearance of thousands of Hadith raised suspicions that many were being fabricated, particularly when they attributed anachronistic ideas or technology to the Prophet. Al-Bukhari, Muslim, and the other great collectors developed critical standards to assess the traditions by examining their internal evidence and weighing the integrity of the individuals who were said to have passed them from one generation to another. The *isnad*, or "chain of transmitters," was the single most important criterion for determining a Hadith's authenticity. The isnad would trace a saying or behavior of the Prophet through a series of well-known persons back to its source, which would ideally be a close companion of the Prophet. The following Hadith is a typical example:

> Al-Bukhari writes: 'Abdallah ibn al-Aswad told me: Al-Fadl ibn al-'Ata' told us: Isma'il ibn Umayya told us on the authority of Yahya ibn 'Abdallah ibn Sayfi that he heard Abu Ma'bad, the freedman of Ibn 'Abbas, say, I heard Ibn 'Abbas say: I asked, Messenger of God, what is the greatest sin? 'It is to make an idol for God, who created you.' Then what? 'To kill your own child from motives of economy.' And then what? 'To commit adultery with your neighbor's wife.'

According to legend, al-Bukhari examined 600,000 such traditions before deciding on the 2700 that he put into his collection. Although many Western scholars are skeptical that a majority even of these vetted traditions are authentic, most Muslims consider them to be as authoritative as the Qur'an.

The new initiative to codify God's will was intended to bring uniformity to the practice of law. Ironically, it multiplied the differences among the various groups of ulama. According to tradition, literally hundreds of "schools" (sing. *madhhab*) of law emerged across the empire during the ninth century. These schools were not colleges, but rather circles of scholars who followed the methods determined by influential local ulama for ascertaining the principles of law. In most of the madhhabs that had a life span of several generations or more, the founding scholar's teachings were modified and elaborated considerably, perhaps even beyond recognition, but each one represented a cohesive social unit as well as an ideological perspective. The madhhabs differed from each other due to their choice of which Hadith to use (many contradicted each other), differences in techniques of Qur'anic interpretation, and differences over the scope that individual reasoning should be allowed in making legal judgments. Moreover, the impact of local, pre-Islamic customs and values on the various scholars did not disappear; even pious men with the best of intentions absorbed elements of their local culture, just as everyone else did. The cleavage among the schools reached its height in the ninth century, when some Muslim scholars who were influenced by Greek philosophy asserted that the human mind is capable of determining which acts are good and which are bad, independent of revelation. The caliph al-Ma'mun (813–833) patronized this group, known as the Mu'tazilites, and he ordered all qadis and other government officials to adhere to their theories. Because the Mu'tazilite position seemed to threaten the primacy of the Qur'an, a scholar named Ahmad ibn Hanbal (d. 857) refused to submit to the ruling, even though he was persecuted as a result. His followers, the Hanbalis, insisted that acts were good or bad because God had decreed them so and that it was impious to reason why or whether they were so. Scholars should rely only on the Qur'an and the Sunna of the Prophet.

The Development of the Shari'a

The numerous schools of religious law caused confusion and consternation among Muslims. How was one to know which most closely reflected God's will? By the middle of the tenth century, a consensus had developed on the broad outlines of a method for determining religious law. As a result, the number of schools rapidly declined and the Shari'a, or Islamic law, became the defining element of Muslim identity.

Hadith: Guides to Living

The thousands of Hadith provide guidance for a remarkably wide range of behavior. The following selections are excerpts from one of the two major collections of Hadith, the Sahih Muslim. *The* isnad, *or chain of transmitters, has been removed from each. Note how each Hadith cites a saying or act of the Prophet as a model for one's own life.*

'A'isha reported, The Messenger of Allah (may peace be upon him) said: Ten are the acts according to Fitra (the ritual acts that enable human nature to reach its potential): clipping the moustache, letting the beard grow, using the tooth-stick, snuffing up water in the nose, cutting the nails, washing the finger joints, plucking the hair under the armpits, shaving the pubes, and cleaning one's private parts with water. The narrator said: I have forgotten the tenth, but it may have been rinsing the mouth. (I, 192–193)

Salman reported that it was said to him, Your Apostle (may peace be upon him) teaches you about everything, even about excrement. He replied: Yes, he has forbidden us to face the Qibla at the time of excretion or urination, or cleansing with the right hand or with less than three pebbles, or with dung or bone. (I, 193)

Jabir said: Allah's Messenger (may peace be upon him) forbade that the graves should be plastered, or they be used as sitting places (for the people), or a building should be built over them. (II, 553)

Jabir b. 'Abdullah reported Allah's Messenger (may peace be upon him) as saying: Do not walk in one sandal and do not wrap the lower garment round your knees and do not eat with your left hand and do not wrap yourself completely leaving no room for the arms (to draw out) and do not place one of your feet upon the other while lying on your back. (III, 1388)

Buraida reported on the authority of his father that Allah's Apostle (may peace be upon him) said: He who played chess is like one who dyed his hand with the flesh and blood of swine. (IV, 1469)

Abu Huraira reported Allah's Messenger (may peace be upon him) as saying: Do you know who is poor? They (the Companions of the Holy Prophet) said: A poor man amongst us is one who had neither dirham with him nor wealth. He (the Holy Prophet) said: The poor of my Umma would be he who would come on the Day of Resurrection with prayers and fasts and Zakat but ... since he hurled abuses upon others, brought calumny against others and unlawfully consumed the wealth of others and shed the blood of others and beat others, ... his virtues would be credited to the account of one (who suffered at his hand). And if his good deeds fall short to clear the account, then his sins would be entered in (his account) and he would be thrown in the Hell-Fire. (IV, 1645)

SOURCE: Imam Muslim, *Sahih Muslim*. Tr. 'Abdul Hamid Siddiqi. 4 vols. Rev. ed. New Delhi: Kitab Bhavan, 2000.

The Synthesis of al-Shafi'i

Although the rationalist school of the Mu'tazilites lost its official patronage by mid-century, it remained active in legal and philosophical circles. Rationalists and Hanbalis engaged in arguments that sometimes resulted in physical violence. By the early tenth century, however, a compromise between the Mu'tazilite position and the Sunna-based Hanbali position began to gain acceptance in many of the law schools. The compromise was based on the work of a scholar, Muhammad ibn Idris al-Shafi'i, who had died a century earlier in 820. On the one hand, he had argued that the Qur'an and Sunna of the Prophet were the sole material sources of the law, a position that sounded much like that of Ibn Hanbal. On the other hand, al-Shafi'i squarely confronted the reality that questions frequently arise in daily life that are not addressed in these sources and therefore require the use of reason. Unlike the rationalists, he did not allow the free exercise of reason or opinion (*ra'y*), but he did allow reasoning by analogy: If a case could be resolved on the basis of an analogy with the ethical principles expressed in the Qur'an, Hadith, or previous legal cases, the decision was valid. When a legal decision became accepted by the consensus of scholars across the Dar al-Islam, it could reasonably be considered to reflect God's will.

Thus, al-Shafi'i's theory actually recognized four sources of law: the two primary sources of the Qur'an and Hadith, and the two derivative sources of analogy and consensus. This new model for jurisprudence was ignored for many decades after al-Shafi'i's death in 820, but it rapidly gained acceptance in the early tenth century. Soon, any jurist seeking a solution to a legal problem was expected to consult the Qur'an and the Hadith first. If these sources did not address it directly, he was to employ an analogy with cases that had already been resolved. The result was a tentative conclusion that rulings of other jurists would substantiate or reject. In the event that it was corroborated by other rulings, it was said to have been confirmed by the consensus of the other ulama.

The growing uniformity within jurisprudence led to a general sense that God's will was being ascertained, and the rules that were developed for living the upright life were called the *shari'a*. The term *shari'a* had been used up to that time in the Arabian Peninsula to denote the beaten path to a watering hole in the desert. If one did not know the path that the camels had taken repeatedly, death could result. Likewise, knowing and practicing God's will as revealed through the disciplined decisions of the ulama brought spiritual life to whoever submitted to it.

Consolidation of the Madhhabs

The Shari'a gradually became an essential element of Muslim life. Then as now, highly trained professionals were less likely to choose to live in rural areas than in cities, and it was thus much harder for peasants and pastoralists to gain access to educated qadis. Nevertheless, everyone was expected to choose which madhhab he would follow. Over the years, the growing uniformity of legal method had the effect of consolidating many madhhabs and reducing the number from which to choose. By the end of the thirteenth century, only a few schools were left. In some large cities, a choice still existed even as the number of schools declined, for one could find qadis from several madhhabs. For most people, however, the school they followed was in effect chosen for them because of the distinctly regional coloration that madhhabs possessed.

Out of the hundreds of schools that emerged during the early period, four have continued into the modern era to represent the majority of Muslims. The tradition from Kufa was named after one of Ja'far al-Sadiq's students, Abu Hanifa (d. 767), and was called the Hanafi school. It dominated in Iraq and Syria, and later spread to Anatolia, Central Asia, and India. The school in Medina was named after one of its greatest early scholars, Malik ibn Anas (d. 796), and is known as the Maliki school. It became paramount in North Africa and the Iberian Peninsula, and it spread into West Africa. The Shafi'i school, claiming descent from the original disciples of al-Shafi'i, prevailed in Egypt, Yemen, East Africa, certain coastal regions of India, and Southeast Asia. The Hanbali madhhab derives its name from Ibn Hanbal, who was known for his theological disputes with the Mu'tazilites. Over the years after his death, his followers developed a madhhab that argued for the primacy of the Qur'an and Hadith literally understood. (Ibn Hanbal is said never to have eaten watermelon, on the grounds that he found no precedent in the example of the Prophet.)

The Hanbalis were so hostile to the use of personal opinion that they placed sharp limits on the use of analogy. Regarded as the most conservative and traditional of the four schools, the Hanbalis nevertheless turned out to be the least bound by tradition. Because they did not feel constrained by the consensus of other scholars, in later centuries they were the most active in making new interpretations of the law to fit changing circumstances. The Hanbali madhhab was influential in Baghdad and Syria until the fourteenth century. It was revived in the Arabian Peninsula in the eighteenth century and remains dominant in Saudi Arabia today. It is also popular among reformist movements all across the Muslim world, whose members regard it to be the most congenial for allowing new interpretations.

The Shi'ites and Ibadis developed their own distinctive madhhabs, although they share much in common with the four discussed above. As we have seen, true sectarian identity took centuries to crystallize, with the result that the major developments in Islamic law took place in an atmosphere in which Muslims of all inclinations were in communication with each other. The Shi'ites maintained three major madhhabs, the most influential of which was attributed to Ja'far al-Sadiq and is thus known as the Ja'fari madhhab. All Muslims agreed that the Qur'an and Hadith are the primary sources of the law, although the collections of Hadith used by the Isma'ili and Twelver schools contain traditions that differ in part from the earlier collections due to an emphasis on the Alid tradition. Likewise, when Shi'ites began developing their own legal methods, they placed less emphasis on analogy and consensus than did the earlier madhhabs, since the decisions of the Imam had authoritative weight.

The Impact of the Shari'a

By the ninth century, the Shari'a was the authorized basis for qadis to make their judgments in court. The Shari'a was not a codification of laws to which a qadi could refer when confronting a case. It was largely a set of norms regarding how to live a life pleasing to God, and it included a remarkably broad range of topics. In it one could find details on the proper way to consummate a marriage or to defecate, as well as regulations regarding contracts, theft, and inheritance. Despite the intent of its architects to provide guidelines for all of life, its primary utility was for issues relating to religious rituals, marriage, divorce, inheritance, debts, and partnerships.

Among the most notable legacies of the Shari'a have been norms regarding the roles and status of women. Like other topics treated by the jurists, the decisions relating to women arose out of an interplay among Qur'anic injunctions, the Hadith, and deeply rooted customs of a given region. The Qur'an itself insists on the essential equality of women and men (3:195, 33:35, 4:124), but it also suggests that God views men to be "more equal" in rights than women (4:34). Because the Qur'an became the chief source of the Shari'a, the jurists followed that lead. In addition, however, a Mediterranean tradition of honor and shame, a centuries-long Greek tradition of keeping women out of public life, the misogynistic teachings of some of the Christian theologians, and a Sasanian culture in which women were second-class subjects were powerful forces in the Fertile Crescent. At the Abbasid court—which was influenced by both Byzantine and Sasanian norms—the women were already being secluded even as the Shari'a began to be delineated. The jurists of Islam worked within societies influenced by one or more of these factors as they interpreted the Qur'an and the Hadith.

According to the Shari'a, a woman was to have a male guardian—father, husband, brother, or uncle—and the marriage contract was technically between the bridegroom and the woman's guardian, not the bride. A father could give his daughter in marriage without her consent if she had not yet reached the age of puberty. Once a young woman had attained puberty, she technically could not be married against her will, but if she was a virgin, consent could be given "by silence," a condition that was often exploited. A woman could marry only one man at a time, whereas a man could have up to four wives and as many slave concubines as he could afford. (The Hanbali school recognized the legitimacy of the marriage contract to stipulate that the husband could take no concubines or additional wives, but the other schools did not allow that provision.) The woman was entitled to a dower and maintenance (food, clothing, and lodging). The amount of the dower was determined by negotiations between the bridegroom and the bride's guardian.

All of the law schools agreed that the husband could divorce his wife unilaterally and for any cause, but the wife's rights to divorce were more limited. According to some legal schools, the husband could divorce his wife by simply stating that he had divorced her in the presence of witnesses, and she did not even have to be present or to be informed of the act. Women, by contrast, could obtain a divorce only by mutual consent or by petitioning a qadi. The Hanafi school allowed a woman to request a divorce on the grounds of impotence, whereas the Maliki school allowed a wife to cite impotence, cruelty, desertion, failure of maintenance, or the threat posed to her by her husband's disease. In the event of divorce, the woman would have custody of the children of the marriage and the duty of bringing them up until they reached a certain age (typically seven for boys and nine for girls) or until she remarried, in which case the children's age was irrelevant. At that point, the father or his family would assume custody of the children.

Women in urban areas from Transoxiana to Andalus did not play an active, visible role in public life either before or after the arrival of Muslims, unless they were from poor families that needed them to engage in trade, services, or the crafts. Most scholars agree that, if anything, the status of women in the area probably rose slightly in the formerly Byzantine and Sasanian territories due to the ethical principle of the spiritual equality of the sexes before God that runs as a leitmotif throughout the Qur'an. Legally, women were guaranteed a share of an inheritance, as well as the right to own and sell property. Many women from prosperous families did engage in business activities, but typically that meant renting out a shop, buying and selling property, and lending money—activities that did not necessarily thrust them into the public eye. On the other hand, the traditions of concubinage and seclusion that both the Byzantines and the Sasanians had practiced prior to the advent of the Muslims continued into the Islamic era and shaped Muslim mores in a profound manner. Women had clearly demarcated roles that left them subservient to those of men.

Qadi courts dealt with criminal cases as well as family issues, but the state increasingly appropriated the responsibility for criminal law because the Shari'a's rules of evidence precluded a qadi from investigating criminal cases. In principle, only oral testimony from reputable witnesses was acceptable. Written evidence was only occasionally acceptable, and circumstantial evidence was not recognized at all. Because of the constraints on the qadi in this regard, the state transferred the greater

FIGURE 5.2 Arabesque is a patterned art form that most often represented the tendrils and leaves of the acanthus plant. It is characterized by repetition and extension, encouraging the eye to move throughout the whole design.

Maria Galan / Alamy Stock Photo.

part of criminal justice cases to the police. Both commerce and taxation were also spheres in which governments increasingly found that they needed a more flexible framework than what the Shari'a provided.

Thus, although the Shari'a became a central feature of Muslim life, it never became a comprehensive law code for all of society's needs. Two parallel systems of law existed in the Islamic world: the Shari'a and one that served the needs of the state. As we have seen, the Shari'a itself arose not from the needs of the state but rather from the sense of moral responsibility that pious Muslims felt toward God. The Shari'a was the guide to living a life acceptable to God. Rulers were willing to accommodate the Shari'a because it served as a guide for judges and its implement-ation gave religious legitimacy to the state that employed it. Nevertheless, governments frequently faced issues that the Shari'a did not address, and they utilized a variety of expedients for resolving their legal problems.

On the other hand, the Shari'a, because of its focus on the issues of marriage, divorce, and inheritance, was much better known to the public than the secular codes, and it was the system that provided a common identity from one end of the Islamic world to the other. The very fact that the Shari'a had not been created to resolve the issues of a given state endowed it with the capacity for universality. When the political unity of the Abbasid empire began breaking up, it was the Shari'a that provided for a commonality among Muslims regardless of their membership within a given state. Governments could come and go without affecting the stability of their respective societies.

The development of the Shari'a also seems to have been instrumental in crystallizing an identity for most of the Muslims who were not Alids. Oddly enough, we do not know when *Sunnis* began to call themselves by that term. However, the expression, *ahl al-sunna wa al-jama'a*, discussed earlier, evoked the confidence that this group had that God's will could be followed when individuals cooperated in emulating the model of the Prophet's life. It set them in contrast to those who relied for such guidance on a supernaturally inspired individual such as the Shi'ite Imam. Those who came to be known as Sunnis argued that God's will could be ascertained in the legal sciences, which were based on guidance from the Qur'an, the Hadith, analogy with similar cases, and the consensus of learned and pious scholars. A Hadith from the Prophet was often cited that expressed this confidence: "My community will never agree on an error." Over the years, more and more of the Muslims who sought religious truth from the consensus of the community referred to themselves as Sunnis to distinguish themselves from the Shi'ites, whose sense of identity was already established.

Early Sufism

While Shi'ism, the Hadith movement, and the Shari'a were emerging during the late seventh and early eighth centuries, a devotional movement arose in Kufa and Basra that eventually became the most widespread and characteristic form of Islamic piety. Because some of its adherents wore the rough woolen garments that had been the characteristic clothing of ascetics in the area for centuries, the movement came to be called Sufism, and its members Sufis (sing. *sufi*, from *suf*, or wool). At the heart of

Sufism was a burning passion to transcend the externals of religion in order to experience the spiritual reality for which rituals and texts were the representation. Although Sufism would come to embrace a wide variety of devotional practices and ways of life, most of the early Sufis sought a personal relationship with God through a combination of asceticism, a concern for ethical ideals, and a mystical form of worship.

The Contemplative Life

For more than a century, many of the most prominent Sufis were among those who were engaged in the gathering of the Hadith in order to have a guide for living according to the will of God. What set many of the early Sufis apart from the other Hadith collectors was their emphatic renunciation of this world. Some favored a mild form of asceticism, while others took self-denial to an extreme. Just as Shi'ism and the Hadith movement contained elements of pious opposition to the Umayyad dynasty, the private piety and asceticism of the Sufis were in many cases expressions of disapproval or even active opposition to governmental authority. Throughout the Umayyad period, more and more individuals shunned the trappings of wealth and sought a highly disciplined life of the spirit that stood in sharp contrast to the increasingly flamboyant way of life of the Umayyad court.

Sufism cannot be reduced to a movement of political protest, however. A movement of pious self-discipline had arisen early within Islam. The Sufis point to the Prophet himself as their model, and he certainly led a simpler life than his political power and access to the community's resources would have allowed him. Moreover, many passages in the Qur'an stress the necessity of focusing on eternal goals rather than on worldly, material ones. Still other verses suggest the nearness of God that complements His transcendence and allows Him to be approached in a personal relationship. One that had a central role in the development of an accessible God was, "Indeed we created man; and we know what his soul whispers within him, and we are nearer to him than his jugular vein" (50:16).

Sufism was an indigenous development within Islam. All the world's great religions include mystics who share in a quest for the purification of the heart, a disregard for—if not renunciation of—worldly concerns, and a search for a deeper knowledge of God. Islam would have developed a mystical tradition even if it had been in a cultural vacuum without contact with other religious traditions. By virtue of Islam's development within Syria and Iraq, though, Muslims who felt the need to cultivate the life of the spirit had a wealth of traditions in their midst from which they could borrow. Many references in Sufi literature make it clear that Muslim, Christian, and Jewish mystics exchanged information on the contemplative life. Christian monks were particularly influential. In eighth-century Iraq and Syria, Christians still outnumbered Muslims, and awareness of monasticism was unavoidable. Indeed, the literary sources make it clear that Muslim mystics deliberately sought out conversations with pious members of the People of the Book who seemed to exemplify genuine spirituality. Even the woolen clothing characteristic of early Sufis was almost certainly a direct borrowing from Christian monasticism.

Interest in a pietistic form of worship was apparent by the beginning of the eighth century. In the urban environment of late Umayyad Iraq, a number of ascetics, itinerant preachers, and individuals referred to as *weepers* called the Muslim community to a more faithful adherence to God's will. The most famous of this group was Hasan al-Basri (d. 728), who had served as a soldier in the military campaigns of the late seventh century. He eventually became a religious scholar as well as a critic of the Umayyad regime who was often in trouble with the Iraqi governor for his remarks. He was noted for his bouts of weeping for his own sins and for those of Muslim society, and people flocked to the mosque when he gave the sermon. One of Hasan's most important themes was his emphasis on the purity of the intention of any religious act. He denigrated as worthless a religious act that was performed out of habit or even from a sense of duty alone.

In the next generation, the celebrated female mystic Rabi'a (d. 801) extended the concept of purity of intent to the attitude of worship itself: "O God, if I worship you from fear of hell, burn me in hell; and if I worship you in hope of heaven, exclude me from heaven; but if I worship you for your own sake, do not withhold your eternal beauty." This theme became a central one in later Sufism, and the movement can be seen in large part as a quest for spiritual and ethical perfection. The Sufis' conviction that purity of the heart is more important than perfunctory ritual or moral behavior was the source of a long-running tension between Sufi adepts and many of the ulama who were concerned to establish the precise acts that God willed and those He forbade. Whereas the ulama would have agreed that intention must be inseparable from the act, Sufis often regarded the ulama's concern for specific behavior to be legalistic, formal, and bereft of true spirituality. Some Sufis

FIGURE 5.3 Geometric designs in Islamic religious art employ a wide variety of polygons, but circles and stars are favorites with artists, as they can suggest perfection, infinity, and the handiwork of God.

Nelly Boyd / Alamy Stock Photo.

actually drifted into a disregard for religious law. The law, they believed, was useful for the masses but was meant to be only symbolic for the spiritually adept.

One of the most compelling features of Sufism for Muslims everywhere was the new emphasis that it placed on the love of God. On the one hand, it is a mistake to overstate the contrast between the Sufi doctrine of God's love and the theme of His wrath or justice because every Muslim frequently made reference to the "merciful and compassionate" God to whom he was devoted. Moreover, the Qur'an has many references to the mercy, love, and kindness of God that lend themselves to a fully developed doctrine. On the other hand, it is clear that the Sufis found love to be a major theme that had not been mined as diligently before. Sufi writers emphasized not only the love of God for His creatures, but also the love of the believer for God. Like Rabi'a, they taught that God should be loved for Himself alone, and that when the pure of heart approached God in this way, God in turn would draw near to the believer.

By the ninth century, the Sufi tradition had matured sufficiently that spiritual masters (sing. *shaykh* in the Arabic-speaking lands and *pir* in the Persian-speaking regions) were writing manuals that described the methods of discipline that had enabled their followers to develop their spiritual potential. The manuals described a progression of the soul toward God that required the completion of sequential stages (*maqamat*) and psychological and gnostic "states" (*ahwal*). Sufi masters might identify as few as four stages or as many as one hundred, but even the most detailed "road maps" for the soul usually followed a basic progression beginning with repentance and moving through stages of asceticism, fear of God, longing for God, and love for God. Most initiates never attained the final stage(s); they remained in a state of arrested spiritual development at one stage or another. Only those who themselves would become shaykhs attained the highest stage. But the passage through even a limited number of stages was more than most humans had experienced, and the seeker who had made any progress felt gratitude to God. In each stage, God granted to the seeker a "state," or spiritual experience, that demonstrated to him the presence of God in a manner not accessible otherwise. The path required a long and arduous journey of many years, during which initiates learned the virtues of patience and gratitude, even for the hardships that came one's way. Gradually, their souls became open to the presence of God, and they developed a longing for intimacy with God. Finally, the way culminated in spiritual knowledge and the loving experience of God.

The characteristic activity for a Sufi was meditation. While the practice of meditation has a multitude of variations, many Sufis began to utilize a devotional practice known as _dhikr_, or the ritual "recollection" or "remembering" of the name of God. Many worshipers simply chanted "Allah" repetitively; others chanted the formula "There is no god but God"; some would recite the ninety-nine names of God, perhaps aided by a rosary; still others would utilize a more complex invocation, accompanied by movements of the body, rhythmic breathing, or even music. Like the mantra of South Asia or the "Jesus prayer" of the Eastern Church, the purpose of the _dhikr_ was to provide a focus for the soul to fix its gaze upon God and to free itself from the distractions of the world. In both the Muslim and Christian cases, the prayer reflected the idea that the name of God is sacred and that the act of invoking it in some sense entails contact with the divine.

Testing the Limits of Transcendence

As the mystical tradition developed, some writers began describing in more detail the experience that awaited the elite mystics at the end of their quest. This spiritual state was unique, characterized by the twin concepts of *fana'* ("passing away" or "annihilation") and *baqa'* ("survival"). After pursuing a difficult discipline of spiritual cleansing and renunciation of the world, mystics would achieve direct knowledge of God and enter a state of joy and rest. A defining characteristic of the mystical experience is that it is ineffable, for it is not accessible to reason or empirical experience. Nevertheless, Sufis attempted to describe the experience as one in which their attributes or characteristics merged with those of God. Their worldly longings and physical nature would pass away, whereas the direct knowledge of God survived. Some mystics described this experience as one of an intoxicating, rapturous union with God in which the self was extinguished and actually united with God.

Appearing for the first time in the eighth century was the doctrine of "friendship" with God, which arose from the desire to seek a personal relationship with God. An adept who had achieved a direct experience of God and had demonstrated superior spiritual insight was regarded as a *wali* ("friend") of God. Whereas the ordinary believer sought out God, God actually sought out His "friends." The term *wali* is often translated as "saint" in English, and if not confused with the term as found in Catholicism, it is a useful concept to express some connotations of the word. Sufis regarded their spiritual teachers as wise, and they revered them for their insights and piety; some followers revered their teachers to such a degree that they considered them to be in some sense a manifestation of the divine being. Some saints practiced alchemy, an avocation that reinforced their reputation as healers and workers of miracles, both during their lifetime and afterward. Their tombs became objects of pilgrimage to which those who had special needs would go to pray and present offerings. The "friends of God" thus became intercessors between ordinary human beings and God.

The quest to bridge the gap between God and mankind became at once one of the great strengths of Sufism and the source of many problems for it. The mystical path has often had difficulty fitting comfortably within the monotheistic religions of Judaism, Christianity, and Islam because of its attempts to overcome the gulf between God the Creator and His human creature. Monotheism places a heavy emphasis on the transcendence, or "otherness," of God, whereas mysticism seeks to bridge that transcendence and to overcome the gulf between the divine and the mortal. Many Muslims regarded the notion of fana' to be heretical, for it seemed to suggest the essential identity of God and humans. The belief that "friends of God" could become intercessors between humans and God also seemed to run counter to original Islamic doctrine and was the target of bitter attacks.

The tension reached its peak in the life and death of al-Hallaj (d. 922), originally from Fars in southwestern Iran. He joined a Sufi group in Iraq but soon quarreled with Sufis there and in his home province. He subsequently devised his own mystical path. He became a missionary to India and Central Asia, and then settled in Baghdad. His reputation for working miracles followed him to that city, and he developed a large popular following. He is widely considered to have uttered the cry "*ana al-haqq*" ("I am the Truth" or "I am the Real"), from which the authorities would have inferred his claim to be one with God. He insisted that ritual acts in themselves were merely perfunctory, and that only their inner meaning had value. The court record of his subsequent trial reveals that his offense was his having asserted that the pilgrimage to Mecca could be performed in his own room. Whatever his actual assertions, he suggested that in some manner he was a manifestation of God. He seems to have sought out condemnation by the authorities, as though to demonstrate that he had not accommodated himself to the worldly order.

Al-Hallaj lived during the unstable time of the rise of the Isma'ilis, the Fatimid takeover of Ifriqiya, and the raids of the Carmathians. His extreme mysticism, coupled with indications that he had Shi'ite leanings, caused the ulama and civil officials to regard him as a threat to their authority. If he and others were able to persuade the common people of the unimportance of ritual acts or that Alids had a more legitimate claim to the caliphate than anyone else, then the entire religious and political order could be jeopardized. In 922, al-Hallaj was executed in a particularly brutal fashion. His enemies and supporters alike agreed that, as his feet and hands were chopped off, he faced death with a remarkable equanimity and asked forgiveness for those who executed him.

The Accommodation of Sufism

As impressive and revered as al-Hallaj was, his defiant disregard for ritual and prescriptive behavior did not represent the future of mainstream Sufism. Whether because of the threat of persecution or because it was increasingly clear to many Sufis that some of the ideas associated with al-Hallaj could not be reconciled with basic Islamic doctrines, his teachings were permanently eclipsed by the path represented by al-Junayd (d. 910) of Baghdad. Al-Junayd, who had been al-Hallaj's teacher for a short time before they quarreled, was a gifted thinker who combined an ascetic mysticism with a quest for moral perfection. He is often referred to as the greatest figure in early Sufism, one who created a synthesis between the scrupulous observance of the Shari'a and a sophisticated theory of mysticism.

Al-Junayd managed to justify the doctrine of a direct experience with God and carefully used the terms fana' and baqa' without claiming the permanent "annihilation" of the human identity. According to him, the mystic's quest is possible only because of God's active enabling power: God guides and strengthens the seeker in his quest to "die to himself" (*fana'*) and "live in God" (*baqa'*). In some sense, the mystical experience recaptures the preexistent state of the human soul as a thought in the mind of God. As a result, the joyous experience of God's direct presence makes it impossible for the mystic to be satisfied with life in this world, and he is constantly yearning for God's presence. On the other hand, precisely because he is in this world, the point of "life in God" is to live everyday life transformed by God's love and guidance. The spiritual experience enables a Muslim to see the world through new eyes and to become a model of piety for others to follow. Even though al-Junayd shared the common Sufi attitude that the law was secondary to the inward life, he stressed that both were essential.

Al-Junayd's synthesis was crucial, for it kept Sufism grounded in the ritual and prescribed behavior that provided the common identity for Muslims everywhere. By the tenth century, Sufism was still a minority movement, and in order for it to be

accepted as a valid Islamic experience, it needed to demonstrate that it was compatible with the rituals and ethic of the evolving norms of the majority. Few could predict at the time that the Sufi approach would come to dominate the inner life of Islam from West Africa to Southeast Asia. That it did so is a testimony to the wisdom of leaders such as al-Junayd. Their great accomplishment was to combine the doctrine of a transcendent God with the experience of an immanent God who is closer to a person than his or her jugular vein.

The Reception of Science and Philosophy

The Arab conquests of the seventh and eighth centuries obliterated the political barriers that had formerly separated the rich and varied cultures of the areas that lay between the Indus valley and the Atlantic. Not only did a massive migration of peoples occur in their aftermath, but they also provided an economic stimulus to both trade and agriculture. More than commodities and luxuries were traded, however. Architectural styles, techniques for making pottery, and concepts in philosophy, mathematics, medicine, and many other intellectual fields now made their way across this vast expanse faster than ever before. The result was that cultural traditions that had developed in isolation from each other now began to interact on a regular basis. The scholars and creative artists in the Dar al-Islam synthesized a wide variety of traditions and made original contributions to them.

Science and Mathematics

When the Arabs conquered Egypt and Syria in the 630s, they entered a cultural zone that had been exposed to Greek intellectual influences for a thousand years, ever since the conquests of Alexander the Great. Iraq, too, was conversant with the Greek heritage. Unlike Syria and Egypt, Iraq had largely lost the Hellenistic patina that it had acquired during the two centuries after Alexander the Great, but in the fifth and sixth centuries a considerable number of Nestorian and Jacobite (Syrian Monophysite) scholars entered Sasanian Iraq to escape Byzantine persecution. They brought with them their Syriac translations of Greek theological writings, medicine, astronomy, and philosophy. Iraqi Christians were welcomed into the Sasanian royal school at Jundishapur, located east of the capital of Ctesiphon. Jundishapur was a particularly exciting intellectual milieu, for it combined Greek medicine and philosophy with a Persian literary tradition and Sanskritic medical and mathematical influences.

The Arabs themselves had a brilliant poetic tradition and an effective tradition of folk medicine, and they could navigate over land and sea by virtue of their knowledge of the heavens. Nevertheless, they were in awe of what they found in the newly conquered territories. Muslim scholars and rulers were fascinated by the knowledge that their subject peoples had of numerous fields of study, but especially of astronomy and astrology (the two were not yet differentiated), alchemy, mathematics, and medicine. As early as the late seventh century, Umayyad princes commissioned the translation of texts in the field of alchemy and were performing their own experiments. Later, the Abbasid caliph al-Mansur (754–775) commissioned the translation of some of the medical texts attributed to Galen and Hippocrates, and a few other texts were translated during the remainder of the eighth century. Not until the ninth century, however, did the government organize a systematic approach to the acquisition and translation of foreign texts. The caliph al-Ma'mun (813–833) institutionalized the translation process by establishing the *bayt al-hikma*, or House of Wisdom. This institution became the focus of a massive translation project and served as a library to hold the newly translated books. Almost all the translators during the next two centuries were Iraqi Christians. The notable exception was the pagan Thabit ibn Qurra (d. 901), who was also the court astrologer and physician to the caliph al-Mu'tadid (892–902). Hunayn ibn Ishaq (809–873) determined the framework for the translation process. He acquired as many Greek manuscripts as he could of a given work, compared them to determine the most accurate version, translated the work into Syriac, and then consulted with Arabic specialists to prepare an Arabic translation.

The first works to be translated were those with an immediate practical application. Mathematics was an essential tool in the huge construction effort taking place across the empire; medicine and pharmacology were required to keep the caliph and others among the elite healthy; and astronomy–astrology made possible the calculation of correct dates for religious festivals and propitious times for officials to implement important policies. Alchemy held out numerous possibilities: Its practitioners explored the relationship of humans to the natural world, devised ways to purify the soul, and sought ways to transmute base metals into gold.

One of the most notable scholars of this period was al-Khwarizmi (ca. 780–ca. 850). As his name indicates, he was originally from Khwarazm, south of the Aral Sea, but he spent his adult career in Baghdad. He is credited with introducing the Indian numerals into the Muslim world, replacing Roman numerals as well as the awkward Hellenic style of using letters of the alphabet to represent numbers. Although Arabs still call the Indian numerals "Hindi," Europeans call them "Arabic" because they borrowed them from the Arabs. The Indian numeric system was not the first to utilize the place value system or to have a concept of zero—both the Babylonians and the Chinese had a place value system and the Babylonians had a blank symbol—but its combination of a decimal system (the Babylonians used a base of 60) and a highly developed concept of zero to signify the "null number"—absolutely nothing—was a powerful innovation and an essential development for modern mathematics. Al-Khwarizmi's most famous mathematical treatise utilized the new system and compiled rules for solutions of linear and quadratic equations, elementary geometry, and the solution of inheritance problems faced in probate cases. No two scholars can agree on an English translation of the book's title, which contains the word *al-jabr*, meaning the restoration and amplification of something incomplete. The book later became so influential in Europe that *al-jabr* gave birth to the word *algebra*. Another of al-Khwarizmi's works was translated into Latin as *Algorismi de numero indorum* ("Al-Khwarizmi Concerning the Hindu Art of Computation"), immortalizing his name in our mathematical term *algorithm*.

Philosophy

Although medicine, mathematics, and astronomy attracted the immediate attention of the Arabs, it was not long before they began to commission the translation of philosophical texts as well. The educational curriculum of the Eastern Christians had for centuries required the study of logic prior to that of theology or medicine, and it quickly became a staple of Islamic education. The majority of the corpus of the known surviving Greek philosophical tradition quickly became available in Arabic versions. Because the fields of study that we know as philosophy and science had not yet been divorced into separate disciplines, Muslim scholars who were interested in the new texts usually combined an interest in both. They were philosopher-scientists, as most of their Greek forerunners had been.

In philosophy, as in the sciences and mathematics, Muslim scholars made original contributions. For the first few centuries, they did so within the tradition known as Neoplatonism. Until the twelfth century, intellectuals in Muslim Southwest Asia and North Africa, as well as in Christian Europe, thought that the premises and logic of Plato and Aristotle were more alike than they actually were (Plato is usually considered an "idealist," whereas his student Aristotle was an "empiricist"). For reasons that are not clear, by the time of the translation project in the House of Wisdom, the Greek tradition had attributed to Aristotle two works that were not Aristotelian at all. They have features in them that are so patently different from the thrust of Aristotle's own work that modern scholars are baffled that they could have been identified with him. Nevertheless, they became central to the subsequent Islamic and medieval Western Christian philosophical enterprise. One was the so-called *Theology of Aristotle*, which was actually a paraphrase of Books IV, V, and VI of the *Enneads* of Plotinus, the third-century philosopher whose writings form the basis for Neoplatonism. The other was the *Book of Causes* (known later in medieval Europe as *Liber de causis*), which was excerpted from the *Elements of Theology*, written by Proclus, a fifth-century Neoplatonist.

Neoplatonism was the substratum for much of the work that was done in Islamic philosophy, and it underlay many of the assumptions within Sufism and Islamic theology, especially that of Shi'ism. Neoplatonism was a complex and sophisticated philosophical current, but it may be characterized as taking as its starting point "intellect" or "consciousness" rather than the material world. It was based on the work of Plotinus, who credited his teacher in Alexandria, Ammonius Saccas, with having provided him the basis for his thought. Plotinus postulates a universe at the head of which is a First Cause, or the One, which so transcends the world we know that Plotinus does not even wish to say that it "exists" or has "being" (which makes it technically incorrect to say that the First Principle "is" at the head of the universe!).

The concepts of the One and of an Unmoved Mover were familiar in the Platonic and Aristotelian systems, but Plotinus's contribution was to suggest that this wholly transcendent First Principle has no direct relation with the material world. He argued that it "emanates" an entity that he calls *nous*, or the intellect, which in turn emanates soul, which in turn contains in itself all particular souls, including human souls. Soul in its turn emanates nature, or the phenomenal world in which we live. Later Neoplatonists made this scheme of emanations much more detailed and linked it to the nine spheres of the Ptolemaic universe.[1] Each sphere, or heaven, had its own intellect and soul, emanated by the previous one. The whole universe is thus the result of a succession of emanations in which each principle produces the next lower principle. Each lower principle is, to the extent that its lower nature permits, the imitation of the higher.

The vision of Plotinus was essentially religious, and in fact his philosophy was one of the great "natural theologies" of history. Rather than depending on prophetic revelation, he found the divine in nature, and it was accessible by human reason. Like Plato, he felt trapped in his corporeal body and thought that the highest joy for man is union with the One, attained by purification and contemplation. In classic mystical fashion, he believed that if a person puts aside his identification with his corporeal self and attains to a state of pure thought, he can "return" in a sense to a union with the First Principle in a process that goes in the reverse direction from that of the emanations. The individual soul loses its identity and submerges itself in the One. As we shall see, this scheme helped to give shape to the later Islamic mystical tradition.

The fact that Neoplatonism was a self-contained philosophical religious tradition made it in one sense a competitor to the monotheistic traditions of Judaism, Christianity, and Islam. It appropriated Aristotelian notions such as the eternity of the universe, the denial of the resurrection of the body, and the rejection of the notion that prophets have a special knowledge inaccessible to reason. Its doctrine that the human soul loses its individual personality upon the death of the body was also a problem for most Muslims and Christians. On the other hand, certain influential Christian theologians, such as Augustine (354–430), found in Neoplatonism a notion of the deity as a creative force, or energy, that was more sophisticated than that of a crudely anthropomorphic Creator. When combined with an allegorical interpretation of the scriptures, the emanationist theory made the traditions about a Creator God philosophically acceptable, and it avoided having to address the knotty problems of creation *ex nihilo* ("out of nothing").

Many Muslim intellectuals faced the same issues that Augustine did. Some of them concluded that the apparent contradictions between scriptural and Neoplatonic views of creation, resurrection, and the personal soul could be reconciled when it was understood that the scriptural versions were allegorical expressions of more complicated philosophical truths. In the hands of Muslim philosophers and mystics, the Aristotelian–Neoplatonic synthesis became progressively more complex and sophisticated as they attempted to correct weaknesses and inconsistencies in earlier versions. Each generation, however, confronted two insuperable obstacles: the basic incompatibility between Aristotle's actual system and the Neoplatonic structure that became enmeshed in it and the inconsistencies between Neoplatonism and doctrines derived from the Qur'an and Hadith.

Some of the translators in Baghdad's House of Wisdom made philosophical contributions of their own, but the first genuine philosopher to write in Arabic was al-Kindi (ca. 800–ca. 870), who gained the nickname "Philosopher of the Arabs." Al-Kindi, impressed by the *Theology of Aristotle*, asserted that the truths revealed through the prophets were metaphysical knowledge; thus, there was no contradiction between philosophy and revelation. Despite his protestations, the emergence of philosophy within the Islamic world during the first half of the ninth century provoked a bitter debate about the role of reason within religion, just as it did within Christianity in various periods. As a result, philosophy almost from its inception among Muslims came under suspicion. With few exceptions, advances in philosophy thereafter took place among informal circles of scholars who knew that they were viewed with mistrust, and their work never became part of the institutions of formal education. Those who supported the use of unfettered reason adduced several Hadith to show that learning had been praised and encouraged by the Prophet—"Seek learning, though it be in China," "The ink of scholars is worth more than the blood of martyrs," and "The search for knowledge is obligatory for every Muslim" were but a few of many such sayings—but to no avail. Their work in science and mathematics was encouraged for its practical value, but because their philosophical speculations risked challenging the literal interpretation of the Qur'an, many Muslims regarded them as heretics, if not apostates.

In the context of the handicaps under which the philosopher–scientists worked, the achievements of this group of scholars are nothing short of awe inspiring. As a result of their work, Arabic, which had been the language of revelation for the Muslims, now replaced Greek as the primary language of philosophical and scientific inquiry for the next several centuries. Numerous scholars made contributions that would be immortalized in the twelfth and thirteenth centuries when their works were translated into Latin. Here we will mention two of the most famous whose work dates from before the middle of the tenth century.

Abu Bakr al-Razi (ca. 865–ca. 932), known as Rhazes to medieval Europeans, was born in the Iranian city of Rayy. He became a physician and head of a hospital there and in Baghdad. He was probably the greatest medical mind of his era in the world. Medieval Europeans venerated him for his compendium of medicine from the Greek, Syriac, and Indian traditions, and for his treatise on smallpox and measles. His treatises were not mere encyclopedias. His work as a practicing physician and his keen attention to the details of symptoms and stages of illnesses infused his work with vividness and a captivating style. Despite the universal respect for his medical contributions, he was widely hated for his philosophical ideas, such as his denial of the eternity of the soul and his rejection of the concept of revelation. He argued that because God had imparted reason to mankind, reason rather than revelation would purify the soul and release it from the chains of the body.

Al-Farabi (ca. 878–ca. 950) was known to medieval Europeans both as Alfarabius and Avennasar. He was born in Transoxiana, probably of Turkic origin, but he grew up in Damascus. Al-Farabi studied in Baghdad under the great Nestorian and Jacobite logicians there, but he soon surpassed them. He was not as extreme as al-Razi in his expression of the relationship of philosophy and revelation, but he made it clear that human reason, as utilized by philosophers, is superior to revelation. Ordinary people, however, cannot be expected to comprehend philosophical truth and so must be provided with the concrete and picturesque images by which religion expresses philosophical truths symbolically. Al-Farabi was the first major Muslim Neoplatonist, and subsequent Muslim philosophers used him as a touchstone to measure their own work.

A major part of al-Farabi's career was devoted to the problem of the correct ordering of the state. As the authority of the Abbasid caliphate was collapsing in the tenth century, he turned back to Plato's *Republic* for inspiration, arguing that the ruler must embody the highest intellectual as well as practical virtues. Reflecting Hellenic values, al-Farabi considered the required qualifications of the ruler to include intelligence, love of knowledge, moderation in appetites, and the love of justice, among others. By implication, he suggested that the political problems of his century were due to the absence of philosophers in the government.

FIGURE 5.5 Abu Bakr al-Razi was known and revered in Europe as Rhazes. Here is a page from a thirteenth-century Latin translation of his work on the diseases of the eye.

Bibliothèque Nationale, Paris, FranceArchives Charmet / Bridgeman Images.

The Development of an Islamic Theology

As is the case in Judaism and Christianity, Islam stresses man's obedient response to the sovereign Word of God. Within each tradition, sacred scriptures are the basis for doctrine, ritual, and pious behavior. As a result, great efforts have been made to preserve the integrity of the scriptures and to ascertain their full meaning. The adherents of all three religions have found, however, that the attempt to live a devout life based upon the guidance provided by the scriptures is beset with complications. Passages in the scriptures can be ambiguous, they can contradict each other (at least in their literal meaning), and they are not comprehensive (that is, they fail to address every issue that a person will encounter in his or her life for which ethical, ritual, or doctrinal guidance is needed). In order to determine the will of God in such cases, pious scholars within each religion have utilized a variety of intellectual devices. They identify principal themes within the scriptures as a whole that clarify ambiguities or that harmonize apparent contradictions within specific passages, and they apply the principles found within the scriptures to specific situations confronted in everyday life.

Within Christianity these attempts led to the development of systematic theology. Islamic theology, like its Jewish counterpart, never developed into the comprehensive field of study that Christian theology did. In part, the reason for that lay in the fact that Christianity developed doctrines that required considerable exploration in order to be comprehensible: original sin, the Trinity, the nature and person of Jesus, the meaning of the crucifixion and resurrection, and so forth. Islam and Judaism are more preoccupied with simply discovering God's will through His law and with following it. Muslims did develop a field of study, *kalam*, which is often translated *theology*. It has focused largely on analyzing the attributes of God and of His creation by means of philosophical reasoning.

The Reception of Rationalism

The introduction of philosophical modes of thought into the Arabic cultural tradition had profound implications for the development of Islamic religious thought. In fact, although developments in science and philosophy were the features of the intellectual achievement of the Muslims that caught the attention of medieval Europeans, Muslims first experienced the Greek impact in the field of theology well before the translation process in the House of Wisdom made possible a philosophical tradition in Arabic. The pressures for the development of an Islamic theology came from disputes within the Umma and from forces impinging upon it from the outside world. Within decades of the Prophet's death, urgent questions confronted the community that had to be addressed.

The Muslims of Syria and Iraq found themselves among large communities of Jews and Christians who had been exploring questions such as free will for centuries. The discussion of these issues was shaped by the concepts and forms of argument developed by the Greek tradition, in both its Hellenic and Hellenistic phases. These communities raised questions that Muslims initially found difficult to answer because of the rhetorical methods employed. Many of the questions with which all of the monotheistic religions of revelation are now familiar were first put into stark relief for Muslims at this time: Are humans autonomous rather than agents of God's will? If we are not autonomous, how can God hold us responsible for our evil acts? Are we judged by our acts alone, or by our faith, or by a combination of them? If our acts matter, do they have to be motivated by good intention? Can we know the standards by which we are judged? If so, does that mean that God is compelled to act according to norms—such as justice—that limit His omnipotence, or can He act arbitrarily, unbound by standards that we can count on? Can God be described by the attributes we use for human beings, such as "just" or "loving"? Is God all-powerful and all-knowing? If so, why does He permit evil?

The evidence suggests that groups of Muslim scholars were employing certain Greek concepts and patterns of argument by the early eighth century, both to defend their religion against the polemics of non-Muslims and to explore theological questions themselves. By the time of the reign of the Abbasid caliph Harun al-Rashid (r. 786–809), a well-organized group emerged that was identified by its friends and its enemies alike as the "partisans of dialectic." These were the Mu'tazilites, whom we have already seen locked in a struggle with Ahmad ibn Hanbal. Based in Basra and Baghdad, they were not the only actors in the discipline of Islamic theology, but they were the dominant group for several generations. Mu'tazilism was the result of a desire to use Greek concepts and methods of argument in defense of Islam. Its scholars were exclusively interested in exploring and defending religious topics. They were motivated by a desire to demonstrate to non-Muslims that Islamic beliefs were in accord with reason, and they tried to defend reason against fellow Muslims who insisted on the sole efficacy of faith. They were the first group of Muslim thinkers to give a systematic, rational treatment of religious beliefs.

The Mu'tazilites were famous for their five basic principles, two of which provoked the most discussion. One was that of "justice," which connoted their doctrine of free will and responsibility. They were convinced that they could vindicate the rationality of God's ways. They argued that good and evil are not arbitrary concepts whose validity is rooted in the dictates of God but rather are rational categories that can be established by the use of reason alone. Hence, if God does not create ethical categories but is, Himself, bound by them, His actions are predictable. If He is indeed just, He cannot condemn a person who is good nor excuse a sinner. If God is just, then He can punish only if humans are responsible for acting in an evil way, and we can receive a reward only if we are capable of doing the good on our own power.

Traditionalists like Ibn Hanbal instinctively felt that such a theology limited the power of God—either He is omnipotent or He is not. They could also point to verses in the Qur'an that supported the idea that God is ultimately responsible for evil as well as for good. Their position was that God determines what is right or wrong at any given time, so that His actions are both arbitrary and right. Hence, a person could live a righteous life and yet God could justifiably condemn him or her to hell. The traditionalists regarded the Mu'tazilites' denial of God's right and power to do as He wills to be an affront to His majesty.

The other Mu'tazilite principle was called God's "unity." It was aimed at both the Manichaeans (dualists who believed that God cannot be responsible for the evil in this world) and Muslims who interpreted literally the anthropomorphic descriptions of God that are found in the Qur'an. With regard to the latter, the question became whether to accept revelation literally or to use reason to interpret revelatory images. The anthropomorphic position was articulated by the jurist Malik ibn Anas with regard to the issue of God's "sitting" on the throne: The "sitting is known, whereas its mode is unknown. Belief in its truth is a duty, and its questioning a heresy." The Mu'tazilite approach to the problem reveals its philosophical underpinnings. To accept literally the attributes accorded to God in the Qur'an threatens God's unity and simplicity, for to posit attributes of God (such as His power, knowledge, life, hearing, sight, or speech) distinct from His essence suggests a plurality of eternal entities. The Mu'tazilites were uncomfortable asserting the eternality of anything but God Himself. They declared that God is pure essence with no eternal names and qualities. His attributes are simply aspects of His essence.

Traditionalists, on the other hand, interpreted the Qur'an literally. They identified the Qur'an with the Word—and words—of God. They argued that, since God is eternal and has speech, then His speech—an attribute—must be eternal. Since the Qur'an is His speech, it is eternal as well. Thus, God's attributes, *contra* the Mu'tazilite position, are coeternal with Him, and the Qur'an is uncreated, not created. They viewed the Mu'tazilite position as an attack on the authority of the Qur'an and, indirectly, on the power of God.

These debates seem as hairsplitting to many of us as the Christian controversies over the nature of Christ that produced Monophysitism and Nestorianism. However, like their Christian predecessors, the principals in these controversies were determined to use the power of the state to enforce their opinion. The crisis came to a head during the caliphate of al-Ma'mun (813–833). Mu'tazilism appealed to him in part because he was a rationalist himself and in part because the doctrine of the createdness of the Qur'an could more easily allow the caliph, like the Shi'ite Imam, to interpret and expand on the meaning of the Qur'an as he felt was necessary. A doctrine that insisted on the literal meaning of the Qur'an restricted the scope of such interpretation. Al-Ma'mun required that Mu'tazilite doctrines be followed by qadis and other officials whose decisions had an impact on policy. In the face of resistance to this decree, he instituted a tribunal in 833 to enforce the Mu'tazilite doctrine. The court used the threat of torture and death to force compliance. Only a few, including Ibn Hanbal, refused to recant the doctrine of the uncreatedness of the Qur'an. The obstinate ones were imprisoned, and some died from the harsh treatment they suffered. The persecution continued intermittently until 849, when the new caliph reversed the policy, and then it became the turn of the Mu'tazilites to be persecuted.

The Critique of Rationalism

The reaction against the Mu'tazilites was vehement. Despite the fact that even their Muslim critics had often commended them for their defense of Islam against attacks by competing religious systems, their arguments seemed to imply that they regarded revelation to be valid only if it is consistent with the workings of reason. Many of their opponents assumed that, like the philosophers, they regarded reason to be the supreme organizing principle in the universe, and that God and His works were subject to the rules of logic, which are devised by human minds. Ibn Hanbal spoke for many Muslims when he asserted that the Qur'an and the Sunna of the

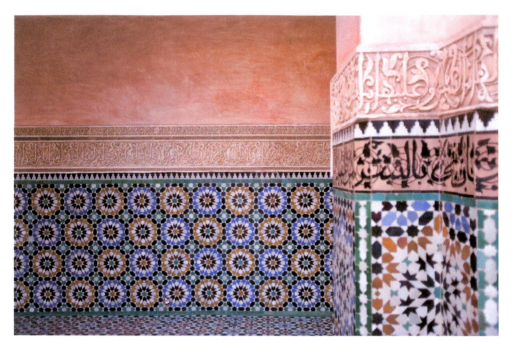

FIGURE 5.6 Not infrequently, all three forms of patterned design were used together when decorating buildings. Here, arabesque is at the top, calligraphy in the middle, and geometric forms at the bottom.

Robert Harding / Alamy Stock Photo.

Prophet were the sole sources of Islamic doctrine and practice. It was the duty of Muslims to accept the literal meaning of the Qur'an at face value "without asking how" (*bi-la kayf*) ambiguous or puzzling doctrines could be reconciled with human reason. Ibn Hanbal's school of law arose as a reaction to the Mu'tazilite controversy. Its purpose was to ensure that the Qur'an—literally interpreted—and the Hadith were the sole basis for jurisprudence.

In the midst of the conflict between the rationalist approach of the Mu'tazilites and the literalist position of their opponents, other thinkers tried to find a middle ground. The most influential was al-Ash'ari (d. 935), whose work eventually became the basis on which subsequent scholars fashioned the theology that became the intellectual rationale for Sunni doctrine. Al-Ash'ari was a former Mu'tazilite who was convinced that the Mu'tazilite emphasis on reason undermined faith. Claiming that he was following in the tradition of Ibn Hanbal, he set about to do battle with the rationalists. The irony of the situation, which was not lost on the Hanbalis, was that al-Ash'ari defended the faith with the very tools of the Mu'tazilites: philosophical terms and dialectical arguments. This came about by the necessity of the age, as al-Ash'ari realized that to defeat the Mu'tazilites he would have to meet them on their own terms.

Al-Ash'ari insisted without equivocation that the Qur'an was uncreated and that God possesses attributes that are in His essence. Realizing the trap that lay in store for him, he cautioned that God's attributes may not be said to be identical with

His essence, nor can they be said not to be identical with it. His attributes—such as speech, sight, and hearing—are not like those of His creatures and must simply be accepted *bi-la kayf*. Al-Ash'ari also argued that humans are incapable of creating their own acts. Unlike the Mu'tazilites, who argued that humans have free will, and the Hanbalis, who claimed that God is the author of all acts despite the fact that man is responsible for his evil acts on the Day of Judgment, al-Ash'ari used the concept of "acquisition" (*kasb*) to try to account for the synergy of God and a person in a given act. At the heart of the concept is the theory that the creation of the world is not a finished act but an ongoing one, in which God is constantly making each moment possible. At each instant, God is the creator of all acts, and yet people in some sense "acquire" them.

Al-Ash'ari's attempt to reconcile God's omnipotence with a person's responsibility for his or her own acts was rejected by Mu'tazilites and Hanbalis alike. The Mu'tazilites saw that it precluded free will, and the Hanbalis were opposed to the use of rational arguments in support of doctrinal points. Moreover, Mu'tazilites could not accept the literalist presuppositions of al-Ash'ari, and Hanbalis refused to recognize that reason had any role in affairs of religion. Al-Ash'ari did have followers, however, and they continued to refine his approach in ways that soon became acceptable to most Sunnis. By the middle of the eleventh century, "Ash'arism" represented a compromise between rationalists and those who placed a premium on faith, and it became the major expression of Sunni theological thought. Hanbalis were a dwindling, if influential, minority, whereas Mu'tazilism practically disappeared among Sunni scholars, although it became popular within Shi'ism. It had become apparent to most scholars that the real conflict was not between rationalism and faith, but over the scope and the validity of reason in faith. The theologians, as opposed to the philosophers, could not accept reason as a source of new and certain knowledge, but they became increasingly sophisticated in their use of reason to demonstrate the truths of revelation.

Conclusion

Just as the middle of the tenth century represents a major watershed in the political history of the Dar al-Islam, it also marks a milestone in the development of Islam as a major religion. By that time, the principles for deriving the Shari'a had been established. As a result, Sunni Islam had its basic organizing principle. Shi'ism had become a sectarian movement, and the majority of its adherents were clustered into two groups. One of them had become known as the Isma'ili or Fatimid movement and had achieved political power in North Africa, allowing it to develop without fear of governmental persecution. The members of the Imami branch of Shi'ism, who heretofore had followed a "visible" and "present" Imam, became "Twelvers" after 874. They awaited the return of the Twelfth Imam, who was being groomed by God to return in triumph from his "occultation." The essential difference between Sunnis and Shi'ites seemed to be that the former sought God's will in a method of inquiry for determining the Shari'a, whereas the latter sought God's will in the first instance from a divinely guided descendant of Muhammad. Shi'ites considered the Shari'a to be a secondary source of guidance to that of the Imam.

Sufism, too, had achieved an important milestone by the middle of the tenth century. The major issues of basic presuppositions and of the methods for achieving spiritual maturity had been established, but Sufism was still in its infancy in terms of organization and literature. It offered new avenues for worshiping God, and its deep spirituality appealed to many. Conversely, it threatened others. Whereas some Sufis understood their quest to be the fulfillment of the Shari'a, others saw it as an alternative to the practice of the Shari'a, with the result that some of the ulama were deeply suspicious of it.

Muslims were also active in science, philosophy, and medicine in this period. The translations of the ninth century, in particular, made available the heritage of the Greco–Roman tradition and of India. Important work by Muslims in medicine, mathematics, and philosophy laid the foundations for subsequent generations of philosopher–scientists to make contributions that are still admired. Other Muslims were beginning to question whether the quest for knowledge independent of the scriptures was either worthwhile or pious.

It is noteworthy that the work of scholars in Iraq was central to the developments within Imami Shi'ism, the Shari'a, Sufism, philosophy, mathematics, and medicine during this period. The Muslims there—Arabs and converts, natives and immigrants—managed to create a tradition that was enriched by its sophisticated environment and yet remained a distinctly Islamic enterprise, inspired by the Qur'an and the example of the Prophet. After the mid-tenth century, the most important intellectual work would take place on the geographical periphery of the Dar al-Islam, rather than in its heartland. The glory days of the Abbasid caliphate were over.

NOTES

1   Ptolemy, the second-century Roman scientist, postulated a model of the universe that would shape the thought of scholars in the Christian, Jewish, and Islamic lands for more than a millennium and a half. Like almost all other intellectuals, he assumed that the earth was at the center of the universe and that surrounding it were spheres containing the various celestial bodies. The sphere nearest the earth contained the moon, the next one the sun, then separate spheres for each of the five known planets, and beyond those was a sphere that contained all the stars, which were equidistant from the earth. The final sphere was what many scholars referred to as the Primum Mobile, or the agency that drives the entire apparatus as a result of the First Cause, or the One.

FURTHER READING

The Origins of Islamic Law

Coulson, N.J. *A History of Islamic Law*. Edinburgh, U.K.: Edinburgh University Press, 1964.

Hallaq, Wael B. *A History of Islamic Legal Theories: An Introduction to Sunni usul al-fiqh.* Cambridge, U.K.: Cambridge University Press, 1997.

Juynboll, Gualterus H. A. *Muslim Tradition: Studies in Chronology, Provenance and Authorship of Early Hadith,* Cambridge, U.K.: Cambridge University Press, 1983.

Schacht, Joseph. *An Introduction to Islamic Law*, Second Impression. Oxford, U.K.: Clarendon Press, 1964.

Schacht, Joseph. *The Origins of Muhammadan Jurisprudence.* Fourth Impression. Oxford, U.K.: Clarendon Press, 1967.

Early Sufism

Arberry, A.J. *Sufism: An Account of the Mystics of Islam.* New York and Evanston: Harper & Row, 1950.

Knysh, Alexander. *Islamic Mysticism: A Short History.* Leiden, Boston, Koln: Brill, 2000.

Peters, F.E. *Allah's Commonwealth: A History of Islam in the Near East 600–1100 A.D.* New York: Simon and Schuster, 1973.

Schimmel, Annemarie. *The Mystical Dimension of Islam.* Chapel Hill, North Carolina: The University of North Carolina Press, 1975.

The Reception of Science and Philosophy

Anawati, G. "Science." In *The Cambridge History of Islam,* edited by P. M. Holt, A. K. Lambton, and B. Lewis, vol. II, 741–779. Cambridge, U.K.: Cambridge University Press, 1970.

Fakhry, Majid. *A History of Islamic Philosophy,* 2d ed. New York: Columbia University Press, 1987.

al-Hasan, Ahmad, and Donald R. Hill. *Islamic Technology: An Illustrated History.* Cambridge, U.K.: Cambridge University Press, 1986.

Hill, Donald R. *Islamic Science and Engineering.* Edinburgh, U.K.: Edinburgh University Press, 1994.

Lindberg, David C., ed. *Science in the Middle Ages.* Chicago and London: The University of Chicago Press, 1978.

Lyons, Jonathan. The House of Wisdom: How the Arabs Transformed Western Civilization. New York: Bloomsbury Press, 2010.

Peters, F.E. *Aristotle and the Arabs: The Aristotelian Tradition in Islam.* New York: New York University Press, 1968.

Turner, Howard R. *Science in Medieval Islam: An Illustrated Introduction.* Austin, Texas: University of Texas Press, 1995.

Ullmann, Manfred. *Islamic Surveys II: Islamic Medicine.* Edinburgh, U.K.: Edinburgh University Press, 1978.

Young, M.J.L., J.D. Latham, and R.J. Serjeant, eds. *Religion, Learning, and Science in the 'Abbasid Period.* Cambridge and New York: Cambridge University Press, 1990.

PART TWO

Civilization vs. Chaos, 950–1260

By 950, Muslims were justified in feeling a sense of satisfaction in the accomplishments of the past. The agreement regarding a methodology for jurisprudence had produced a comprehensive set of rules and laws that satisfied the vast majority of Sunnis; after a bumpy start, the mystical life was becoming attractive to more and more believers; science and philosophy were being selectively incorporated into the Islamic framework; and a far-flung commercial network was increasing wealth and stimulating creative solutions to everyday problems. The result was the emergence of a civilization that could compare favorably with any that had existed in history.

Despite these achievements, many thoughtful Muslims shared a sense of foreboding about the future of the Dar al-Islam. In 950, three rulers claimed the title of caliph, a position that had traditionally laid claim to leadership of all Muslims. The competing claims of authority were exacerbated by differences in religious creeds: The caliph in Cordoba was a Sunni; the one in Mahdiya was a Fatimid Shi'ite; and in Baghdad, the Sunni caliph was powerless, whereas the Buyid sultan—who exercised the real power in the Abbasid caliphate—supported Twelver Shi'ism. The sense of lost unity, both spiritual and political, has haunted Muslims ever since, and it has been a major factor in the rise of reform movements for more than a millennium.

As it turned out, the next three centuries would confirm both the highest hopes and the worst fears of the mid-tenth century. The period from 950 to 1260 witnessed major cultural achievements—many historians judge its cultural productivity to have been one of the most spectacular in world history—but it was punctuated by shocking violence and disorder. The first three centuries of Muslim history experienced violence, as we have seen, but it was episodic and most of it occurred between armies. In the second period, by contrast, we witness numerous examples of factional conflict among the inhabitants of the same city, persecution of subjects by their rulers, and "total war" tactics by invading armies, in which farmers and city dwellers alike suffered from ruined property or death, simply for being in the way.

The political history of the period 950–1260 can be divided in half to illustrate some important differences. The first half, 950–1100, provides a rough approximation for the period during which most of the violence was that of Muslims against other Muslims. This is the subject treated in Chapter 6. From eastern Iran to Andalus, new political dynasties came to power, and they did so in the only way they could, which was to overthrow the existing rulers. The second half of the period, roughly 1100–1260, is the subject of Chapter 7. The degree of the violence intensified and tended to affect noncombatants more than previously. The origin of most of the violence was from outside the Dar al-Islam and was initiated by non-Muslims. This is the period of the Reconquista in the Iberian Peninsula, the Crusades in Anatolia and Syria, and the Mongols in Iran and Iraq. Overlapping both of these periods is the in-migration of tens of thousands of Turkic warrior–herdsmen. Some of their leaders were devout Muslims and sophisticated leaders of great ability, but the vast majority of their followers were illiterate, only nominally Muslim, and in search of plunder. Their initial impact was destructive, too, but the long-term effect of the irruption of the Turks into the Dar al-Islam would be not only constructive, but decisive, in shaping the character of Islamic civilization.

Chapter 8 returns to the topic of religious and intellectual developments that we last explored in Chapter 5. By the mid-tenth century, Muslim scholars were sufficiently familiar with the Greek and Indian cultural legacies to begin making major contributions of their own, and some of the most famous intellectuals in Muslim history produced their work during the next three centuries. Their achievements in science and philosophy were so impressive that Western Europeans began a major translation process to transfer Arabic learning into Latin. On the other hand, a consensus developed among Muslims that the exercise of reason, unless guided by revelation, was a dangerous force in society. Increasingly, intellectuals who might have pursued a path in philosophy became mystics instead. Indeed, this was the period in which the most distinctive Sufi institutions—the lodge and the order—emerged.

Chapter 9 surveys the state of the Dar al-Islam as it was in the mid-thirteenth century, employing the concept of "commonwealth" that some scholars have adopted to characterize this vast region of the planet which, for all its differences, constituted a single civilization. The scale of the violence of the period could have spelled the end of Islam. Islam's enemies, in fact, counted on that to happen. Precisely the opposite happened. Muslims proved to be highly resourceful, developing new social institutions that enabled them to weather the storms that afflicted them both physically and emotionally. They had created a civilization that would not only survive, but thrive, under the most severe conditions.

CHRONOLOGY

969	Fatimids conquer Egypt
998–1030	Reign of Mahmud of Ghazna
c.1000–1037	Career of Ibn Sina
1034–1060	Norman conquest of port cities in Ifriqiya
1058	Tughril Bey secures Baghdad for Saljuqs
1050s–1147	Almoravid Empire
1060–1091	Norman conquest of Muslim Sicily
1066	Norman conquest of England
1071	Battle of Manzikert
c.1085–1111	Career of al-Ghazali
1085	Toledo falls to Reconquista
1092	Civil war begins among Great Saljuqs
1094	Musta'li-Nizari schism among Fatimids; "Assassins" become notorious
1099	First Crusade conquers Jerusalem
1130	Hafizi-Tayyibi schism among Fatimids
1140s	First Gothic cathedral (Saint Denis)
1144	Edessa falls; first Crusader state to do so
1147–1269	Almohad Empire
c.1160–1198	Career of Ibn Rushd
c.1170	Emergence of Sufi lodges
1171	Saladin takes power in Cairo, ends Fatimid caliphate
1176	Battle of Myriokephalon
1187	Battle of Hattin
1189–1193	Third Crusade
1180–1225	Caliphate of al-Nasir, who attempts a renaissance of Abbasid power
c.1200	Emergence of Sufi tariqas
c.1200–1240	Career of Ibn al-'Arabi
1204	Fourth Crusade results in sack of Constantinople and creation of Latin Kingdom
1212	Battle of Las Navas de Tolosa
1215	Magna Carta issued in England

1219–1222	Chinggis Khan's campaigns in Muslim world
1236–1266	All of Andalus except Granada falls to Reconquista
c.1240–1273	Career of Rumi
1241	Batu leads a Mongol army in Eastern Europe
1250	Mamluk era begins
1258	Hulagu destroys Baghdad
1260	Mamluks defeat Mongols at 'Ayn Jalut
1261	Byzantines regain Constantinople from Latin Kingdom
1269	Marinids replace Almohads in Morocco

CHAPTER 6

Filling the Vacuum of Power, 950–1100

In 950, three cities claimed to be the seat of the legitimate caliphate. The next century and a half proved that each claim merely demonstrated that the Muslim world was hopelessly divided, both religiously and politically. The inherent weakness of each polity, and the emerging social strains in each region, rendered their claims ephemeral. Their petty concerns and evident weakness encouraged other ambitious leaders to make bids for power, with the result that the period witnessed frequent clashes.

The year 1100 is a convenient one with which to close the period. In the east, the Buyids fell in 1055 to a group of invaders called the Saljuq Turks. The Turks' entry into the heartland of the Muslim world heralded the arrival of a dynamic ethnic group that would dominate large parts of the Dar al-Islam for centuries to come. A dynastic struggle for power within their ranks in the 1090s, however, left the Mediterranean coastline vulnerable to the invasion of the Frankish Crusaders at the close of the decade. In North Africa, the Fatimid Empire became the greatest of the Muslim powers in the eleventh century, but it suffered a debilitating schism in 1094, also just before the Crusaders showed up to seize Palestine from it. In the west, the Reconquista claimed its first major triumph in 1085 by taking Toledo, but a new Berber dynasty known as the Almoravids immediately came across the Strait of Gibraltar from North Africa to prevent any more of Andalus from falling under Christian control. By 1100, the Almoravids had incorporated most of Andalus into their North African empire.

The Buyid Sultanate

In Baghdad, one of the first orders of business for the Buyids when they seized power in 945 was the regularization of pay for the military. They inherited from the

Abbasid regime a practice that had begun as early as the ninth century of substituting "tax farms" for the salaries due to officers. Because tax collection was so inefficient, the government was often short of cash to pay military officers and high civilian officials. The new technique entailed granting to officials the right to collect the taxes themselves from specific villages or districts. The system under the Abbasids had had only limited success due to its intermittent practice and the fact that the officers in charge of the revenue of a district sometimes would not forward to the government the amount in excess due to the officer himself. The Buyids codified the practice, guaranteeing officers that if their assignment was inadequate, another would be exchanged for it. They also implemented audits that secured the amount due the government. The grant of a tax district is known as an *iqta'*, and it proved to have a long life in Southwest Asia. Its theoretical appeal to government officials is understandable, but in practice it proved detrimental to the economic productivity of the areas in which it operated. The officer in charge of local revenues was often tempted to extract more taxes than were due him whenever he saw any accumulated wealth. As a result, peasants and merchants soon learned that they had no incentive to improve their farms or businesses.

The early Buyids wore their Zaydi convictions lightly, and they quickly became devoted Twelver Shi'ites. On the one hand, they did not force their sectarian identity on their subjects, and they never threatened the Sunni caliph. On the other hand, they did protect and encourage the practice of Shi'ism, which had been crystallizing in Iraq even before the Buyids assumed power there. Hasan al-'Askari, the eleventh Imam of Twelver Shi'ism, was in Samarra when he died in 874, and the scholars who began developing the idea of the Hidden Imam in the 940s were centered in Baghdad. During the 960s, the Buyid regime in Baghdad inaugurated two ceremonies that became central to the ritual life of subsequent Twelver Shi'ism. One was Ashura, which memorializes the death of Husayn at Karbala. *'Ashura'* literally means "tenth," referring to the tenth day of the month of Muharram, when Husayn was killed. Over the next several centuries, the observance of the martyrdom eventually developed into an elaborate ten-day observance involving prayer, Qur'anic recitations, reenactments of the battle at Karbala, and, in some localities, self-flagellation by the pious as a way to share in Husayn's suffering.

The other festival that Shi'ites began to observe at this time was Ghadir Khumm, the celebration of Muhammad's designation of 'Ali to be his rightful successor. The fundamental assumption of pro-Alids all along had been that 'Ali and his family were the most qualified to rule. The early Shi'ites claimed that the Prophet had designated 'Ali to be his successor at the pool (*ghadir*) of Khumm. Now, under a Shi'ite regime, that tradition could be publicly celebrated. When the celebrations were held, however, clashes between Sunnis and Shi'ites were common.

Throughout the period of Buyid rule, Baghdad lagged behind both Rayy and Shiraz economically and politically. Shiraz was the wealthiest city of the Buyid confederation, and Rayy became a thriving commercial center on the east–west caravan route. Baghdad did house the caliph, its physical size was still impressive, and scholarly life continued, but it was in the grip of perpetual economic and political crises. Daylami and Turkic soldiers frequently fought pitched battles in the streets, and the countryside was plagued with banditry.

In addition, the tenth and eleventh centuries witnessed a reassertion of nomads throughout the Fertile Crescent and western Iran. The Umayyads and early Abbasids had controlled the movements of nomads by means of a policy that combined the incentive of subsidies and the threat of force. The bedouin lost their subsidies by the ninth century and were displaced from the Abbasid army by the tenth century. In order to compensate for their economic losses, they began raiding settlements in Syria and Iraq. They discovered that the decline of central authority and of economic stability enabled them to engage in attacks almost with impunity. Several local Arab and Kurdish families seized control of cities during this period and created short-lived dynasties. By the end of the tenth century, competing Arab and Kurdish families ruled northern Iraq, northern Syria, the middle Euphrates valley, and eastern Anatolia. The most famous of the new ruling groups was the Shi'ite Hamdanid confederation, which controlled Mosul and Aleppo for most of the tenth century. The Hamdanids actually controlled a larger area than did the caliph or his Buyid "Commander of Commanders." They demonstrated their wealth and sophistication by patronizing famous artists and scholars. The Hamdanid ruler of Aleppo, for example, became the primary patron of the philosopher al-Farabi.

Compounding the disorder caused by the "bedouinization" of Syria and Iraq during this period was a century-long revival of Byzantine military power. The Byzantines began capturing Arab settlements in eastern Anatolia in the 930s, driving out the population. In the 960s, they retook Crete, captured Antioch and Tarsus, and sacked Aleppo. Aleppo was subjected to nine days of pillaging, and 10,000 Muslim children were said to have been dragged into captivity. Although the Hamdanids subsequently regained their position as rulers of Aleppo, they served thereafter at the sufferance of the Byzantines and had to pay tribute to them.

Under pressure from the street preachers and ulama, the Buyid regime in Baghdad attempted to mobilize against the Byzantine threat in the early 970s. Factions within the Turkic units of the Buyid army seized this chance to rebel against their masters, however, leading to a civil war that lasted from 972 to 975 and devastated Baghdad. The instability in Baghdad allowed the Byzantines to eliminate vast expanses of Muslim settlement in the frontier zone along the Taurus Mountains. Refugees flooded into Syria and northern Iraq, causing the Buyids and the caliphate to lose considerable prestige for their failure to stem the tide of the Christian army's incursions.

A resurgent Byzantine empire was ominous for the Buyids, but the security problem was intensified by the rise of yet another threat, this time from the east. After 1030, isolated groups of Turkic sheep herders and war bands began to filter into Azerbaijan and northern Iraq from Transoxiana. Themselves the victims of warfare in the east, they were desperately poor, seeking green grass for their sheep and plunder for themselves. Their arrival touched off chronic warfare between them and the local inhabitants. One group of these herdsmen temporarily captured Mosul in 1044. Challenged from the east and from the west, the authority of the Buyids by the middle of the eleventh century extended little farther than the environs of their three main cities. Even in the cities the sight was not pretty. Travelers reported that Baghdad had degenerated into a congeries of fortified hamlets, separated from each other by the desolate ruins of what once had been the greatest city in the world west of China.

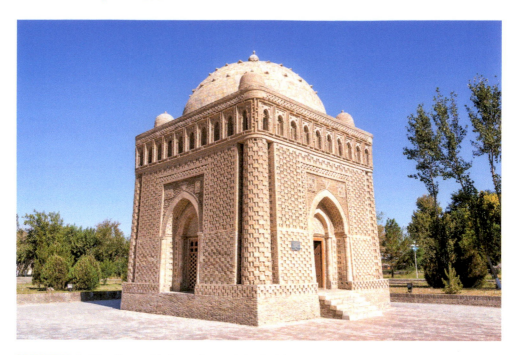

FIGURE 6.1   The Samanid dynastic tomb in Bukhara, tenth century. The Samanids were known for their fine decorative brickwork, and the tomb exhibits their skill on both the exterior and interior walls.

Melvyn Longhurst / Alamy Stock Photo.

The Advent of the Turks

By the middle of the eleventh century, the Buyids were suffering from a series of escalating challenges from the Byzantines, bedouin, and Turks. A clear-headed military analyst in Baghdad in the early eleventh century would have emphasized the need to concentrate Buyid military resources against the Byzantines and bedouin. They were, after all, formidable local threats. The Turks, fearsome as they might be, were based a thousand miles away in Transoxiana. Such a clear-headed analysis would have been wrong, as even rational calculation sometimes can be in the face of the unexpected. As it turned out, the Turks dispensed with the Buyids, Byzantines, and bedouin as though they were leaves before the wind. The coming of the Turks into Southwest Asia in the mid-eleventh century heralded a profound transformation in the relations of power in the Dar al-Islam.

The Turks were a new addition to the linguistic quilt of the Umma. Whereas Arabic is part of the Semitic language family and Persian is one of the Indo–European languages, the Turkic languages are part of the Ural–Altaic language group, which includes the languages of the Mongols and Koreans. Like the Arabs before them, the Turks quickly conquered a vast, sedentary, and urban-based society. Unlike the Arabs, whose language and religion transformed the civilization of the conquered areas, the Turks were quick to appropriate the languages and religion of the societies into which they moved. But even though they recognized that the culture of the new areas was superior to theirs, they had a sense that they were destined to be rulers over wide areas of the earth. Politically and militarily, they would prove to be the dominant ethnic group within the Umma for most of the next nine centuries.

For as long as we have historical evidence, there have been several Turkic groups. Today these include the Turks of Turkey as well as the Azeris, Turkmen, Uzbeks, Kazakhs, Kyrgyz, and others. There are about forty recognized Turkic languages. Today, ethnologists like to reserve the term *Turkish* for the language and culture of the Turks of Turkey, whereas the term *Turkic* can apply to all those who speak a related language. The Turkic peoples enjoy varying degrees of mutual intelligibility, similar to ranges of intelligibility among speakers of Romance languages or Slavic languages. In this book, *Turkish* will be used for the Oghuz group who settled Anatolia and southeastern Europe, and *Turkic* will be used for other related groups or Turks in general.

Origins

Between the seventh and eleventh centuries, most Turks lived in the area north of the Syr Darya River and the Aral Sea. They were divided into some two dozen competing confederations. A few Turkic groups—among them the Bulgars, Khazars, Cumans (the western Qipchaqs), and Pechenegs—made their way westward early in this period and played an important role in the early medieval history of Eastern Europe. Others, notably the Qarluqs, Oghuz, and eastern Qipchaqs, remained in the area north of Transoxiana.

From the early ninth century, Turks had interacted with the Dar al-Islam in different ways. Individual Turks entered the region as adventurers, slaves, mercenary soldiers, and merchants. The Samanid amirate (819–999), with its capital in Bukhara, was the Muslim principality that had the most contact with Turkic peoples. Even though it was a self-consciously Persian regime, its military force was composed largely of Turkic mamluks. Furthermore, although the economic base of the Samanid regime was the irrigated agriculture of Transoxiana, a large part of its wealth derived from the commerce of the slave trade in Turks, for the states of Southwest Asia had by the tenth century developed an insatiable appetite for slave soldiers.

In 961, one of the Samanid ruler's Turkic mamluks seized from his master the city of Ghazna (modern Ghazni) in what is now Afghanistan, where he proceeded to build a power base. In 994, his successor cooperated with the Samanid ruler of the time to repel an invading force of Turks from the Qarluq confederation, and as a reward he received control of Khorasan. Thus, by the end of the tenth century, Ghazna (its ruling dynasty has come to be known as the Ghaznavids) had virtually independent control of the territories south of the Amu Darya. This empire was inherited by Mahmud of Ghazna (998–1030), who became famous for his wide-ranging military campaigns. He made at least seventeen major raids into India for treasure, striking as far south as Gujarat, plundering and destroying Hindu temples. The most successful—and infamous—of his conquests was the plundering of the immense temple complex of Somnath in 1025–1026, which resulted in the massacre of thousands of Hindus and the extraction of incalculable wealth. Mahmud boasted of how his troops smashed to pieces the golden idols there; he did not emphasize that the gold was then carried back to the treasury at Ghazna for him to enjoy.

The emergence of the Ghaznavid state had long-lasting repercussions. As an aggressive Muslim regime in what are today Afghanistan and eastern Iran, it was poised to be a base for the future expansion of Islam into South Asia, as we shall see in subsequent chapters. Culturally, it was equally influential. Mahmud's capital at Ghazna is obscure to most of us today, but prior to the thirteenth century it ranked among the three or four most culturally advanced cities in the entire Dar al-Islam. It attracted not only Turkic warriors but also many scholars and literary figures who were conversant in both Persian and Arabic culture.

The Ghaznavids were Persianized Turks. Although members of the ruling elite were ethnic Turks, they continued the patronage of Persian art and literature that the Samanids had begun in Transoxiana decades earlier. The greatest literary work of the era was the *Shah-nameh*, or *Book of Kings*. This monumental epic of some 60,000 verses is an intriguing example of the Persian revival of the period. While it is not anti-Islamic, it is a celebration of pre-Islamic Iran and can be read as an implicit criticism of the Arab conquest of Iran. Its author, Ferdowsi, is said to have worked on the poem for thirty years. For most of that period he lived under Samanid rule, but he presented the manuscript to Mahmud in 1010.

Mahmud also commissioned several outstanding architectural works which had a long-lasting influence. Iranian mosques were already beginning to incorporate into their design a Sasanian feature, the *eyvan*, or large vaulted hall closed on three sides and open to a court on the fourth. Several large mosques of this type were constructed in Ghazna. The motif of a court surrounded by four eyvans came to dominate Turkic monumental architecture in Iran and Central Asia for centuries to come.

Mahmud's large army, augmented by armor-plated war elephants, struck terror into the hearts of all his opponents. Although his raids may appear to the observer to have been largely in quest of loot, Mahmud insisted that he was championing the cause of Sunnism against both paganism and Shi'ism. He gained a reputation in the Muslim heartland as a champion of Sunni Islam, and although he was a brutal and exploitative ruler, scholars praised him for his patronage of the arts and sciences. Sunnis who chafed under Buyid rule looked to him as their potential deliverer. To their delight, he turned his armies westward late in his career. He captured Rayy from the Buyids in 1029 and harassed Buyid holdings in Kirman and Fars. At his death in 1030, he controlled an empire that extended from the border of Azerbaijan to the upper Ganges and from the Amu Darya to the Indian Ocean.

The Birth of Rostam

Speakers of Persian still revere Ferdowsi's Shah-nameh, *and many of them know by heart large numbers of its verses. The figure from the poem who remains the most popular with Iranians is Rostam, a great hero who fought continually for the defense of Iran. The selection that follows relates details from the circumstances surrounding his birth and provides a flavor of the tone and style of the poem, even though the translation is in prose.*

The incident requires some background: The great ruler Sam had abandoned his infant son Zal at birth because the baby's hair was entirely white. The child was placed on the top of a remote mountain to die, but a great bird, the Simorgh, brought Zal to her nest and raised him as her own. Eventually, Sam learned that Zal had survived to become a towering figure himself and came for him. As Zal was leaving the mountain with his father, the Simorgh gave him one of her feathers and told him that, should he ever encounter trouble, he should burn the feather, and she would come to his aid. Zal soon met the beautiful princess Rudaba, and, as the poem relates, their love grew, and wisdom fled: She was soon pregnant with their son, Rostam. The pregnancy, however, was difficult, and Zal was afraid that Rudaba would die. Remembering the feather, he burned it, and the Simorgh instantly appeared.

The Simorgh inquired, "What means this grief? Why these tears in the lion's eyes? From this silver-bosomed cypress, whose face is as the moon for loveliness, a child will issue for you who will be eager for fame. Lions will kiss the dust of his footsteps and above his head even the clouds will find no passage. Merely at the sound of his voice the hide of the fighting leopard will burst and it will seize its claws in its teeth for panic. For judgment and sagacity he will be another Sam in all his gravity, but when stirred to anger he will be an aggressive lion. He will have the slender grace of a cypress but the strength of an elephant; with one of his fingers he will be able to cast a brick two leagues.

"Yet, by command of the Lawgiver, Provider of all good, the child will not come into existence by the ordinary way of birth. Bring me a poniard of tempered steel and a man of percipient heart versed in incantation. Let the girl be given a drug to stupefy her and to dull any fear or anxiety in her mind; then keep guard while the clairvoyant recites his incantations and so watch until the lion–boy leaves the vessel which contains him. The wizard will pierce the frame of the young woman without her awareness of any pain and will draw the lion–child out of her, covering her flank with blood, and will sew together the part he has cut. Therefore banish all fear, care and anxiety from your heart. There is an herb which I will describe to you. Pound it together with milk and musk and place it in a dry shady place. Afterwards spread it over the wound and you will perceive at once how she has been delivered from peril. Over it all then pass one of my feathers and the shadow of my royal potency will have achieved a happy result."

Speaking thus she plucked a feather from her wing, cast it down and flew aloft.

(*Zal took the feather and obeyed his instructions. When his son was born, he named him Rostam.*)

Ten foster-mothers gave Rostam the milk, which provides men with strength and then, when after being weaned from milk he came to eating substantial food, they gave him an abundance of bread and flesh. Five men's portions were his provision and it was a wearisome task to prepare it for him. He grew to the height of eight men so that his stature was that of a noble cypress; so high did he grow that it was as though he might become a shining star at which all the world would gaze. As he stood you might have believed him to be the hero Sam for handsomeness and wisdom, for grace and judgment.

SOURCE: *The Epic of the Kings: Shah-Nama the national epic of Persia.* Translated by Reuben Levy. (1967) 47–48.

While the Ghaznavids were securing their power in Afghanistan during the second half of the tenth century, clans from two of the Turkic confederations—the Qarluq and Oghuz—began crossing the Syr Darya into Transoxiana. The Qarluq group, led by the Qara-khanid dynasty, converted en masse to Islam about 960. In 992, the Qara-khanids seized Bukhara from the Samanids, and seven years later they took Samarqand. The Amu Darya served as the boundary between the Qara-khanids and their rivals, the Ghaznavids.

Like the Ghaznavids, the Qara-khanids ruled over a largely Persian-speaking populace at first, but Transoxiana experienced a continual in-migration of Turks. Again, like the Ghaznavids, they patronized literature, but in this case, it was a new Turkic literature based on Arabic and Persian models, with the result that Turkic speakers had access to a wide range of Islamic literature. Qara-khanid unity soon splintered into several rival petty states, but the rulers of these chiefdoms signaled their transition from a nomadic lifestyle to an urban environment with their financial support for hospitals, mosques, schools, and caravanserais in Transoxiana.

The Saljuq Invasion

Not long after the Qarluqs entered Transoxiana, the Oghuz followed. The most famous of the Oghuz clans is that of the Saljuqs. They left the region north of the Aral Sea and entered Transoxiana in the 980s, when the Samanids requested their assistance against other Turkic invaders. Still more migrated into the area in the early eleventh century when various branches of the Qara-khanids sought outside aid in their own civil war. Thus, the Saljuqs came into Transoxiana by invitation. It is not known if they had converted to Islam before they entered Transoxiana or after, but, like the Qarluqs, they converted collectively—the religion of the leader became the religion of the tribe.

In 1035, a drought in Transoxiana forced a band of Saljuqs, led by the brothers Chaghri and Tughril, across the Amu Darya into Khorasan in search of grazing land for their sheep. Khorasan was still part of the Ghaznavid domain, but Mahmud's son Mas'ud had succeeded him as ruler at the former's death in 1030. Mas'ud had no sympathy for the Saljuqs' plight and treated them harshly. The Saljuqs struck back and defeated him. Mas'ud then granted them a small territory for grazing purposes, but their victories had emboldened them, and they were no longer willing to act as supplicants. They allowed their sheep to graze unrestricted in the oases of the northern Khorasan, with the result that crops were damaged. They also intercepted caravans and harassed the villages and towns of the region.

The inhabitants of the major cities of Merv and Nishapur had already been chafing under the heavy taxation of the Ghaznavids, and now their discontent increased as it appeared that Mas'ud was not going to deliver them from the uncouth and dangerous nomads who did what they pleased. Despairing of any help from the government in Ghazna, Merv surrendered to the Saljuqs in 1037, followed the next year by Nishapur. In 1040, Mas'ud finally attacked the Saljuqs, only to be soundly defeated. The Ghaznavid Empire lost Khorasan forever and was thereafter centered on Ghazna and Lahore.

As the new rulers of Khorasan, the Saljuqs were in a position to carve out a large empire. They conquered Khwarazm on the lower Amu Darya, in 1042. The Saljuq leaders found much to admire in the Persian culture that permeated the new areas

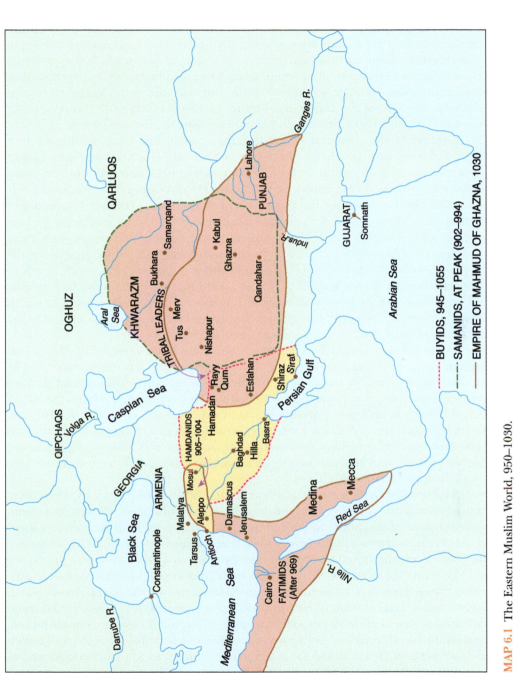

MAP 6.1 The Eastern Muslim World, 950–1030.

they ruled. Although they and their successors always remained proud of being Turks, they began to adopt certain features of the new culture for their own purposes. They saw the advantages of an efficient bureaucracy with a tax-gathering mechanism, and they admired the Persian literary tradition and architectural styles. They began recruiting Khorasani bureaucrats, the most talented of whom was Nizam al-Mulk, whose achievements we shall examine later. They also began to incorporate into their army a unit of slave soldiers. Within two decades or so, mamluks would constitute the core of the Saljuq army, although the majority of the troops at that time were still free Turks, often accompanied by their families and herds.

Soon after the conquest of Khwarazm, Tughril and Chaghri agreed on a division of labor. Leaving Chaghri in charge of Khorasan, Tughril began a campaign of conquest westward across Iran. He captured Rayy in 1043, and over the next seven years he also captured Hamadan and Esfahan. He discovered that he had to rely increasingly on his mamluks and less on his nomadic Turks. Typically fractious and independent, these Turks' priority was the acquisition of loot and good grazing grounds for their herds. Tughril knew that he could not discipline them sufficiently to control their looting, but he did try to channel their looting into regions outside the provinces for which he had taken responsibility to protect. As a result, bands of Turks not directly under Tughril's control raided into Armenia, eastern Anatolia, and northern Iraq. As long as they were not causing havoc in the areas in which Tughril wanted his authority recognized, they served a useful purpose in weakening the administrative authority of potential enemies.

From Esfahan, Tughril began negotiating for the surrender of Shiraz and Baghdad by their Buyid rulers. Baghdad, characteristically, was riven at the time by sectarian strife between Sunnis and Shi'ites, bedouin depredations, and schisms within its own army. Now it faced the Saljuq army. The faction aligned with the caliph invited Tughril to take over the city from its Buyid overlords. In December 1055, he did so, with little effort. Soon, however, he faced two serious challenges. The first was a revolt by one of his brothers, who managed to secure a large following by charging Tughril with having lost his authentic Turkish identity by associating too closely with urban Arab and Iranian elites.

The second challenge was a threat from a Shi'ite conspiracy. By the 1050s, Fatimid missionaries had achieved considerable success in Iraq, as villagers and townspeople sought an alternative to their unbearable conditions. Fatimid agents pointed to the deteriorating conditions as evidence that the time was ripe for God to deliver the Iraqi people through the agency of his Imam. When Tughril took over the capital in 1055, many Iraqis were suspicious and even contemptuous of the Saljuq leader, whom they regarded as dangerous and uncivilized. Among the group that opposed Tughril was a Turkish mamluk officer in Buyid service called al-Basasiri. Al-Basasiri had become one of the most powerful members of Baghdad's military establishment. As such, he was determined not to become subject to what he regarded as a bunch of sheep herders. He consulted with a Fatimid missionary as he planned to recapture Baghdad, only this time in the name of al-Mustansir, the Fatimid caliph-Imam.

Taking advantage of Tughril's absence when the Saljuq leader had to subdue the revolt by his brother, al-Basasiri inflicted a major defeat on the Saljuq army in 1057 and entered Baghdad in triumph the following year. He handed the Abbasid caliph over to Arab tribesmen for safekeeping, instituted the Shi'ite form of the call to prayer, and said the sermon in the name of al-Mustansir. Thus, for almost a year, Baghdad formally acknowledged the authority of the Fatimid caliph. For purposes that are now obscure, the Fatimid wazir abruptly cut off aid to al-Basasiri. Tughril, having crushed his brother's revolt, turned back to Baghdad. Upon defeating al-Basasiri, he carried out an intense persecution of Iraqi Shi'ites, both Twelver and Isma'ili. The attempted Shi'ite coup d'ètat left the Saljuq regime permanently hostile to any form of Shi'ism.

Tughril's recapture of Baghdad was a momentous occasion. For many Sunnis who had become concerned about the political dominance of Shi'ism in Iraq, Egypt, and scattered provincial dynasties, it was a ray of hope that the caliph's authority would be restored. In fact, although the Sunni Saljuqs respected the caliph as the Shi'ite Buyids could not, they had no intention of turning political or military control over to him. On the other hand, by destroying the Buyids, challenging the Fatimids, and in general persecuting Shi'ites, the Saljuq administration did play a major role in the consolidation of Sunni dominance over Shi'ism in most of Southwest Asia during the next century.

Tughril's consolidation of power was also a dramatic expansion of a process that had been underway since the beginning of the century: the growing importance of Turkic political and cultural power in the Muslim world. Many of the urban sophisticates of the era were contemptuous of Tughril's achievement, viewing it as an ephemeral power grab by a mob of unruly nomads. In fact, however, his arrival marked the advent in Southwest Asia of Turks as creators of empires rather than as mere soldiers. As empire builders, they would create some of the most powerful states in the world during the next several hundred years, controlling territory from the middle Danube in Europe to the mouth of the Ganges in South Asia.

The Great Saljuqs and the Saljuqs of Rum

With the recapture of Baghdad in 1058, Tughril secured control of Iraq and western Iran. A year or two later, his brother Chaghri died in Khorasan and was succeeded by his son Alp-Arslan. Then, when Tughril died in 1063, a council of elders chose Alp-Arslan to inherit the entire empire, from Iraq to Khorasan. Although Baghdad remained important as the seat of the Abbasid caliphate, and hence of the legitimacy of Saljuq rule, Esfahan became the seat of most of the Saljuq bureaucratic apparatus. Alp-Arslan left most matters of civil administration to Nizam al-Mulk, his Khorasani *vizier* (the transliteration for the Turkish pronunciation of *wazir*).

Alp-Arslan spent little time in Esfahan, for he was a tireless military campaigner. He secured regions that had been bypassed during the original campaign, disciplined renegade followers, and conducted campaigns in Armenia and Georgia designed to secure his borders against Byzantine threats. He also had to suppress a major revolt by one of Tughril's cousins, Qutlumish, who challenged Alp-Arslan's right to rule the entire empire. Alp-Arslan's rapid rise to power had created a crisis. He had not acted illegitimately, but the Saljuqs had no regularized process of succession to power. Like their fellow Turks, they followed a tradition that every member of the ruling dynasty had an inherent right to rule. Influential elders could agree on a successor to the dead ruler, but any member of the family could legitimately challenge the selection. The advantage of the system was that it prevented the accumulation of power in a

FIGURE 6.2 The *Shah-nameh* was popular everywhere that Persian culture became influential, including the Indian subcontinent. Here, in a fourteenth-century painting from India, Rustam is shown killing the White Dragon.

Museum of Fine Arts, Boston, Massachusetts, USA Denman Waldo Ross Collection / Bridgeman Images.

single lineage. The disadvantage was that most Turkic domains were frequently embroiled in struggles for leadership.

The Byzantine Empire, for which the Saljuqs borrowed the Arabic name *Rum* (for Rome, pronounced "room"), now came under unrelenting Turkish pressure. The reason for this did not lie in policies of state: Alp-Arslan was not interested in conquering the Byzantine Empire. In the wake of the Saljuq conquests, however, a constant stream of Turks flowed into western Iran, northern Iraq, and Azerbaijan. With their families and herds in tow, they renewed the raiding of Azerbaijan and Byzantine Armenia and began extending their forays even into central Anatolia and northern Syria. Rarely were these raids authorized by Alp-Arslan. Many of the participants were even his enemies, including the sons of Qutlumish, who formed a cohesive group of raiders that grew steadily more powerful.

Nevertheless, the raids were rationalized as attacks on the infidel, in accordance with a long tradition of warfare on the frontiers of the Dar al-Islam. From the perspective of the Turks, Rum was a territory in which towns and villages could be looted, the dominance of Muslims could be asserted, and refuge could be sought from the hands of a central Saljuq authority that was becoming progressively alienated from its nomadic masses. From the perspective of Alp-Arslan himself, the more unruly nomads who could be diverted into Rum, the fewer problems he had to worry about as he began laying the foundation for a powerful state. Thus began a tradition of Turkish *gazis*, or raiders, who harassed non-Muslim territories on the Muslim Turkish frontier.

The Byzantine authorities became increasingly concerned about the rising scale of the raids, particularly when one campaign took raiders to the heart of Anatolia at Iconium (Konya). Negotiations between the emperor and the sultan took place sporadically, but Alp-Arslan had nothing to gain from antagonizing thousands of Turks by limiting their raiding. The Byzantines suspected that he was secretly encouraging the raids, and when, in 1071, he embarked on a military campaign to capture Syria, the leaders in Constantinople decided to take advantage of his absence by attacking Azerbaijan. The sultan, who had advanced to Aleppo, had to turn back to protect his empire. He met the Byzantine army at Manzikert (Malazgirt), near Lake Van.

The Byzantine emperor, Romanus IV Diogenes, had assembled almost the entire Byzantine army to confront the sultan, but the bulk of his forces now consisted of foreign mercenaries, including the Norsemen of the Varangian Guard, Normans and Franks from Western Europe, Slavs, and even Turks, including some from the Oghuz group itself. The various units were feuding among themselves, and key commanders even of the Greek units despised their emperor. The result was that up to one-half of the army deserted on the eve of the battle, and the Saljuqs obliterated the proud imperial military force. The Battle of Manzikert, remembered thereafter by the Byzantines as "that terrible day," ranks as one of history's most decisive battles. The units of the vaunted Byzantine army either were destroyed in the battle or melted away into fragmentary and ineffective components.

Rum now lay open to invasion, utterly undefended. Conquest of the area was the last thing on the mind of Alp-Arslan himself: Confronted with a threat by the Qara-khanids on his Amu Darya frontier, he launched a campaign to invade Transoxiana. Turks on the Anatolian frontier, however, *were* interested in Anatolia, and now they encountered no effective resistance to their encroachments into Rum. Once in the area, they had no reason to leave after raiding. More and more of them entered the peninsula in search of grazing areas and raiding opportunities. Some Turks even entered by invitation from Byzantine factions competing for power in the aftermath of Manzikert. In 1078, the new emperor was struggling to cling to power against nobles who coveted the throne for themselves. He requested military aid from the Saljuq group led by the sons of Qutlumish. When they succeeded in securing his power, he then enlisted them to defeat a European rival. In return for their invaluable services, he gave them access to the city of Nicaea (modern Iznik), sixty miles from Constantinople. The Saljuqs turned it into the capital city of what came to be known as the Sultanate of Rum. Thus, in a remarkable irony, the Byzantines themselves encouraged Turkish immigration into central and western Anatolia, even providing the Saljuqs with cities to use as their bases. It would be several centuries before Turks constituted the majority of the population of Anatolia. But with their rapid dominance of its cities, it is little wonder that, in little over a century, the Franks of the Third Crusade would be calling the area Turkey.

Alp-Arslan met an untimely end during his campaign in Transoxiana. A prisoner was brought to his tent, and somehow the man was able to stab the sultan, mortally wounding him. The sultan was succeeded by his teenage son, Malik-Shah (1073–1092), for whom Nizam al-Mulk continued to serve as vizier. Like Alp-Arslan and Tughril, Malik-Shah was an able military leader. Early in his career, he suppressed revolts by relatives who challenged his leadership, and he repulsed a Qara-khanid attack. Thereafter, however, he combined diplomacy and intrigue with his military skills. He expanded Saljuq power into parts of Qara-khanid territory in Transoxiana, captured most of Syria and Palestine from the Fatimids; and occupied parts of Yemen and the Persian Gulf. The army that brought him victories and made his diplomacy effective continued to evolve. Alp-Arslan had increased the number of slave soldiers in it, and at the height of Malik-Shah's career, the nucleus of his army was slave. Almost all the rest were now mercenaries rather than nomadic Turks.

The composition of the army was only one example of the assimilation of the Saljuq elite into the Perso–Islamic culture of the period. Malik-Shah's name is another. Whereas Tughril and Alp-Arslan are Turkish names, the name Malik-Shah derives from the new environment: *Malik* is the Arabic word for "king," and *shah* is Persian for "emperor." The young ruler was a patron of literature, science, and art, and he ordered the construction of beautiful buildings in his capital at Esfahan. Nizam al-Mulk, the native Iranian vizier, worked hard to impose traditional Iranian administrative practices within the Saljuq court and partially succeeded. He, too, was instrumental in providing patronage for great works of architecture and in establishing colleges of higher learning in Iraq and Syria that emulated similar institutions in his home of Khorasan.

Malik-Shah died in 1092, and with him died the unity of his empire. The open-ended Turkic policy of succession now created a crisis. Contrary to Nizam al-Mulk's conviction that an autocratic regime was the highest expression of good government, the Saljuq state had continued to be administered in a decentralized fashion in deference to the traditional Turkic conception that the family as a whole should participate in the wielding of power. The provinces were granted a considerable amount of autonomy under the leadership of close relatives of the sultan. When Malik-Shah died, the family could not agree on his successor, and various princes fought each other with the armies at their disposal. For more than a decade, civil war raged as two of Malik-Shah's sons struggled for the sultanate. One of the sons died in 1105, worn out at the age of twenty-five, leaving Muhammad (1105–1118) the sole ruler. Muhammad, however, relied on a surviving brother, Sanjar, to govern Khorasan for him. Muhammad's dynasty came to be referred to as the Great Saljuqs, to be distinguished from the Saljuq Sultanate of Rum at Nicaea in Anatolia. Headquartered at Esfahan, Muhammad had hardly noticed that, during the civil war with his brother, Frankish warriors had taken control of his father's Mediterranean coastline.

The Fatimid Empire

The secretive and underground Isma'ili sect surfaced in the ninth century and made a bid for political power as a force known to history as the Fatimids. In 910, the Fatimids seized power in Ifriqiya, and within a few decades they established their capital in Egypt. Fatimid Egypt quickly blossomed into one of the most advanced societies in the world, posing a serious threat to its Sunni rivals. Almost as quickly, however, it faded to second-rate status. By the end of the eleventh century, it occupied space but was nearly irrelevant as a geopolitical factor.

The Conquest of Egypt and Palestine

When we last saw the Fatimids, their plans to attack Egypt were foiled yet again by the Berber revolt of 943. A revolt of this magnitude had not occurred in two centuries, since the Great Berber Revolt of 740 initiated the collapse of the Umayyad caliphate of Damascus. The Fatimid regime had to fight for its life at a time when it might have been able to take advantage of the Buyid seizure of power in Baghdad. The Sunni governors of Egypt acknowledged the legitimacy of the Abbasid caliph but had cool relations with the Buyid military leaders. Had the Fatimids been able to attack Egypt in the late 940s, the chance that they would not have confronted Buyid reinforcements was good.

It took almost twenty years for the Fatimids to restore their control over the Maghrib. By the 960s, they were once again prepared to turn east. Having failed three times to capture Egypt, the regime prepared carefully for the campaign of 969. One decision was ideological: It changed the official genealogy for the Fatimids in order to attract the support of the far-flung Isma'ili community. The regime's founder, 'Abd Allah al-Mahdi, had claimed descent from Ja'far al-Sadiq's son 'Abd Allah. Without great fanfare, his grandson al-Mu'izz (953–976) consistently claimed descent from Isma'il instead, making the Fatimids "Isma'ilis" again.

Al-Mu'izz was fortunate to have as his chief of armies one of the greatest generals of the age, Jawhar al-Rumi, a former Greek slave. Jawhar developed a formidable army. Its core was composed of the Kutama Berbers, but it was supplemented by growing numbers of Sudanese, Slavic, and Greek troops. This army put down the Berber revolt and recaptured Sijilmasa and Fez between 958 and 960. With North Africa pacified, al-Mu'izz set his sights on Egypt. This time the Fatimids won a surprisingly easy victory in 969.

Jawhar administered Egypt until the caliph-Imam al-Mu'izz arrived in 973. One of Jawhar's first official acts was to found a new capital city for his master. The existing capital, Fustat, had been a garrison for the Arabs since its founding in 640. Jawhar's task was to create an imperial city that reflected the glory of the new dynasty. He laid out the boundaries of the new capital some three miles to the northeast of Fustat, calling it al-Qahira al-Mu'izziya, "Victorious (City) of al-Mu'izz," or Cairo. Surrounded by high walls, it was to be the center of government and of the Fatimid religion. For many years, it was composed almost exclusively of palaces, mosques, and barracks for the troops.

The new government initially sought to challenge Baghdad for the allegiance of the world's Muslims, but it ran into problems when its army began occupying territories in Palestine. The indigenous Carmathians of Syria called upon the aid of their compatriots in Bahrain, and the two groups joined together to thwart the eastward expansion of Fatimid rule. For eight years, they fiercely resisted their fellow Isma'ilis. The Carmathians seriously impeded the Fatimid consolidation of power in Palestine, and they invaded Egypt twice before being decisively defeated. The

FIGURE 6.3   The Bab al-Futuh city gate in the original, tenth-century Fatimid city wall of Cairo.
JTB MEDIA CREATION, Inc. / Alamy Stock Photo.

Fatimids did manage to have the prayers in the holy cities of Mecca and Medina said in the name of the Fatimid caliph, but otherwise their expansionist aspirations were largely disappointed. At its height at the beginning of the eleventh century, the Fatimid caliphate directly controlled Libya, Egypt, Palestine, and the upper Red Sea coast. Al-Mu'izz was content to rule Ifriqiya indirectly through the Zirid dynasty, a Berber family that had been rewarded for its loyalty with the governorship of the region when al-Mu'izz departed for Egypt.

Religious Policies

In light of the resources that the Fatimids had devoted to missionary activity and the expansion of territory under their control, it would have been reasonable to expect that the new regime would attempt to turn Egypt into an Isma'ili society from which to convert the rest of the Muslim world. Their actual policies were somewhat surprising. On the one hand, the Fatimids did promote Shi'ism within their realm. They quickly adopted the observance of Ghadir Khumm and Ashura from the Buyids. By the early twelfth century, they had introduced a festival of their own: Mawlid al-Nabi, the birthday of the Prophet. Although Ghadir Khumm, for obvious reasons, remains a distinctly Shi'ite festival, both Ashura and Mawlid al-Nabi are widely celebrated among both Sunni and Shi'ite communities today.

On the other hand, the Fatimids became surprisingly tolerant rulers in Egypt. For over fifty years, the Fatimids had persecuted Ibadi Kharijism and Sunni Maliki jurists in Ifriqiya in a brutal campaign of terror and extortion. The campaign did scatter the Ibadis, but the martyrdom of Maliki ulama only increased the hostility of Sunnis toward the regime. By the 970s, the new leaders of the regime appear to have learned something from that experience. Although the Fatimid Imams continued an active and wide-ranging missionary program all across the Muslim world, their religious policies in Egypt were benign. Isma'ili missionary activity, based on the model of a master and his initiates, was intended to bring about the conversion of spiritual adepts, not the masses. Prayers in the mosque were given for the Fatimid caliph, but otherwise Sunni prayers, doctrines, and ritual were hardly affected. During the first few decades of Fatimid rule, Fatimid law was dominant and held sway in the event of conflicts with Sunni schools, but by the middle of the eleventh century the Sunni schools were given equal status.

Fatimid authorities were, indeed, vigilant in monitoring Sunnis regarding their pro-Abbasid sympathies, and they were reluctant to allow them to serve in the government. Jews and Christians, on the other hand, enjoyed unique opportunities in Fatimid Egypt, and many of them served in large numbers in the government. Twice—under al-'Aziz (976–996) and al-Hafiz (1131–1150)—Christians served as wazir. Jews served in high offices in such numbers that Abbasid partisans claimed that the Fatimids were actually a Jewish dynasty. During the Fatimid period, Copts were the majority in many of the rural areas and in towns that specialized in the manufacture of textiles. Whereas Sunni rulers (and insecure Fatimid wazirs) occasionally felt compelled to respond to the sensitivities or fears of the masses regarding religious minorities, the Imams, as divinely appointed agents, felt no such compulsion. Imams were even known to visit churches and monasteries and to observe Christian festivals such as Epiphany and the Coptic New Year. With one exception, Imams did not persecute Christians or Jews. The street crowd, however, could become dangerous. In 996, at the death of Imam al-'Aziz, who appointed a Christian wazir and otherwise showed toleration of Jews and Christians, a Sunni mob in Cairo plundered churches and murdered several Christians.

The caliph-Imam who violated the policy of toleration was al-Hakim (996–1021), the son of al-'Aziz. For this reason he is, unfortunately, the most famous of the Fatimid rulers. Eleven years old when he succeeded his exceedingly able father, he killed his regent four years later and ruled on his own authority. During the remainder of his reign, he ordered the execution of several thousand people, many of whom were important officials in the government who never knew why they were targeted. He issued edicts that required the markets to be open all night, and he forbade the consumption of watercress and fish without scales. Once, he ordered that representations of the Christian cross not be shown in public, only to issue an order shortly thereafter requiring Christians to wear the cross. He ordered the destruction of many churches and synagogues, including the Church of the Holy Sepulcher in Jerusalem.

A little over halfway through his reign as Imam, al-Hakim became the center of a new religious movement. By that time, the Fatimids had been in power in Egypt for nearly half a century, and the apocalyptic expectations of many Isma'ilis that the regime would enact a radically new order had been disappointed by what appeared to be nothing more than yet another mundane regime. About the year 1010, certain religious leaders in Cairo began teaching their initiates that al-Hakim was an incarnation or manifestation of the deity. The most visible spokesman for the cause was Muhammad al-Darazi, but soon devotees of the movement were to be found in considerable numbers all the way to Aleppo. They were called *al-duruz* (the Druze), a plural noun meaning "the followers of al-Darazi," apparently because of the active role that al-Darazi played in the teaching of the new doctrines. Al-Darazi paid for his notoriety: He was assassinated in 1019, but it is not clear whether soldiers or jealous rivals within his own movement were responsible for his death.

In 1021, al-Hakim failed to return from one of his customary nighttime wanderings into the desert. Some suspected foul play, while those who worshiped him insisted that God had placed him in concealment. His successor as caliph persecuted the movement mercilessly, and soon the remaining members were living only in the mountains of Syria–Lebanon. The Druze, who call themselves *al-Muwahhidun,* or Unitarians, number about 300,000 today. They are not regarded as Muslims because of their unique doctrines and rituals.

In light of the apparent goal of the Fatimids while in Ifriqiya to dominate the known world, their subsequent actions in Egypt seem strangely unambitious. Aside from a persistent determination to maintain control of Palestine and the Hijaz in the face of various local and outside threats, the Fatimid government did not appear to be interested in territorial expansion. In fact, after the reign of al-'Aziz (976–996), it maintained peaceful relations with the Byzantines throughout most of Fatimid history. In 1038, one of the many treaties concluded between the two governments allowed the Byzantines to rebuild the Church of the Holy Sepulcher. The regime's ambitions became focused on spreading its teachings. The famous mosque of al-Azhar, which was constructed in 970, became the setting for public lectures on the Isma'ili school of law. Within the palace itself, the famous *dar al-hikma* (often translated as "House of Wisdom," but "Repository of Wisdom" is probably closer to the intended meaning) trained missionaries for the purpose of spreading Isma'ili doctrines throughout the Muslim world. Fatimid missionary activities reached their peak during the reign of al-Mustansir (1036–1094), with agents active in Iraq, Fars, Khorasan, Transoxiana, and India. Al-Basasiri's short-lived coup in Baghdad in 1058 appeared to be a major triumph for these efforts at first, before the fatal breakdown in relations between al-Basasiri and the Fatimids.

The New Egyptian Economy

Despite the eccentricities and distractions of the reign of al-Hakim, the Fatimid state continued to thrive for several decades. From the late tenth century until the middle of the eleventh, it was the preeminent empire in the Mediterranean basin and in the Muslim world. Its wealth was based on the agricultural productivity of the rich Nile valley, but commercial contacts with areas as far apart as Morocco and India supplemented the economic base. The empire's own conquests in the Maghrib had established links there, and its missionary work resulted in the presence of numerous Isma'ili merchants in Sind and Gujarat, who worked to funnel as much as possible of the trade from those important commercial centers to Egypt.

The Fatimids had become established in Egypt at a fortuitous time in economic history. First, Western Europe, which had been a poverty-stricken hinterland for the previous five centuries, was slowly developing a stable economy on the foundations of the medieval agricultural revolution. This in turn spawned the emergence of towns where the new agricultural surplus could be marketed. The nobility and the new merchant class, their pockets brimming with newfound wealth, were developing a taste for luxury goods from the East. It turned out that both Christians and Muslims overcame their religious scruples when it came to trade, for the emerging Italian maritime city-states and the Fatimids eagerly sought each other's trade.

Second, as we saw in Chapter 4, the Fatimids were the beneficiaries of changes in major trade routes. Much of the trans-Saharan trade shifted from Ifriqiya to Egypt when the Fatimids' traditional sub-Saharan suppliers saw that the new imperial market in Egypt was much more lucrative than the provincial markets of North Africa. The Fatimids also benefitted from the turmoil that began in Iraq during the late ninth century during the Zanj revolt. South Asian merchants who had been accustomed to shipping goods through the Persian Gulf and across Iraq and Syria now looked for a trade route that could guarantee them safety and a demand for their goods. They found it in the Red Sea route, where the Fatimid navy controlled both the Red Sea and the eastern Mediterranean. A portage of one hundred miles from the Red Sea carried goods to Cairo, which was linked to the Mediterranean via the Nile. Spices, perfumes, and fabrics from South Asia and Southeast Asia were in heavy demand all around the Mediterranean, and in return the Indian Ocean suppliers received the products of the Mediterranean hinterland: fine glassware, cloth, furs, and gold. Egypt itself was famous for producing remarkably high-quality fabrics, jewelry, pottery, and crystal ware.

Ominous Developments

At the middle of the eleventh century, the Fatimids began to experience a series of jolts that shook the very basis of their regime. The first was a factional conflict within the military. The Fatimid army had begun as a mixed force based on a Kutama Berber lance-bearing cavalry supplemented by Slavic and Greek infantry. The conflict with the Carmathians in Syria during the 970s, however, had demonstrated to Fatimid commanders that Berber lancers were vulnerable to mounted archers. As a result, the regime soon began importing both slave and free Turkic cavalry as mounted archers. Moreover, the change in the regime's base from Ifriqiya to Egypt meant that it was now more economical to employ Daylamis and black Sudanese in the infantry than Slavs and Greeks, who were more difficult to obtain.

Within a few years, two major rifts within the military began to reveal themselves. One was that the Turks threatened the privileged position of the Kutama, and the tensions were expressed by violent encounters between the two groups. The second was that the infantry, which achieved parity in numbers with the cavalry, began to demand more equitable treatment. Both conflicts had ethnic overtones. Within the ranks of the cavalry itself, Turks and Berbers were clashing as early as 1044 over scarce resources, and a civil war between units of Turkic cavalry and black infantry erupted in 1066. Cairo suffered extensive damage, and the violence in the countryside caused fields to be unattended, a factor contributing to a seven-year-long famine. As if these miseries were not enough, a plague struck Egypt in 1063, and in 1069 the governor of Mecca and Medina transferred his allegiance to the Saljuqs and had prayers said in the name of the Abbasid caliph.

The turmoil within the Fatimid military at midcentury led to such destruction and economic distress that, in 1073, the caliph-Imam al-Mustansir was forced to seek the assistance of his governor in Palestine, Badr al-Jamali. Badr went to Cairo, where he combined the role of wazir with full military powers. Badr, a converted Armenian, was a forceful personality who realized that drastic steps had to be taken to save the regime. He brought with him thousands of his own Christian Armenian troops to be the core of his military force, and he began replacing the troublesome Turkic mamluks with Sudanese infantry, a trend that continued over the next century until the Sudanese units became the largest contingent in the army.

Badr al-Jamali's promotion achieved al-Mustansir's immediate goal, but it had two major drawbacks. First, the withdrawal of the Armenian troops from Palestine allowed the Saljuq ruler Malik-Shah to seize most of Palestine with ease. Second, Badr never yielded the reins of power in Egypt until his death in 1094, leaving al-Mustansir as subservient to his military leadership as the Abbasid caliphs had been to military officers since the early tenth century. The position of the caliph-Imam in Egypt never regained its prominence.

The Nizaris ("Assassins")

The Saljuq court had been hostile to the Fatimids ever since the latter had supported al-Basasiri in his attempt to overthrow Tughril. Nizam al-Mulk, in particular, became increasingly concerned about the Fatimid threat because of a new militancy among the Isma'ilis of Iran. In 1090, the former quietism of that group gave way to a policy of assassinating public officials. The architect of the new policy was Hasan-i Sabbah, an Iranian from the city of Qum. He had studied in Cairo at the Dar al-Hikma and then returned to Iran, probably in the late 1070s. The Isma'ili message seems to have gained new strength in the aftermath of the Saljuq invasion, combining the traditional demand for social justice with a heightened sense of Iranian ethnicity that emerged in reaction to the Turkish invaders. Isma'ilis were to be found all across Iran by the closing decades of the century, and Hasan found particularly strong support in the traditionally Shi'ite region of Daylam.

In 1090, Hasan acquired Alamut, a fortress in the Elburz range that proved to be impregnable for more than a century and a half. Hasan began a campaign against the Saljuqs, who were doubly despised as advocates of Sunnism and as outsiders. Recognizing that winning pitched battles against the Saljuq army was not a realistic goal, he began a policy of assassinating Saljuq officials. The legend arose that the agents who were sent out from Alamut for the purpose of murdering officials were administered hashish during a ritual. No evidence supports the idea that the drug was used in this way, but the agents nevertheless gained the nickname of *hashishin*, or hashish users. The English word *assassin* derives etymologically from this word, with the result that Hasan's followers have been known as the Assassins for centuries. After killing several minor officials, the Assassins made a spectacular "hit" in 1092 by killing their old nemesis, Nizam al-Mulk, possibly in collusion with none other than Malik-Shah, who was clearly chafing after twenty years of the old Iranian's imperious tutelage.

Hasan's career took a turn in 1094, when a schism developed within the Fatimid movement. The Fatimid caliph-Imam al-Mustansir died a few months after Badr al-Jamali's death in 1094. Confusion over the succession process followed. The new

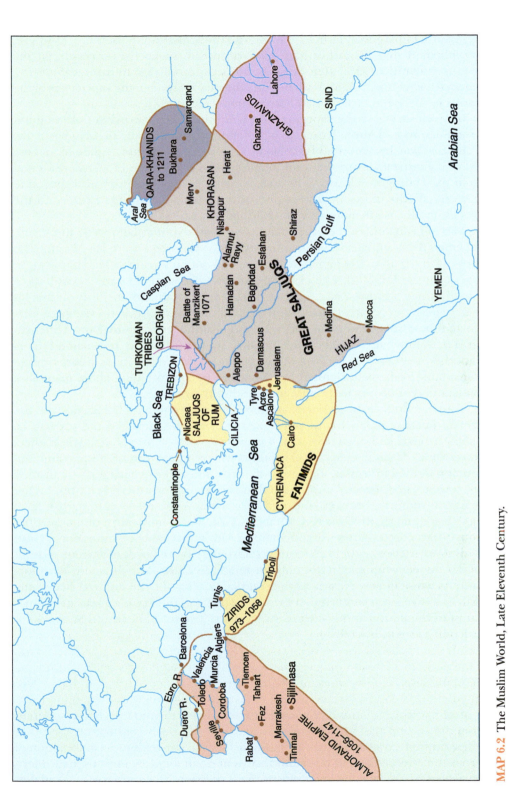

MAP 6.2 The Muslim World, Late Eleventh Century.

wazir, Badr's son al-Afdal, favored the youngest son, al-Musta'li, but the eldest son, Nizar, claimed that his father had designated him to be his successor. In the subsequent conflict, Nizar fled Cairo but was captured and murdered by being entombed within a wall. Al-Musta'li became the new Imam, but the supporters of the two sons formed rival factions that became bitter enemies.

The schism within the Fatimid ruling family in Cairo reverberated throughout the Isma'ili world. Al-Musta'li came to be recognized by most Isma'ilis in Egypt, many in Palestine, and by almost all Isma'ilis in Yemen. The Sulayhid regime in Yemen, ruled by the capable queen al-Sayyida al-Hurra al-Sulayhi (1084–1138), played a vital role in expanding the Musta'li branch of Isma'ilism. She sponsored extensive missionary activity in the Gujarat region of India on behalf of the cause, and the Musta'lis became permanently well-established there.

Hasan-i Sabbah, on the other hand, sided with Nizar's claim to be the Imam. He claimed that a son of Nizar had somehow been safely sequestered at Alamut. The masses of Nizaris never saw him, but Hasan served until his death in 1124 as the *hujja*, or agent, of the Imam who he claimed was in safekeeping. Hasan's considerable personal authority influenced many Isma'ilis in Syria and the vast majority of Isma'ilis in Iran to become "Nizaris." The upshot was that the "Musta'lis" had a visible caliph–Imam to follow, but one who was under the actual authority of al-Afdal, the Armenian wazir. The Fatimid state had become a hollow shell by this time. It remained intact for another century only because of a peculiar set of international affairs that we shall examine in the next chapter. The Assassins, by contrast, were about to embark upon a period of history that would immortalize their name.

Hasan, therefore, by 1094 led a movement opposed to both the Saljuqs and the Fatimids. Because of his highly publicized activism, he attracted the support of Isma'ilis throughout Iran and Syria, and he soon came to rule over what was in effect a Nizari "state." It was not a territorial country with borders; instead, it was composed of widely scattered fortresses, together with surrounding farms, villages, and, in a few cases, towns. The fortresses were located in eastern and southern Iran, the Elburz and Zagros mountain ranges, and northern Syria. Although occasionally a local Isma'ili leader might disagree with a policy adopted at Alamut, most of the time the various Nizari communities worked together with remarkable coordination. Hasan and his seven successors were commonly referred to as the Lords of Alamut. Alamut itself developed a reputation not only for terror, but also for being an intellectual center. As we shall see, Nizaris were remarkably active in the cultural life of the twelfth and thirteenth centuries. Alamut housed one of the world's greatest research libraries of the period and hosted many scholars. Twelver Shi'ites and Sunnis were as welcome there as Isma'ilis.

The Muslim West

The Muslim coastal regions of the western Mediterranean enjoyed a halcyon period during the second half of the tenth century. The eleventh century, on the other hand, witnessed a profound change in the fortunes of the region. A combination of internal conflicts and foreign invaders threatened the very existence of the western wing of the Dar al-Islam and led to the permanent loss of Sicily and parts of Andalus.

Norman Invasions of Muslim Territory

A major theme in the history of the western Mediterranean basin in the eleventh century was the advent of a people known as the Normans. The Normans, who are more famous in northwestern Europe for William the Conqueror's exploits of 1066 at Hastings, had made a name for themselves years earlier in the warmer climes of the Mediterranean. They were the vanguard of an expansive Europe that was undergoing an economic revival and a "baby boom." Abundant food, commerce, cities, and education were finally coming to Western Europe. The wealth and power of that society expressed itself in the military expeditions of the eleventh century by the knights of the various Norman conquests, the Reconquista, and the Crusades. The earliest triumphs were by the Normans, and they inflicted territorial losses on the Muslims that have lasted to the present.

Beginning in the early eleventh century, small groups of Norman adventurers began entering southern Italy in search of their fortune. In that welter of small, feuding states they sold their services to local lords and then took over from their erstwhile masters. Some of them took advantage of Zirid weakness as early as 1034 and began occupying port cities in Ifriqiya. Of much greater interest to them, however, was Sicily, which had the appeal both of proximity to the Italian Peninsula and great wealth.

Sicily had been under Muslim control for two centuries. The Aghlabids of Ifriqiya had slowly conquered the island from the Byzantines during the period 827–878. As an Aghlabid possession, Sicily served as a base for Muslim raids into Italy, the most famous of which was the sack of the basilicas of St. Peter and St. Paul in 848. In 909–910, the Fatimids conquered the Aghlabids and thereby became the masters of Sicily. By midcentury, when the great Fatimid general Jawhar was preoccupied with reestablishing control over the Berbers of Ifriqiya and with planning the conquest of Egypt, the island had become in effect an autonomous province under a local Muslim dynasty.

Throughout its two centuries as a Muslim-controlled island, Sicily played an important political and cultural role. Like every other Mediterranean state of the period, its relations with its neighbors, Christian and Muslim alike, included piracy, wars, trade agreements, and cultural exchanges. The island's agriculture, like that of Andalus, achieved unprecedented prosperity as a result of new irrigation techniques, the breaking up of large land holdings, and the introduction of new crops such as citrus fruits, sugar cane, new vegetables, and date palms. Castles, palaces, mosques, and gardens patterned after Iranian models changed the landscape, and poetry, law, and Qur'anic studies flourished. Sicilian Christians and Jews assumed the typical status of dhimmis, paying the poll tax but enjoying freedom of worship.

After about 1040, two developments led to the destruction of Muslim Sicily. First, the authority of the ruling Muslim dynasty was eroded, and Sicily fragmented politically. Then, in the 1060s, Robert Guiscard and his brother Roger began consolidating Norman power in southern Italy and eventually formed an alliance with the pope. They conquered Byzantine territories in Italy, and in 1081 Robert began an anti-Byzantine campaign in the Balkans that the Byzantine emperor defeated only with Venetian help.

Meanwhile, Roger, acting as his brother's vassal, began conquering Sicily in 1061. As in the case of the Muslim conquest of the island two centuries earlier, the task required several decades. It was finally completed in 1090. Roger's son, Roger II, brought about the unification of the Norman territories of Sicily and the Italian mainland in 1127, creating the new Kingdom of Sicily. The first Norman rulers were intrigued by Islamic civilization, and under their patronage a flourishing synthesis of Islamic, Jewish, and Christian civilization occurred. In the twelfth century, however, the Reconquista and Crusades created a hostile climate for Muslims and Jews. Sicily was lost to the Dar al-Islam.

The "Hilali Invasion" of Ifriqiya

Muslims in Alid-ruled Ifriqiya were concerned about a Norman conquest there as well. During a period of twenty-six years after 1034, the Normans methodically captured Tripoli, Jerba, Sfax, Sousse, Mahdiya, and Tunis. Whatever the Norman ambitions in Ifriqiya were, however, the invaders soon learned that a large-scale conquest was out of the question. The Norman army was not large enough to garrison all the cities and had to make alliances with local tribes for security purposes. Moreover, the foreigners soon learned that the region was not as prosperous as it had been earlier. Ifriqiya still had the aura of its former glory under the Aghlabid (800–909) and Fatimid (910–973) regimes, which had stimulated a lucrative, long-distance caravan trade across the Sahara. Their lavish courts had placed a premium on luxury goods, and their possession of Sicily facilitated commerce with European ports. The creation of a commercial network that linked Europe and Ghana had made merchants in many ports in Ifriqiya wealthy during the ninth and tenth centuries.

Sicily, however, became autonomous during the Fatimid wars to suppress the Berber revolts of the mid-tenth century, and its commercial links with Ifriqiya were loosened. Subsequently, the departure of the Fatimid court for Egypt in 973 diverted much of the Saharan trade from Ifriqiya to the much larger metropolitan area of Fustat–Cairo. Thus, by the eleventh century, Ifriqiya was already feeling the effects of a decline in the long-distance trade that had once crossed the region. Information about the Norman presence in Ifriqiya is sketchy, but it is clear that the serial seizure of the port cities after 1034 was accompanied by raids into the hinterland and agreements with local tribes to secure cities for them. Agriculture may well have suffered from the raids and from the free hand given to the local nomads.

The diversion of the trade routes to Egypt, the Norman capture of the most important ports, and the crisis in Sicily after the Norman conquest began there in 1061 might well have been sufficient to leave a permanent scar on the economic history of North Africa. All those developments, however, have been overshadowed in the annals and in epic poetry by yet another incident at midcentury. In 1051, the Zirid leader of Ifriqiya, whose regime had been autonomous under the Fatimids for decades, bowed to the pressure of his Maliki ulama and publicly humiliated the Fatimids by declaring his allegiance to the Abbasid caliph. In view of the Abbasid caliph's abject weakness in both religious and political affairs at the time (these were the last days of the Shi'ite Buyid regime in Baghdad), this declaration was particularly galling to the Fatimid court and was viewed as a blatant insult. According to legend, the Fatimid wazir persuaded Imam al-Mustansir to punish the disloyal Zirid ruler and simultaneously rid his realm of a domestic problem: He encouraged a number of bedouin tribes that were posing a threat to villages in the Nile valley to migrate into Ifriqiya. The Banu Hilal and the Banu Sulaym were the most famous of the bedouin tribes that migrated westward.

The "Hilali invasion" has long been blamed for the economic decline that undoubtedly occurred in Ifriqiya during the eleventh century. It has inspired Arab epic poetry and shaped our historical understanding of the period. Recent research on the economy of the era and the impact of the Norman raids, however, has modified that picture considerably. There is no evidence that the Fatimids actually sent bedouin into Ifriqiya. The Banu Hilal and Banu Sulaym were Arab tribes grazing their herds to the west of the Nile, and they seem to have migrated west about the time that the Zirids made their declaration. The Banu Sulaym settled in Cyrenaica (eastern Libya), but the Banu Hilal continued to Ifriqiya. There they harassed the Zirids during the 1050s, forcing the ruling family to abandon Qayrawan and move to the better-fortified city of Mahdiya.

Other Arab tribes continued to move into the coastal plain of North Africa during this period. Some stayed north along the Mediterranean coast, and others migrated along the eastern slopes of the High Atlas into southern Morocco. These incursions coincided with continued Norman raids along the coast of Ifriqiya. From Ifriqiya to Morocco, agriculture on the coastal plains was disrupted; the city of Qayrawan was largely abandoned and its economic and cultural influence plummeted; and Arab tribesmen feuded among themselves and with Berber tribes, making travel and commerce even riskier than before. The Normans soon drove the Zirids out of Mahdiya and captured the city. They also conquered Tunis and contracted with a Berber chief to rule the city for them. They now controlled the important ports from Tripoli to Tunis.

The Arab nomads were no doubt destructive, just as they were in many other regions of the Dar al-Islam at one time or another. Their impact now seems to have been cumulative, however, rather than decisive. They were one factor, along with the slowing of long-distance trade and the Norman invasions, that led to the economic decline of North Africa. On the other hand, regardless of the precise economic role of this second Arab invasion, it did have a significant cultural legacy. It accomplished what the Umayyad conquest of North Africa had not: the displacement of Berber by Arabic as the lingua franca of the North African coastal plain. The growing number of powerful Arab tribes caused their language and customs slowly to become dominant on the coastal plain, so that the region became in many ways a cultural extension of the Arab East. The majority use of Berber languages became confined to the mountains and the desert regions.

A Berber Empire

The Maghrib west of Ifriqiya was without a major state during the three centuries between the time of the Great Berber Revolt of 740 and the middle of the eleventh century. During that period, the region witnessed the rise of numerous petty principalities, such as Tahart, Sijilmasa, Tlemcen, and Fez. Most were Berber, while Fez was the notable Arab-led ministate. By the middle of the eleventh century, however, a religious movement among a Berber tribe in southern Morocco gave rise to the Almoravid Empire, a state that would play a major role in the geopolitics of the era and help to lay the foundation for modern Morocco.

The seventh-century Arab conquest in North Africa had followed closely the contours of Roman settlement. In order to protect those areas from Berber incursions and Byzantine naval attacks, Arab leaders established garrisons in forts along the lines of settlement and along the coast. Such forts in Andalus and Ifriqiya came to be known as *ribats*. Often local citizens would supplement the regular soldiers in the forts as a civic and religious duty. During the ninth century, the long campaign by the Aghlabids to conquer Sicily had intensified this process, as garrisons kept watch for signs of the Byzantine fleet, which occasionally attacked in retaliation. The men who lived in the forts—and especially the civilians who did so—were known as *murabitun* (sing. *murabit*). Thus, in the coastal areas of the western Mediterranean, as along many other frontiers of the Dar al-Islam (including the Andalusi–Christian frontier and the Turkish–Byzantine frontier), "warriors for the faith" had become a familiar feature of daily life.

As the military threat receded along the coasts, the ribats of Ifriqiya lost their military importance, and their combined military–religious function evolved into a religious one. They often developed into centers where men came to strengthen their devotional life through prayer and spiritual exercises. In Morocco, the process was almost the reverse: The term *ribat* had been used for centers of religious instruction since the ninth century, even in cases where there had not been a fort. Because they were usually situated in tribal markets or on former religious sites, they were nodes of interaction among various groups, some of whom were mutually hostile. The spiritual leaders tried to play a mediating role, but clashes did happen. Over time, the ribats of Morocco became fortified in order to provide the local population with a secure refuge. They were fortified religious schools.

From the late ninth century on, many of the murabitun moved from the coasts of the Atlantic and Mediterranean into the Atlas Mountains and into the plains along the desert edge, where they could spread their faith among Berber villagers. There, because of their isolation from the trade routes, many of the Berbers had never encountered Islam or were only vaguely familiar with the rituals and doctrines of the faith. The murabitun taught the fundamentals of the faith, made charms and amulets for the sick and the lovelorn, and served as spiritual advisors. For many of the secluded villages, the murabitun were the first tangible contact with the world of Islam that they had ever experienced.

It was among the Sanhaja Berbers, who lived south of the High Atlas Mountains and north of the Senegal and Niger rivers, that a spiritual movement began that would transform the history of both the Maghrib and Andalus. The Sanhaja had been only lightly Islamized by the early eleventh century, but one of their chieftains returned from the pilgrimage to Mecca about the year 1035 accompanied by a young religious teacher. The teacher, 'Abdullah ibn Yasin, imposed a strict religious and moral discipline on his followers and began to implement the Maliki law code in their affairs. Because of his emphasis on the importance of the Shari'a, his movement—at least in the eyes of its critics—developed a tendency toward legalism. For a decade, the leaders of the new movement used force to spread their version of Islam among fellow Sanhaja groups. They closed taverns, destroyed musical

FIGURE 6.4   The ribat at Monastir, Tunisia. It was founded in the late eighth century, but the Aghlabids and Fatimids expanded it.

instruments, and abolished illegal taxes. Because their religious fervor reminded others of the men of the ribat, they became known as *al-murabitun*, a term that has been anglicized as Almoravids.

During the 1050s, the movement began expanding into southern Morocco, and it gained a new leader in 1061 in the figure of Ibn Tashfin. He was a talented military and political leader, and under him the movement enjoyed tremendous expansion. In 1062, he established Marrakesh as his capital, and by 1069 he had control of Morocco. By 1082 his rule extended from the southern Sahara to the Mediterranean and from the Atlantic to Algiers. For the first time in history, this area was subject to a single political authority. Later in the decade, the power of this new state expanded into Andalus, as we shall see later in this chapter.

The Collapse of the Umayyad Caliphate of Andalus

The strong rule of 'Abd al-Rahman III (912–961) provided hope to some (and fear to others) that a powerful central government had at last been established in Andalus. Events were soon to demonstrate once again, however, that stability in the peninsula was dependent upon the personality of a charismatic ruler. By the last quarter of the century, the number of converts to Islam had swelled dramatically compared to a few decades earlier and so had the number of Berbers and Slavs, both brought in by 'Abd al-Rahman III and his successor to bolster their armies. The society became splintered into factions. Arab tribes maintained feuds whose origins were often obscure, the social cleavage between Arab and non-Arab Muslims persisted, and Berbers who had been born in Andalus resented the arrival of recent Berber immigrants. Outbreaks of violence among the various ethnic groups were frequent, and the most commonly heard complaint was that of the arrogance of the Arabs. Many of the "Arabs" of Andalus in fact had mothers who were Eastern European slave girls, but they continued to trace their origin patrilineally and claimed high status by virtue of their Arab lineage.

When a weak ruler came to the throne in 1002, the stage was set for the various cleavages in society to widen irrevocably. The civil war that many had anticipated broke out in 1009 and did not end until 1031. By the conclusion of the conflict, the withered authority of the Umayyad dynasty had altogether disintegrated. The traditional political fragmentation of the peninsula reasserted itself, and the Umayyad caliphate's authority was replaced by more than three dozen independent Muslim city–states. Arab historians have called the rulers of these tiny states *muluk al-tawa'if*, or "party-kings," suggesting that they were the instruments of one interest group or another. Some of these party-kings were Arabs; others were Berbers and Slavs. Even a prince of the Berber Zirid family that ruled Ifriqiya went to Andalus to fight on behalf of the caliph during the civil war. He eventually took control of Granada in 1012, and his descendants ruled it until 1090. The Zirids of Granada became famous for their alliance with the Jewish Nagrella family, which provided the chief administrators for the state.

Several of the small new states experienced unprecedented economic prosperity due to the fact that their surplus was no longer being siphoned off to Cordoba. The economic boom generated a cultural efflorescence that made the eleventh and twelfth centuries the golden age of Andalusi arts and letters, just as the tenth century had been the pinnacle of its political power. Cordoba's wealth, however, had depended on the surplus extracted from other regions, and now that it was no longer able to obtain it, the city began to decline. Toledo, Zaragoza, and Seville benefitted the most from Cordoba's displacement. Of those three, Seville became the preeminent city of Andalus for the next two centuries.

The collapse of the Umayyad caliphate of Cordoba entailed a reversion to the status quo that had prevailed during most of the previous three centuries: political fragmentation in Andalus. Many, if not most, Muslims of the peninsula seem to have been more content with less power at the political center. As we have seen, the loss of political centralization even enhanced, rather than harmed, the economic and cultural life of eleventh-century Andalus. On the other hand, the feuding of the city-states seems to have exacerbated the deeply rooted ethnic tensions of Andalus. In some Arab-dominated cities, Muslim Berbers were subjected to the sumptuary laws intended for Christians and Jews but rarely enforced on them. Berbers were even prohibited from riding horses or carrying arms. This humiliation was followed by an anti-Berber pogrom in Cordoba that spread to other cities, and in some clashes between Berbers and Arabs, acts of ritualistic cannibalism were committed on both sides. A revealing insight into the problems of Andalusi society is found in the plight of the last Zirid ruler of Granada, who, although totally Arabized, felt stigmatized by Arabs to the end of his life because of his Berber origins.

The disintegration of the caliphate played into the hands of the Christian kingdoms to the north, which were growing in strength. They had been prospering ever since the identification in 813 of a site in the extreme northwest of the peninsula as the tomb of St. James. It was soon christened Santiago de Compostela, and it became the third greatest object of Christian pilgrimage (after Jerusalem and Rome) during the Middle Ages. Because of the pilgrimage traffic, Asturias and Navarre increased in wealth. Investing its new wealth in its military forces, Asturias pushed to the south as far as the Duero River and then consolidated its power westward to the Atlantic. By the tenth century, it was increasingly known by the name of its southern region, Leon. Its dramatic rise to power was cut short in the middle of the tenth century, however, when its eastern province, Castile, broke away and became a rival kingdom. For the remainder of the century, Leon and Castile—as well as Navarre and Barcelona—were on the defensive against the caliphate and suffered repeated invasions from 'Abd al-Rahman III and his immediate successors.

The eleventh century witnessed a reversal of the balance of power between the Christian north and Muslim south. The political fragmentation of the Muslims after their civil war (1009–1031) provided Christian states the opportunity to exact tribute from the weaker Muslim rulers just as the caliphate of Cordoba had exacted tribute from the Christians in the tenth century. Castile, in particular, became the beneficiary of Muslim weakness after the civil war. Many party-kings now paid tribute in the form of "protection money" to persuade Castile not to attack them. Muslim states not infrequently even allied with one or more of the Christian kingdoms against their Muslim rivals. The wealth of the Christian kingdoms expanded dramatically as the tribute money from Muslim states poured in and as agricultural lands were opened up in the Duero valley once the caliphate was no longer a threat to Christian settlement there.

By the third quarter of the eleventh century, Castile had come to expect tribute as a right, and Muslim cities that refused to pay could expect a punitive campaign directed against them. The Muslims of Andalus had not been able to overcome their ethnic divisions and develop a cohesive identity within the framework of the Umma, even in the face of the growing menace to the north. They had gained temporary local freedom only at the expense of military weakness, which meant that in the long run they would fall victim to outside political control.

The Incorporation of Andalus into the Maghrib

While Ibn Tashfin was conquering the vast territory between the Atlantic and Ifriqiya under the Almoravid banner, Castile and Leon intensified their campaigns against the party-kings of Andalus, who belatedly realized the vulnerable position of their mutually hostile city–states. In 1082, the ulama of several cities in Andalus appealed to Ibn Tashfin to aid them in thwarting the designs of King Alfonso VI of Castile. Ibn Tashfin, however, considered the urban Muslim elites of Andalus to be a decadent class, hardly more worthy of aid than were the Christians. He was not surprised when, in 1085, Alfonso took over Muslim Toledo, practically without a fight. This large city, which had represented the first line of defense against the Christian powers for the other Muslim city–states, had been under the "protection" of Alfonso for some years. Alfonso had actually buttressed the authority of its inept and corrupt ruler against his fellow Muslim challengers, and he had had to intervene several times to save the ruler from his own mistakes and crimes. Tired of expending energy in order to protect such incompetence, Alfonso decided to take over the city directly.

Despite Ibn Tashfin's dislike for Andalusi society, he viewed the Christian capture of Toledo as an assault on the Dar al-Islam that he could not ignore. He crossed the Strait of Gibraltar for the sake of Islam but not to save the party-kings, for whom he did not bother to hide his contempt. In 1086, his Berber army defeated Alfonso's Castilian forces, and he laid siege to Toledo. During the siege of Toledo, Ibn Tashfin applied to the Abbasid caliph—at that time under the leash of Malik-Shah and Nizam al-Mulk—for recognition as ruler of the Maghrib and for the right to use the title *amir al-muslimin*, or "commander of the Muslims." The title was remarkably close to the caliph's own title of *amir al-mu'minin*, or "commander of the faithful." The caliph, however, flattered to be recognized as possessing authority and desperate to exercise it, eagerly granted him both requests. Moreover, he could not be unaware of the fact that, thanks to the Almoravid movement, the Friday prayers in the Maghrib were being recited in the name of an Abbasid caliph for the first time in more than 300 years.

Although Ibn Tashfin had defeated Alfonso in the field, he could not retake Toledo by siege. Moreover, relations between him and the party-kings deteriorated quickly from suspicion to hostility. He and they belonged to two radically different cultures: He was pious and ascetic and they were worldly and self-indulgent. He was a rustic Berber and spoke Arabic with difficulty; they were sophisticates who valued elegance, education, and refinement. He and his male followers wore veils whereas their women did not; this scandalized the menfolk of Andalus, whose women were veiled. When the party-kings failed to cooperate with Ibn Tashfin's military campaigns, his first impulse was to abandon them to their fate at the hands of the Christians, and he returned to Morocco. After several months of reflection in the quiet of his palace, however, his sense of responsibility for defending the Umma overcame his dislike for the Andalusi elites. He became convinced that it was his calling to keep the Christians out of Andalus and to reform the society along the lines laid out by Ibn Yasin. He returned to Andalus, and from 1090 until his death in 1106, Ibn Tashfin methodically captured all the city–states but Zaragoza, which did not fall to the Almoravids until 1110. Although he managed to capture and unite the Muslim city–states, he was not able to win back any significant territory that the Christians had captured prior to his arrival in Andalus.

Conclusion

By 1100, the Umayyad caliphate of Andalus was as dead as its namesake in Damascus. The Fatimid caliphate was under the control of its wazir–military general, just as the Abbasid caliphate was under the control of the Saljuq sultan. The institution of the caliphate had lost its aura for many Sunnis. The caliph was not a source of religious leadership. Doctrinal and ethical leadership was to be found among private scholars—the ulama—who discovered God's will by means of jurisprudence. A deeper, personal relationship with God was to be found by seeking out the guidance of a Sufi master (who, increasingly, might also be one of the ulama). The caliph was also not the model of the Just Ruler. The government itself was increasingly viewed as remote, oppressive, and interested in its subjects only for the taxes they owed. Shi'ites, on the other hand, were convinced that the problems of society were caused precisely because the majority of Muslims had not recognized that the only legitimate caliph was to be found in the lineage of Muhammad through 'Ali. That the Twelvers, Musta'lis, Nizaris, and Zaydis all disagreed over who the legitimate caliph-Imam should be was a stumbling block for the Sunnis, but it did not shake the confidence of the Shi'ites themselves.

The violence of the late tenth and eleventh centuries had been exhausting and destructive. The bedouin and Turkish nomads enjoyed the skirmishes, but all pious urban Muslims, at any rate, could agree that the struggle among ambitious warlords was an affront to God's desire for order and justice and that invasions by nomads and by Christian Europeans were detrimental to the development of a cultured and stable life. What they could not know at the end of our period was that the violence of the previous 150 years was minor compared to what lay ahead.

FURTHER READING

The Buyid Sultanate

Kraemer, Joel L. *Humanism in the Renaissance of Islam: The Cultural Revival during the Buyid Age,* 2d ed. Leiden: Brill Academic Publishers, 1992.

Mottahedeh, Roy P. *Loyalty and Leadership in an Early Islamic Society.* Princeton, New Jersey: Princeton University Press, 1980.

The Advent of the Turks

Bosworth, C.E. *The Ghaznavids.* Edinburgh, U.K.: Edinburgh University Press, 1963.

Bosworth, C.E. "The Political and Dynastic History of the Iranian World (A.D. 1000–1217)." In John A. Boyle, ed., *The Cambridge History of Iran,* vol. 5, *The Saljuq and Mongol Periods.* Cambridge, U.K.: Cambridge University Press, 1968.

Cahen, Claude. *Pre-Ottoman Turkey.* Tr. J. Jones–Williams. New York: Taplinger, 1968.

Cahen, Claude. *The Formation of Turkey.* Tr. and ed. by P. M. Holt. Harlow, U.K.: Longman, 2001.

Sinor, Denis, ed. *The Cambridge History of Early Inner Asia.* Cambridge, U.K.: Cambridge University Press, 1990.

The Fatimid Empire

Brett, Michael. *The Rise of the Fatimids: the World of the Mediterranean and the Middle East in the fourth century of the Hijrah, tenth century C.E.* Leiden, Boston: Brill, 2001.

Halm, Heinz. *The Fatimids and Their Traditions of Learning.* London: I.B. Tauris in association with The Institute of Ismaili Studies, 1997.

Lev, Yaacov. *State and Society in Fatimid Egypt.* Leiden: E. J. Brill, 1991.

The Nizaris

Daftary, Farhad. *The Isma'ilis: Their History and Doctrines.* Cambridge, U.K.: Cambridge University Press, 1990.

The Muslim West

Abulafia, David. *Italy, Sicily and the Mediterranean, 1100–1400.* London: Variorum Reprints, 1987.

Abun-Nasr, Jamil M. *A History of the Maghrib in the Islamic Period,* 3d ed. Cambridge, U.K.: Cambridge University Press, 1987.

Safran, Janina M. *The Second Umayyad Caliphate: The Articulation of Caliphal Legitimacy in al-Andalus.* Cambridge, Massachusetts: Harvard University Press, 2000.

Wasserstein, David J. *The Caliphate in the West.* New York: Oxford University Press, 1993.

Wasserstein, David J. *The Rise and Fall of the Party-Kings: Politics and Society in Islamic Spain, 1002–1086.* Princeton, New Jersey: Princeton University Press, 1985.

CHAPTER 7

Barbarians at the Gates, 1100–1260

In the previous chapter, we saw that the Dar al-Islam suffered from major episodes of violence from the mid-tenth to the end of the eleventh centuries. Worse was yet to come. As the eleventh century waned, the Dar al-Islam began shrinking for the first time due to attacks from non-Muslims. Prior to that period, Muslims could rationalize the Byzantine resurgence of the tenth century, the Norman conquest of port cities in Ifriqiya (1034–1060) and of Sicily (1061–1090), and the Castilian conquest of Toledo (1085) as temporary defeats in the great ebb and flow of warfare to which everyone had become accustomed in frontier areas. In the twelfth and thirteenth centuries, such rationalizations would not come so easily.

What had not been evident in the eleventh century was Western Europe's growing strength, which had been made possible by a more productive agricultural sector and a surge in international trade. The balance of power was slowly but surely tilting in favor of Western Europe and against the Muslim-ruled areas of the Mediterranean basin. In Iberia, the tiny Christian kingdoms of the north grew steadily throughout the eleventh and twelfth centuries, and they would conquer almost all of Andalus by the mid-thirteenth century.

Meanwhile, Western Europeans from north of the Pyrenees began sending "armed pilgrims" to the eastern Mediterranean in a series of military engagements that were later given the name of the Crusades. These Frankish conquests were ephemeral: The Crusaders were eventually evicted, unlike the Normans in Sicily and the Castilians in Toledo. What is far more significant, however, is that the Crusaders required the services of the merchant fleets of Italian city-states to transport them to their destination and then to supply them. Taking advantage of this opportunity, these commercial powers soon dominated the maritime trade of the entire Mediterranean. Muslim navies and commercial vessels would not be able to compete again until the Ottoman navy asserted its power in the sixteenth century. More ominous than the Christian Crusaders were the pagan Mongols, who obliterated the eastern Iranian cultural area in the early thirteenth century. A few decades later, a second Mongol campaign conquered Iraq and threatened the very

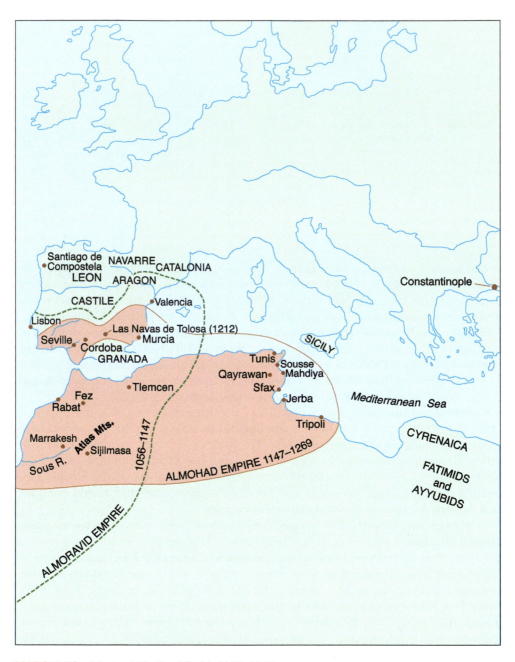

MAP 7.1 The Western Muslim World, 1100–1260.

existence of the Muslim heartland. These events mark a major turning point in Muslim history.

The Loss of Andalus

As we saw in Chapter 6, the early eleventh-century civil war in Andalus resulted in the collapse of the Umayyad Caliphate of Cordoba in 1031 and its replacement by some three dozen feuding city-states under the so-called "party-kings." The fragmentation of Muslim political and military power could not have come at a worse time for the Muslim community because the Christian kingdoms in northern Iberia were beginning to share in the general economic expansion of eleventh-century Europe. In the absence of the caliphate, the Duero River valley now became open to Christian settlement. Moreover, the northern Christian kingdoms asserted their power over the party-kings, first by demanding tribute and then by trying to conquer them. The capture of Toledo in 1085 was the first major success in a campaign of expansion that was later called the *Reconquista,* or "Reconquest." The term is misleading, since the military campaigns against the Muslims of Andalus were not a reconquest in the strict meaning of the word, since these kingdoms were not heirs of the Visigothic kingdom that the Muslims had conquered in the early eighth century. In fact, at the time, the Christian kings did not use the term; rather, they justified their wars to their subjects and the pope as wars to evict Muslim rulers and establish Christian rule. As a result, the papacy offered financial and spiritual support for them, including the offer of indulgences (the remission of temporal punishment for sins) to warriors who participated in them. Thus, fully twenty years before the First Crusade in the eastern Mediterranean, "crusades" had already begun in the western Mediterranean.

Provisional Solutions: The Great Berber Empires

Had it not been for outside factors, Alfonso VI of Castile might well have brought the Reconquista to a successful conclusion at the end of the eleventh century. His stunningly easy victory at Toledo in 1085 was an ominous portent for the smaller Muslim principalities of Andalus. The emergence of back-to-back Berber empires, however, postponed the day of reckoning for most of the Andalusian party-kings until the thirteenth century.

For more than 1500 years, the Berbers of North Africa's coastal plains had been subject to imperial powers that had conquered them. The Carthaginians, Romans, Byzantines, and Arabs had taken possession of these fertile areas, and few Berbers had been allowed to hold important positions in any of the empires, even at the provincial level. Some Berber groups, notably the Kharijite ministates of the eighth to tenth centuries, managed to create small, autonomous societies on the fringe of the vast desert to the south, but not until the eleventh century did a Berber empire appear. We saw in the previous chapter that the Almoravids created a huge empire in the Maghrib and then annexed Andalus. They were followed by yet another Berber empire, led by the Almohads. These two empires changed the course of history in the western Muslim world. They intensified the process of the Islamization of the Maghrib, they delayed the progress of the Reconquista by a century or more, and they set a precedent for large-scale political structures in the region.

The Almoravids

The key to understanding the new dynamism of the Berbers may lie in the role of the holy men, or murabitun, who extended the process of Islamization into central and southern Morocco. As we have seen, these were areas that were initially untouched by the Arabs, whose own settlements and influence extended along the Mediterranean and Atlantic plains and along the foothills of the High Atlas. The Arabs regarded the interior of Morocco and the regions south of the Sous River as hostile, pagan territory.

When Ibn Yasin began his crusade to reform the Sanhaja along the lines of a strict adherence to the Maliki school of the Shari'a, this group of Berbers gained an ideological advantage comparable to that of the Arabs who swept out of the Arabian Peninsula in the 630s. Like the earlier movement, it combined the motivation of acquiring wealth with the desire to obey the perceived will of God. The result was a powerful complex of martial qualities: ambition, discipline, and fearlessness in the face of possible death in battle.

With this motivated force, Ibn Tashfin conquered the western Sahara, the Maghrib, and Andalus. The consequences were immense. The presence of this large political unit stimulated trade all across the region. Of particular note was the intensification of commercial links with the gold- and salt-producing areas of West Africa. In later centuries, these links led to the Islamization of the western Sahara and sub-Saharan regions. Morocco, which had been largely neglected under the Arabs, became a commercial and urbanized society for the first time. Andalus, for the first time since the 730s, once again became an appendage of the Maghrib.

Unlike many rulers who used Islam as a cloak for their personal ambitions, Ibn Tashfin accorded respect and power to the ulama. He created an advisory council composed exclusively of them, and he took them on his campaigns. The Almoravid regime was, above all else, a regime of the Shari'a as interpreted through the Maliki tradition. The jurists in the other three major madhhabs (the Hanbali, Hanafi, and Shafi'i) regarded the Maliki jurists as mavericks. The most influential Maliki practitioners still did not stress the importance of the prophetic Hadith to the degree of the other three major schools, preferring to rely more on their school's own body of legal precedent.

In the eleventh century, however, a reform movement was afoot in Andalus and in parts of the Maghrib. With the collapse of the Umayyad caliphate of Cordoba, legal scholars who wanted to reform Maliki practice by adopting the Shafi'i consensus of emphasizing the Hadith found it easier to engage in such labor since they could migrate to whichever of the new city-states would allow it. Both the reforming scholars and their tolerant rulers tended to be either Andalusi Berbers or indigenous converts to Islam (muwallads), since the well-established Arab families tended to be conservative in this regard. The Almoravids sided with the conservatives and resisted reform.

Under Ibn Tashfin's son 'Ali (1106–1143), discontent with the Almoravid regime began to mount. The expectation on the part of many Andalusis that

Almoravid rule would increase the social mobility of non-Arabs in general to the higher political and religious positions was not fulfilled. On the contrary, the Almoravids reserved the highest military and political positions for themselves and allowed the Arab elites of Andalus to dominate the high religious offices. The legal reformers were becoming increasingly frustrated with what they considered to be the narrow literalism of Maliki techniques of Qur'anic interpretation and the neglect of the Hadith in the interpretation of law. They identified several weighty issues that they considered to be in urgent need of reform, but a relatively minor one was a powerful symbol of what they thought was deeply flawed about the current state of Maliki law as practiced by the Almoravids: The Sanhaja males who claimed to be upholding the Shari'a were veiled, whereas their women walked about in public with their faces uncovered. The Almoravids, in turn, regarded such criticism to be an attack on the legitimacy of their political power rather than a sincere attempt to join a universal consensus regarding the methodology of determining the Shari'a, and they began a policy of suppressing dissenters.

Many Andalusis were also critical of the rank-and-file Sanhaja troops. Not surprisingly, many of the troops had joined the Almoravid army to escape boring and poverty-stricken peasant lives and to live a life of high adventure. Many of them now became infamous for their indiscriminate looting. Both the muwallads and the "old" Andalusi Berbers rapidly became disillusioned with the "new," rough Berbers who were ruling them. For Jews and Christians, the regime was even more problematic. They were frequently victims of persecution and extortion, with the result that thousands fled to the north, to the Christian-ruled states. 'Ali accused the Jews and Christians of Andalus of secretly aiding the Christian kingdoms, and he deported thousands to Morocco.

'Ali's policies have tarred the Almoravids with the charge of being hostile to Jews and Christians, but his policy toward the People of the Book in Andalus stands in stark contrast to his policy in North Africa. In the latter region, he hired Western European Christian mercenaries (especially Catalans, from the area of modern Barcelona, who were ostensibly among his bitterest enemies) to serve in his cavalry, many of the empire's civil servants were Andalusi Jews and Christians, and many Christian artisans worked as free laborers in the construction of mosques in Morocco. His discriminatory policies in Andalus appear to have been provoked by fears of having fifth columnists in his ranks, since the threat from the north was so great.

The Almohads

'Ali's rule seemed secure, but during his reign a rival group of Berbers known to history as the Almohads began to challenge the Almoravid leadership. In part, this challenge was due to tribal differences, for the challenge came from the Masmuda Berbers in southern Morocco. It was also, however, based on religious differences. About the time that 'Ali began to rule the Almoravid Empire in 1106, a young man from southern Morocco made his way to Mecca to perform the hajj. This pilgrim, Ibn Tumart, stayed in the east for about a decade, studying with religious scholars in Saljuq-ruled Baghdad and Damascus. He returned to the Maghrib in 1118 with visions of Islamic reform. (It is worth noting that, despite the fact that the crusading Franks were in occupation of western Syria throughout his entire stay in Damascus, there is no evidence that their conquest concerned him.) The twin themes of his program were the transcendence and oneness of God and the rejection of pagan Berber customs that had been assimilated into Islamic practice. His emphasis on the oneness of God gained for his followers the nickname, the Almohads (*al-Muwahhidun*, or "the Unitarians").

Ibn Tumart derived two major corollaries from the theme of God's transcendence and oneness. The first was that the passages in the Qur'an that described God's characteristics should be interpreted figuratively rather than literally. He argued that the anthropomorphic interpretations characteristic of Almoravid Qur'anic studies infringed on doctrines of God's unity and oneness, for they made him manlike rather than transcendent. The second doctrine was that the legalism of the Almoravids was misguided. Ibn Tumart taught that only the Qur'an and Hadith should be accepted as guides for living a life pleasing to God, and he rejected all four schools of law.

Ibn Tumart's attacks on anthropomorphism and legalism, combined with his tirades against the Almoravid custom of allowing the women of the ruling family to be seen in public unveiled, put him on a collision course with the ruling regime. He found a responsive audience among his own people, the Masmuda Berbers of the western High Atlas Mountains. They were sedentary Berbers. As peasants, they had historically been victims of raids at the hands of nomads who coveted their livestock and grain. As a result, they had been suspicious of the Almoravids, whose base of support was the nomadic Sanhaja tribe. Ibn Tumart established a ribat at Tinmal in the foothills of the High Atlas, some seventy miles south of Marrakesh. From there, he began consolidating his power in the area by subduing rival tribes.

Ibn Tumart shared the Prophet's desire to overcome tribalism with the universal creed of Islam, but he was acutely aware of how powerful tribal identities were. Accordingly, he sought to amalgamate various Berber tribes into an alliance that employed existing tribal institutions and customs, but that focused primary loyalty upon the one God as revealed by the Prophet. Ibn Tumart even created a genealogy for himself that traced his descent from the Prophet, and he completed his ideological challenge to the Almoravids (and to all other existing political authorities) by claiming to be the expected Mahdi.

Ibn Tumart died in 1130 and was succeeded by 'Abd al-Mu'min, a Berber from the Zanata tribe who had gained Ibn Tumart's confidence. The fact that 'Abd al-Mu'min was not a Masmuda Berber is significant. It was the result of Ibn Tumart's efforts to honor tribal identities while subsuming them to Islam. 'Abd al-Mu'min, who continued to insist that Ibn Tumart had been the Mahdi, assumed the title of Ibn Tumart's caliph. He concentrated on taking over Almoravid territory during his thirty-three years as leader of the Almohads. From 1130 to 1147, he conquered Morocco, capturing Marrakesh in 1147 and making the Almoravid capital his own.

'Abd al-Mu'min's successes against the Almoravids encouraged the opponents of the Almoravids in Andalus. As early as 1140, some of the cities there were evicting their Almoravid garrisons and becoming independent. As a result, in 1143, the Christian kingdoms in Iberia began taking advantage of the chaos to lay siege to many of the weak Muslim city-states. The most notable Christian victory of the period was the campaign led by the king of the nascent Portuguese state, who invited a combined force of English, Flemish, and Norman troops to join his Portuguese soldiers in a siege of Lisbon. The city fell to the Christian alliance in 1147. Upon the fall of Lisbon, 'Abd al-Mu'min invaded Andalus, and the Muslim city-states now faced the prospect of capture by the Christian kingdoms or by the Almohads. Several surrendered to 'Abd al-Mu'min, and several others put up only perfunctory resistance to him. As a result, during 1147–1148, 'Abd al-Mu'min came into possession of most of the southwestern quadrant of the peninsula. He then turned to the North African coast, where the Normans and their Berber allies were entrenched between Tunis and Tripoli. He won Ifriqiya from them in 1160, and his son and grandson captured the Andalusi cities in Murcia and Valencia in the 1170s.

The Almohad Empire was at the height of its power from about 1175 to about 1210. It was never totally at peace due to Berber rebellions in North Africa and wars against the Iberian Christians, but these disturbances were on the fringes of the empire. Most of the interior region enjoyed peace and economic prosperity for extended periods of time. Marrakesh became the capital of an empire that stretched from the central Iberian Peninsula to Tripolitania (western Libya). Despite its origins among peasants, it had a complex government bureaucracy, and—perhaps precisely because it arose among peasants—it developed a sophisticated and fair system of land taxes. With the wealth derived from its control of the Saharan trade routes, the Almohad regime commissioned several spectacular architectural monuments that still inspire awe, especially in Marrakesh, Rabat, and Seville. Almohad caliphs patronized scholars from Andalus, the Maghrib, Egypt, Syria, and the Hijaz. A literary and intellectual culture flourished in North Africa as never before. It was centered in Fez, but serious learning spread as far south as Sous—south of the Atlas Mountains—for the first time.

The Almohad Empire seemed secure against its divided Christian neighbors, particularly after its decisive victory over Castile and Leon at Alarcos in 1195. For several years after the battle, the Castilian king would not attack Almohad forces even when the latter marched through his territories around Toledo. The line that demarcated Muslim territory from Christian-controlled areas ran from just below Lisbon to just below Barcelona and seemed impregnable to Christian attack. Despite appearances, however, the Almohad Empire had lost much of its legitimacy by the beginning of the thirteenth century. Its leadership had become increasingly restricted to the Masmuda tribe, alienating many erstwhile supporters. Internal instability occurred at a time when external forces became more of a threat than ever. Its sudden collapse would toll the death knell of Andalus.

The Disintegration of the Almohads and of Andalus

The Almohad regime was not popular in Andalus, and it was the target of continuous revolts by Berbers and Arabs in its distant hinterlands in the Maghrib. Sophisticated as its tax machinery was, no one likes to pay taxes. Regardless of how open the regime was theoretically to other Berber tribes, acceptance into leadership roles was predicated on accepting Almohad doctrine, and many Muslims strongly rejected elements of it. The teaching that Ibn Tumart had been the Mahdi seemed blasphemous to some, and advocates of legal reform wanted to bring Maliki law into line with the methodological consensus of the other madhhabs, not to ignore the Shari'a altogether, as Ibn Tumart had. Even within Almohad ruling circles, the teachings of the founder

FIGURE 7.1 The Giralda of Seville. The Almohads excelled at monumental architecture. The Giralda, constructed during 1184–1198, was originally the minaret for the congregational mosque. In the fifteenth century, the Castilians transformed it into the bell tower for Seville's new Christian cathedral, adding the Renaissance-style superstructure to what had been a flat top.

© KenWelsh / Bridgeman Images.

came into question. In 1229, the Almohad caliph al-Ma'mun (1229–1230) proclaimed that there was no Mahdi other than Jesus. He also officially reintroduced Maliki law, naming members of the reform movement to positions as qadi.

Such attempts at reform came too late. In 1212–1213, the Almohads suffered almost simultaneous attacks from the north and the south. Throughout the whole period of their occupation of Andalus, they had benefitted from quarrels among the Iberian Christian kingdoms that made it impossible for the Reconquista to resume. With the accession to the papacy of Innocent III (1198–1216), that changed. Using both persuasion and the threat of excommunication, Innocent organized a truce among the Christian kingdoms, emphasizing their duty to engage in war with non-Christians on behalf of Christianity. Moreover, a powerful new Christian kingdom had emerged during the first half of the twelfth century. Aragon, heretofore merely a province of Navarre, subsequently incorporated Catalonia and its largest town, Barcelona. In 1212, with Innocent's active financial support, Aragon allied with Castile and the other Christian kingdoms in a war against the Almohads. The alliance shattered the Almohad army at the battle of Las Navas de Tolosa, some seventy miles east of Cordoba. Fortunately for the Almohad ruler, the victors fell to squabbling among themselves again and did not take advantage of their opportunity to seize Andalus.

The following year, the Almohad caliph died, leaving no adult son. In Marrakesh, disputes flared over the succession, and a Berber group known as the Banu Marin, or Marinids, took advantage of the confusion to advance into the empire. The Marinids, pastoralists who lived in southeastern Morocco on the edge of the Sahara, had never submitted to Almohad control. Now they replicated the Almoravid and Almohad pattern of piecemeal conquests of the Maghrib and, in 1269, captured Marrakesh. The Marinids moved their capital to Fez, and their leader took the title of caliph in the early fourteenth century. They remained the dominant power in Morocco until 1465.

In the wake of the devastation of the Almohad army at Las Navas de Tolosa in 1212, the Christian kingdoms were afforded the luxury of being able to quarrel for more than a decade, secure in the knowledge that Almohad attention was focused on the Marinid threat. With the reunification of Leon and Castile in 1230, however, the foundation was laid for the definitive end of Muslim rule in the area. In the absence of the Almohad army and with the Muslim city-states fighting each other again, Castile conquered Cordoba in 1236 and Seville in 1248 (the latter with the aid of 500 men sent by the king's vassal, the Muslim ruler of Granada!). The Muslim inhabitants of the two cities were then expelled and forced to find new homes. When Aragon took the city of Valencia in 1238 after a two-year siege, the Muslims there, too, were expelled, leaving a practically empty city for Christians from Aragon to settle.

Over the course of the next two decades, Aragon systematically absorbed the rest of the province of Valencia, and in 1266 Murcia fell. Meanwhile, between 1234 and 1249, the Portuguese crown took over all the lands south of Lisbon and west of the Guadiana River, leaving Portugal with the shape that it has retained to this day. Of the former territory of Andalus, only Granada remained as a Muslim-ruled province. Throughout its remaining history of two and one-half centuries, it was rarely independent. For most of the time, it was a vassal of Castile and was required to pay tribute; when it failed to do so, it suffered punitive raids.

Of all the regions won by the Umayyad conquests of the seventh and eighth centuries, Andalus was the only one to be lost permanently from the Dar al-Islam. The Muslims had established a vibrant economy and culture there, but they could never transcend their ethnic and kinship rivalries, despite their shared religious values. By creating a myriad of rival city-states, they replicated the experience of the Greek city-states of the mid-fourth century B.C.E., which were absorbed by a less sophisticated, but more unified and motivated, Macedon.

The Muslims who now found themselves subjects of Christian kings, however, were in a much more difficult position than were the Greeks under Philip II's Macedon. How, they wondered, could they be good Muslims in the Dar al-Kufr? A widespread belief among Muslims was that they had an obligation to emigrate ("perform hijra") to a Muslim-ruled land if non-Muslims took over their country. Tens of thousands did leave, mostly for North Africa, but many hundreds of thousands remained. Emigration to a distant country is expensive, and if done under duress, it is emotionally devastating: Leaving one's home, family, and friends is wrenching in itself, but in addition to those strains is the anxiety over economic security and personal safety. The individuals who left Andalus for North Africa were wealthy or so highly skilled that they were confident of finding employment in a distant land, or zealous enough in their faith to overcome both emotional and financial obstacles. Those who stayed could rationalize their decision by arguing that God would likely not allow the alien rulers to remain long. Moreover, the Muslim population in some areas was very large, providing a comfortable support group. Muslims may well have constituted the majority of the population in the Guadalquivir valley, and they were almost certainly the majority in the provinces of Valencia and Murcia. Only a minority initially found the situation so unbearable that they felt compelled to leave for an unknown destination. Moreover, the kings of Castile and Aragon were intent on developing their new territories; they had no interest in deporting some of their most valuable subjects. Muslims had a reputation as skilled artisans and farmers, while the Jews were known as able administrators, physicians, and merchants.

Muslims who remained under Christian hegemony eventually came to be known as *mudejars*, a term derived from an Arabic word (*mudajjan*) that can mean "permitted to remain" but which also suggests "domesticated" or "put to use." The experience of the mudejars differed from kingdom to kingdom and even among regions of the same kingdom. In general, however, during the thirteenth century their status was similar to that of the <u>dh</u>immis under Muslim rule. Just as the first generation of Muslim conquerors had turned some churches into mosques, in many cities the Christian rulers seized the major mosques and turned them into churches. They left most small mosques unmolested and allowed Muslims to continue practicing their religion. The call of the muezzin still rang out, the faithful observed the daily prayers, the state recognized tax exemption for properties supporting religious purposes, religious schools stayed open, pilgrims were allowed to go to Mecca, and Islamic marriage and burial practices continued unchanged. Shari'a courts continued to function, and when Muslims testified in Christian courts, they were allowed to swear on the Qur'an.

On the other hand, the mudejars had to contend with restrictions on their freedom that made them second-class subjects of their rulers. The most shocking was the experience of the Muslims in about six cities who were expelled from their homes and had to take residence outside the walls. In many places, Muslims were required to wear distinctive clothing that set them apart from Christians; they were subject to certain annual dues and taxes paid to the crown; they had to pay tithes to the Church for property that they bought from a Christian; in some cities they were required to live in separate quarters of their own; city authorities often set aside separate days for the use of municipal bathhouses by Christians, Jews, and Muslims; Christian families were not allowed to employ Muslim or Jewish girls as caretakers for their children; sexual relations between Christians and members of the other two groups were punished savagely; mudejars were expected to abstain from work on Sunday; Muslim proselytizing was strictly forbidden, and in both Aragon and Castile, Christian converts to Islam were executed; and a mudejar who mocked the doctrine of Jesus as the Christ or who took the name of the Virgin in vain would be whipped for the first two offences and have his tongue cut out for a third. These policies remained in force for the next three and one-half centuries. As oppressive and humiliating as they were, Iberian Muslims of the early seventeenth century would look back upon this period as "the good old days."

The Period of the Crusades

For several centuries, European rulers, popes, and private individuals launched numerous armed "crusades" against Muslims in a variety of locations. Usually, however, the phrase "the Crusades" denotes a series of Western European military expeditions directed against targets in Syria and Egypt (and one against Christian Constantinople) during the century and a half after 1096. Only the first Crusade was an unambiguous success. The others were attempts to regain lands lost to Muslim counterattacks or, in the case of the Fourth Crusade, a looting operation against fellow Christians. By the early thirteenth century, the Crusaders remained in possession of only a few isolated castles; by the end of that century, they had all been evicted.

The First Crusade

Saljuq rule in Southwest Asia resulted in persecution for Shi'ite Muslims, but not for Christians and Jews. Some Christians—Armenians and adherents of other minority creeds—actually preferred Muslim authority to that of Orthodox Byzantines. The Christians of Anatolia, to be sure, suffered at the hands of Turkish raiders before the battle of Manzikert (1071) and, in that battle's aftermath, they continued to suffer from lawless banditry. However, they were not singled out for attack in the later period. Muslim peasants and townsmen who happened to be in the way of Turkish bandits suffered as much as Christians. In areas under the effective control of either the Saljuqs of Rum or the Great Saljuqs, Christians and Jews actually praised the enlightened policies of Saljuq policies toward them. It is true that Orthodox Christianity declined and ultimately disappeared in central Anatolia during the next several centuries, but that was due in large part to its isolation from Orthodox urban centers on the coast rather than to a policy of persecution. Moreover, the Byzantines viewed the Saljuqs of Rum to be their rivals, rather than as implacable enemies. The two states engaged in trade and cultural exchanges, and they occasionally even aided each other militarily.

The Christians under Saljuq rule, then, did not call on Western Europe for help. The Crusades were the result of a number of developments taking place within Constantinople and Western Europe that coincided in the last decade of the eleventh century. In Constantinople, a new emperor, Alexius Comnenus (1081–1118), came to the throne ten years after the disastrous loss at Manzikert and began taking steps to bring stability to his empire. His first order of business was to arrange a truce with the Saljuqs of Rum, who already had a history of allying with various Byzantine princes and emperors. In the course of the next decade, he secured his realm in the Balkans from Norman invaders and, with the help of Cuman (western Qipchaq) Turks, he became the first Byzantine emperor to inflict a decisive defeat on the Pechenegs, a Turkic group that had been marauding in the basin of the Danube River since the tenth century.

With his borders secure, Alexius could begin to build a solid foundation for a revival of Byzantine glory. One of his goals was to recruit mercenary soldiers from Western Europe. Frankish and Norman heavy cavalry and armored infantry were among the most effective military forces of the age and had been important units in the Byzantine army until Manzikert. Having them in the army again would come in handy against future threats, whether from Normans or Turks. With that goal in mind, Alexius dispatched a delegation to Italy in 1095 to seek the pope's aid in recruiting soldiers.

The response was not at all what Alexius had in mind. Rather than simply helping to recruit soldiers for the Byzantine army, Pope Urban II gave a sermon to a large crowd at Clermont, France, in November 1095. In it, he called on European Christians to deliver the holy sites in Jerusalem from infidel hands. The sermon had an explosive impact. Western Europe was in the midst of an unprecedented wave of religious enthusiasm as a result of papal and monastic reforms that had been implemented during the preceding decades. Moreover, the younger sons of the Western European nobility were experiencing economic hardship due to the "baby boom" that had begun in the eleventh century: Despite a growing urban economy, the inheritance rules of the prevailing feudal system meant that a nobleman's younger sons had few economic opportunities in the rural economy. Many of them were raiding churches, monasteries, and landed estates in search of plunder. The Church had been forced to issue several edicts against such raiding. Now, as Urban's sermon spread by word of mouth throughout an overwhelmingly illiterate Europe in the winter of 1095–1096, many knights interpreted it to mean that Christians who helped deliver Jerusalem from the hands of infidels would not only be entitled to haul away whatever loot they could gather during the military campaigns, but also to receive a full indulgence from the pope, thus avoiding purgatory when they died. Instead of being poverty-stricken and possibly excommunicated by the Church for attacking its property, they could become rich spiritual heroes. It was a win-win situation.

Although Western Christians in general were moved by the appeal, local conditions determined the nature of the response. The Normans as a whole were already preoccupied. The descendants of William the Conqueror were still trying to consolidate power over the Anglo–Saxons thirty years after his victory at Hastings.

Other Normans were busily conquering or consolidating their hold over territories in southern Italy, Sicily, North Africa, and the Balkans. The Germans were wracked with civil strife in the wake of the recent monumental conflict between their King Henry IV and Pope Gregory VII, and the Christians of the Iberian Peninsula were preoccupied with their conflict with the Almohads and the Muslims of Andalus.

Individuals from all those areas would go to the Holy Land, but it was the Franks, from the area we now know as France, who formed the bulk of the volunteers who went east on the first "armed pilgrimage." (The term *crusade* was not coined until centuries later.) Scattered throughout their various duchies, counties, and kingdoms, they had a variety of motivations. Many were prompted by deeply felt religious sentiments; others were interested primarily in the opportunity to gain glory and wealth; and most embarked upon the venture for a combination of motives and saw no contradiction in doing so.

Numerous groups headed off toward Constantinople, including the remarkable horde that followed Peter the Hermit. Others were little more than gangsters, who robbed and plundered their way across Europe until they themselves were robbed or killed. The primary force that is identified with the First Crusade, however, went to Constantinople in four groups, arriving between December 1096 and April 1097. Emperor Alexius was stunned by the arrival of the huge contingents, none of whom intended to give up their autonomy by submitting to his leadership. The land route to Jerusalem passed by Nicaea, the capital of the Saljuqs of Rum. By a stroke of good luck, it was practically undefended, for the young Saljuq Sultan, Qilij Arslan, had recently left the city and led his army several hundred miles to the east in order to fight Turkish rivals who had challenged his power. He was unable to return in time to enter Nicaea, and his light cavalry lost a pitched battle with the Frankish heavy cavalry. The Byzantine emperor actually organized a clandestine rescue mission for the sultan's family and reunited them to him. He also claimed the city for himself when its population surrendered to him rather than to the Franks.

The Franks, who had come to fight "infidels," felt betrayed by Alexius's actions and could not understand the nuances of the working relationship that the Byzantines and Saljuqs of Rum had established. They were convinced that their initial suspicions of the integrity of Orthodox Christians were vindicated. They got their revenge a year later: When the city of Antioch finally fell after an eight-month siege in June 1098, the Franks refused to turn the city over to Alexius despite their earlier commitment to do so. Even before the First Crusade had accomplished its mission, relations between the Byzantines and Franks had become cold at best and were often hostile. The original intent of the expedition was long forgotten, and the Byzantines and Franks would never trust each other again.

Meanwhile, the Fatimids, who were recovering from the Musta'li-Nizari schism of 1094, were watching the campaign of the Franks with interest and curiosity. The wazir, al-Afdal, thought that it represented the beginning of a combined Byzantine–Frankish campaign to push back the Saljuqs, a prospect he found gratifying. He sent a note of congratulations to Alexius upon the fall of Nicaea and sent a delegation to the camp of the Franks during their siege of Antioch, offering a partition of Syria. He received no response to the offer, and he became increasingly uneasy. When, in the summer of 1098, he learned that Antioch had fallen, he seized several garrison

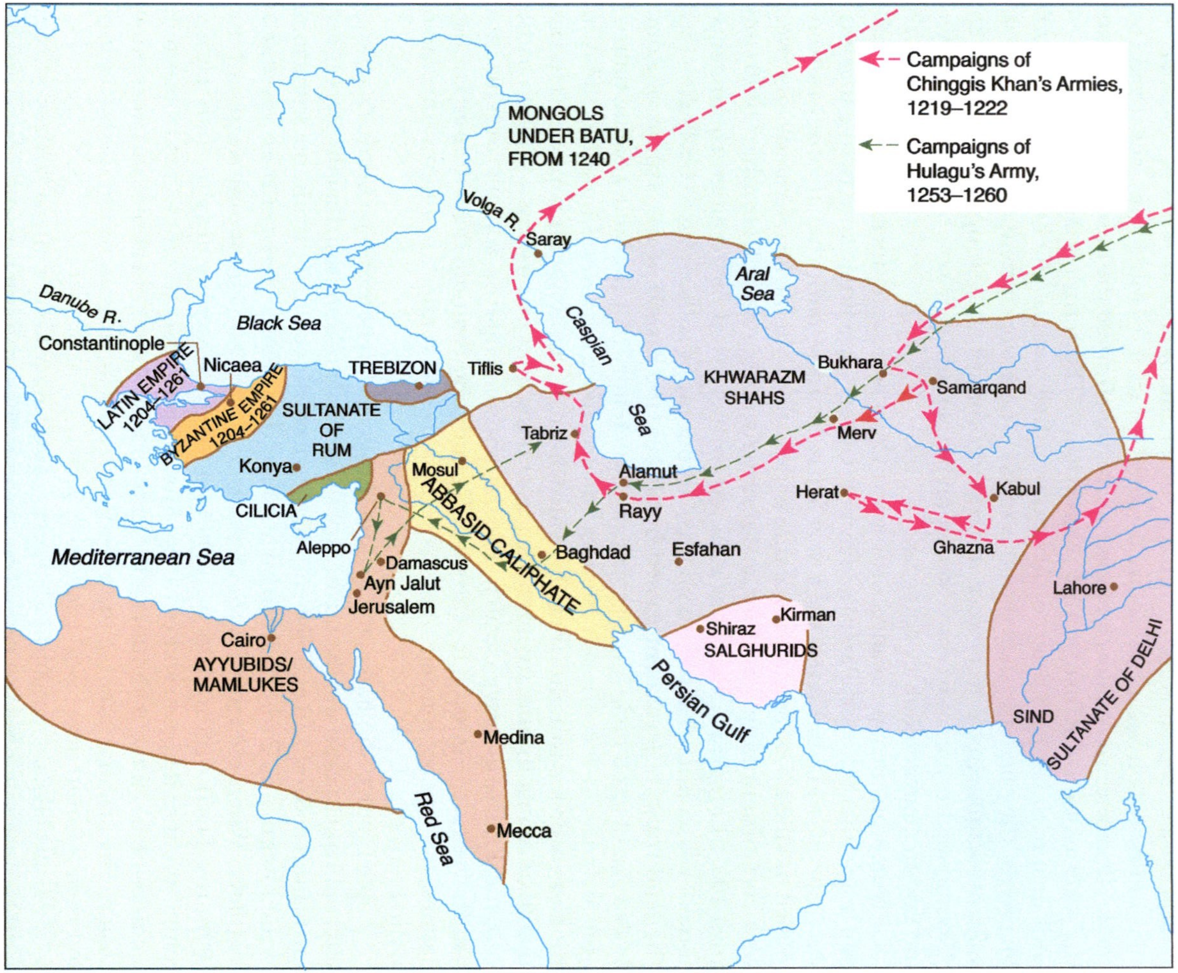

MAP 7.2 The Muslim East, 1200–1260.

Legend:
- Campaigns of Chinggis Khan's Armies, 1219–1222
- Campaigns of Hulagu's Army, 1253–1260

Map labels:
- SULTANATE OF DELHI
- SIND
- Lahore
- Kabul
- Ghazna
- Samarqand
- Bukhara
- Merv
- Herat
- Kirman
- Shiraz
- SALGHURIDS
- KHWARAZM SHAHS
- Esfahan
- Aral Sea
- Alamut
- Rayy
- Baghdad
- Persian Gulf
- Caspian Sea
- Tabriz
- ABBASID CALIPHATE
- Mosul
- Medina
- Mecca
- Tiflis
- Saray
- Volga R.
- MONGOLS UNDER BATU, FROM 1240
- TREBIZON
- Damascus
- Ayn Jalut
- Jerusalem
- Red Sea
- Black Sea
- SULTANATE OF RUM
- Nicaea
- BYZANTINE EMPIRE 1261–
- Konya
- Aleppo
- CILICIA
- Cairo
- AYYUBIDS/MAMLUKES
- Mediterranean Sea
- LATIN EMPIRE 1204–1261
- Constantinople
- Danube R.

cities in Palestine that the Fatimids had lost to Malik-Shah some two decades earlier. He left the area poorly defended, however, and the towns and garrisons of Palestine surrendered quickly in the spring of 1099 to the European invaders. Even Jerusalem, which the Fatimids thought was secure, fell to the Franks in July 1099 after a siege of only one month. In keeping with the pattern of previous sieges, the Crusaders massacred a large number of the population of the city without regard for their religious affiliation. Al-Afdal sent an expeditionary force into Palestine to try to save the situation, but the Franks mauled it. He did not challenge them again.

The Franks had fought their way to Jerusalem, but they had yet to consolidate their gains. Over the next thirteen years, they secured the entire coast of the eastern Mediterranean, except for the two Fatimid-held cities of Tyre (finally captured in 1124) and Ascalon (captured in 1153). The conquered area was organized into four states. The County of Edessa was the least well defined territorially and the most vulnerable. It lay inland in northern Syria, straddling the Taurus Mountains as far east as the upper Euphrates valley. The storied city of Antioch became the focal point of the new Principality of Antioch, which lay on the upper Mediterranean coast from the Taurus Mountains to a point several miles north of the present Lebanese border. The County of Tripoli lay in the northern half of present-day Lebanon, and the Latin Kingdom of Jerusalem encompassed the territory included today within the borders of Israel and southern Lebanon.

The Europeans set up a society on the basis of what they knew, which was the Frankish feudal structure. It was not an exact replica, for the European landlords lived in towns in Syria, not in castles on their holdings, and the cash economy of Southwest Asia forced a revision in the pattern of service obligations to which the Franks had been accustomed in Europe. The local landowning class was completely replaced by Franks, and in each of the new states, Franks ruled over a mixed population of Muslims and Christians. In several large areas, the indigenous Christians were the majority. The Catholic Franks characteristically regarded the local Orthodox and other Christians as suspect as the Muslims.

One indignity the Muslims had to endure was the payment of a head tax, which had been the obligation of non-Muslims in the area for the previous four centuries. But in the towns, the indigenous merchants and craftsmen—Christians, Jews, and Muslims—retained some rights, just as their urban counterparts in Europe had obtained in the eleventh century (although Jews were not allowed to resettle Jerusalem for more than a century). Some Christian Arabs even succeeded in becoming members of the knightly class, but such assimilation to Frankish elite culture was the only non-military interaction that interested the Franks. Whereas the Franks of Syria adopted certain features of local dress, medicine, and creature comforts, they had no interest in a cultural symbiosis. In this regard, they were quite different from their contemporaries, the Normans of Sicily and the Christians of the Reconquista in the Iberian Peninsula, who often took an avid interest in the scholarship and arts of the Muslims. Only a tiny number of the Franks even learned to speak Arabic.

The success of the expedition to Jerusalem left the Franks confident of their superiority over their Muslim neighbors, but their new states were much more fragile than they realized. They feuded with each other, the leaders and soldiers were in a culture they did not understand, and they were surrounded by rival states. Perhaps most problematic for them was their dependence for leadership and protection on men who viewed their service in the region as temporary. As a result, Frankish manpower had to be constantly replenished just to keep the numbers stable. The Italian city-states of Venice, Pisa, and Genoa took advantage of this need to increase their seaborne trade in the eastern Mediterranean. Their fleets had assisted in the provisioning of the military expedition of 1098–1099 and even blockaded the besieged Muslim ports. Thereafter, their role was invaluable in bringing to the feudal states supplies, soldiers, and pilgrims who had money to spend.

Muslim rulers in the region were slow to respond to the Frankish challenge. They had been accustomed to defending their power against fellow Muslims rather than against foreigners. After the death of Malik-Shah in 1094, the Saljuq rulers of Damascus, Hama, Homs, Aleppo, Mosul, and other cities were rivals of each other as well as of their fellow Turks across the Taurus Mountains. Among the latter were the Sultan of Rum (who had relocated to Konya after his defeat at Nicaea) and his Turkish enemies in eastern Anatolia. Thus, the Crusaders had embarked on their enterprise with exquisite timing. Normally at each other's throats in Europe, they had united militarily just as the Saljuqs had splintered into a decentralized system that resembled feudal Europe in many respects. Had the Franks invaded Syria during Malik-Shah's reign, they might well have met with disaster. Instead, they were able to pick off the jealously independent city-states along the coast. Almost all proved to be relatively easy to subdue.

In addition to their rivalry with each other, the petty Saljuq rulers were also determined not to become subservient to the Great Saljuq sultan again. Although theoretically still appointed to their positions by him, the local rulers of Syria were autonomous and had everything to lose by allowing troops from Esfahan to occupy their cities. The Great Saljuqs themselves were actually more interested in Iran than Syria, but religious leaders, Sunni and Twelver Shi'ite alike, managed to inflame public opinion against the Frankish invaders. Demonstrations in Baghdad—still the seat of the Abbasid caliphate—forced the Saljuqs to respond. Sultan Muhammad, whom we last saw as the victor in the Saljuq war of succession after the death of Malik-Shah, organized several limited campaigns against the Franks beginning in 1110. These, however, were handicapped by lukewarm support from the local rulers in Syria. In 1115, a campaign sent by the sultan actually found the Muslim princes of Damascus and Aleppo allied with the Franks against him. After this betrayal, Muhammad vowed that he would not intervene against the Franks again.

The politics of the area were immensely complicated. Several times during the first twenty-five years of the Frankish occupation, Muslim rulers allied with one or more Frankish rulers against fellow Muslims. In addition, local communities of Nizaris gained influence with the rulers of both Aleppo and Damascus and encouraged them to cooperate with the Franks, seeing the European newcomers as tools to be deployed against both the Fatimids and Sunni rulers. The Fatimids themselves, although in possession of the wealth of Egypt, had been severely weakened by bouts with famine and plague and the schism of 1094. They never threatened the Latin Kingdom. From the time of Badr al-Jamali (the Armenian wazir from 1073 to 1094) until the end of the Fatimid state in 1171, the authority of the caliph-Imam was minimal. Most of the caliphs were minors when they came to the throne, and they were never allowed to assume full powers. Al-Afdal, Badr's son and successor as wazir (1094–1121), even abolished the distinctively Shi'ite festivals and closed the Dar al-Hikma, where missionaries had been trained. The Fatimid state was living on borrowed time.

Franks through Muslim Eyes

Few Muslims, even in Andalus, had had contact with Franks prior to the era of the Crusades. A widespread assumption among educated Muslims was that the Franks must be slow-witted and boorish, for they lived in a cold climate and had contributed nothing noteworthy to the sciences. Syrian Muslims who were forced to live under Frankish rule after the First Crusade found little reason to change their opinion of them. In the passage that follows, a Syrian Muslim describes the Frankish custom of trial by combat. Under this legal process, the accused could challenge his accuser to a fight, and the community believed that God would favor the righteous person. A logical extension of this theory made it possible for either party to name someone else to take his place in the combat, for God would not give the advantage to the unjust, even if he were stronger. To a Muslim acquainted with the highly developed rules of evidence and procedure in the Shari'a, this system would seem bizarre.

I attended one day a duel in Nābulus between two Franks. The reason for this was that certain Moslem thieves took by surprise one of the villages of Nābulus. One of the peasants of that village was charged with having acted as guide for the thieves when they fell upon the village. So he fled away. The king [of Jerusalem] sent and arrested his children. The peasant thereupon came back to the king and said, "Let justice be done in my case. I challenge to a duel the man who claimed that I guided the thieves to the village." The king then said to the tenant who held the village in fief, "Bring forth someone to fight the duel with him." The tenant went to his village, where a blacksmith lived, took hold of him and ordered him to fight the duel. The tenant became thus sure of the safety of his own peasants, none of whom would be killed and his estate ruined.

I saw this blacksmith. He was a physically strong young man, but his heart failed him. He would walk a few steps and then sit down and ask for a drink. The one who had made the challenge was an old man, but he was strong in spirit and he would rub the nail of his thumb against that of the forefinger in defiance, as if he was not worrying over the duel. Then came the viscount …, i.e., the seignior of the town, and gave each one of the two contestants a cudgel and a shield and arranged the people in a circle around them.

The two met. The old man would press the blacksmith backward until he would get him as far as the circle, then he would come back to the middle of the arena. They went on exchanging blows until they looked like pillars smeared with blood. The contest was prolonged and the viscount began to urge them to hurry, saying, "Hurry on." The fact that the smith was given to the use of the hammer proved now of great advantage to him. The old man was worn out and the smith gave him a blow which made him fall. His cudgel fell under his back. The smith knelt down over him and tried to stick his fingers into the eyes of his adversary, but could not do it because of the great quantity of blood flowing out. Then he rose up and hit his head with the cudgel until he killed him. They then fastened a rope around the neck of the dead person, dragged him away and hanged him. The lord who brought the smith now came, gave the smith his own mantle, made him mount the horse behind him and rode off with him. This case illustrates the kind of jurisprudence and legal decisions the Franks have—may Allah's curse be upon them!

SOURCE: Ibn Munqidh, Usama. *An Arab–Syrian Gentleman and Warrior in the Period of the Crusades: Memoirs of Usāmah ibn-Munqidh (Kitāb al-I'tibār)*. Translated by Philip K. Hitti. Princeton, New Jersey: Princeton University Press, 1987, pp. 167–168.

The Franks on the Defensive

The Franks enjoyed a period of almost half a century before they were seriously challenged. The first real threat came from a father-and-son team of Turkish warlords who built up power in northern Iraq and Syria and then captured Egypt. A protégé of this family, Salah al-Din, continued the work of centralization and delivered a near-fatal blow to the Crusader states. His successors in Cairo groomed Egypt to become the preeminent power in the Sunni Muslim world for the first time.

The Zengis

In 1127, 'Imad al-Din Zengi became the ruler of Mosul, in northern Iraq. He captured Aleppo one year later, unifying northern Iraq and northern Syria. In 1144, he attacked and captured the city of Edessa, the first of the Frankish-held cities to be retaken by Muslims. Before he could follow up on the victory, he was murdered by a Frankish slave in 1146. Zengi's exploits appeared to have died with him, as his state was divided between his two sons.

The fall of Edessa prompted the call for the Second Crusade. This expedition, however, was as disastrous as the first one had been successful. Edessa proved to be impossible to retake, so in 1148 the Crusaders decided to conquer Damascus, instead. Some of the Franks who had lived in the area for years objected to the decision because the leaders of Damascus had been in a tacit alliance with the Kingdom of Jerusalem against the Zengi family for almost a decade. The Crusaders had their way, however, and laid siege to Damascus. Now, faced with a hostile takeover by Jerusalem, the Damascenes looked to Aleppo to help them. Imad al-Din's son Nur al-Din Zengi was the ruler there, and he was gratified for the opportunity to extend his influence where his father's had never reached. When he began marching toward Damascus, the Crusaders abandoned their siege. Five years later, the Franks of Jerusalem finally captured Ascalon from the Fatimids, prompting Damascus to submit voluntarily to Nur al-Din for protection from the aggressive Franks.

Christian Jerusalem and Nur al-Din's holdings in Aleppo and Damascus were now the two major powers in Syria. For either of them to dislodge the other would require the acquisition of further resources. Those resources seemed ripe for the taking in the Nile valley, where the Fatimids were growing ever weaker. Amalric, who became king of Jerusalem in 1163, made every effort to conquer Egypt, and Nur al-Din matched him step by step. Both led several expeditions into Egypt and even fought each other there. The Fatimid wazir, realizing how weak his country had become, played one power off against the other in an attempt to remain independent. He pretended to favor one side and then the other; he promised tribute to both (and then would not pay); and he allowed envoys to view the Fatimid court ceremony, which even in the last, sad days of the caliphate left observers impressed.

Salah al-Din (Saladin)

Despite the best efforts of the wazir, Nur al-Din's army gained control of Cairo in January 1069. Rather than dismantling the regime immediately, Nur al-Din authorized the commanding general of his army, Shirkuh, to become the new

Egyptian wazir. When Shirkuh died a few weeks later, his nephew Salah al-Din, better known in Europe as Saladin, took his place. For over a year and a half, Salah al-Din ruled Egypt without deposing the irrelevant Fatimid caliph-Imam. In September 1171, the caliph-Imam died, and Salah al-Din took over as governor of Egypt. He formalized the change in the nature of the state by ordering that the Friday services in the mosques be said in the name of the Abbasid caliph. The Fatimid Empire was at an end, after more than 250 years of existence.

Nur al-Din, who had expanded his power to include Mosul in 1170, was now in possession of a large empire that extended from Mosul through eastern Syria and up the Nile valley. Despite the confidence that he and his father had invested in Salah al-Din's family (both Shirkuh and Salah al-Din's father Ayyub had served as governors for the regime), he became suspicious of Salah al-Din's ambitions and had evidence that he was withholding tribute from Aleppo. As he was preparing a campaign to bring Salah al-Din to heel, Nur al-Din died in Damascus in 1174, leaving Salah al-Din the independent ruler of Egypt.

Shirkuh, Ayyub, and Salah al-Din were members of the Kurdish ethnic group, which has long been concentrated in the mountainous areas of northeastern Iraq, northwestern Iran, and eastern Anatolia. Kurds are members of the Iranian peoples and speak dialects closely related to Persian. Salah al-Din is the most famous Kurd in history due to his consolidation of political power, his severe crippling of Crusader power, and his founding of a dynasty that ruled Egypt for several decades.

Salah al-Din was faced with the task of reuniting the Muslims of Syria and Egypt, for upon the death of Nur al-Din, his hard-won empire collapsed into feuding

FIGURE 7.2   The walls of the citadel at Cairo. Salah al-Din began their construction using the labor of Crusader prisoners of war.

city-states again. Salah al-Din now tried to reunite them under his own control. He gained Damascus easily in 1174, and it soon became his base of operations. The areas of northern Syria and northern Iraq resisted him ferociously, however, and it was not until 1186 that he was in effective control of both Aleppo and Mosul.

Meanwhile, Salah al-Din had a few minor clashes with Jerusalem, but he remained on peaceful terms with that kingdom for most of the time. The notorious Reynald of Chatillon changed that relationship in the late 1180s. Reynald, master of the castle known as Karak on the Dead Sea, was a hothead who began attacking Muslim pilgrims and repeatedly violated agreements regarding the security of caravan routes that connected Egypt with the Hijaz and Syria. When Salah al-Din demanded that Reynald pay restitution for his attacks, the latter contemptuously refused. Salah al-Din declared war, and at the Battle of Hattin, fought in 1187 west of Lake Tiberias (the Sea of Galilee), Salah al-Din destroyed the Frankish army. With most of the Frankish fighting force killed or captured, the Latin kingdom lay practically defenseless before Salah al-Din. He took Jerusalem and several other cities, and by the end of the year, only Tyre was still in Crusader hands.

The Third Crusade (1189–1193) was the European response to Salah al-Din's victory, but despite its initial all-star cast of European monarchs and the famous campaigns of Richard the Lionheart, its gains were disappointing for the Crusaders. A few coastal towns were regained, including Acre, which became the new capital of the Latin kingdom, but Jerusalem remained in Muslim hands. Moreover, European chroniclers came to the shocking conclusion that Salah al-Din conformed more closely to their ideals of chivalry than even their great hero, Richard. After months of campaigning that resulted in a stalemate, Richard and Salah al-Din signed a truce in 1192. It provided a coastal strip for the Crusaders and gave Christian pilgrims free access to the holy places. Richard left for an eventful trip home, whereas Salah al-Din died in 1193.

The Ayyubids

Salah al-Din's dynasty—the Ayyubids—ruled Egypt, Syria, the Hijaz, and Yemen until 1250. The Ayyubids built a powerful state based on a military core of mamluks, most of whom were Qipchaq Turks from the region north of the Black Sea and Caspian Sea. The family distributed power widely: The sultan ruled all of Egypt directly, but he allowed relatives to rule as governors of the half-dozen major Syrian cities.

The Ayyubids oversaw a major rise in the status of Egypt in the Sunni world. Egypt had been blessed with rich agricultural resources for millennia, but under the Umayyads and Abbasids it had filled a distinctly secondary rank in status to Syria, Iraq, and Khorasan, which surpassed it in long-distance trade and cultural production. During the Fatimid period, when it was the center of an empire rather than the periphery of one, Egypt made significant gains. We have seen how it surpassed Baghdad as a channel for trade between the Mediterranean Sea and the Indian Ocean. Most historians believe that under Fatimid rule the majority of the Egyptian urban population had become Muslim, even though the Fatimids had not applied pressure to do so. Arabization of the country had also occurred, and the use of the Coptic language declined dramatically. Ayyubid rulers now set out to establish Cairo as a major center of Sunni learning. They actively recruited scholars from Syria, Iraq, and Iran—all of which had heretofore produced far more scholars of note than Egypt—and their efforts were aided by the flight of scholars from Khorasan when the Mongols attacked in 1219. By midcentury, Cairo became the cultural capital of the Muslim world, a status sealed in 1258 when the Mongols sacked long-suffering Baghdad. For almost three centuries thereafter, Cairo remained preeminent as the center of Islamic scholarship.

Salah al-Din's campaigns finally convinced Europeans that Egypt held the key to the control of Palestine. Accordingly, the Fifth and Seventh Crusades were launched against the Ayyubids on their own ground, but neither was successful. The Fifth Crusade centered on the coastal city of Damietta during 1218–1221, but it was expelled. The Seventh Crusade occurred during 1249–1250 and was led by the great Louis IX of France. It, too, began at Damietta, but the Crusader army was trapped and encircled as it made its way to Cairo. It was the last of the major Crusades.

The Seventh Crusade marked an important transition in Egypt's political history. The Ayyubid sultan, al-Salih Ayyub (1240–1249), died in November 1249, just as Louis was leading his army to Cairo from its base at Damietta. His widow was a Turkic woman, Shajar al-Durr ("String of Pearls"), who had been his concubine, but whom he had married when she gave birth to his son. She and two of al-Salih's trusted advisors ruled as a triumvirate until al-Salih's eldest son, Turanshah, could assume the throne three months later. Only a few weeks after assuming power, however, Turanshah was murdered by a group of his father's mamluks. They then took the remarkable step of naming Shajar al-Durr to be their sultana, making her the first female to rule Egypt since Cleopatra, more than a millennium earlier.

At this point, the Syrian branch of the Ayyubid family, who had been chafing under the dominance of their relatives in Cairo, seized the opportunity to assert their power. Challenging the legitimacy of Shajar al-Durr's rule on the grounds of her gender and former slave status, they threatened to invade Egypt. The Egyptian mamluks, realizing they had created a political liability for themselves by naming a woman as their ruler, forced her to abdicate in July 1250, and a power struggle began among various cliques within the mamluk organization. Over the next decade, many prominent individuals were murdered, including, in 1257, Shajar al-Durr herself.

In 1260, a mamluk named Baybars seized power. For the next seventeen years, he showed that it was possible for the system of military slavery actually to rule the country. Because the Egyptian military slaves never relinquished power to a member of the Ayyubid family and subsequently created an empire, they are the only group of mamluks whose name is honored with uppercase letters: Mamluks. We will examine their history in more detail later, but here it is appropriate to close out the history of the Crusades by noting that Baybars and his successors waged war against the few remaining Crusader outposts in Syria until 1291, when they utterly destroyed the last ones.

Additional European military expeditions attacked various territories within the Dar al-Islam over the next two centuries, and most were conducted explicitly as Christian wars against Islam. They were all failures, and none of them reached "the Holy Land." Most historians regard them in a separate category from the expeditions that were focused on Palestine and Egypt between 1096 and 1291 and are known as "the Crusades." The Crusades accomplished little that can be called positive. Western Europeans did become more familiar with geographical place names in the eastern

Mediterranean, and they learned better techniques for building castles while residing in Syria.

Most of the consequences of the Crusades, however, were negative. The Franks made no effort to learn Arabic or understand Islam and made no contribution to cross-cultural understanding. The Muslims themselves were not unified in a countercrusade against the Franks. Individual Muslim rulers led campaigns against the Franks out of their own ambition, while Muslims not directly affected by the Crusaders had little interest in the conflict. Not surprisingly, Muslim attitudes toward local Christians hardened as a result of the Crusades. In some areas, particularly in northern Syria, indigenous Christians cooperated with the Crusaders, leading the Mamluks to regard their Christian subjects in general as potential fifth columnists. The great irony of the Crusades is that, whereas they began ostensibly as a relief effort by Western Christianity to aid Eastern Christianity, they created a permanent rift between the two communities. The Fourth Crusade, in 1204, attacked and sacked Constantinople. It created an undying hostility among Orthodox Christians toward Catholics, and the wanton destruction of the attack permanently damaged the ability of the city to defend itself.

Realignment in the East

During the period of the Reconquista and the Crusades, major developments were also transforming the eastern Muslim world. On the positive side, the Saljuqs of Rum achieved the pinnacle of their culture in the first half of the thirteenth century, and the Nizaris achieved a peaceful modus vivendi with the Sunni world. Among the negative developments in the region, the Great Saljuqs collapsed in the face of revolts from their own Oghuz people. A new Muslim power, the ruler of Khwarazm, took the place of the Great Saljuqs. Like many other high achievers who have won their success quickly, the new ruler of Khwarazm tended to be arrogant in his dealings with others. Unfortunately for him and millions of other Muslims, he offended a man named Chinggis Khan.

The Collapse of the Great Saljuqs

While Christians and Muslims at both ends of the Mediterranean were involved in clashes that increasingly came to be seen as holy wars, the Saljuqs of Esfahan were preoccupied with their own affairs. As we have seen, the Great Saljuq, Muhammad, tried to organize resistance to the Crusaders from 1110 to 1115, but he became disgusted with his cousins who ruled Damascus and Aleppo when they stood with the Crusaders against him. From that time on, the Great Saljuqs had little to do with affairs in Syria. After Muhammad's death in 1118, in fact, the Saljuqs of Esfahan had little influence over affairs even in Iraq and western Iran. Family members ruling in those areas were embroiled in constant conflict with each other and deferred to Muhammad's brother Sanjar, who, after Muhammad's death, ruled Khorasan as the Great Saljuq.

The turmoil in the western part of the empire resulted in a shattered economy. The chronic fighting stripped cities of their wealth, rampaging armies routinely confiscated peasants' crops and livestock, and combatants often pursued a

FIGURE 7.3 Saljuq rulers invested heavily in infrastructure that supported commerce. Pictured here is the interior of the enormous Sultan Han caravanserai of the Saljuqs of Rum, northeast of Konya.

imageBROKER / Alamy Stock Photo.

scorched-earth policy to deprive their opponent of provisions. By midcentury, the western capital was moved from Esfahan to Hamadan, but the Saljuqs were increasingly overshadowed by other provincial rulers and even by a revived Abbasid caliphate. Growing assertiveness by caliphs who took advantage of Saljuq divisiveness was capped by the career of the Abbasid caliph al-Nasir (1180–1225). He was able to brush off Saljuq control entirely, and he carved out a small province in Iraq over which he was supreme military and political ruler. In 1194, Tughril, the Saljuq prince of Hamadan, tried to reestablish his family's control over Baghdad, but al-Nasir sought assistance from the ruler of Khwarazm. In the ensuing battle at Rayy, Tughril was killed, bringing an end to the Great Saljuq presence in western Iran.

By contrast, the Sultanate of Rum recovered from its loss of Nicaea to the Crusaders and established its capital at Konya in 1116. Hemmed in by the Crusaders to the west and Turkish rivals to the east, it was weak for several decades. By 1141, however, its chief Turkish rivals had collapsed, and Konya's power began to increase. In 1176, the Byzantine Empire made the mistake of attacking the sultanate at Myriokephalon, resulting in a defeat almost as spectacular as that of Manzikert a century earlier. The victorious sultanate now had access to ports on the Aegean again, and within a few decades, Konya took over ports on the Black Sea and the Mediterranean as well. Relations with the Byzantines soon improved. The Fourth Crusade in 1204 had Egypt as its announced goal, but its "armed pilgrims" sacked and captured Constantinople instead. As the Byzantine government relocated to Nicaea, it and the Sultanate of Rum once again became natural allies, united in their opposition to the Europeans and the Armenians.

The sultanate continued to expand, and by the second quarter of the thirteenth century, it encompassed almost the whole of Anatolia. At its height, from 1205 to 1243, the sultanate impressed visitors by its economic vitality, high level of urbanization, impressive architecture, generous patronage of the sciences, and religious toleration. Of particular interest was this Turkish dynasty's conscious appropriation of Persian culture. The rulers of the period all had Persian names, and the chancellery used the Persian language in its documents.

Far to the east, in Khorasan, Sanjar ruled longer than any other Saljuq in history. His older brother Muhammad had appointed him governor of Khorasan in 1097 when he was only about twelve years old. After proving himself as an adolescent governor, he became the Great Saljuq after the death of Muhammad in 1118. He was a successful military leader, but he was also a generous patron of culture, and his capital city of Merv became a center of the arts and the intellect. In 1141, however, the Mongol tribe of the Qara-khitai defeated Sanjar's Qara-khanid vassals in Transoxiana, and Sanjar was unable to retake the province. In 1153, some of his own Oghuz troops revolted against him, defeated him in battle, and held him captive for two years. The Oghuz engaged in an orgy of violence, during which many Khorasani cities were sacked and the great library at Merv was burned. Sanjar was released in 1155, but he was broken in health and died the next year. Oghuz chieftains and Saljuq amirs took advantage of his capture and his death to assert their own power, and Khorasan fragmented into a patchwork of competing principalities, much as Syria had done after the death of Malik-Shah more than half a century earlier.

The resulting power vacuum allowed a former vassal of Sanjar, the governor of Khwarazm, to build up his power. Khwarazm's location on the lower Amu Darya River allowed it to derive extensive wealth from irrigated agriculture, and it benefitted from a trade route that connected Khorasan with the valley of the Volga River. Khwarazm's rulers, known as the Khwarazm-Shahs, built up a strong power base in the late twelfth and early thirteenth centuries while in principle subject to the Qara-khitai. Tekish, the Khwarazm–Shah from 1172 to 1200, absorbed western Khorasan during the 1180s in a series of destructive campaigns, building up his reputation sufficiently for the caliph al-Nasir to call upon him in 1194 to help him defeat the last of the western Saljuqs. By 1212, his son Muhammad defeated the Qara-khitai Mongols and began annexing Transoxiana. Muhammad, however, had developed a reputation as a ruthless and rapacious tyrant, and many of the Muslim inhabitants of Transoxiana preferred the rule of the pagan Qara-khitai to the prospect of rule by him. They resisted his attempts to take them over, and Muhammad engaged in a particularly brutal campaign to subject the population. He fought outside Transoxiana as well, and soon his empire incorporated territories from Afghanistan to Azerbaijan.

Sunni–Nizari Rapprochement

The disintegration of Great Saljuq power in Iraq and western Iran after the death of Muhammad in 1118 was the fulfillment of the dream of the Nizaris, but the consequences were not what they might have expected. The constant squabbling and warfare among the various branches of the Saljuq family, and between them and their subjects, caused the Assassins to lose their raison d'être. Their political murders no longer caught the public's attention amid the constant mayhem of the era, and yet they were not powerful enough to take advantage of the chaos by seizing power themselves. They became inactive for several decades.

The major exception to the lower profile of the Assassins during this period was the career of the head of the Syrian community. Known to the Crusaders as the Old Man of the Mountain, he was Rashid al-Din al-Sinan, a native of Basra, whom the fourth Lord of Alamut had sent to lead the Syrian Nizaris in 1162. He remained the head of the community there until his death in 1192. Thus, he was a contemporary of the great Nur al-Din of Syria and northern Iraq, Amalric of Jerusalem, and Salah al-Din. In typical Nizari fashion, he considered Nur al-Din and Salah al-Din, who were Sunnis, potentially greater threats to his movement than the Crusaders were. Although he made enemies with the aggressive Knights Hospitallers among the Crusaders, in general he maintained peaceful relations with the Crusaders while making several attempts on the life of Salah al-Din. Sinan was also often at odds with the leadership at Alamut. Despite the difficulties of communication among the widely flung Nizari "state," Alamut's policies were carried out uniformly everywhere within the Nizari network except in Syria; Sinan was the only regional leader who occasionally pursued policies that ran counter to those of the central command.

The changed conditions of the region may well be responsible for two radical shifts in Nizari doctrine during the next half-century. In 1164, the Lord of Alamut, Hasan II, announced the arrival of the Last Day, the end of history. The exact meaning of Hasan's announcement is still debated. Most scholars agree that it entailed the long-awaited Last Judgment, when individuals would be assigned to paradise or to hell, and apparently at least some Nizaris understood it to mean the abrogation of the Shari'a. Many of Hasan's followers also inferred that he was claiming to be the Imam rather than merely his deputy. A year and a half later, one of his former followers stabbed him to death, but his son who succeeded him made explicit the claim that his father was a descendant of Nizar and not merely a deputy or spokesman for him. From then on, the Nizaris recognized the Lord of Alamut as their Imam.

Thus, the Nizaris and the Muslim world at large were taken aback in 1210 when their new Imam, Hasan III, repudiated Nizari doctrine and proclaimed the adherence of his community to Sunni Islam. The Abbasid caliph al-Nasir did not hesitate to welcome a potential ally in his effort to reassert caliphal authority against the Saljuqs, and many other Sunnis cautiously followed his lead in accepting the new "converts." Nizari leaders invited Sunni ulama from across Southwest Asia to the regional Nizari centers in order to instruct members of the community in Sunni doctrine. Most Nizaris, however, assumed that the reason for the apparent conversion was a severe threat to the community and that this was really an instance of *taqiya,* or divinely sanctioned dissimulation. They were convinced that the professed adherence to Sunnism was merely a tactic for the survival of the Nizari community and that they should continue to recognize the Imam as such in private.

These conservatives were reassured in 1221, when Hasan III's successor, Muhammad III, reclaimed the position of Imam. Many Sunnis felt that their cynicism had been vindicated, but, in fact, relations between Nizaris and Sunnis from this point on were not as hostile as they had been. Assassinations of political and religious leaders were no longer automatically assumed to be the work of Nizaris, particularly since that tactic served no useful purpose in the revised doctrines of the community. Moreover, all Muslims, regardless of doctrinal affiliation, had a more important foe to fear: The Mongols had arrived.

The Mongol Campaigns

However presumptuous and brutish the Crusaders were and however shocking the Reconquista had proved to be by 1248, the Mongol campaigns of 1219–1222 and 1253–1260 were far more destructive. Between the Mediterranean and Central Asia, only Syria, Egypt, and the Arabian Peninsula remained free of Mongol destruction and subsequent occupation. The arrival of the Mongols marks a major turning point in the history of the Muslim world east of the Maghrib.

The Campaign of Chinggis Khan, 1219–1222

In the late twelfth century, a Mongol warlord by the name of Temuchin began asserting his dominance over the tribes of Mongolia near the Sea of Baikal. The process was largely completed by 1206, and Temuchin immediately began preparing for a campaign against China, the traditional target of Mongol nomads. By 1215, Temuchin, who gained the title of Chinggis (Genghis/Jengiz) Khan, had pushed as far south as the modern city of Beijing, and he began securing his borders to the west.

Chinggis established diplomatic contact with the Khwarazm–Shah, Muhammad. As we have seen, Muhammad had just defeated the Mongol Qara-khitai of Transoxiana and had rapidly expanded his territories. His achievements were genuinely spectacular, and he wanted to be recognized for them. Unfortunately, in the letter of diplomacy that Chinggis sent to him, Chinggis stated that he viewed the Khwarazm–Shah as he did his own sons. Muhammad, not knowing that he should be flattered, took offense at the remark. A few months later, when a delegation arrived from Chinggis protesting the massacre of several hundred merchants at the hands of one of Muhammad's governors, Muhammad ordered the execution of the Mongol envoys. This act was not only a brazen violation of a basic element of diplomatic protocol; it was also one of history's greatest miscalculations of relative strength.

Chinggis began an offensive against Muhammad in 1219 with an army that may well have numbered 150,000–200,000 men. He took Transoxiana in the winter of 1219–1220, razing the great cities of Bukhara and Samarqand in the process. After resting during the summer heat, he pursued a scorched-earth policy in Khorasan during the period from late autumn of 1220 into late autumn of 1221. Nishapur, Merv, Herat, and other cities were destroyed stone by stone and their inhabitants massacred. The Mongol destruction of the eastern Iranian world is one of the great catastrophes of world history. Even when placed in the context of the region's violent history, it still elicits wonder and shock. The farmers and townspeople of Iran had been accustomed to destruction. During the 200 years since the advent of the Saljuqs, they had experienced the wanton and irrational destruction of property by Turkish raiders, and the subsequent clashes of great armies among the regional powers had inflicted great losses on the area. Cities had been sacked, large numbers of civilians killed, and libraries burned. But nothing had prepared the inhabitants for what the Mongols would visit on them.

When cities resisted Chinggis Khan's army, his policy was to destroy the walls and buildings and massacre the inhabitants. Eyewitnesses from the era report that, after the destruction, the army would leave behind it pyramids constructed of as many as 40,000 heads of the victims. It is true that we have to evaluate critically the reports of chroniclers, whose estimates of the size of armies and populations were not tempered with modern concern for statistical accuracy. In this case, however, the reports come from numerous sources and many locations and are supported by what we know of the subsequent economic and social history of the area.

Eventually, the residents of cities learned that, if they did not resist, a general massacre was not likely, but during the campaign of 1219–1221 that was not widely known, and the destruction to the cities and to the agricultural infrastructure was almost total. Thousands of ulama, secular scholars, merchants, and artisans fled in advance of the danger, seeking refuge farther west or even east. Many scientists and philosophers found refuge within Nizari communities, while others fled all the way to Konya, Damascus, and Cairo in the west, and Lahore and Delhi in the east. The Mongol armies split into two major units. One claimed Central Asia for Mongol rule, and the other pursued Muhammad's son, who had succeeded him as Khwarazm's ruler, all the way to Delhi and then westward to the Caucasus Mountains, where he was killed.

Chinggis returned to Mongolia, where he died in 1227. His son Ogedai became the Great Khan, and his other three sons inherited the areas of Mongolia and the lands between China and the Caspian. In 1235, Ogedai authorized his nephew Batu to lead a campaign into the west, and he subdued western Russia during the next few years. By 1241, Batu commanded two armies in Europe. One defeated a Polish army at Liegnitz (modern Legnica, Poland) in April 1241. The other conquered Buda and Pest, two towns on opposite banks of the Danube that had not yet united into one city. As Western Europe trembled in the expectation of further devastating attacks, Batu abruptly reversed course and headed back to the east. The reason is not clear; he had received word that Ogedai had died, and he may have intended to return for the great council to choose a successor but then changed his mind. It may be that he simply exhausted his resources in men and available grazing ground for his horses after so many battles. At any rate, Batu set up his command post on the lower Volga River. A settlement known as Saray grew up around it, and it became the commercial and administrative capital of an empire known to Europeans as the Golden Horde.

Having established control over the Russian steppes, Batu now focused on securing control over the Caucasus. In doing so, his armies came into contact with the Sultanate of Rum, which had expanded by this time into eastern Anatolia. In 1243, one of Batu's generals informed the sultan of Rum that he needed additional grazing land for his army. The sultan, realizing that any concession would result in Mongol dominance, challenged Batu militarily. At Kose Dagh, the Mongols routed the Saljuqs, and for the next several decades, the sultanate was a vassal state of the Mongols. It soon became embroiled in a civil war and collapsed before the end of the century.

The Campaign of Hulagu, 1253–1260

In 1253, the Great Khan sent Chinggis's grandson Hulagu to conquer Southwest Asia. Hulagu made it clear that the destruction of Alamut was a high priority. He laid siege to Alamut in 1256 and promised safe passage to those who surrendered. The Nizari Imam stalled for several weeks, hoping for the onset of winter weather. During this period, he tried to appease the Mongol leader by authorizing the destruction of scores of his castles. Eventually, however, the Imam had no choice but to surrender. Hulagu sent him and his family on the road to Karakorum, the Mongolian capital, ostensibly to the court of the Great Khan. En route to the Mongol capital, his escorts killed him and his family, and Hulagu also violated the terms of the surrender by massacring the Nizaris in his custody. Muslim scholars who accompanied Hulagu received permission to salvage some manuscripts of the immense library at Alamut, but most of it was destroyed. Other Nizari fortresses fell in the next fifteen years, sometimes after sieges of a decade or more.

After destroying Alamut, Hulagu proceeded to Baghdad, where he demanded the surrender of the city. The city resisted for four weeks and then surrendered. When the inhabitants left the city as demanded, however, Hulagu ordered them to be massacred, and the city was pillaged. The last caliph of Baghdad was then executed, either by being smothered in a carpet or by being rolled up in a carpet and trampled by horses.

FIGURE 7.4 Qalaat Masyaf, the Assassin castle in Syria that served as the headquarters of Rashid al-Din al-Sinan, the Old Man of the Mountain.

dbimages / Alamy Stock Photo.

By early summer 1260, Hulagu's troops were in Gaza, preparing for an invasion of Egypt. He sent an insulting ultimatum to the slave–soldiers who were still engaged in their ten-year-old, often violent, factional quarrels regarding who should lead the others. Many people, both inside and outside Egypt, were impatiently waiting for some dynasty to take control of the state and bring these unruly Turks to order. The mamluk who held effective power at the time, Qutuz, showed no interest in seeking the advice of a nonslave master to deal with the Mongols, however. He took the initiative of prudently arranging a temporary truce with the few remaining Crusaders in Syria in the face of a Mongol threat that concerned both sides. Then, rather than waiting for the Mongols to attack, he moved toward them, advancing into Palestine.

As the two armies were preparing to meet each other in a showdown that would determine the fate of the Muslim world, Hulagu received a message that the Great Khan had died. Almost twenty years earlier, a similar message had saved Europe from Batu; now Hulagu headed eastward at once with most of his army, perhaps intending to present himself as a candidate for the vacant throne. He left the remaining Mongol force under the command of his general, Kit-buqa. Halfway across Iran, Hulagu received word that the succession crisis had been resolved, and he turned back. Before he could reinforce Kit-buqa, however, Qutuz met the latter at a site near Lake Tiberias called 'Ayn Jalut. The result was a crushing defeat for the outnumbered Mongols and the death of their general. Qutuz himself had only a few days to relish his victory until Baybars murdered him and seized power in Egypt.

Meanwhile, Batu's brother Berke succeeded to the throne of the Golden Horde and converted to Islam. He was now exerting great efforts to secure his hold on the Caucasus. Hulagu knew that if he were to control Southwest Asia he would have to possess Azerbaijan, and so he based himself there in order to block Berke's expansion. From there he sent a second army against Egypt. It, too, was defeated. Rather than challenge the Mamluks again, he set about consolidating his power in Iran and Iraq from his capital on the east side of Lake Urmia, in northwestern Iran. His empire would become known as the Il-khanate.

Conclusion

By the middle of the thirteenth century, the expansionist designs of Muslim states and neighboring powers alike seem to have been replaced by a focus on the consolidation of power. In the West, the Reconquista had achieved more in the twelve years from 1236 to 1248 than it had in the previous 300. Granada was the single remaining Muslim principality in the Iberian Peninsula, but the Christian kingdoms would not make another serious effort to capture it for more than two centuries. The Marinids were in secure control of Morocco, and they would also remain in power for two centuries.

Egypt, Syria, and the Holy Cities were under the rule of the slave–soldiers, who would rule there until 1517. The Mamluks were the most powerful Muslim regime in the Dar al-Islam in the thirteenth century, and their prestige was higher than perhaps any Muslim government in history due to their defeat of the Mongols at 'Ayn Jalut. They moved quickly to certify their place in the Sunni world by installing a member of the Abbasid family as the new caliph in Cairo. Like most of his grandfathers, he turned out to be merely an ornament for a military court.

The Mongol states of the Muslim world—the Il-khans, the Golden Horde of Russia, and the Chaghatay Khanate of Central Asia—were likewise relatively stable compared with the irresistible aggression their people had shown for half a century. They did send out raiding parties and the occasional expedition, but none of them ever again conquered significant territory. The conversion of Berke of the Golden Horde to Islam held out the hope that other Mongol rulers might yet convert.

As it happened, these Mongol newcomers were turning out to be not so unfamiliar, after all: Both the Golden Horde and the Il-khanid armies had assimilated numerous ethnic groups as their campaigns progressed. Both had a majority of Turkic warriors by the time they began to consolidate their power at their respective capital cities. It was not lost on the public who anxiously watched the events unfold at 'Ayn Jalut that the battle between the "Mamluks" and the "Mongols" was in fact a clash for control of Southwest Asia between two Turkic armies, one of which represented a Muslim regime and the other did not.

FURTHER READING

General

Lewis, Archibald R. *Nomads and Crusaders,* A.D. *1000–1368.* Bloomington and Indianapolis, Indiana: Indiana University Press, 1988.

The Loss of Andalus

Abun-Nasr, Jamil M. *A History of the Maghrib in the Islamic Period,* 3d ed. Cambridge: Cambridge University Press, 1987.

Bennison, Amira. *The Almoravid and Almohad Empires.* Edinburgh, U.K.: Edinburgh University Press, 2016.

Brett, Michael. *Ibn Khaldun and the Medieval Maghrib.* Aldershot, Hampshire/Brookfield, Vermont: Ashgate/Variorum, 1999.

Brett, Michael and Elizabeth Fentress. *The Berbers.* Oxford and Cambridge, Massachusetts: Blackwell, 1996.

Burns, Robert J. *Islam Under the Crusaders.* Princeton, New Jersey: Princeton University Press, 1973.

Cornell, Vincent J. *Realm of the Saint: Power and Authority in Moroccan Sufism.* Austin, Texas: University of Texas Press, 1998.

Fletcher, Richard. *Moorish Spain.* New York: Henry Holt and Company, 1992.

MacKay, Angus. *Spain in the Middle Ages: From Frontier to Empire, 1000–1500.* New York: St. Martin's, 1977.

Scales, Peter C. *The Fall of the Caliphate of Córdoba: Berbers and Andalusis in Conflict.* Leiden: E.J. Brill, 1994.

Wasserstein, David. *The Rise and Fall of the Party-Kings: Politics and Society in Islamic Spain, 1002–1086.* Princeton, New Jersey: Princeton University Press, 1985.

The Period of the Crusades

Gabrieli, Francesco. *Arab Historians of the Crusades.* Translated from Italian by E. J. Costello. Berkeley and Los Angeles, California: University of California Press, 1984.

Hillenbrand, Carole. *The Crusades: Islamic Perspectives.* New York: Routledge, 2000.

Hitti, Phillip K. *An Arab–Syrian Gentleman and Warrior in the Period of the Crusades: Memoirs of Usamah Ibn-Munqidh.* Princeton, New Jersey: Princeton University Press, 1987.

Holt, P.M. *The Age of the Crusades: The Near East from the Eleventh Century to 1517.* London and New York: Longman, 1986.

Maalouf, Amin. *The Crusades Through Arab Eyes,* Jon Rothschild. Tr. New York: Schocken Books, 1984.

Powell, James M., ed. *Muslims Under Latin Rule, 1100–1300.* Princeton, New Jersey: Princeton University Press, 1990.

Realignment in the East

Daftary, Farhad. *The Assassin Legends: Myths of the Isma'ilis.* London: I. B. Tauris, 1994.

Daftary, Farhad. *The Ismailis: Their History and Doctrines.* Cambridge, U.K.: Cambridge University Press, 1990.

McLynn, Frank. *Genghis Khan: His Conquests, His Empire, His Legacy.* Boston, Massachusetts: Da Capo Press, 2015.

Morgan, David. *The Mongols.* Oxford, U.K.: Basil Blackwell, 1986.

CHAPTER 8

The Consolidation of Traditions

The turmoil of the period from 950 to 1260 inevitably had an impact on cultural life. The fracturing of political unity, the militarization of society, and the repeated invasions meant that it was unlikely that large-scale, state-sponsored intellectual projects such as al-Ma'mun's House of Wisdom would be funded again. Moreover, as a result of the conflicts, libraries were often burned and looted, patron-rulers were killed, and scholars themselves were sometimes kidnapped or killed. On the other hand, the very proliferation of small states meant that petty rulers wanted to enhance their status in the pecking order by patronizing the arts and sciences. A similar situation emerged in the eighteenth and early nineteenth century when the rulers of dozens of small German principalities extended patronage to musicians, artists, and writers as a way of elevating their rank. It is possible that more scholars and artists were funded under the political decentralization of the period that we are considering than would have been possible under centralization.

Thus, despite the hardships of the era, the period from the tenth through the thirteenth centuries was an era of impressive cultural production in the Muslim world. Scholars built on earlier developments in science and philosophy, theology, and Sufism, enabling them to achieve an unprecedented level of sophistication. They also devised new institutions to conserve and expand the knowledge that was being produced. The achievements were so striking that scholars and rulers in Western Europe exerted great efforts to translate the results of the new knowledge from Arabic into Latin.

Science and Philosophy

The ninth century had witnessed al-Ma'mun's monumental project of translating Greek and Syriac texts into Arabic. During the next several centuries, Muslim scholars worked out the scientific, philosophical, and religious implications of those texts. Many of the scholars became famous throughout the Dar al-Islam for their original work in science, mathematics, and philosophy, and they gained even wider fame in Europe during the twelfth and thirteenth centuries when their own work was translated into Latin. On the other hand, it became clear that elements of the philosophical legacy from Greece were incompatible with certain interpretations of Islamic doctrine. The Aristotelian tradition, in particular, posed problems for Muslim intellectuals the way it would in the thirteenth century for European Christian intellectuals.

Mathematics and the Natural Sciences

One of the great mathematicians and physicists of the period from the tenth through the thirteenth centuries was Ibn al-Haytham (known later to the Latins as Alhazen), who was born in the Iraqi city of Basra about 975. He was well educated in religious studies and obtained a position as an administrator. He became so disgusted, however, with the religious bickering of the period—this was the time when Iraqi Sunnis and Shi'ites were particularly intolerant of each other—that he resigned from his position and devoted himself to science. Apparently a Shi'ite himself, he won a reputation for his scientific achievements in Basra and then went to Egypt during the reign of al-Hakim, the Fatimid caliph-Imam. Ibn al-Haytham is famous for advances he made in geometry, astronomy, the theory of light, and number theory, but he is best known for making the first significant contributions to optical theory since Ptolemy, the second-century Roman scientist. He is the first to have used the camera obscura, and his name is best known in the context of "Alhazen's problem," which he stated as follows: "Given a light source and a spherical mirror, find the point on the mirror where the light will be reflected to the eye of an observer." He contradicted Ptolemy's and Euclid's theory of vision that the eye sends out visual rays to the object of the vision; according to Ibn al-Haytham, the rays originate in the object of vision and not in the eye. He published theories on refraction, reflection, binocular vision, the rainbow, parabolic and spherical mirrors, spherical aberration, atmospheric refraction, and the apparent increase in the size of the moon and sun near Earth's horizon. He died in 1039.

A contemporary of Ibn al-Haytham was al-Biruni (973–1048), a native of Khwarazm. In an age of multitalented scholars, many considered him to have been the most erudite scholar of the period. He obtained positions in several Iranian courts, where he measured latitudes between cities and measured solar meridian transits. In 1017, he was back home when Mahmud of Ghazna conquered Khwarazm. Al-Biruni was one of the many captives taken to Ghazna, and he remained a virtual prisoner of Mahmud for the rest of that ruler's reign. He was forced to accompany Mahmud on several campaigns to India, but he made the most of the experiences and subsequently wrote a massive and perceptive description of Indian society and culture. He mastered Turkish, Persian, Sanskrit, and Arabic, and he published numerous works in physics, astronomy, mathematics, medicine, history, and what we might call anthropology. He introduced techniques to measure the earth and distances on it using triangulation. He estimated the radius of the earth to be 3930 miles, a value not obtained in Western Europe until the sixteenth century. His wide range of abilities is demonstrated in his having translated Euclid's works into Sanskrit.

'Umar Khayyam (ca. 1048–1122) was born in Nishapur. He is most famous in the English-speaking world for Edward FitzGerald's 1859 translation of the *Rubaiyat*, a collection of quatrains, only some of which can be attributed to him with certainty. He was an even greater mathematician and astronomer than he was a poet, however. Like al-Biruni, Khayyam complained of the difficulties that the constant wars caused for the scholarly life, and yet, like him, his accomplishments would have been notable even for a scholar in the most serene of circumstances. His first appointment was in Samarqand, but his achievements in music theory and algebra were already so great by the age of twenty-five that the young Saljuq sultan Malik-Shah invited him to help set up an observatory (without telescopes, which would be used for the first time in the seventeenth century) in Esfahan. For eighteen years, he was the leader of a team of observers that developed important astronomical tables. He also began work on calendar reform and calculated the solar year to be 365.24219858156 days. (Today it is said to be 365.242190 days.) When Sanjar became the supreme sultan of the Great Saljuqs in 1118, Khayyam moved to his capital at Merv, which Sanjar was turning into a great center of Islamic learning. Among Khayyam's achievements is a complete classification of cubic equations with geometric solutions found by means of intersecting conic sections. He also realized that a cubic equation can have more than one solution.

Philosophy

The most influential of all the Muslim philosopher–scientists was Ibn Sina (980–1037), known later in Europe as Avicenna. He was born in Samanid Bukhara into an Isma'ili family, although he appears not to have remained one. His father held a position in the Samanid regime, and Ibn Sina grew up having access to the royal library. He was a child prodigy, mastering Islamic law and medicine, and he became a practicing physician at the age of sixteen. He then began a study of metaphysics. His study of philosophy was interrupted by Mahmud of Ghazna's defeat of the Samanids. He escaped the fate of al-Biruni (with whom he had exchanged much correspondence) and headed west rather than east in search of patrons to support his intellectual pursuits. He spent the rest of his life serving in the courts of provincial Shi'ite rulers: first in Khorasan, then at the Buyid court in Rayy, and then successive posts in Qazvin, Hamadan, and finally in Esfahan. He served as court physician and twice was wazir, but the political intrigues endemic in the courtly life led to his being imprisoned at least once and his life endangered several times.

Remarkably, this man of affairs was one of the most productive scholars in history, and he left a permanent mark on both medicine and philosophy. *The Book of Healing* is a vast philosophical and scientific encyclopedia that treats logic, the natural sciences, the four disciplines that the Latins called the quadrivium (arithmetic, geometry, astronomy, and music), and metaphysics. His *Canon of Medicine* is the most famous book in the history of medicine in both the East and the West. Although some scholars regard it as advancing very little beyond the medical compendium of al-Razi, its great accomplishments were its clarity, its comprehensiveness, and its classificatory system. As a result, it was used in the medical colleges of Western Europe into the seventeenth century.

FIGURE 8.1 An illustration from a fourteenth-century Latin edition of Ibn Sina's *Canon of Medicine*. The book was used in Western European universities from the thirteenth through the seventeenth centuries.

Bibliothèque Nationale, Paris, FranceArchives Charmet / Bridgeman Images.

As great as his influence was in medicine, Ibn Sina is also widely regarded as having been one of the world's greatest philosophers. Basing his own work on that of al-Farabi, which had been the most sophisticated Neoplatonic work before the eleventh century, he took advantage of the fact that Greek thought had been a part of the Arabic tradition for two centuries. His writing is more confident and original than that of his predecessors and, as a result, has been more influential. He infused the existing Neoplatonic system with more Aristotelian content, including a subtle discussion of the difference between necessary and possible being. He also tried to prove that it was possible, despite the insistence of the Neoplatonic tradition, that a personal soul would survive death (rather than losing its identity in the One). Although he tried to reconcile Islamic doctrines and philosophy, the brilliant system that he created posed serious challenges to the revealed message of Islam, precisely because it was so persuasive to intellectuals.

The defense of the traditional religious doctrines fell to al-Ghazali (1058–1111), whom Europeans would later call Algazel. Born in Tus, near Mashhad in Khorasan, he was educated in schools near the Caspian Sea and in the Nishapur area, and he moved to Baghdad about 1085. In 1091, Nizam al-Mulk, the Saljuq vizier, appointed him to the new Nizamiya college there, where he became a popular lecturer in jurisprudence and theology. Although possessed of a keen philosophical mind, his theological commitments made him hostile to the legacies of Neoplatonism and Aristotelianism. He wrote a summary of the views of al-Farabi and Ibn Sina entitled *Intentions of the Philosophers*. Designed to help his students understand Neoplatonism so that they could begin to criticize its weaknesses, it was so lucid and objective that thirteenth-century Europeans misunderstood his intentions and concluded that the book reflected al-Ghazali's own views; they believed that he had worked in the same tradition as al-Farabi and Ibn Sina. The sequel to this book was a criticism of Neoplatonism entitled *The Incoherence of the Philosophers*, which was not translated into Latin. It was, however, highly influential in the Islamic world. In it, al-Ghazali challenged the philosophers' denial of the resurrection of the body, their postulate of the eternality of the world, and their notions of causality, which had diminished the concepts of God's sovereignty and omnipotence and had rendered Him subject to necessity.

Al-Ghazali's attack on philosophy triggered a response by Ibn Rushd (1126–1198), known in Europe as Averroes. By the twelfth century, some of the greatest advances in philosophy in the world were taking place in Andalus. Ironically, this was the period of the Almoravids and Almohads, who have a reputation today for anti-intellectualism. Ibn Rushd was well versed in the work of the great Andalusi Neoplatonist Ibn Bajja (ca. 1095–1138), known in Europe as Avempace, and he was the student and protégé of Ibn Tufayl (ca. 1100–1185), known to the Latin world as Abubacer. Ibn Rushd came from a family of jurists, and he himself was trained in medicine, the religious sciences, and philosophy. He was a qadi as well as a physician in Cordoba and Seville under the Almohads. He then became court physician to the caliph in Marrakesh in 1182.

As we have seen, the official religious ideology of the Almohad state made the Qur'an and Hadith the only sources of truth, a position which would seem to create a hostile environment for philosophy. The two caliphs whom Ibn Rushd knew, however—Abu Ya'qub (r. 1163–1184) and his son Abu Yusuf (r. 1184–1199)—were genuinely interested in philosophical speculation. Except for one brief period after 1194, when Abu Yusuf was compelled by popular agitation to send Ibn Rushd back to Andalus and burn his books publicly, the patronage and respect of the Almohad rulers saved Ibn Rushd from the anger of his more traditionally pious critics.

A member of the ulama as well as a philosopher, Ibn Rushd was determined to construct a case for philosophy that would not violate the norms of true religion. Ibn Rushd's philosophical role was to champion true Aristotelianism and to extricate it from Neoplatonism. His profound, yet lucid, commentaries on the texts of Aristotle earned him in Europe the nickname "the Commentator." He swept away the concept of successive emanations from the One and argued for a restoration of the original Aristotelian concept of the First Cause or Unmoved Mover, by which it can be argued that a multiplicity of Intelligences can come directly from God, rather than in successive emanations. He upheld the Aristotelian concept of the eternity of the world but pointed out that this does not mean that the world is eternal by itself, leaving room for a way to finesse the problem of creation. Ibn Rushd also argued for personal immortality, even though medieval Europeans misunderstood him on this point until the fourteenth century.

In addition to numerous commentaries and original works, Ibn Rushd wrote the *Incoherence of the Incoherence*, a response to al-Ghazali's attack on philosophy. Al-Ghazali had equated philosophy with the Neoplatonism of al-Farabi and Ibn Sina, but Ibn Rushd was not interested in defending Neoplatonism. Rather, he wanted to demonstrate that the conclusions of philosophy, if well understood, were an infallible source of truth in harmony with revelation. If there are apparent conflicts between revelation and philosophical reasoning that has no mistakes in assumptions and logic, then the scriptures are meant to be interpreted allegorically.

Ibn Rushd said that there are three types of learners: those who can reason philosophically, those who are convinced by dialectical arguments (the theologians), and those who are convinced by preaching, inspiration, or coercion. The Qur'an was intended for all three, but the meaning of the Qur'an is not readily apparent to all persons. Those who are endowed with the ability of philosophical reasoning are under a divine obligation to pursue philosophy, and they are not obligated to change the demonstrable truths obtained by that means just because they contradict the opinions of theologians. Theologians, who rely on dialectic and rhetoric, are in no position to argue with the superior conclusions of philosophy. Moreover, the theologians are wrong to make public the various interpretations of ambiguous verses, for it could confuse or raise doubts in the minds of the masses. Ibn Rushd thought that al-Ghazali, as a mere theologian, was out of place to be scolding philosophers. His discipline lacked the rigorous methods and concepts that characterized philosophy, and he should have ensured that theology yields to philosophy, rather than the reverse.

Ibn Rushd is often regarded as the last great philosopher in the Islamic world. Such a judgment has to be qualified. Brilliant Muslim minds would continue to work out highly sophisticated systems of thought for centuries to come, but after Ibn Rushd, such systems were developed only within a theological context and are best described as philosophical theology. Ibn Rushd's defense of an open-ended quest for truth by rational means had little resonance in the Dar al-Islam. East of the Maghrib, al-Ghazali's attack on philosophy had persuaded scholars that reason needed to be disciplined by the doctrines taught by the religious establishment rather than given free rein. In the Maghrib and Andalus, domestic and foreign affairs combined in the early thirteenth century to bring a halt to the exuberant philosophical tradition that had taken root there in the twelfth century. The Maghrib continued to be a hostile environment for philosophy, and Andalus collapsed under the impact of the Reconquista. Only Granada was not under direct Christian control, and it was forced to pay tribute. Under those circumstances, Granada's population was averse to intellectual creativity. The ablest minds and the wealthiest patrons left the peninsula for permanent exile. After the early thirteenth century, the Muslims of the peninsula never again produced literature that interested Muslims outside that beleaguered community itself.

The Sunni Resolution to the Tension between Reason and Revelation

Although most Muslim intellectuals remained suspicious of metaphysics, philosophical modes of reasoning and arguing made a lasting impact on Sunni Islam. At the beginning of the twelfth century, the new Islamic theology, in the person of al-Ghazali, had gone head to head with philosophy's most articulate exponent, Ibn Sina, and to most observers, the fight ended in a draw. Al-Ghazali's arguments were often better than those of either Ibn Sina or the later Ibn Rushd, and many of his critics and supporters alike noted that he had attempted to demonstrate the inadequacy of philosophy on philosophical grounds. Moreover, he admitted that he found many of the methods and results of philosophers to be highly useful; he conceded that they had made valuable contributions in logic, mathematics, ethics, and politics. Ironically, although al-Ghazali attacked Neoplatonism, his own metaphysics were shaped by Neoplatonism. He did not deny emanationism, for example, and he assumed the existence of the Universal Intellect and the Universal Soul.

Al-Ghazali was followed by two theologians who, if anything, were even more influenced by philosophy than he was: al-Shahrastani (ca. 1080–1153), who spent most of his career in his homeland of southeastern Iran, and Fakhr al-Din al-Razi (1149–1209, not to be confused with Abu Bakr al-Razi the physician, whom we saw in Chapter 5), originally from Rayy, but who spent most of his career in what is today Afghanistan. Both scholars used arguments that employed new philosophical conceptions and logical methods, and the organization of al-Razi's work reveals his philosophical bent. In the first part of his theological book, he establishes the logical and epistemological framework for his work; then he discusses metaphysical issues such as being, necessity, and possibility; and only then does he discuss the doctrine of God and other religious topics.

By the thirteenth century, a student could not expect to embark upon a course of study in theology without becoming thoroughly familiar with philosophical concepts and forms of argument as well as the long history of the doctrine itself. Even the great Hanbali teacher Ibn Taymiya (1263–1328), who was unsparing in his criticism of philosophers and theologians for their use of philosophical reasoning, used his own profound command of both philosophy and kalam to attack his targets. By the fourteenth century, most of the ulama regarded kalam in the same way that al-Ghazali had: Theology could not lead to certainty in spiritual truths, but it was a useful tool for polemics and apologetics.

FIGURE 8.2 Europeans of the Renaissance revered Ibn Rushd. Raphael, in his *The School of Athens*, suggests that Ibn Rushd (left foreground, wearing a turban) ranked alongside the greatest of the Greek intellectuals.

Vatican Museums and Galleries, Vatican City / Bridgeman Images.

Consolidating Institutions: Sufism

The period from the tenth through the thirteenth centuries was decisive in shaping the organizational and conceptual framework for Sufism. The tenth century was a pivotal time for the mystics of Islam. As we saw in Chapter 5, al-Hallaj's lack of caution not only cost him his life, but it also forced many other Sufis into a defensive position. In the aftermath of al-Hallaj's execution in 922, Sufi leaders began justifying their manner of worship. Over the next two centuries, they wrote books explicating Sufi tenets in an effort to allay the anxieties and suspicions of the ulama, and most Sufis gave careful thought to the balance that they should strike between everyday ritual and the mystical path. Most found the writings of al-Junayd to be helpful in this regard. Some Sufi intellectuals began viewing their enterprise as a religious science just as law was, and they wrote manuals that explained methods and technical vocabulary. As a result, by the eleventh century, Sufism had become much more acceptable to the majority of the ulama, many of whom were now Sufis themselves. Hanbali traditionalists continued to hurl invectives at Sufism, but by the twelfth century the cultivation of the inward life had become an accepted part of the Sunni experience. Sufism offered a wide range of options. A practitioner could use it to develop self-discipline, cultivate gnostic insight, or pursue ecstatic experiences.

A powerful endorsement of the Sufi path appeared at the beginning of the twelfth century in the person of al-Ghazali, whose name is as closely linked with the history of Sufism as it is with philosophy and kalam. On the one hand, it is useful to point out that he was not a philosopher, that his contribution to kalam was less than other thinkers, and that he added almost nothing to the content of Sufism itself. On the other hand, his passionate engagement in the debates of his day contributed to the future direction of all three fields of thought. In 1095, al-Ghazali resigned his teaching post in Baghdad, apparently with the intention of abandoning his career as a jurist, theologian, and professor in order to serve God more completely as a Sufi. He apparently suffered from a severe emotional crisis that almost incapacitated him. Whether his crisis derived from a conviction that the intellectual life that he had led did not produce certainties after all, from revulsion at the worldliness of his fellow ulama, or from some other cause is unclear. Whatever the reason, he lived for short periods of time in several cities of Syria (on the eve of the arrival of the Crusaders in Palestine) and Iraq before returning home to Tus. There he lived the life of an ascetic and mystic and attracted a group of followers. The Saljuq vizier persuaded him to lecture in Nishapur for three years, but he returned again to Tus, in northeastern Iran, where he died in 1111.

During this post-Baghdad period, al-Ghazali wrote a major work entitled *The Revival of the Religious Sciences*. In it, he argued that it was not by theological learning that one attained heaven, but rather by a life of moral uprightness and closeness to God, which could be attained through Sufi methods. Whereas theology was a necessary safeguard for true belief in its role of defending the faith, the truly pious life was the fusion of religious obligations and the mystical experience. Prior to al-Ghazali, many Sufis and critics of Sufism alike considered that the Sufi way of life began where the Shari'a ended, but his contribution was a persuasive demonstration that, on the one hand, the truly Sufi life embraced the faithful observance of all these duties, and on the other, that the inner meaning of the Shari'a was fulfilled in the Sufi life.

Al-Ghazali's profound influence in this regard can be seen in the fact that the Almoravid regime implemented a policy of hunting down copies of his *The Revival of the Religious Sciences* and burning them publicly. Al-Ghazali had become a hero to the dissenters in the Almoravid empire because of his defense of the mystical life and his insistence on the importance of the Shafi'i consensus in law. As a corollary of his defense of Sufism, he asserted that all learned Muslims, not just the official ulama, had a right to be heard on the issues of ethics and law. His rationale was that the combination of piety and learning was what qualified people to make public judgments, not scholastic credentials. In the conservative, highly stratified Almoravid society, such ideas were considered seditious. As a result, his followers were persecuted and his works were banned.

The Emergence of Lodges and *Tariqa*s

As Sufism became more widely practiced, it made an important transition from an individual exercise to an organized, collective effort. The first step in this direction was the widespread appearance of residential lodges. In the first few centuries of Sufism, a student in a city typically studied with several spiritual masters. He might visit them in their homes or travel widely in order to learn from as many as possible.

On the frontiers and in the rural areas, however, it was the Sufi masters who tended to be itinerant. It was there that mosques, forts, and other structures became meeting places for Sufis, and many of the buildings (except for the mosques) became temporary residences for students who would stay with the master for as long as he remained in the area. As we have seen, many of the fortresses, or ribats, of North Africa assumed this role, and soon the term *ribat* had both military and Sufi connotations. By the second half of the eleventh century, such lodges were making their appearance in large cities such as Baghdad and soon could be found throughout the cities of the Dar al-Islam. At first, they were used for a variety of religious purposes, but by the end of the twelfth century they were exclusively Sufi institutions. Such a lodge was usually called a *ribat* in North Africa, a *khanaqa* in Iran, a *zawiya* in most of the eastern Arabic-speaking lands, and a *tekke* in Turkic areas.

The next important step in the development of Sufism was the emergence of the *tariqa*, a term that is usually translated as "brotherhood" or "order." Literally meaning "path," the tariqa was a unique spiritual discipline and an accompanying set of rituals that constituted the identity of a group associated with a particular zawiya. The tariqa consisted of a structured set of spiritual exercises for the student to learn and master. These exercises were designed to bring the Sufi into direct communion with God and therefore became the focal point of the student's concentration. The exercises included a dhikr as well as the ascetic or contemplative practices that a novitiate struggled to master on his ascent to a personal experience with God. Both the dhikr and the spiritual exercises distinguished one tariqa from another.

We know very little about the origins and spread of either the lodges or the orders, but it appears that the very presence of multiple lodges in a given city produced a momentum for each lodge to become associated with a particular master's spiritual discipline. Once the concept became fixed that a student belonged to a particular order, the practice of initiation into that order became the norm. Sufis were now allowed to practice the method of an order only in return for a pledge of spiritual loyalty to the master or the local representative of a given order.

Like the lodges themselves, tariqas appear to have developed first outside the major cities. They began developing in the twelfth century but became prominent only during the first half of the thirteenth century. The Abbasid caliph al-Nasir (1180–1225), who was attempting to rebuild the authority of his office, appointed 'Umar al-Suhrawardi (1145–1234) *shaykh* ("leader" or "master") of a zawiya with the proviso that the membership associated with it be limited to those who accepted the teachings of Suhrawardi's great uncle, Abu al-Najib al-Suhrawardi. Abu al-Najib was revered as the formulator of a spiritual discipline, and it was believed that he had a spiritual genealogy that could be traced back to the Prophet—that is, he had been taught by men who had been taught by men who had been taught by the Prophet himself.

This spiritual genealogy, or *silsila*, became a distinguishing feature of Sufi orders, just as the isnad was of authentic Hadith. It guaranteed the soundness of the method by showing that it had been transmitted from one Sufi to another ever since the Prophet's generation. The master himself had received it in its pure form, and his successors passed it on to future generations, its authenticity attested to by the collective membership. The orders themselves gained their names from the names of the master who supposedly founded them, although often, as in the case of the

Suhrawardiya order, the organization was founded after the master's death. Another such posthumous order was the Qadiriya, named after 'Abd al-Qadir al-Gilani of Baghdad (d. 1165).

The development of the orders marked a new stage in the history of Sufism. To that point, the mystical tradition had encouraged an independence of spirit and creativity, but the crystallization of the orders meant the imposition of a rigorous discipline on those who sought spiritual enlightenment through them. No longer were the teacher and his students in a mere relationship of instructor and pupil; now they were in a relationship of spiritual guide (*shaykh* or *murshid* in the Arab world; *pir* in the Persian-speaking regions) and disciple (*murid*). Disciples were to submit themselves unquestioningly to their master. As one Sufi put it, the disciple was to be as a dead body in the hands of its washer.

Because of the new sense of discipline, generation after generation of members of a particular lodge followed the same tariqa (albeit with modifications over time). By doing so, they developed a group identity. They were persuaded that the teachings associated with the order could be traced back through the generations of masters, the order's founder, and eventually to the Prophet himself. Mystical wandering mendicants, healers, and spiritual advisers continued to be found throughout the Dar al-Islam, but henceforth the characteristic Sufi approach would be that of a disciple who belonged to a community led by a spiritual master.

Merchants or scholars who visited a city might join an order for a few months or years and then return home and begin a branch of the order there. By this process, some of the orders gained adherents over huge areas. By the seventeenth century, the Qadiriya tariqa could be found from North Africa to India. Sometimes the branches remained remarkably faithful to the original tariqa, but in many cases local conditions and traditions led to slight modifications in the ritual. As a result, many suborders emerged within the Sufi movement. By adapting to local needs, lodges enabled Sufism to become a mass movement. The orders encouraged those who could to live in the lodge and engage in the fully dedicated life of an adept, but many of them also encouraged those who had families and full-time jobs to participate as much as they could, if only to engage in the dhikr once or twice a week. Moreover, the masters freely gave of their spiritual guidance to anyone in need of reassurance and healing. As a result, the masses revered them during their lifetime and sought out their tombs after their death.

A Handbook for Sufi Novices

Abu al-Najib al-Suhravardi (1090–1168), after whom the Suhravardi (in Arabic: Suhrawardi*) order was named, wrote a guide addressed to novices and laymen who wished to learn the rules of conduct of a Sufi. The handbook contains less material on the stages and states of the Sufi mystical path than it does on such matters as companionship, hospitality, and specific rules dealing with* *particular situations. It is a revealing insight into the importance that most Sufi orders placed on adab, a term that suggests good manners, refinement, and proper behavior. The section reproduced here deals with the adab of eating.*

121. The ethics and manners of eating. (Qur'an 7:31 is quoted.) One should give the poor to eat from what one is eating. One should say at the beginning of the meal "In the name of God." If one forgets to say "In the name of God" at the beginning, he should say this when he remembers....

122. One should not be concerned about the provisions of livelihood nor should one be occupied in seeking, gathering, and storing them. (Qur'an 29:60 quoted.) The Prophet did not store anything for the morrow. One should not talk much about food because this is gluttony. In eating one should intend to satisfy hunger and give one's soul its due but not its pleasure. The Prophet said, "You owe your soul its due." Food should be taken like medicine [as an unpleasant necessity]. Gluttony should be avoided. One should not find fault in any food nor should one praise it.

124. Sufis eat only food whose source they know. They avoid eating the food of unjust and sinful people. A Hadith: "The Prophet forbade us to accept an invitation to dinner by sinful persons." The Sufis refuse to accept the gifts of women and to eat at their meals.

125. The Sufis do not disapprove of conversation during the meal. More of their rules of conduct in eating: to sit on the left leg, to use the formula "In the name of God," to eat with three fingers, to take small bites and chew well, to lick the fingers and the bowl. One should not look at the morsel taken by a friend. When he finishes his eating, he should say, "Praise be to Allah who has made the provisions of our livelihood more plentiful than our needs." It is not polite to dip one's hand in the food because one can get soiled with it [one should dip only three fingers].

126. [On eating in company.] A Sufi saying: "Eating with brethren should be with informality (insibat); with foreigners, with nice manners; and with the poor (fuqara'), with altruism." Junayd said, "Eating together is like being nursed together, so you should carefully consider the persons with whom you eat." The Sufis prefer to eat in company.... When one eats in company, he should not withdraw from eating as long as the others are eating, especially if he is the head of the group. When the Prophet was eating in company, he would be the last one to finish.

130. Three obligations of the host and three of the guest. The host should present only licit food, keep the times of prayer, and should not withhold from the guest whatever food he is able to give. The guest should sit where he is told by the host, be pleased with what is given to him, and should not leave without asking permission of the host. The Prophet said, "It is a commendable custom (sunna) to accompany the guest to the door of the house."

SOURCE: *A Sufi Rule for Novices: Kitab Adah Al-Murzdzn of Abu Al-Najib Alsuhrawardi*, an abridged translation and Introduction by Menahem Milson, pp. 57–59. Copyright © 1975 by the President and Fellows of Harvard College.

In large cities, members of lodges were in close contact with the mosque system, and the shaykh might even be the imam of a major mosque. Thus, "middle-class" Sufism usually maintained practices and doctrines that did not run afoul of the developing cosmopolitan consensus regarding the acceptable doctrines and practices in Islam. Among the illiterate in the cities, and especially in rural and frontier areas, however, Sufi practices could include features quite unrelated to the written tradition of Islam. Some of these practices came into Sufism from local pre-Islamic traditions and were initially viewed by Sufi masters as harmless baggage that enabled new converts to make the transition to Islam. Howling, fire eating, sword swallowing, and juggling became associated with the rituals of some orders.

The result was a syncretism that made some Muslims uneasy. On the one hand, the persistence of pre-Islamic religious elements facilitated the conversion of vast numbers of people who otherwise might not have found the religion attractive. By combining these elements with piety and faith in God's love, Sufism made important contributions. On the other hand, some ulama were aghast at features that suggested ancestor worship or idolatry, as well as an ignorance of the Shari'a. The highly charged tension continued between those who assumed the role of guardians of the Qur'an and Hadith on the one hand and those who were willing to make compromises in order to expand the Umma on the assumption that converts would gradually assimilate into correct practice.

Speculative Mysticism

Although the mystical experience itself cannot be subjected to rational analysis or description, many so-called "speculative" mystics have tried to understand how the mystical experience is possible at all and what it can reveal about the nature of God and of the human soul. As a result, many Sufis were attracted to the new sciences and philosophy that became available as a result of the translation movement of the ninth and tenth centuries. Alchemy was highly popular among Sufis. Sometimes its practitioners attempted to transform base metals into gold, but they were even more concerned to transform imperfect souls into perfect ones through the spiritual discipline that alchemy offered. Some Sufis became well known for both their spiritual exercises and their elixirs.

Philosophy, however, had an even more powerful impact on the mystical expression of Islam. Certain features of Neoplatonism and of gnosticism appealed to many mystics for the same reason that they had been popular among pagans, Jews, Christians, and Muslim rationalists. Neoplatonism not only furnished the cosmology that allowed mystics to explain their progress toward union with the One in the reverse order of the emanations, but it also had a complex theory of the divisions of the human soul that enabled them to explain their spiritual progress in mastering one aspect or another of their lower selves. Gnosticism taught that spiritual elites were in possession of a special knowledge that was different from knowledge gained by the masses or from empirical observation. Moreover, this knowledge was different from (and better than) even what passed as wisdom: It was obtained by direct contact with God's presence.

Neoplatonism and gnosticism provided the framework and concepts for the development of ideas that played an important role in Sufism for hundreds of years.

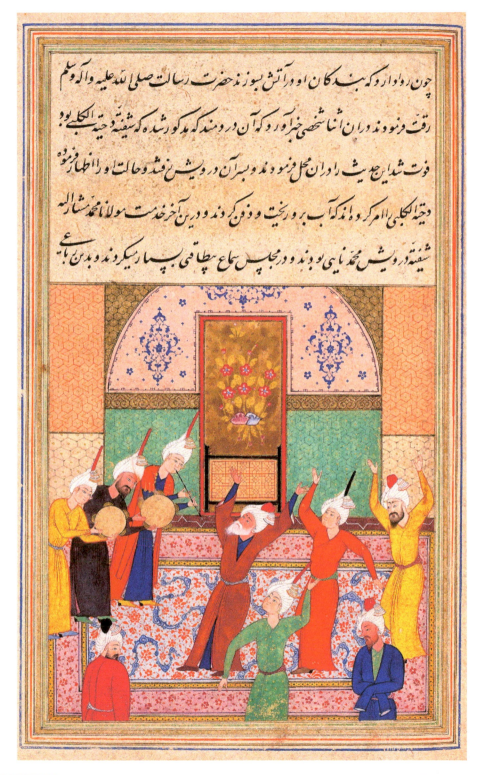

چون رو بود از و که بنده کان او در آتش بسوز نذ حضرت رسالت صلی الله علیه واله وسلم

رقت فرمود ند در ان اثنا شخصی خبر آورد که آن درومند که مذکور شده که شفیقه دحیة الکلبی بود

فوت شد در این حدیث را در ان محل فرمود ند و بر آن درویش رقت و حالت او را اظهار فرمود

دحیة الکلبی الامر که روه انذ که آب بر و ریخت و فوکر دند و در این آخر خدمت مولانا محمد مثال الله

شفیقه درویش محمد نایبی بودند و در مجالس سماع قطاعی بسیار میکرد ند و بدین بایع

FIGURE 8.3 A sixteenth-century Persian painting of a Sufi pir dancing with his disciples.

The Bodleian Library, University of Oxford MS. Ouseley Add. 24, fol. 119r.

A major example is the understanding of the significance of the Prophet himself. The earliest Muslims viewed Muhammad to be a prophet and a warner, but his image inevitably acquired additional characteristics due to his role as the model of the pious life. With the aid of Neoplatonic concepts, the doctrine of the preexistence of Muhammad and the concept of Muhammad as the Perfect Man emerged, developments that run parallel to the Hellenistically influenced Christian ideas of Jesus of Nazareth as preexisting Logos and Perfect Man. The doctrine of the *mi'raj*, or the ascent of the Prophet to heaven (from Jerusalem), became fully developed during this time. Based on an ambiguous passage in the Qur'an (17:1), it soon was fleshed out in the Hadith and further elaborated among Neoplatonic Sufis. For the latter, it became a powerful paradigm for their own spiritual ascent into the presence of God.

Another legacy from Neoplatonism and gnosticism was the development of the concept of *al-Qutb*, "the Pole" or "the Axis," introduced by the Sufi theoretician al-Tirmidhi (d. 932). Al-Tirmidhi (who was nicknamed al-Hakim, the term used to refer to Greek philosophers), wrote that saints, or walis, govern the universe. They are ranked in a hierarchy, according to their spiritual insight, with al-Qutb at the pinnacle. Over the next few centuries, these ideas were developed in great detail, and many people considered walis to be responsible for everything that happens in this world. Several Sufi masters claimed to be the Qutb of their generation, and some Sufis believed that a Muslim had to know the Qutb of his era or be regarded as an infidel. Al-Qutb was also known as the Seal of the Saints, a concept that disturbed some ulama because it could be construed to detract from the status of Muhammad as Seal of the Prophets.

In the twelfth and thirteenth centuries, several speculative mystics produced works that have been a source of inspiration for Sufis to the present day. Three are of particular importance for our purposes. Shihab al-Din Yahya al-Suhrawardi (1153–1191) was from the same town and had a similar name as the man who created the Suhrawardiya order, but he is nicknamed al-Maqtul ("the murdered") to distinguish him from the other one. As a young man, he settled in Aleppo at the court of Salah al-Din's son, Malik al-Zahir. Al-Suhrawardi attempted to create a philosophical base for an Islamic mysticism that combined elements of Neoplatonism, Zoroastrianism, and gnosticism. The central theme of his work is the metaphor of God as Light. With the help of this image, al-Suhrawardi could substitute illumination for the Neoplatonic concept of emanation; both the creation and the sustaining of the universe are the result of the constant production of light that characterizes God. The mystical experience itself is understood as a process of illumination, and the soul's fate after death depends on the degree of illumination that it obtained during life in the body.

Al-Suhrawardi was critical of Aristotelian categories, and he dismissed all definitions and categories as mental constructs. For him, all reality was a single continuum, possessed with more or less of a degree of Being. God is pure Being, whereas nature has less Being. This interpretation of the universe is variously called pantheistic or monistic, for it suggests that nothing exists except God. By suggesting that the world is in some sense God, and that there is no distinction between God and His creation, al-Suhrawardi undercut a basic tenet of revealed monotheism. His ideas were too bold for the leading ulama of Aleppo, and they prevailed upon Malik al-Zahir to have him imprisoned and then killed. His ideas of Illuminationism, however, have survived to influence mystics of the Persian-speaking world for centuries.

Meanwhile, in Andalus, a young man was reaching maturity who would have an even wider influence. Ibn al-ʻArabi (sometimes rendered "Ibn ʻArabi") was born in Murcia in 1165. Sometime between 1198 and 1201, he set out on the hajj and never returned to Andalus. He remained in Mecca for several years and then visited many other cities over the next quarter of a century. He finally settled in Damascus in 1223, where he died in 1240. Ibn al-ʻArabi's ambition was to give philosophical expression to the important mystical doctrines that had been developed to that point. Like al-Suhrawardi, Ibn al-ʻArabi employed ideas from gnosticism and Neoplatonism, and his erudition was formidable. His output, which included both poetry and prose, was prodigious, but his writings have always been difficult to understand. Much of his work drew upon sources with which his readers were not familiar; he was fond of metaphors; and many of his ideas seem to contradict each other. As one can imagine, modern readers who grapple with his books in translation find his thought to be quite obscure. But precisely because his work combines a brilliant philosophical scheme with provocative imagery and ambiguous concepts, generations of Sufis have been able to find within his work many passages that reflect their own transcendental experience.

At the center of Ibn al-ʻArabi's thought is a God who is inconceivable and unknowable, and whose only attribute is self-existence. And yet, God wishes to be known, and so He created the world. The universe exhibits His characteristics, serving in a sense as a mirror for His attributes. Longing to be known by individual souls, He makes His names known to us, that we may at least know Him in part. This partial self-revelation explains why each individual has a different conception of God, and why the various religions describe Him in different ways.

Just as Ibn al-ʻArabi became *al-shaykh al-akbar* ("Great Master") for subsequent generations of speculative mystics, another thirteenth-century Sufi genius became known as *Mevlana* ("Our Master" in Persian and Turkish) for the unsurpassed beauty of his poetry. Jalal al-Din al-Rumi (1207–1273) was born in Balkh, in modern Afghanistan. Leaving home just before the onslaught of Chinggis Khan, his father led his family on a circuitous route westward, eventually settling in Konya. Thus, Jalal al-Din grew up under the Saljuqs of Rum and, as a result, this poet who hailed from the eastern Islamic world has forever been known as Rumi. Rumi succeeded his father as a teacher of the religious sciences in Konya, and he also became a Sufi master, leading a circle of devoted disciples. In 1244, he met a wandering mystic named Shams al-Din, whom many found to be boorish. Rumi, however, discovered in him the Divine Beloved. He became totally preoccupied with his relationship with Shams, and his family and disciples finally drove "the Beloved" from Konya. Rumi fell into a depression, and his family summoned Shams back to the city. Rumi's single-minded obsession resumed, however, and in desperation, his jealous disciples and children killed Shams.

The death of Shams was a life-changing event for Rumi. The experience of loss and love turned him into a poet, and he developed a passionate interest in music and dance. He produced a collection of poetry dedicated to his beloved, and then, in 1249, he met a goldsmith whose deep spirituality reestablished for him a relationship similar to the one he had had with Shams. After the goldsmith's death, he formed a similar relationship with Husam al-Din Chelebi. Husam became the inspiration for Rumi's most famous work, the *Masnavi*, which contains 26,000 couplets. The *Masnavi* was inspired by the music of the world around Rumi—formal music, the music of nature, and music of the everyday world of work, such as the ringing of the coppersmith's hammer. The *Masnavi* contains fables, stories, proverbs, and the poetic evocation of the spiritual nature of the everyday world. For Sufis of the Persian-language world, it is second in importance only to the Qur'an as an inspirational text. At Rumi's death, Husam succeeded him as the leader of his spiritual circle and was in turn succeeded by Rumi's son Sultan Walad. Sultan Walad created the order that became known as the Mevlevi order, better known in the West as the Whirling Dervishes, whose musical, mesmerizing dance recapitulates the ecstasy and joy of Rumi's life and spiritual quest.

Ibn al-'Arabi, Rumi, the Egyptian Ibn al-Farid, and other Sufi poets of the thirteenth century produced one of the most powerful literary traditions in history. Rhythmic, sensuous, lucid, and yet deliberately obscure, it has provided pleasure and spiritual inspiration. (It has also provoked a powerful opposition to it from those who sense that it goes beyond the bounds of acceptable forms of worship.) Since the mystical experience cannot be described but can only be communicated through metaphor and analogy, poetry was found to be a far more appropriate medium for it than prose. In addition, the symbols and evocative imagery that are more easily expressed through poetry can also convey the mystical perspective that transcends the categories of rational thought. In their meditations upon the divine, Sufi poets borrowed subjects and themes from secular poetry to create allegories. A discussion of divine love could include a quatrain such as the following:

> Last night my idol placed his hand upon my breast,
> he seized me hard and put a slave-ring in my ear.
> I said, "My beloved, I am crying from your love!"
> He pressed his lips on mine and silenced me.[1]

In much the same way that Jews and Christians have found in the Biblical *Song of Songs* a metaphorical expression of the love between God and humans, so Sufis found in images of human love, of nature (the rose, the nightingale, and the ocean), and even of forbidden pursuits (idols, wine, taverns, and temples) ways to express the ineffable truths of God's relationship to His creatures. The beloved represents God, who is usually portrayed in Persian poetry as a beautiful boy. Occasionally, in Arabic poetry, the beloved is a female, as in the works of Ibn al-Farid and in Ibn al-'Arabi's love lyrics in Mecca, composed under the spell of a young Persian-speaking lady. The idol, too, represents God; wine expresses the intoxication of God's love; the tavern can be the divine presence (where the lover drinks the wine of God's love); and the tavern keeper often represents the Sufi master. Puckishly, whereas the tavern and tavern keeper are positive symbols, the mosque and preacher usually represent hypocrisy or, at best, legalistic and empty religiosity. Not surprisingly, many of the non-Sufi ulama found such lyrics reprehensible, but many others found them profound, enjoyable, and inspirational. Particularly in their Persian form, they influenced the literature not only of Southwest Asia but of Central Asia and South Asia as well, in lasting ways.

Consolidating Institutions: Shiʿism

The tenth and eleventh centuries were heady days politically for the Shiʿites, for they controlled a large part of the Dar al-Islam. The Carmathians were a threat in the Persian Gulf from their base in Bahrain from the early tenth century until 1077; the Buyids ruled parts of Iraq and western Iran from 945 until 1055; the Fatimids controlled Ifriqiya and then Egypt and parts of Syria from 909 until 1171; the Ismaʿili dynasty of the Sulayhids ruled Yemen from 1063 until 1138; the Hamdanids were a northern Syrian power in the second half of the tenth century; and the Assassins were a feared presence in Iran and Syria from 1090 until 1256. In addition, small Shiʿite states were scattered throughout remote areas of the Dar al-Islam.

The period also witnessed important developments in Shiʿite theology and organization. As we have seen, this remarkably fragmented and inchoate movement coalesced into four major branches. The Zaydi community remained remarkably unchanged. Concentrated on the periphery of the major states in mountainous regions such as Daylam and Yemen, its members created small states but had little interaction with the major powers of the region. The Fatimid movement split in 1094 into the Nizari and Mustaʿli branches. The Imamiya, who fragmented upon the death of the eleventh Imam in 874, regrouped by the early tenth century around the doctrine of the Occultation of the Twelfth Imam. The dissolution of the Yemeni and Egyptian Ismaʿili states in the twelfth century and the persecution of the Nizaris in the thirteenth century after the Mongol invasion left the Twelvers the largest single group of Shiʿites.

Twelver Shiʿites

We have seen that, from the 870s to the 940s, the leaders of what had been known as the Imamiya stated that the Hidden Imam was communicating with his community through certain spokesmen. Because the Hidden Imam was regarded as the twelfth and final leader of the Imamiya, the movement has become known as Twelver Shiʿism. After about seventy years of this so-called Lesser Concealment, the doctrine changed to that of the Greater Concealment, according to which the Imam no longer has an official spokesman. The transition from the period of the Lesser Concealment to that of the Greater Concealment occurred about 941, shortly before the Buyids seized power. Under their patronage, the Twelver Shiʿites flourished in Iraq and western Iran for a century.

During the Buyid period, Twelver scholars developed doctrines that answered some of the vexing questions that accompanied the end of the period of a present, or visible, Imam after 874. They taught that the twelfth Imam continues to provide guidance to his community despite his concealment. Although he has no single spokesman or agent, he does communicate through dreams and visions to highly-educated, spiritual ulama. When the Saljuqs retook Baghdad from Fatimid-supported al-Basasiri in 1058, they took revenge on all Shiʿites. As a result, the leading Twelver intellectuals moved to Hilla, in southern Iraq, to escape persecution. There they developed the doctrine that the Imam had delegated his judicial authority to those who had studied jurisprudence. Thus, he continued to serve as a guide to his community, as well as to intercede with God for his followers. Because he is also the Mahdi, shortly before the Day of Judgment he will return to bring justice to this corrupt world. After a cataclysmic conflict with the forces of evil, he will rule the earth for several years. Then Jesus and the first eleven Imams will come, as well as prophets and saints who have previously brought the word of God and who have striven to establish righteousness on earth.

The doctrine of the Concealment of the twelfth, or hidden, Imam had important repercussions for the Twelver Shi'ites. One was that it provided stability to the movement for the first time. During the first two centuries or more of Shi'ite history, the Imamis had been less organized and less ideologically identifiable than the Isma'ilis, and they had actually been in danger of fragmenting irretrievably in the late ninth century. However, during the tenth and eleventh centuries, they began to rally around the doctrine of the Hidden Imam and to develop doctrines

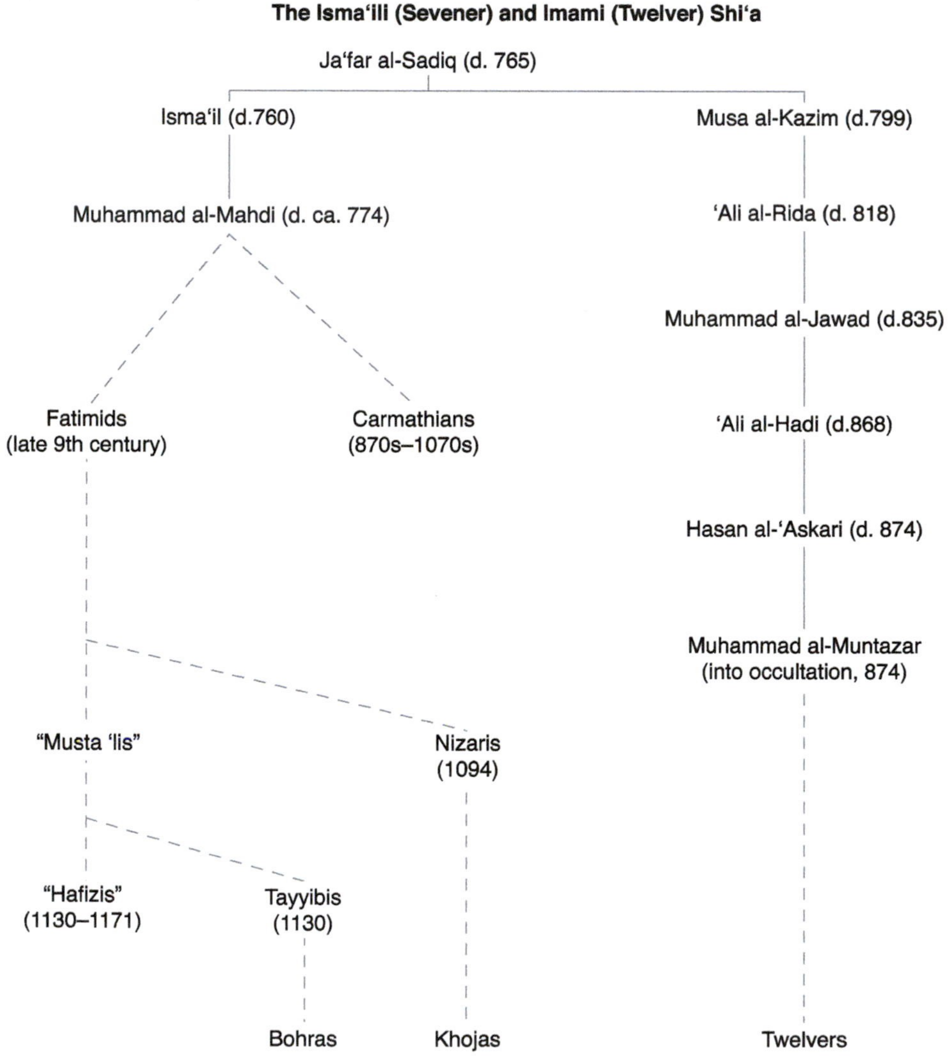

The Isma'ili (Sevener) and Imami (Twelver) Shi'a

FIGURE 8.4 The Isma'ili (Sevener) and Imami (Twelver) Shi'a.

and institutions that provided them with continuity and a stronger identity than before.

A second consequence of the new doctrine was that Sunni persecution of the sect became less pronounced. Until the doctrine of the Occultation was developed, the various Imams had been at least potentially political as well as religious figures. Although the Imams themselves had not led political uprisings since the time of Husayn, several pro-Alid agitators had proclaimed revolts in their name, and the Imams were suspect in the eyes of the political authorities because of these revolts and those of Zaydi activists. Any "present" or "visible" Imam would inevitably be perceived to be a political threat to the established order. As we have seen, several were persecuted, and others died under mysterious circumstances. After 874, with the removal of the twelfth Imam from the political arena, Sunni authorities did not consider Twelver Shi'ism to be a threat and were able to coexist with it much more easily than they could Isma'ilism for several centuries. By the thirteenth century, Twelver Shi'ism was clearly the strongest and largest of several Shi'ite groups.

The Isma'ilis

The Isma'ilis enjoyed a period of great influence and power in the eleventh and twelfth centuries. In the first half of the eleventh century, the Fatimid empire was rivaled in the Muslim world only by the Ghaznavid empire under Mahmud. The factional conflicts and famines that began to afflict the empire during the 1060s greatly weakened it, but the schism of 1094 that resulted in the Musta'li-Nizari rift paradoxically left the perception that Isma'ilism was even more powerful than before. To many Sunnis and Twelver Shi'ites, it appeared that Hasan-i Sabbah's fortresses in Iran and Syria were simply an extension of the Fatimid state and that Isma'ilism was poised to dominate most of the Dar al-Islam. In reality, of course, the Fatimid movement had become greatly weakened, and it was saved from disintegration only by the fragmentation of the Saljuq Empire (1092) just before the Fatimid schism (1094).

In 1130, the Fatimid movement suffered yet another blow. In that year the Fatimid caliph al-Amir was murdered, and yet another schism developed that would have a lasting impact. A cousin of the murdered caliph claimed the throne under the name al-Hafiz, and he was accepted by the Fatimid faithful in Egypt and Syria. In Yemen, however, where the policies of the Fatimid wazir al-Afdal were increasingly regarded as oppressive, many of the Musta'lis refused to accept al-Hafiz. Under the leadership of their queen, al-Sayyida al-Hurra al-Sulayhi (1084–1138), who had upheld the claims of al-Musta'li in 1094, the Yemenis asserted that an infant son had been born to al-Amir shortly before the caliph's murder, and that the infant, named al-Tayyib, was the legitimate ruler.

Because al-Tayyib never appeared in public in Yemen, his followers, the Tayyibis, claimed that he had gone into concealment. They asserted that the Imamate passed from him to his son, then from father to son thereafter. In the meantime, during the concealment, his guidance is administered through the *da'i mutlaq* (literally, "chief missionary"). The Tayyibi Isma'ilis, who seemed insignificant at the time compared to the center of the Fatimid movement in Cairo, outlasted the Fatimids. The latter group disappeared after Salah al-Din seized control of Egypt in 1171, whereas the Tayyibis have continued to thrive to the present. The Tayyibi community in Yemen remained strong for several centuries. Over the years, many of them migrated to Gujarat, where they became wealthy by virtue of their involvement in international trade.

The widely scattered Nizari Isma'ili state of the Assassins lasted from 1094 until 1273, when its last remnants were destroyed through the combined efforts of the Mongol conqueror Hulagu and the Mamluk leader Baybars. Although the Nizaris established their fortresses in remote, rustic areas, they cultivated a remarkably sophisticated intellectual life. Alamut, in particular, had become famous for its research library, and its leadership encouraged non-Isma'ili Muslim scholars to study there. The fall of Alamut to Hulagu and the subsequent murder of the Imam were tremendous blows to the Nizari community. Most of its members came to believe that the Imam's son had been hidden for safekeeping, and for the next two centuries Nizaris and their Imams lived secretively under the Mongols and successor dynasties. Discovering the Sufi relationship of master and pupil to be a useful cover for their own hierarchical structure, they pretended to be adherents of one Sufi brotherhood or the other. Because of continuing persecution, however, many Nizaris gradually migrated to South Asia. Thus, by the end of the thirteenth century, the two main surviving groups of Isma'ilis were the Nizaris and the Tayyibis, and both were gravitating toward the western coast of India.

The Impact of "the Foreign Sciences" and Jurisprudence

Shi'ism was profoundly influenced by the new intellectual currents of the ninth and tenth centuries. By the early tenth century, the Isma'ilis were incorporating Neoplatonism into their thought, enabling them to conceptualize the distinction between the exoteric (*zahir*) and esoteric (*batin*) features of the scriptures and of Isma'ili doctrines. This distinction allowed the leadership to justify their position as a spiritual elite who had a monopoly on the knowledge of the deep spiritual truths essential to salvation. The masses needed the Imam and the hierarchy of teachers that he installed in order to provide the allegorical interpretation of the scriptures and of Isma'ili literature which came to be the distinctive feature of Isma'ilism. The Fatimids backed away from this extreme position, however. By the time they had secured their position in Egypt, they insisted on the equal importance of the exoteric and the esoteric, and they were more careful than the Carmathians and their own descendants, the early Nizaris, to insist on the fulfillment of the requirements of the Shari'a.

Isma'ili and Twelver Shi'ite intellectual life took somewhat different directions from that of the Sunni community because of the centrality of the Imam in their doctrine. Philosophy and gnostic thought, under a cloud in the Sunni community, flourished among both of the main Shi'ite groups. Of the two communities, the Isma'ilis were more attracted to complex cosmological doctrines adapted from Neoplatonism and even Indian philosophical systems. On the other hand, commentaries on the Qur'an are absent from Isma'ili literature of the period, for the Imam was the ever-present interpreter. The Fatimid Imam was often referred to as the "speaking Qur'an," whereas the book was known as the "silent Qur'an." Commentaries on the Qur'an were also rare within the Imami community until the doctrine of the Hidden Imam became firmly established. When the Imam was no longer present to interpret the scriptures, however, a demand arose for them.

The Imamis/Twelvers began as a Hadith-based movement, but they made a wrenching change to a rationalist one. Whereas the early Imamis agreed with Sunnis that the Hadith were a second source of law along with the Qur'an, they had quite different criteria for judging the authenticity of Hadith. Because of their hostility toward the first three caliphs and their supporters, as a rule they accepted only those Hadith that had been transmitted through a descendant of Husayn. The major center for Shi'ite Hadith collection and analysis in the ninth century was Qum, in Iran. The scholars there refused to accept consensus and analogical reasoning as secondary sources of the law. They also espoused a view of God that was as anthropomorphic as that of the conservative Sunni Ibn Hanbal, and they were as convinced as he was that the fate of individual humans was determined in advance by God. Many also insisted that the Qur'an had been tampered with; otherwise, they said, it would be clear how central the role of 'Ali and his family was meant to have been.

Under the Buyids, Twelver scholars found a welcome home in Baghdad. In that cosmopolitan capital, a Twelver rationalist school of thought arose that challenged the traditionalism of Qum. It was in Baghdad that Mu'tazilism made its comeback after it lost support among the Sunnis. Although the Imamis and the Mu'tazilites had been associated together during the reign of the Abbasid caliph al-Ma'mun because of his patronage of both groups, their actual linkage was not firmly established until the early eleventh century. By that time, Mu'tazilism had become thoroughly discredited within Sunnism because of the ascendancy of Ash'arism, but Twelver scholars in Baghdad began to adopt it. Under Mu'tazilite influence, the anthropomorphic elements of the Qur'an began to be interpreted allegorically, humans were declared to be responsible for their own actions, and reason was accorded an important role in the development of theology. The Qur'an in its existing text was recognized as legitimate, albeit in need of esoteric interpretation.

Several eleventh-century Twelver scholars argued that the fundamental truths of religion are derived in the first instance from reason alone and that it is indefensible to rely exclusively upon the teaching of religious authorities for knowledge of them. They clearly took Twelver Shi'ism beyond the Sunni consensus that reason is to be used to defend and justify doctrine. They also made no attempt to disguise their contempt for the anthropomorphism and predestinarianism of the scholars of Qum, and they ridiculed their reliance on Hadith, claiming that the traditions were full of obvious forgeries. Later scholars recognized the importance of selected Hadith, but the victory of the rationalist school was so complete in the eleventh century that the Hadith scholars had to wait until the seventeenth century to challenge it successfully.

In practical terms, the doctrine of the Imamate and the greater Shi'ite regard for reason resulted in surprisingly few major differences between Shi'ite and Sunni versions of the Shari'a. A few differences in prescribed rituals developed. Until the twentieth century, the Friday midday service was not as important for most Twelver Sh'ites as for the Sunnis because of the absence of the Hidden Imam, the legitimate prayer leader. Twelver legal rulings sanctioned the growing practice of visiting the shrines of Imams, and for some pilgrims these trips were as important as the hajj. The most important shrines were those of 'Ali at Najaf and of Husayn at Karbala (both in Iraq) and of 'Ali al-Rida at Mashhad (in northeastern Iran). Most of the significant differences in legal practice, however, lay in provisions for marriage and inheritance. The most famous of these was the practice of temporary marriage among Twelvers:

Couples can contract a marriage for a day or longer, explicitly stipulating that it is meant to be a temporary marriage. Historically, travelers have been the most likely to contract a temporary marriage, although couples initiate it for a variety of reasons.

The Transmission of Knowledge

The ferment of ideas in the Muslim world had major consequences for the Dar al-Islam and parts of the Dar al-Kufr alike. Within the Dar al-Islam, new institutions emerged in order to preserve and transmit to future generations the knowledge that was becoming the cultural legacy of a new civilization. In the twelfth and thirteenth centuries, Europeans engaged in a massive effort to transmit the achievements of Islamic civilization to the Latin Christian civilization.

Schools

As a community based on scriptures, Islamic society had always valued education. Study was regarded not merely as an intellectual endeavor, but also as an act of piety and worship. In the earliest period of the Umma in Medina, the Prophet's compound served as his home, the communal place for prayers, and a site for religious, moral, and legal instruction. In later years, as Muslims erected mosques in the new territories that they conquered, the mosque remained the primary locus for religious instruction. Teachers would occasionally offer instruction in their homes to eager pupils, but the mosque, as the community center, offered the advantage of a large space, a central location, and the appropriately spiritual atmosphere. Mosques were usually the location where one could find the local *kuttab* or *maktab* (a school for Qur'anic instruction) and, for advanced students, courses in Hadith and grammar.

As cities grew, a distinction arose between the small, neighborhood mosques and the large, official mosques to which much of the populace and the ruling elite would repair for the main Friday noon service. The term for a mosque in general is *masjid*, from the Arabic root, *s-j-d*, meaning "to prostrate oneself" (in prayer, in this case). Most mosques are called masjids, but an officially designated central mosque is called a *jami'*, which suggests a place where a large group gathers. It is sometimes referred to as a congregational mosque, to distinguish it from the masjid, which can be quite small. The imam of a congregational mosque delivered the weekly sermon and invoked the name of the ruler and caliph, acknowledging his legitimacy. A major city such as Baghdad or Damascus had a handful of congregational mosques (although Cairo had more) and hundreds of regular masjids.

Instruction could take place in masjids, but the congregational mosques naturally assumed the most prominent role in education beyond the level offered by the kuttab. In some cases, the government appointed teachers to posts in the congregational mosques. Many teachers, however, were beneficiaries of the largesse of wealthy patrons, while others relied on the income from the tuition they charged their students. Students from out of town usually lived in a hostel, often called a *khan*, and might be the fortunate recipients of a stipend provided by a benefactor who had set up a religious endowment (*waqf*) for that purpose. Although the Shari'a prescribed how a person's estate should be allocated to his heirs, it allowed people to designate part or all of their estate to be a waqf. By setting aside part of one's estate as a waqf that would result in the construction and maintenance of a public service such as a mosque or khan, a person was gaining favor with God and prestige for his family within the community.

By the tenth century, a new type of school emerged in Khorasan that offered advantages over the mosque-school model. Perhaps originally of Buddhist origin in Central Asia, in the Islamic world it came to be called the *madrasa* (*medersa* in the Maghrib). In essence, it was a boarding school that combined teaching halls with a prayer hall and living quarters for the students, visiting scholars, and perhaps for the professor. The madrasa achieved widespread dissemination throughout the Islamic world in the second half of the eleventh century, when the Saljuq vizier Nizam al-Mulk established his Nizamiya madrasa in Baghdad and then provided the patronage for several others throughout the Saljuq realm. The institution eventually made its way across North Africa and into Andalus.

The madrasa never displaced the mosque as an educational institution. In fact, Muslims were never precise in distinguishing between the two, because education and worship took place in both. (Even the Sufi khanaqa, as a center of formal learning, was occasionally referred to as a madrasa.) The madrasa was not government-sponsored school. All madrasas were the result of personal patronage. Wealthy individuals would either provide a grant during their lifetime or leave a bequest stipulating that after their death the funds be applied toward the construction of a madrasa. A madrasa might enroll as few as ten students or as many as several hundred. The young scholars often received tuition scholarships. Sometimes they enjoyed stipends as well, but more often than not they had to pay for room and board.

Students did not seek out madrasas or mosques on the basis of an institution's reputation. Instead, students sought out individual scholars under whose tutelage they wished to study. Madrasas and mosque schools were not characterized by a formal curriculum and did not offer an institutional degree. Most schools had a single lecturer, but several scholars were available on and off campus for private study. Students came to a school not to master a given curriculum, but to deepen their mastery of a certain field of study by working closely with a prominent scholar in the field. Some students might choose to focus on Arabic grammar and would therefore explore grammar, philology, and literature. Others might focus on Qur'anic exegesis, in which case they would also mine the most influential commentaries on the Qur'an as well as become experts in Arabic grammar. Others might focus on mastering the field of Hadith studies, in which case they would study the various collections of Hadith and the biographies of the transmitters of Hadith.

Madrasas and mosques rarely taught the "foreign sciences" (science and philosophy), although many of their libraries provided interested students access to the Greek legacy, and a few professors taught them in courses that were listed under the rubric of Hadith or grammar. Usually, however, the scholars who were proficient in any of the sciences or philosophy held positions as advisors, astrologers, or physicians at the courts of rulers in the Dar al-Islam. Students who wished to learn science or philosophy usually had to seek out a scholar in the privacy of his home. The disadvantage of this system was that science and philosophy had no institutional structures within which they could develop. The critique of one's ideas and the sharing of knowledge that a community of scholars can provide were limited by the need to travel to

FIGURE 8.5 The Medersa Attarine in Fez was constructed during the 1320s by the Marinids. The madrasa gets its name from its proximity to the Souk al-Attarine, the city's spice and perfume market.

Boaz Rottem / Alamy Stock Photo.

visit other, like-minded scholars or by sending manuscripts by courier to scholars at a distance. Philosophers, in particular, were vulnerable to politically influential critics and to the whims of patrons. By the late twelfth century (the period of Ibn Rushd), they encountered greater difficulty performing their work. Religious authorities and pious scholars were relentless in their insistence on the limitations, and the dangers, of knowledge that was not intended solely for the glorification of God.

Students who engaged in advanced studies in mosques and madrasas were all respected for their knowledge of the religious sciences, but it is probably fair to say that the "stars" of the religious colleges were those who were engaged in the study of the Shari'a. After mastering the religious and linguistic subjects, they studied the sources and methodology of the law; the body of decisions arrived at in one's own school of law; differences of opinion within one's own school of law and between one's school and the other schools; and *jadal*, or dialectic, the mode of argument that in Western Europe became the heart of Scholasticism.

The typical classroom activity in learning the law involved the raising of a question—real or hypothetical—by one person (often the professor) and the reasoned response to it by another, using precedent and logic. Then, another student would attempt to rebut the reply, resulting in a "disputation." The goal of this method was to produce legal scholars who were masters of massive amounts of facts and who could organize the material into a logical manner consistent with the spirit of the Qur'an and Hadith. This practical activity, however, often carried over into public. Since there was no Nobel Prize in those days to recognize intellectual achievement, many of the legal experts felt the need to put their hard-won skills on display. Like two swordsmen, it was not uncommon to see two scholars contesting a point in an arranged public debate, each trying to bolster his reputation by defeating the other in argument.

Islamic education was based on the relationship between the student and the teacher. The students sought a license from an individual scholar, not the institution. A student might develop his skills by spending a few months with a teacher and then move on to another, or he might spend as long as twenty years with a particular scholar. When a teacher was convinced that his student had mastered the books he was studying, he granted him an *ijaza*, or imprimatur—a written statement certifying that he had placed his stamp of approval on the student. Thus, the former student had established his link in the chain of authorities stretching back to the Prophet that authenticated the texts at the core of Islam. He could go on to study with other scholars, or he could attract younger ones to himself on the basis of the seal of approval that he had gained. The silsila, or chain of authorities, was as important in the certification of scholars as it was in Sufism and the authentication of Hadith.

The students who attended mosques and madrasas were males, but education was not limited to males. Indeed, because education was perceived as a form of worship, the quest for knowledge was widely regarded as a duty of every Muslim, male or female. Some males opposed the education of female students, just as many European males opposed female education into the late nineteenth century, but such opposition was not a majority opinion. We know of no female professors or students in madrasas who taught or studied along with men; many women nevertheless received ijazas. Due to the injunctions regarding sexual propriety, it was more convenient for women to gain ijazas from relatives, who could instruct them informally rather than in a classroom setting. Nevertheless, many women studied with scholars who were not family members and received ijazas from them. Some of the scholars they studied with were men, but others were women. The daughters of the learned elite sometimes became famous Hadith transmitters themselves and were visited by students from all over the Muslim world. They bestowed ijazas upon men and women alike.

The Legacy to Europe

Although the study of science and philosophy was increasingly constrained within the Dar al-Islam, the scientific and philosophical contributions of Muslims began to be noticed by a Western Europe that was slowly recovering from the sustained economic crisis of the early medieval era. Medieval Europe had preserved very little from its Greco–Roman heritage. A few of Aristotle's treatises on logic and Plato's *Timaeus* survived in monasteries, but little else. Europeans knew Islamic culture through their acquaintance with Andalus and Sicily. As early as the tenth century, monks from France crossed the Pyrenees to study "Arabic learning." In the tenth and eleventh centuries, later generations of monks began to translate texts from Arabic to Latin. The most important of these efforts were translations of Arabic versions of Galen's medical treatises, which were done by Constantine the African in the third quarter of the eleventh century.

During the last quarter of the eleventh century, two developments in Christian Europe provided the stimulus for a wholesale appropriation of Arabic texts. The first was Europe's economic revival. The new urban centers were enjoying a building boom, universities were emerging, and a middle class was growing. The second development was the European military expansion that began annexing formerly Muslim territories. Normans established their kingdom in Sicily and southern Italy between 1060 and 1091. In Palermo, Roger established a cosmopolitan court where Greek, Arabic, and Latin were all in use, and he patronized several Muslim scholars. Southern Italy and Sicily had maintained their commercial contacts with Constantinople, and the international atmosphere in the new Norman kingdom stimulated the translation of numerous Greek and Arabic texts into Latin.

When Toledo fell to the Reconquista in 1085, a more massive process of translation began that matched the accomplishments of Baghdad's House of Wisdom two centuries earlier. Although not formally organized in the way that al-Ma'mun's institution had been, the production of Latin translations of Arabic texts in the Iberian Peninsula attracted scholars from all over Europe, and it soon became systematized. Translation centers were established in the Ebro valley, Pamplona, and Barcelona, among other places, but the most famous was at Toledo. The Toledan translation institute developed after 1165 under the leadership of Gerard of Cremona and was most notable for its translation of the works of Aristotle. The translation technique that became characteristic of these institutes entailed two steps. First, native scholars who were fluent in Arabic (a few were Muslims but most were Jews) would translate a text into a Romance dialect (usually Castilian or Catalan), and then a Latin specialist would translate it into Latin. Alternatively, since much of the corpus of Arabic texts had already been translated into Hebrew by the Jewish community of Andalus, texts were rendered directly from Hebrew into Latin. The translators found that many of the Arabic terms used in the philosophical, mathematical, alchemical, agricultural, and other texts (some of which had themselves been borrowed from Greek or Persian) had no equivalents in Latin or in the spoken languages of Europe. As a result, they were included in the Latin texts almost unchanged, introducing numerous new words into Europe (for examples of English words that are derived from Arabic, see the list in the accompanying table).

Hundreds of texts were translated. The first Latin Qur'an was produced in 1143, and two years later al-Khwarizmi's algebra appeared in Latin. The works of Aristotle, Ptolemy, Euclid, Galen, and other Greek scholars were finally available to medieval Europeans, and the Muslim scholars who elaborated upon their work, such as al-Razi, Ibn Sina, and Ibn Rushd, were acknowledged to be as authoritative as the Greeks themselves. By the thirteenth century, the pace of translation from Arabic decreased in Iberia, whereas it increased in Italy and Sicily due to the patronage of Frederick II (1198–1250).

The results of the translations were explosive. As in the Dar al-Islam, the introduction of Aristotle's works into Christian Europe caused an uproar. The primary battleground was the University of Paris, where the faculty of liberal arts fought the faculty of theology over the issue. Aristotle, Ibn Sina (Avicenna), and Ibn Rushd (Averroes) were intellectual heroes to the former and villains to the latter. In 1210, a council of bishops met in Paris to denounce heretical doctrines deriving from Aristotelianism, such as the eternity of the universe. In 1215, the university prohibited the teaching of Ibn Sina's recently translated commentaries on Aristotle, upon pain of excommunication from the Church. Despite the dangers, groups such as the

TABLE 8.1 English Words Derived from Arabic

A Select List			
admiral	azure	jar	satin
adobe	camel	jasmine	sequins
albatross	candy	lemon	sherbet
alchemy	carafe	lilac	sine
alcohol	carat	lute	soda
alcove	caravan	magazine	sofa
alfalfa	cipher	marzipan	spinach
algebra	coffee	mascara	sugar
algorithm	cotton	mask	syrup
alkali	crimson	mattress	taffeta
almanac	damask	monsoon	talc
amalgam	divan	mummy	tambourine
amber	elixir	muslin	tariff
apricot	gazelle	myrrh	tarragon
arsenal	ghoul	nadir	zenith
artichoke	giraffe	orange	zero
assassin	guitar	racquet	
azimuth	hazard	saffron	

"Aristotelians" and "Latin Averroists" sprang up. The scholars Albertus Magnus and Roger Bacon championed the reception of Aristotle's works, but the most famous Aristotelian of the period was Thomas Aquinas. Although he tried to mediate between the Averroists and those who adhered to the Platonic–Augustinian tradition, the masters of Paris condemned twelve of his own Aristotelian theses in 1277, three years after his untimely death.

The rigorous demands of scientific rationalism confronted Christians in Europe just as they had Muslims several centuries earlier. It would require several centuries for the dust to settle, but the course of events took a different turn in Western Europe from that of the Muslim world. Eventually, a Western philosophical tradition emerged that was independent of theology, and the Scientific Revolution is widely regarded to be at least in part the ultimate result of the assimilation of an Aristotelian attitude that takes the material world more seriously than did the Platonic one. Those developments are far too complex to be accounted for here, but some scholars suggest that they were made possible in part because of the institutional structure of education in Western Europe. In Western Europe, universities began to emerge out of cathedral schools in the twelfth century. Their basic curriculum was that of the seven liberal arts: the trivium (grammar, rhetoric, and logic) and the quadrivium (geometry, arithmetic, music, and astronomy). Further study could be pursued in law, theology, and medicine.

Unlike the madrasa, then, the cathedral school and the university provided an institution within which scientists, philosophers, and theologians studied in adjacent facilities. As a result, intellectuals in all disciplines were forced to grapple with issues raised in the others. Just as important in the long run was the fact that both the cathedral schools and the universities were legal corporations whose rights were guaranteed by charters. As a result, the faculties were able to set their own curriculum regardless of who endowed the school. As a consequence of these two factors, science and philosophy were able to continue to develop with institutional support despite vehement objection from critics who felt that vital religious principles such as God's absolute sovereignty were at risk. As we shall see, science and philosophy by no means disappeared in the Dar al-Islam, but the lack of a nurturing institutional environment imposed handicaps on their further development.

Conclusion

The period 950–1260 was crucial to the development of doctrines and institutions that we identify with Islam today. It is important to recognize that fact, and it is important not to distort it. Some historians have called this the Golden Age of Islam, as though the centuries after 1260 represent a decline. Others have assumed that Islam attained a fixed form during this period and has not changed significantly since then. Neither of these positions is tenable. The history of Islam shows strong parallels with the history of Christianity, in which the first three centuries were crucial for narrowing the possible routes of development of doctrine, and the next three centuries witnessed the development of its most characteristic institutions and doctrines. Both traditions continue to evolve and adapt to changing circumstances.

The period from the tenth through the thirteenth centuries is notable for the great intellectual achievements that were made in the teeth of upheavals and destruction. At a time when Europe and China were enjoying long periods of immunity from invasion, the Dar al-Islam experienced repeated episodes of destruction. Despite these obstacles, the life of the mind flourished. The impact of al-Ghazali's work in the Almoravid Empire is illustrative: Al-Ghazali wrote his *The Revival of the Religious Sciences* in the first decade of the twelfth century in Tus, and within fifteen years it was causing an upheaval in Morocco and Andalus, 3700 miles and many frontiers away. A similar rate of transmission and assimilation of a book across a comparable distance is inconceivable in any other part of the world at the time. A more well-known testament to the creativity of Muslim intellectuals during this period was the intense engagement with their thought that took place in European universities after the century-long process of translating their works into Latin.

The violence of the period may not have been without its cultural consequences, however. The rise of the khanaqa coincided with the decrease in the scope allowed for philosophical exploration among Sunnis. Some scholars have suggested that the flourishing of Sufi lodges and the proliferation of tariqas were responses to the grim security conditions of the twelfth and thirteenth centuries. Sufi brotherhoods, or orders, can be viewed as voluntary support groups that provided material and spiritual sustenance and were often linked to the *futuwwa*, the self-defense groups often found in city quarters in the eastern half of the Dar al-Islam. When the civil and military institutions failed to provide security, the brotherhoods provided spiritual comfort, collective defense, and communal aid.

Philosophical reasoning, on the other hand, was viewed by many people as a threat to the community rather than as an instrument of defense and security. That has been a common reaction in every society from the time of Socrates until now. It is a particularly characteristic response in societies whose religion is based on divine revelation because of the difficulties in defining the proper scope of reason as opposed to that of revelation. The thirteenth-century uproar in Western Europe that resulted when Aristotelianism was introduced from Andalus is a case in point. The contrast between the fate of philosophy in Western Europe (where it subsequently thrived) and in the Dar al-Islam (where it subsequently struggled) is quite striking. No definitive explanation is possible at this time, but it is useful to keep in mind that Christians in Western Europe no longer worried about the survival of their civilization. They were actually confident and aggressive. Muslims of the thirteenth century, on the other hand, had to wonder what God had in store for them next. From Andalus to eastern Iran, entire societies had been destroyed or were under siege. This was a time to conserve what was certain and not to speculate on the possible, particularly when such speculation could injure the faith.

A striking characteristic of this period is that Iraq ceased to be the center of intellectual creativity. Important work continued to be produced there, but the intellectual "stars" tended to come from Andalus and the Persian cultural area. Particularly noteworthy is the Persian language renaissance of this period. This was a movement that began in the mid-ninth century but gained momentum only under the Samanids in the late tenth century. Thereafter, work in the Persian language became highly creative. For the first time, the religion and culture of Islam became available in a language other than Arabic. Most of the powerful Turkic dynasties that ruled large areas of the Dar al-Islam for the next seven centuries adopted the Persian culture for their court, with the result that Persian styles became dominant from Anatolia to India. Arabic continued to be the primary language of the religious disciplines and of science and philosophy, but Persian became the language of belles-lettres and was increasingly used as a language of scholarship as well.

NOTES

1 From *The Shambhala Guide to Sufism*, by Carl W. Ernst Ph. D., ©1997 by Carl W. Ernst. Reprinted by arrangement with The Permissions Company, Inc., on behalf of Shambhala Publications Inc., Boulder, Colorado, www.shambhala.com. The discussion on pp. 157–178 is particularly useful. For another excellent discussion of Sufi poetry, see Annemarie Schimmel, *Mystical Dimensions of Islam* (Chapel Hill, North Carolina: The University of North Carolina Press, 1975), 287–343.

FURTHER READING

Science and Philosophy

Nasr, Seyyed Hossein. *Three Muslim Sages: Avicenna, Suhrawardi, Ibn 'Arabi*. Delray, New York: Caravan Books, 1976.

Peters, F.E. *Allah's Commonwealth: A History of Islam in the Near East 600–1100 A.D.* New York: Simon and Schuster, 1973.

Starr, S. Frederick. *Lost Enlightenment: Central Asia's Golden Age from the Arab Conquest to Tamerlane*. Princeton and Oxford, U.K.: Princeton University Press, 2013.

Turner, Howard R. *Science in Medieval Islam: An Illustrated Introduction.* Austin, Texas: University of Texas Press, 1995.

Watt, William Montgomery. *Islamic Philosophy and Theology: An Extended Survey.* Reprint Edition. Edinburgh, U.K.: Edinburgh University Press, 1996.

Watt, W. Montgomery. *The Formative Period of Islamic Thought.* Edinburgh, U.K.: Edinburgh University Press, 1973. http://www-history.mcs.st-andrews.ac.uk/Indexes/Arabs.html

Consolidating Institutions: Sufism

Cornell, Vincent J. *Realm of the Saint: Power and Authority in Moroccan Sufism.* Austin, Texas: University of Texas Press, 1998.

Ernst, Carl W. *Sufism: An Introduction to the Mystical Tradition of Islam.* Boston and London: Shambhala, 2007, 2011.

Knysh, Alexander. *Islamic Mysticism: A Short History.* Leiden, Boston, Koln: Brill, 2000.

Schimmel, Annemarie. *Mystical Dimensions of Islam.* Chapel Hill, North Carolina: The University of North Carolina Press, 1975.

Trimingham, J. Spencer. *The Sufi Orders in Islam.* Reprint, intro by Voll. New York: Oxford University Press, 1998.

Consolidating Institutions: Shi'ism

Daftary, Farhad. *The Ismailis: Their History and Doctrines.* Cambridge, U.K.: Cambridge University Press, 1990.

Madelung, Wilferd. *Religious Trends in Early Islamic Iran.* Albany, New York: Persian Heritage Foundation, 1988.

Momen, Moojan. *An Introduction to Shi'i Islam.* New Haven, Connecticut: Yale University Press, 1985.

The Transmission of Knowledge

Berkey, Jonathan. *The Transmission of Knowledge in Medieval Cairo.* Princeton, New Jersey: Princeton University Press, 1992.

Chamberlain, Michael. *Knowledge and Social Practice in Medieval Damascus, 1190–1350.* New York: Cambridge University Press, 1994.

Colish, Marcia L. *Medieval Foundations of the Western Intellectual Tradition, 400–1400.* New Haven and London: Yale University Press, 1997.

Halm, Heinz. *The Fatimids and Their Traditions of Learning.* London: I.B. Tauris in association with The Institute of Ismaili Studies, 1997.

Huff, Toby E. *The Rise of Early Modern Science: Islam, China, and the West.* Cambridge, U.K.: Cambridge University Press, 1995.

Lyons, Jonathan. *The House of Wisdom: How the Arabs Transformed Western Civilization.* New York: Bloomsbury Press, 2010.

Pedersen, Johannes. *The Arabic Book.* Trans. Geoffrey French. Princeton, New Jersey: Princeton University Press, 1984.

CHAPTER 9

The Muslim Commonwealth

The Arabs who participated in the conquests of the first century of Islamic history had been driven by an esprit de corps that allowed them to dominate their huge empire for a century despite serious internal feuding. By the Abbasid period, however, no single ethnic group could generate a similar dynamism. Moreover, the fact that the new empire attempted to base its legitimacy on a monotheistic religion practically guaranteed eventual fragmentation. Whereas polytheism offers a wide range of religious expression for a society's members and can defuse conflicts over religious issues, monotheism is typically plagued by clashes over the correct interpretation of the one true faith. Ethnic, religious, and purely personal factors splintered the political unity of the Muslim Umma within a short time.

On the other hand, among many Muslims the sense of belonging to a single community provided a powerful bond that transcended linguistic and other cultural differences that could have proved ultimately divisive. A Muslim empire ruled by an Arab oligarchy was gradually replaced by what some scholars call a "Muslim commonwealth" in which individual Muslims found a common identity with others all across the Dar al-Islam. The fact that there were multiple caliphs did not create sharp divisions among the mass of Muslims except among zealots. The Qur'an was the common text of all Muslims regardless of sect, and one's devotion to it made him or her a self-conscious member of a well-defined community, clearly set apart from those who did not recognize it. It was written in the Arabic language, which also served as the medium of commentaries on the Qur'an, devotional materials, and legal thought. Despite the decline in political importance of the Arabs themselves, their language permeated the entire Dar al-Islam as the primary language of learning, even in the face of the persistence—and even revival—of certain local languages. By mastering Arabic, an individual could converse with educated Muslims everywhere and could take advantage of a valued skill that could lead to high-status careers in law or education in general.

The Muslim world developed a cultural unity despite the overthrow of the Arab empire of the Umayyads and the rapid disintegration of Abbasid power. From the tenth through the thirteenth centuries, Shi'ites, Sunnis, and shamanists held power in several different areas of the Muslim world; Iranians, Berbers, Turks, Kurds, and Mongols replaced Arabs as the ruling ethnic group in several polities; and utter devastation occurred in several areas. Nevertheless, the development of a distinctive Islamic culture continued without interruption. Just as the Shari'a had developed independently of state patronage, so the economic, social, and cultural life of the Muslims continued to develop without reliance on any given political order.

Remarkably, the rise of numerous independent Muslim states did not result in a reassertion of the barriers that had hindered commerce and cultural exchanges between Byzantines and Sasanians. Although Muslim states feuded with each other, they did not erect obstacles to travel, trade, or the pilgrimage to Mecca. Scholars, missionaries, merchants, and pilgrims traveled widely throughout the Dar al-Islam and communicated developments in law, science, engineering, devotional material, etiquette, and numerous other facets of the various evolving Islamic societies over vast distances. The different regions of the Muslim world retained unique characteristics inherited from their pre-Islamic culture, but they were increasingly able to share a common Islamic culture as well.

Frontiers and Identities

Today, after two centuries of experience with nationalism and the nation–state, we take for granted clearly demarcated boundaries, checkpoints, passports and visas, nationalist emotions, patriotism, and numerous other characteristics of nationhood. These paraphernalia of the modern nation–state are, in historical terms, recent phenomena. When studying the premodern history of any region of the world, it is important to understand that boundaries and personal identities functioned quite differently from the ways they do now.

Frontiers Defining the Dar al-Islam

When nation–states became defined in the modern period, physical features such as rivers, mountain ranges, and straits were convenient and easily recognized markers that could serve as fixed borders for the countries that shared them. In the premodern era, such phenomena were not viewed as dividing lines. The Strait of Gibraltar, for instance, which so "obviously" separates Africa and Europe to modern eyes, was not viewed as a border by the inhabitants of Iberia or North Africa in the period under review. The Umayyads of Andalus, the Almoravids, the Almohads, and later, Spain, considered the strait a water highway.

Rather than relying on borders, rulers had a sense of where their effective power lay and where it diminished. Cities were the seat of power for Muslim rulers, and in their vicinity their troops wielded effective control (as long as they were not rioting themselves), but the further away from the city, the less control was exercised. This was particularly the case when the territory at a distance from the capital was mountainous or arid. Such areas were too unproductive to justify the expense of administration, and they provided havens for rebels. Much as the illuminated areas of individual street lamps at night fade imperceptibly into the penumbra that lies between them, so there existed "penumbras of power" between rival polities where legitimate authority was ambiguous and where warlords, bandits, or adventurers of various types operated with considerable impunity. The best that the central government could hope to do was to play one group in these penumbras against another. This would effect at least temporary cooperation by means of bribes or punitive expeditions.

There were two types of land frontiers: one separated the Dar al-Islam from the Dar al-Kufr, and the other separated the realm of one Muslim ruler from another. The former, of course, was usually the most dramatic, because the jurists agreed that Muslims were under an obligation to conduct jihad into lands unfortunate enough not to be under the guidance of the Shari'a. Raids were not only permitted, but encouraged, into the Dar al-Kufr, and only there could one enslave people. The land frontier of the Dar al-Islam was thousands of miles long, and conditions varied from region to region. Along the Saharan frontier in North Africa and in the region now occupied by Pakistan and Afghanistan, Muslims did not face major competing powers due to huge expanses of desert or formidable mountain ranges. In the northeast, the frontier beyond Transoxiana was highly active and proved to be a conduit for numerous nomadic Turkic and Mongol groups. For almost a thousand years, the Central Asian frontier would prove to be a lucrative route to China, a source of manpower renewal and ethnic diversity for the Umma, and the origin for occasionally catastrophic blows to lives and property.

At both ends of the Mediterranean, a quite different frontier evolved from that in North Africa and on the eastern edges of the Iranian cultural zone. In Andalus and Anatolia, Muslim and Christian powers faced each other for centuries across frontiers that might vary from ten to one hundred miles wide. The frontier in either zone would shift from time to time and, due to almost constant raiding and skirmishing, some parts of it were depopulated. When an army from one side attacked the other, it departed from heavily populated areas defended by forts and passed through less densely populated areas. Eventually, the troops encountered only widely scattered, impoverished settlements, interspersed with gradually decreasing numbers of friendly fortified outposts. The army then began confronting enemy outposts, more and more enemy settlements, and then the enemy's populated regions.

For more than two centuries, the Duero River valley in the Iberian Peninsula served as the center of the frontier between Muslim and Christian authority. This no man's land was subject to sudden raids by murabitun from the Muslim side and their counterparts from the Christian side. Little is known of the nature of the Christian irregulars along the frontier during the early centuries of the history of Andalus, but the advent of the Almohads spurred the Christian kingdoms to approve the creation of three monastic orders of knights (Santiago, Alcantara, and Calatrava), which were modeled after the murabitun.

Nevertheless, the dynamic of life along the frontier was not characterized by unremitting hostility toward the other side. Despite the demands of distant popes to conquer the entire peninsula, Christian rulers operated within specific local restraints and opportunities, and people who lived on the frontier often found that they had much in common with the "enemy" who lived in their vicinity. The Umayyads of Andalus were usually preoccupied with subduing recalcitrant petty Muslim rulers rather than trying to expand into Christian territory. As we have seen, Muslim rulers sometimes allied with Christian rulers against fellow Muslims, and Christians allied with Muslims against fellow Christians.

Even some of the greatest heroes of the faith on both sides reveal a striking ambiguity of cultural, and even religious, loyalty. The most famous of these was probably El Cid, or Rodrigo Diaz de Vivar, one of the most celebrated figures of the Reconquista. A Christian nobleman from Castile, he lost favor in Castile and moved to Zaragoza, where he served the Muslim ruler there for a decade, fighting both Christian and Muslim rivals of his master. During the mid-1080s, he refused to become involved in the critical campaigns against the invading Almoravids when they posed a genuine threat to the existence of an independent Christian presence in the peninsula. When he had the chance, he seized the Muslim city of Valencia in 1094 and ruled it independently until his death in 1099, defying rival Muslim and Christian rulers. Diaz's ambivalent identity is apparent in the honorific by which he is known —"El Cid"—which derives from the term *al-sayyid*, an Arabic term of respect and honor. The legend that grew up around El Cid over subsequent centuries, portraying him as a champion of Christianity against Islam, was the result of a highly selective approach to his career.

A similar situation existed along the Anatolian frontier. The Taurus Mountains, as well defined as they are, did not suggest to either the Muslims or the Byzantines a natural border between the Dar al-Islam and the Byzantine Empire. Although the Arab conquests did not push westward of them by much, Arab settlements did slowly extend onto the Anatolian plateau. The Arabs also swept to the northeast of the Taurus into Azerbaijan. As early as the reign of the Abbasid caliph al-Mansur (754–775), volunteers from Khorasan moved to this Byzantine frontier in order to engage in both commerce and jihad. Most of the Arab settlers lived in towns, the largest of which were Malatya and Tarsus, the home of the Apostle Paul.

Both Malatya and Tarsus served as bases for attacks on the Byzantines, but Tarsus presents a special case. For the first two centuries of the Abbasid era, the city's economy was dependent on the institutionalization of jihad, or *ghaza*, as it was sometimes rendered. The latter term was an Arabic word used to refer to bedouin raids in the Arabian Peninsula. A raider in such an attack was a *ghazi*. Although jihad—usually understood as a war of conquest for the propagation of Islam or a war in defense of Islam against an outside threat—technically has a different connotation from ghaza, the chroniclers who reported on the activities of the Arab–Byzantine frontier used the two words interchangeably.

By the tenth century, the concept of jihad had become central to Muslim identity and had endowed frontiers with cosmic significance. By this time, the Shari'a divided the world into two realms, the Dar al-Islam and the Dar al-Harb. A dweller in the realm of war was an enemy to whom the law offered no protection. Muslims had an obligation to attack him in his own realm, and if he entered the realm of Islam and was killed, no one was held culpable. Conflict with the inhabitants of the Dar al-Harb was assumed to last until the end of time. A permanent peace with the infidels was, therefore, an impossibility. A ruler could arrange a temporary truce if it served the interests of the Umma, but it was not legally binding. Jihad was understood to be a *collective* obligation: A group of Muslims had to be fighting at all times, or the community was guilty of a sin against God. Jihad became an *individual* obligation only when the Muslim ruler mobilized an army in response to an enemy invasion.

Jihad was a serious matter of shedding blood, and so the jurists framed it with numerous qualifications. A Muslim ruler could not declare jihad without first calling on the target population to accept Islam or pay the head tax as a mark of tributary status. It was permissible to kill infidel warriors, but not women, children, old men, the blind, or lunatics, unless they were unexpectedly engaged in warfare. A Muslim commander was given wide latitude in his choice of disposing of male prisoners. He could kill them, enslave them, or free them as tributary subjects, but he could not allow them to return to the realm of the infidel. Women and children could only be enslaved or freed as tributary subjects. The rationale for these options was that returning a non-Muslim to the Dar al-Harb would extend the length of time necessary to conquer it, and the Shari'a did not provide for the possibility of an infidel's permanent residence in the realm of Islam other than as a slave or tributary subject.

To be a *mujahid* ("one who engages in jihad") was a matter of high status because it entailed the risk of martyrdom in service to God. Thus, although young men were obligated to engage in jihad only in order to ward off an invasion, many engaged in it voluntarily as a rite of passage. Many engaged in raids for a short time before entering their intended careers as craftsmen, merchants, or scholars. Doing so not only gained them religious merit but also raised their standing in society. Other ghazis were Sufis who saw jihad to be the outward expression of their inward quest. Still others made an occupation of raiding (some of them became quite wealthy from the spoils of war). The largest cities of the empire—particularly those on the Iranian plateau—financed the construction of ribats in Tarsus where their young men could stay while engaging in jihad/ghaza. They also supplied them with food and spending money until they acquired spoils from their raids. Muslims clearly viewed Tarsus as a permanent base for raiding Byzantine lands, and the expansion of territory was not the objective. This phase of ghaza ended in 965, when the Byzantines embarked on their reconquest of the area and depopulated Tarsus.

The Byzantine frontier again became the scene of institutionalized raiding under the Turks a century later. As we have seen, the first bands of Turkish herdsmen who entered the Buyid realms of the Dar al-Islam in the early eleventh century caused havoc in Iran, Iraq, and Azerbaijan. When the Saljuqs replaced the Buyids at mid-century, they tried to direct the herdsmen's attention to Anatolia and away from Muslim territory. After Manzikert, in 1071, most of the Anatolian plateau lay open to the herdsmen. Christian villagers remained the majority population on the Anatolian plateau for two or three more centuries, but the constant threat from raiders increasingly concentrated the Christian population along the edges of the peninsula. During the twelfth and thirteenth centuries, Armenian Christians were concentrated in eastern Anatolia and in south-central Anatolia around the bend of the Mediterranean (Cilicia), while Orthodox Christians were concentrated in the extreme western littoral and along the Black Sea coast. As the Sultanate of Rum grew in power at Konya from 1116 until its defeat at the hands of the Golden Horde in 1243, Turkish raiders operated in the zones between the Sultanate of Rum and the Christian societies.

The Turkish raiders of the no man's land between Muslim and Christian polities were known as *gazis* (the Turkish language does not have the guttural *gh* of

Arabic). The Turks of Central Asia, like the bedouin of the Arabian Peninsula, regarded raiding as part of their pattern of subsistence, to supplement the meager return from their herds of animals. When they arrived in Anatolia, they typically did not immediately settle down but rather continued to herd and raid. They soon learned that, whereas raids on Muslim neighbors resulted in unpleasant punishment from the central authorities, those same authorities encouraged the raiding of nearby Christian territories.

The Turks, like the Arabs before them, rationalized their raids as a religious act, and other Muslims came to understand them as such. The frontier society of the gazis offered an adrenaline rush to adventurers, a sense of freedom to those who felt oppressed under a centralized government, the possibility of wealth to the needy, and a ripe field of untutored souls to the missionary. Like most frontier areas, it was egalitarian in the sense that if a man could contribute to the goals of the group, he was accepted into it. Despite the fact that gaza (the Turkish version of *ghaza*) was increasingly rationalized as a specifically Islamic religious act, identities and loyalties were as fluid as on the Iberian frontier. Occasionally, Christians who had been victimized by gazas sought to join a gazi band, in a classic example of the attitude expressed by the phrase, "if you can't beat them, join them." Gazis not only accepted non-Muslims (and non-Turkish Muslims) as compatriots but also shared the spoils equally with them. A Christian ruler (ostensibly defending his realm against the Muslim threat) who was fighting a fellow Christian would occasionally invite gazis to join him in a campaign, and gazis would occasionally seek alliances with Christian rulers against "wayward" fellow Muslims.

Jihad in the Shari'a

This selection regarding the rules pertaining to jihad comes from a legal treatise by the Egyptian Shafi'i scholar Ahmad ibn al-Naqib (d. 1368). Jurists from the other schools of law differed over details (some would reject the permissibility of destroying property of the enemy, for example), but this text reflects a widespread conception of jihad: The Dar al-Islam is in a constant state of potential or actual war with the Dar al-Harb; actual conflict should be taking place somewhere at all times; the engagement in jihad by a few Muslims relieves the obligation on the Umma as a whole; jihad is viewed as both a defensive reaction against hostile non-Muslims and as an aggressive act that follows a rejected ultimatum from a Muslim ruler to non-Muslims in the Dar al-Harb to accept Islam or pay the poll tax.

Jihad is a communal obligation. When enough people perform it to successfully accomplish it, it is no longer obligatory upon others. Jihad is personally obligatory upon all those present in the battle lines. Jihad is also obligatory for everyone when the enemy has surrounded the Muslims. Those called upon are every able-bodied man who has reached puberty and is sane …

It is offensive to conduct a military expedition against hostile non-Muslims without the caliph's permission.

Muslims may not seek help from non-Muslim allies unless the Muslims are considerably outnumbered and the allies are of goodwill towards the Muslims.

The caliph makes war upon Jews, Christians, and Zoroastrians until they become Muslim or else pay the non-Muslim poll tax [and thereby become dhimmis]. The caliph fights all other peoples [idolaters] until they become Muslim.

It is not permissible to kill women or children unless they are fighting against the Muslims. Nor is it permissible to kill animals, unless they are being ridden into battle against the Muslims, or if killing them will help defeat the enemy. It is permissible to kill old men and monks [who fight Muslims]. It is unlawful to kill a non-Muslim to whom a Muslim has given his guarantee of protection provided the protecting Muslim has reached puberty, is sane, and does so voluntarily.

Whoever enters Islam before being captured may not be killed or his property confiscated, or his young children taken captive. When a child or a woman is taken captive, they become slaves by the fact of capture, and the woman's previous marriage is immediately annulled. When an adult male is taken captive, the caliph considers the interests [of the community] and decides between the prisoner's death, slavery, release without paying anything, or ransoming himself in exchange for money or for a Muslim captive held by the enemy. If the prisoner becomes a Muslim then he may not be killed, and one of the other three alternatives is chosen.

It is permissible in jihad to cut down the enemy's trees and destroy their dwellings.

A free male Muslim who has reached puberty and is sane is entitled to the spoils of battle when he has participated in a battle to the end of it. After personal booty, the collective spoils of the battle are divided into five parts. The first fifth is set aside, and the remaining four are distributed, one share to each infantryman and three shares to each cavalryman. From these latter four fifths also, a token payment is given at the leader's discretion to women, children, and non-Muslim participants on the Muslim side. A combatant only takes possession of his share of the spoils at the official division.

As for personal booty, anyone who, despite resistance, kills one of the enemy or effectively incapacitates him, risking his own life thereby, is entitled to whatever he can take from the enemy, meaning as much as he can take away with him in the battle, such as a mount, clothes, weaponry, money, or other ….

SOURCE: Ibn al-Naqib, Ahmad ibn Lu'lu'. *Reliance of the Traveller: A Classic Manual of Islamic Sacred Law.* Edited and translated by Nuh Ha Mim Keller. Revised edition. Beltsville, Maryland: Amana Publications, 1999, 600–606.

Since gazis accepted non-Muslims into their raiding societies, it is not surprising to learn that they were more tolerant of religious differences than most urban Muslims were. On the one hand, they became much more active as missionaries than the ulama in any time or place have been; on the other hand, they commonly venerated the shrines of local Christian saints, just as Christians of the rural areas visited Muslim spiritual teachers and venerated the shrines of Muslim saints. Gazi society was characterized by folk religion rather than by the intellectualized and formal Islam of the cities. As such, its version of Islam was often scorned by the ulama. Illiteracy was high in rural areas anywhere; the uncertainties and fluidity of the frontier could only exacerbate the situation. Inevitably, religion on the frontier was different from its urban cousin, and it was syncretistic, whether among Christians or Muslims. The Turkish nomads and semi-nomads themselves were originally shamanists. As they passed through Iran and into Anatolia, they picked up their knowledge of Islam from popular preachers, Sufi adepts, and members of persecuted sects who sought the safety of remote regions out of fear of persecution. In the process, they combined elements of their original spiritual practices with Shi'ism, Sunnism, popular Christianity, and other local religious legacies.

Frontiers within the Dar al-Islam

If hostile empires failed to demarcate exact boundaries between each other, the separation of Muslim polities from each other was even more imprecise. Like the frontiers that surrounded the Dar al-Islam, internal frontiers were a function of the diminishing power that cities exerted over their hinterland. Deserts, mountains, and sheer distance ultimately reduced the power of a Muslim ruler until he had to cooperate with regional strongmen, who in turn had to negotiate with rulers on their other frontiers. Thus, travel among the various Muslim polities required flexibility and adaptation to changing circumstances, but it was rarely complicated by legal obstacles.

In order to understand the achievements of the peoples of the Muslim world prior to the formation of nation–states, it is important to realize that they were able to travel remarkably freely, regardless of their religious affiliation. When traveling from one part of the Muslim world to another, they would be recognized as *different* from the indigenous inhabitants, but they were not regarded as *alien*. Linguistic barriers were not a major concern, either, since traveling scholars and merchants of any of the three main religions knew at least some Arabic, which played the role of an international language throughout the Dar al-Islam just as Latin did in Western Europe. Due to the patronage of Persian literature by the Samanids and Ghaznavids, the Persian language increasingly became the lingua franca from Iran to South Asia.

The major challenge that travelers faced was posed not by powerful Muslim rulers but rather by the absence of such power in the frontier regions. It was there that scholars, merchants, pilgrims, and others who were traveling overland were most likely to be attacked by bandits. If they survived the hazards of the less secure areas, they would not know when they had passed definitively from one "country" to another until they approached towns and cities dominated by a different amir. Upon entering the gates to the town, they would encounter customs booths and other signs of official monitoring. Local authorities would check the travelers' papers. In spite of the technical legal vulnerabilities of inhabitants of the Dar al-Kufr who ventured into the Dar al-Islam, they were rarely harassed if they followed protocol. Whereas passports were not required, officials would make sure that foreigners from the Dar al-Kufr paid for the protection that they would enjoy and that Christians and Jews from other regions in the Dar al-Islam were carrying documentation that they had paid their taxes in their home regions.

Identities

Prior to the spread of the nationalist idea in the nineteenth century, the concept of "nationality" or "citizenship" was extremely rare, with the Roman Empire being one of the few exceptions. Otherwise, people conceived of their personal identity in terms of family lineage, residence in a particular village or city, participation in the rituals of a given religion, and the language they spoke. Within the Dar al-Islam, the most important identities were those defined and addressed by the Shari'a. Among these were religious affiliation, gender, and slavery. The issues of religious identity and the status of women are discussed in other sections of this book, but, at this point, a few observations on slavery are in order. In addition, the issue of ethnicity bears some exploration. Although it was not an issue of concern to jurists, it played an important role in the perceptions of others, in self-perception, and in the development of cultural expressions.

Slavery

Until the modern period, slavery was practiced in almost every known society. No one wanted to be a slave, but hardly anyone had ethical objections to its practice in principle. The scriptures of Islam, like those of Judaism and Christianity, assumed the existence of the institution of slavery and did not condemn it. On the contrary, the scriptures and their commentaries addressed slaves and slave owners alike, providing them with guidance in how to relate to each other. Although the Shari'a condoned slavery, it prohibited the enslavement of both Muslims and dhimmis. Unlike the Christian world, the Umma also forbade the imposition of slavery as a punishment for debt or crime. Thus, to be a slave in the Muslim world one was born to slave parents, captured in campaigns of conquest, or purchased from abroad. Like the Roman and Greek worlds but unlike the plantation slavery of the early modern period, slaves in the Muslim world were used primarily for domestic purposes or in the military and less in agriculture and mining. Slaves were not unknown in large-scale agriculture and mining: The late ninth-century Zanj revolt in southern Iraq was the best-known case of the agricultural use of slavery, although slaves were also used on a few large estates in Andalus and North Africa. Crews of slaves were also doomed to the brutal and hopeless conditions of salt mines in the Sahara and gold mines of Nubia. Nevertheless, nothing in the records available to us now suggests that agriculture and mining were reliant to a large degree on slave labor. Slaves were used primarily in homes, shops, and the military, and as tutors and entertainers in the palace.

Most of the earliest slaves owned by Muslims were captured in warfare, but by the Abbasid period, that source dried up considerably. The raids of Mahmud of Ghazna once again brought in a vast quantity of slaves, this time from India—contemporary accounts report a figure of over 50,000 Indian captives as part of the pillaging in the raid of 1018 alone—but conquest ceased being a primary source of slaves. Most slaves originated from outside the Dar al-Islam, and they were purchased at huge slave markets. Many came from Africa, but even more came from Europe. The European slaves were usually referred to as Greeks or Slavs. Andalus became a thriving entrepôt of the European slave traffic, and it was serviced primarily by Catalan

FIGURE 9.1 The mud wall around old Sana'a, Yemen. In arid climates, both buildings and city walls could be kept in good repair even when made of mud.

and Italian merchants. Egypt, too, had a famous slave market, which offered for sale slaves from Africa and Europe alike. With the increasing demand for Turks in the many Muslim armies of the Dar al-Islam, Transoxiana became a major market in the long-distance slave trade. From the Samanid regime until the end of the fifteenth century, the trade in Turkic slaves became an important pillar of the economy of the region.

Muslims viewed slavery with ambivalence. On the one hand, jurists ensured the legal existence of the institution by formulating a myriad of regulations that became enshrined in the Shari'a. Slaves were legally property and could not own or inherit property themselves. Courts of law usually did not accept their testimony. A slave owner had unlimited sexual access to his female slaves. According to Sunni legal schools, slaves were not to hold jurisdiction over freemen and were not to exercise religious functions.

On the other hand, the Shari'a admonished slave owners to treat their slaves humanely, and families commonly adopted their slaves. The Qur'an and Hadith made clear that the manumission of slaves was a commendable act, and the Shari'a provided various ways for manumission to happen. A master who stated in the presence of a witness, even in jest, that his slave was free would have to give him his freedom. Slaves could purchase their freedom if their masters were willing to part with them. A concubine who gave birth to the children of her master could not be sold thereafter; on his death, she and her children were free, and her children had a legal right to his property on the same basis as the children of his wife or wives. The concubines of caliphs were in a particularly ambiguous position. Technically slaves, their sons could become caliphs. The last two Umayyad caliphs were the sons of slave mothers, and all but the first Abbasid caliph were the sons of concubines.

Like concubines, eunuchs held an ambiguous social position. The Qur'an forbade the mutilation of slaves, and the Shari'a reinforced the stricture. As a result, it was illegal to castrate individuals within the Dar al-Islam, but a thriving trade developed for individuals who were emasculated on the frontiers. Most eunuchs were either Slavs or Africans, and although they are most famous for their role in the harems of powerful men, they also served as custodians of the Ka'ba and the tombs of famous individuals. Moreover, within the Fatimid Empire some eunuchs managed to gain a certain revenge for their mutilation as they became powerful military or political figures who wielded enormous authority over free Muslims. Jawhar not only served as commander of the Fatimid armies but also exercised absolute power in the process of consolidating Fatimid power over Egypt in preparation for the arrival of al-Mu'izz. Several other eunuchs were Fatimid military leaders, governors of towns and provinces, chiefs of police, and muhtasibs.

The most distinctive feature of slavery in the Muslim world, however, was the widespread use of slave armies. Between the early ninth century, when the Abbasid caliph al-Mu'tasim began building his slave units, to the thirteenth century, most armies between Egypt and Central Asia became organized around a nucleus of slaves. The Abbasids sought to avoid having to depend on the bedouin, who had provided the support for the Umayyad regime; a few decades later, they wanted to dispense with the Khorasani guard, which had begun to expect extra consideration for its role in the destruction of the Umayyads. The Buyids needed Turks to supplement their own Daylami infantry, and the Fatimids needed units of various types in order to be able to compete as a great power. Slave armies were, indeed, dependent on their patron and usually fanatically loyal. On the other hand, they perceived how vulnerable they were in the event of a cutoff of support, and they could turn on their master in a moment. For them to seize power themselves was hardly a possibility that al-Mu'tasim or any other of the early rulers could have entertained, but it was a logical step for the Ghaznavids and Mamluks.

Ethnicity

The strength of ethnic identities varied with period and place. During the Umayyad period, non-Arab Muslims discovered that their ethnic identity automatically classified them as inferior to the Arabs, and it is clear that during the Abbasid period, ethnic tensions within the armies were a major cause of strife. Because of their dependence on the ruler, slave soldiers were sensitive to any signal that another group was gaining an advantage over them, for such a development could be life-threatening. Within the larger society, ethnic identity remained important, if not as divisive as during the first century of Islam. In Andalus, Berbers felt that the Arabs never fully accepted them, right down to the end of the Reconquista. Like the Arabs, the Turks who invaded Southwest Asia in the eleventh century considered themselves superior to the peoples whom they conquered. The Saljuqs, in particular, made it clear that they were proud of their Turkish heritage even while they were adapting to the mores and customs of their Iranian and Arab subjects.

Perhaps the most impressive instance of ethnic assertion, however, was the revival of certain aspects of Persian culture in the ninth and tenth centuries. The Arabic language had been the medium of religious scholarship for Muslims from the beginning, it had become the language of administration in the late Umayyad and early Abbasid regimes, and it had rapidly become a lingua franca for commerce and poetry throughout the Dar al-Islam by the ninth century. However, Persian remained the spoken language east of Iraq, and it soon became a major literary vehicle. The Tahirid regime, which served as governors for the Abbasid caliphate (821–873), began patronizing Persian literature; the Saffarid state (867–963) continued the tradition; and the Samanid state (892–1005) developed a special interest in the cultivation of Persian literature at its court in Bukhara. Dialects of Persian had long been the language of commerce for the overland trade in Central Asia, and with the aid of court patronage, the Dari dialect of Persian now became a language of high culture.

In part, the revival of the Persian language was an expression of Iranian pride and resentment against Arab domination, causing a controversy as early as the eighth century that pitted proponents of Iranian culture against defenders of Arab preeminence. The poets and writers whose creativity produced the new Persian language, however, were not reluctant to borrow Arabic themes, styles, and vocabulary, as well as the Arabic alphabet. Except for the Qur'an itself, the texts of Islam became available in a language other than Arabic for the first time. By the thirteenth century, some of the greatest Sufi literature would be written in Persian.

Because Arabic continued to be the dominant language of religious scholarship even in Iran, it was in the secular arts that the Persian themes particularly flourished. Numerous lyric poets attained a high degree of proficiency, but perhaps the most famous of the medieval Persian works of literature was Ferdowsi's *Shah-nameh* (1010). Sasanian values and styles were also revived in political writings, inscriptions and coins, court ceremonies, architecture, and painting. The glittering culture impressed Turkic newcomers, who, although proud of their own identity, readily accepted the Perso–Islamic elite culture for their own purposes. Ferdowsi's dedication of his masterpiece to a Turkic ruler, consequently, was not merely in default of having a Persian-speaking regime to which to give it. Both the Ghaznavid and Saljuq regimes cultivated the Persian culture and adopted Persian as the language of administration (except for use in the Shari'a courts). Their patronage of Persian culture laid the foundation for it to become the elite culture of South Asia for several centuries.

The City and the Countryside

Throughout history, cities have served as the centers of government, commerce, and culture for most societies. They had higher death rates than did the villages because disease was more likely to be spread from person to person in the crowded cities. Many rural folks might also view the cities as dens of vice or as enclaves for the rapacious classes that sought to enrich themselves at the expense of the peasants. Nevertheless, cities possessed the allure of wealth, power, and entertainment for rural inhabitants, and other than during periods of catastrophe, the migration pattern tended to be from the village to the city.

The City

As in all premodern civilizations, only a minority of the population of the Dar al-Islam lived in towns and cities. On the other hand, only China, among other regions of the world, could claim to have as many large towns and cities as the Muslim world did. The new patterns of trade and expansion that the Arab conquest helped to create had a powerful impact on the region's urban life. Not all cities shared the same experience. The truncation of the Byzantine Empire and the long-term, intermittent naval warfare in the eastern Mediterranean had a negative impact for three centuries on cities such as Alexandria and Antioch; a few interior cities, such as Hira, lost their raison d'être altogether and disappeared; others, such as the caravan cities of Rayy and Hamadan, experienced an economic boom because of the stimulus for overland trade; whereas numerous others, such as Kufa, Basra, and Sijilmasa, were created for the first time.

Cities in the Muslim world had their own "personalities," just as cities such as London and Paris differ today. They were located in a wide variety of settings. Access to water inevitably shaped the city's contours: Some were on the coast, while others were on rivers, in oases, in the plains, or nestled in hills. Most were in arid to semiarid climates and used primarily mud-brick construction, but some were located in areas of moderate rainfall and needed to use stone as the primary building material. Mud-brick construction tended to result in low skylines, but some stone towns and villages, particularly in Yemen and southern Morocco, contained buildings that rose ten or more floors. The legacies of Indian, Sasanian, Hellenistic, Byzantine, Roman, and Visigothic cultures, among others, influenced elements from architectural styles to the prevalence of bathhouses, churches, synagogues, gardens, and plazas. Some cities appeared from a distance as colorless as the earth that surrounded them, while others were highlighted with glittering tiles or whitewash that covered the entirety of congregational mosques and other public buildings. As a result, travelers often remarked on the distinctive appearance of cities from one region of the Dar al-Islam to the other.

The center of public life in Muslim cities was the mosque. Cities contained numerous neighborhood mosques in which the pious would perform their daily devotions, but the officially designated congregational mosques were the preferred venue for the Friday noon prayer and sermon. They were also the setting for primary schools and higher education, they served as a forum for deliberations and the expression of public opinion, and they were restful havens when the crush of urban life created the need for repose and quiet. Their minarets might be thin or thick, round or square, but they served as a beacon to prayer and a reassurance of the Islamic character of the society in which the traveler found himself.

The congregational mosque was necessarily surrounded by a large public space or square. Typically, the square connected the mosque with the central market. Muslim cities had one or more major markets, and most of the quarters of the city had smaller local markets. The large market might be either open air or enclosed. Some enclosed markets in capital cities were huge, and over the centuries they might grow until they extended for a mile or more. The markets were usually organized according to the product being sold, so that the merchants of rugs and carpets would be consolidated in one area, while those who sold pots and pans of copper, brass, and other metals would be clustered together, and the sellers of glass objects operated their shops in their own sector. Often the shops in which the articles were sold also served as the workshop in which they had been produced. The butchers, tanners of leather, and blacksmiths, however, were almost always confined to the outskirts of the city for hygienic purposes or to reduce noise. Likewise, caravansaries tended to be located at the city's edge. In some important caravan cities, thousands of camels, donkeys, and other beasts of burden might be constantly coming into the city's environs, and the local inhabitants thought it best to keep both the animals and the foreign merchants at a distance.

European visitors to thirteenth-century Andalus and fourteenth-century Muslim India commented on the attention to cleanliness characteristic of the cities in those regions. All across the Dar al-Islam, cities boasted numerous bathhouses. The public bath, of course, was not unique to the Muslim world. It was a legacy of Roman and Hellenistic societies. Islamic insistence on ritual purity before prayer, however, ensured that the institution would flourish in the Muslim world. Muslim cities from Andalus to India enthusiastically adopted the bath, modifying its layout and function according to their needs. Because of its primary purpose, the larger baths were usually adjacent to the congregational mosques. Muslims soon had to admit that, quite apart from its function in providing the required ablution, the bath was admirably suited for the objectives for which the Romans most valued it: relaxation and social interaction. Muslims devoted much energy and attention to the construction and maintenance of baths, washing facilities, drains, and latrines, even as these amenities declined in use in Western Europe after the collapse of the western Roman Empire.

Cemeteries were usually situated outside the walls of the town. Their layout reflected the Muslim preference to be buried facing Mecca. They tended to be active social areas. Groups of Sufis might live adjacent to the tomb of the master who began their method of achieving spiritual insight, and the tomb might well attract pilgrims, who often lent a festive air to the vicinity. Townspeople often visited the graves of family members and used the cemetery as picnic grounds and strolling areas. Also located outside the city walls might be a *musalla*, or place to perform the salat, for festivals or other occasions when such a huge number of worshipers assembled together that even the congregational mosque was not large enough to hold them.

Residential neighborhoods in Muslim cities were nearly self-contained quarters. Pre-Islamic towns in the Arabian Peninsula had been organized by families and clans, so it was natural that garrison cities such as Kufa and Basra were organized along the same lines. Arab immigrants who settled in existing cities in Iraq, Syria, and Egypt followed a similar pattern. Even as more and more of the dhimmis converted to Islam in places as far apart as North Africa and Khorasan, most—but not all—cities in the Muslim world became organized into quarters that were based on kinship, ethnic group, religion, or occupation. They might contain a few hundred or a few thousand residents, and each would typically be served by a local mosque, market, public bath(s), and perhaps its own cemetery.

Cities in the Dar al-Islam did not develop municipal institutions that assumed responsibility for the governance of a legally defined urban area. Thus, the inhabitants of each quarter had to provide essential services such as the adjudication of conflicts, security, sanitation, and the delivery of tax revenues to the authorities. Facilities such as hospitals, neighborhood mosques, fountains, madrasas, khans, and public baths were usually funded by waqfs, the religious endowments provided by private individuals. Although some of the services that a quarter provided—most obviously the provision of water and sewerage facilities—required cooperation with other sections of the city, the quarters nevertheless were self-reliant and had a sense of territoriality and identity.

A city's residential quarters were not easily accessible by the wider public. The wide streets in the vicinity of the main mosque, which had to accommodate hundreds, if not thousands, of persons, branched off into smaller arteries that in turn branched off into still narrower lanes that twisted and turned and finally came to an end as culs-de-sac in front of the doors of a handful of residences in the residential quarter. The streets in most cities anywhere in the world at the time would seem labyrinthine to modern observers, but the layout of cities in the predominantly Muslim world had a special character. When thirteenth-century Aragonese (whose cities would seem claustrophobic and mazelike to us) began consolidating their hold on Valencia, they expressed their astonishment at the narrow, twisting streets and confusing layout of the Muslim cities there.

In part, this pattern can be explained by the fact that wide streets were not required in a society almost utterly devoid of wheeled vehicles. In addition, streets usually followed the contours of the elevation in order to facilitate drainage after rains. In many cases, too, individuals tended to associate with family members, members of the same craft or occupation, or fellow members of a religious sect or ethnic group in a particular neighborhood and deliberately set it off from other

FIGURE 9.2 The corridor-like streets of a residential neighborhood in Fez, Morocco.

Georg Gerster / Science Source.

neighborhoods. Modes of transportation, terrain, and affinity groups explain only part of the unique layout of Muslim cities, however. In the Iberian Peninsula, where one could expect continuity in the shape of cities over time, the Reconquista brought about a striking change: When the Portuguese, Castilians, and Aragonese built over preexisting Muslim cities, the new cities included twenty-five percent more public space than the Muslims had provided.

Clearly other forces were at work, whether in Iberia or India. Some are attributable to Islam and others are not. One is a concern with privacy and gender segregation, which has both pre-Islamic and Islamic roots. Pre-Islamic housing in North Africa, for example, was characterized by an absence of ground-floor windows and few windows on the upper floors. In part, this was a function of the heavy walls needed to insulate rooms and the need to reduce the amount of light entering the house. Courtyards allowed the occupants access to fresh air and sunshine without having to be in the public eye. This concern for privacy extends even to the tents of nomads, where it seems likely that male and female spaces were demarcated even before the advent of Islam.

Instances of this pre-Islamic concern for privacy could no doubt be multiplied across the vast world of Islam. On the other hand, certain features of the Qur'an, Hadith, and Shari'a also encouraged a consciousness of privacy that was given expression in the design of buildings and streets. In order to ensure family privacy and modesty, qadis frequently ruled on the height of buildings, the placement of windows, and the comportment of individuals. Not all Muslims lived in courtyard houses, but the Islamic concern for privacy and gender segregation reinforced any preexisting parallels, affecting the whole range of housing from one-room structures to vast palatial complexes. In addition, qadis tended to favor the individual's property rights over concerns for the collective good except in the case of an overriding moral principle such as privacy. As a result, property owners had relatively free rein in their wish to build. Thus, buildings were allowed to infringe on public space, transforming streets into narrow, twisting defiles. The maze of streets created in effect an informal zoning system, which kept public activities and strangers away from most residential homes.

The labyrinthine nature of the streets also contributed to the security of a residential quarter. Anyone crossing a city kept to the public areas; a stranger who wandered into a residential area would be immediately noticed and monitored, if not accosted. During normal times, the head of the leading family of the quarter was responsible for maintaining order. His job was made easier by the presence of a massive gate that closed off entry to a quarter at night. During periods when the central authority was weak, neighborhood security in cities from Anatolia through Iran was often assumed by groups of local youths. These were called *futuwwa* orders (sometimes also called *'ayyar* in the Arabic-speaking regions and *ahi* in the Turkish-speaking regions). *Futuwwa* in Arabic literally means "youth," and the motivation for the earliest futuwwa orders was a moral one. Most of them had a code of behavior stressing altruism, generosity, patience, gravity, and justice. Many of their members were models of the best civic and moral behavior. As a result, Sufi orders often became linked with them, and Sufis as far away as Morocco would later adopt their regimen as part of their own code of behavior.

Some of the futuwwa orders promoted sports activities, others were related to specific crafts, and others were mutual aid societies. The perceived obligation to help others contributed to the evolution of some futuwwa orders into militias when the power of the amir or sultan was weak and troops or police might not be reliable. Unfortunately, the young men could sometimes act more like youth gangs than disciplined militias, and they could be more of a threat to the local residents than they were a source of security. As a result, the term '*ayyar* is often used by the chroniclers to mean "brigands" or "troublemakers."

The futuwwa thus had an ambiguous status in society and an ambivalent relationship with the social and political authorities. They could be a force for cohesion or for disruption. On the whole, they tended to express the energies and causes of the disadvantaged and could applaud what they saw as "Robin Hood" behavior. The Abbasid caliph al-Nasir (1180–1225), who gained his autonomy from the Saljuqs, tried to institutionalize the futuwwa movement to further his own cause of social and political reform, but the destruction of the Abbasid caliphate soon thereafter ended whatever progress he may have made in that direction.

By the thirteenth century, cities all across the Muslim world were slowly assuming a variation of the same pattern. There was no blueprint for such a Muslim city—as we have seen, Baghdad began as a meticulously planned, circular city. Esfahan, Herat, and Shiraz also began as circular cities, but their original plans were submerged under the pattern that became the dominant model throughout the Dar al-Islam by the thirteenth century. Hamadan's original, square design was likewise lost to the characteristic model. Cities otherwise as culturally distinct as Herat in Afghanistan (founded by Alexander the Great), Baghdad in Iraq (carefully planned as the imperial capital of a Muslim empire), and Fez in Morocco (established by refugees from Arabia) all slowly adapted in their own way to the model.

The Countryside

The vast majority of people in the Dar al-Islam lived in rural areas. Most lived in villages, and their livelihoods were tied to agriculture. In some areas, such as Yemen, Lebanon, and Morocco, villages could be built in remote mountainous areas and the peasants tilled fields that had been carved out of the sides of the mountains as terraces. Perched on precipices and constructed out of local stone or even lava, such villages were virtual fortresses that discouraged attacks from their neighbors. Aside from perpetual feuds with neighboring villages, the lives of their inhabitants were relatively unmolested. Most peasants, however, lived in the fertile river valleys or plains, where they were subject to outside intervention. The food and fiber that they produced were essential to the survival of the local town and city, and therefore the local governor exerted considerable efforts to ensure that they were under his control.

Villages throughout the Dar al-Islam had traditionally been autonomous in the sense that they were self-governing. Christian and Jewish villages were allowed to practice their own preferred system of law. The villagers in Iraq and Iran were the first to feel the effects of the iqta' in the tenth century. As we have seen, the Buyids introduced the iqta' into Iraq. Later, the Saljuqs, Ayyubids, and Mamluks adopted the practice. An iqta' was originally a specified tract of land (usually agricultural land and the villages that supplied the manpower for it) temporarily assigned to a military officer in return for equipping, paying, and supplying a number of soldiers to the service of the sultan. The holders of the early iqta's knew that their possession of the land was temporary, and their sole interest was to exploit it. Typically, they neglected maintenance of the irrigation systems and extracted exorbitant taxes from the unlucky peasants. The consequences for agriculture were catastrophic in some areas. Because of the debts that cultivators amassed under such conditions, they could be tied to the land as securely as the serfs in Western Europe. When the Saljuqs made iqta's inheritable, peasants reaped the benefits, as managers began to take an interest in long-term investments.

In addition to the exploitation that they usually experienced at the hands of local elites, many of the peasants from North Africa to Transoxiana were subject to the depredations of nomads. Most of the time, peasants and nomads lived in a symbiotic relationship with each other. The pure nomads required the grains, fruits, and tools that peasants could provide, while the peasants purchased draft animals, wool, and hides from the nomads. Many of the bedouin were not pure nomads but seminomads who cultivated fields for part of the year and spent the rest of the year in pastures. Because of their wanderings, both types of nomads often encroached on the fields of peasants. In the ensuing quarrels, the nomads had the upper hand in mobility and martial training, and the peasants usually lost. The temptation for bedouin to raid the storage sheds of cultivators was always great, and because of the nomads' ability to subsist in harsh environments, it was difficult, if not impossible, for central authorities to punish them.

With the widespread breakdown in central authority during the tenth and eleventh centuries, the bedouin increased their depredations in the area from Iraq to Morocco, with the result that large tracts of cultivated land were abandoned. The twelfth century witnessed the violence caused by several Crusades, the Almoravids, the Almohads, and the endemic warfare of the late Saljuq period; it was followed by the two thirteenth-century Mongol invasions. The voiceless people of the countryside endured a degree of suffering that most of us cannot even imagine.

Nomads and peasants had little access to education or formal religious instruction. The bedouin, in particular, were scorned by urban populations for their irreligion. Groups such as the Almoravids and the Almohads, who conquered under the banner of Islam, were regarded with jaundiced eye by many merchants and artisans, who regarded their versions of Islam with suspicion and condescension. These Berber peoples at least had been instructed in the faith; most nomads were quite ignorant of the basics of Islam. Muslim peasants almost always had access to a village mosque, but their imam was unlikely to be well educated. Many of the parents in the village would be satisfied if he could teach their children the Arabic alphabet and drill them until they had memorized the Qur'an. Because villagers and nomads had an uncertain grasp of the doctrines of Islam, they were even more likely than their low-income cousins in the city to have recourse to pre-Islamic religious practices that the ulama condemned. They, however, turned to whatever could help them find meaning in an otherwise crushing existence.

Conversion to Islam

A major development in world history was the achievement by 1300 of a Muslim majority in the region from North Africa to Iran. This outcome is not surprising, but it was also not inevitable. Muslim military conquests outside the Arabian Peninsula were never followed by rapid widespread conversion. The mere imposition of Muslim political rule was sufficient to change the status of a country from the Dar al-Kufr to the Dar al-Islam. The Shari'a recognized the existence of non-Muslim populations within the Muslim state and granted them a wide degree of autonomy in the application of their law and customs, as long as they paid their taxes. The government's need for the taxes was a major reason why it did not encourage large-scale conversions.

A Muslim Minority

Conversion rates were slow during the Umayyad caliphate of Damascus and for some time thereafter in most parts of the Umma. The Umayyads themselves were in part responsible for this. They assumed that Islam was for Arabs and that it was better for non-Muslims to pay taxes rather than to convert and not pay taxes. Other factors were at work as well. Christians and Jews continued to have access to important government offices for centuries in various parts of the Islamic world. As long as lucrative and prestigious employment was possible and conversion was optional, it was natural to continue with one's traditional religion. Christians dominated the financial bureaucracy of the Egyptian bureaucracy until the late nineteenth century, and more than one Christian served as wazir in the Fatimid state. Jews, especially, served as personal physicians to Muslim rulers from Andalus to Iran. Personal physicians to rulers had unusually open access to the center of power, and their broad education often made them the most qualified officials in the palace. Some of them wielded considerable influence (and a corresponding vulnerability when things went wrong).

One's place in the social structure also played a role in rates of conversion. Peasants in most areas of the empire had little contact with the culture of the conquerors except with the hated and feared tax collector. As a result, they were even slower to convert than urban dwellers. Terrain also played a factor. The formidable mountains of the Taurus, Zagros, Elburz, Lebanon, and Anti-Lebanon ranges in the east and the Atlas and other ranges in North Africa were home to many peoples who were there precisely because they wished to avoid contact with the central authority. Shielded by the rugged terrain, they were more trouble to subdue than they were worth to any imperial government until the late twentieth century. As a result, they remained unconverted for centuries. If and when these groups did convert, it was often to a minority version of Islam, such as Shi'ism or Kharijism, and the mountainous areas in southwestern Asia and North Africa have remained refuges of minority groups to the present day.

The continuing presence of large numbers of dhimmis within the Dar al-Islam did not lead to anything comparable to the European Christian social pathology known as anti-Semitism. Large numbers of Christians and Jews in Muslim-ruled societies were an unwelcome reminder that not everyone had recognized Muhammad as the Prophet, just as the presence of Jews in Europe were a reminder that not everyone recognized Jesus as the Christ. But whereas Christian anti-Semitism in Europe was widespread, continuous, and often resulted in violence against Jews, severe discrimination against dhimmis was rare in the Dar al-Islam. There were, indeed, fanatical members of the ulama who demanded that amirs or caliphs enact harsh measures against <u>dh</u>immis, but rulers rarely listened to them. Occasional discrimination against Christians and Jews did occur, most notably under the Fatimid Imam al-Hakim, during the Zirid regime in Granada, and under the late thirteenth-century Mamluks. Overall, however, Jews and Christians fared much better under Muslim rule than Jews did under Christian rule. As we will see, most of the Jews who fled Christian Spain in 1492 fled to Muslim-ruled territories.

<u>Dh</u>immis were, to be sure, distinct from the Muslim population. In many cities, they tended to be concentrated in certain quarters of the city (although rarely were they the exclusive residents of a given quarter). They paid the poll tax, and ulama developed sumptuary laws to regulate their behavior. These laws were irregularly enforced: The Umayyad caliph of Damascus 'Umar II and the Fatimid caliph al-Hakim were exceptional precisely because they enforced such laws. Nevertheless, they were on the books and were a constant reminder to Jews and Christians that they were subject, if protected, peoples. Examples of such regulations were the requirement to wear distinctive dress and to avoid wearing colors—particularly green—associated with the Prophet, a prohibition against carrying arms and riding horses, and a prohibition against building new places of worship and repairing old ones without permission.

Although some of the later Shi'ites believed that eating with, or perhaps even touching, <u>dh</u>immis would obligate a Shi'ite to perform full ablutions in order to remove the taint, most Muslims enjoyed unrestricted interaction with Christians and Jews and often celebrated their holidays with them. The Sunni schools of law agreed that meats prepared by Jews according to kosher practices satisfied the ritual prescriptions of the Shari'a. On the other hand, apostasy from Islam to Judaism or Christianity was punished severely and often resulted in death. Muslim men could marry non-Muslim women (many marriages in the ruling class were of this type), but a Muslim woman could not marry a non-Muslim man. Implicit in this custom, of course, was the assumption that the male was the head of the family and that his religion would influence the rest of the family's members.

The Pace of Conversion Quickens

Forces were at work that did encourage conversion, however. Some were what may be termed negative factors. Christians or Jews might seek to escape paying the <u>dh</u>immi tax, to gain legal equality with Muslims, or to improve their social status. It is significant that the weakening of central authority seems to have played a role in mass conversion. In Iraq, for example, the Nestorian community had maintained excellent relations with both the Umayyad and Abbasid administrations and had avoided subjection to the more onerous features of the sumptuary laws. That changed with the caliphate of al-Mutawakkil (847–861), who was confronted with his fractious army, the expensive new capital at Samarra, and the explosive debate between the Mu'tazilites and Hanbalis over the relative merits of reason and revelation. The caliph, desperately seeking allies in his struggles, yielded to the demands of the antirationalist Hanbalis and enforced harsher regulations. After the middle of the ninth century, the quality of life for Nestorians deteriorated markedly, and conversion rates rose.

The "bedouinization" of large parts of Iraq and eastern Syria during the tenth and eleventh centuries also accelerated the conversion process. The reassertion of bedouin autonomy in Syria and Iraq occurred simultaneously with the Hilali invasion of North Africa and bedouin predations in Egypt. The result was the raiding of villages and towns and the disruption of agriculture. The poor, as always, suffered, but in the long run it was the ruin of the landowning and merchant elite and of the monasteries that broke down the institutional structures of the Christian and Jewish communities in these areas and led to their replacement by Islamic institutions.

On the other hand, it is highly unlikely that most converts to Islam left their original religious affiliation for "negative" reasons. Some did so primarily because they had been impressed by the piety and spirituality of individual Muslims or because they found the simple, yet profound monotheism of Islam a more convincing model of the meaning of the universe than any other religion with which they were familiar. Many converts, no doubt, changed their religious affiliation for reasons they would have had difficulty articulating, because the change simply seemed like the natural thing to do. A variety of factors, positive and negative, would accumulate in their experience, and the impulse to convert was less explicit and conscious than tacit.

Today, many of us find it difficult to understand how individuals could change religions without coercion. Religious identity in premodern societies, however, was typically not a matter of an individual commitment to a set of doctrines. Rather, it was the product of one's community and involved ritual and the body of laws that guided one's life. When one's social situation changed, it was appropriate to change one's religion. In some cases, individuals made the switch, but we see many incidents in which whole families or communities voluntarily converted en masse.

The military garrison cities played a major role in this process of gradual conversion. Founded in order to isolate the Arabs from the surrounding population, they quickly became centers for the dissemination of the Arabic–Islamic culture instead. Whether in Egypt, Iraq, or Khorasan, the large cantonments served as magnets for local craftsmen, traders, household servants, entertainers, and scholars. The policy of cultural insulation collapsed as economic symbiosis became a fact of life. Some non-Muslims became acculturated to the norms of the dominant cultural group by having learned the Arabic language and having adopted new habits of dress and manners. The adoption of the Arabs' religion was a next, natural step. For others, the process was reversed: Adoption of Islam led to cultural assimilation.

The process of assimilation was never a one-way process, however, as we saw when the Arabs adapted many Byzantine and Sasanian governmental practices to their own purposes. On the individual level, as well, one adapted to one's environment. In Khorasan, where tens of thousands of Arab warriors settled during the last third of the seventh century, Arabs assimilated to the local culture more dramatically than elsewhere. Not only were Arab soldiers placed in the garrison city of Merv, but they also settled in numerous small Iranian communities. Ordinary villagers and townsmen mixed frequently with Arabs, and the two cultures assimilated. The two groups engaged in a high degree of intermarriage, Arabs adopted Iranian dialects, and many Khorasanis converted to Islam during the early eighth century. Arab and Khorasani Muslims were already making common cause when Abbasid propaganda began to appeal to them, and ethnic distinctions became less and less apparent.

Later, the rise and increasing independence of the Tahirid, Saffarid, and Samanid dynasties from about 820 on seems to have accelerated the conversion process not only within Khorasan but also throughout the Persian cultural area. These Iranian dynasties were explicitly Muslim, and yet they encouraged the development of a new Persian literature. The new literature used the Arabic alphabet and borrowed motifs from Arabic poetry, but it glorified themes from pre-Islamic Iranian history and myth. By reasserting an Iranian cultural identity within an explicitly Islamic context, this literary and cultural movement seems to have been particularly effective in enabling Iranians to make the transition from Zoroastrianism to Islam seem less of a betrayal of one's tradition and identity.

The rate at which conversion took place is not known, because chroniclers of the day did not comment on it. Richard Bulliet's statistical analysis[1] of the history of the adoption of Muslim names in Iran makes a strong case for assuming that, by the mid-ninth century, half the population of Iran had converted to Islam and that, by 882, half the population of Iraq was Muslim. He concludes that, by the beginning of the eleventh century, perhaps eighty percent of the population of Iran was Muslim. This method of calculating the rate of conversion is useful, but while the evidence for certain cities has to be taken seriously, generalizations can mask local variations. The cities in the regions of Fars, Jibal, and Kirman in Iran, for example, remained strongholds of Sasanian and Zoroastrian loyalties until at least the middle of the eleventh century. The populations of the major mountain ranges do not appear to have become Muslim before the twelfth century.

FIGURE 9.3 A typical residential street in old Tunis, Tunisia, illustrating the emphasis on privacy to be found throughout most of the Dar al-Islam.

No agreement exists on when the population of other areas of the Dar al-Islam became a Muslim majority. Many scholars would agree that Syria and Egypt became majority Muslim societies sometime between the twelfth and fourteenth centuries but cannot be more specific than that. That would be 500 to 700 years after the Arab conquests. Regions as distant as Andalus, as we have seen, present special problems. The proclamation of the caliphate suggests a self-confident and dominant Muslim community, and yet scholars cannot agree on whether Islam was ever the majority religion there. Christianity seems to have disappeared from North Africa by the end of the eleventh century—the century of great disorder in Ifriqiya—but Judaism continued to maintain a viable presence there.

As the proportion of Muslims in the population increased and the influence of the ulama over the people and the rulers was consequently enhanced, the position of dhimmis deteriorated. The ulama tended to insist that rulers enforce sumptuary laws as a matter of obedience to the will of God. Mobs could put pressure on the political authorities to remove non-Muslim officials, and the safety of other members of the non-Muslim communities would be threatened by association. During periods of distress, large numbers converted to escape the humiliating conditions and the physical dangers they entailed.

The Issue of Authority in the Muslim World

Ironically, the process of conversion to Islam seems to have contributed not only to social tension but also to the breakdown of political unity in the Dar al-Islam. As long as the Muslims were a minority ruling elite, they had a vested interest in maintaining ties of affinity with each other across great distances. Whenever the percentage of Muslims in a given society approached half the population, the Muslims found themselves pulled by a variety of identities—familial, social, and ethnic—that often competed with their sense of being a part of the Umma. Just as social clashes among the Muslims within each polity increased, so did the likelihood of breaking from a caliph's political authority.

The office of the caliphate was a unifying factor in the early history of Islam, for it was the locus of political and religious authority for most Muslims. It proved to be a combination of fragility and durability over the first six centuries of Islam. It emerged as an ad hoc measure to carry on the work of the Umma in the absence of the Prophet. It was not a constitutional office—it was explicitly provided for neither by the Qur'an nor by the Prophet's instructions—and two issues remained controversial: the responsibilities and powers of the office, and the provision for succession to the office in the event of a vacancy.

A significant minority within the Umma rejected the Umayyad and Abbasid caliphs as illegitimate on the grounds that they were not lineally associated with 'Ali, whom they believed to have been the Prophet's choice to have been his successor. The numerous factions that adhered to this conviction were collectively known as Shi'ites, and they followed their own candidates as the true Imam/caliph. Increasingly, as it became clear that their Imams (with the exception of the Fatimids) would have little or no chance to wield political power, the figure of the Imam became one of heightened spirituality, a figure to whom God had granted spiritual insight available to no other mortal.

By contrast, the Sunni caliphal dynasties increasingly accentuated their worldly power by means of constructing finer palace complexes, devising ornate ceremonies, and taking on the trappings of a monarchy in general. Some of the early Abbasid caliphs did make at least implicit claims for more than mere temporal power: al-Mahdi (775–785); al-Hadi, "the Guide" (785–786); and al-Ma'mun, "the Trustworthy" (813–833)—who introduced the title of Imam for all subsequent Abbasid caliphs— were obviously attempting to compete with the Shi'ite doctrine of the Imamate. Nevertheless, they never took the task seriously enough to initiate a doctrinal change.

The true status of the Sunni caliphate became clear as early as 756, when the new Umayyad regime in Andalus refused to recognize the Abbasid caliph. Rather than being considered apostates for having rejected God's deputy, the Umayyads of Andalus were considered merely political rebels. Moreover, the Umayyad princes of Andalus did not feel compelled at the time to claim the caliphate for themselves. They claimed only the title of *amir* ("commander" or "prince"), leaving the relationship between the Muslims of Andalus and the caliph in suspension. The Abbasid caliph had no political or economic claim on the Muslims of Andalus and had no way of imposing religious doctrines or rituals on them. Iberian Muslims in effect had no caliph, and yet they were not the less Muslim for that. Thus, the Abbasid caliphate from its beginning revealed itself to be a dynastic monarchy, despite its appeal to Islamic legitimacy.

In the early tenth century, two new caliphates in North Africa and Andalus arose to contest the monopoly of an increasingly beleaguered Abbasid caliphate. By the middle of that century, the Abbasid caliph was a mere figurehead for a military regime that administered affairs in Iraq and western Iran. After three centuries, Muslim society was further away than ever from achieving a synthesis between Islamic political ideals and Islamic political practice. The Umma had fragmented into such conflicting groups that a consensus regarding the structure and functioning of governance appeared impossible. Kharijites argued that a caliph was not even necessary if God's law was being followed; the various Shi'ite groups agreed that the Abbasids and Umayyads should not be caliphs but disagreed over who should replace them as the Imam/caliph; the Fatimids, the one Shi'ite faction that did install its chosen Imam, soon settled in Egypt but did surprisingly little to transform their society; and Sunnis were dispersed throughout the three competing caliphates as well as in several autonomous provinces whose rulers paid only lip service to the Abbasid caliph.

Shi'ite scholars were greatly preoccupied with defining the meaning and importance of the Imam, who was central to their whole belief system. Sunnis, however, devoted surprisingly little scholarship to the topic of the caliph. Most references to the office appear in the work of legal scholars who were trying to connect the implementation of the Shari'a to his office. The first major systematic work that analyzed the nature of the Abbasid caliphate appeared only in the eleventh century, from the pen of al-Mawardi (d. 1058). His *The Rules of Governance* was written during the caliphate of al-Qa'im (1031–1075), who began asserting some independence of action against his Buyid amir. Al-Mawardi's book boldly declared that the caliph was still the chief executive of the Umma and was entrusted by God for a wide range of responsibilities: protecting the traditional interpretation of Islam from the designs of innovators, enforcing the provisions of the Shari'a, defending the borders of the

Dar al-Islam, combating unbelievers until they accept Muslim rule, levying taxes, regulating public expenditure, and appointing qualified people to public office. Most of these functions, of course, were performed by the Buyid amir, but al-Mawardi blithely argued that this was due to the fact that the caliph had the prerogative of delegating his powers; if these responsibilities were usurped or otherwise corrupted, the caliph had the right of summoning aid to restore his rightful powers.

Al-Qa'im welcomed the advent of the Saljuq conqueror Tughril Bey in 1055, but any anticipated liberation from the restricted role that the Buyids had imposed upon him turned out to be chimerical. The Sunni Saljuqs were no more willing than the Shi'ite Buyids to allow al-Qa'im or any other caliph to reassert the power of his Abbasid predecessors. The cleavage between al-Mawardi's vision and political reality continued under the Saljuqs. Their leaders adopted the title of *sultan*, which derives from the Arabic word *sultah*, meaning "power." The sultan claimed to wield power at the pleasure of the caliph, just as the Buyid amirs had. Resigning themselves to the fact that it was unlikely that the caliph would be actively involved in their governance, Sunni jurists accepted al-Mawardi's idea of the delegation of powers by the caliph to justify the system that was in place. Scholars such as al-Ghazali (d. 1111), who was born the year that al-Mawardi died, insisted on obedience to governmental authority in the absence of a regularly constituted caliphate. His widely quoted argument was that the anarchy that would result from a rebellion against an unjust ruler would be more detrimental to the purposes of God than the ruler himself was.

We do not have a clear understanding of how Andalusi Muslims viewed the religious authority of their Umayyad caliph. At any rate, their caliphate disintegrated early in the eleventh century, and during its span of a century, it had almost no effect on the lives of Muslims outside the Iberian Peninsula. The Fatimid caliphate, although in theory invested with a high degree of religious and political authority, shrank to insignificance after little more than a century of its conquest of Egypt. Although the Abbasid caliphate under al-Nasir (1180–1225) did manage to regain control over a small state in Iraq for a short time during the twelfth and thirteenth centuries, it played no active role in most Muslims' lives after the ninth century due to the political disintegration of the empire. This is an important point, because many general history books portray the Abbasid caliphate as though it led a powerful empire until 1258 and discuss Hulagu's destruction of the caliphate as though it had dire repercussions throughout the Muslim world.

The Abbasid caliphate lost both political and religious power in the ninth century, but it did play an important *symbolic* role in the lives of many Sunnis in the Muslim East (and to a lesser extent in North Africa) for a long time after that. Despite the caliph's de facto inability to impose his political or religious authority on anyone, Sunni religious teachers taught that he was the supreme head of all the Muslims. In the minds of the faithful, he represented an unbroken line of succession of authority and served as a symbol of Muslim unity from the time of the Prophet himself. He continued to serve as a source of legitimacy for many provincial rulers, as many Muslim rulers from the Maghrib to India sought an official document from the caliph certifying that they had been "appointed" or "delegated" to rule on behalf of the caliph. These same rulers usually minted coins bearing the name of the caliph as well as themselves, and they ordered that the name of the caliph be recited at the

Friday sermon. The weaker the caliph was, the more convenient regional rulers found it to acknowledge his theoretical suzerainty. Hulagu's brutal destruction of the Abbasid caliphate was no doubt temporarily troubling to many Sunnis at the personal level, but it had no effect on the political order in the Dar al-Islam outside the environs of Baghdad.

Conclusion

The enormous ambition of the Arab empire of the early eighth century was radically scaled down by Abbasid times. There was no single "Islamic" empire even at the start of the Abbasid period due to the loss of much of North Africa and Andalus. By the end of the ninth century, most of the remainder of the old Umayyad empire had slipped from Baghdad's control as well. The chances that the physical dimensions of the original Arab-dominated empire could have remained intact, of course, were practically nonexistent. The breathtaking size of that empire challenged any attempts to provide security, and the plethora of cultures that the conquests had brought together complicated the task of identifying a common interest. And yet, a culture grew up across the breadth of the Muslim world that facilitated travel, commerce, scholarship, and technological innovation.

Perhaps the most interesting and ultimately determining feature of the Muslim commonwealth was that, in the absence of a single leader who combined both religious and temporal authority, the importance of the legal schools and their scholars became magnified. In an unusual development, the "law" that most people felt compelled to obey was not developed by their government but by independent scholars: the jurists. A few of them served as qadis for the various rulers, but most remained private citizens, engaging in frequent discussion with others like themselves in an attempt to reach agreement on the finer points of living a life pleasing to God. Some of them traveled widely, sharing thoughts with other jurists in distant parts of the Dar al-Islam. As a rule, they were much more respected than government officials themselves. As we have seen, the rulers developed their own set of commercial and criminal laws to supplement the Shari'a, but these had little impact on the majority of Muslims. Muslims expected their governments to enforce the Shari'a, but they knew that governments had not created it—it came ultimately from God, mediated through the jurists. A tension existed between the governments and the interpreters of the law that would shape Muslim history for centuries to come.

NOTES

1 Richard Bulliet, *Conversion to Islam in the Medieval Period: An Essay in Quantitative History*. Cambridge, Massachusetts: Harvard University Press, 1979.

FURTHER READING

For a good discussion of the concept of a Muslim commonwealth see Garth Fowden, *Empire to Commonwealth: Consequences of Monotheism in Late Antiquity*. Princeton, New Jersey: Princeton University Press, 1993, passim, and Hugh Kennedy, *The Prophet and the Age of the Caliphates: The Islamic Near East from the Sixth to the Eleventh Century*. London and New York: Longman, 1986, 200–211.

Frontiers and Identities

Bonner, Michael. *Aristocratic Violence and Holy War: Studies in the Jihad and the Arab–Byzantine Frontier*. New Haven, Connecticut: American Oriental Society, 1996.

Brauer, Ralph W. *Boundaries and Frontiers in Medieval Muslim Geography*. Transactions of the American Philosophical Society. Vol. 85, Pt. 6. Philadelphia: The American Philosophical Society, 1995.

Chabbi, J. "Ribāt." In *The Encyclopedia of Islam, New Edition*. Vol. VIII. Leiden: E.J. Brill, 1995.

Goitein, S.D. *A Mediterranean Society*. Vol. I. Berkeley, California: University of California Press, 1967.

Hambly, Gavin R.G., ed. *Women in the Medieval Islamic World: Power, Patronage, and Piety*. New York: St. Martin's Press, 1998.

Imber, Colin. *Ebu's-su'ud: The Islamic Legal Tradition*. Stanford, California: Stanford University Press, 1997.

Lewis, Bernard. *Race and Slavery in the Middle East: An Historical Inquiry*. New York: Oxford University Press, 1990.

Mélikoff, I. "Ghāzī." In *The Encyclopedia of Islam, New Edition*. Vol. II. Leiden: E.J. Brill, 1983.

Peters, Rudolph. *Jihad in Classical and Modern Islam: A Reader*. Princeton, New Jersey: Markus Wiener, 1996.

Wink, Andre. *Al-Hind: The Making of the Indo–Islamic World*. Vol. I: *Early Medieval India and the Expansion of Islam, 7–11e*. Leiden: E.J. Brill, 1990.

The City and the Countryside

Abu-Lughod, Janet L. "The Islamic City—Historic Myth, Islamic Essence, and Contemporary Relevance." *International Journal of Middle East Studies*, 19 (1987), 155–176.

Ahsan, Muhammad Manazir. *Social Life Under the Abbasids*. London and New York: Longman, 1979.

Brown, L. Carl, ed. *From Madina to Metropolis: Heritage and Change in the Near Eastern City*. Princeton, New Jersey: The Darwin Press, 1973.

Burns, Robert J. *Islam Under the Crusaders*. Princeton, New Jersey: Princeton University Press, 1973.

Hourani, Albert, and S.M. Stern, eds. *The Islamic City: A Colloquium*. Oxford, U.K.: Bruno Cassirer, 1970.

Insoll, Timothy. *The Archaeology of Islam*. Oxford, U.K.: Blackwell Publishers, 1999.

Lambton, Ann K.S. *Continuity and Change in Medieval Persia: Aspects of Administrative, Economic, and Social History, 11th–14th Century*. Albany, New York: State University of New York Press, 1988.

Wheatley, Paul. *The Places Where Men Pray Together: Cities in Islamic Lands, Seventh Through the Tenth Centuries*. Chicago and London: University of Chicago Press, 2001.

Conversion to Islam

Bulliet, Richard. *Conversion to Islam in the Medieval Period: An Essay in Quantitative History.* Cambridge, Massachusetts: Harvard University Press, 1979.

Gervers, M. and R.J. Bikhazi, eds. *Conversion and Continuity: Indigenous Christian Communities in Islamic Lands, Eighth to Eighteenth Centuries.* Toronto: Pontifical Institute of Mediaeval Studies, 1990.

Levtzion, Nehemiah. *Conversion to Islam.* New York: Holmes & Meier, 1979.

Lorenzen, David N., ed. *Religious Change and Cultural Domination.* Mexico, D.F.: El Colegio de Mexico, 1981.

The Issue of Authority in the Muslim World

Fowden, Garth. *Empire to Commonwealth: Consequences of Monotheism in Late Antiquity.* Princeton, New Jersey: Princeton University Press, 1993.

Kennedy, Hugh. *The Prophet and the Age of the Caliphates: The Islamic Near East from the Sixth to the Eleventh Century.* London and New York: Longman, 1986.

Mikhail, Hanna. *Politics and Revelation: Mawardi and After.* Edinburgh, U.K.: Edinburgh University Press, 1995.

Safran, Janina M. *The Second Umayyad Caliphate: The Articulation of Caliphal Legitimacy in Al-Andalus.* Cambridge, Massachusetts: Harvard University Press, 2000.

PART THREE

Mongol Hegemony, 1260–1405

The Mongol conquests dwarfed those of the Arabs, which had occurred some six centuries earlier. Between 1206 and 1260, the Mongols subjugated northern China, Central Asia, Iran and Iraq, eastern Anatolia, the Caucasus, and the vast steppe region from Mongolia to the area now occupied by eastern Poland. By 1279, they completed the conquest of southern China as well. On the one hand, then, their achievement is greater than the Arabs on sheer scale. On the other hand, the Mongols did not create a civilization, and most of their conquests were lost within three generations.

The Mongols are not easy to dismiss as a destructive, one-time wonder, however. In spite of the fact that they soon lost control of their possessions, their legacy was remembered, revered, and emulated for centuries thereafter throughout much of the vast region they had conquered. In Western and Central Europe, too, the legacy lingered, but in a peculiar fashion: Rumors that a great force in the East had brutalized part of the Muslim world during 1219–1222 sparked hope in Europe that a potential ally, perhaps even a Christian king, existed outside Europe who would help destroy Islam. This was the origin of the legend of Prester John, a great Christian king in the East with whom the Europeans should join forces against Islam. The hope was so strong that when, in 1238, the Nizari Imam at Alamut and the Abbasid caliph in Baghdad jointly dispatched an embassy to Europe, appealing for help against the Mongols, they were rebuffed. Europe, particularly in the person of the pope, was pursuing a diametrically opposed policy of attempting to form a great Christian alliance with the Mongol Great Khan—whom some thought to be Prester John—against the world of Islam. Even the crushing Mongol defeat of European knights three years later at Liegnitz did not dissipate the fantasy of Prester John, who continued to fascinate and lure Europeans for centuries to come.

But the Mongols were not merely the stuff of memory and legend. They transformed enormous areas of Eurasia. These horsemen from the steppes, who destroyed so many cities, began to rebuild urban economies once they assumed power. Agriculture, unfortunately, languished, but long-distance trade flourished as never before. From the Pacific to the Black Sea, the Mongols held bandits in check, built caravanserais, and established diplomatic networks. The famous career of the Venetian Marco Polo in the last third of the thirteenth century would be unthinkable without the Mongols. He and his father and uncle traveled from Constantinople to Beijing and back with less fear for their lives or property than they would have felt had they journeyed anywhere in the Mediterranean basin. Taking advantage of the *pax Mongolica*, Venice quickly established a vast trade network that extended from the Pacific to Scandinavia.

The Mongol Empire affected the histories of all its neighbors as well as of peoples beyond their immediate reach. The history of a large part of the Muslim world was irrevocably altered. The Mongols and their desperately ambitious scion Timur Lang dominated Southwest Asia for only a century and a half, but Mongol hegemony had such a profound influence on the course of Muslim history that it merits a separate section in this book. Chapter 10 establishes the historical framework for the period. It examines the history of the three Mongol states whose rulers eventually converted to Islam, traces the rise of three other powerful Muslim states during this period, and explores the destructive effects of the plague and Timur Lang on Southwest Asia. Chapter 11 examines the cumulative effects of these and other events on Muslim intellectual and religious life. The evidence undermines the widely held view that the Mongol era caused Islamic civilization to decline. Despite frequent outbreaks of political chaos and the long-lasting economic depression of some regions, Islamic culture continued to thrive and break new ground in a wide variety of fields. More striking still, the period marks a transition from an era of several centuries during which the frontiers of the Muslim world had remained largely static to an era of expansion into far-flung regions. The period of Mongol hegemony would be followed by the rise of three powerful Muslim empires and the spread of Islam into areas that now contain half the followers of the Prophet Muhammad.

CHRONOLOGY

1210–1236	Reign of Iltutmish, founder of Delhi sultanate
1219–1222	Campaigns of Chinggis into Muslim world
1240s	Batu founds Saray, begins to administer the Golden Horde
1250	Mamluks seize power in Egypt and Syria
1253–1260	Hulagu's campaign
c.1250–c.1290	Career of Hajji Bektash
1260	Mamluks defeat Hulagu's army at 'Ayn Jalut
1260–1265	Hulagu is first ruler of Il–khanate, establishes Maragha observatory
1261	Byzantines regain Constantinople from Latin Kingdom
1269	Marinids replace Almohads in Morocco
1271–1295	Marco Polo's adventures in the Mongol Empire
c.1280–1326	Career of Osman, founder of Ottoman dynasty
c.1280–1334	Career of Shaykh Safi al–Din
1291	Mamluks capture the last Crusader castle in Syria
c.1290–1327	Career of Ibn Taymiya in Mamluk Empire
1310–1341	Third, and most successful, reign of Mamluk ruler, al–Nasir Muhammad
1313–1341	Reign of Uzbeg and the Islamization of the Golden Horde
1325–1351	Reign of Muhammad ibn Tughluq of Delhi
1325–1349	Ibn Battuta's journey east; serves Ibn Tughluq seven years
1326–1362	Reign of Orhan of Ottoman sultanate
1334	Schism in Chaghatay Khanate, Transoxiana is lost
1335	Collapse of Il–khanate
c.1335–1375	Career of Ibn al–Shatir
1347	First wave of plague
c.1350–1390	Career of Hafez
c.1350–1398	Career of Baha al–Din Naqshband
c.1350	Consensus has been achieved in most *madhhab*s that, theoretically, *ijtihad* is no longer permitted
1359–1377	Civil war in Golden Horde; Toqtamish secures control
c.1360–1406	Career of Ibn Khaldun
1368	Ming dynasty overthrows Yuan dynasty of the Mongols in China
1370	Timur's career begins in Transoxiana
1381–1402	Timur's campaigns from Ankara to New Saray to Delhi
1405	Death of Timur

CHAPTER 10

The Great Transformation

By 1248, the Christian kingdoms of the Iberian Peninsula had seized all Muslim territory north of the Strait of Gibraltar except for the small principality of Granada. Almost immediately thereafter, a similar process of conquest and consolidation of power was taking place in the eastern Muslim world. During the 1250s, the second major Mongol invasion of Southwest Asia took place. Millions of Muslims were now under the rule either of Christian Europeans or of pagan Mongols. For the first time since the Islamic calendar began, half or more of the world's Muslims were subject to governments dominated by non-Muslims.

In spite of the similarities, the situation in the eastern Muslim world differed from that of the Iberian Peninsula. The challenges facing Muslims in Iberia were insidious and chronic, but those in the east were violent and episodic and transformed the eastern Muslim world in profound ways. Whereas the Iberian Muslim community slowly suffocated under increasing restrictions, Muslims in three of the four Mongol empires rejoiced at the conversion of their rulers to Islam by the early fourteenth century. Their joy was short lived, for all three dynasties suddenly lost their grip on power in the middle third of the fourteenth century. Anarchy and widespread destruction became the order of the day. As the dynasties were collapsing, the worldwide epidemic of plague began its deadly work, leaving large areas of the Muslim world underpopulated. The first wave of the plague had hardly subsided when a half-Turk, half-Mongol warlord named Timur Lang began his career. His inexplicably vicious campaigns ranged from Delhi to Damascus and caused the horrors of Chinggis and Hulagu to pale by comparison. From 1380 to 1405, the very mention of his name sent panic into the hearts of multitudes, and his conquests laid waste to vast regions. The region from the Aegean Sea to the Ganges River had been violently shaken, with consequences that would reverberate for centuries.

The Mongol Khanates

Shortly before his death in 1227, Chinggis Khan gave each of his four sons a portion of his great empire. He did so in accordance with the ancient Mongol custom of establishing a home for the eldest son at the furthest distance and assigning the youngest to tend the family hearth. Accordingly, Jochi, the eldest, received the steppe land that lay north of the Aral Sea and extended westward "as far as the hooves of Mongol horses have reached," whereas Tolui, the youngest, received the ancient Mongol homeland that is now eastern Mongolia. The second son, Chaghatay, and the third, Ogedai, divided the lands that lay between those extremes. Ogedai succeeded his father as Great Khan, and his son Guyuk replaced him in the 1240s. In 1251, Tolui's eldest son Mongke became the Great Khan.

From his capital at Qaraqorum in modern Mongolia, Mongke (1251–1259) planned a new campaign of expansion. Leaders of Christian Europe hoped that he was Prester John, and they appealed to him to join them in a crusade against Islam, but he was unwilling to do so unless the Christian rulers and the Pope submitted themselves to him. Confident that the Lord of the Sky had entrusted the world to the Mongols, he embarked upon an ambitious campaign of conquest on his own terms. He sent one brother, Qubilai, to conquer the Sung dynasty in southern China and another brother, Hulagu, to subjugate Southwest Asia. When Mongke died, he was succeeded by Qubilai (1260–1294), who completed the conquest of China and is regarded as the first ruler of the Yuan dynasty (1279–1368) in China. He symbolized his new status by moving his capital from Qaraqorum to Beijing.

During the rule of Mongke and Qubilai, the Mongol domains became more or less institutionalized: The Great Khan ruled over Mongolia and China; Jochi's son Batu and his successors ruled over the Golden Horde in the vast steppe that extended from north of the Aral Sea almost to the Baltic Sea; the Chaghatay Khanate ruled over the area that now comprises the Chinese province of Xinjiang and eastern Afghanistan, as well as the territory north of the Amu Darya River; and Hulagu's Il-khanid regime comprised Iraq, eastern Anatolia, the southern Caucasus, and Iran to just east of Herat.

The Golden Horde

Europeans from the sixteenth century on referred to the domain of Batu's successors as the Golden Horde. The origin of the name is lost in obscurity. The English word *Horde* derives from the Mongol word *ordu*, meaning "camp" or "domain," but the meaning of the term *Golden* has spawned considerable debate, with no consensus having emerged. The name Golden Horde is commonly used in English to refer to the entire period of the dominance of the Mongols on the Eurasian steppes. Europeans have also frequently referred to the people of the Golden Horde as *Tatars*, a word that has been very loosely used throughout history. Understood in its linguistic sense, however, it has some value, because the various Tatar dialects belong to the Qipchaq division of the Turkic languages. In fact, the Golden Horde's neighbors in the east knew it as the Qipchaq Khanate, which is a more appropriate name for it. For ease of reference, this discussion will refer to the khanate as the Horde.

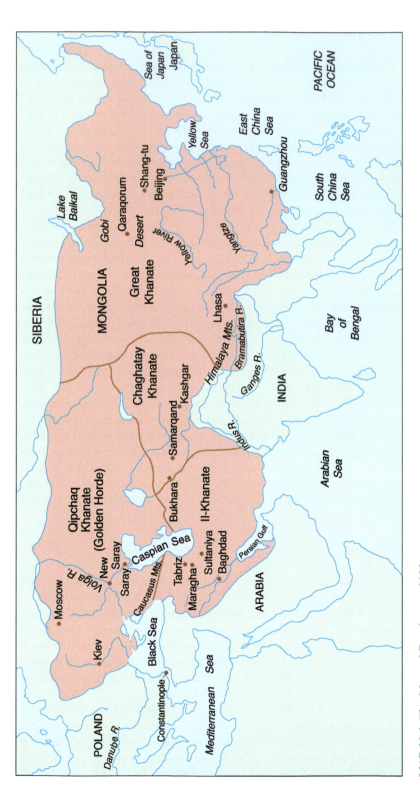

MAP 10.1 The Mongol Empire, ca. 1300.

At its height, the Horde dominated the area from eastern Poland to the Siberian forests. The core was the vast, grassy plain known as the Qipchaq steppe that extended from northwest of the Black Sea to northeast of the Caspian Sea. This sea of grass was broken by three of the great rivers of Russia: the Dnieper, the Don, and the Volga. Batu had no doubt immediately recognized that the level, endless plains were ideal for his horse culture. The rivers complicated travel on an east–west axis but facilitated travel and trade on a north–south axis.

This core region of the khanate was populated by numerous ethnic groups but was dominated by the Qipchaq Turks. Batu's followers quickly became assimilated into the majority Turkic culture when their Mongol leaders intermarried with local Qipchaq elites and adopted the local language. The "Mongol" elite of the khanate always boasted of their lineal ties with Chinggis Khan and retained certain aspects of their Mongol culture, but they were soon indistinguishable from their Qipchaq subjects.

Our knowledge of the first century and a half of the history of the khanate is frustratingly scanty, due to Timur Lang's destruction of its cities and written records in the 1390s. What we know about it is derived largely from the observations of outsiders and from archaeological evidence. It began with Batu, whose invasion in the late 1230s inflicted major damage on parts of Russia. Cities that resisted his initial call to surrender were pummeled into ruins by catapults and battering rams, and thousands of people were slaughtered. Cities that surrendered immediately were usually spared. The Horde exercised direct control over the Qipchaq steppe, but it exacted tribute in a system of indirect control over the forested north and west. The latter region covered a vast area that included Russian, Ukrainian, Polish, Lithuanian, and Latvian cities. The most important among these were Kiev, Novgorod, and Moscow. The ruling elite preferred to remain nomadic, whereas the majority of the population lived in towns and villages. Unlike the Mongols in China and Iran, who assimilated to the local culture, the Qipchaqs did not live among the Russians or in any way become integrated into Russian society. On the whole, the rulers resisted the urge to raid and loot their territory, but retribution for failing to pay the heavy tribute was typically severe. Armies of the Horde often engaged in slave raiding even in areas that had not been targets of punishment.

The economy of this new empire was quintessentially Mongol, based on pastoralism and long-distance trade; the leaders of the Horde were interested in agriculture only insofar as it generated the revenue among the Russians that enabled them to pay tribute. Pastoralism was the means of subsistence that most Mongols wanted to retain, but they recognized the benefits that long-distance trade could bring. The security that the various Mongol regimes successfully enforced across the huge region from the Pacific Ocean to the Black Sea enabled merchants of all nationalities to benefit from the new commercial possibilities. Batu, like other Mongol rulers, was interested in trade, which would augment the revenues derived from taxes on peasants and townsmen. In pursuit of this objective, he established his capital of Saray near the Volga delta, situated at the crossroads of trade routes that connected China with Eastern Europe in one direction and Scandinavia with Iraq and Iran in the other. It rapidly became a commercial center with a distinctly international air. From the forested zones to the north came amber, furs, timber, Russian slaves, and honey, to be exchanged for textiles, tools, and scientific instruments from the Muslim heartland and for spices from the East.

Merchants from all nations were encouraged to live in the capital, and a wide variety of religious missionaries—Muslim, Catholic, Russian Orthodox, Greek Orthodox, and Nestorian—were tolerated. The Horde established correct relations with the Byzantines once the latter had recaptured Constantinople from the Italians in 1261, but they also welcomed Italian traders to Saray. The regime encouraged trade with both the Latin Catholics and the Greek Orthodox, despite their hostility toward each other. The Mamluk regime took particular pains to foster good relations with the government at Saray because of the abundance of Qipchaq boys available to be shipped to Egypt as mamluks. Many Egyptian and Syrian craftsmen made their way to Saray to create objects of art in the Mamluk style. By contrast, the Horde's relations with its fellow Mongol regime, the Il-khanids, were hostile throughout the thirteenth century due to competing claims over the Caucasus. Several expensive wars drained the resources of both Mongol powers.

Too much can be made of the fact that Batu's brother Berke (1257–1267) was the first Mongol khan to convert to Islam. He did not pressure the remainder of the Mongol elite to convert, and he tolerated the Christian missionaries who proselytized in his realm. Until the early fourteenth century, only one other khan converted to Islam, and shamanism remained the focus of the religious life of the masses. Nevertheless, Islam slowly became the dominant religion in the khanate. The caravans that plied the long-established routes between Syria and the lower Volga provided a means for Muslim merchants, scholars, and craftsmen, as well as wandering preachers, to make their presence felt in the realm. Mosques, the call to prayer, Ramadan observance, and numerous other signs of a growing Muslim presence provided strong witness to a vibrant Islam.

The definitive turning point in the religious history of the Horde was the conversion in 1313 of the khan Uzbeg (1313–1341). Like Berke, he did not force other members of the elite to convert, and Christianity maintained a strong and tolerated presence. Uzbeg did, however, expel shamanistic priests. During his reign, Islam became the dominant religion, at least in the urban centers. Muslims coming from Syria or Egypt would have felt comfortable in the larger cities, particularly the capital, which Uzbeg moved upriver to New Saray on a site near the present city of Volgograd. By the end of Uzbeg's reign, the new city had large mosques and madrasas, and qadis were dispensing justice in Shari'a courts.

Uzbeg's rule represented the height of the Horde's wealth and prestige. Under him the Horde had become an international power feared and respected by other nations. Even during Uzbeg's lifetime, however, his Eastern European vassals were becoming restless. During the reign of his two sons, Lithuania gained its independence and other regions began challenging Mongol power. With the death of Uzbeg's son Berdi-beg in 1359, the last of Batu's descendants was gone. Rival leaders within the Horde began fighting each other, and in the midst of the chaos, Moscow refused to pay tribute. A distant cousin of Berdi-beg, Toqtamish of the White Horde, seized New Saray in 1377. He crushed Novgorod and Moscow, and by 1383 he had restored Mongol control over Russia. The Horde seemed as strong as it had ever been, but Toqtamish's ambitions exceeded his good judgment. He unwisely challenged Timur Lang, who was building his power in Transoxiana. As we shall see, Timur would administer a defeat to the Horde that would shatter its mystique in the eyes of its subjects, and it would never again be so formidable.

FIGURE 10.1 An illuminated manuscript from the Il-khanid period, revealing Chinese influences.

The Morgan Library & Museum, New York.

The Il-khanate

Hulagu proved to be a gifted administrator in the areas he had just devastated in his campaign of 1253-1260. He established his headquarters in northwestern Iran immediately after the destruction of Baghdad, and his state came to be known as the Il-khanate. The name comes from *il-khan*, meaning "subject khan," in the sense of being subject to the Great Khan in China. The Il-khanate maintained closer ties with the Great Khan in China than did the Horde, whereas the Chaghatay Khanate was on hostile terms with all three other Mongol empires.

Like Qubilai and the leaders of the Horde, Hulagu valued the wealth that trade generated. He realized that he needed thriving cities in order to benefit from trade and that he would need a strong agricultural sector to feed the population of those cities. The southern half of Iran had not been harmed by the Mongol invasions of 1219–1222 and 1253–1260, but the northern half was in ruins. The irrigation system of qanats in Khorasan had not been rebuilt since the destruction of Chinggis Khan, and the riverine system of irrigation in Iraq had been destroyed during Hulagu's own campaign. He ordered the rebuilding of cities and the restoration of the irrigation works, but he was able to accomplish little in the five years remaining in his life. During his short reign, he did lavish patronage on art and architecture, inaugurating a policy that his successors would follow. He also built an astronomical observatory at Maragha, some sixty miles south of Tabriz, which became the most highly regarded scientific institute in the Muslim world.

Hulagu's efforts to rebuild Iran were handicapped by the fact that he was surrounded by enemies. The Mamluks, the Horde, and the Chaghatay Khanate were all hostile to him, forcing him to disperse his troops to confront them. The greatest threat was the Mamluk Empire. Hulagu initiated contacts for an alliance with Louis IX of France against it, beginning a diplomatic correspondence between France and the Il-khans that lasted well into the next century. Hulagu's death in 1265 interrupted his plans to revive the economy that he and his predecessors had shattered so thoroughly in their conquests.

Hulagu's son established the Il-khanid capital at Tabriz, which was a wise decision. Otherwise, he and the next several rulers of the Il-khanid realm were notable for their lack of ability. For thirty years, the khanate was subject to constant infighting among the ruling elite and was the victim of neglect of the economic infrastructure. The population had suffered a catastrophic decline due to a combination of mass murder, famine, and flight, and it remained low. The peasants suffered particular hardship, for the Il-khanid rulers actually increased the taxes on villages compared to pre-conquest levels, even though both population and production had fallen precipitously. Mongol nomads stole peasants' livestock and grazed their horses on what had been prime cultivated fields. Most towns on both sides of the Euphrates were deserted, and Marco Polo described Baghdad as a mere "trading town" when he passed through it in 1272. Other major cities such as Nishapur lay in ruins until the early fourteenth century.

The early Il-khans were hostile to Islam. They had come out of a shamanistic background, but several of the leaders found Buddhism attractive. Many Buddhist monks came with Hulagu's expedition, and others arrived soon after Tabriz became the capital. Buddhism remained strong among the male Mongol ruling elite, but many of the rulers, from Hulagu on, had Nestorian wives or concubines. For the first several decades of Il-khanid rule, the rulers clearly were more sympathetic to Buddhism and Christianity than to Islam. During this period, the Nestorian and Jacobite churches thrived across Iran as never before.

From the accession of Ghazan in 1295, those policies were reversed, and Christianity and Buddhism went into irreversible decline in the Il-khanid realm. Ghazan (1295–1304) was the greatest of the Il-khans after Hulagu. A Buddhist, he proclaimed his conversion to Islam in the first year of his rule and ordered the destruction of churches, synagogues, and Buddhist temples throughout the realm. He initiated many reforms in order to build up his regime's wealth and prestige. He began the restoration of irrigation systems, reduced taxes and exchange rates, and reformed the system of weights and measures. The agricultural economy began a slow recovery, and for over two decades, tax revenues showed a steady increase despite the lowering of the tax rate.

In contrast to the agricultural decline throughout the thirteenth century, the Il-khanid regime boasted a sparkling urban life in certain areas. Hostile relations with the Mamluks had interrupted the historic long-distance trade with Syria and Egypt, but trade with China intensified. The Il-khans were also as eager to please

Italian and other European merchants as were their cousins in the Horde. Tabriz thrived on the new commercial life. Its location placed it on excellent trade routes. Iranian and Iraqi scholars and artists who had not fled to other lands in the face of the Mongol conquests made their way to Tabriz to enhance their careers. Hulagu's astronomical observatory at Maragha, near Tabriz, became famous for thousands of miles. Nasir al-Din al-Tusi (1201-1274), a Persian Shi'ite who had joined Hulagu's retinue at the siege of Alamut, was its first director. Al-Tusi was a man of many talents who wrote more than 150 books in mathematics, astronomy, logic, and other fields. He was perhaps the most original astronomer between Ptolemy in the second century and Copernicus in the sixteenth. He, like many other Muslim astronomers, struggled to modify some of Ptolemy's ideas about the universe in light of centuries of empirical observations that had been made after the great Roman scientist's death. Al-Tusi is best known for his "Tusi couple," which demonstrated that a circle revolving within another one that has a radius twice the length of the smaller one produces a back-and-forth motion that describes a straight line even though it is moving in a perfect circle. The Tusi couple enabled astronomers to simplify Ptolemy's model of the universe, which required "epicycles," or orbits that were centered on yet other orbits. The Maragha observatory attracted astronomers and mathematicians from as far away as Andalus and China. It surpassed anything that Europe would offer until the career of Tycho Brahe in the late sixteenth century.

Under Uljaytu (1304–1316), Il-khanid literature, history, architecture, and painting blossomed. He constructed a new capital at Sultaniya, for which he commissioned magnificent tombs, mosques, bazaars, and schools. Because of close trading relations with the Great Khan in China, Chinese styles and techniques began to influence the plastic arts of the Il-khanate. The Chinese influence is particularly striking in the manufacture of porcelains and in the emergence of Persian miniature painting.

Just as it appeared that the Il-khans had established a regime that would enable them to create a stable administration and a thriving economy, family feuds broke out into the open. Uljaytu's son Abu Sa'id (1316–1335) was a devout Muslim, fluent in Arabic and Persian, musically talented, and determined to continue the rehabilitation of his empire's economy. In 1335, however, he was poisoned, and anarchy broke out as ambitious chieftains struggled for supremacy. By midcentury, Iran and Iraq had been carved up by numerous successor states headed by Mongol, Turkic, Iranian, or Arab families. The populace once again sank into poverty and despair, and then, as we shall see, the northern arc of Iran was devastated by Timur Lang. Not for two centuries did the area begin to recover economically.

The Chaghatay Khanate

The Chaghatay Khanate was separated from the Il-khanid realm by the Amu Darya River and a line of fortresses east of Herat. In the northwest, only the grazing areas of some Mongol and Turkic pastoralists separated it from the territory of the Horde. In the east, its territory extended into modern Xinjiang province in China, which encompasses the Tarim Basin.

The Tarim Basin consists largely of an absolutely barren desert the size of the state of Texas. The desert is surrounded by a series of oases that served not only as fertile crop-producing areas but also as rest areas for the southern Silk Road. The oases exploit the fertile alluvial soil that has been washed down over the ages from the mountains ringing the basin on three sides. These are some of the most formidable mountain ranges in the world. To the west are the Pamir Mountains, to the north are the Tien Shan Mountains, and to the south are the Kunlun Mountains. All three ranges are covered perpetually in snow and are laced with numerous glaciers. Their average altitude is over 20,000 feet, and all have peaks that exceed 24,000 feet. The Pamirs have subranges that run east and west and others that run north and south; merchants on the southern Silk Road often experienced dizziness and nausea while crossing it. The Tien Shan are formidable barriers to transit between the Tarim and Mongolia, but predatory bands found ways to get through. The Kunlun, on the other hand, constitute an impenetrable barrier to Tibet in the south.

The Chaghatay Khanate thus extended over vast steppe land, some of the world's most inaccessible mountains, and the sophisticated urban oases of Transoxiana. The khans themselves retained the original features of the Mongol traditions more than did their cousins in the Horde, Il-khanate, or Yuan dynasty. Whereas the Yuan and Il-khan dynasties became urbanized quickly and the Horde fostered the development of mercantile interests in their capital of New Saray, the Chaghatays remained nomadic in lifestyle and outlook. The ruling family did not settle down in one of the great cities. The closest to a capital that it had was an encampment between Lake Balkhash and the Tien Shan Mountains. Members of the ruling family never lost their contempt for urban life, and they treated cities as fields to be harvested. The khans plundered and looted their own cities more than once. The fate of Bukhara is representative. Within twenty years of its destruction in 1220 by Chinggis Khan, it had largely recovered its prosperity. By the early 1270s, Marco Polo, passing through Khorasan, heard that it and Samarqand were the most splendid cities in Iran. However, in 1273 and again in 1316 the Chaghatay rulers sacked, burned, and depopulated Bukhara.

Kebek (1318–1326) was the first Chaghatay to prefer urban life to a nomadic existence, and under him Samarqand and Bukhara enjoyed a modest revival. Despite his efforts at rebuilding those cities, however, as early as 1334 the great Moroccan traveler Ibn Battuta found many of the mosques, colleges, and bazaars of Bukhara in ruins. Because of the antipathy of most of the Chaghatays to urban life, we have little evidence to indicate that any of the rulers other than Kebek patronized literature and the arts. On the other hand, it is clear that long-distance trade continued to be conducted through Transoxiana throughout the thirteenth and fourteenth centuries. The repeated rebuilding of the cities of Transoxiana and the pronounced Chinese influence on Il-khanid arts speak eloquently of a well-established commercial life linking China and Southwest Asia that refused to die even in a hostile cultural environment.

The ruling elite of the Chaghatay Khanate was a loose coalition of Mongols, Turks, and Uighurs (a Turkic-speaking people who inhabited the oases of the Tarim), in addition to a few Muslim Iranians who were appointed governors of Transoxiana. As in the Horde, Turkic culture soon became predominant. Shamanist religious practices remained strong among the nomadic population, although Buddhism made inroads, particularly among the nomads of the Tarim. The Uighurs, on the other hand, gradually Islamized, as did the Turkic nomads who migrated to Transoxiana.

In 1326, a new khan, Tarmashirin (1326–1334) came to the throne. He had been a Buddhist ("Tarma" in his name derives from *dharma*), but he became the first

FIGURE 10.2 The tomb of the Il-khan ruler Uljaytu (1304-1317), in Sultaniya.

Tuul and Bruno Morandi / Alamy Stock Photo.

Chaghatay ruler to convert to Islam. When he converted, he required all the important leaders in the khanate to follow suit. The order antagonized his chieftains in the east, and they became restive. When Tarmashirin was unsuccessful in his attack on Delhi in 1327, these chieftains seized the opportunity to revolt. After seven years of civil war, the khanate split in 1334. The Tarim basin and the area north of the Tien Shan Mountains were paired in an unlikely entity that became known as Moghulistan. It remained a regional political actor for two more centuries, and members of the House of Chaghatay exercised at least nominal authority in the area into the twentieth century. Ironically, the remaining area, wealthy Transoxiana, was bereft of a central government. A handful of tribes dominated the area, and the towns and cities once again became prey to the raids of nomads and seminomads. The merchants and ulama of Samarqand and Bukhara could only hope for a leader to arise who would restore to their cities the vitality and glory of their fabled past. By the last quarter of the century, they would find him in Timur Lang.

Thus, all four of the Mongol empires collapsed or were gravely weakened within a period of just over thirty years. The Chaghatay Khanate splintered in 1334, leaving only a minor principality behind in remote Moghulistan; the Il-khans disappeared in 1335; the Horde suffered a civil war between 1359 and 1377; and in Beijing the Chinese overthrew the Yuan dynasty of the Great Khan in 1368. The only descendant of Chinggis Khan who still exercised authority was in Moghulistan. The Horde survived after being taken over by Toqtamish in 1377, but his lack of descent from Chinggis Khan was a distinct liability in an era that stood in awe of the Chinggisid bloodline.

New Centers of Islamic Culture

For 600 years, the most influential forces shaping the legacy of the Qur'an and the Hadith into an Islamic civilization had been the creative communities of Iraq and Iran. Their decline had begun even before the Mongol threat, but the invasions of Chinggis Khan and Hulagu, followed by decades of Mongol misrule, were devastating in their effect. Now, as Iran and Iraq suffered, Muslim military power and cultural vibrancy shifted to the geographical fringes of the historic heartland. The Mamluk Empire, the Delhi Sultanate, and the Ottoman Sultanate assumed the dominant roles for the Islamic world in the thirteenth and fourteenth centuries. All three of them left permanent legacies for Islamic history.

The Mamluk Empire

The Mongol invasions profoundly altered the geopolitics of the eastern Mediterranean. Egypt now rose to a position of influence that it had not enjoyed since Hellenistic times. By virtue of its triumph over Hulagu's army at 'Ayn Jalut in 1260, the Mamluk Empire gained the respect and gratitude of Muslims everywhere. The regime continued to enhance its reputation for military prowess by repelling an Il-khan invasion of Syria in 1281, eradicating the last of the Crusader strongholds from the Syrian mainland by 1291, and preventing further Il-khan attempts to annex Syria during the period 1299–1303. As a result, it achieved the control over Syria that rulers in Cairo had aimed for since early Fatimid times, and it occupied the Holy Cities of the Hijaz.

The Mamluk Empire wielded one of the most formidable military forces in the world from the thirteenth through the fifteenth centuries. Although that fact alone would merit its place in history, it attracts attention primarily because of its unusual recruitment policy. Muslim governments had relied on slave soldiers since the early ninth century, but the Mamluk regime is distinguished by the fact that the rulers themselves were of slave origin. The staffing of the highest positions in the state relied upon a well-organized system of slave importation and training. Slave merchants combed foreign markets—primarily in the Qipchaq steppe—for young boys ten to twelve years of age. They sold the boys to the sultan and several dozen amirs who were the most powerful men in the empire other than the sultan himself. These included the vizier, other chief court officials, provincial governors, and military officers. Each official then provided several years of training for the boys.

The "curriculum" included instruction in the basic rituals of Islam and rigorous drilling in the cavalry arts of the bow and lance. The sultan, of course, was able to provide the most elaborate program. His slaves lived together in barracks, were drilled in the arts of cavalry warfare, and were taught basic literacy. They learned that their survival depended on loyalty to their master and to their fellow recruits. Upon completion of the training, their master granted them their freedom and gave them an estate to supply the revenue to maintain the expenses of their horses, arms, and armor.

The graduates of the sultan's school became members of the "royal mamluks," who numbered 5000–6000 during the late thirteenth and early fourteenth centuries.

Enjoying the highest status of all the troops, they demanded to be stationed in or around Cairo rather than at posts remote from the center of power. The mamluks of the amirs were stationed in the provinces and at the homes of their masters. The Mamluk army, then, was characterized by an organization not unlike a feudal army of contemporary Western Europe. At its core were the sultan's troops, who were loyal to him; supplementing them were the dozens of regiments that were loyal to their respective amirs, who in turn were loyal to the sultan. When the various corps of mamluks were supplemented by cavalry of the auxiliary units (freeborn troops who included local Egyptians, Syrians, and foreign soldiers of fortune), the regime could mobilize 40,000–50,000 cavalrymen, in addition to infantry.

Regardless of who their master was, mamluks were intensely loyal to him and to their brothers in arms. This loyalty, by virtue of which the master was viewed as the mamluks' father and they called each other brothers, also meant that it was almost impossible for a mamluk who was transferred from one amir to another to be accepted by the new group. The sense of exclusivity also meant that the mamluks always felt a social distance between them and the society they ruled. They passed laws prohibiting civilians (Muslim as well as non-Muslim) from riding horses. They also adhered to a policy of marrying slave women (usually from the areas where they themselves came), and even their concubines were not of local origin. Some exceptions occurred, but local marriages were rare. Because mamluks' sons by such wives and concubines were not slaves, they did not receive the training of the slave boys and found themselves overlooked in the competition for the best positions. They could serve in the lower-status auxiliary units, but with the exception of several of the sultans' sons and brothers, they did not advance to the highest ranks. Thus, the perpetuation of the regime required the continual purchase of new slaves.

The Mamluk system is intriguing for its combination of power and latent anarchy. On the one hand, it fostered an esprit de corps among its soldiers that, combined with the high level of training, resulted in a formidable military force. On the other hand, the system of purchasing and manumitting slave troops created a system of cliques and factions that was a constant threat to peace and security. The system was most vulnerable during the process of succession to the leadership of the state. Each sultan wished to pass his office to his son, but the amirs demanded the right to ratify the choice of the next sultan. The amirs were not being presumptuous: They were adhering to the traditions of their common Turkic background, and they were well aware that the new sultan's "family" of troops would expect to displace the existing bureaucratic and military officials. Those who were threatened with the loss of their positions in the existing government sought allies among the other amirs, and those aspiring to office did the same. Such a transition of power almost always led to fighting and scores of deaths.

The dynamics of this process were in evidence from the early years of the empire. Baybars, a talented and ruthless sultan, ruled for seventeen years (1260–1277). He named his son to succeed him, but his son was overthrown by Baybars's own troops. In 1293, another sultan was overthrown by a conspiracy of amirs, and his ten-year-old brother, al-Nasir Muhammad, was installed on the throne by yet another faction. He was deposed a year later, reinstalled in 1299, only to be deposed again in 1309. By this time in his mid-twenties, the young ex-sultan seized the throne himself in 1310 and enjoyed the longest and most successful rule in Mamluk history

(1310–1341). The nature of the Mamluk system guaranteed political instability, and its entire history was punctuated by frequent violence among the mamluks themselves. Fortunately, although the Egyptian and Syrian subjects of the Mamluk Empire were occasionally harassed and often exploited by the slave soldiers, they were not frequent victims of the political violence, which was largely restricted to the ruling elite themselves.

The mamluks who seized control of Egypt and Syria in 1250 from the Ayyubid dynasty were Qipchaq Turks. Their homeland was the Qipchaq steppe, which, as we have seen, had become the domain of the Horde a few years before the coup d'état in Cairo. The Mamluk regime needed a constant supply of slave soldiers, but the traditional supply route for them by 1260 lay through hostile Il-khanid territory. Baybars began a two-pronged diplomatic effort to develop a new supply route. In a fortuitous development for him, the Byzantines now reappeared in diplomatic affairs for the first time in several decades. The Byzantine royal family had been living in exile in Nicaea ever since the Venetians conquered Constantinople in the so-called Fourth Crusade of 1204. After decades of Byzantine frustration, the emperor Michael VIII Palaeologus (1259–1282) recaptured Constantinople from the Venetians in 1261. Threatened by the Venetians to the west and Turkish raiders to the east, the emperor needed to be on good terms with both Berke of the Horde and Baybars of the Mamluks. He agreed to facilitate the slave trade between the Horde and Egypt, and he refurbished an Umayyad-era mosque in Constantinople as a gesture of good will to Baybars. He even made a promise to give Egypt military aid if needed.

Baybars also cultivated diplomatic relations with the Horde. The alliance became progressively easier to maintain because the Horde was continually assimilating to the Qipchaq culture into which the Egyptian mamluks had been born, and the two empires had no reason to quarrel over territory. Both empires had hostile relations with the Il-khans, and so the natural trade routes through Iran and Iraq were never accessible to them. Both the Horde and the Mamluk Empire therefore maintained good relations with the Christian Byzantines in order to keep the shipping route open between Egypt and the Black Sea. The trade route opened up opportunities for merchants to purchase boys who were of Greek, Georgian, and Slavic origin as well, some of whom became mamluks. Beginning in the late thirteenth century, however, most of the non-Turkic mamluks were Circassians, members of an ethnic group whose origin was the area of the Caucasus on the northeastern shore of the Black Sea.

Baybars was as careful to develop economic ties as he was to cultivate diplomatic contacts. Mediterranean trade in the thirteenth century was dominated by Europeans. The fleets of Italian city–states by that time had obtained a near monopoly of naval power. By virtue of Baybars's campaigns against the Crusader ports of Syria and Palestine, however, the once-flourishing Italian trade with Syria was destroyed. Baybars realized that he could redirect that trade to Egypt. Despite papal condemnation of trade with Muslim powers, several Italian maritime cities negotiated treaties with Baybars. Egypt's maritime commerce grew steadily in volume over the next century, and Alexandria experienced an economic boom as a result. The Mamluk Empire regained the dominant position in the trade between the Mediterranean and the Indian Ocean that Egypt had lost during the era of the Crusades. It maintained good relations with Venice and Genoa, whose ships transported most of the slaves from the

Black Sea and whose merchants purchased the spices that came to Egypt from India and the East Indies.

Realizing the need for a vibrant economy to support their military machine and their high standard of living, the Mamluks supported the crafts and manufacturing as well as trade. During the early fourteenth century, they invested in huge paper-making factories and sugar refineries. They encouraged the export of sugar to Italy, southern France, Catalonia, Flanders, England, and the Baltic Sea. The most important Egyptian industry continued to be the manufacture of cotton and linen textiles, both of which were in great demand during this period in both the Muslim world and in Europe.

With their wealth, the Mamluks patronized learning and the arts. During the Mongol devastation of Iran and Iraq in the first half of the thirteenth century, both Damascus and Cairo had welcomed scholars and merchants fleeing the destruction of their homelands. Due to the influx of Iranian and Iraqi scholars and the destruction of Baghdad in 1258, the two cities became the greatest centers of Islamic learning during the late Ayyubid period. As the capital city of the Mamluk Empire, Cairo surpassed Damascus in importance and imperial stature, and it remained the cultural capital of the Muslim world at least until the late fifteenth century. Through patronage of culture, Mamluk sultans attempted to legitimize their rule by winning favor with the ulama and the masses alike. One time-honored way for rulers to impress upon the public the grandeur of their reign is through the construction of impressive buildings, and the Mamluks were no exception in this regard. They vied with their predecessors in endowing magnificent madrasas, mosques, Sufi lodges, and hospitals, in addition to constructing enormous tombs for themselves. Some of the most impressive buildings to be found in Syria and Egypt to this day are the result of Mamluk patronage of monumental architecture.

Baybars installed a member of the Abbasid family as caliph in Cairo after he consolidated his power. It is impossible to assess the actual impact of this symbolic act, although it is clear that the new caliph had even less power and prestige than his predecessors in Baghdad had possessed. On the other hand, his presence was politically useful for the government and perhaps psychologically important for many Egyptians and Syrians. More tangible were changes that the regime made in the patronage of the religious institutions. Previous Muslim regimes had favored one or another school of law, but the Mamluks were the first to endow all four schools and to appoint qadis for each one.

The period 1260–1341 was the high point of Mamluk history, and the third reign of al-Nasir Muhammad (1310–1341) was its apogee. During al-Nasir's reign, there were neither famines nor plagues in the empire, a stark contrast with the late Fatimid and early Ayyubid periods. The population grew, and prosperity soared. Beginning in the last decade of the thirteenth century, however, ethnic rivalry between the Qipchaq and Circassian mamluks had already begun, and fierce clashes broke out when al-Nasir Muhammad died. Struggles between the two groups caused chronic violence for the next forty years. Members of al-Nasir's family held the office of the sultanate during that time, but they were puppets of the factions who placed them on the throne. Thus, political instability in the Mamluk Empire occurred simultaneously with the collapse of the Mongol khanates.

To complicate matters, the plague, or Black Death, struck the Mamluk realm with at least the level of ferocity in 1348 that it did Europe, killing one-fourth to one-third of the population in its first wave. For the next century and a half, the epidemics recurred at a rate of more than once per decade, causing the population to continue to decline. As agriculture and commerce plummeted, a clique of Circassian mamluks seized power in 1382, and the Qipchaq era was over. The Circassians dominated Egypt for the next 135 years, until their defeat at the hands of the Ottomans in 1517.

The Delhi Sultanate

The Arab conquest of Sind in 711–713 established a Muslim presence in the middle and lower Indus valley, but in terms of both geography and influence, the settlements there remained on the periphery of the Islamic world for several centuries. The Abbasids lost control of the area in the ninth century, and several of the towns in the valley soon came under the control of Isma'ilis who looked to Fatimid Cairo for guidance. In the eleventh century, however, Mahmud of Ghazna expanded his aggressive and predatory Muslim state into the upper Indus valley. The Ghaznavids inaugurated an era of seven centuries that would witness a series of powerful, autonomous Muslim states in South Asia (the area south of the Hindu Kush and Himalaya mountain ranges). Usually ruled by Turks or Afghans, each dynasty attempted to maintain an identifiably Muslim court in an overwhelmingly Hindu society. The model they found most congenial was the Islamic–Persian style that developed in northeastern Iran with the Samanid court of the tenth century. Until the advent of the Mughals, the greatest of these Muslim states was the Delhi Sultanate.

Mahmud of Ghazna laid the foundations for a powerful Muslim presence in South Asia. He raided the Punjab as early as 1002 and captured Lahore in 1030. When the Saljuqs chased Mahmud's successor out of Khorasan ten years later, Lahore increasingly became the most important city in the remaining area of the Ghaznavid Empire, and it developed into a thriving center of Islamic culture.

In 1173, an Afghan family from the region of Ghur seized power in Ghazna and began a systematic conquest of Ghaznavid holdings in the Punjab. That task was accomplished by 1192. Not content with the Punjab, these Ghurids conquered the small town of Delhi in 1193 and occupied areas as far east as Bihar on the lower Ganges River. Their military power can be gauged by the fact that, while they were conquering the Punjab and the Ganges, they were also winning Khorasan from the shahs of Khwarazm, often regarded as the greatest Muslim military power of the day until their defeat by Chinggis Khan. The Ghurid realm grew until it extended from Bihar through Khorasan. But just as the Ghurids were poised to create a major state in South Asia, their ruler was assassinated in 1206, leaving no son to inherit the throne. The general who had conquered Delhi for the Ghurids took over the reins of power in both Delhi and Lahore. But he in turn died in a polo accident in 1210. One of his Turkic mamluks, Iltutmish, then seized power. Iltutmish (1210–1236) is considered to be the founder of the Delhi Sultanate, although it was over a decade before he made Delhi preeminent over Lahore.

Although the Delhi Sultanate was composed of several different dynasties, it is regarded as a single period in Muslim–Indian history because of the continuity of the ruling elite. Historians disagree on the issue of its duration. Some point out that it was the dominant state in South Asia from 1210 to 1398 and limit their treatment of the sultanate to the three dynasties of that period. Other historians include two later dynasties, in which case the sultanate's history is considered to last until the arrival of the Mughals in 1526. Regardless of how one defines the period of the sultanate, each dynasty began with either Turkic or Afghan founders. Like almost all other Muslim regimes (the major exception was that of the Mamluks), the rulers might choose wives or concubines of strikingly different ethnic origin, but the patrilineal system of tracing one's ancestors made it natural for each generation to see itself as the heir to the founder of the dynasty and to identify with his ethnic origin.

The early Delhi Sultanate experienced the same degree of political turbulence that the Mamluk regime did. The entire period from 1210 to 1320 was one of political tumult among the ruling elite itself. Powerful amirs attempted to check the power of others, and violence often resulted. Between 1236 and 1296, ten sultans reigned, eight of whom averaged a reign of less than three years. Only one of the ten is known to have died a natural death. Despite having to confront almost constant challenges within the elite and violent changes of dynasties in 1290 and 1320, the sultanate successfully withstood threats from the Mongols. A Mongol expedition did sack Lahore in 1241, but between 1290 and 1327, Delhi repulsed attacks by the Chaghatay Khanate at least nine times.

In the periods between internal clashes and Mongol attacks, the sultanate expanded its area of control. By 1230, Iltutmish dominated a wide arc based on the Indus and Ganges river valleys. In that year, he sought and won recognition from the Abbasid caliph in Baghdad as the legitimate Muslim ruler of the area. By the early fourteenth century, the sultanate had extended its authority to Gujarat and the Deccan Plateau, in addition to controlling the upper and middle Ganges valley and the Punjab. Until the 1320s, the regime exercised authority in the conquered areas by a variety of policies. The sultanate ruled directly in some areas, and in other areas it exacted tribute from Hindu or Muslim princes who were allowed to rule with little oversight.

The most influential of the Delhi dynasties was that of the Tughluq family, whose effective rule was from 1320 to 1388, although members of the family remained on the throne until 1413. Muhammad ibn Tughluq (1325–1351) was the most famous of the dynasty. He was a fascinating figure of undoubted intellectual and creative talents, but his administration was a disappointment. On the one hand, he continued his father's military campaigns and managed to extend the authority of the sultanate over almost all of South Asia. His domain extended from the Himalayas almost to the southern tip of the peninsula, and from the Punjab to Bengal. He also defeated the Chaghatay ruler Tarmashirin at the very gate of Delhi in 1327, the event that indirectly resulted in the division of the Chaghatay Khanate into Transoxiana and Moghulistan. He was an accomplished scholar, proficient in both Arabic and Persian, and he recruited numerous new qadis from abroad in a major effort to facilitate the implementation of Islamic law. Toward his Hindu and Jain subjects, he practiced a conciliatory policy of offering them high positions in the government, allowing them to build new temples, and inviting them to court to debate philosophical and theological issues.

Although these policies seem like the strategy of an accomplished politician, Muhammad actually found it difficult to devise realistic policies for some important issues. His obsessive need for symmetry made it impossible for him to tolerate the variety of relations that existed between the central government and the multitude of provinces that were at least nominally subject to it. He instituted a uniform policy of direct rule for all regions, provoking widespread resentment in the areas that had been allowed a degree of autonomy by previous Delhi sultans. The biggest problem was in the Deccan. The region was hundreds of miles south of Delhi, and the Hindu rulers there had no intention of yielding on the issue of indirect rule. Muhammad thought that he could resolve the problem of distance by moving the capital from Delhi to the more centrally located site of Dawlatabad in the Deccan, but the change was implemented in a heavy-handed fashion that provoked resentment among his own followers.

These, and other unpopular measures, were followed by a catastrophic drought and famine in the Punjab and the Ganges valley during the years 1335–1342. The suffering brought on by the drought became the pretext for widespread rebellions throughout the northern tier of the sultanate, forcing Muhammad to lead his army on repeated campaigns to the northern as well as southern provinces of his realm. He responded to the uprisings, and even to the whispering of criticism of his policies, with brutal punishment that caused him to develop a reputation for cruelty. By the end of his rule, he had lost control of his southern possessions, including Bengal, and the support of most of his remaining subjects.

The reign of Muhammad's cousin Firuz (1351–1388) stood in sharp contrast to that of his own. Firuz practiced clemency where Muhammad had been brutal, although he responded to Muslim criticisms of his cousin's religious toleration by destroying newly built Hindu temples and promoting proselytizing efforts among the Hindu majority. He made a concerted effort to assist the agricultural sector of the economy by constructing irrigation projects, and he promoted employment by building a new capital city near Delhi. In the end, however, he had not made a convincing case for the continuing authority of Delhi. When Firuz died in 1388, a power struggle broke out among his sons and grandsons. Many of the Hindu and Muslim rulers of the provinces took advantage of the confusion to renounce their allegiance to the dynasty, plunging the sultanate into a civil war that lasted a decade.

Delhi was not on a major trade route and probably would never have become the center of the sultanate had it not been for the Mongol threat. Chinggis Khan's return route to Mongolia in 1222 passed through the Punjab, persuading Iltutmish to establish his headquarters at Delhi rather than at the Ghurid capital of Lahore. On the other hand, the valley of the Indus, the Punjab, and the Gangetic plain were all rich agricultural regions that supplied Delhi with wealth, and the acquisition of Gujarat granted the city access to the wider world of commerce. Gujarat was famous for its fine cotton cloths as well as for its role as an entrepôt. Commodities shipped to there from Southeast Asia or East Africa would be transshipped to yet another port, such as Hormuz in the Persian Gulf.

As the capital of a rich and powerful regime, Delhi attracted soldiers, merchants, craftsmen, scribes, and scholars. Like Cairo and Damascus, it was a haven for refugees fleeing the depredations of Chinggis Khan and Hulagu. The Delhi sultans welcomed and offered patronage to foreign scholars and artisans, whose work enhanced the glory of the regime. Outstanding ulama were appointed to serve as qadis and administrators in the government, particularly during the reign of Muhammad ibn Tughluq, who seems to have been willing to trust foreign officeholders more than local ones. Most of the intellectuals who emigrated to Delhi came from Khorasan and Transoxiana, reinforcing the Persianate cast of the elite culture that had been bequeathed by the Ghaznavids to the Punjab. Poetry, music, and historical works composed in Persian flourished under the regime. Architecture, likewise, reflected the styles that had been developing in Iran and Central Asia. Magnificent mosques, Sufi lodges, madrasas, tombs, and palaces incorporated the vaulted halls, pointed domes, blue faience tiles, and gold plating of the Persian-speaking region. Only contemporary Cairo among Muslim cities exceeded the architectural splendor of Delhi.

The sultanate shared many common characteristics with those of Muslim regimes to the west, but it was distinctive in one major feature: Not in several centuries had the Muslim rulers of any other major state represented such a small minority of the population. The population of the sultanate at its height (ca. 1310–1340) was remarkably complex linguistically. More than one thousand languages and dialects were spoken in South Asia. From the perspective of a Muslim government, however, the issue of religion was more vexing than that of language. During the thirteenth and fourteenth centuries, the Muslims of the sultanate were a tiny minority of the total population. The ultimate responsibility for any Muslim ruler was the protection and advancement of the faith. Among those duties were the expansion of the Dar al-Islam, the enforcement of the Shari'a, the toleration of Jews and Christians within prescribed guidelines, and the eradication of polytheism.

In the Delhi Sultanate, the tension between the religious duty of the ruler on the one hand and the social reality on the other reached a level inconceivable in the

FIGURE 10.3 The Alai Darwaza, constructed in 1311, is the main entrance to the Quwwat al-Islam mosque of Delhi. Commissioned by a ruler of the Delhi Sultanate, it is the first example of architecture in India that has arches and a dome.

Bjanka Kadic / Alamy Stock Photo.

rest of the Islamic world. The sultans depended on millions of polytheistic Hindu laborers, peasants, troops, bureaucrats, carpenters, masons, metallurgists, bankers, and merchants. The Ghaznavids, Ghurids, and early sultans at Delhi exploited the religious issue when they raided Hindu towns and temples, but as the later sultans began to consolidate their holdings, they followed a more pragmatic policy. The fourteenth-century rulers Muhammad ibn Tughluq and his successor Firuz exemplify the range of possibilities available to the Muslim rulers of South Asia in their treatment of non-Muslims. The former's generosity to Hindus and Jains was criticized by devout Muslims, and the latter's punitive measures against non-Muslims contributed to the outbreak of the civil war that followed his death in 1388. As we shall see, the disorder of that period exposed northern India to perhaps the greatest catastrophe that it has ever experienced: the invasion of Timur Lang.

The Ottoman Sultanate

The third of the great Muslim states to emerge on the periphery of the Islamic heartland in the thirteenth century was that of the Ottomans. During the second half of the fifteenth century, it achieved the status of an empire, and it went on to become one of the greatest and most durable states in world history. It collapsed only after World War I. During the period prior to the fifteenth century, when its territory was relatively compact and its reputation was only regional, its status may best be described as that of a sultanate.

Until the Saljuq defeat of the Byzantines at Manzikert in 1071, Anatolia was hostile territory to Muslims and represented a seemingly impenetrable barrier to Muslim expansion. After the battle, the entire peninsula lay open to unlimited Turkish migration for a quarter of a century. In 1098, the knights of the First Crusade discovered that Nicaea (Iznik), just a few miles east of Constantinople, was the capital of the Saljuq Sultanate of Rum. They forced the sultanate back onto the Anatolian plateau, where the Saljuqs established their capital at Konya.

For the next two centuries, the pattern of settlement in Anatolia did not change much. The Turks controlled the central plateau and the east. The majority of the population under their control remained Christian peasants, although conversions and emigration ensured that the Christian population slowly declined throughout this period. Three independent Christian states lay on the periphery of the peninsula. On the southern shore was the Armenian kingdom of Cilicia (sometimes known as Lesser Armenia). In the extreme west was the Byzantine state, which moved its capital to Nicaea when the soldiers of the Fourth Crusade captured and sacked Constantinople in 1204. The Byzantines returned the capital to Constantinople when they retook the city in 1261, but their former subjects in Trebizon, on the Black Sea coast, refused to recognize the new emperor and insisted on their independence. The zones between the three Christian states and the Turkish-controlled area were the domain of the frontier warriors known as gazis.

The Sultanate of Rum was the dominant Turkish power in the peninsula. It frequently cooperated with its neighboring Christian states, and as an urban society, it sometimes had tense relations with the gazis on its frontiers. Occasionally, it restrained gazis when their activities caused problems for their diplomatic relations with the Christian states. Despite the often peaceful relations with its neighboring

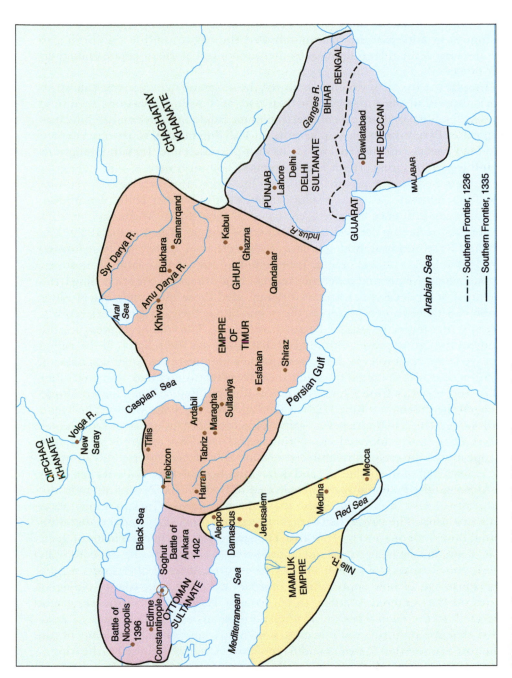

MAP 10.2 The Eastern Muslim World, Late Fourteenth Century.

Christian kingdoms, however, the history of the sultanate was punctuated by violence. For several decades, it had to contend for primacy with several other Turkish dynasties in the area, and after having established its supremacy, it had to subdue challengers. In addition, the dynasty followed the Saljuq tradition according to which the sons of the ruler fought each other for control of the sultanate upon their father's death.

Despite the frequent violence, however, the sultanate managed to establish an urban culture that was more vibrant than had been seen in Anatolia in several centuries. It synthesized several cultural traditions. Saljuq monumental architecture incorporated Byzantine styles, an emerging Turkish Sufi musical repertoire adapted Orthodox Christian musical themes for its own purposes, and Turkish immigrants were influenced by local customs and manners in countless ways.

Persian models of government, art, and literature also influenced the culture of the Rum sultanate. The early sultans admired the Persian cultural tradition, but the Persian influence became even stronger when Konya became a haven for Iranian refugees fleeing the destruction caused by Chinggis Khan in the 1220s. The products of the newly-arrived scholars, architects, and craftsmen transformed Konya into a lively cultural center. It became famous for its beautiful mosques, madrasas, caravanserais, and other monuments, as well as for the mesmerizing lyrics of the great Sufi poet Rumi, whose career unfolded there. Although non-Muslims probably constituted ninety percent of the population in the early thirteenth century, Konya's prestige aided the Islamization of the sultanate. The visibility of mosques, the ubiquity of the call to prayer, and the fact that Islam was the religion of the ruling elite played important roles in the growing Islamic identity of the Anatolian plateau.

Mongol armies shattered the sultanate as decisively as they had destroyed other regimes and societies from China to Central Europe. Batu of the Golden Horde challenged the sultanate at Kose Dagh in 1243 and won a decisive victory. The Saljuq army disintegrated, and Konya never again wielded effective influence outside its own environs. The sultanate withered away during several decades of tortured civil war until it disappeared in the early fourteenth century. In 1260, Hulagu asserted his authority in the eastern half of the peninsula, and that region became part of the Il-khanate.

Although the Il-khanid regime continued to nourish the Persian strain in the high culture of eastern Anatolia, it also sparked a new wave of Turkish immigration into the peninsula. The second half of the thirteenth century witnessed the migration of tens of thousands of Turks into the area. Hulagu's conquests had left many of them displaced and in desperate straits; others had served as troops during the conquests and were now in search of further military adventures; and still others were simply taking advantage of new opportunities that had arisen in the wake of Hulagu's victories. As they entered Anatolia, the process of Turkification of the peninsula accelerated. In the central region, neither the Il-khans nor the Sultanate of Rum wielded effective authority, and it became a no man's land of anarchy. Many of the new immigrants resorted to sheer banditry to survive. Others continued to the fringes of the peninsula, where they augmented the existing groups of gazi fighters.

The Turkish migration began just as the Byzantines gained their revenge on their Latin enemies. When Michael Palaeologus unexpectedly recaptured Constantinople from the Venetians in 1261, the Byzantines eagerly anticipated a revival of imperial power. Unfortunately for them, they now faced a conjunction of challenges. To the west, rival Christian states—both Orthodox and Catholic—were planning to seize the wealthy Byzantine capital, and to the east, the new Turkish migrants were swelling the ranks of the gazis. The gazis were discovering that, when the Byzantines had relocated their capital to Constantinople, they had neglected their defense structure around Nicaea. After mid-century, the ambitious gazi chieftains who until then had been held in check by both Nicaea and Konya began to carve out independent principalities in the western third of the peninsula. Many of the Turkish newcomers joined the ranks of the successful raiders, enabling some of the chieftains to establish thriving bases of power even along the Aegean coast. By the end of the century, some were hiring renegade Byzantine sailors to help them raid Aegean islands. Although the Byzantine emperor's diplomacy had protected his realm from the Sultanate of Rum, the Horde, the Mamluks, and the Il-khans, it was futile against the gazi tradition, which had gained a new life with the arrival of large numbers of Turkish immigrants.

One of the gazi regimes was led by a chieftain named Osman, who was born about 1260. He developed a power base at Soghut, only a few miles east of Bursa. From there, Osman had opportunities to tax merchants who were using the trade route that connected the Aegean with Central Asia, and he could raid Byzantine territory. By virtue of his successful raids, he attracted a growing number of gazis and adventurers. Many of the latter included Christians. Thus, the early Ottomans reflected the typical gazi band, which was not a group related by kinship ties, but rather a mixture of many different peoples, Turkic and Turkicized, who chose to participate in a dynamic organization.

At some point (possibly long after Osman's death), Osman's group became known as Ottomans, or "followers of Osman." Taking advantage of the Byzantines' deadly rivalries with the Bulgars, Serbs, Venetians, Genoans, and other Christian powers, they laid an extended siege to Bursa and took it in 1326, just after Osman died. His son Orhan (1326–1362) made Bursa his capital city, and from there he captured Nicaea (1329; later renamed Iznik) and Nicomedia (1337; later renamed Izmit), the last major Byzantine cities in Anatolia.

Osman and Orhan, like all contemporary successful leaders of volunteer military forces, had to provide outlets for the energies, appetites, and religious fervor of their followers. Success necessitated further success, for victories generated new recruits who expected glory and treasure, and veterans of previous campaigns soon felt the need for new exploits. There is little doubt that Orhan would have eventually crossed the Dardanelles on his own, due to the fact that beyond it lay a vast territory that was Christian, wealthy, and increasingly riven by conflicts among weak states. As it turned out, however, in 1345, he was invited to cross by a Byzantine faction vying for power in the capital city, just as earlier Byzantines had invited the Saljuqs into western Anatolia at the end of the eleventh century. After enabling his Byzantine ally to gain the throne, Orhan remained interested in the Balkans. By 1361, he had captured territory that extended from the Dardanelles to the old Roman capital of Adrianople (modern Edirne), which became the new Ottoman capital.

The Ottomans arrived in the Balkans at an opportune time for their ambitions. The Byzantine Empire had shrunk to a mere shadow of its former self and comprised little more than the suburbs of Constantinople; the Serbian Empire of the great Stephen Dushan had lost most of its vitality at his death in 1355; and the peoples of the Balkans were suffering from the constant warfare of numerous petty states. Few of the inhabitants of the area, powerful or weak, were loyal to a Balkan state at the time. Many of them sensed that the prospect of Ottoman overlordship could be no worse than what they were already experiencing. Due to the chaotic conditions, Orhan was able to recruit Christian knights to serve in his army, and in some battles, still more Christians defected to the Ottoman side. Many Orthodox noblemen and soldiers of fortune made successful careers out of service to the Ottoman state. Many Christian peasants and townsmen benefitted from the stability offered by the Ottomans of this era, in contrast to the anarchy and exploitation characteristic of the Balkan Christian states of the fourteenth century.

Orhan's son Murat I (1362–1389) took advantage of the vacuum of power in the region. He consolidated his hold on Thrace, conquered Macedonia and southern Bulgaria, and forced the Byzantines to pay tribute to, and provide troops for, Ottoman campaigns. In 1389, his army, composed of Turks and Christian vassals, defeated a far larger force of Serbs and their allies at Kosovo. Murat was killed in the battle, and his son Bayezit (1389–1402) became sultan.

Murat and Bayezit laid the foundations for the future Ottoman Empire. Murat had begun the process of building a more reliable army than that of either the gazis or Turkish tribesmen in general, both of whom he regarded as unpredictable and independent minded. He created a unit of soldiers who were prisoners of war, and he instituted a centralized bureaucracy in order to collect the taxes required to support his growing empire. Bayezit expanded these initiatives. He implemented a levy of male children on Christian villages in the Balkans, who were then educated as Muslims and trained for either the military or the civilian administration. This recruitment mechanism was known as the *devshirme* system. The slaves in the military served in what came to be known as the Janissary corps (from *Yeni Çeri*, or "New Force"). The Janissaries rapidly became the Ottoman army's primary infantry unit and were stationed around the sultan on the battlefield. Originally armed with pikes and bows and arrows, they later became famous for their effective use of gunpowder weapons.

As a result of his policies and leadership ability, Bayezit became a successful conqueror. Relying on the loyalty of his Christian vassals and Janissaries, he quickly conquered the western half of Anatolia from Turkish rivals, acquired large areas north of the Danube, and, in 1395, laid siege to Constantinople itself. By this time, all of the major European leaders had become aware of the potential threat of the Ottomans to their security, and they responded to the appeal of the Byzantine emperor for aid. The king of Hungary organized a huge army that attracted knights from France, Burgundy, England, Germany, and the Netherlands. This military force moved down the Danube in 1396, destroying Ottoman forts along the way. At the fortress of Nicopolis, however, Bayezit confronted the coalition's army and utterly destroyed it, sending a wave of terror throughout Europe.

While the siege of Constantinople continued, Bayezit turned to Anatolia again in 1397 and began conquering its eastern regions. By this time, the defunct Il-khanate's domain in eastern Anatolia had been replaced by several Muslim Turkish overlords. Bayezit won battle after battle until he had conquered the bulk of the peninsula. His territory, extending from the Caucasus to the Danube, was poised to become an empire. His brutal Anatolian conquests, however—accomplished with the aid of large numbers of Balkan Christians—had alienated many Turkish families in Anatolia, whose own hopes for leadership had been destroyed. They looked to Timur Lang to get their revenge.

Scourges

The fourteenth century was a difficult one for much of the world's population. The travails of the inhabitants of Europe are justly famous: famine, wars, the schism within the papacy, and the plague, which reduced the population by thirty to fifty percent. China suffered from epidemics during this century as well. For much of the predominantly Muslim world, however, the second half of the century was probably more wretched than for any comparably sized area on the planet.

Plague

The plague swept into Southwest Asia and Europe in 1347. Known in Europe as the Black Death, its origins are unclear despite enormous efforts by biologists, epidemiologists, anthropologists, and historians to understand how and where it emerged. Recent research can trace it back only to Caffa, a Black Sea port in Crimea. From there it spread with astounding rapidity to Constantinople, Iraq, Iran, and port cities in the Mediterranean and along the Atlantic coast of Europe. From the ports, it spread inland. It had a high mortality rate, and it recurred frequently during the next several centuries, keeping the population unnaturally low in the areas where it struck.

The Dar al-Islam suffered a serious blow from the pestilence. The Mamluk Empire's experience with the plague is the best-documented case in the Muslim world, and it suggests a population loss by the end of the century of at least one-third, a rate comparable to that of Europe. Rural and urban areas alike suffered depopulation, and the disease killed the livestock upon which agriculture and transport depended. Because of the depopulation of rural areas, orchards and crops were neglected and food production dropped. Disease spread even more rapidly in the cities; the chronicles report a continuous procession of the dead being carried out the city gates to the cemeteries. Many of Cairo's neighborhoods were abandoned and had fallen into ruin by the end of the century. Hardest hit of all, it seems, were the royal mamluks. Refusing to leave the capital city and living in the close quarters of their barracks, the mamluks suffered huge losses. The struggle between the Qipchaqs and the Circassians had become intense by the time of the first appearance of the plague; what role it played in shifting the balance of power to the Circassians (who seized power in 1382) is a matter of speculation.

The Mamluk Empire entered a period of sustained decline in population, wealth, and military power. For reasons not understood, the pneumonic variety of the plague recurred repeatedly in the Mamluk Empire, and as a result, the mortality rates of several of the later epidemics were as high as the first one. At least fifty epidemics struck the empire over the next 170 years. The population of Syria and Egypt did not regain their preplague levels for several centuries. The regime's military power declined markedly due to the high rate of death among the royal mamluks.

Mamluk agriculture remained in a centuries-long state of depression, and the thriving industries of the fourteenth century went into steep decline. The one bright spot amid the gloom of the plague was that the Mamluk Empire did witness a boom in construction. New buildings, particularly madrasas, mosques, fountains, and tombs, went up in large numbers. Many of these may have been endowed by individuals hoping to escape the plague by their good works and by others grateful for having been spared from the plague. At any rate, as a result of the increased opportunities for constructing and decorating such buildings, urban artisans who survived the epidemics were well paid. In addition, Egypt continued to benefit from its role as an entrepôt in the international spice trade. Its spice merchants joined the artisans as the only groups who prospered during the period from the mid-fourteenth to late fifteenth century.

The ports of North Africa and of Granada were also hit hard by the epidemic. The disease struck the Iberian Peninsula during a war between Granada and Castile. It hit Granada's army before that of Castile, causing some Muslims to consider converting to Christianity as a prophylactic. Fortunately for their faith, the disease was soon raging among troops of Castile as well. Alfonso XI, the king of Castile, was the only ruling monarch of Europe to die of the Black Death. The Ottomans crossed the Dardanelles in 1345 in order to aid their Byzantine ally in his struggle for the throne, but we do not know how the plague of 1347 affected them there. Constantinople suffered grievously from it, as did all the Aegean and Mediterranean port cities. The Byzantines recorded ten major plague epidemics between 1347 and

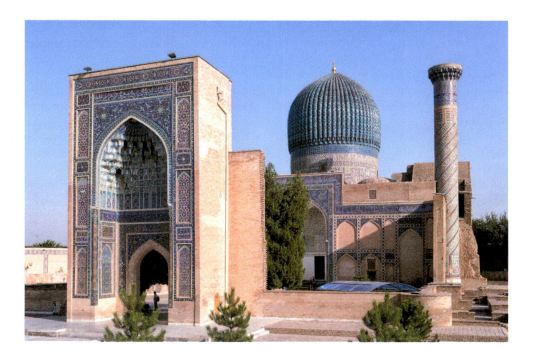

FIGURE 10.4 The Gur-i Amir in Samarqand. Timur began its construction in 1398, and it became the tomb for him and several of his illustrious Timurid descendants.

B.O'Kane / Alamy Stock Photo.

1440, but little is known about the plague's effects on the Ottomans until after they conquered Constantinople in 1453. Whereas England suffered periodic bouts with the plague through 1665 and France endured its last epidemic in 1720, the Ottomans suffered frequent waves of it into the nineteenth century.

The Conquests of Timur Lang

Shortly after the first incidence of the plague, another destructive scourge struck Southwest Asia. This was the army of the warrior Timur Lang, known to Europe as Tamerlane (*Temur Leng* is more accurate as a Turkic rendering of his name, but it is less widely used). The ferocity and wanton destructiveness of his campaigns still provoke amazement and horror, and the victories of his undefeated army changed the course of history for numerous regimes. He came of age as the Mongol states were collapsing, and he found the heirs to those states to be easy prey. More impressive was the ease with which he defeated the Mamluks, the Delhi Sultanate, and the Ottomans.

Timur (1336–1405) was born in the immediate aftermath of the schism within the Chaghatay Khanate that erupted during the reign of Tarmasharin. He grew up near Samarqand, where the settled population was dominated by nomadic and semi-nomadic Turko–Mongol tribes. Timur himself claimed descent from the Mongols through his mother and from Turks through his father. During the 1360s, he developed a series of alliances with local chieftains and became a powerful actor in the affairs of Transoxiana.

About 1370, Timur seized control of Samarqand and declared his intention of restoring the glory of the Mongol Empire. He spent the next decade securing control of the frontiers of Transoxiana. True to the classic model, victories begat victories, for the vanquished armies became the reservoir for new recruits into his own army, and his forces grew exponentially. Unlike the armies of light cavalry characteristic of the Chinggisid conquests, however, Timur's armies gradually became a composite force. One element that made him such a formidable opponent was that he realized the advantages of combining the mobility of light cavalry with the shock force of heavy cavalry. He also utilized infantry when it served his purposes, and he adopted the new Chinese technology of rockets.

In 1381, Timur began the conquests that made his place in history. His own explanations for the campaigns are not recorded, and historians have had to speculate on his motivations. To some observers, the needless bloodshed and physical destruction of the campaigns suggest that they were simple plundering operations, carried out to keep his volatile troops satisfied with booty. Other historians have speculated that the campaigns were begun in order to create a great commercial network that would allow Samarqand to recapture its glory, and that the accompanying violence was a technique to intimidate the subject populations to submit to his authority.

Whatever Timur's motives may have been, by 1385 he had captured Herat, Khorasan, and all of eastern Iran, and during the course of the next year he conquered Esfahan and Hamadan, thus destroying the petty dynasties that had emerged in the aftermath of the collapse of the Il-khanid regime. Over the next nine years, he conquered Iraq and the Caucasus. During the 1390s, he led two punitive expeditions against Toqtamish of the Horde. Toqtamish, self-confident after having seized power over the Horde in 1377, dared to encroach upon Timur's territory in Transoxiana. Timur retaliated and punished him in battle, but Toqtamish foolishly challenged Timur again in Azerbaijan. This time, Timur systematically destroyed all the commercial cities in the Horde from the Black Sea to the Aral Sea. Although Timur was not able to capture Toqtamish, the latter's reputation was destroyed, and the destruction of the cities of the steppes caused irreparable harm to the economy of the Tatars.

During Timur's campaign against Toqtamish, revolts broke out all over Iran against his occupation. He brutally suppressed them. Whole cities were destroyed, their inhabitants massacred, and towers were built of their skulls. After reestablishing control of Iran, Timur invaded the Delhi Sultanate in 1398. The Indian army, exhausted by the decade of civil war that followed the death of Firuz, was crushed. The killing and wanton destruction that characterized the Delhi campaign may be unsurpassed in history. The chroniclers report that Timur ordered the execution of tens of thousands of Hindu captives before and after the battle for Delhi. Thousands of them are said to have been skinned alive. The sack of Delhi went on for several days before the city was set afire and left in smoldering ruins. Members of the Tughluq dynasty continued to claim sovereignty in Delhi until 1413, but the city remained devastated. Over the course of the next century, Delhi slowly established itself as a regional power, but it would take more than a century for it to eclipse its rival Hindu and Muslim states again.

Timur returned to Samarqand in 1399 with a vast amount of wealth with which to enhance the only city that he appears ever to have appreciated. He also brought back a herd of Indian war elephants, a novel weapon that he wanted to add to his arsenal. As usual, he spent only a few days inside the walls before retiring to his rural pavilion. Before the end of the year, he set out on a campaign to the west, and he again secured control over Azerbaijan. While there, he received emissaries from Turkish chieftains in Anatolia who were under his protection and learned that Bayezit had invaded their territories. Bayezit's action was an affront to Timur's honor and resulted in a tense confrontation between two of the most powerful men in the world. Neither one had a clear picture of the other's power, and both were reluctant to force the issue without more intelligence. Timur sent a diplomatically worded dispatch to Bayezit, warning him to keep his distance from areas under Timur's authority. Bayezit replied not only arrogantly, but insultingly. Timur then attacked and destroyed the Ottoman outpost of Sivas, which had been under the command of one of Bayezit's sons.

Assuming that he had taught Bayezit his lesson, Timur then turned to the Mamluks and attacked the city of Aleppo in 1400. The Circassian Mamluks, reeling from the effects of recurring bouts with the plague, famines caused by inadequate floods of the Nile, and a worsening balance of trade with Europe, were in no position to contest the mighty Timur. Aleppo fell, and in 1401, Timur moved on to Damascus. The young Mamluk sultan had assembled his army near that city, but he abandoned it and hastily returned to Cairo on the pretext that a rebellion had broken out there. His leaderless army straggled back to Cairo in disarray. The inhabitants of Damascus, now defenseless, agreed to pay Timur a heavy ransom not to be attacked. Once inside the walls, however, Timur increased the ransom demand tenfold. When the citizens protested, he ordered the city to be sacked, and the inhabitants were massacred. He spared the city's artisans, whom he sent to Samarqand.

By the fall of 1401, Timur was no longer concerned by a potential threat from the Mamluks, and he headed toward the Caucasus for the winter. Learning of a rebellion in Baghdad, he ordered the hapless city destroyed. Leveled for the second time in little more than a century, it would require more than four centuries for the city to become even a regional town again. Once in the Caucasus, Timur received news of Bayezit's continuing challenge to his claims in eastern Anatolia, and he resolved to decide the issue the following season. In July 1402, the two armies met at modern Ankara. Timur used his Indian war elephants to launch the attack. Once the battle had been joined, Bayezit's Turkish allies abandoned him, leaving him to fight Timur with his Balkan Christian vassals. He was defeated and captured, and he died in captivity eight months later. Timur's army pursued the remnants of the Ottoman army all the way to the Dardanelles, where the Ottoman survivors were ferried across (for a price) by boatmen from Genoa and Venice.

Bayezit's sons began fighting each other for control of the Ottoman holdings, and they almost caused the destruction of everything that their ancestors had achieved. For the next nine years, their civil war allowed most of the local leaders in Anatolia and in the Balkans to regain their political independence, and both areas lapsed into near anarchy. To contemporaries, it appeared that the Ottomans were finished.

In the Presence of Timur

Anyone trapped within a city besieged by Timur would be consumed by anxiety of the worst kind. Such a fate befell one of the era's greatest scholars, Ibn Khaldun, when Timur besieged Damascus. The scholar's experience with Timur soon became "up close and personal" when the conqueror announced that he desired to see him. Timur received Ibn Khaldun graciously and then informed him that he wanted him to write a detailed description of the Maghrib. Ibn Khaldun spent the next five weeks in Timur's camp writing his report, and he left a record of his experiences during that time. Foregoing an opportunity to portray Timur as a monster, he reveals a human side to Timur as well as his own obsequiousness in the presence of absolute power.

[After asking for the report on the Maghrib] he gave a signal to his servants to bring from his tent some of the kind of food which they call "rishta" and which they were most expert in preparing. Some dishes of it were brought in, and he made a sign that they should be set before me. I arose, took them, and drank, and liked it, and this impressed him favorably. [Then] I composed in my mind some words to say to him which, by exalting him and his government, would flatter him....

The news was brought to him that the gate of the city had been opened and that the judges had gone out to fulfill their [promise of] surrender, for which, so they thought, he had generously granted them amnesty. Then he was carried away from before us, because of the trouble with his knee, and was placed upon his horse; grasping the reins, he sat upright in his saddle while the bands played around him until the air shook with them; he rode toward Damascus....

(Continued)

When the time for Timur's journey approached and he decided to leave Damascus, I entered to him one day. After we had completed the customary greetings, he turned to me and said, "You have a mule here?"

I answered, "Yes."

He said, "Is it a good one?"

I answered, "Yes."

He said, "Will you sell it? I would buy it from you."

I replied, "May Allah aid you—one like me does not sell to one like you; but I would offer it to you in homage, and also others like it if I had them."

He said, "I meant only that I would requite you for it with generosity."

I replied, "Is there any generosity left beyond that which you have already shown me? You have heaped favors upon me, accorded me a place in your council among your intimate followers, and shown me kindness and generosity—which I hope Allah will repay to you in like measure."

He was silent; so was I. The mule was brought to him while I was with him at his council, and I did not see it again....

Then on another day I entered to him and he asked me: "Are you going to travel to Cairo?"

I answered, "May Allah aid you—indeed, my desire is only [to serve] you, for you have granted me refuge and protection. If the journey to Cairo would be in your service, surely; otherwise I have no desire for it."

He said, "No, but you will return to your family and to your people."

SOURCE: *Anthology of Islamic Literature: From the Rise of Islam to Modern Times,* with an introduction and commentaries by James Kritzeck. New York: Holt, Rinehart and Winston Inc., 1964, 281–284.

Timur now began to prepare for the climax of his career: a campaign against the Ming dynasty in China. He set out from Samarqand in December 1404 but fell seriously ill as he approached the Syr Darya River. He died in February 1405. Contrary to Muslim practice, his body was embalmed and sent to Samarqand, where it was buried in the impressive tomb that he had constructed for that purpose, the Gur-e Amir. At his death, his sons and grandsons fought over the succession and lost all the territories that Timur had conquered except for Transoxiana and western Afghanistan.

Timur's legacy would boast of impressive cultural achievements in Samarqand and Herat over the next century. Timur himself adorned Samarqand with beautiful buildings, gardens, and a national library where books were copied, illustrated, bound, and stored. Elsewhere, however, the result of Timur's career was sheer destruction. The area from Delhi to Damascus had been laid waste, and combined with the effects of the plague in Syria and Iraq, the communities of a huge area experienced suffering and despair beyond comprehension.

Some historians have pointed out that Chinggis Khan and his Mongol successors usually employed cruelty as a means to gain submission. Timur, like Alexander the Great, seems to have simply enjoyed watching rivers of blood flow. What makes

Timur's cruelty more difficult to explain is that all of his opponents were Muslim regimes. If he had been a pagan like his Mongol ancestors, his barbarity might be dismissed as a symptom of his hostility to an alien culture. Timur, however, like many of his fellow Turks and Mongols in Central Asia, easily combined residual shamanism with a commitment to Islam. In the name of Islam, he systematically destroyed the Jacobite church in northern Syria and western Anatolia, as well as the Nestorian church in Central Asia. He also claimed to be serving the cause of Islam in invading the Delhi Sultanate, which of course was ruled by Muslims. But his motives for the utter destruction of large numbers of Muslims across a wide swath of territory remain obscure.

Conclusion

The fifteenth century dawned on an eastern Muslim landscape utterly transformed from its contours of the early thirteenth century. From Syria and the Russian steppes in the west to India in the east, the whole order had been reworked several times in a century and a half. Muslim regimes, Mongol regimes, civil war, the plague, and Timur Lang had transformed the political and social order the way a tornado scrambles anything in its path. The Mongol conquests of the thirteenth century inflicted catastrophic damage upon Iraq and Khorasan. They had also inadvertently boosted the fortunes of the nascent Mamluk, Ottoman, and Delhi regimes by causing tens of thousands of intellectuals, craftsmen, and artists to flee to those havens. In the fourteenth century, the plague and Timur's campaigns laid waste once again to Iran and Iraq, but they also threatened the very existence of the Mamluk, Ottoman, and Delhi states and societies. By the time of Timur's death in 1405, Delhi had been reduced to the status of a local pretender, and Ottoman power appeared to be destroyed. The Circassian Mamluks had been humiliated by their failure to defend Damascus, and recurring waves of the plague kept them weaker than their Qipchaq predecessors.

The Mongol conquests, it should be remembered, were only the latest wave of violence and suffering to afflict the Muslim world. On the other hand, they were so destructive that they caused mass migrations of peasants, nomads, craftsmen, intellectuals, and merchants to areas not under the immediate threat of Mongol attack. One important consequence was that the ethnic composition of many parts of the Muslim world would be changed for centuries to come. Moreover, regions which up to that time had been peripheral to mainstream developments in the Dar al-Islam now became thriving centers of commerce and culture due to the influx of refugees from the Mongol advance.

The period 1260–1405 represents a major watershed in Muslim history. It witnessed a degree of destruction and suffering that can hardly be imagined, and yet the thoroughness of the changes that took place created opportunities for new societies to assert themselves. The cumulative effect of this period was that, by the beginning of the fifteenth century, the political structures of the central and eastern sections of the Dar al-Islam had been so shaken that a contemporary outside observer could be forgiven for wondering if Islamic civilization had a future. As it turned out, that civilization was about to rise, phoenixlike, and become the most dominant force in the world for several centuries.

FURTHER READING

The Mongol Khanates

Adshead, S.A.M. *Central Asia in World History*. New York: St. Martin's Press, 1993.

Allsen, Thomas T. *Culture and Conquest in Mongol Eurasia*. Cambridge, U.K.: Cambridge University Press, 2001.

Kwanten, Luc. *Imperial Nomads: A History of Central Asia, 500–1500*. Philadelphia: University of Pennsylvania Press, 1979.

Morgan, David. *The Mongols*. Oxford, U.K.: Basil Blackwell, 1986.

Vernadsky, George. *The Mongols and Russia*. New Haven, Connecticut: Yale University Press, 1953.

New Centers of Islamic Culture

Ahmed, Aziz. *Studies in Islamic Culture in the Indian Environment*. Oxford, U.K.: Oxford University Press, 1962.

Ayalon, David. *Islam and the Abode of War*. London: Variorum, 1994.

———. *Outsiders in the Lands of Islam: Mamluks, Mongols and Eunuchs*. London: Variorum Reprints, 1988.

Cahen, Claude. *The Formation of Turkey*. Translated and edited by P. M. Holt. Harlow, U.K.: Longman, 2001.

Canfield, Robert L., ed. *Turko–Persia in Historical Perspective*. Cambridge, U.K.: Cambridge University Press, 1991.

Ikram, S.M. *Muslim Civilization in India*. Edited by Ainslie T. Embree. New York and London: Columbia University Press, 1964.

Inalcik, Halil. *The Ottoman Empire: The Classical Age, 1300–1600*. Translated by Norman Itzkowitz and Colin Imber. New York and Washington: Praeger Publishers, 1973.

Kafadar, Cemal. *Between Two Worlds: The Construction of the Ottoman State*. Berkeley, California: The University of California Press, 1995.

Irwin, R. *The Middle East in the Middle Ages: The Early Mamluk Sultanate (1250–1382)*. Carbondale, Illinois: Southern Illinois University Press, 1986.

Jackson, Peter. *The Delhi Sultanate*. Cambridge and New York: Cambridge University Press, 1999.

McCarthy, Justin. *The Ottoman Turks: An Introductory History to 1923*. London and New York: Longman, 1997.

Scourges

Adshead, S.A.M. *Central Asia in World History*. New York: St. Martin's Press, 1993.

Dols, Michael. *The Black Death in the Middle East*. Princeton, New Jersey: Princeton University Press, 1977.

Manz, Beatrice Forbes. *The Rise and Rule of Tamerlane*. Cambridge, U.K.: Cambridge University Press, 1989.

Varlik, Nükhet. *Plague and Empire in the Early Modern Mediterranean World: The Ottoman Experience, 1347–1600*. New York: Cambridge University Press, 2015.

CHAPTER 11

Unity and Diversity in Islamic Traditions

In 1325, a young Moroccan named Ibn Battuta embarked upon the hajj. Others from his hometown who had traveled to Mecca before him had usually been away for two to three years. Thus, he knew that he would be gone for an extended period, but it is doubtful that he had any idea at the time just how long it would be before he saw home again. In fact, after he had completed the rituals of the pilgrimage, he decided to travel the extent of the Muslim world. He sailed along the coast of East Africa, ventured into the realm of the Horde in southern Russia, lived for seven years in India, and may even have sailed through the straits of Southeast Asia on his way to China. He did not return home until 1349. His return trip was fraught with numerous perils, for he had to make his way through the collapsing states of the mid-fourteenth century as well as avoid becoming a victim of the plague, which was ravaging much of the world at the time.

Ibn Battuta's career opens a window upon Muslim cultures of the fourteenth century. Muslim states, as a rule, proved ephemeral in the face of the cataclysms of the thirteenth and fourteenth centuries. More impressive was the strength of the ideas and institutions that had evolved within the Muslim world over the previous several centuries. Scholars in many disciplines had not ceased producing original work, and Ibn Battuta visited many whose fame was spread all across the Dar al-Islam. The Shari'a provided cultural continuity when states failed, and Ibn Battuta financed his travels by serving as an itinerant qadi: Everywhere he went, his credentials qualified him to adjudicate disputes according to Islamic law, and grateful Muslims paid handsomely for his services. Ibn Battuta also benefited from the fact that, by the mid-fourteenth century, Sufi lodges and orders were widespread throughout the Dar al-Islam. He visited many different Sufi masters, enjoyed the hospitality of numerous Sufi lodges, and marveled at the variety of Sufi expression wherever he went.

Intellectual Life in the Fourteenth Century

The inhabitants of the Dar al-Islam suffered widespread and repeated violence during the thirteenth and fourteenth centuries. The sudden gains of the Reconquista, the widespread elimination of Muslim states by the Mongols, the collapse of the newly Islamized Mongol regimes themselves, the catastrophe of the plague, and the utter ruthlessness of Timur were spectacularly destructive and severely demoralizing. Many European historians of the nineteenth and twentieth centuries, viewing the Muslim experience of this period through the prism of the subsequent rise of Europe to world dominance, found it easy to assume that Islamic civilization had been shattered and left moribund. That view can no longer be defended.

The End of the "Golden Age"?

Unlike early medieval Western Europe after the collapse of Roman administration, the Muslim world never suffered from a cessation of its cultural life. As had happened earlier during times of great turmoil, Islamic law continued to function, precisely because it was not dependent upon the stability of any particular regime. Also as before, the new states, even the transitory ones, attempted to gain legitimacy for themselves by patronizing scholars and artists who exemplified the best of Islamic civilization.

Even though Islamic civilization did not collapse in the fourteenth century, Europeans gradually ceased envying it. Until the thirteenth century, the level of intellectual production in the Muslim world had been vastly superior to that of Europe. With the work of scholars such as Albertus Magnus, Robert Grosseteste, and Roger Bacon (all of whom were inspired by translations of Arabic manuscripts), however, European thought caught up with the natural science being practiced in the Dar al-Islam. The twelfth- and thirteenth-century translation of Arabic versions of Greek texts prompted a desire to read the Greek originals. In the process of searching for them, European scholars discovered previously unknown texts by Plato, Aristotle, and other intellectuals. Although philosophy remained largely within the framework set by the Church for three more centuries, numerous new currents in philosophy emerged, laying the foundation for humanism and other secular developments of the fifteenth and sixteenth centuries.

From the thirteenth to the seventeenth centuries, European scientific and philosophical thought was on a rough parity with its counterpart in the Dar al-Islam. Although Copernicus proposed his heliocentric (sun-centered) theory in the 1540s, it was not widely accepted even among scientists until the late seventeenth century. Even those of us who still speak of the sun "rising" and "setting" have a difficult time grasping how incredulous the vast majority of people were that anyone could seriously propose that the earth revolved around the sun. The new theory flew in the face of the everyday experience of seeing the sun rise and set, and it is hard not to take our sensory experience seriously, particularly when everyone else registers the same results that we do every day. But heliocentrism also challenged the authoritative, geocentric (earth-centered) Ptolemaic model of the universe. Ptolemy, the great second-century geographer and astronomer, had established the basis for determining latitudes on earth, and his geocentric model of the universe rapidly became the paradigm accepted by the greatest scientific authorities for more than a millennium. Moreover, it was soon evident that the Copernican model was less successful in predicting eclipses and explaining the movements of the celestial bodies than the Ptolemaic one. Finally, the Copernican model flatly contradicted the Biblical worldview. The Church considered the new theory both nonsensical and heretical, and it threatened its proponents with execution for teaching it. Not until the end of the seventeenth century was the heliocentric theory conclusively accepted in scientific circles (after considerable revisions of Copernicus's ideas), but the Catholic Church had so much institutional prestige invested in opposing it that it continued to forbid its teaching in Catholic-majority countries until 1860. In science and mathematics, therefore, we can say that Protestant Europe began to move beyond Muslim achievements only in the late seventeenth century. It was also during this period that European universities finally began to discard Ibn Sina's 700-year-old book of medicine in favor of new knowledge of anatomy and physiology that owed much to the discoveries of Vesalius and Harvey.

The reversal of fortunes in the scientific and philosophical productivity of Europe and the Muslim world has given rise to much speculation about "what went wrong" for the Dar al-Islam. Often forgotten in the discussion is the fact that Europe's subsequent development was unique and unpredictable. Its science and technology eventually dwarfed that of all other regions of the globe, not just the predominantly Muslim regions. The cultural systems of China, India, Southeast Asia, and the Americas all contained elements that had been more sophisticated than their European counterparts, but by the late eighteenth century, their technological prowess was eclipsed. The European aberration is actually the topic that needs explanation, and we still cannot provide an adequate one. Much of the speculation has been based on misplaced assumptions about historical inevitability and progress, rather than on a careful analysis of how history actually takes place.

The contrasting trajectories of the intellectual history of Europe and the Muslim world are of particular interest due to their common heritage. They shared many features: Their monotheistic traditions were remarkably parallel, and they enjoyed the same access to the Greco–Roman traditions of architecture, philosophy, engineering, medicine, and political thought. The advantages that the Muslim world enjoyed were a more direct access to the creative traditions of China and India and not having to overcome the disastrous collapse of Roman administration that Western Europe suffered after the fourth century. A major advantage for Western Europe was that it no longer suffered from outside invasions after the mid-tenth century. It subsequently enjoyed a period of economic growth that resulted in political centralization and cultural sophistication. The Muslim world, by contrast, began suffering from sustained violence from the same, mid-tenth century period.

Muslim religious scholars became increasingly intolerant of speculative thought. Innovation (*bid'a*) in religious affairs had always been frowned upon due to the perceived obligation to act strictly in accord with the Qur'an and the Prophet's own behavior, but the charge of "bid'a" was increasingly effective in limiting the scope of intellectual inquiry. By the thirteenth century, when Muslims felt hemmed in by aggressive Christian enemies to the west and ruthless pagan Mongol enemies to the east, philosophical speculation had practically ceased.

Today, it is as difficult to explain adequately the growing conservatism of Muslim intellectuals as it is to explain the increasing creativity of European intellectuals. A multitude of factors played a part in both cases, and perhaps we will never be able to identify the most important ones. It does seem useful, however, to keep in mind two elements of the Muslim experience. One is the conjunction between the sense of collective insecurity, on the one hand, and the growing reluctance to allow challenges to established religious doctrine, on the other. A confident society is likely to allow more scope to intellectual inquiry than one that fears for its future. The other element is the fact that Muslim philosopher–scientists required the patronage of ruling families for their economic support, whereas, by the twelfth century, European scholars were beginning to organize autonomous universities. European scientists and philosophers enjoyed legal protection as communities of scholars. They benefitted from the exchange of ideas and the criticism that came from belonging to a faculty, and they could respond to threats to their livelihood by going to court. Muslim scholars, however, were attached individually to the palaces of ruling dynasties. They shared ideas with fellow scholars, but at a distance. If their ideas were criticized by local religious leaders or by public opinion, the patron usually found it expedient to dismiss them. Under those conditions, it was next to impossible for a school of thought to develop based on an original idea.

Thus, it is possible to say that the period of Mongol hegemony represents a period during which Muslim philosophical thought practically disappeared except as an adjunct to theology and law. The fields of prose, poetry, the sciences, and mathematics, however, continued to boast the work of outstanding talents, and the visual arts were entering their most spectacular period. Scientists and mathematicians continued to make important revisions to existing knowledge, but their isolation from each other and their dependence on the goodwill of a ruler limited the scope of their work. Their plight was similar to that of the vast majority of intellectuals in the world at the time.

Against All Odds

A notable feature of the period that featured both the Mongols and Timur is the vibrancy of the religious, artistic, and intellectual life of the Muslim world. The cultural and intellectual life of the Dar al-Islam showed that it had securely established itself across a wide area, and even the hammer blows of the fourteenth century could not destroy it. As we have seen, even the Mamluk Empire, which experienced the effects of the plague as severely as any other region in the world, made contributions to art and architecture that are still regarded with awe. The intellectual life of Muslims, too, continued to flourish. Philosophy continued to be suspect because of its association with challenges to the authority of revelation, but the use of disciplined reason was highly valued in most theological and legal circles. Historical and scientific studies also continued to flourish wherever manuscripts survived or were copied and where patronage made scholarship possible. Sometimes these conditions made vibrant scholarship possible in the most unlikely of settings.

Ibn Taymiya

One of the greatest Muslim religious scholars of the fourteenth century was Ibn Taymiya (1262–1327). He was born in the city of Harran, located near today's border between Syria and Turkey. Fearing the effects of the onset of Hulagu's rule, his family moved to Damascus while Ibn Taymiya was a small child. For the rest of his life, he lived under Mamluk rule. Through a combination of formal education and independent study, he mastered the disciplines that focused on the study of the Qur'an, Hadith, jurisprudence, rational theology, philosophy, and Sufi metaphysics. His keen intellect, his deep knowledge of the religious sciences, and his forceful personality combined to create one of the most influential thinkers in Islamic history.

Ibn Taymiya's career was committed to the cause of Islamic reform. He was convinced that certain doctrines and practices had arisen that were not sanctioned by the legitimate sources of the faith, and he became a tireless advocate of the need to return to what he regarded as the purity of early Islamic history. He argued that the two sources of all religious truth are the Qur'an and the Hadith as interpreted by the first generation of Muslim scholars. As a member of the Hanbali school of law, he believed that whatever is commanded in those sources must be obeyed, and whatever is not mentioned in them must not be required. Although he was proficient in the methods of philosophy and rational theology, he was bitterly critical of the conclusions that philosophers and theologians drew from them.

He was particularly critical of philosophers who asserted that scripture had been deliberately couched in metaphors and pictorial images so that common people could understand it. He also found fault with certain features of Sufism, although he was not opposed to Sufism as such. He did, however, object to common Sufi practices such as the pilgrimages that were made to the tombs of saints, and he rejected the monism of Ibn al-'Arabi. One of his greatest contributions to subsequent Islamic history was his criticism of fellow jurists for accepting without question the decisions of jurists of previous generations. He was convinced that scholars of the Shari'a had an obligation to continue interpreting the will of God as it applied to contemporary society, provided that all such decisions were firmly grounded in the two major sources of law, extended where necessary by analogical reasoning.

Ibn Taymiya was what today we would call a "public intellectual." He brought his passionate concerns to the attention of both the public and the authorities, not just to the small group of his fellow intellectuals. Because some of his criticism was directed at other intellectuals, popular religious leaders, and government officials, he became the center of controversy and conflict. From at least 1298 until his death in 1327, he was repeatedly brought before the courts on various charges—"anthropomorphism," his attacks on rituals at saints' shrines, and his support of a revision to the Shari'a that would make it more difficult for a man to divorce his wife, among others—and was jailed several times for a total of at least five years for his "offenses." His funeral attracted thousands of admirers, many of whom he had criticized for un-Islamic practices but who respected him for his courage, brilliance, and integrity.

Ibn Taymiya's moral courage and his uncompromising dedication to truth as he understood it has made him a role model for many Islamic reformers to the present day. He is particularly remembered today for his evaluation of Ghazan, the Il-khan ruler whose army occupied Damascus for a year after defeating the Mamluks in 1300. Ghazan, as we have seen, was a professed Muslim, but Ibn Taymiya never forgot that the Mongols had destroyed much of the civilization of the Islamic world and had frightened his family out of their home in Harran. He also pointed out that Ghazan continued to apply the Mongol code of law (the Yasa). He led an opposition group to the Mongol occupation of his adopted city, and afterward he wrote extensively on the duty of believers to oppose rulers who professed to be Muslim and performed the basic rites, but who in fact failed to apply the Shari'a. As a result, he is revered today by Muslim activists who challenge the oppressive and corrupt governments of their countries and advocate the creation of an Islamic state.

Ibn al-Shatir

Until the late twentieth century, the focus of historians of astronomy on the Copernican tradition caused them to ignore the original work of Muslim astronomers. In fact, from the tenth century on, a large number of Muslim astronomers recorded important observations and made significant contributions to astronomical theory. Some of the most important Muslim astronomers lived during the period from the thirteenth to the sixteenth centuries, an era when many Western historians assumed that Islamic scholarship had died. One of the most important astronomers in history was Ibn al-Shatir of Damascus (1306–1375), whose career spanned the last, turbulent decades of the Qipchaq period of Mamluk rule. He was a young man in Damascus when Ibn Taymiya died there. Ibn al-Shatir was the *muwaqqit*, or timekeeper, for the congregational mosque of Damascus, and he was chief of the mosque's muezzins. He designed and constructed his own versions of several observational and computing instruments, including the quadrant and sundial. His large sundial for the congregational mosque of Damascus still stands, and a portable one is preserved in the Aleppo Museum.

Even more impressive is Ibn al-Shatir's work in astronomy. He stands in the tradition of what has come to be known as the "Maragha school" of astronomy. As we have seen, Hulagu's observatory at Maragha attracted scientists from China to Andalus. The astronomers at Maragha engaged in much observational work but are best known for their revision of existing astronomical theory. Although the Maragha observatory had been abandoned after the collapse of the Il-khanate, Ibn al-Shatir continued its modifications of Ptolemy's work. Muslim astronomers did not offer a heliocentric theory because, at the time, such a theory was contrary to the evidence of the senses as well as unnecessary, due to the usefulness of the Ptolemaic model. What concerned them (and European astronomers) was the inconsistency between Ptolemy's model and the mechanics that he proposed to explain how it worked. A major problem was that Ptolemy assumed for theoretical purposes that celestial orbits were perfectly circular, but actual observation demonstrated that they acted in an elliptical fashion. He had attempted to explain the discrepancy by proposing that spherical orbits moved uniformly around an axis that did not pass through the center of the sphere (an "eccentric" circle, rather than a "concentric" one).

Another problem was that, over the centuries, astronomers found that the assumption of the perfect uniformity of the velocity of planets ran counter to their observations. Planets appeared to wander in random patterns, and they seemed to speed up and slow down. Rather than abandoning the Ptolemaic model, however, astronomers proposed that a given planet actually moves in a small circular orbit (an "epicycle"), which is itself centered on the rim of an orbit around the earth. This corollary seemed adequate until so many epicycles had to be proposed that the entire model became unwieldy. When the dozens of epicycles were combined with the eccentric orbits, the Ptolemaic model was beginning to look like a Rube Goldberg machine. The Copernican Revolution was triggered in part because Copernicus could not believe that God had designed such an awkward instrument.

Ibn al-Shatir, too, was concerned with the problems of the eccentrics and the epicycles. Like all other astronomers of the fourteenth century, he saw no need to challenge Ptolemy's basic model. The task was to make it internally consistent. Starting with the assumption that celestial orbits are the result of a succession of uniform circular motions, he developed models of orbits of the moon and the planets that did not require eccentrics. His highly sophisticated geometry allowed him to accomplish what the master Ptolemy could not. His geometric models, which assume a geocentric universe, show up in a revised form 200 years later in the heliocentric model of Copernicus. Since the late 1950s, when Ibn al-Shatir's manuscripts were discovered by European scholars, historians of science have been wrestling with how to explain the similarity of the models of Ibn al-Shatir and Copernicus. They are aware that just because Ibn al-Shatir came up with such models prior to Copernicus does not mean that someone else could not devise them independently, but two considerations cause them to think that they must have been transmitted in some form to Central Europe, where Copernicus could have had access to them. One reason is that no such models existed in the European tradition from which Copernicus could borrow. The other is that it is inconceivable that Copernicus would come up with the models himself, since they cause, rather than solve, problems for his theory. The lack of a theory of gravity in the Copernican model renders Ibn al-Shatir's models problematic in a heliocentric context: Without gravity, Copernicus has no explanation for why celestial bodies orbit the sun, whereas the Ptolemaic model utilized the Aristotelian theory that planets and the moon "desire" the earth. The discovery of a "missing link" between Ibn al-Shatir and Copernicus would provide a fascinating glimpse of late medieval intellectual history.

Ibn Khaldun

Ibn Khaldun (1332–1406) was descended from one of the great families of Seville. His great-grandparents fled the city just before its fall to Castile in 1248 and settled in Tunis, where Ibn Khaldun was born. As the scion of a wealthy and powerful family, he received the best education possible but was forced to emigrate in 1352 after the plague epidemic took the lives of his parents and teachers. For most of the rest of his life, he served as a government minister. He found advisory positions in the Marinid capital of Fez, and then at Granada and several small principalities in modern Morocco and Algeria. Life as a government minister in that era was notoriously unpredictable and dangerous, but Ibn Khaldun seems to have had a knack for making enemies that made his own career even more unpredictable and dangerous than most: In every position that he held, he was either jailed or forced to leave town. Perhaps seeking a more stable career line, he sailed for Egypt in 1382,

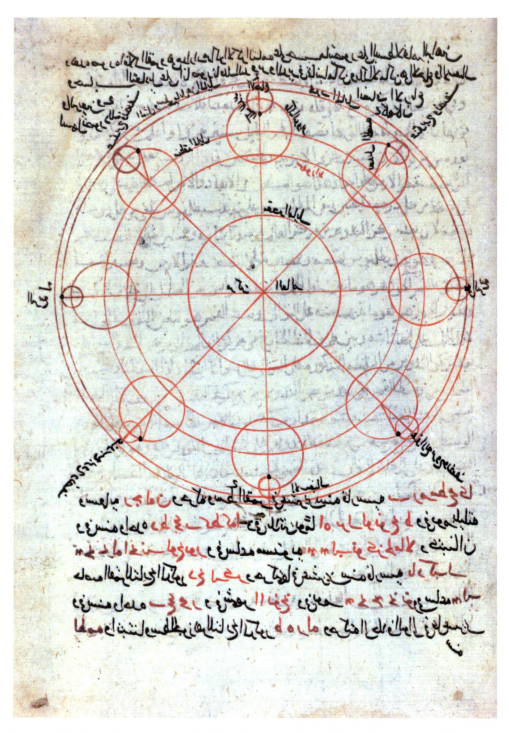

FIGURE 11.1 A solution proposed by Ibn al-Shatir to the problem of the moon's orbit around the earth.

The Bodleian Library, University of Oxford, MS. Marsh 139, fol. 16v.

the same year that Sultan Barquq seized power and inaugurated the Circassian period in Mamluk history. Barquq, recognizing Ibn Khaldun's achievement as a scholar and jurist, appointed him professor of Maliki law and then to be the senior Maliki qadi of Egypt. Even in Egypt, Ibn Khaldun encountered political problems and temporarily lost his posts. Because he was so adept at establishing contacts with important patrons, however, he always regained his positions.

Soon after Barquq's death in 1400, Timur began his invasion of Syria. The new Mamluk sultan insisted that Ibn Khaldun join his entourage as he went to Damascus to repel the attack. When the sultan returned in haste to Cairo, however, and his army straggled after him, he left Ibn Khaldun behind in the defenseless city. Timur asked to see him. Ibn Khaldun was thereupon lowered over the city's walls by ropes in a scene strikingly evocative of an episode in the life of the Christian theologian and missionary Paul fourteen centuries earlier. He spent five weeks in Timur's camp, serving as "scholar in residence." Ibn Khaldun recorded his experiences in the camp in a remarkably informal style. (See the extract in Chapter 10.) Timur wanted detailed knowledge of the Maghrib, and Ibn Khaldun presented enormous quantities of oral and written information, but in a way that portrayed the area as strong and united, rather than as the weak and divided region that it actually was. Whether the information he provided had anything to do with the fact that Timur did not venture south of Damascus is a matter of conjecture. Ibn Khaldun managed to obtain a safe conduct for himself and several of his friends, but he witnessed the murderous sack of the city and the burning of the great congregational mosque for which Ibn al-Shatir had served as timekeeper. Ibn Khaldun died in Egypt in 1406, a year after Timur.

Ibn Khaldun is best known for the *Muqaddima*, or "Introduction," to his history of the Arabs and Berbers. In 1374, after a particularly exhausting period of government service in North Africa, Ibn Khaldun had sought refuge with a Berber tribe in what is now Algeria. He stayed with them for four years, and it was during this time that he wrote the *Muqaddima*, a massive introduction (the English translation is in three large volumes) to an even larger work of history. Its originality and profundity have had a major influence on Egyptian historians of the fifteenth century, Ottoman historians, and social scientists and philosophers of our own time. Many consider it to be the first work of genuine social science. While it is too complex to be summarized in a few dozen words, mention can be made of its most famous features. It includes a survey of the full range of Islamic learning, but it focuses on the dynamics of historical change. Ibn Khaldun's positivism is revealed in his blistering critique of the metaphysics of philosophy and is expressed again in his theory of history, which he believes to be governed by rational or natural laws. He stresses the role of climate, geography, economics, and ecology in creating the distinctive characteristics of given societies.

Ibn Khaldun's most famous idea is a theory of historical change that was based on his understanding of North African history: An aggressive and simple nomadic community conquers an existing state and then develops a dynamic community characterized by ethnic, religious, or lineal solidarity. As the nomads become assimilated into the urban society that they have conquered, however, the second generation becomes corrupted by the vices of urban civilization. That generation gradually rejects the loyalty-based political authority that had made the state possible in the first place. The third and final generation loses both its solidarity and its martial spirit and becomes easy prey to yet another vigorous nomadic community. Ibn Khaldun offered numerous examples from the time of the Arab conquests through the Berber dynasties of the Almoravids, Almohads, and Marinids to support his theory. The campaigns of Timur, which occurred after he wrote his book, could only have made him feel that his theory had been validated.

Hafez

The rebirth of Persian literature that began in the ninth century produced numerous talented poets. The epic poet Ferdowsi (ca. 940–1020) and the mystical poets Farid al-Din 'Attar (ca. 1120–ca. 1220), Sa'di (ca. 1193–1292), and Jamal al-Din al-Rumi (1207–1273) are still revered in Iran. Speakers of Persian, literate and illiterate alike, can recite from memory numerous verses of their poetry, and they can harmonize Ferdowsi's celebration of pre-Islamic Iran with the religious themes of the others. As beloved as these poets are, however, the favorite poet of many Iranians is Hafez (ca. 1325–ca. 1390). Widely regarded as the greatest lyric poet in Persian, Hafez honed his craft in the midst of the chaos of the immediate post-Il-khanid era.

Hafez lived almost his entire life in Shiraz. When he was about ten years old, the Il-khanid ruler Abu Sa'id was poisoned, and the Il-khanid regime disintegrated. Various chieftains throughout the former empire seized power in the provinces. In Shiraz and western Iran, political violence was common throughout Hafez's life, and Shiraz changed hands several times. Hafez's family was not prominent in the community, but he managed to acquire a deep knowledge of the Islamic sciences, Arabic, and Persian literature. He is said to have written several commentaries on religious texts and to have taught the Qur'an. (His name is actually an honorific title, deriving from the Arabic word *hafiz*, which literally means "memorizer," specifically one who has memorized the entire Qur'an.)

Hafez was a deeply spiritual Sufi, but he was not an ascetic. He saw no contradiction between a love for God and a robust delight in the pleasures of the senses, and he composed poetry celebrating both. He became so renowned for his verses that he became a court poet for the Muzaffarid dynasty that ruled Shiraz for several decades, although he fell out of favor with them in 1368. His sensual lifestyle and love of wine provoked the ulama to criticize him, and at his death, some of them did not even want him buried in a regular cemetery.

Hafez specialized in the type of poetry known as the *ghazal*, a lyric poem of six to fifteen couplets. By the fourteenth century, Arabic and Persian poetry had developed certain conventions that were beginning to make poetry stilted and formal. Hafez deliberately chose to write about everyday experience in simple and colloquial language, avoiding artificial display. The listener detects a remarkably humane and honest spirit in the poet. Unlike most court poets, he wrote few panegyrics, and even when he satirized hypocrites, he did not use the insults commonly hurled by other poets.

Hafez continued the Persian Sufi tradition of allusive images. His poetry contains many references to lovers (both male and female), wine, idols, mosques, birds, flowers, and other potent symbols. On the other hand, even at its most materialistic, it is often couched in Islamic terminology. Western students of his poetry have often wondered whether his language is allegorical and needs to be "decoded" for its spiritual message or whether it is simply the sly musings of a profligate. Neither approach is adequate for the great Persian poets. Ambiguity of meaning is intrinsic and essential to their poetry. The cultivation of ambiguity was born in the midst of political and religious tension. Iranians chafed under the political dominance first of Arabs and then of Turks and Mongols. Iran was a religious cauldron as well. Both Zoroastrianism and Manichaeism (a religion that arose in the third century, became highly popular in Southwest Asia and Europe, and was severely persecuted by both Christians and Muslims over the next millennium) contained elements that still appealed to some Iranians. As a result, literal-minded interpreters of the Qur'an suspected philosophically or mystically inclined Muslims of being

The People's Poet

The poetry of Hafez, like that of many of the great Persian poets, can be read on at least two levels. Its literal meaning expresses the values of the secular sophisticate, but its words can be interpreted as metaphors for Sufi mystical theology. After Hafez's death, his poetry became popular even in the Ottoman Empire and in Muslim India, where Persian literature benefitted from court patronage. On the level of popular culture, many people used his poems for divination: They would open a copy of his collection of poetry, the Diwan, *at random and place their finger on a poem, expecting it to give them guidance for the day.*

THE BODY'S CUP

Last night I saw angels knocking at the tavern door;
they shaped and cast a winecup from Adam's clay,

and I was drunk with potent wine poured
by ascetic angels who dwell behind the sacred veil.

The sky couldn't bear that burden of love along,
so they cast the dice and my poor name came up.

Seventy-two sects bicker over fairy tales;
forgive them, they don't know the truth.

Thank you God for making peace with me;
the Sufis dance and raise their cups to you.

The candle laughs flame, but the true fire
harvests bodies of countless ecstatic moths.

The brides of poetry have combed my hair.
Only Hafiz has ripped the veil from wisdom's face.

Source: Barnstone, Tony; Barnstone, Willis. *Literatures of the Middle East*, 1st Ed., ©2003. Reprinted by permission of Pearson Education, Inc., New York, New York.

seduced by the older religions. In this political and religious hothouse, poets with serious themes learned to express themselves through double entendre, symbol, and metaphor. Everyday experience became inextricably entwined with the mystic's hunger for union with God.

Ibn Battuta

Ibn Taymiya, Ibn al-Shatir, Ibn Khaldun, and Hafez were intellectuals of the first order whose work is still the object of scholarly inquiry. Other intellectuals of similar stature could be treated here who worked in the natural sciences, historical studies, and religious studies. It seems appropriate to close this section, however, with Ibn Battuta (1304–1368) who was a minor intellectual but whose career, as suggested at the beginning of this chapter, demonstrates the scope and depth achieved by Islamic civilization by the fourteenth century. Ibn Battuta may have qualified as the most widely traveled individual prior to modern times. Born in 1304 in Tangier, he had the typical education of a young man who was preparing for a career as a qadi. Like many other young scholars, after his preparatory training he was ready to seek certificates from the more celebrated ulama in the great centers of Islamic studies. Thus, he embarked upon the hajj in 1325, planning to combine the fulfillment of that religious duty with the experience of studying with some of the more famous scholars of the two Holy Cities and of the Mamluk Empire. By the time he had completed the hajj, however, he had developed a passion for seeing the world. Over the next two decades, he became a citizen of the world; before returning to Morocco in 1349, he had traveled at least 60,000—and perhaps as many as 75,000—miles.

Ibn Battuta could not have timed his travels better if he had had the hindsight of history and returned in a time machine. He passed through Cairo during the third reign of the Mamluk sultan al-Nasir Muhammad and thus saw Egypt and Syria at their most prosperous and stable period for centuries before or after that time. He sailed south along the African coast as far as modern Tanzania. Later, he was introduced to Orhan, the Ottoman leader; to Abu Sa'id, the last of the Il-khan rulers; and to Uzbeg, the great khan of the Golden Horde. (He even accompanied one of Uzbeg's wives—a Byzantine princess—to Constantinople so that she could give birth to her child in her father's palace.) He took advantage of Muhammad ibn Tughluq's generosity to foreign scholars and served the Delhi Sultanate as a qadi and administrator of a huge mausoleum complex. After serving the sultan for seven years, he spent several months as a qadi in the Maldive Islands and may have traveled as far east as China, although features of the account of his trip to Sumatra and Beijing cause some scholars to think that this section was composed by the editor of his book.

On his way back to Morocco from the Indian Ocean basin, Ibn Battuta began to see evidence of the problems that would have made his trip impossible had he begun it later. As he came through Iran and Iraq, he had to dodge the chaos and anarchy that followed the death of Abu Sa'id, and in Syria he witnessed the devastation of the plague. By the time he reached Cairo, it, too, was reeling from the epidemic as well as from the violence that had begun to diminish the quality of life there since the death of al-Nasir Muhammad seven years earlier. He returned home to Morocco in 1349, but his travels were not over. During the remaining twenty years of his life, he visited both Granada and Mali.

The significance of Ibn Battuta's career goes well beyond the actual number of miles that he traveled. A contrast with the extensive travels of Marco Polo, which had taken place some fifty years earlier, is instructive: Whereas Polo's travels took place almost entirely in cultures that were strange and alien to him, Ibn Battuta always found a Muslim community in which his skills were valued. Polo could not possibly have traveled as extensively as he did had he remained within a Christian, Latin, or Greek culture. By contrast, Ibn Battuta found mosques, schools, Sufi communities, and acceptance of the Shari'a as the legal norm in an uninterrupted zone from Morocco to the steppes of Russia and Central Asia, and all around the rim of the Indian Ocean basin. Everywhere he went, he found that his mastery of the Arabic language was useful to him, either as a lingua franca or as a skill that qualified him for remunerative positions as a religious specialist. He found the areas on the periphery of the Islamic heartland to be the most rewarding, for there he was invariably given a lavish welcome, including money, robes, horses, and wives. In those areas, the members of the Muslim community were eager to have a religious authority who could advise them on how to follow the Shari'a, and the local rulers were eager to have their own authority legitimized by their patronage of specialists in the Islamic sciences. Ibn Battuta's career reveals in strikingly personal and concrete detail that, despite the catastrophes of the thirteenth and fourteenth centuries, the Dar al-Islam had become the largest cultural continuum in the world.

Law

The most honored intellectual activity in the Dar al-Islam was jurisprudence, or *fiqh*. This valuation was justified: Not only did Muslims believe that Islamic law reflected God's will, but the independence of Islamic law from any given regime enabled societies to continue even when their governments were destroyed. Thus, the Shari'a was one of the most important elements in the "glue" that held Islamic civilization together. As the law books proliferated, however, many jurists began to question what their role was. If they did not make the law but only inferred from the sources what God's will was, would there come a time when they had no more original work to do?

The Queen of the Sciences

The delineation of Islamic law had begun at the initiative of private scholars, and it continued to be elaborated in the same, unofficial manner. The judges, or qadis, it is true, were appointed by specific regimes, and their jobs depended on the good will of those regimes. The existence and perpetuation of the Shari'a itself, however, was totally independent of the patronage of governments. A myriad of "schools," or traditions of interpretation, arose in the eighth century, but most of them failed to attract a sizable following and disappeared. The number of viable schools continued to decline, and by the end of the tenth century a consensus had been established that no new schools could emerge. The appearance of a new school, after all, would imply a rejection of the methods of fiqh that had been used up to that time.

By the fourteenth century, the Sunni community had consolidated into four main traditions. Until the thirteenth century, it was not uncommon to hear of riots between the followers of competing law schools; thereafter, such clashes were less likely to happen. Despite the differences among them, their adherents came to recognize the legitimacy of the others. Ibn Battuta's experience was typical in this regard. He was trained in the Maliki school of North Africa, and yet his services were always welcomed in communities in which the Hanafi, Hanbali, or Shafiʻi traditions predominated.

The public accorded high respect to a *faqih*, a scholar who engaged in fiqh. Since scholarship of any kind was regarded as a form of worship of God, the study of jurisprudence was considered to be one of the highest acts of piety. The faqih was also respected for his intelligence and perseverance: One was accepted as a faqih only after a long and rigorous course of study. He had to demonstrate that he could derive a legal ruling from the Qur'an or Hadith, know when to stress the literal rather than the metaphorical meaning of a text, realize whether a general rule fit a specific case, and refer to the entire corpus of his school's literature in order to cite a precedent.

Despite the insistence of all the schools that their work was not man-made but rather the methodical deduction of the will of God from the Qur'an and Hadith, all the schools tacitly admitted that the process of fiqh involved at least some degree of *ijtihad*, the "effort" or "exercise" of one's judgment or reasoning. Everyone acknowledged that such judgment had to be employed when interpreting texts or assessing the authenticity of Hadith, and the jurists who defended its use in fiqh argued that it had to be exercised when extending the principles established by the Qur'an and Sunna to problems not directly addressed by those texts. These faqihs had been careful to point out that they advocated the use of reasoning only when it was subordinate to the dictates of divine revelation. Some early faqihs, notably in the Hanbali madhhab, campaigned vigorously against analogical reasoning. By the twelfth century, however, even the members of the Hanbali school (as we have seen in the case of thirteenth-century Ibn Taymiya) had come to realize that the practice of finding analogies between cases was unavoidable and that the logic and good sense of the faqih had to come into play.

The period of the most original work in fiqh was the eighth through the twelfth centuries. Most of the problems of ritual, family law, and criminal law had been identified during the first three centuries, but the eleventh and twelfth centuries witnessed an increase in the sophistication of legal concepts as well as a growing precision in the use of language. As the issues to be addressed declined in number and the actual work of the faqih became that of framing legal issues with more clarity and subtlety, it was becoming clear that some faqihs were more original than others. Some were able to recast an issue in a new light, while others were more comfortable simply applying the results of a precedent to a current case.

The "Closing of the Gate of Ijtihad"?

During the twelfth century, the fact that fewer faqihs were doing original work led some Sunni scholars to voice the opinion that the era of engaging in ijtihad was now past. In the rhythmic and rhyming style so popular in Arabic prose, this sentiment was often expressed in the phrase "*insidad bab al-ijtihad*," or the "closing (blocking) of the gate (door) of ijtihad." Those who expressed this opinion regarded the earlier members of their legal schools to have been intellectual and spiritual giants and felt that it was disrespectful and even impious to think that further ijtihad could be exercised. This sentiment was expressed most frequently by members of the Hanafi and Maliki schools.

Other legal scholars insisted that the exercise of juristic judgment was a continuing need. They argued that there was no reason to think that intellectual abilities and spiritual qualities had declined over the generations. Moreover, by then there was more legal knowledge available to scholars precisely because of the work of those past generations of jurists. Therefore, there were more opportunities to make wise judgments than ever before, assuming that jurists made the effort to apply sound reasoning to their decisions. Most members of the Shafi'i school took this position, and Hanbalis after the twelfth century were the most adamant in their insistence on the necessity of practicing ijtihad.

The issue of the closing of the gate of ijtihad slowly grew more controversial within the Sunni community. In the thirteenth century, some scholars began ranking each other in terms of their proficiency in exercising original judgment. Some rankings included up to seven grades of proficiency, ranging from very original to extremely imitative. The rankings provided ammunition to some scholars to argue that the number of genuine *mujtahid*s (practitioners of ijtihad) was decreasing, that the day would soon come when no qualified scholars would be alive, and that ijtihad could no longer be practiced. The Hanbalis were contemptuous of this position. They argued that ijtihad was an obligation imposed on the totality of Muslim scholars and that to stop exercising it would be a sin. This was the position of Ibn Taymiya, and his difference with other faqihs over this issue was a major irritant for many of his critics.

By the second half of the fourteenth century, the majority of Sunni scholars had come to agree that ijtihad was no longer an option for faqihs. They argued that *taqlid* ("imitation" of previous scholars) was the only option for "modern" jurists. Taqlid came to be understood as the unquestioning acceptance of a previous decision or doctrine without inquiring into the reasons and evidence that were the basis for them. Most Hanbalis and a few Shafi'is continued to claim the right to practice ijtihad, but they were in a conspicuous minority. Their position became more and more peripheral. The Hanbali school was largely confined to lightly-populated desert regions, whereas the Hanafi school eventually became the official fiqh of both the Ottoman and Mughal empires, providing it with institutional and demographic clout.

The sentiment that led to the near consensus to terminate ijtihad can be appreciated in light of a conservative understanding of Islamic law. Most jurists would have agreed that the Shari'a, as God's law, is ultimately unknowable. Fiqh, they would argue, represents the efforts of jurists to discover God's law, and thus the jurists' writings are works of jurisprudence rather than statements of God's law. In daily life, however, with concrete decisions having to be made, it was easy to slip into the habit of assuming that the statements of the jurists *were* the Shari'a: The jurists needed to feel that what they were doing was worthwhile, and the community needed to have confidence in the rules they were accepting. A Hadith that quoted the Prophet as saying that his community would never agree upon error reassured them that they in fact had approximated God's will. Since God's will does not change, one did not have to worry about revising laws; besides, revisions would smack of human agency rather than divine decree.

In practice, of course, ijtihad could not stop. Legal experts, even Hanafis, continued to employ it, but few faqihs admitted that they were doing so, and those who witnessed it pretended not to see it. New problems continued to arise that needed ijtihad in order to be solved. Jurists who were active in solving those problems understood their work in a different light from that of the outspoken advocates of taqlid. They believed that the work of all jurists throughout Islamic history had been approximate and had been achieved within a specific time and region. Circumstances, they knew, change from time to time and from society to society, and therefore ijtihad was necessary. Their work can be seen most vividly in the careers of the most preeminent jurists in Muslim societies, who were called upon to give rulings (*fatwas*) on vexing questions that other jurists could not provide. Such a legal authority, usually known as a *shaykh al-islam* or *mufti*, could issue thousands of fatwas on a wide variety of issues during his career.

The very fact that fatwas from muftis were necessary because other jurists could not agree on an issue may seem to the eyes of the twenty-first century to be evidence that ijtihad continued. Nevertheless, taqlid became the official practice of the period after the fourteenth century. As a result, the fundamentals of the law did not change for centuries. The legal concepts that had developed during the creative eleventh and twelfth centuries remained unchanged until the nineteenth century. Discussions among jurists tended to be about hypothetical cases or even about issues that had once been important but were no longer relevant. The occasional mujtahid did make revisions in practice when necessary, and sometimes a mufti's defense of his novel decision entered into the corpus of juristic tradition. On the whole, however, jurists understood that their primary mission was not to codify the law or to make the process of adjudication more streamlined and efficient. They continued to learn the body of decisions that had been recorded in the legal books and tried to apply them to their own circumstances with as little innovation as possible. Social pressure and the demands of piety restrained them from making original contributions to the science of fiqh.

Twelver Shi'ite law faced similar issues but underwent a different evolution. The Shi'ite jurists who advocated ijtihad won an eleventh-century victory over those who opposed the exercise of reason. The opponents of ijtihad would have to wait until the late seventeenth century to (temporarily) "close the gate." Advocates of the use of reason continued to develop more sophisticated arguments for its employment. During the fourteenth century, when Sunnis were achieving a near consensus on agreeing that ijtihad was no longer possible, the great Shi'ite jurist 'Allama al-Hilli was reorganizing jurisprudence so as to make reasoning its central feature.

The practical results of the apparent contrast between Sunni and Shi'ite jurisprudence were not as great as one might think, however. Shi'ite experience after the fourteenth century was the mirror image of that of the Sunnis: Whereas Sunnis claimed that ijtihad was no longer acceptable but found to their embarrassment that they continued to practice it, Shi'ites claimed to practice it but found that the scope within which reason could be exercised was quite limited. That was because they were obligated to accept as authoritative all pronouncements attributed to the first eleven Imams. Shi'ite jurists understood that they must exercise what they called

FIGURE 11.2 Cairo's Sultan Hasan madrasa-tomb-mosque complex (on the left), constructed 1356-1363. Elements of this Mamluk monument's style appear to be due to the influence of architects who fled Iran after the collapse of the Il-khan regime some two decades earlier.

SuperStock / SuperStock.

"prudence and caution" in their decisions in order not to stray from the path of the Imams.

The Varieties of Religious Expression

The adherents of any major religion exhibit a wide variety in their patterns of belief and ritual behavior. Protestants, Catholics, and Orthodox Christians all belong to the same religion and yet differ considerably from each other. Even within Protestantism or Catholicism, the range of expression is great: If a Catholic bishop from Paris were to spend a month in the home of fellow Catholics in a village in Haiti, he might well experience moments when he would wonder what religion his hosts practiced, after all. Muslims are equally diverse in their beliefs and practices. Muslims from North Africa, Central Asia, and the littoral of the Indian Ocean inevitably received the Islamic tradition through the filter of their respective cultural heritages. The remarkable fact about Islam is that it has a common identity at all. Unlike most monotheistic traditions, it has no institution with the authority to enforce orthodoxy. During the period of Mongol hegemony, many of the myriad expressions of Islam were becoming organized into institutional form and would be prepared to affect history in profound ways over the following centuries.

"Orthodoxy" and "Heterodoxy"

Throughout history, the various Christian denominations have enforced orthodox doctrines and practices within their respective churches. Persons who claim to be within a particular tradition but who preach or teach contrary to orthodoxy ("correct doctrine") and engage in other than orthopraxy ("correct practice") are labeled "heretics." In earlier centuries, heretics were severely disciplined, often by execution. Since the Enlightenment, the typical response of the officials of the Church in question has been to exclude the person from membership. Islam does not have the equivalent of a pope or patriarch who can enforce conformity. Several individuals have claimed such a role, to be sure: During the first two centuries of Islamic history, some of the Umayyad and Abbasid caliphs attempted to enforce correct religious practices; the Imams of the various Shi'ite groups served such a function; and subsequent caliphs of many splinter groups all over the globe claimed such authority. In every case, however, the actual authority of a given leader extended over a limited territory or period of time. The majority of Muslims were unaffected.

Islamic history has witnessed many instances in which the charge of *kufr* ("unbelief," the equivalent of "heresy") has been leveled at various individuals and groups who claimed to be Muslim. The seventh-century Kharijites stimulated one of the most intense of these crises, for they regarded all Muslims who disagreed with them to be outside the pale, while other Muslims considered that attitude itself to be un-Islamic. This conflict gradually resolved itself over the next couple of centuries as the extreme Kharijites died out in the battles they provoked, and the surviving Ibadi Kharijites of North Africa and Oman were known primarily for their puritanism and reluctance to interact with outsiders, rather than for their aggression.

Early Shi'ites who elevated 'Ali (or other individuals) to the status of a divinity were considered to have compromised the monotheistic status of Islam. The extremist Shi'ites were gradually marginalized when the major Shi'ite groups officially denied deifying 'Ali or anyone else. Two important groups that were excluded from the Umma in this fashion still play important roles in the countries of the eastern Mediterranean. The Druze, who deified al-Hakim, the eleventh-century Fatimid caliph, were forced by popular pressure to seek refuge in the mountains of Lebanon and southern Syria. Farther north, the Alawis sought refuge in the mountains of the Lataqiya province of western Syria. Alawis were the followers of the ninth-century figure Ibn Nusayr, who had preached that the eleventh Imam had no heir. Thus, Alawis were not Twelver Shi'ites. Alawis worship a divine trinity of 'Ali, Muhammad, and Salman the Iranian, in which 'Ali takes precedence as the God of the Qur'an. The name *Alawi* derives from this worship of 'Ali. Alawis worship in homes instead of mosques, do not observe Ramadan or the hajj, drink wine at religious services, and hold to the doctrine of transmigration of souls. For these reasons, both Sunni and Twelver Shi'te Muslims have frequently persecuted Alawis as heretics. (Since 1970, members of the Alawi ruling elite of Syria have claimed to be Twelver Shi'ites for reasons of political expediency.)

Early Sufis who claimed to have experienced union with God during their mystical experiences were also ostracized. Once again, the central issue at stake was the compromising of the doctrine of the unity of God, which to most scholars also entailed a radical distinction between the Creator and his creatures. Al-Hallaj, the most famous of the extreme Sufis, was even executed by the state in 922 as a threat to public peace. Sufi leaders then began working toward a consensus on the doctrine that union with God was not a legitimate claim for the mystical experience.

With the exception of the execution of al-Hallaj, these examples of spiritual disciplining were largely collective affairs in which private religious scholars managed to win a consensus among other scholars and influential men of affairs to exclude (and even persecute) groups that had violated basic Islamic tenets. The key to understanding the continuity of Sunni Islam is an appreciation of the insistence upon fidelity to the text of the Qur'an and the Sunna ("practice") of the Prophet as revealed in the Hadith. The various schools of Islamic law insisted on the centrality of those two sources; theologians condemned the practice of philosophical speculation not limited by the truths of revelation; and Sufi orders developed traditions that reputedly linked their practice to the practice of the Prophet. The Sunni tradition was one of self-censorship. It was inevitably conservative and traditional in spirit, leading to the withering of an independent philosophical tradition and the closing of the gate of ijtihad in most of the schools of law.

In order to maintain a consensus across the vast Muslim world, scholars corresponded frequently with each other about their own work. They went on journeys to study with scholars greater than themselves. Most importantly, the practice of the hajj ensured that scholars would travel from every part of the Muslim world to Mecca, where they would be kept up to date on current thinking on theology and practice. Meccan scholars served as the touchstone for piety. They had absolutely no authority to enforce any doctrine or practice on anyone in any region, but pilgrims who came to Mecca seeking to study under such scholars for a period of time could learn whether their home community practiced a version of Islam that reflected the Meccan standard. Many pilgrims throughout history returned to their homes to begin reform movements, having been jolted by their experience on the hajj. This Sunni tradition of self-censorship was somewhat different from the attainment of a consensus within the various Ibadi and Shi'ite traditions. The Ibadis comprised a relatively small number of Muslims, but they were scattered from Oman to North Africa. They engaged in a high level of scholarly activity and maintained communications over vast distances in order to stay current with each other. Their political leaders were religious authorities, as well, and they maintained an effective discipline within their oases.

The Shi'ite communities that had the good fortune of being led by a "visible" Imam had direct access to the keeper of the consensus, for the Imam by definition possessed the authority to define truth. He could enforce any doctrine and maintain tight discipline. The communities that had a "hidden" Imam were a step removed from that sense of certainty but still had confidence that the Hidden Imam maintained at least indirect communication with their religious scholars. As we have seen, the dominant school of religious scholars within the Twelver Shi'ite community during the period under review did not share the opinion of most Sunnis that the gate of ijtihad had closed. When they were left without a visible Imam, they were confident that pious, consecrated reason was capable of determining the will of the Hidden Imam. They developed the doctrine that the Hidden Imam would never allow his community to be misled by an erroneous ruling. If it should ever happen that (1) two jurists' rulings be in opposition, (2) one be totally wrong, and (3) the methods of jurisprudence not be able to detect the error, the Hidden Imam would intervene in person. Since he has never intervened, the members of the Twelver community can be confident that no rulings have ever been in error.

Thus, Islam had no Vatican, synod, or rabbinate to determine orthodoxy or orthopraxy. Scholarly consensus served as an effective method for obtaining cohesion among large groups of Muslims across a vast swath of the planet. The achievement is all the more impressive when one remembers that the vast majority of Muslims were illiterate. Just as it is impossible to appreciate Luther's accomplishments in the years after 1517 without realizing that most contemporary Europeans were illiterate and lightly Christianized, one cannot appreciate the fact that Islam exists today without understanding the far-flung, multiethnic, decentralized, and largely illiterate society in which the small group of private scholars labored to conserve the heritage of the Prophet.

Cohesion and a common sense of identity did not mean homogeneity, of course: Muslims developed distinctive differences in the expression of their faith. Sunnis, Shi'ites, and Ibadis formed three quite distinct groupings. Subsects formed within each of these traditions and yet were regarded to be within the bounds of acceptable doctrine and practice. Some Muslims were persuaded that a scrupulous performance of ritual was the height of piety; others felt that ritual had to be balanced by a spiritual communion with God; and yet others regarded ritual as the mere outward expression of piety, placing emphasis on a mystical experience. The Qur'an and the Hadith (Sunni or Shi'ite) remained central, however.

The Proliferation of Sufi Groups

Historians assume a linkage between the upheavals of the twelfth and early thirteenth centuries on the one hand and the rise of Sufi lodges and orders during those centuries on the other. In the face of the sufferings and uncertainties of the period, the small communities established by Sufis provided spiritual and material support as well as the possibility of common defense. The subsequent disasters of the Mongol era from the mid-thirteenth century to the end of the fourteenth century were accompanied by a rapid increase in the number of Sufi organizations and an even larger increase in the percentage of Muslims who practiced Sufism. Once again, it appears that Sufism responded to a deep need. In damaged and leaderless societies, the new Sufi orders (tariqas) satisfied social and religious needs that were not met in any other way. The lodges (variously known as ribats, zawiyas, khanaqas, and tekkes) became centers of local worship, teaching and healing, and politics.

Sufism Triumphant

Sufism first appeared in the eighth century in Syria and Iraq. By the beginning of the tenth century, it was established in Andalus. By the fourteenth century, Sufism had become integrated into the everyday religious life of many—perhaps most—Muslims. Believers performed the ritual and moral duties of the Shari'a obediently and willingly and understood them to be the public expression of their faith and commitment. The Sufi dimension was the inner, emotional, personal relationship that they sought with their Creator God. Sufism could assume a wide range of expressions: Some adherents lived permanently in a lodge following the teachings of the founder of the tariqa, and others were wandering mendicants. Most, however, lived ordinary lives at home with their families and occasionally attended meetings of the local chapter of an order in order to recite mystical litanies.

Along with the work of intellectuals and artists and the consensus of the Shari'a, Sufism was one of the critical universal features that held the Umma together in the absence of a central authority. Each order had its own distinct devotional practice and ethical system that were followed in lodges and mosques wherever the order was found. A given order's common tradition, authoritative texts, network of lodges, and distinctive lifestyle became elements that the culturally and ethnically diverse societies of Islam shared in common.

Sufism was also important because it provided women an acceptable avenue of both religious expression and religious leadership. Over the centuries, mosques had practically become preserves of males. The increasing exclusion of women from urban public spaces, coupled with the requirements of modesty during the ritual of the prescribed prayers, resulted in a consensus in most parts of the Muslim world that the community was better served if women performed their prayers at home. The expression of women's religious needs therefore frequently took the form of maintaining folk cults and performing pilgrimages to local shrines. Certain pious women themselves became the objects of intense veneration: In Cairo, both al-Sayyida Zaynab (daughter of 'Ali) and al-Sayyida Nafisa (great-great-granddaughter of 'Ali, celebrated for her learning and piety) are revered in magnificent tomb–mosques. (*Sayyida* is an Arabic word normally meaning "lady" or "Mrs"; here, it implies both lineal descent from the Prophet and the status of sainthood.)

Sufism did not shatter gender barriers, but in most locales it did encourage women's participation in Islamic rituals. Some Sufi preachers ministered primarily to women, a few lodges that served a largely male clientele were staffed primarily by women, women held their own Sufi meetings, some women became preachers, and other women were accorded the status of saint. It is clear that a number of women were initiated into Sufi orders. One young fourteenth-century male even received from his grandmother a *khirqa*, the robe that a Sufi novice received from his mentor.

Sufi masters—the heads of lodges and the teachers of the mystical path—rarely limited their services to their formal disciples. Usually known as *shaykhs* in the Arabic-speaking communities and *pirs* in Persian-speaking regions, they served the entire community, whether urban or rural. They provided spiritual guidance, mediation, and medical cures. Their primary function was to serve as a religious specialist, teaching their students how to achieve the mystical experience. For local residents, however, they also served as spiritual counselors, led prayers in mosques, and helped as needed at times of special rites such as circumcision, marriage, and funerals. Some of the shaykhs, particularly in Morocco, were well versed in the Shari'a and issued definitive rulings on legal matters.

Sufi shaykhs also mediated disputes. They provided arbitration in disagreements among local residents and between local residents and the conquerors that came and went with dizzying frequency. Their zawiyas became busy centers where disciples lived and learned; local inhabitants depended on them for religious services, spiritual counsel, and food; and local tribesmen came to have conflicts settled. Lodges were often located at an intersection of trade routes or near water sources, making them easily accessible to as many people in the area as possible. In rural areas, they were usually fortified in order to provide a refuge for local residents from raiders.

Religious specialists throughout history have often been called on to provide aid to those in need of medical attention, since they are believed to be able to intercede with God. That was particularly true in the premodern period, when modern medicines were not available. Sufi shaykhs were believed to have the power to heal persons and animals and to bestow blessings that enabled petitioners to become prosperous, bear children, and restore affection in a marriage relationship.

A Sufi shaykh with outstanding spiritual gifts might become revered as a *wali*, or "saint." The status of saint, or "friend of God," was accorded to notable martyrs, Shiʻite Imams, companions of the Prophet, and noteworthy ascetics. Sufi shaykhs achieved the distinction by their combination of exceptional piety, ecstatic states, power of intercession, and miracles. Most saints were credited with the gifts of clairvoyance and telepathy. Some were said to be able to fly, to be in two places at once, to ride rainbows, and to end droughts.

People far and near sought out saints in order to share in the power of their spiritual gifts. Their authority was enhanced even further when they combined evidence of spiritual power with an esteemed genealogical descent, either from a notable local family or, especially, from the Prophet's family. Saints were thus in a good position to provide an alternative source of authority in the absence of a strong central government. By virtue of their personal qualities and, perhaps, their family lineage, they possessed an authority that enabled them to keep the peace within an impressive radius of their lodge, intercede for the poor with wealthy landowners, and assure that travelers could enjoy both hospitality and safety.

A saint's service to his community did not end with his death. He was usually buried at the site of his lodge, and his tomb would usually become the object of pilgrimages, as individuals continued to look to him as a source of aid. The shrine was considered to be the repository of the spiritual power (*baraka*) that inhered in the saint in death as in life. Pilgrims came to shrines to ask for healing and the other blessings that the saint had provided during his lifetime. They touched or kissed the tomb, made small gifts or sacrifices, attached written requests to the shrine, celebrated the major religious festivals of the year, and observed the death day of the saint.

After the saint's death, the lodge complex might actually increase in importance, for it boasted the attraction of the shrine in addition to the services of the saint's successor and his disciples. Its influence might then spread into an even wider radius, providing the services of a market, religious education, the settling of tribal disputes, and the distribution of food to the poor. Over time, the shrine would typically receive gifts from grateful local residents and develop a large endowment that would enable it to exercise even greater spiritual, political, and economic power.

Sufism as Social Critique

The practice of pilgrimage to shrines did not attract much controversy before the eighteenth century. The veneration of holy men and women—or of sacred places and objects—is a phenomenon common to all the major religious traditions and should be seen as a normal aspect of premodern Islam. It was the Muslim parallel to the contemporary Western Christian traffic in relics and visits to shrines such as Canterbury, Santiago de Compostela, and Jerusalem. The practice was validated by mainstream Sufism and sanctioned by most jurists, who cited passages from the

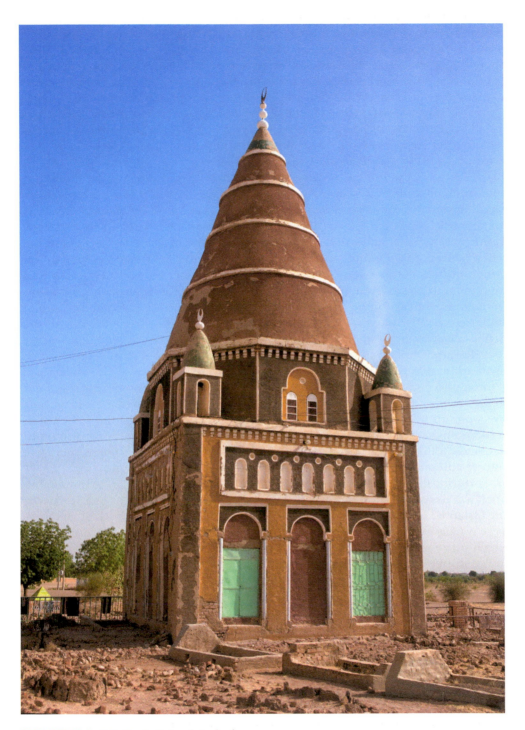

FIGURE 11.3 A Sufi saint's tomb in Sudan.

Eric Lafforgue / Alamy Stock Photo.

Qur'an and the Hadith supporting the doctrine that some individuals have superior spiritual power. A handful of religious scholars opposed the veneration of saints, however: Ibn Taymiya vehemently attacked the practice as a flagrant violation of the Shari'a. The great Hanbali scholar practiced Sufi meditation techniques himself and did not oppose Sufi spirituality. On the other hand, he regarded shrine visits to be a remnant of pre-Islamic idolatry, and he accused supplicants at shrines of being "grave worshipers." His diatribes had no impact on the practice and only landed him in jail. The masses, the majority of religious scholars, and government officials (throughout the Dar al-Islam, not just the Mamluks) agreed that the veneration of living and dead saints was a valid Islamic practice.

The veneration of saints drew the ire of Ibn Taymiya because he thought it compromised features of Islamic monotheism. Other critics of Sufism focused on the fact that some of the movement's features had taken on the trappings of a fully mature social institution. Indeed, the more elaborate shrines were eloquent testimony to the power, wealth, and systematization that had come to characterize much of the Sufi experience by the thirteenth and fourteenth centuries. This development was criticized by some individuals who were aware that ascetics had begun the Sufi movement in part as a critique of the material and institutional elements of society. In the thirteenth century, a rejection of mainstream Sufism appeared in the form of "Sufi deviancy." It was characterized by mendicancy, celibacy, asceticism, and the deliberate tweaking of what today would be called middle class sensibilities.

Forms of deviancy had manifested themselves throughout most of Sufi history. From at least as early as the tenth century, individuals known as the *malamatiya* ("those who draw blame upon themselves") were Sufis who were so concerned not to parade their virtue that they deliberately invited the contempt of their neighbors by committing unseemly, and even unlawful, acts. Most other Sufis, however, recognized that, while the malamatiya might be overzealous and overly conscientious in obeying the precept to avoid trying to impress the world of one's purity, they were sincere and pure of heart.

During the thirteenth century, Sufi deviancy became a much larger movement, but it was viewed with hostility by much of society. Several groups emerged, including the Qalandars, Haydaris, Abdals, Bektashis, and Madaris. Their individual members were usually called *dervish*es. *Dervish* is the Turkish form of the Persian word *darvish*, which suggests "wandering mendicant." Dervishes first appeared in Syria and Egypt in the thirteenth century, but they soon became more characteristic of the region that includes Anatolia, Iran, and India.

In some ways, the life styles of dervishes suggest parallels with the Cynics, who became notorious in the Hellenistic world of the eastern Mediterranean beginning in the fourth century B.C.E. Typically, dervishes showed their contempt for social conventions by rejecting family life and choosing celibacy, rarely bathing, wearing unusual clothing (such as turbans with horns) or abandoning clothing altogether and going nude, shaving all bodily and facial hair (a practice that went contrary to the Shari'a), and using forbidden hallucinogens and intoxicants.

Beyond the obvious characteristics shared by many of the dervishes lay differences in their attitudes toward communal life. Some were solitary mendicants, who tended to exhibit the more extreme of the unconventional traits we have described. It is these individuals that European travelers and novelists of the nineteenth century made famous as "wild-eyed dervishes." Others also wandered across the countryside, but did so as a group of disciples who followed their shaykh. Still others maintained a permanent community, but their lodge was distinctively decorated, and they themselves were clearly marked off from their fellow townsmen by their clothing and behavior.

The cultural elite of Muslim societies consistently identified the dervishes as the riffraff of society and frequently accused them of being impostors and frauds. In fact, a considerable number of dervishes were sons of the elite. They rejected the comfortable and staid world of their fathers and engaged in behavior that scandalized and disappointed their families. Like the Cynics (and hippies), they were engaged in a countercultural critique of dominant social norms. Unlike those two groups, most of the dervishes were also sincerely seeking a close spiritual relationship with God. They thought that establishing a relationship with God required severing their ties with the world of conventional morality.

Sufism, Syncretism, and Shi'ism

During the Mongol period, Sufi deviancy was most likely to be found in Anatolia, northern Iran, and northern India. The arc that stretched from Anatolia across northern Iran was also the setting for the rise of Sufi groups that would exercise much more influence on subsequent Muslim history than did the Sufi deviants. Their story is the result of the Turkic migrations into the area.

During the century of Mongol rule of Iran, the composition of the population underwent a significant change. Under the Il-khanate, Iran was opened to the migration of large numbers of Turkic and Mongol peoples. Many of them made the long journey all the way into western Anatolia, where they played important roles in the early history of the Ottoman Sultanate. Most of those who entered the Iranian cultural area, however, settled in Transoxiana and in the region that comprises both Azerbaijan and eastern Anatolia. In both Transoxiana and Azerbaijan/eastern Anatolia, the Turkic-speaking peoples gradually came to outnumber the speakers of Persian. One result of this change in the ethnic composition of the area was a significant modification of the economy. Because many of the Turkic immigrants continued their nomadic existence, large areas of Iran, Azerbaijan, and eastern Anatolia were converted from agriculture into grazing areas for the service of a pastoral economy. In order to adjust, many erstwhile villagers began to practice semipastoralism: They cultivated the valleys that remained under cultivation and took herds of sheep into the mountain highlands during the summer for grazing. Other than the short-lived reforms of Ghazan (1295–1304), the agricultural economy of the region from the Amu Darya River to the headwaters of the Euphrates River suffered alternate bouts of destruction and neglect for several centuries.

The decline of urban life and the long-term absence of state security institutions encouraged the development of new forms of social and religious organization in the region. With the decline of central governments, the traditional social organization that the Turks brought with them from Central Asia remained unchallenged. This structure was based on what has been called a household state: A chief ruled over a large group of people related by kinship ties or alliances. He was aided by his family and lesser chiefs who had their own followers, whose support he won by his leadership ability and martial skills. The system was financed by raiding and by extorting revenues from nomads, peasants, and towns under its control. It was very unstable, however, for the authority of the chief was constantly challenged by ambitious subordinates. Rebellions were common, and the ensuing violence wreaked havoc among defenseless subject populations.

It was within this unstable and violent environment that Sufism began making inroads. As early as the twelfth century, Sufis had been working among the Turks of Transoxiana. The most revered of these Sufi missionaries was Ahmad Yasavi (d. 1166). Yasavi met with considerable success due to his technique of setting religious and moral education to music, using the lute as an accompaniment. From the mid-thirteenth to mid-fourteenth centuries, several other Sufi-led movements appeared among both peasant and nomadic communities from Transoxiana into rural Anatolia. There, shaykhs served the functions mentioned earlier: They were healers, mediators, and religious guides, and they resisted the oppression and exploitation of the poor by the household states.

Given the insecurity and oppression that characterized the era, it is understandable that the doctrines that flourished in the Sufi communities stressed a longing for deliverance by superhuman spiritual figures. Among the anticipated saviors were the Mahdi, who would come at the end of time to create a just order, and the Qutb, the figure in Sufi circles who served as the axis for the world and a haven for oppressed peoples. 'Ali, the Prophet's closest companion, cousin, and son-in-law, gained even wider appreciation during this period than he had in earlier centuries. His combination of religious piety and martial valor provided a role model for serious young men. 'Ali was particularly popular among Sufis of this era, and many of the newly emerging Sufi orders constructed *silsilas*, or spiritual genealogies, that traced their teachings back to him. For some groups, 'Ali became as prominent as Muhammad, although these groups seem not to have viewed themselves as Shi'ite. Unlike the urban Sunni and Shi'ite scholars, distinctions such as "Sunni" and "Shi'ite" do not seem to have been important to them.

Of the many Sufi groups that emerged at this time among the primarily Turkic-speaking peoples, four are particularly worthy of notice because of their subsequent historical importance. The Naqshbandi order, whose founding was attributed to Baha al-Din Naqshband (1318–1398) of Bukhara, later became highly influential in Southwest, Central, and South Asia. One of its distinguishing characteristics was the teaching of a "silent dhikr": Whereas most orders practiced a communal, vocal dhikr, the silent dhikr enabled an individual to recite it mentally, making it possible to recite under practically any circumstance and at any time. The order arose in the highly sophisticated atmosphere of Bukhara, and despite its subsequent dissemination among the rural population of the Ottoman realm, Central Asia, and India, it was always characterized by a careful attention to normative ritual and doctrine. As a result, it became famous (and infamous) for the reform movements that it initiated.

By contrast, several groups that emerged at this time exhibited syncretistic qualities that reflected their origins in the multireligious and multiethnic rural area between central Anatolia and Azerbaijan. After the battle of Kose Dagh in 1243, when Batu of the Horde defeated the Sultanate of Rum, the region's cities went into decline. With Hulagu's creation of the Il-khanate in 1259, the region was inundated by Turkish and Mongol immigrants. The influence of the Shari'a-minded ulama was no longer as strong as it had been. In contrast to the strict adherence to the Shari'a practiced by the Naqshbandi order and the rural shaykhs of Morocco, Sufi leaders of eastern Anatolia and Azerbaijan tended to stress the universal aspects of Islam in their preaching. They relaxed their ritual requirements, making it easier for shamanistic Turks and local Christian peasants alike to make the transition into their communities.

One example of this trend was the career of Hajji Bektash. Scholars have traditionally thought that Bektash lived until 1337, but recent research suggests that he died in the last quarter of the thirteenth century. He was a learned Sufi shaykh who emphasized the importance of the mystical way and taught his followers that the details of the Shari'a, including the daily prayers, were not important. As a result, his original movement is regarded as an example of Sufi deviancy. Over the next two centuries, as the Bektashi movement developed in the melting pot of Anatolia and Azerbaijan, it acquired many doctrines and practices that, had it not been so secretive, would almost certainly have caused it to be ostracized or even persecuted. Nevertheless, it became highly popular all across Anatolia and eventually in the Balkans.

Similarities between the mature Bektashi order and the Alawi sect are striking. Its members considered many elements of Islamic ritual and worship, such as performance of the salat and observing the fast during the month of Ramadan, to be unimportant. Bektashis did not attend mosques but rather held a communal weekly prayer in a private home. Ostensibly Sunni, the Bektashis revered the Twelve Shi'ite Imams, but they scandalized Twelvers by their extremist practice of worshiping 'Ali as the center of a trinity of 'Ali, Muhammad, and "God." They denied the doctrine of the resurrection of the body and taught instead that souls are reincarnated into other bodies. They initiated new members with a reception of wine, bread, and cheese, a practice that seems to have been borrowed from a heretical Christian group of Anatolia called the Paulicians.

The Bektashi tariqa was usually found in towns and cities. A similar group, the Alevi (the Turkish spelling of *Alawi*) movement, was closely related to it and seems to have been the result of a schism in the historical development of Hajji Bektash's group. The Alevis tended to be rural, located in central and eastern Anatolia, and on the whole less educated than the Bektashis. Their practices and doctrines were almost identical to those of the Bektashis, however. Because they were scattered among farming villages and nomadic tribes, they were not as cohesive as the Bektashis, who looked down upon them for their rustic ways. Millions of modern Turks identify with these two groups, but the Bektashis became famous in Ottoman times for their association with the Janissaries, as we shall see in the next chapter.

Of the other Sufi groups that emerged at this time, one stands out for its role in creating an empire. Shaykh Safi al-Din (1252–1334) created a Sufi community in Ardabil, near the southwestern shore of the Caspian Sea. In acknowledgment of his founding role, his organization has come to be known as the Safavid movement. During the fourteenth century, the order developed schools and residences in Ardabil and expanded its missionary activities among the Turkic-speaking populations of Anatolia and Azerbaijan. In the fifteenth and early sixteenth centuries, the Safavids and Alevis shared a wide range of doctrines and practices and were almost indistinguishable. At the beginning of the sixteenth century, the Safavids caught the attention of the world when they created an empire in what is now Iran. We will explore that achievement in a later chapter.

Conclusion

By the end of the fourteenth century, the majority of the population from Morocco to eastern Iran was Muslim. Numerous new clusters of Muslims were beginning to form all around the Indian Ocean and south of the Sahara Desert. Their mosques, Shari'a courts, schools, and fraternal organizations provided networks of support that proved to be decisive for surviving crises. In the areas that the Mongols captured, those institutions proved to be strong enough to survive the severest of challenges, confirming the work of centuries of laborious effort on the part of pious scholars and activists. Individual Muslims were able to maintain their identities and ways of life precisely because the major Islamic institutions were independent of government control. The destruction of a given regime, therefore, did not entail the destruction of the judicial, educational, or religious traditions of the society in question.

Muslim societies survived the era of Mongol hegemony from 1260 to 1405. They were more conservative and cautious at the end of it than they had been at the beginning, but they also had more reason to be confident that, having survived the fourteenth century, they could survive anything. In fact, Islam was about to enter upon a period of dynamic expansion into Africa, Central Asia, and Southeast Asia, when a group of Muslim states were among the superpowers of the world.

FURTHER READING

Intellectual Life in the Fourteenth Century

Dunn, Ross E. *The Adventures of Ibn Battuta: A Muslim Traveler of the 14th Century.* Berkeley and Los Angeles: University of California Press, 1986.

Ibn Khaldun. *The Muqaddimah: An Introduction to History.* Tr. Franz Rosenthal, Vol. 3 2d ed. London: Routledge and Kegan Paul, 1967.

Kennedy, E.S. and Imad Ghanem, eds. *The Life & Work of Ibn al-Shātir.* Aleppo, Syria: The University of Aleppo, 1976.

Laoust, Henri. "Ibn Taymiyya." In *Encyclopedia of Islam, New Edition.* III. Edited by Bernard Lewis, et al. Leiden: E.J. Brill; London: Luzac & Co., 1971.

Mahdi, Muhsin. *Ibn Khaldūn's Philosophy of History.* Chicago and London: University of Chicago Press, 1957.

Saliba, George. *A History of Arabic Astronomy: Planetary Theories During the Golden Age of Islam.* New York University Studies in Near Eastern Civilization. New York and London: New York University Press, 1994.

Law

Hallaq, Wael B. "Was the Gate of Ijtihad Closed?", *IJMES*, Vol. 16, No. 1 (March 1984), 3–41.

Imber, Colin. *Ebu's-Su'ud: The Islamic Legal Tradition.* Stanford, California: Stanford University Press, 1997.

Stewart, Devin J. *Islamic Legal Orthodoxy: Twelver Shiite Responses to the Sunni Legal System.* Salt Lake City, Utah: The University of Utah Press, 1998.

The Varieties of Religious Expression

Cornell, Vincent J. *Realm of the Saint: Power and Authority in Moroccan Sufism.* Austin, Texas: University of Texas Press, 1998.

Karamustafa, Ahmet T. "Early Sufism in Eastern Anatolia." In *Classical Persian Sufism: From its Origins to Rumi,* ed. Leonard Lewisohn. London and New York: Khaniqahi Nimatullahi Publications, 1993, 175–198.

———. *God's Unruly Friends: Dervish Groups in the Islamic Later Middle Period, 1200–1550.* Salt Lake City, Utah: The University of Utah Press, 1994.

Knysh, Alexander. *Islamic Mysticism: A Short History.* Leiden, Boston, Koln: Brill, 2000.

Moosa, Matti. *Extremist Shiites: The Ghul t Sects.* Syracuse, New York: Syracuse University Press, 1988.

PART FOUR

Muslim Ascendancy, 1405–1750

It is no exaggeration to describe as catastrophic the blows suffered by the Muslim world in the thirteenth and fourteenth centuries. Soon after Timur's death, however, the course of Muslim history was reversed. For the next three centuries, the twin themes of Muslim history were expansion and dynamism. The frontiers of the Muslim world expanded dramatically as Islam became deeply rooted in regions as diverse as West Africa, East Africa, Central Asia, South Asia, and Southeast Asia. The stage was set for South Asia and Southeast Asia to become the world regions that now contain more than half the world's Muslims. In addition, new Muslim states arose that wielded enormous political and military power. By the early sixteenth century, the Ottoman, Safavid, and Mughal empires extended in an unbroken arc from the Danube River to the foothills of Nepal.

The period treated in Part Four provides the foundation for understanding the formation of the modern Muslim world. Many of the ideas, institutions, and practices that we now associate with both Sunni and Shi'ite Islam date from this period. It was also a period of major innovations in the fields of military technology, art, economic organization, and political systems. Given the importance of this period, it is all the more remarkable how little the general outline of its history is known in Western Europe and the Americas. It has the disadvantage of competing for attention with topics in contemporary European history such as the Renaissance, the Age of Discovery, the Protestant Reformation, the Scientific Revolution, the Enlightenment, and the emergence of modern states, economies, and ideologies. These topics claim our attention in part because they so clearly shaped the world on both sides of the Atlantic and in part because we seek in them an explanation for the global dominance of Europe in the nineteenth and twentieth centuries.

What is lost in this approach to the study of history is the realization that, throughout the era under review, no one could have been confident that Europe would eventually dominate the globe. To the contrary, at least until the end of the seventeenth century, Europeans feared being overwhelmed by Muslim power. Not until well into the eighteenth century were some individuals within both Europe and the Muslim world becoming aware of how the balance of power had shifted in dramatic fashion. In fact, what is emerging in recent research is that many important changes that took place in the Muslim empires between the fifteenth and seventeenth centuries echo developments in contemporary Central and Western Europe. Among the most notable were the triumph of regional political claims over universal ones, challenges by new religious groups to the dominant religious traditions, new relationships between the religious establishment and governments, and the increasing use of vernacular languages in religious literature.

The Dar al-Islam doubled in geographical extent during the period from the fifteenth to the eighteenth centuries. The addition of numerous new cultures to the realm of Islam renders the concept of "Islamic civilization" progressively more problematic as a unit of historical analysis for these centuries. The previous chapters of this work were an attempt to show how an Islamic civilization arose over a period of several centuries. As long as the literature of that civilization remained almost exclusively in the Arabic and Persian languages, a case can be made for the notion of an Islamic civilization that was a stage in the ongoing development of Middle Eastern civilization. However, as indigenous Muslim communities arose in Java, Bengal, Xinjiang, the Horn of Africa, and Hausaland, religious literature began appearing in local languages as well as in Arabic. Mosques and their decorative motifs assumed the forms of local architectural traditions, and many Islamic concepts and doctrines were interpreted in light of indigenous religious and moral traditions.

By the seventeenth century, the Muslim world extended across several civilizations. From that time on, we can continue to speak of the Muslim world, but probably not of Islamic civilization. Islam had become multicivilizational. That is not to say that the Muslim world no longer had a sense of identity or that its members could not communicate well with each other. On the contrary, scholars of all lands continued to communicate in Arabic or Persian much as medieval European scholars communicated in Latin. They travelled extensively and studied with each other, exchanging ideas and views. Muslims continued to view themselves as members of the Umma—the community of believers—and they recognized their common allegiance to a core of values and beliefs and their common grounding in a particular historical tradition.

In Part Four, then, we will see that most of the Muslim world experienced cultural and economic dynamism and territorial expansion during the fifteenth, sixteenth, and seventeenth centuries. Some societies, naturally, were not so fortunate. Muslim community life was almost annihilated in the Qipchaq steppe, where a weak tradition of urban life rendered Islamic institutions vulnerable to civil disorder, and in Kerala and the Philippines, where Iberian Christian crusaders made a determined effort to destroy Islam. The most significant setback, however, was in the Iberian Peninsula itself, where Muslim society had flourished for centuries. Granada, the only Iberian Muslim principality to survive the thirteenth century intact, fell to Spain in 1492, the same year that witnessed the expulsion of Iberian Jews. For the first time in almost eight hundred years, no independent Muslim state existed in the peninsula.

Shortly afterward, Spain began persecuting its large Muslim minority. By 1614, the country's rulers had expelled the entire Muslim population.

It is understandable that not all regions of the Muslim world experienced growth during the period from the fifteenth through the seventeenth centuries. What is harder to understand is why, after three centuries of robust expansion, the bulk of the Muslim world rapidly declined in economic and political power during the few decades prior to the mid-eighteenth century. During this period, the Ottoman Empire lost its dominant position in Eastern Europe and both the Safavid and Mughal empires suddenly collapsed. Simultaneously, the economies of Southeast Asia and Central Asia withered. The political and economic declines did not march in tandem—several areas remained generally prosperous while they fragmented politically—but the pattern of a rapid loss of political power throughout the Muslim world is striking. Each region had its own unique factors that created political or economic crises, but the overall trend suggests a general crisis that has not yet been adequately described or explained.

CHRONOLOGY

1405	Death of Timur Lang
1407–1447	Reign of Shah Rukh of Herat
1413	Mehmet I begins to reconstruct the Ottoman imperial project
1451–1526	The Lodi period, the last dynasty of the Delhi Sultanate
1453	Mehmet II captures Constantinople
1484–1525	Fragmentation of Bahmani Kingdom in the Deccan Plateau
1492	Spain expels its Jews and captures Muslim Granada
1493–1528	Reign of Askia Muhammad of Songhay
1498	Vasco da Gama sails into the Indian Ocean for Portugal
1501–1524	Reign of Shah Isma'il I of Iran
1511	Afonso de Albuquerque captures Melaka
1514	Battle of Chaldiran
1520–1566	Reign of Suleyman the Magnificent
1526–1530	Babur lays the foundation for the Mughal Empire
1520s	Era of Mediterranean corsairs begins
1552–1556	Fall of Kazan and Astrakhan to Muscovy
1556–1605	Reign of Akbar of Mughal Empire
1558–1603	Reign of Elizabeth I of England
1580	Spanish–Ottoman truce in the western Mediterranean
1582–1598	Shaybanid period in Transoxiana
1587–1629	Reign of Shah 'Abbas I of Iran
1596–1608	Most intense period of the Jelali Revolts in the Ottoman Empire
1602	Founding of the Dutch United East India Company (VOC)
1609–1614	Spain expels Moriscos
1620	English Separatist Puritans known as the Pilgrims sail to Plymouth
1631–1654	Taj Mahal under construction
1658–1707	Reign of Aurangzeb of the Mughal Empire
1699	Treaty of Karlowitz, the first significant loss of territory by the Ottomans
1722	Fall of Esfahan to Mahmud Ghilzai of Qandahar
1729	Jai Singh's scientific delegation spends a year in Europe
1739	Nadir Shah's sack of Delhi
1747	Ahmad Durrani founds the Durrani dynasty in Afghanistan
1755	The VOC's mediation of a civil war in Mataram gives it effective control of Java

CHAPTER 12

The Central Muslim Lands

During the period 1405–1750, the region that extends westward from the Persian Gulf to the Gulf of Sidra in Libya and northward from the Arabian Sea to the steppes of Russia was the central zone of the Muslim world. The region was central in several senses of the word. Historically, it is where Islam began. Geographically, it was still the demographic center of the Muslim world; the current demographic weight of the Muslim population in South and Southeast Asia was a development of the nineteenth and twentieth centuries. Religiously, it was the area where Mecca was located. Muslims in all parts of the globe turned five times daily toward Mecca for their prayers and tried to make the hajj at least once. Like Jerusalem in medieval Jewish and Christian cosmology, Mecca was the center of the world for Muslims, both in their devotional lives and on the world maps that they drew.

The central Muslim lands lay at the crossroads that linked Africa, Asia, and Europe. Cultural influences, world trade, and the ambitions of great states all converged here. This chapter will illustrate those themes by exploring three developments that took place during the period under investigation. The first is the dramatic rise of the Ottoman Empire from the ashes of Timur's attack. The Ottomans created an empire that spanned all three continents within its reach and lasted into the twentieth century. The empire's strength, strategic location, and self-styled role as protector of Islam involved it in events as far afield as Morocco and Southeast Asia. The second is the important role played by several dynamic cities on the fringes of the Arabian Peninsula. Most of the peninsula is extremely inhospitable to human life, and yet cities along its Red Sea and Indian Ocean coasts served vital functions in commerce and the transmission of culture. The third development was the fragmentation of the Golden Horde. The groups that splintered from it represented the last major challenge by Eurasian steppe warriors to the peasant societies of Eastern Europe.

The Ottoman Empire

The Ottoman sultanate appeared to be dead after Timur Lang smashed its army in 1402. It quickly recovered, however, and by the early sixteenth century it had become the most powerful empire in the world other than China. Its social and religious institutions influenced large areas of the Muslim world for centuries, and its struggles with Spain, the Habsburg Empire, Russia, and the Safavid Empire of Iran gave rise to a large number of today's cultural and political boundaries.

The Creation of an Empire

After Timur's defeat of Bayezit, the Ottoman sultanate nearly disintegrated. As Bayezit was dragged off to die in captivity, his four sons began to contest for leadership of the realm. In a replay of the fratricidal conflicts that crippled the Saljuqs from the eleventh to the thirteenth centuries, the brothers fought each other in a brutal civil war for more than a decade. It was the perfect opportunity for a European attack to have delivered a fatal blow against the Ottomans, but the European nations were too preoccupied with fighting each other to focus on their common enemy. Some of the Ottomans' vassals in both Rumelia (the Ottoman holdings in Europe) and Anatolia did assert their autonomy, but they proved to be unpopular rulers with their subjects. They fought numerous wars with each other, and they also imposed higher taxes than the Ottomans had levied. Merchants and peasants alike wistfully recalled the "good old days" under the Ottomans.

By 1413, Bayezit's son Mehmet I defeated all his brothers and became the new sultan. Under his aggressive leadership, the Ottoman army recaptured western Anatolia and much of the territory in Rumelia that had been lost in the chaos of the civil war. His son Murat II succeeded him in 1421. He was an able ruler, but he had to devote his energies more to the defense of the sultanate than to its expansion. By this time, Hungary and Venice were the primary European states that threatened the Ottomans, and they began a series of attacks on the Ottoman western front during the 1430s and 1440s. By 1444, the Hungarians and their allies had driven the Ottomans out of several areas of the Balkans. Under pressure, Murat signed a treaty that renounced several Ottoman claims there. At that point, when the morale of the Europeans was at its highest, Murat abdicated the throne in favor of his twelve-year-old son, Mehmet II.

The reason for Murat's abdication is still a puzzle, although there is evidence that it may have been the result of a state of psychological depression. At any rate, it left the realm vulnerable to an opportunistic attack. Indeed, the Pope promptly called for a crusade, and in the summer of 1444 knights and foot soldiers by the tens of thousands gathered in Hungary for war. The Ottoman response to the crusade demonstrated how the administrative structure of the government at Edirne had evolved since Osman's day. The Ottoman elite comprised several competing ethnic and social groups: Turkish chieftains, devshirme recruits, and Balkan Christian nobility. Previous Muslim regimes had deliberately kept such ethnic military groupings separate in order to play one off against the other. In the event of a crisis, the groups would often fall upon each other in a desperate struggle for survival, and the regime would collapse. This time, when the Europeans threatened a state headed by a twelve-year-old boy, the powerful groups at the top of the Ottoman hierarchy did not fragment. Their interests had become fused with a centralized bureaucratic structure. Imperceptibly, they had accepted an Ottoman identity and helped to create a state that would continue to exist even in the face of unexpected changes in leadership. Now, confronted with a potentially fatal threat, all sides within the ruling elite agreed to ask Murat to come out of retirement, if only to lead the army against the Europeans. He did so, and in November 1444, the Ottomans shattered the invading force at Varna. Murat once again retired, but a unit of the Janissaries refused to serve under the boy-emperor, Mehmet II. Murat was persuaded to resume his sultanate in 1446.

Despite having been deposed, the teenage Mehmet benefited from his father's resumption of the sultanate. During the next five years, he gained administrative experience as well as intensive academic training. In 1451, his father died, and Mehmet II inherited the throne as a talented and well-trained nineteen-year-old. Two years later, he achieved what Muslim leaders had failed to do for seven centuries: He captured the legendary city of Constantinople and turned it into his capital. The conquest was the result of meticulous planning. Mehmet built a fort on the European side of the Bosporus that matched the one that the Ottomans already held on the Asiatic side, he constructed a fleet to blockade the city from reinforcements, he contracted with a Hungarian gunsmith to provide huge cannons to bombard the walls of the city, and he assembled an army that is soberly estimated to have been composed of 100,000 troops. After a furious bombardment that lasted two months, the huge walls caved in. The defenders, who were outnumbered more than ten to one, had no chance once the walls were breached.

Some historians curiously downplay the significance of the conquest. They note that the Byzantine Empire had long ceased to exert meaningful political influence beyond the immediate environs of the city itself and that the city's population had shriveled to a tenth of its former size. It is true that the conquest would have been much more difficult had Mehmet faced the metropolis that Constantinople had been in its glory days, but the achievement was nevertheless monumental in both symbolic and practical terms. For centuries, Constantinople had been the epitome of Christian urban life. Despite its shrunken population, no other city in Europe could compare with its physical dimensions or cultural heritage. It was also a shield for Christian Europe against Muslim armies due to its potential role as an enemy military base behind Ottoman lines. Its fall in 1453 was both a severe psychological blow and a genuine military liability for Christendom. For Muslims, on the other hand, the capture of the city resulted in profound euphoria. The Byzantine city had always been a major obstacle to the expansion of Muslim power. Its fall appeared to be a harbinger of a glorious era for Islam. The Ottoman Empire thereafter enjoyed immense prestige for having been the power that captured Constantinople and transformed it into its capital, Istanbul.[1] For Ottoman administrative purposes, the capture of the city removed a serious obstacle to Ottoman communications between Rumelia and Anatolia, and it secured imperial control over the overland trade routes from east to west as well as the water route from the Black Sea to the Mediterranean.

The capture of Constantinople was Mehmet II's most prestigious military victory, but two other contests were just as important strategically. One, in the west, was the defeat of the Serbs in 1459, which led to the definitive annexation of Serbia. The other, in the east, was the defeat in 1473 of Uzun Hasan's White Sheep (Aq-Quyunlu) confederation. Uzun Hasan was a powerful Turkic chieftain who ruled eastern Anatolia and most of Iraq and Iran. Ambitious and sophisticated, he purchased muskets from the Venetians and other European powers for use against the Ottomans. By 1472, he felt strong enough to march against Bursa. This was a miscalculation, for Mehmet launched a major attack on him and drove him back into central Anatolia before utterly defeating him on the upper Euphrates River in 1473. Mehmet's victories between 1453 and 1473 secured a vast territorial base for the Ottoman Empire. Mehmet was also responsible for outfitting the Ottoman army with gunpowder weaponry. Although the Ottomans may have used muskets and cannon as early as the Anatolian campaigns of Murat I in the 1380s, it was Mehmet II who made muskets and artillery the standard equipment of the corps.

By the early sixteenth century, this new composite army of cavalry, infantry, and artillery had developed into one of the most formidable in the world. Its effectiveness was first demonstrated in a war against Iran that was precipitated by Ottoman anxiety over the ambitions of the Safavid Sufi order. The Safavids had actively recruited among the population of central and eastern Anatolia since the mid-fifteenth century. Their message had received an enthusiastic response from many Anatolian Turks who feared Ottoman expansion. In addition, many pastoralists felt a genuine attraction to Safavid religious teachings and practices, which bore striking similarities to the Bektashi and Alevi movements with which they were already familiar.

In 1501, Isma'il, the charismatic young leader of the Safavids, won a string of impressive military victories in Azerbaijan. He then assumed the title of shah, declaring his intention of implementing a temporal empire. Soon he controlled eastern Anatolia and eastern Syria. Almost immediately, pro-Safavid revolts began occurring within the Ottomans' Anatolian realm. For several years, numerous pro-Safavid rebellions flared up as far west as the Aegean coast. Ottoman sultans became increasingly concerned about Isma'il's influence among their subjects. Bayezit II (1481–1512) killed thousands of Shi'ites and deported large numbers of others to the Greek Peloponnesus in 1502, but the revolts continued. In 1511, a huge, pro-Safavid revolt erupted near Antalya. Bayezit sent an army to suppress it, but thousands of Ottoman soldiers defected from the army and joined the rebels. When the revolt's leaders gained control of central Anatolia, they began leading an army toward Bursa with the intention of besieging the city. An Ottoman army intercepted the expedition and defeated the rebels only after a major battle.

The growing disorder prompted several of Bayezit's sons to begin revolts against their father. Isma'il contributed to the confusion by aiding two of the brothers, thus incurring the wrath of a third brother, the ruthless and taciturn Selim. In 1512, Selim deposed his father, becoming Sultan Selim I (1512–1520). Then, in accord with Turkic tradition, he killed his brothers in order to preclude the risk of sibling rivalry. After securing his position, he began making plans to strike a decisive blow against the Safavids themselves. In the spring of 1514, he led his army through Anatolia, punishing pro-Safavid Turkmen. Selim even had to purge his own army of Safavid sympathizers during the campaign.

The Ottomans and Safavids finally met each other at Chaldiran, in the extreme northwestern corner of modern Iran. Some 70,000 Ottoman soldiers—including

12,000 Janissaries wielding muskets and cannons—faced some 40,000 Safavid cavalrymen. The Safavids chose not to use gunpowder weapons, although they were familiar with them: The Safavids and Uzun Hasan had employed muskets on a limited basis, but the mountainous terrain of Azerbaijan rendered the transport of cannons a practical impossibility. Besides, in the hands of the skilled Safavid cavalryman, the arrow and saber were devastatingly effective.

The Safavids routed the Ottoman army's left wing, but the musketry and 200 cannons of the Janissaries finally took their toll on the Safavid cavalry. Both sides suffered horrible losses, but it was the Safavid army that retreated from the field. The Ottomans continued unopposed to the Safavid capital of Tabriz, which they occupied. Shortly thereafter, they pulled back to the region of Lake Van. Although the Safavids remained dangerous enemies of the Ottomans, they were never again able to challenge them for supremacy in Anatolia.

Selim made military history again two years later. In August 1516, he led a campaign into Syria, which the Mamluks had retaken shortly after Timur's death in 1405. The Mamluk Empire, which had begun in 1250, was still intact. It also still ruled Syria and the Holy Cities as well as Egypt. By the time of Selim's invasion, however, the empire was much weaker than it had been at its peak in the early fourteenth century. Egypt and Syria were still reeling from continued epidemics of the plague. The population in both provinces had continued to decline, and their economies were weak. The fine products that had made the Mamluks famous— textiles, glassware, and inlaid work—deteriorated in quality during this period to the extent that the local inhabitants began to import such items from Europe. This economic weakness accelerated during the first decade of the sixteenth century after Portugal became established in India in 1500. The Portuguese tried to divert all trade between India and Europe around the tip of southern Africa by attacking Muslim shipping and capturing port cities in the Indian Ocean. The result was a temporary but precipitous drop in tariff revenues in Egypt from long-distance trade.

Ominously, too, the Mamluk ethos did not easily accommodate gunpowder weapons into its system. Like the Safavids, the Mamluks had experimented with artillery and muskets as early as the 1480s, but they did not revise their military organization in order to incorporate the weapons into their order of battle. Unlike the Safavids, the Mamluks did not have the argument of mountainous terrain to justify not using muskets and artillery: Egypt and the most valuable regions of Syria were situated on plains that would have accommodated wheeled artillery. The Mamluk army resisted gunpowder weapons because its decision makers were cavalrymen, and gunpowder transferred the striking power and the weight of the economic resources of any army to the infantry.

As a consequence, Selim's army faced Mamluks who, as a point of honor, insisted on making cavalry charges directly into the teeth of musket and artillery fire. Courageous as the Mamluks were, they were literally blown away during battles in Syria and Egypt, and by January 1517, the Mamluk Empire was gone, its territory now securely within the Ottoman fold. As spectacular as the conquest of Constantinople had been in raising the prestige of the Ottomans, their conquest of the Mamluks enhanced their prestige even more. Because Mecca and Medina were part of the Mamluk domain, Selim became the ruler of the Holy Cities and the guardian of the pilgrimage routes.

The conquest of Constantinople, the defeat of the Safavids, and the annexation of the Mamluk Empire transformed the Ottoman state into an empire. Its expansion did not stop there, however. Selim's son, Suleyman I (1520–1566), captured Iraq from the Safavids, annexed Hungary, captured the island of Rhodes from the Knights of St. John, and occupied much of the North African coast. He laid siege to Vienna in 1529 and might well have captured the city had winter weather not forced him back to his own capital. By the end of his reign, the empire comprised the Balkans south of the Danube River; autonomous provinces in modern Hungary, Romania, and southern Russia; all of Anatolia; and almost the entire Arab world to the frontier with Morocco. In the eastern Mediterranean, it included all the Aegean islands. (Cyprus and Crete were later acquisitions: The former was taken in 1571, and Crete was laboriously conquered between 1645 and 1669).

Society

For roughly two centuries, the Ottoman Empire was one of the world's greatest powers. At the beginning of the seventeenth century, it occupied an area of 800,000 square miles and contained twenty-five to thirty million people. (By comparison, the British Isles had approximately seven million people in 1600, France had almost nineteen million, and Spain had about ten million.) The population of the Ottoman Empire was diverse, containing large numbers of Turks, Armenians, Magyars, Arabs, Greeks, Slavs, and Berbers, as well as many smaller groups.

The empire also comprised many religious groups, including Sunni and Shi'ite Muslims, several Christian denominations, and Jews. The Muslim and Christian communities, in particular, were further distinguished by their various social classes and their urban or rural identities: The differences between the urban and rural expressions of these religions could be quite striking. As in every major society of the era, the majority of the population were peasants. Only a small minority were nomads, but in eastern Anatolia, Iraq, the Arabian Peninsula, and North Africa, their influence was considerable. Compared to Europe, the empire had a much higher percentage of the population living in huge cities (such as Istanbul and Cairo) and large cities (such as Edirne, Izmir, Aleppo, and Damascus).

The status of free women in the Ottoman Empire changed over time, particularly among the upper social strata. Among the early Ottomans, the manners and customs of their Central Asian heritage prevailed: Women moved about freely, left their faces uncovered, and played an active role in the economic production of the household. As the Ottomans became urbanized, wealthy, and influenced by urban Islamic values, however, women's public roles changed just as they had throughout Muslim history. On the one hand, women's public roles became more circumscribed; on the other hand, women's legal rights were formalized due to the impact of the Shari'a.

These two developments became evident during the reign of Suleyman I (1520–1566). By that time, the wealthy Muslim women of Istanbul did not have the freedom of movement of local Christians. Some men even stipulated in the marriage contract that their wives would never be allowed to step outside their homes. Even when they were allowed to leave the home, their faces were covered by a veil that made it impossible for anyone to see their features. Such women, however, might be quite powerful individuals. In the palace, the mothers of the sultan's sons exerted tremendous influence, whether they were wives or concubines. They lobbied to obtain for their sons the most powerful positions possible, they advised the sultan (whether consort or son) on policy decisions, and they granted huge sums of money for the construction of mosques, hospitals, and schools.

Even women outside the palace could wield considerable power. Unlike their contemporaries in Europe, they were able to buy, own, use, and sell property without any restrictions by their male relatives. They could lend or borrow money, enforce their rights in court when necessary, and serve as executors of wills. Legally, they could not be forced into marriage, although family pressures are known to have infringed on this right. As in many other societies (such as that of the Byzantines), their sequestration was a sign of their families' wealth—it showed that their labor was not necessary for the maintenance of the family. Sequestration and veiling were also regarded as demonstrations of piety, but they were characteristics primarily of prosperous families. Poor women, on the other hand, whether in the city or in the village, often appeared in public without their faces covered, for they were actively involved in labor.

Ottoman society, like most other premodern societies, exploited a large slave population. The trade in slaves was a major element in the Ottoman economy. Istanbul's slave markets were enormous, siphoning human chattel from a huge Afro-Eurasian hinterland. Some of the slaves were captured in war by the regular army, others were captured by pirates in the Mediterranean or Black Sea, and still others were transported into the empire as "commodities" of long-distance trade. We are accustomed to thinking of slaves as being forced into the most menial and oppressive types of work, but it should be obvious by now that this was not always the case in the Ottoman Empire. Slaves played an even more visible role in the Ottoman Empire than they did in the Mamluk Empire, where they were technically manumitted at the end of their training. The recruits of the Ottoman devshirme remained slaves all their lives, and yet they joined the highest ranks of administrators in the land. The Shari'a forbade the offices of the sultan and the highest religious dignitaries from being held by slaves, but the vizier, other top government officials, military officers, and many provincial governors were lifelong slaves who wielded enormous power. Viziers and other powerful slaves in the civilian and military administration possessed their own slaves.

Most slaves, of course, did not occupy powerful positions. On the other hand, few provided cheap labor for agriculture or industry (although they were used extensively in the navy's galleys). Most were personal servants and bodyguards, and there was a thriving trade in concubines. Like many Muslim rulers before them, Ottoman sultans had concubines as well as wives, and most of the sultans were themselves children of concubines. A glance at the family tree of the sixteenth-century sultans demonstrates that their Turkish gene pool had been overwhelmed by the Slavic element of their mothers, grandmothers, and great-grandmothers. When one remembers that the heads of government bureaus and the military were also largely of Slavic origin by way of the devshirme, that the language of the elite was heavily Persianized and Arabized, and that the large cavalry force was primarily Turkish, the cosmopolitan nature of the Ottoman enterprise comes quickly into focus.

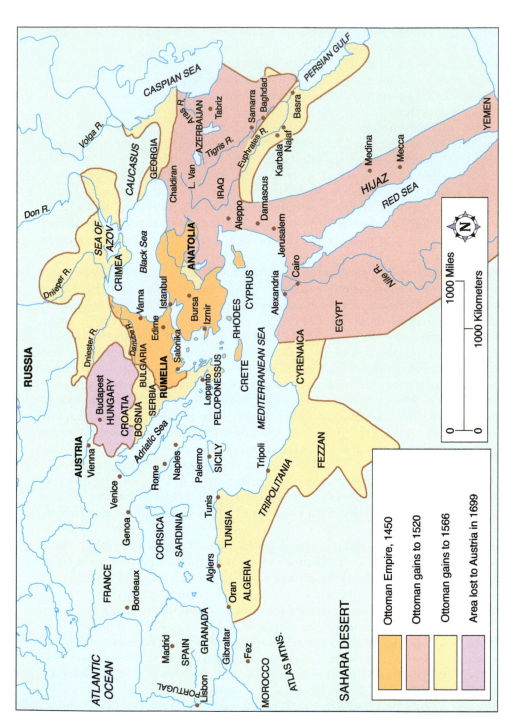

MAP 12.1 The Ottoman Empire to 1699.

Ottoman Empire, 1450

Ottoman gains to 1520

Ottoman gains to 1566

Area lost to Austria in 1699

1000 Miles

1000 Kilometers

RUSSIA

ATLANTIC OCEAN

FRANCE

Bordeaux

SPAIN

Madrid

PORTUGAL

Lisbon

GRANADA

Gibraltar

Fez

MOROCCO

ATLAS MTNS.

SAHARA DESERT

Genoa

Venice

Rome

Naples

Palermo

CORSICA

SARDINIA

SICILY

Tunis

Algiers

Oran

TUNISIA

ALGERIA

Tripoli

TRIPOLITANIA

FEZZAN

CYRENAICA

AUSTRIA

Vienna

Budapest

HUNGARY

CROATIA

BOSNIA

SERBIA

BULGARIA

Adriatic Sea

RUMELIA

Salonika

Lepanto

PELOPONESSUS

CRETE

MEDITERRANEAN SEA

Danube R.

Dniester R.

Dnieper R.

Don R.

Volga R.

CAUCASUS

GEORGIA

CASPIAN SEA

SEA OF AZOV

CRIMEA

Black Sea

Varna

Istanbul

Edirne

Bursa

Izmir

ANATOLIA

RHODES

CYPRUS

Chaldiran

L. Van

AZERBAIJAN

Tabriz

Aras R.

Tigris R.

IRAQ

Aleppo

Damascus

Jerusalem

Alexandria

Cairo

EGYPT

Nile R.

Euphrates R.

Samarra

Baghdad

Karbala

Najaf

Basra

PERSIAN GULF

HIJAZ

Medina

Mecca

RED SEA

YEMEN

The State

The success of the Ottoman Empire during its first two and one-half centuries was due in large part to its sophisticated administrative system. It incorporated elements from its Iranian, Byzantine, and Saljuq predecessors, and it continually adapted to changing circumstances. Because the early Ottomans were constantly conquering new territory that contained non-Muslims, the Ottomans thought it only natural to tolerate Christians and Jews, who formed the majority of the population for several centuries. The state's institutions were profoundly affected by the relationship of the ruling class with its non-Muslim subjects.

The Sultan

The first ten Ottoman sultans were men of unusual ability. They were highly charismatic, and they all personally led their armies and civil administrations. Before they occupied the throne, they were trained by long service in various administrative and military positions. Until 1611, the sons of sultans succeeded to the throne in the traditional Turkic manner of a struggle among the brothers. Each gathered an army and fought the others until one emerged triumphant. Any surviving losers were garroted. This ruthless process of natural selection seems, in fact, to have resulted in the survival of the fittest.

In 1421, Mehmet I added the title of *caliph* to his long string of honorifics. He was not claiming a unique status in the Muslim world. Numerous rulers all across the Dar al-Islam had appropriated the title ever since it was cheapened in the tenth century, when three caliphs contested for power. Since 1260, the Mamluks had retained the services of a descendant of the Abbasid family upon whom they conferred the title of caliph as well. He had no power and was simply a puppet of the state. Mehmet laid claim to the title only because he knew that fellow Muslims would not take him seriously as a chief of state without it.

When Selim went to war against the Safavids and Mamluks during 1514–1517, he was in the awkward position of making war on fellow Muslims rather than engaging in jihad against infidels. Like many rulers before and after him, he justified his wars against Muslim states by claiming that they were heretics, but he knew that such a claim rang empty in many quarters. His defeat of both powers, however, provided him with the opportunity to secure his preeminent status. Upon defeating the Mamluks, he dismissed the puppet caliph in Cairo and began to emphasize his own responsibility for the sacred precincts of Mecca and Medina.

Despite the rapid ascent of Ottoman power between the capture of Constantinople in 1453 and the annexation of the Holy Cities in 1517, sultans knew that they could not aspire to be the spokesman for the entire Muslim world. Like sixteenth-century Safavid and Mughal rulers, Ottoman sultans faced a vastly expanded Muslim world that made a mockery of universal claims. Despite occasional wars among these rulers, they recognized that the others had their respective spheres of influence. They often engaged in formal diplomatic relations with each other as equal powers. None of those rulers claimed that, by virtue of his office, he held hegemony over the others. The Muslim world had been multipolar from very early in its history: No single power was in a position to dominate the entire Dar al-Islam from the time of the Great Berber Revolt of the 740s. By the sixteenth century, the emergence of three powerful Muslim empires should have forced a reassessment of the meaning of the caliphate, but the topic was too sensitive for political and religious theorists to touch it.

The irrelevance of the caliphate was not a controversial issue as long as empires were vibrant, for religious scholars and the masses alike could assume that their respective leaders were fulfilling the caliphal function by virtue of their success. Awkward moments did occasionally arise in the matters of war and peace, however. Rulers confronted two major complications. One was that wars with other Muslim empires were problematic from the perspective of Islamic law because fighting fellow Muslims was hard to justify except on the basis of stamping out heresy.

The other problem was that the doctrine of jihad became less and less consistent with political reality. The Shari'a prohibited the making of peace with non-Muslim states except under extraordinary circumstances. Theoretically, the normative relationship between the Dar al-Islam and the Dar al-Harb was supposed to be continual jihad. The collective duty of jihad was to respond to the caliph's call to go to war against non-Muslim neighbors. The individual duty of jihad was to defend the Dar al-Islam if it were attacked, regardless of whether a caliph was present to lead. Muslim monarchs, however, discovered that they occasionally had to go to war with fellow Muslims to accomplish their goals and that they occasionally needed alliances with non-Muslim states for the same reason. When a Muslim ruler concluded a treaty of alliance with a non-Muslim ruler, his partner in peace expected him to restrain zealous subjects from engaging in jihad. Thus, like earlier Muslim dynasties, the Ottomans, Safavids, and Mughals had amicable relations with both Muslims and non-Muslims and fought both Muslims and non-Muslims. The practice of international relations in Muslim countries was hardly distinguishable from that of European nations. The concept of jihad lost its clarity, and individuals in later generations would reinterpret it to serve their own purposes.

Whatever Muslims themselves might think about jihad and the caliphate, the Ottomans ruled over a large population of non-Muslims who had little interest in those issues. As a result, Ottoman sultans worked hard to establish justice as the principle that legitimized their rule in the eyes of all of their subjects. In addition to their lavish support of the court system that enforced the Shari'a, they paid careful attention to issues that fell outside the purview of Islamic law. All Muslim regimes employed non-Shari'a laws to fill gaps that the Shari'a did not cover. These laws included new regulations that the state needed in order to carry on its business as well as traditional laws that the empires' subjects—both Muslim and non-Muslim—were accustomed to following. Ottoman administrators were more diligent than previous ones had been in compiling provincial law books that reflected customary usage in a given area. This body of non-Shari'a law, or *kanun* (a term borrowed from the *canon* law tradition of the Romans and Byzantines), gradually became very large, and it occasionally contradicted the Shari'a. When Ottoman administrators codified kanun regulations into books, the differences between them and the Shari'a became more obvious. The muftis during the reign of Suleyman resolved many of the inconsistencies between the two systems of law, and Suleyman received the credit: Although Europeans know him as Suleyman the Magnificent, Muslims refer to him as Suleyman the Law-Giver.

The *Devshirme*

As impressive as the sultans were as individual leaders, even they realized that without a stable and efficient bureaucratic apparatus, the Ottoman regime was unlikely to be any more durable than that of the Saljuqs had been. A sophisticated administrative system distinguished the Ottomans from the many short-lived dynasties that preceded them. At the dawn of their own history, they had been a loosely organized band of independent-minded gazis, but over the decades their leaders gradually created a complex administration. It proved to be a hybrid bureaucracy, having emerged under the guiding hands of religious specialists and administrators from the cities of the old Sultanate of Rum, the Byzantine Empire, and the Mamluk Empire, as well as from the Ottomans' own innovation of the devshirme.

A sophisticated bureaucracy began to emerge as early as the reign of Murat I (1362–1389). Prior to the capture of Constantinople, Turks played the most important role in the army and the administration, but Mehmet II attempted to balance the power of the Turks in both institutions by expanding the levy of Christian children (devshirme) that Bayezit I (1389–1402) had instituted. Under Mehmet II (1451–1481) the devshirme became the recruiting mechanism for some of the most powerful figures in the empire. Agents went out into the villages to seize (by force, if necessary) the brightest and hardiest Christian boys between the ages of eight and eighteen. They escorted the boys to Istanbul, where they were tested for a variety of abilities. The most promising ten percent or so were sent for training to the palaces of Edirne and Istanbul, whereas the majority were assigned to Turkish farmers. Those who lived with the farming families learned the Turkish language and the rudiments of Islam. When they became sufficiently acculturated, they were enrolled in the ranks of the Janissaries, where they received training in the use of muskets and artillery. The Janissaries owed supreme loyalty to the sultan. They were his personal slaves, and few retained any ties with their homelands.

The devshirme recruits who had been sent for palace instruction began a rigorous program of education and training. They studied the Qur'an and the various religious sciences; became fluent in Arabic, Persian, and Turkish; and engaged in physical training such as wrestling, archery, and horsemanship. In addition, each trainee acquired a professional artistic skill like miniature painting or bookbinding. At the end of the program the candidates were subject to a second screening. The majority (probably about ninety percent) entered high-status positions in the sultan's household cavalry, administrative positions throughout the empire, or the profession of military engineer (for the all-important task of conducting siege operations). The elite ten percent who survived this second screening became the most powerful civilian and military officials in the empire. These included the governors, the highest officers of the army, the heads of departments in the central government, and the vizier, or chief minister to the sultan. Like the Janissaries, these officials were the personal slaves of the sultan.

By the early sixteenth century, devshirme recruits had become the dominant element of the ruling class. They held the leading civilian and military offices, and they were the only recruits allowed to enter the most elite unit of the army: the musket-wielding Janissaries. The size of the Janissary corps rose from 6000 men at the end of Mehmet II's reign to 12,000 at the end of Suleyman's reign. The influence of the Turks, who had dominated Ottoman affairs in the early years, declined, but they remained a powerful force. They formed the bulk of the cavalry, which numbered as many as 50,000 in a single campaign (with many more in reserve) by the sixteenth century. The cavalrymen were known as *sipahis*. The Ottomans granted to a sipahi a *timar*, or the agricultural tax revenue derived from a specific region. The more important the sipahi was, the larger his timar. This correlation was not mere favoritism: A sipahi was responsible not only for his own military service, but also for perhaps several dozen troops in addition to their armor, tents, and supplies. The powerful Turkish sipahis continued to be the influential local lords in the countryside despite the growing authority of the devshirme in the cities.

One of the factors accounting for the dynamism of the Ottoman Empire during the fifteenth and sixteenth centuries was its merit-based system of administration. The most powerful offices in the empire, whether in the cavalry or the devshirme system, were achieved through competence. The hereditary principle was certainly not absent among the Turks, for they were proud of their lineage, but it did not provide an automatic entrée into the ruling elite as it usually did in contemporary Europe. The most powerful posts in the empire were open to talent, and they were almost always held by men of proven ability. Moreover, the tension between the devshirme and the sipahis resulted in a balance that ensured both the sultan's security and the welfare of the peasants who lived on the timars: The devshirme officials, who themselves had been recruited from peasant families, set the policies that the sipahis had to follow with regard to the peasants who worked their land.

Bureaucratizing Islam

The Ottoman administration was the first Muslim government to develop a fully bureaucratic structure for the religious institutions of its society. From the Umayyad period (661–750) on, the ulama and the state maintained an uneasy relationship. The ulama mediated God's will to society through their jurisprudence, while the state granted society a reasonable degree of physical security in return for taxes. The ulama officially recognized the legitimacy of the government in return for a pledge of governmental nonintervention in the affairs of religion. The degree of mistrust between the ulama and their governments was often high. Governments were usually so despised for their corruption and brutality that members of the ulama who did agree to serve as qadis when the state asked them to do so were frequently held in contempt by their fellow ulama, even though qadis were indispensable for the operation of the religious courts. Prior to the period of the Ottomans, the Mamluks had made the most concerted effort to control religious institutions. They attempted to gain influence with Sufi orders and madrasas by endowing their institutions, and they appointed qadis for all four schools of Islamic law (it had been customary to favor one school) so that none would be outside their system of patronage.

The Ottomans were even more systematic and thorough than the Mamluks had been. They sought to control the religious establishment by creating an elaborate hierarchy of learned offices held by appointment. Although they did not succeed in making all important ulama state employees, their comprehensiveness was unprecedented. Religious functionaries, from the highest-ranking specialist in the capital city to the lowliest preachers in the villages, were tied into the system. Lavish patronage of schools, hospitals, Sufi lodges, and mosques all over the empire facilitated the efforts to make local religious leaders dependent on the government. Many of the waqfs (religious endowments) throughout the empire were centralized under the administration of a new bureaucracy staffed by ulama.

The ulama who served the government were now powerful government officials. They possessed high status, honors, and privileges, and they could pass their wealth and status to their children. Some of the ulama realized that the state was using Islam as a means to legitimize its own sovereignty and policies, and they regarded government service as unethical. Most, however, rationalized such service as a way to standardize the norms of the Istanbul-based ulama throughout the entire empire. They eagerly sought the new opportunities.

The ruling elite were particularly concerned to monitor Sufi brotherhoods, because the spiritual authority of the Sufi masters was a potential threat to the government's monopoly of power. Some of the tariqas, especially the Naqshbandiya, were not considered a threat because of their adherence to the norms of the Shari'a. The degree to which an order neglected the Shari'a was considered a barometer of its potential to threaten the government. Sufis considered spiritual authority to be higher than temporal authority (the government), and many of them regarded the Sufi engagement in spiritual communion to be superior to the emphasis on correct doctrine and ritual (which they associated with the ulama). Justice and morality were almost universal norms among the Sufis (the dervishes, as we have seen, defined "morality" in their own way), and they judged the worthiness of any government by the degree to which these two ideals were implemented.

Government officials knew that the discipline, obedience to the master, and organizational sophistication of the Sufi orders provided a potential source of worldly power to Sufi masters that could be mobilized whenever such a leader felt that justice and morality were being neglected. Even after Selim's defeat of the Safavids in 1514, Sufi-inspired rebellions continued to erupt in Anatolia. Suleyman was forced to alternate his campaigns of conquest with bloody suppressions of such revolts throughout his reign. In the middle decades of the seventeenth century, the ulama–government alliance engaged in several purges of Sufi orders during periods of economic hardship.

An intriguing exception to the governmental enforcement of the Shari'a's norms was the case of the Bektashi Sufi movement, which was closely identified with the Janissaries. For the first century or so of the existence of the Janissary organization, the esprit de corps of its members was enhanced by a prohibition against marriage. The emotional needs of the Janissaries were sublimated through Sufi organizations, and the Bektashi order became the official order within the corps. As we have seen, the Bektashi movement was characterized by doctrines and practices (such as the use of wine in initiation ceremonies and belief in the trinity of God, Muhammad, and 'Ali) that scandalized most of the ulama. Because of the special relationship between the Janissary corps and the sultan, however, the ulama learned not to inquire too closely into the doctrines and practices of the Bektashi tariqa.

On the other hand, the Bektashi order was well suited to facilitate the transition of rural Christian boys into an officially Islamic society. Reports from contemporary observers reveal that many Christian Balkan villagers could not explain the Eucharist or recite any prayers; in 1453, the Orthodox Church felt compelled to issue a

FIGURE 12.1   The interior of the Selimiye Mosque, Edirne. Commissioned by the Ottoman Sultan Selim II, the mosque was constructed during 1568–1574. The great architect Sinan considered it his masterpiece due to the uncluttered interior space and unusual degree of illumination that the huge windows provide.

Ayhan Altun / Alamy Stock Photo.

condemnation of the practice of bowing to the sun and moon and addressing prayers to them. Boys from such backgrounds would not require intense indoctrination to enter an organization that was indifferent to the specifics of the Shari'a. Furthermore, the order taught that apparent contrasts between Christianity and Islam were due to metaphorical language used in both religions. Bektashi shaykhs taught that their mystical path was superior to any of the rituals and rules of the organized religions, including the Islam of the mosques and madrasas. Thus, many members of the Janissary corps found that, apart from the circumcision ceremony that awaited them upon their arrival from their home village into the capital, their transition into Muslim society was quite painless.

The *Millet* System

For the first two centuries of their history, the Ottomans often incorporated non-Turks and non-Muslims into their enterprise. During that period, the majority of the population in the empire (in both Rumelia and Anatolia) were Christian, and there were considerable numbers of Jews in some areas. By the turn of the sixteenth century, access to powerful civilian and military positions was largely closed to non-Muslims, but the government continued to cultivate good relations with its various religious communities. Like all governments of the day, the Ottoman administration was primarily interested in finances. Most aspects of government not directly associated with exploiting the wealth of empire were left to the subjects to organize as they wished. In the Ottoman context, that meant that the government's relations with non-Muslims would be guided by both custom and the Shari'a. The Ottoman administration integrated these guidelines in a unique manner that enabled the various religious communities to live together with the least possible friction while ensuring that the state treasury was the beneficiary of taxes paid by non-Muslims.

In the Ottoman Empire, all subjects were regarded as belonging to a certain religious community, or *millet*. Mehmet II began the practice of organizing the administration of the millets soon after the conquest of Constantinople. Originally, the official millets included only the Orthodox, Armenians, and Muslims, although the Jews were always treated as a de facto millet. The Ottomans eventually recognized as millets the communities of the Jacobites, Copts, and Maronites, as well. Each millet was allowed internal self-government according to its own laws and traditions, and each was directed by its own religious leader, who was responsible for civil as well as religious matters. In many ways, then, the millet system gave non-Muslim religious leaders more power over their flocks than they had under previous regimes.

The most important non-Muslim millet was that of the Orthodox Church, which was by far the largest non-Muslim group in the empire. Its membership outnumbered even the Muslims until the incorporation of the Arab lands in the sixteenth century. The two largest ethnic groups among the Orthodox Christians were the Greeks and Slavs, but there were significant numbers of Arabs and other ethnic groups as well. In fact, the inclusion of the various ethnic groups within the single millet remained a grievance for many of the Orthodox Slavs because the Bulgarians and Serbs had maintained their own Slavic-language churches prior to the Ottoman conquest. In the single millet, they had to be subject to a Greek Orthodox administration, with deleterious consequences for their Slavic culture.

The fortunes of the Orthodox Church were decidedly different in Rumelia from what they were in Anatolia. In Anatolia, the Orthodox Church was challenged by the Armenian Church, which the Orthodox regarded as heretical. The Armenians continued to thrive in the eastern and southern areas of the peninsula, but the Orthodox population of the central plateau gradually disappeared. In part, this decline was no doubt due to harassment by Turkish nomads, who raided Christian settlements whenever they could. The larger problem, however, seems to have been a gradual breakdown in the Church's institutional network across the peninsula after the Saljuqs took over Anatolia in the late eleventh century. The Church had always been an instrument of the Byzantine state, and when state control broke down across Anatolia after the Battle of Manzikert, the Church was not as prepared to service the needs of the Christian population that was scattered across Anatolia as the Catholic Church had been in Western Europe after the collapse of Rome's political authority. It became more and more difficult to maintain a Christian identity in the rural areas, and the poorer members of the church sought assistance from Muslim welfare institutions in the absence of aid from the Church. As a result, the Orthodox community in those regions lost its cohesion and an individual Christian's gradual assimilation to Islam was not hindered by the many social constraints from family, friends, and church that prevailed in other areas.

In Rumelia, by contrast, the Orthodox population continued to thrive due to Ottoman recognition and an active, well-organized support network directed by the patriarch. Whereas Anatolia had suffered from repeated waves of incursions, warfare, and destruction over a period of four centuries, the Balkans were conquered in relatively short campaigns. Ottoman rulers rapidly incorporated the area into a well-organized and stable administrative system, for they disliked the predatory raiding of the gazis as much as anyone. Ottoman policy favored Christian nobles and churches as vehicles of Ottoman administration. In turn, at least until the late seventeenth century, Orthodox Christians openly expressed their preference for Ottoman administration to that of any Catholic power that coveted the Balkans, for they believed that they would suffer less religious persecution under the millet system than under Catholic rule.

The Catholics in the Ottoman Empire did not fare as well as Orthodox Christians did. Catholics were placed within the Armenian millet. This was a much more serious situation for Catholics than the merging of the Slavic and Greek Orthodox churches: Catholics regarded Armenians as heretics, and yet they were subject to the Armenian patriarch. This humiliation may have been a deliberate ploy on the part of the Ottomans, whose attitude toward the Catholic Church was one of suspicion and occasional hostility. The Ottoman attitude was largely a reaction to the hostility toward the Ottomans on the part of the Catholic powers of Venice, Hungary, and the Habsburg Empire (which included Spain and Austria during most of the sixteenth century). During the sixteenth century, the Ottomans did develop close diplomatic ties with predominantly Catholic France, but France was a long distance away and shared certain foreign policy objectives with the Ottomans. The French and Ottomans cooperated diplomatically and militarily, and both were determined to ensure that the Habsburg rulers of Spain and Austria did not become dominant in Europe.

At the urging of the French Catholic king, Suleyman maintained diplomatic correspondence with an alliance of German Protestant princes who were fighting the Catholic Habsburg emperor, Charles V. He encouraged them and assured them of Ottoman support. Apart from his desire to harass Charles, Suleyman also seems to have had a genuine religious appreciation for the Protestant revolt because of the destruction of religious statuary and images in stained glass windows that some of the Protestant groups practiced. The continuous Ottoman military threat directed against the Habsburgs between 1521 and 1555 forced the Habsburgs to grant concessions to the Protestants and was a factor in the final official Habsburg recognition of Protestantism. A common saying in the German-speaking lands of the time was *Der Türke ist der lutheranischen Glück* ("the Turk is Lutheran good fortune").

The contrast between the Jewish experience in the Ottoman Empire and Christian Europe is striking. The growth of virulent anti-Semitism in Europe brought increasing numbers of Jews to the empire during the fifteenth and sixteenth centuries. When Spain expelled its Jews in 1492, tens of thousands of refugees emigrated to Ottoman territories. Sultan Bayezit II issued orders to his officials throughout the empire to welcome them. Some of the refugees achieved success quickly. A famous example is Joseph Hamon, who left Granada in 1493 and served Bayezit II and Selim I as court physician for a quarter of a century. Jews from Spain settled in many parts of Ottoman territory but were concentrated in Istanbul and Salonica (Thessaloniki), the two largest commercial port cities. They eventually became the majority population of Salonica, which was often referred to as "the Jewish city." It was also known as "La Madre de Israel" in recognition of its eminence as a center of Jewish learning.

The millet system was a means by which the Ottomans could continue the traditional Muslim administrative practice of religious toleration toward Jews and Christians while simultaneously reaping financial advantage from them in the form of the religious head tax. Conversions to Islam did occur in the Balkans under Ottoman rule, but the evidence suggests that most were voluntary rather than the result of coercion.[2] The most dramatic example of large-scale conversion took place in Bosnia. Like the Croats, Slovenes, Serbs, and Bulgarians, most inhabitants of Bosnia were Slavic, descendants of the Slavs who migrated into the area in the seventh and eighth centuries. During the medieval period, the Slavs of the western half of the Balkans (the Croats and Slovenes) came under Habsburg influence and shared with their Austrian rulers the Catholic faith and the Latin alphabet. The Slavs in the eastern half of the peninsula (the Serbs and Bulgarians), however, gravitated to the Orthodox faith and used the Cyrillic alphabet, which had been developed by Byzantine missionaries. The Slavs in Bosnia, between these two regions, were in a frontier area where the Latin–Catholic culture competed with the Cyrillic–Orthodox culture. In these remote valleys' there were few churches and even fewer priests, with the result that Bosniaks were even more notorious for their ignorance of the fundamentals of Christianity than other rural Balkan residents. The Bosniak nobility rapidly converted to Islam in the fifteenth century, taking advantage of the opportunities to hold high military and civil offices. Many villagers followed soon thereafter, with the Bektashi order particularly active in winning over converts. Bosnia and Albania became Bektashi strongholds.

The Economy

Agriculture was the foundation of the imperial economy. The conquest of Syria and Egypt in 1517 enhanced the value of this sector. The empire was nearly self-sufficient in the production of foodstuffs and made a profit from exporting grain to markets around the Mediterranean basin. The so-called "Columbian exchange"—the worldwide diffusion of plants and animals that took place after the European discovery of the Western Hemisphere—had a less pronounced effect on Ottoman society than it did in Europe and Africa, but it resulted in the introduction of some important products. The tomato entered the cuisine of the empire just as it did the other Mediterranean societies. Maize also made an impact, but it was valued as animal fodder, not as a staple of the human diet. Tobacco made its appearance in Istanbul about 1600 and spread rapidly throughout the empire. Men soon discovered the pleasure of smoking a hookah, or water pipe, in the coffeehouses that had recently become fashionable.

Long-distance trade was an important supplement to agriculture. The Ottomans took over an area that had been a crossroads of commerce for millennia. Their first capital, Bursa, had been a terminus for the caravan route that brought raw silk from Iran to supply the European demand for that valuable commodity. Aleppo was a spice market for the trade route from Southeast Asia that ran through the Persian Gulf, while Cairo was the equivalent market on the Red Sea route. Istanbul, of course, was the preeminent market in the empire due to its size and its status as the capital city.

Much of the Ottoman interest in expanding into the Black Sea, Aegean Sea, and Mediterranean Sea stemmed from the desire to compete with the Venetians and Genoese, who had dominated those regions for centuries. Genoa's economy suffered the most from the Ottoman conquest of Constantinople, for it had dominated the Black Sea trade since the thirteenth century. In 1484, the Ottomans placed a virtual prohibition on non-Ottoman shipping in the sea.

While the Ottomans were consolidating power in the Black Sea and eastern Mediterranean, Portugal was seeking to control the commerce of the Indian Ocean. After Vasco da Gama's arrival at Calicut in 1498, one of the Iberian power's explicit goals was to destroy Muslim commerce in the Indian Ocean. At first, the Portuguese were successful, as their aggressive attacks on Muslim shipping in the ocean caused the spice trade through the Red Sea to contract severely. The Ottomans conquered the Mamluk Empire in 1517, just as the supply of spices coming into Cairo was starting to diminish due to the Portuguese blockade. In order to counter the Portuguese threat, the Ottomans seized Aden, on the southwestern coast of the Arabian Peninsula. Ottoman possession of this strategic port revived the Red Sea spice trade, and both the Ottomans and the Venetians benefitted. The Ottomans invested heavily to protect their trade routes from the Europeans. They fought the Portuguese in the Persian Gulf and along the African coast, and even sent ships, supplies, and soldiers to aid Muslims against the Portuguese on the Malabar Coast of India and on the island of Sumatra in Southeast Asia.

Ottoman officials valued international trade so highly that they granted foreign merchants a set of special privileges called *Capitulations*. These privileges were similar to the content of what we call diplomatic immunity today: They entailed exemption from Ottoman law and taxes. Special privileges had been granted to certain merchants from Italian city–states in the fourteenth and fifteenth centuries, but the first major Capitulations were granted to the French in 1536, a year after France and the Ottoman Empire signed a formal alliance against the Habsburgs. In effect, the Capitulations bestowed on the French merchant community in the Ottoman realm the status of millet. In the sixteenth century, the Capitulations were reciprocal—Ottomans received them in France—but in later centuries, they proved to be instruments that enabled Europeans to gain important leverage in the Ottoman Empire.

Culture

The Ottomans always took pride in their origins as Central Asian Turks, but it had taken only a few decades for their culture to differ substantially from that of their nomadic ancestors. First at Bursa, then at Edirne, and finally at Istanbul, the Ottomans created an imperial presence that impressed visitors and subjects alike. The most spectacular period of Ottoman cultural history began with Mehmet II's capture of Constantinople. The storied city had shrunk to a population of some 50,000 at the time of the conquest, and after the sack of the city it appears to have contained only 10,000 souls. Mehmet was determined to restore the city's stature as a great imperial capital, and he immediately began a program of repopulation and construction. He provided incentives for Christians, Jews, and Muslims alike to move to the city; when necessary, he forcibly settled his subjects in the capital.

Embellishment of the city was the greatest economic project in Ottoman history. It required the construction of schools, hospitals, baths, caravansaries, bazaars, and shops of all kinds. Mehmet II's reign alone witnessed the construction of more than 200 mosques, thirty-two public baths, and twenty-four schools. Engineers made repairs to the aqueducts, sewers, and other components of the city's infrastructure. Having turned Justinian's imposing, 900-year-old church, the Hagia Sofia, into the greatest mosque in the world, Mehmet soon commissioned the construction of a new mosque to rival it (it was destroyed by an earthquake in the eighteenth century).

Mehmet II also built two new palaces in the city, the most famous of which was the Topkapi. It began rising on 150 acres of land situated on the promontory overlooking the Bosporus Strait. Future sultans would continue to add on to it until it became one of the largest palace complexes in the world. The city that contained it was correspondingly large: By the end of Mehmet's reign in 1481, the population of Istanbul had risen to almost 100,000. By the end of Suleyman's reign in 1566, the city boasted 400,000–600,000 inhabitants, which was a population twice as large as either London or Paris could claim.

Mehmet II was a highly cultured ruler, even if many of his subjects found him to be arbitrary and cruel in his dealings with those who displeased him. A talented poet, he had eclectic cultural tastes. He gathered Italian humanists and Greek scholars at his court, and he ordered the Orthodox patriarch to write a credo of the Christian faith that he could study. He filled his palace library with works in Greek and Latin, and he commissioned Gentile Bellini to come from Venice to paint his portrait. Mehmet also recruited painters, astronomers, and mathematicians from Central Asia to his court.

Ottoman culture is most famous for its monumental architecture, and the greatest of the Ottoman architects was Sinan (1489–1588). A product of the devshirme, Sinan began as an officer in the artillery and then became a designer of military bridges and fortifications. He built his first nonmilitary building in 1539 and served as the chief imperial architect for the next forty years. He is credited with dozens of mosques and palaces as well as numerous public baths, tombs, madrasas, caravansaries, hospitals, aqueducts, and fountains.

Sinan's most famous works are the Suleymaniye mosque in Istanbul and the Selimiye mosque in Edirne. Using the Byzantine church as his inspiration, Sinan adapted the design to meet the needs of Muslim worship, which requires large open spaces for communal prayer. The huge central dome remained the focal point around which the design of the rest of the structure was developed, but he was able to reduce the bulk of the weight-bearing piers and buttresses, resulting in thinner walls that contained more and larger windows. The square-sided, domed mosque, punctuated with several pencil-shaped minarets, became the model for subsequent Ottoman religious architecture.

The Ottomans were also active in creating a new literary tradition. The Persian language had enjoyed an important role in the diplomatic correspondence and Sufi poetry of the Sultanate of Rum. As a result, even Osman's generation had been powerfully influenced by Persian literary motifs. The continuous migration of

Persian-speaking bureaucrats and scholars into the Ottoman Empire consolidated the importance of Persian literature for Ottoman elites. Several of the sultans—most notably Selim I—were accomplished poets in Persian.

The Ottomans also used the Persian language for international correspondence, and under its influence they developed a new literary Turkish language that every bureaucrat was expected to use. Ottoman Turkish was based on Turkish grammar, but its vocabulary was supplemented by Persian words and, like Persian, it used a modified version of the Arabic alphabet. After the conquest of the Arab lands by Selim and Suleyman, Arabic vocabulary became another important influence on Ottoman culture. By the second half of the sixteenth century, a majority of words in Ottoman poetry were Persian and Arabic loanwords.

Calligraphy continued to be a major form of the decorative arts under the Ottomans. It embellished manuscripts, monumental architecture, and objects as varied as bowls and swords. A major Ottoman innovation in calligraphy was the *tuğra*, a highly stylized signature or logo for the sultan. At the beginning of each reign, calligraphers would design the tuğra, which would then appear on all official documents and correspondence and on coins minted during the sultanate. By the time of Suleyman, the tuğra included the sultan's name, his father's name, and the phrase "ever-victorious": Suleyman Shah the son of Selim Shah Khan, ever victorious.

The writing of history flourished under the Ottomans. As early as the middle of the fifteenth century, sultans were commissioning histories of the dynasty, establishing a tradition of valuable historical writing that persisted for centuries. Major contributions were also made in cartography. The work of the admiral Piri Reis (d. 1553) is the most famous today. In 1513, he produced a map of the known world. Among his sources were several European maps showing the discoveries of Portuguese and Spanish mariners, including Columbus. His most important work was a detailed description of the natural features of the Mediterranean that contained 129 separate maps of the sea's basin.

Medicine and astronomy flourished in the sixteenth century. The Suleymaniye mosque complex included a madrasa complex that broke with tradition and emphasized medicine and mathematics over the religious sciences. Numerous hospitals were constructed all over the empire in which physicians developed new surgery techniques and conducted original research in physiology and the treatment of disease.

The fields of mathematics and astronomy boasted some first-class intellects under the Ottomans. The leading astronomer under Mehmet was 'Ali Kuscu (d. 1474). 'Ali had directed a famous observatory in Samarqand and then moved to Tabriz to serve Uzun Hasan, the leader of the White Sheep. Uzun, in an effort to impress Mehmet, sent 'Ali to Istanbul as his ambassador, but 'Ali was so impressed with Istanbul that he entered Mehmet's service. There he wrote a number of important works on mathematics.

Taki al-Din Mehmet (1521–1585) was the greatest Ottoman astronomer of the sixteenth century. He made important corrections in existing astronomical tables and secured the construction of an observatory in Istanbul. The new edifice had hardly been completed, however, when it was razed in 1580 due to agitation on the part of the highest member of the ulama, the Shaykh al-Islam. Like some other members of the ulama, he identified astronomy with astrology, which he regarded

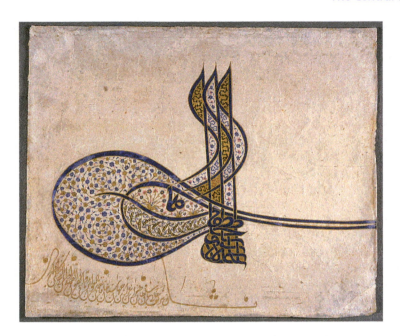

FIGURE 12.2 The *tuğra*, or calligraphic seal, of Suleyman the Magnificent.

© 2017. Digital Image Museum Associates / LACMA / Art Resource NY / Scala, Florence.

as a violation of God's sovereignty. Unfortunately, the publicity surrounding the destruction of the observatory cast astronomy into disrepute, and thereafter little was accomplished in that discipline within the empire.

The razing of the observatory reflected a broader cultural retrenchment that began during the late sixteenth century. During the fourteenth and fifteenth centuries, Ottoman rulers annexed a wide variety of societies and were open to an equally wide variety of cultural influences. Mehmet II exemplified this period, inviting scholars from Central Asia and Italy to his court. During the sixteenth century, by contrast, the campaigns against the Safavid Empire and Shi'ite groups within Ottoman territories led to a suspicion of new ideas. The sultan's status as the guardian of the pilgrimage route to Mecca and the incorporation of ulama into the governmental hierarchy strengthened the case for the government to become the defender of Shari'a-based Sunni values. The eager encounter with other cultures, characteristic of the fifteenth century, was replaced by a suspicion of new ideas in the seventeenth century. Not until the early eighteenth century did the elites begin to sample selected features of a neighboring culture again.

From Dominance to Parity

The reign of Suleyman I (1520–1566) was the culmination of an impressive revival and expansion of Ottoman might after Timur's crushing defeat of Bayezit I in 1402. Suleyman's power and the opulence of his court profoundly impressed contemporary Europeans, who called him Suleyman the Magnificent. No single European state would dare to attack his empire, and even coalitions of powers would think twice before doing so. The potential for further Ottoman expansion struck fear into the hearts of Europeans everywhere. The peoples of central Europe lived in constant fear of "the Terrible Turk," and even the rulers of powerful Spain, at the far end of the Mediterranean, were nervous about a possible invasion. Spain's Muslim minority fervently pleaded with the Ottomans to invade their country. Concentrated on the Mediterranean coast, the Muslims of Spain would have posed a critical security problem for Madrid in the event of such an attack.

During Suleyman's reign, however, the dynamic phase of Ottoman history came to an end. The momentum of the first half of the sixteenth century suddenly stalled during the great sultan's last few years, and his successors could never regain the momentum. One oft-noted feature of the period is that, with Suleyman's death, a period of almost two centuries of outstanding sultans (interrupted only by the civil war that followed Timur's defeat of Bayezit) came to an end, and a period of more than two centuries began during which all but one or two sultans were of inferior ability. A factor in the decline of the quality of leadership was a change in the training of Ottoman princes. Until the last quarter of the sixteenth century, princes of the dynasty were sent to the provinces for administrative experience. After Suleyman's death, they were confined to the palace instead. As a result, they not only failed to gain administrative experience, but they also were remarkably ignorant of any experience outside the highly artificial routines of the harem.

The limited experience of young sultans was not the only difference between the earlier period and the one after Suleyman. The first period was one of military expansion, when the most important trait of a sultan was military leadership, whereas the second period required the creativity to reorganize the empire's institutions and the determination and resourcefulness to implement the required changes in the face of determined opposition. Moreover, sultans faced enormous problems of inertia and inefficiency within the empire's vast bureaucratic structure, which was officially headed by the vizier. The demands on sultans and viziers alike had changed dramatically. The fact remains that the empire's leadership, whether focused on the sultan or generalized at the level of the ruling class, was not equal to the challenges facing the empire from the mid-sixteenth to mid-eighteenth centuries. By the end of the period, the empire had lost its preeminent position in Europe.

Strategic and Military Challenges

The most striking change that catches our attention is the abrupt end to territorial expansion. Suleyman's conquests brought the empire to the limits that its army could go on a campaign and return the same year. The campaigning season was normally from April to October in order to avoid the brutal winter weather and the prohibitive expenses that year-round provisioning would entail. This constraint forced the Ottomans to recognize limits to their sphere of activity. Taking terrain into account, Budapest and Lake Van were each a march of more than 800 miles from Istanbul, and Baghdad was more than 1000 miles. An army of 50,000–70,000 troops, complete with the tens of thousands of war horses and pack camels necessary for such a venture, could normally travel only twelve to fifteen miles per day. An expedition to Budapest or Lake Van would require four months just for the round-trip march, apart from any military action. It is significant that the only important annexations after Suleyman's death (of Cyprus in 1571 and of Crete, 1645–1669) were the result of naval operations, not long overland expeditions.

The end of the conquest phase was a serious matter, because the entire administrative structure had been based on the assumption of territorial expansion. The military organization, civil administration, tax structure, and landholding system were all affected by the new development. Still, if the Ottoman elite had been faced only with reorganizing the system in order to deal with stable borders, they might have had the time and resources to make adjustments without wrenching changes. As often happens in real life, however, they were faced with a constellation of challenges simultaneously.

The cessation of territorial expansion took place during a period when both the empire and Europe faced rapid population growth and inflation. Population estimates are notoriously difficult to make for any region in the world in the sixteenth and seventeenth centuries, but it is clear that the population of Europe and the Ottoman Empire grew rapidly from the early sixteenth century to the early seventeenth century. During this same period, overall prices also increased. The experience of inflation in the Ottoman Empire occurred simultaneously with a similar phenomenon in Europe known as the Price Revolution, which is linked to the impact of a larger silver supply, both from domestic sources and from Spain's colonies in Latin America. Until recently, historians of the Ottoman Empire believed that Europe's increased silver supply and Ottoman inflation were closely linked in terms of cause and effect. The accepted explanation was that, when prices for commodities began skyrocketing in Europe, European merchants sought to purchase cheaper grains, metals, and wool from the Ottomans. The export of those commodities to Europe caused shortages of them in the Ottoman Empire, causing prices to rise there as well. Today, economic historians agree that the export of commodities to Europe did feed inflationary flames, but that even more important for the rising prices were the debasement of Ottoman currency (the reduction of the silver content in coins) and the rising use of coins in the Ottoman economy.

The Ottoman administration was also undergoing disruptions due to its efforts to reorganize the army. In part, the need for military reform stemmed from the fact that inflation was making it impossible for many timar holders to equip their cavalrymen for combat. As a result, when imperial military campaigns were organized, the cavalry units would frequently be understaffed or poorly equipped. In addition, Ottoman military authorities were beginning to recognize that their army was losing its technological advantage in battle. Clashes with Austria in the late sixteenth and early seventeenth centuries demonstrated that European armies were rapidly shifting their resources to musket-carrying infantry, giving them an advantage over the relatively small Janissary corps. Ottoman cavalrymen found that their horses would not charge into the disciplined formations of European infantry and that the repeated discharge of thousands of European muskets produced a devastating effect on horses and armored men alike. The Ottomans found themselves in the unaccustomed position of having fallen behind in both military technology and strategy.

To its credit, the government began to make changes in its military structure. Doing so, however, caused unforeseen problems for the system as a whole. Recruiting enough musketeers to match the Europeans could not be accomplished through the devshirme system, and so Muslim peasants began to be admitted into the army alongside the slave soldiers. Once the breach had been made in the devshirme system, ambitious Muslim families that wanted their sons to have a career as an army officer began asking why the devshirme should exist at all. It was gradually abandoned during the seventeenth century. From then on, military needs were filled by conscription of young men from Muslim families, and civilian offices were filled by competition among leading families. The army began to increase the number of its infantrymen, expanding the number of soldiers in its Janissary corps from some 12,000 in 1570 to some 40,000 by the middle of the seventeenth century. By the beginning of the eighteenth century there were at least 80,000 on the rolls, although they were never mustered together at once.

While the infantry units were growing in size, the cavalry remained a large force. Sipahis, however, became caught between the pressures of rising prices and the government's need to pay cash to its professional foot soldiers. When a timar holder could not afford to fulfill his military duties, the government seized his property and turned it over to a government official or wealthy landowner as a tax farm. As a timar, the property's revenues had been used to equip cavalrymen, but as a tax farm its revenues were forwarded to the central government, minus any extra taxes the holder of the tax farm could collect. The system was obviously ripe for abuse, particularly since a tax farm was theoretically assigned to an individual for a specified period (usually three years, although tax farms later became hereditary). Since the administrator had no incentive to develop the property's value, he was tempted to squeeze out of it what he could in a short time.

These changes in military structure had major repercussions. Three are worth noting here. First, the transition from timars to tax farms came at the expense of public support of the regime. The low taxes that the Ottomans had levied in the fourteenth and fifteenth centuries were a major reason that the Balkan peasantry had acquiesced in Ottoman rule. During the seventeenth century, however, peasants discovered that their standard of living was declining due to the avarice of the tax farmers. Starvation or eviction from the land was the fate of many families who could not meet the demands of rapacious tax farmers. Both Rumelia and Anatolia were affected, but peasant discontent in Rumelia, populated largely by Christians, was of particular importance in the long term. By the end of the eighteenth century, nationalist leaders would be able to take advantage of the discontent for their own purposes.

Second, the abandonment of the timar system reduced the number of loyal cavalrymen in rural areas. As a result, administrative and police authority declined in the countryside. Combined with the increasing resentment expressed by the peasant class, this development had serious consequences for centralized control. Until the last decade of the sixteenth century, rural revolts had been a recurring feature of Anatolian life, but the army had always been able to suppress them. Beginning in the 1590s, such revolts were far more difficult to contain. Between 1596 and 1608, the famous Jelali revolts produced a state of anarchy in large parts of western and central Anatolia. The earliest Jelali leaders were former cavalrymen who had been dispossessed of their livelihoods. The rebels looted villages, drove many peasants from their lands, and threatened to sack even the largest cities. The uprisings forced the government to incur the expense of establishing permanent garrisons of Janissary troops in the troubled regions. Sporadic Jelali revolts continued into the 1640s. By that time, the upheavals had led to disruptions in trade and agricultural production. The empire's population, which had been increasing for a century, began to decline.

A third consequence of the reforms was that the Janissary corps of the seventeenth and eighteenth centuries was quite different from the unit that had been formed of slaves. In the seventeenth century, the Janissaries who were assigned to provincial garrisons to keep the peace gradually melted into the local civilian population and became shopkeepers, butchers, and bakers while still retaining their membership on the military rolls. Many refused to report for service when needed in the wars against Austria, citing their responsibilities in their businesses. Unable to count on its own troops to report for duty, the central government had become stretched to the limit in order to fight external wars and suppress internal rebellions. It was forced to cede responsibility for local governance to landlords and merchants who, as local notables, carried out the functions of the state with or without the sanction of the central government. The Ottoman state was in the process of decentralization and fragmentation of authority precisely at the time when European rulers were centralizing control into their hands. The consequences of these opposing trends would be revealed in the eighteenth century.

Portrait of an Ottoman Gentleman

Turkish ethnicity was not a requirement for admission into the ranks of the Ottoman ruling elite, but a mastery of Ottoman culture and manners was. We can catch a glimpse of the Ottoman ethos in a description of one of the most powerful men in seventeenth-century Ottoman life, Melek Ahmed Pasha (1588–1662). Melek was a member of the Abkhazian ethnic group in the Caucasus. His father was an important military officer whose connections enabled him to find a sponsor who presented Melek to the court when Melek was fourteen. His talents proved to be worthy of the recommendation, and he eventually married Kaya Sultan, the daughter of Sultan Murat IV (ruled 1623–1640). He was governor in several sensitive posts, and he served as the empire's grand vizier in 1650. One of Melek's protégés, Evliya Çelebi, wrote this description of his patron, who had died several years earlier.

At no time did a falsehood issue from his lips. He spoke little and wept much and laughed sparingly. In his councils he never allowed idle talk and malicious gossip. But if a tasteful witticism was uttered in his presence, he would smile so broadly that you could see his teeth.

He was so scrupulous in his dress that he only wore garments sanctioned by religious law—various cotton stuffs, and those silken weaves and other splendid stuffs not forbidden by the Shari'a. And he was so clean and neat and elegant and refined, that he was famous among the viziers—his skirts were cleaner than the collars of his peers.

Indeed, Melek Pasha was clean-skirted (*i.e.*, chaste) in every respect, and was pure in every respect. He was very upright and pious, learned in religious sciences and active in

(Continued)

carrying out religious prescriptions; he was virtuous and abstinent; a perfect *gazi* and brave vizier, the likes of Asaf son of Barakhya (the vizier of Solomon). . . . He was very skilled in archery, which is a Sunna of the Prophet, and in such sports as javelin throwing, swordplay, mace, and spear. And among his peers only Ipşir Pasha and Seydi Ahmet Pasha could rival him in horsemanship and cavalry exercises. Being a strong and courageous champion, he was also unexcelled in wrestling, familiar with seventy branches of that science: very few champions could bring his back to the ground. But sometimes he would have nice wrestling matches with his wife Kaya Sultan, for the propagation of the species. In the end he would overcome Kaya Sultan and bring her down. He engaged in this sort of "greatest jihad" forty-eight times a year—he did not indulge overmuch in sexual intercourse.

He read a good many books on the science of grammar; and was without equal in the science of canon law, particularly the laws of inheritance. He had by heart over 800 problems of the Shari'a and over 1000 prophetic Hadiths. Because he was inclined to the dervish path, he had on the tip of his tongue several thousand verses of the noble *Mesnevi* of Mevlana (Rumi) and the *Manevi* of Ibrahim Gülşeni, plus Persian and Turkish odes and mystical ghazels that he could recite at appropriate occasions.

In the science of calligraphy he . . . had been authorized by Sultan Murat IV to draw the illustrious *tuğra*, and under his tutelage he learned to draw it in a manner that rivaled the pens of Bihzad and Mani. Koca Nişancı Ankebut Ahmed Pasha, Nasuh-paşa-zade, Ömer Beg, and our head of chancellery Ginagı Efendi—all stood agape at Melek's *tuğra*.

Never did he accept bribes or allow others to accept them, nor did he get posts by means of bribery. Rather, he accepted dismissal from office. Of course, he did use to send some of the specialities of the regions he was governing, or some thoroughbred horses, as gifts to the imperial stirrup [the sultan] and to the viziers and deputies.

SOURCE: Reprinted by permission from *The Intimate Life of an Ottoman Statesman: Melek Ahmed Pasha (1588–1622): As Portrayed in Evliya Celebi's Book of Travels*, pp. 277–281, translated by Robert Dankoff, the State University of New York Press ©1991, State University of New York. All rights reserved.

Religious Unrest

The decline of central power was accompanied by the weakening of the personal authority of the sultan himself. The military and administrative legitimacy of the sultans through the reign of Suleyman had been unquestioned, but in the seventeenth century sultans were forced to engage in continual plots and schemes in order to thwart conspiracies by powerful factions that had agendas of their own, including the removal of a sultan. One reason for the more vulnerable position of the sultans was the previously noted decline in the quality of leadership among the sultans. Another factor was the dismantling of the devshirme system. Important posts that had formerly been filled by loyal products of the devshirme slaves went to members of powerful Ottoman families instead. These families sought to improve their position both at court and in the provinces by creating coalitions to put pressure on the sultan and vizier to achieve a desired goal. Coalitions were particularly effective when they included Janissaries: In the seventeenth century, palace coalitions involving the Janissaries deposed and even killed sultans. As a result, sultans found it expedient to ally themselves with whatever interest groups could help them weather political storms. During the 1630s, a religious reform movement offered the young Murat IV (1623–1640) a welcome ally.

Murat inherited the throne at the age of twelve, after the deposition of the mentally ill Mustafa (1618), the deposition and murder of Osman II (1622), and a second deposition of Mustafa (1623). Murat's mother served as his regent during the 1620s, when wars with the Safavids were a constant drain on the treasury. The nearly constant warfare, inflation, and violence in the countryside took their toll on the psyche of much of the population. In 1632, Janissaries forced Murat to dismiss some of his highest officials and to execute another. The following year, a fire burned one-fifth of Istanbul. Social unrest was common. It was then that the religious reformers seized the opportunity to exert influence with the sultan.

The reformers were from among the lower-ranking members of the ulama. They were led by Kadizade ("Son of a Qadi") Mehmet Efendi, an influential mosque preacher. Because of his role, the movement came to be known as the Kadizadeli movement. Mehmet Efendi and his followers were angered by a massive rise in the popularity of Sufism. Their hostility toward Sufism took two tracks. One was the perennial criticism that literal-minded ulama levelled against any practice that could not be justified by the Qur'an or the Sunna of the Prophet. The reformers condemned the use of rhythmic movements and music in Sufi rituals, and they criticized the popular practice of visiting tombs of Sufi saints in order to obtain a blessing (*baraka*). The increased popularity of Sufism may well have been due to the need that people felt for a spiritual refuge in times of trouble, but to the Kadizadelis, Sufi tariqas themselves were a major cause of the troubles that the empire was suffering: God was no doubt punishing the empire for the sins of the Sufis. The second element of the Sufi movement that caused the Kadizadelis to be alarmed was that several popular Sufi leaders were taking over the pulpits of some of the major mosques. In the elaborate bureaucracy of the Ottoman Empire, men from the upper social classes dominated the higher echelons of the ranks of the ulama, much as the nobility dominated the ranks of the higher clergy in contemporary Christian Western Europe. The lower ulama knew that they would never be considered for the high religious offices in the government, and so they jealously guarded their access to the pulpits of the large congregational mosques. The competition of the Sufi leaders for these positions compounded a genuine religious difference with a social threat.

The Kadizadelis also noted that many Sufis drank coffee and smoked tobacco, activities that took place in their lodges as well as in newfangled coffeehouses. Coffee had been introduced to Istanbul from Yemen by 1555, and coffeehouses soon followed. Tobacco came to the capital city from the Americas in 1601 (even before it was cultivated at Jamestown, in Virginia). By portraying coffee and tobacco in a negative light, the reformers cast Sufis into disrepute: Coffee and tobacco were reprehensible products on the grounds that they were mind-altering drugs; the practice of smoking tobacco could easily be blamed for the 1633 Istanbul fire; and the coffeehouses were suspected of encouraging loitering, gossip, and illicit behavior.

For most of the period between 1633 and 1683, the Kadizadeli movement exercised influence on domestic policy. Mehmet Efendi convinced Murat IV that Sufi deviations had led to a weakened society, leaving the empire vulnerable to its foreign enemies, and that coffeehouses were centers of sedition where plots were hatched to overthrow the government. In 1633, Murat IV closed the coffeehouses of Istanbul and made smoking a capital offense. During the remainder of the decade, thousands of Ottoman subjects were dismembered or impaled for the crime of smoking tobacco. After Murat died in 1640, the Kadizadelis continued to win favor at the palace. They razed a Sufi lodge in 1651 and obtained a fatwa to ban music and dancing in Sufi ceremonies. When they tried to kill a Sufi leader in 1656, however, a new vizier banned their leaders.

Sufis had a respite from the reformers for only five years. In 1661, one of the recurring waves of the plague was worse than usual, killing tens of thousands of people in Istanbul. In a desperate search for remedies, yet another vizier allowed the Kadizadelis to return to the palace. Sufis had to exercise caution for the next two decades until the Kadizadelis began to overreach again. They demanded that non-Muslims be forced to wear distinguishing clothing, be prohibited from producing and selling wine, and be forbidden to live in Istanbul. The sultan refused all of these demands, and patience with the group began to wane. In 1683, the Kadizadeli leader's prayers and exhortations at the siege of Vienna not only failed to win a victory for Ottoman troops but were followed by a catastrophic loss. He was banished, and the Kadizadeli movement withered away.

The Tide Turns

Despite the turmoil of the seventeenth century, it was not clear for some time that the empire had actually been weakened compared to its rivals. During the first half of the seventeenth century, the Ottomans signed a treaty with their archenemy, the Safavid regime of Iran, and light skirmishes with Austria in western Hungary did not reveal major problems in the military's condition. It was only during the last quarter of the century that it became clear that the empire was no longer the dominant power that it once had been. Economic slumps and social unrest prompted the Ottoman vizier to attack Vienna in 1683 as a way of shaking the empire out of its malaise. The siege of the city was broken, however, by a coalition of European armies that came to Vienna's rescue, and the Ottoman army was routed. The Austrians quickly seized Hungary from Istanbul's control and joined with Venice, Poland, and Russia in an alliance against the Ottomans. The empire had to fight in the Aegean Sea, Central Europe, and the northern coast of the Black Sea, slowly exhausting its resources. In 1699, in the Treaty of Karlowitz, the Ottomans formally recognized the loss of Hungary and Transylvania to Austria. They ceded southern Greece, islands in the Aegean, and the eastern coast of the Adriatic Sea to Venice. Russia gained a foothold on the Black Sea. The Ottomans had lost their aura of invincibility, but everyone at the time realized that it had required a coalition of European powers fighting for sixteen years to force a treaty from them. The empire remained a dangerous foe throughout the first half of the eighteenth century. It defeated Russia's Peter the Great in 1711, and although it lost to the Austrians in 1718, it defeated them in 1739.

Europe was obviously becoming more dynamic, and features of its culture began to intrigue many leading Ottomans. The most conspicuous borrowings from Europe during the 1720s and 1730s took place among the social elite, who became fascinated with European furniture styles, clothing fashions, and gardens. A reforming vizier acquired a printing press and announced sweeping military reforms patterned after European models. The proposed reforms, however, came to nothing at the time. The ulama forced the removal of the printing press, and the Janissaries, realizing that the reorganization, new weapons, and rigorous training programs would undermine their privileged position, used violence to force cancellation of the military reforms.[3]

The victory over Austria in 1739 seems to have calmed the unease among the Ottoman ruling class that the empire had lost its competitive ability. Reform movements that had been producing a momentum for change during the previous half-century were allowed to wither and die at the very time that European nations were developing new technologies and organizational techniques that would create a severe imbalance of power between them and the Ottomans. Although Western and Eastern Europe developed in quite different ways during the eighteenth century, both regions pulled ahead of the Ottomans in military and economic power by the mid-eighteenth century. The stage was set for a series of catastrophic setbacks for the Ottoman Empire beginning in the second half of the century.

The Arabian Peninsula

Islam appeared first in Mecca, in the Arabian Peninsula. The Prophet later established the seat of his Islamic state at Medina, some 200 miles to the north (see Map 12.2). After the Prophet's death in 632, Medina served as the de facto capital of the Muslim world until 661, when the Umayyad dynasty began its rule at Damascus. Thereafter, despite the peninsula's location as the geographic center of the Dar al-Islam, large areas of its vast expanse were at the margins of economic and cultural developments that were taking place within Muslim society. Some of the peninsula's regions were so remote and so rarely visited that they became refuges for Muslims who rejected the decisions taken by the far larger Sunni and Twelver Shi'ite movements. On the other hand, a few cities were the object of heavy international traffic, either for religious or commercial reasons.

The Holy Cities

Mecca and Medina were obvious exceptions to generalizations about the remoteness of the peninsula. Both cities were located in the Hijaz, the plateau that slopes eastward from the northern half of the peninsula's Red Sea coastline. Mecca was the goal of the hajj, or pilgrimage, that each Muslim is expected to perform at least once if possible. Travel was so slow and dangerous until the twentieth century that only a tiny minority of Muslims were actually able to perform the hajj. Nevertheless, tens of thousands of pilgrims arrived in Mecca each year, straining facilities and resources to the limit. Medina, as the seat of the Prophet's government and his burial site, was usually included on the itinerary of pilgrims who performed the pilgrimage.

The hajj is not merely a ritual obligation. Especially for the faithful who live a long distance away, performing the pilgrimage is a deeply emotional, and occasionally life-changing, experience. The effect is felt immediately upon arriving at the boundaries of the sacred precinct around Mecca, when the pilgrim performs ritual ablutions and exchanges his or her clothing for the white simple cloth required by

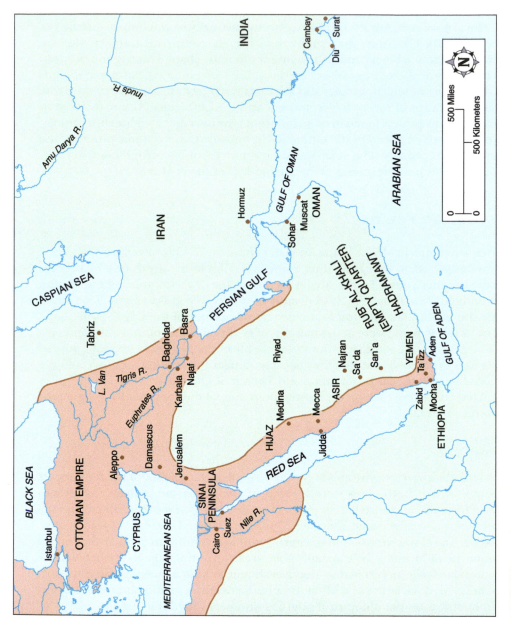

MAP 12.2 The Arabian Peninsula in the Mid-Sixteenth Century.

the rituals. Having entered a state of sanctification, the pilgrim's spiritual antennae become much more sensitive than ever before. To touch the Ka'ba—previously only the imagined object of the direction of one's prayers—during the circumambulation of that venerable structure, to walk where the Prophet himself walked, and to stand where the Prophet preached his last sermon are simultaneously humbling and joyous experiences. The faithful are intensely aware that they are not only at the center of the Muslim world, but also at the very birthplace of the faith. It is unusual not to feel that one has encountered the holy in that place or to leave without recommitting oneself to God's will.

Mecca and Medina developed a reputation for being centers of scholarly activities. Because of the sanctity of the cities, many scholars from all over the Muslim world chose to live in one or the other city for extended periods. Like Ibn Battuta, many pilgrims spent periods of several months to many years in the area in order to study with scholars who had developed international reputations for their legal or theological expertise. As these pilgrims returned home, the teachings of the scholars radiated out to many different parts of the Muslim world.

Mecca and Medina were centers for the diffusion of new products as well as ideas. Merchants constituted a significant percentage of pilgrims. The demands of their business might well bring them onto trade routes flanking the peninsula, and thus they were better placed to make the hajj than most other Muslims were. They were also more likely than other Muslims to be able to afford the trip. Many of them brought something to sell in order to help finance their journey. As a result, international transactions of many kinds were carried out in the two cities. Techniques, inventions, information, and crops were disseminated from them to a multitude of other places.

Yemen and Oman

Mecca and Medina prospered only because of their religious status. Other than these holy sites, the interior of the peninsula contained no attractions for outside visitors. By contrast, international trade was active on the seas that bordered three sides of the peninsula. Several ports along the coasts were highly attractive to Indian Ocean merchants. Whereas most of the peninsula remained isolated from important cultural and economic developments, two regions located on corners of the peninsula—Yemen and Oman—played significant historical roles during our period.

Yemen

Yemen had been wealthy in pre-Islamic times, but the waning international demand for its incense left it to wither economically by the seventh century. Its precipitous mountain ranges and remote valleys provided refuges for two religious minorities that flourished for centuries. During the late ninth century, the Zaydi and Isma'ili movements became established in Yemen and have maintained a presence there ever since. The Zaydis became associated with the northern city of Sa'da, whereas the Isma'ilis found their strongest support in the central region between San'a and Ta'izz.

In 1174, Salah al-Din (Saladin), the ruler of Egypt, sent an army to conquer Yemen. The Ayyubid dynasty that he founded subsequently acquired all but the most

FIGURE 12.3 The home of a wealthy seventeenth-century merchant in Mocha, Yemen.

inaccessible Zaydi regions of northern Yemen, but it left no lasting imprint in the country. The Ayyubids were distracted from Yemen by the third, fifth, and sixth Crusades as well as by family quarrels. One of their governors in Yemen, 'Umar ibn al-Rasul, took advantage of Cairo's preoccupation with other matters. He became independent in 1228, inaugurating the two most flourishing centuries in Yemeni history during the Islamic period.

The Rasulid capital was Ta'izz, but the dynasty placed a premium on developing the Red Sea coast as well as the port of Aden, on the southwestern tip of the peninsula. The Red Sea had long had a reputation as a dangerous region to sail due to its many coral reefs and pirate dens. As a result, sailors on vessels that plied the Indian Ocean were reluctant to enter the sea. That reluctance enabled Aden to become a major port of call. Located at the entrance to the Red Sea, its distinguishing feature was a gray and black volcanic crater ringed by red, jagged cliffs, which created one of the finest harbors in the world. Numerous ships docked there every year. Those carrying goods from the Indian Ocean basin unloaded their cargoes and replaced them with goods from Egypt. Other ships then took the goods that had been off-loaded at Aden and embarked on the risky voyage to Egypt.

Aden developed a reputation for handling the greatest volume of cargo and most lucrative trade in the world. It was the indispensable axis in the maritime trade of the western half of the Indian Ocean. The port linked Suez, Calicut, Cambay, and Hormuz with Kilwa and Mogadishu, as well as with Jidda, the city where pilgrims to Mecca disembarked. Aden offered travelers in the Indian Ocean banking services, transportation in every direction, and a wide variety of goods for sale. North of Aden, in a fertile and well-watered section of the Red Sea coast, the city of Zabid attracted a considerable number of wealthy merchants and became an international center of scholarship, especially in the field of Shafi'i law. It had so many schools that it came to be known as "the city of universities."

Rasulid power began slipping away during the first half of the fifteenth century, and Yemen became fragmented once again. The primary beneficiaries of the changes were the Zaydis, who reasserted their power in the northern and central regions. The Rasulids were finally overthrown in 1454. Little more than four decades later, the Portuguese entered the Indian Ocean, and a new era of struggle for Yemen began. Vasco da Gama sailed to India in 1498, and the Portuguese quickly seized control of numerous ports all along the ocean's rim.

Afonso de Albuquerque, who soon became governor of Portuguese possessions in India, sought to destroy Muslim commerce in the Indian Ocean. He placed a premium on seizing Aden. Albuquerque led an attack on the city in 1513 but failed to capture it. He then sailed into the Red Sea, hoping to make contact with Prester John, the king who, in the European imagination, would join forces with Europe to defeat Islam. Each generation had identified Prester John with a different region and monarch, much as each generation identified the Anti-Christ with a different individual or institution. By the early sixteenth century, it was clear that the Great Khan of the Mongols was not Prester John, but surely the King of Ethiopia was. Joining forces with him had been a major objective of Prince Henry the Navigator, who organized the series of Portuguese explorations along the western coast of Africa early in the fifteenth century that laid the foundation for da Gama's voyage.

Albuquerque's discovery that the Ethiopian ruler was a mere chieftain and that his reputedly fabulous kingdom was actually a primitive and unstable society was disillusioning and disappointing. The Portuguese and Ethiopians did collaborate several times against Muslim forces in the Red Sea region, but their cultural differences resulted in a bitter split in 1634. The shattering of the Prester John myth brought an end to one of the most durable and motivating of medieval European collective fantasies. It also removed the major remaining reason that Europeans viewed the East with awe and respect. Henceforth, Europeans ventured into the Indian Ocean with the expectation that they could compete with anyone on at least an equal footing.

Upon annexing Syria, Egypt, and the Holy Cities in 1517, the Ottomans became a Red Sea power. They began to monitor the Yemeni coast to ensure that the Portuguese did not threaten it again. In 1538, when Suleyman captured the Iraqi city of Basra from the Safavids, he discovered that the Portuguese, having taken Hormuz in 1515, threatened every ship that entered or left the Persian Gulf. The Portuguese threat to the shipping of both the Red Sea and the Gulf placed the Ottomans in a vulnerable position. Suleyman ordered a fleet to be organized in the Red Sea. The ships set out from Suez and conquered the Red Sea coast of Yemen en route to Aden. At Aden, the sailors and soldiers launched a surprise attack against the local dynasty that controlled it. They succeeded where the Portuguese had failed, and they secured Aden for their empire. Then the fleet sailed for Gujarat with the intention of capturing the Portuguese base at Diu. The fortress there, however, was impregnable, and the siege failed. The Ottomans and Portuguese engaged in several more conflicts in the Arabian Sea, but neither was able to evict the other from the region.

During the decades that the Ottomans were increasingly focused on Yemen as a security issue, a beverage from the region rapidly became an international sensation. Coffee, which grew on the well-watered mountain slopes of Yemen and Ethiopia, had been used since the mid-fifteenth century by Yemeni Sufis to help them stay awake during their evening devotions. The drink spread to Egypt and Mecca by the beginning of the sixteenth century, and Ottoman chronicles document that it was in Istanbul at least by 1555. Its use in the Holy Cities and in the larger urban centers of the Ottoman Empire provoked a fierce debate that lasted more than a century. Opposition to the drink was generated in part by its status as a stimulant: Some jurists saw an analogy with wine, the use of which is prohibited in Islam.

Perhaps even more problematic, however, was that the beverage came to be enjoyed as a social drink. Soon, coffeehouses sprang up. The coffeehouse was a brand new secular institution, and its potential for mischief was the feature that was uppermost in the minds of both moralists and government officials. Restaurants had not yet come into being, and night life to that time had been limited to the tavern, gambling house, or Sufi lodge. The convivial conversations, gossiping, board games, and live entertainment of coffeehouses led many pious observers to conclude that the coffeehouse was the moral equivalent of the clearly disreputable tavern and gambling den. Moreover, it became clear that the coffeehouse could provide a setting for plots against the government. This was the pretext that Murat IV used when he closed the coffeehouses of Istanbul. They remained closed in the capital city for more than forty years, to the anguish of many.

The use of coffee quickly spread to Europe. European demand for the product revived the Yemeni economy. Because the city of Mocha (Mukha) became the exclusive point of export for coffee, its name became forever associated with the beverage. Huge quantities of coffee were shipped to the warehouses of Cairo for distribution all over the Mediterranean and to Northern Europe. Mocha became a fashionable and cosmopolitan city. English, French, Dutch, and Hindu merchants competed with Yemenis in building fine homes that graced the otherwise bleak landscape around the city.

The Ottomans captured San'a in 1547, but they never had a secure hold on Yemen outside the major cities. The Zaydis fiercely resisted Ottoman attempts to expand. They even captured and ruled San'a and Aden temporarily. Because of them, Yemen developed a reputation as a graveyard for Ottoman soldiers. In 1598 a new, charismatic Zaydi Imam began a concerted effort to evict the Ottomans, and by 1631 the empire retained only a small area on the coast around Zabid. Istanbul soon ordered the evacuation of all Ottoman soldiers. For the next three centuries, Zaydi Imams were the effective power in the highlands of Yemen.

Zabid and Mocha, both on the coastal plain, continued to be important cities into the eighteenth century. Zabid played an important role in the diffusion of religious ideas throughout the Muslim world. Scholars from as far away as Southeast

Asia and western China came to Zabid to study, and they took home with them ideas that transformed their societies. Mocha's coffee trade grew until it peaked in the period 1720–1740. By then, the Dutch realized that their control over several volcanic islands in Southeast Asia provided them with an ideal setting for growing duty-free coffee. Java soon replaced Yemen as the world's primary source of coffee and joined Mocha as a moniker for the beverage itself. After the decline of Mocha and Zabid in the late eighteenth century, the interior of Yemen became one of the most isolated places on earth, having almost no contact with the outside world until the second half of the twentieth century.

In stark contrast to the growing isolationism of the interior of Yemen, the southern rim of the Arabian Peninsula maintained active contact with ports all around the Indian Ocean basin. Hadramawt, the eastern extension of modern Yemen, was engaged in international commerce from at least as early as 1000 B.C.E., when it was a major source of frankincense. During the period from the fifteenth through the eighteenth centuries, Hadramawti families migrated to East Africa, South Asia, and Southeast Asia in search of commercial opportunities. In each of the regions, individual Hadramawtis played important roles in commercial, political, or religious affairs.

Oman

International commerce thrived in the Persian Gulf. The history of the Gulf has been shaped by the fact that the Arabian coast is not as well suited to receive shipping as the Iranian coast. The water off the Arabian coast is shallow and littered with shoals and reefs. Fresh water is in short supply, and there are no natural harbors. For most of recorded history, the population of the interior was sparse and poor. Other than the pearls that local divers retrieved at great risk to their lives, the coast did not offer foreign merchants products they could not find more easily elsewhere. The Iranian coast, by contrast, had deep water, several natural harbors, slightly better access to fresh water, and advanced societies in the interior that desired to engage in long-distance trade. A succession of wealthy trading cities appeared on the coast—or on islands just off the coast—in the Strait of Hormuz. By 1300 the dominant city was Hormuz, located on a barren, salt-encrusted island that had to have water brought from the mainland. Despite its lunar landscape, the city was wealthy and cosmopolitan, attracting merchants from all around the Indian Ocean basin.

During the thirteenth and fourteenth centuries, the rulers of Hormuz were Arabs from Oman. Oman, located just outside the Gulf, was oriented toward the Indian Ocean. It has been described as an island, for it is surrounded on three sides by the ocean and on the northwest by the Rub' al-Khali, or Empty Quarter. The Empty Quarter is the most formidable of all the deserts in Arabia. Its gigantic sand dunes and waterless wastes served for centuries as a defense shield for Oman against invasion from the interior. On the Omani coast, the port of Sohar was the most important until the fifteenth century, when Muscat began to eclipse it. Both were well situated to take advantage of the maritime traffic that plied the coastal waters between Hormuz and Aden.

Because Oman was isolated from the rest of the peninsula except by sea, it was attractive to the Ibadis, who arrived in the middle of the eighth century. The Ibadis were the result of a development within the Kharijite group, which gained a reputation in the first Islamic century for regarding all Muslims who did not agree with them as infidels who deserved to be killed. Because of their intolerance and aggressiveness, the Kharijites were feared and hated by the majority of Muslims. The Ibadis formed a community of Kharijites in Basra, but they rejected the violence of the larger group. They began to wrestle with the issue of how to live peacefully among a majority whom one regarded to be impious. They tended to retreat to remote areas of North Africa, Khorasan, and Oman, where they could escape persecution as well as spiritual contamination by contact with sinners. In Oman, they established themselves in the interior of the country, away from the port cities. Individual Ibadis lived on the coast, but the ports were typically controlled by outsiders. The Ibadis became famous for their horse breeding. They supplied huge numbers of horses to India, especially to Delhi, after the thirteenth century. Hindu merchants set up holding pens in Muscat to ship the animals to India.

Oman's strategic location caught the attention of Albuquerque, who was determined that Portugal would control its coast. In 1507, he seized the important Omani port cities, and within a few years the Portuguese constructed the two picturesque forts that still stand high above Muscat's harbor. With the seizure of Hormuz in 1515, the Portuguese seemed to be in total control of the Gulf. The Ottomans, who captured Basra from the Safavids in 1538, made periodic attempts to evict the Portuguese, but their long imperial frontiers made too many demands on them to focus on their Iberian rivals. They sacked Portuguese-held Muscat twice, in 1551 and 1581, but did not secure it.

In 1624, Ibadi elders elected a new Imam who considered it his mission to evict the Portuguese from Oman. The Omanis captured Sohar in 1643 and Muscat in 1650, establishing Ibadi power on the coast for the first time. For the next several decades the Omanis were at war with the Portuguese at sea. They attacked the Portuguese on the Malabar Coast of India, on the Iranian coast, and in East Africa. In several East African ports, they replaced the Portuguese as colonial powers.

This first attempt to create an Omani empire was not a success. Portuguese privateers and naval vessels harassed Omani shipping, and Muscat was not able to establish a profitable commercial network among its various holdings in Oman and East Africa. The Omanis were also unable to establish a respectable reputation among international merchants. They were unable to break the habit—which they had developed during the war against the Portuguese—of attacking and seizing other nations' merchant ships. Between 1680 and 1730, Oman developed an international reputation as a den of pirates.

In 1719, a dispute over succession to the Ibadi leadership resulted in the outbreak of vicious fighting among the tribes. Over the next thirty years, tens of thousands of Omanis died in a civil war. The chaos allowed the ruler of Iran to seize much of the Omani coast, including Muscat and Sohar. Ahmad ibn Sa'id became famous for his resistance against the Iranians and claimed the credit for their final expulsion in 1748. In the following year, Ahmad ibn Sa'id was elected ruler, and he began to consolidate power. He laid the foundations for a regional empire that flourished in the nineteenth century. His dynasty, the Al bu Sa'id, has continued to rule Oman to the present.

FIGURE 12.4 The two seventeenth-century Portuguese forts, al-Jalali and al-Mirani, still stand guard over the port at Muscat, Oman.

Hemis / Alamy Stock Photo.

The Eurasian Steppes

Unlike the Ottomans, the Golden Horde was not able to recover from Timur's onslaught. During the 1390s, Timur systematically destroyed the trading cities of the steppe from the Black Sea to the Aral Sea. New Saray and Astrakhan were among those that he demolished. Long-distance trade was diverted permanently northward into Russia and southward into Iran. Moreover, the merchant and artisanal classes were shattered, with catastrophic results for cultural life and technology. Literature, art, and architecture never recovered, and the Horde lost its ability to manufacture firearms, just as its enemies were equipping themselves with them. In 1408 Moscow refused to pay tribute, and the Horde was unable to force it to do so. A new era had begun in Russia.

The Horde remained a dangerous force in Russia for several decades due to the quick-strike ability of its horse-mounted warriors, but it was never able to recover the territories that it had lost. In the fourteenth century, the Horde had ruled over the Qipchaq steppe as well as Ukraine. It also exacted tribute from numerous Russian cities outside its area of direct control. By the fifteenth century, only the steppe remained, and even it was threatened from the east by a cluster of Mongol–Turkic clans from Siberia. These were the Uzbeks, who migrated southward to the valley of the Syr Darya River during the first decades of the fifteenth century.

The loss of tribute from the forested areas and the constriction of the steppe led to clashes among leading families regarding the distribution of resources. The Horde

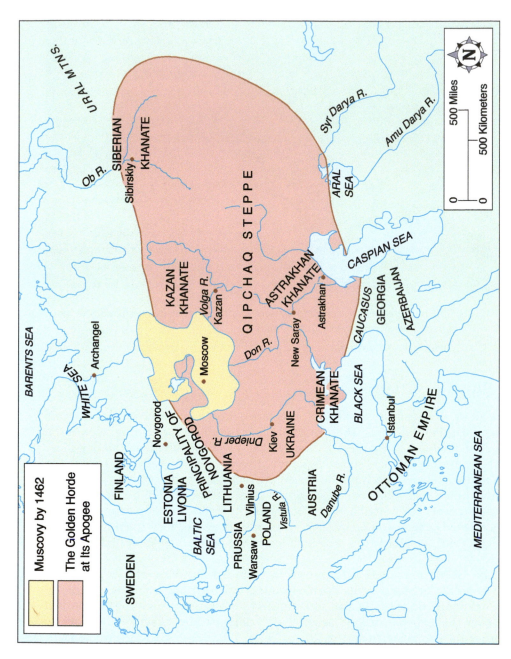

MAP 12.3 The Golden Horde and Its Successors.

Muscovy by 1462

The Golden Horde
at Its Apogee

BARENTS SEA

URAL MTNS.

SIBERIAN
KHANATE

Ob R.

Sibirskiy

Syr Darya R.

Amu Darya R.

QIPCHAQ STEPPE

ARAL
SEA

CASPIAN SEA

WHITE SEA

Archangel

KAZAN
KHANATE

Volga R.

Kazan

ASTRAKHAN
KHANATE

Astrakhan

GEORGIA

AZERBAIJAN

Moscow

Don R.

New Saray

CAUCASUS

PRINCIPALITY OF
NOVGOROD

Novgorod

FINLAND

Dnieper R.

CRIMEAN
KHANATE

BLACK SEA

Istanbul

ESTONIA

LIVONIA

Kiev

UKRAINE

OTTOMAN EMPIRE

LITHUANIA

Vilnius

BALTIC
SEA

AUSTRIA

Danube R.

MEDITERRANEAN SEA

SWEDEN

PRUSSIA

Warsaw

POLAND

Vistula R.

N

0   500 Miles

0   500 Kilometers

rapidly fragmented. During the 1430s and 1440s, it broke into four major independent khanates: the nomadic khanate of Sibir, which later gave its name to Siberia; the city-based khanates of Kazan and Astrakhan on the Volga; and the khanate of Crimea. The Horde itself was relegated to a nomadic existence west of the Volga. It gradually withered in importance until the Crimean khanate destroyed it in 1502. As the final destruction of the Horde suggests, the new khanates did not cooperate with each other. The Crimean khans, when they were not raiding Muscovy, consistently supported the Orthodox Muscovites against Muslim Astrakhan, and Astrakhan supported the Catholic Lithuanians against the Muscovites and the Crimeans.

The breakup of the Golden Horde coincided with the rise of Muscovy. A tribute-paying province of the Horde since the time of Batu, Muscovy had prospered during the thirteenth and fourteenth centuries. It took advantage of the warm relations between the Horde and the Byzantines to establish close commercial ties with Constantinople, and its capital of Moscow became the primary seat of the Orthodox Church in Russia. Its economy benefitted from Timur's destruction of the Horde's cities, for it lost rivals and gained the commerce that they had handled.

With the fragmentation of the Horde in the first half of the fifteenth century, Muscovy no longer had to worry about domination by Tatars. Beginning with the reign of Ivan IV, "The Terrible" (1547–1584), Muscovy went on the offensive against them. It conquered and annexed Kazan and Astrakhan in 1552 and 1556, respectively. Ivan attacked Sibir in 1582, and the khanate fell to Muscovy by 1600. Long-held grievances against the Tatars resulted in a Muscovite policy of expulsion of Tatars from cities, distribution of their land among Russian nobles and the Russian church, and colonization of the annexed regions by Russian peasants. Muscovite rulers destroyed mosques and closed Qur'an schools. For the next 200 years, many of the rural rebellions in Russia contained elements of Muslim desperation and anger against Muscovite policies. For the Russian elite, however, the instability was a small price to pay for removing the obstacles that had lain between them and expansion to the Pacific.

Of the four successor khanates, the one in the Crimea survived the longest. Founded about 1440, its history extended across more than three centuries. Like all the other khanates that broke away from the Horde, it retained little trace of its Mongol heritage except for the ruler's claim of descent from Chinggis Khan. Otherwise, it was a Qipchaq Turkic, or Tatar, society. Just over a decade after its founding, the Ottoman Sultan Mehmet II captured Constantinople and his empire became a Black Sea power. In the 1470s, Mehmet captured the Crimean coast but allowed the khans to rule autonomously as vassals. The Ottoman sultan gained the right to confirm the choice of the Crimean khan and to use Crimean troops in his military campaigns, and the Crimeans enjoyed the protection and commercial advantages of the powerful Ottoman Empire. For the next 200 years, tens of thousands of Crimean Tatars served as scouts, couriers, and raiders in Ottoman armies as far away as Hungary and Iran.

The khanate thrived on a mixture of agriculture and slave trading. Unlike the Golden Horde in its heyday, which worked out a tribute system with the cities of the Eastern European steppes, the Crimean Tatars viewed such cities as fields where slaves could be harvested. Crimean slave raids penetrated as far as Vilnius and Moscow. One historian has estimated that the Crimeans sent two million inhabitants of Poland, Lithuania, and Muscovy to the Ottoman slave markets between 1500 and 1700.[4] As a result, the Qipchaq steppe, never densely populated, became a no man's land where few dared to live. By the early sixteenth century, the only communities to be found there were self-governing villages along the Dnieper and Don rivers inhabited by Cossacks. *Cossack* is a Slavic derivation of the Turkic *kazakh*, which means "adventurer" or "free person." The term was originally applied to semi-independent groups of Tatars on these rivers, but by the end of the fifteenth century it was also applied to Slavic peasants who fled from serfdom in Poland, Lithuania, and Muscovy. The latter group eventually became exclusively identified with the term.

Cossacks fished and hunted, engaged in limited agriculture, and raided neighboring territories. They owed allegiance to no government and proved to be a threat to Tatars, Poland, and Muscovy alike. During the second half of the sixteenth century, several of the Cossack groups worked out arrangements with Poland and Muscovy to protect their frontiers from the Tatars. The decisive event that led to the cooperative relationships seems to have been a devastating Tatar raid on Moscow in 1570. After looting the city, the Tatars set it on fire. Thereafter, both Muscovy and the Polish nobility sought arrangements with the Cossacks, who began a systematic policy of raiding Tatar communities and intercepting Tatar raiding parties on their return from the north.

Because of its development of agriculture and its close contacts with the Ottoman Empire, Crimea became the most sedentary and Islamic of the Tatar khanates. Some of the Crimean khans became famous as poets and patrons of the arts. Islam permeated the majority culture: Property that had been consecrated to religious or charitable purposes (*waqfs*) amounted to one-fourth of all the land in the khanate. By 1783, Crimea had 1500 mosques and a large number of religious scholars. From its earliest history, the khanate had a diverse population of Genoese, Iranians, Greeks, and Armenians in addition to its majority Turkic population. As in the Ottoman Empire, non-Muslims operated most trading, shipping, and banking enterprises.

During the seventeenth century, the balance of power shifted decisively away from the Tatars and toward the Russians. Under Peter the Great (1689–1725), Muscovy became known as Russia, and it began a program of military modernization. Russia resumed the expansionist program that had made Muscovy so dynamic in the fifteenth and sixteenth centuries. It soon cowed Sweden, Lithuania, and Poland, and it was determined to extinguish the Muslim threat to the south and gain access to the Black Sea. The Russians also began to adopt agricultural techniques developed in northwestern Europe during the Middle Ages. The moldboard plow, larger plow teams, and new property concepts made cultivation of the steppe more practicable and investment in the region more attractive. The Cossack "screen" that had slowed the Tatar raids was now supplemented by the development of a Russian standing army, and the line of Russian settlement expanded inexorably southward.

The defeat of the Ottomans by the European alliance at the end of the seventeenth century and the resulting Treaty of Karlowitz were major blows to the Tatars. The treaty obligated the Ottomans to pledge that they and the Tatars would cease their raiding into Russia. The Tatars ignored the provision and continued their raids, but without Ottoman support they were not powerful enough to escape retribution for the raids. As a result, their economy experienced a serious decline. Russia's expanding control of the steppe gradually exhausted the Khanate of Crimea, and Catherine the Great annexed it in 1783.

Conclusion

The Ottoman Empire brought a long period of stability to a wide arc of territory around the eastern half of the Mediterranean basin and the Black Sea. At its height, it brought prosperity and security to a diverse set of linguistic and religious groups. Its frontiers, bureaucratic structures, and artistic traditions remained powerful forces for centuries. In the seventeenth century, however, its inability to cope with an array of financial, demographic, and social challenges left its central government weakened. No longer able to protect the Balkan peasantry from rapacity and violence, the empire's legitimacy became vulnerable to challenges by local leaders who championed ethnic or religious identities. The Ottoman loss at Vienna in 1683 showed that the empire was becoming more vulnerable to outside threats as well. The Treaty of Karlowitz sixteen years later ended a period that had lasted three centuries, during which Europeans had to form a coalition if they hoped to defeat the "Terrible Turk." During the eighteenth century, its neighbors regarded it merely as one of several powerful European states competing for resources.

The disintegration of the Golden Horde and its successor khanates entailed the loss of a huge swath of the Dar al-Islam. Culturally, the loss was not as severe as the fall of Andalus because its urban life was much weaker, but it had major consequences. The revival of the Horde after Timur's death resulted in the development of several major centers of Islamic culture, such as Astrakhan, Kazan, and Bakhchysarai, but these were vulnerable to the rising power of Muscovy/Russia. After their absorption by Russia, never again would Muslims on the steppe be confident that they could practice their religion.

From a geopolitical standpoint, the collapse of the Horde was momentous. Just as the Ottomans and Mamluks had blocked European expansion into the Dar al-Islam through Southwest Asia, the Horde had confined Eastern European powers from expanding into the steppes. In the absence of the Horde, the way was open for Russia to expand eastward all the way to the Pacific and southward into Crimea, the Caucasus, and Central Asia. The weakening of the Ottoman Empire and the disintegration of the Horde left many Muslim areas vulnerable to subsequent European imperialism.

NOTES

1 The official name of the city during Ottoman times was Kostantiniye, but in colloquial speech, a variety of ethnic groups referred to the city by a term that evolved into *Istanbul*. The most widely accepted etymology for the name is that it derived from the phrase *eis tên polin*, which in the colloquial Greek language meant "to the city." Not until 1930, almost a decade after the collapse of the Ottoman Empire, was *Istanbul* used by the postal authority of the Republic of Turkey. Because the name was widely used for centuries in speech, however, it seems fitting to use it to refer to the city after 1453. Not only had the urban area that had once been the greatest capital city of the Christian world become the greatest capital city of the Muslim world, but it had also experienced an immediate economic, demographic, and cultural rebirth after Mehmet II's conquest.

2   See the discussion on the historiography on conversion in the Balkans in Dennis Hupchick, *The Balkans: From Constantinople to Communism*, New York: Palgrave, 2002, 151–156.

3   Francis Robinson makes a convincing argument that the opposition to the printing press in the eighteenth-century Ottoman Empire was due to its disruption of the personal manner in which knowledge was transmitted. Traditionally, Muslims had not assumed that the meaning of a text is self-evident; the purpose of the chain of transmission from scholar to scholar, and the significance of the *ijaza* that a successful student received, was to ensure that the author's meaning had in fact been conveyed in discussion. See Francis Robinson, "Technology and Religious Change: Islam and the Impact of Print," in *Modern Asian Studies* 27, 1 (1993): 229–251.

4   Darjusz Kołodziejczyk, "Slave Hunting and Slave Redemption as a Business Enterprise: The Northern Black Sea Region in the Sixteenth to Seventeenth Centuries," *Oriente Moderno* n.s.25:1 (2006): 151–152.

FURTHER READING

The Ottoman Empire

Barkey, Karen. *Bandits and Bureaucrats: The Ottoman Route to State Centralization.* Ithaca, New York: Cornell University Press, 1994.

Brummett, Palmira. *Ottoman Seapower and Levantine Diplomacy in the Age of Discovery.* Albany: State University of New York Press, 1994.

Hupchick, Dennis. *The Balkans: From Constantinople to Communism.* New York: Palgrave, 2002.

Imber, Colin. *The Ottoman Empire, 1330–1650: The Structure of Power.* Houndmills, U.K., and New York: Palgrave Macmillan, 2002.

Inalcik, Halil, Suraiya Faroqhi, Bruce McGowan, Donald Quataert, and Sevket Pamuk. *An Economic and Social History of the Ottoman Empire.* 2 vols. Cambridge, U.K.: Cambridge University Press, 1994.

Itzkowitz, Norman. *Ottoman Empire and Islamic Tradition.* New York: Alfred A. Knopf, 1972.

Murphey, Rhoades. *Ottoman Warfare 1500–1700.* New Brunswick, New Jersey: Rutgers University Press, 1999.

Pamuk, Sevket. *A Monetary History of the Ottoman Empire.* Cambridge, U.K., and New York: Cambridge University Press, 2000.

———. "The Price Revolution in the Ottoman Empire Reconsidered." *International Journal of Middle East Studies* 33 (2001): 69–89.

Peirce, L.P. *The Imperial Harem. Women and Sovereignty in the Ottoman Empire.* New York: Oxford University Press, 1993.

Petry, Carl. *Protectors or Praetorians? The Last Great Mamluk Sultans and the Waning of Egypt as a Great Power.* Albany: State University of New York Press, 1994.

Robinson, Francis. "Technology and Religious Change in Islam and the Impact of Print," *Modern Asian Studies* 27 (1993): 229–251.

Zilfi, Madeline C. *The Politics of Piety: The Ottoman Ulema in the Postclassical Age (1600–1800).* Minneapolis: Bibliotheca Islamica, 1988.

The Arabian Peninsula

Bidwell, Robin L. *The Two Yemens.* Boulder, Colorado: Westview Press, 1983.

Hattox, Ralph S. *Coffee and Coffeehouses: The Origins of a Social Beverage in the Medieval Near East.* Seattle: Distributed by University of Washington Press, 1985.

Peters, F.E. *The Hajj: The Muslim Pilgrimage to Mecca and the Holy Places.* Princeton, New Jersey: Princeton University Press, 1994.

Risso, Patricia. *Oman & Muscat: An Early Modern History.* New York: St. Martin's Press, 1986.

Silverberg, Robert. *The Realm of Prester John.* Athens: Ohio University Press, 1972.

Wilkinson, John C. *The Imamate Tradition of Oman.* Cambridge, U.K.: Cambridge University Press, 1987.

The Eurasian Steppes

Halperin, Charles J. *Russia and the Golden Horde.* Bloomington: Indiana University Press, 1985.

Hartog, Leo de. *Russia and the Mongol Yoke: The History of the Russian Principalities and the Golden Horde, 1221–1502.* London and New York: British Academic Press and I. B. Tauris Publishers, 1996.

Khodarkovsky, Michael. *Russia's Steppe Frontier: The Making of a Colonial Empire, 1500–1800.* Bloomington and Indianapolis: Indiana University Press, 2002.

Yemelianova, Galina M. *Russia and Islam: A Historical Survey.* Houndmills, U.K., and New York: Palgrave, 2002.

CHAPTER 13

The Umma in the West

The Maghrib and Andalus were the only major regions of Muslim settlement not directly affected by the Mongols and Timur. The thirteenth century was, nonetheless, as significant in the history of these areas as it was in the eastern Muslim world. The Christian kingdoms of northern Iberia swept to stunning victories over most of the Muslim cities of Andalus, and the great Berber empire of the Almohads dissolved in North Africa. These events created the backdrop for the momentous development when the Strait of Gibraltar became a cultural barrier for the first time in history. As Portugal and Spain sought to expand their spheres of influence into Africa, and as the Ottoman Empire attempted to contain those efforts, the inhabitants of Iberia and the Maghrib developed a deep-seated hostility toward each other.

Meanwhile, south of the Sahara, scattered, tiny communities of Muslim merchants and scholars had existed since the eleventh century. By the fifteenth century, they were having a major impact on the political history of a wide swath of the continent. During the period under review, the region of Africa between the Sahara and the equatorial forests became Islamized. It became tied into the trans-Atlantic world due to an expansion of the slave trade, and its ties with the predominantly Muslim world became stronger.

The Iberian Peninsula

Muslims dominated the southern half of the Iberian Peninsula from the early eighth century until 1212. In that year, a temporary coalition of Christian powers from the northern half of the peninsula surprised the peoples of the western Mediterranean by defeating the army of the Almohad Empire, which ruled Andalus and the Maghrib. The battle, fought at Las Navas de Tolosa, did not result in an immediate Christian takeover of Andalus: The rival Muslim principalities enjoyed a short reprieve while the Christian kingdoms quarreled among themselves for a quarter of a century. When the Christians did begin to cooperate again, they seized Cordoba, Valencia,

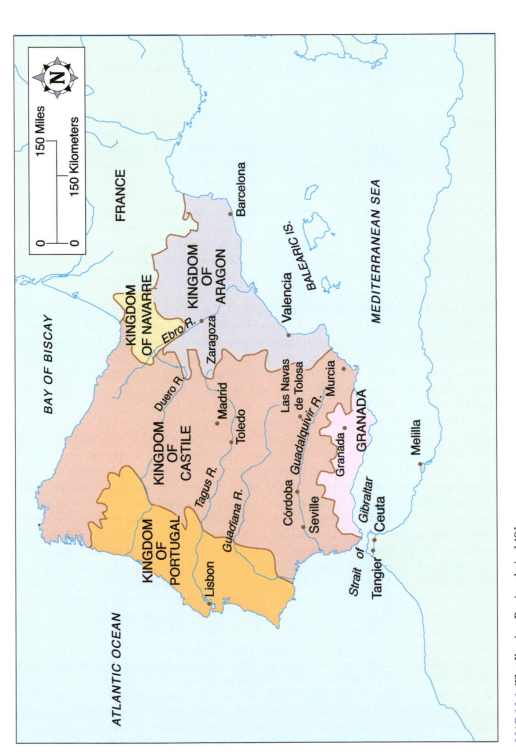

MAP 13.1 The Iberian Peninsula in 1491.

Murcia, and Seville in rapid succession between 1236 and 1248. For the next two and a half centuries, the majority of the peninsula's Muslims were under Christian governments and were referred to as Mudejars, or "the domesticated." Only Granada remained independent of Christian control, but even it was subject to an annual tribute paid to Castile.

Mudejars

Throughout the thirteenth century, Muslims continued to compose the majority of many of the provinces from Zaragoza in northern Aragon to Seville in southern Castile. They dominated the agricultural sector and were in great demand as skilled artisans in the traditional Andalusian crafts of plaster, tile, woodworking, and textiles. Among the wealthy Muslim landowners, there were signs that the patterns of life had not changed a great deal. Just as Iberian Christian adventurers had fought in the service of Almoravid and Almohad rulers in North Africa without compromising their loyalties and identities, Muslim lords and foot soldiers served in the armies of both James of Aragon and Alfonso X of Castile. Muslims even joined with the Knights Templar to combat other Muslims.

Valencia, conquered by James of Aragon (1213–1276), remained predominantly Muslim for at least two centuries. Because Muslims there were so numerous, James granted them generous terms in the hope of establishing a stable rule. The generation that surrendered to Christian forces in the thirteenth century retained many familiar structures of life. Mudejars continued to worship with minimal interference, they were allowed to retain their Shari'a court system, and they remained under the guidance of their market inspectors and qadis.

The tolerable living conditions confronted many Muslims with a dilemma. On the one hand, some of the most respected religious scholars taught that it was incumbent upon pious Muslims to perform hijra (emigrate) to Muslim-controlled territory in emulation of the Prophet's trek from heathen Mecca to Medina, and that it was a sin to remain in a land that was not under Muslim authority. Tens of thousands who could afford to leave the county did so. On the other hand, the disruption of the wars and the flight of many Muslims created a labor shortage in the newly conquered lands. King James offered economic inducements to discourage emigration, and Muslims who stayed found ample opportunities for employment.

At first glance, the various Iberian kingdoms appear to have been pluralistic and harmonious. Alongside the Muslim population in the peninsula was a large, highly educated Jewish community. The Christian monarchs had a great stake in maintaining good relations with their non-Christian subjects due to the skills and knowledge that they possessed. In Aragon, the Mudejars were even known as the "Royal Treasure." They were allowed their own institutions as well as practices such as polygyny and the performance of the hajj to Mecca. In actuality, however, each kingdom contained parallel societies that harbored a great deal of mistrust toward each other. Mudejars found that, in spite of the royal decrees that were issued for their benefit, their lives became increasingly constrained by forces beyond the monarch's control. As the number of Christians in a given region reached a critical mass, conditions for the Mudejars often became intolerable. As Christian immigrants settled in Muslim-majority areas, the authority of Muslim market inspectors and qadis diminished, to be superseded by the jurisdiction of royal judges, bailiffs, magistrates, and bishops. Muslims who were under the feudal or legal jurisdiction of local Christian lords often had no appeal to the monarch. Kidnappers frequently seized them and held them for ransom or summarily sold them into slavery. Severe laws governed relations between the sexes of the two communities: A Christian woman who slept with a Muslim male was theoretically liable to being burned, and the man was subject to being drawn and quartered or burned. A Christian man who slept with a Muslim woman, on the other hand, was liable to no penalty at all, but the woman was invariably sold into slavery.

The Mudejars of Valencia may have faced the most difficult conditions, despite the intentions of King John. Only a few decades after the conquests, they were legally forbidden from emigrating, leaving them exposed to numerous types of repression. The Christian lower classes frequently rioted against the presence of the Mudejars, for they regarded them as threats to their economic well-being. At the time of the Black Death in the mid-fourteenth century, many Christians held the Mudejars to be responsible for the plague (a charge made against the Jews in other parts of Europe) and managed to enact restrictions on their ability to travel in an effort to limit their "poisonous" work. Several popes applied pressure on both the Aragonese and Castilian monarchs to convert their Mudejars. The Mudejars who did convert to Christianity, however, discovered that conversion solved no problems for them. Like the Muslim Arabs of the Umayyad period, many Christian lords were determined that they not lose the taxes or the forcible service that they could glean from members of the "protected" religion and refused to recognize their conversion. In addition, many of the so-called Old Christians were suspicious that the new converts were only pretending to have converted. The new converts were often called Christian Mudejars.

The Mudejars desperately tried to maintain their identity in the face of increasing pressures, but they found themselves in a position similar to that of their contemporaries, the Orthodox Christians of Turkish-dominated Anatolia. Both peoples experienced the loss of their cultural elites and of a strong institutional support structure. As a result, their identity and their numbers disintegrated in the face of a more aggressive culture. Many of the Muslim elites had fled Valencia at the time of the conquest, and most of the others who could afford to slip away to North Africa over the following generations did so. The Mudejar community gradually lost its scholars and natural leaders. By the middle of the fourteenth century, Arabic was still the spoken language of the majority in Valencia, but it was difficult to find Mudejars outside Valencia who could speak or read the language. In Castile and northern Aragon, a new religious literature began to evolve among Mudejars that came to be called Aljamiado. Used for translations of the Qur'an and for devotional literature, it was written in the Arabic script, but its vocabulary was that of the local Romance dialect. The loss of the Mudejars' linguistic identity was paralleled by the loss of their economic importance. As the Christian population increased in formerly Muslim territories, the new immigrants learned the skills that had originally made the Mudejars economically valuable, and the Muslims found their opportunities for gaining a livelihood increasingly limited. Gradually, Mudejars sank in status and were treated with derision by Christian society.

Granada

Neither the city of Granada nor the principality that shared its name had played a major role in Andalusian history prior to the thirteenth century. It had been a region of the second rank, languishing in the shadows of Toledo, Cordoba, and Seville. For two and a half centuries after the fall of Seville and Cordoba, however, the principality of Granada became famous as the last redoubt of Muslim independence in Iberia. Most of Granada was barren and mountainous, but it managed to attain a surprising degree of prosperity. It traded sugar, figs, raisins, and almonds for the grain and olives that it imported from the Maghrib. Its manufactures—particularly its silk and ceramics—were also in high demand throughout North Africa as well as in sub-Saharan Ghana, where merchants were eager to trade gold for them.

In retrospect, it is easy to assume that Granadans must have been constantly preoccupied with the Christian threat from the north after the fall of Toledo in 1085. While there is no doubt that the fear of Christian conquest had to be in the back of everyone's mind after the eleventh century, the rulers knew that there were ways to keep the Christian powers at bay. Granada, like most of the other Muslim principalities of the time, occasionally allied with Christian powers against fellow Muslims. The principality even came to the aid of Castile in its decisive siege of Seville in 1248.

The disappearance of all the other Muslim principalities in the peninsula after 1248 did not alter the fact that Granada continued to ally at certain times with Christians against Muslims and at other times with Muslims against Christians. Because of the power imbalance in the peninsula after 1248, Granada was contractually bound to pay a tribute to Castile. In order to assert its independence, however, its rulers occasionally refused to pay, incurring Castile's wrath. Granada would thereupon seek the assistance of the Marinid dynasty, which had replaced the Almohads in the Maghrib. When, on the other hand, the Marinids made unwanted demands, Granada sought the assistance of Christian Castile against the Muslim Marinids.

Although the rulers of Granada felt compelled to follow policies that maintained their independence from neighboring states, whether Christian or Muslim, their subjects were influenced by the fact that their society had become isolated and vulnerable as the only Muslim principality on the northern shore of the Strait of Gibraltar. Their knowledge that several popes and many other Christian clerics called for crusades to eliminate Granada as a Muslim presence only heightened their anxieties. As a result, Granada developed a more self-consciously Islamic and Arabized society than any that had been known in Andalus. Unlike the Mudejars, the Muslims of Granada spoke and wrote only in Arabic. Rulers zealously enforced Maliki law, and Muslims who were not conscientious adherents of ritual detail were subject to punishments. Whereas Jews were allowed to live and work in Granada, Christians were not. In stark contrast to most of the Muslim regimes of Andalus from the eighth to the thirteenth centuries, which had been a stimulating mixture of various races and creeds, Granada began expelling Christians as early as the twelfth century. By the thirteenth century, there is no evidence that any lived in the province.

The second half of the fourteenth century was the high point of Granada's history. Castile and Aragon became embroiled in a series of bloody wars with each other. The Marinid state in the Maghrib was in a state of decline and could not seriously threaten Granada. With Granada's three main rivals preoccupied, it was able to divert some of its wealth from its military forces to internal improvements. Much of the Alhambra palace complex, the most famous architectural monument of the Granadan era, was the work of Muhammad V (1354–1391), the ruler through-out most of this period. His court boasted the presence of several outstanding poets as well as that of two of the world's greatest historians of that era: Ibn Khaldun and Ibn al-Khatib.

We know remarkably little about Granada during the fifteenth century. After Ibn Khaldun and Ibn al-Khatib passed from the scene, no capable historian took their place. Our knowledge of the period derives largely from Arabic narrative poems and reports by Christians from Castile and Aragon. What is clear about Granadan society itself is that long-time rivalries among the great families became even more bitter and divisive. In foreign affairs, the balance of power in the region shifted decisively against Granada. The Marinid sultanate was no longer a factor in international affairs by the fifteenth century and was finally overthrown in 1465. For the first time, Granada was left without a potential ally in North Africa in the case of a crisis on its borders. Meanwhile, Aragon and Castile consolidated their power during the fifteenth century and became more stable and prosperous. In 1469, Ferdinand, the sixteen-year-old heir to the throne of Aragon, married Isabella, the princess of Castile. By 1479, Ferdinand and Isabella were the joint rulers of their respective kingdoms. Legally, Aragon and Castile remained separate kingdoms for several more decades, but it is useful to begin the history of Spain from the union of the two crowns in 1479.

Moriscos

One of the problems the two young Christian monarchs faced was the growing tension between their Christian and Jewish communities. The dynamics of this conflict, as well as its denouement, foreshadowed that of the subsequent conflict between Christians and Muslims in Spain. Whereas most Mudejars were peasants, workmen, and artisans, Jews had long held positions in the Iberian Christian kingdoms as wealthy merchants, government administrators, and physicians. Their status as wealthy and influential non-Christians provoked an anti-Semitic reaction, just as it did in most of the rest of Christian Europe. On the one hand, the monarchy and the nobility needed their skills and their wealth; on the other hand, many common people resented the high status enjoyed by some Jews. Crowds periodically vented their frustrations in riots. The most severe pogrom occurred in 1391 when mobs sacked the Jewish quarters of Toledo, Cordoba, Seville, Valencia, and Barcelona. Thousands of Jews were killed.

Out of fear of further persecution, many Jews converted to Christianity. These converts, known both as Marranos and Conversos, took advantage of the opportunities that the identity of "Christian" conferred on them. They enjoyed great success in gaining high offices in the municipal and royal governments as well as in the Church. The most spectacular case may well have been that of the rabbi of Burgos, Samuel Levi, who later became the bishop of the same city under the name Pablo de Santa Maria. The assimilation of Jews into Iberian Christian society was so successful that a government report of the mid-fifteenth century stated that almost all of the peninsula's Christian nobility had Converso relatives or ancestors. King Ferdinand

FIGURE 13.1 The Court of the Lions of the Alhambra palace, Granada. The most admired sections of the Alhambra date from the reign of Muhammad V (1354–1391), a century before Granada's capture by Spain.

© 2017. DeAgostini Picture Library / Scala, Florence.

himself had Jewish blood in his veins. Many of the "Old Christians," however, were jealous of the success of the "New Christians" and suspicious of their sincerity. They noted that many of them continued to live in the Jewish quarters of the cities, would not eat pork, stayed home on Saturday, and named their children after Old

Testament figures. Some Conversos were even openly returning to the faith of their ancestors.

The defection of a minority of Conversos back to Judaism was a threat to the position of genuine Jewish converts to Christianity. The issue only compounded Christian suspicions of the genuine Conversos and exacerbated Christian jealousy of the material success of many Conversos. There is evidence that influential Conversos at court and in the Church hierarchy pressed for the creation of the Inquisition to investigate the sincerity of New Christians in order to ferret out those who were likely to become apostates. Genuine Conversos felt that only by this process would their own position be secure. The Inquisition was created in 1478. Its leader was Tomas de Torquemada, himself a descendant of Conversos.

In 1492, the anti-Converso movement expanded into hysteria against Jews in general. During the same year that Columbus sailed in the name of Queen Isabella, the crown demanded that the Jews of Spain choose between baptism and expulsion. An estimated 50,000 Jews submitted to baptism, even though they knew that Conversos were subject to intense scrutiny and suspicion. Estimates of the number of Jews who refused baptism and went into exile range from 40,000 to ten times that number, but most historians today agree that 100,000–200,000 had to leave. Ferdinand and Isabella pressured their fellow monarchs to expel their Jews as well. Portugal complied in 1496, and Navarre followed in 1498. Perhaps 20,000 of the exiles died; some of the survivors found refuge in Italy or Greece, but the vast majority of them settled in the Muslim lands of North Africa, the Mamluk Empire, or the Ottoman Empire. They and their descendants are known as Sephardic Jews because their name for Iberia was Sefarda. (The Jews of Eastern and Central Europe and Western Europe north of the Pyrenees are known as Ashkenazi Jews.) An estimated 300,000 Conversos or descendants of Conversos remained in Spain. Despite continued persecution, they made major contributions to sixteenth-century Spanish culture, both secular and religious. Included among them were a novelist (Mateo Alemán), perhaps the greatest jurist of the age (Francisco de Vitoria), and a mystical saint who is best known today for having been immortalized in stone by Bernini (Teresa of Avila).

In the fifteenth century, Mudejars did not elicit popular fury among the general Christian population the way Jews and Conversos did. Christian hostility was focused on Granada instead. From 1431 on, Castilian rulers began seizing Granadan frontier towns. Tension between the two powers increased after the Ottomans captured Constantinople in 1453. The pope insisted that a retaliatory blow should be struck for Christendom against the powers of Islam. With pressure rising for decisive action, many Christians in the peninsula began asking why Granada was still allowed to exist. In 1481, Granada launched a raid against Spain. This was only the latest in a series of hundreds of such attacks over the previous centuries, but it provided the pope with the pretext for a crusade. For more than a decade, the papacy and various European powers supplied Spain with arms and money for the final campaign to capture Granada.

Even in their hour of greatest peril, the great families of the last independent Muslim state in the peninsula could not maintain solidarity. The ruler of Granada fell out with his brother and his own son, and a civil war raged among the three family members even as Spanish forces closed in. The ruler's son, Abu 'Abd Allah (known in European romances as Boabdil), made a secret agreement with Spanish authorities that would allow him to gain control of Granada and then turn it over to Spain. He seized power but refused to surrender the city as promised. After a huge Spanish army laid siege to Granada, Abu 'Abd Allah agreed to surrender the city in January 1492. He then went into exile in North Africa.

Granada was granted generous terms of surrender, including the possession of property and freedom of worship. Thousands of Muslim Granadans, however, chose to emigrate to the Maghrib rather than live under Christian rule. They would be glad they did: The expulsion of the Jews in the same year as the fall of Granada seems to have affected the perception of Mudejars by many Christians. A new sense of impatience at the failure of Muslims to convert to Christianity became palpable. In 1499, Archbishop Cisneros of Toledo dismissed the bishop who had been responsible for the sensitive treatment of Muslims in Granada. He assumed control of religious affairs in the province and immediately announced a policy of compulsory conversion of Muslims. He forcibly baptized 3000 Granadans on a single day, imprisoned many Muslims who refused to convert, and burned thousands of Arabic books. Granada responded with a major revolt that was quelled only in 1501.

In retaliation for the uprising, the monarchy issued a decree demanding that all Granadan Muslims choose between conversion and expulsion. In 1502, the royal court forced the small minority of Mudejars in Castile to make a similar choice. Local Christian authorities, already suffering economically from the expulsion of the Jews, often refused to allow Muslims to leave. They forced them to remain and be baptized. Satisfied with carrying out the formal requirements of the edict, the Spanish authorities pronounced that no Muslims remained in Granada or Castile. The great majority of the "converts," of course, continued to practice Islam secretly.

The authorities soon extended the provisions of the conversion decree to the rest of Spain. In Navarre, local Christians had enjoyed a history of good relations with their Muslim neighbors for centuries. The Muslims of Navarre were prosperous and continued to hold important positions in the army and government. In 1512, however, Spain annexed the country and Muslims began to suffer discrimination. By 1516, the Muslim community ceased to exist. In Aragon, the province of Valencia posed a difficult problem for the monarchy because Muslims composed an estimated one-third of the population even after 300 years of Aragonese control. Valencia did not see large numbers of conversions to Christianity until after 1525.

Muslims who converted to Christianity were called Moriscos, or "little Moors." The term itself reveals that, even more than Conversos, they were not regarded as genuine Christians. In fact, many Moriscos made little pretense of having converted, for they deeply resented the flagrant violation of the promises of their original conquerors. Throughout the sixteenth century, their relations with the dominant Christian society were strained. They were subject to numerous strictures with regard to their dress, family life, and social institutions. Local courts often ignored illegal seizures of their property by Christians. The Inquisition punished Moriscos who were brought before it on charges of not eating pork. Ascetic Spanish monks who valued bodily dirt as a sign of spiritual purity were successful in closing the public baths that were integral to the Muslim hygienic regimen. In 1566, an edict demanded the surrender of all Arabic books and forbade women to wear a veil. The pressures in Granada became so intolerable that a massive revolt broke out in 1568. The army quelled it in late 1570 only with the aid of Austrian troops. King Philip II ordered all Granadan Moriscos dispersed throughout Castile. Although historians estimate that some 60,000–150,000 Moriscos managed to remain in the south, even larger numbers were dumped, homeless and unemployed, in the towns and villages of Castile.

The tensions between the parallel societies of Spain were heightened by developments within the Mediterranean basin. Spain's ambition to be the premier power in Europe and in the Mediterranean received several challenges during the sixteenth century. The Protestant Reformation, the machinations of the French monarchy, and the rapid expansion of the Ottoman Empire under Selim I and Suleyman made Spaniards nervous. The Ottomans were the most formidable threat. Selim conquered Egypt and Syria in 1517 and Suleyman attacked Habsburg Vienna in 1529. Meanwhile, the Ottomans were sending Janissaries, ships, and funds to support sailors in North Africa who were harassing Spanish shipping. The growing Ottoman involvement in the Maghrib was an intolerable threat to Spanish security.

Increasingly, Spanish Christians regarded the Moriscos as a potential fifth column who would thwart the unity of the country and collude with Spain's enemies. In fact, many Moriscos made no secret of the fact that they hoped that the Ottomans would sooner or later deliver them from oppression. Serious discussions concerning the prospects for expelling the Moriscos were held at the royal court in Madrid as early as 1582, but the obvious difficulties involved in such a project caused the plan to stall. Developments between 1588 and 1609, however, created the climate of opinion that made expulsion a viable political option: The defeat of the Armada by the English in 1588 was a grievous blow to the Spanish self-image, high taxes and currency devaluations led to acute economic problems by the early seventeenth century, and in 1609 the government was forced to sign a truce with the rebellious Dutch because of the near-bankruptcy of the treasury.

The Spanish king signed the royal decree ordering the expulsion of the Moriscos on the same day that he signed the truce with the Dutch. The expulsion was carried out in stages over a five-year period in order to avoid a sudden depletion of the labor force. Estimates of the number of Moriscos who were expelled range from 275,000 to 500,000. Most of them settled in Morocco, Algeria, and Tunisia, but they were not welcomed into economies that could not even support their own populations. Just as they had been regarded as Muslims in Spain, they were often called "Spanish Christians" in North Africa. Thousands died of exposure and malnutrition, and most of the first generation of refugees never fully assimilated into local society. Had they known, they might have derived some satisfaction from learning that their departure entailed the loss of essential economic skills in Spain. The deportation contributed to the decline of the port city of Seville, agricultural disaster in the Ebro valley, and long-term economic stagnation in Valencia.

As late as the early eighteenth century, individuals were still being hauled before the Spanish Inquisition on charges of practicing Islam. For all practical purposes, however, Islam ended in Spain in 1614 after a 900-year presence in the peninsula. The influence of Arab–Islamic culture on Spanish place names, the language itself, art and architecture, and manners and customs was profound, although few Spaniards were willing to admit it until the late twentieth century. The dominant historiography portrayed the peninsula's history as Christian and Spanish, interrupted by an unfortunate and easily disregarded period of "Moorish" presence that was reclaimed by the Reconquista. Spanish historians are now making great strides in integrating the Muslim period into the continuum of the peninsula's history and making that history more intelligible and meaningful. What is still unclear is how the tragedy that befell the Jews and the Muslims could have been avoided, given the assumptions and prejudices of all the communities of the day.

The Maghrib

A heavy mist often envelops the Strait of Gibraltar, but when the sun breaks through, sailors enjoy the spectacle of the Rock of Gibraltar to the north and her sister peaks in North Africa—Jabal Acha and Jabal Musa—to the south. These European and African promontories are separated by only fourteen miles. To the ancient Greeks and Romans, they were the Pillars of Hercules and symbolized the edge of the world, beyond which a ship might simply fall into an abyss. The perception that danger lay in wait beyond the Pillars was not far-fetched. Heading west through the strait, sailors left an inland sea for the apparently boundless Atlantic, whose titanic waves could crush or flip a vessel designed for the Mediterranean.

Historically, the strait was a barrier only to east–west travel. It was a bridge, rather than an obstacle, to north–south relations. The migrations, cultural interchange, and maritime trade of the region served to reinforce that fact for centuries. The fifteenth century, however, reversed the relationship. Developments in shipbuilding and navigation enabled European navies to ply the waters of both the Mediterranean and the Atlantic with the same vessels, and the Atlantic became the theater for a vast enterprise of exploration. Simultaneously, relations between Iberian Christians and their Muslim neighbors in the Maghrib deteriorated, generating hostile attitudes on both sides of the strait that made communication and trade difficult. The strait became a cultural as well as a political boundary between Europe and Africa for the first time.

The Land

The Maghrib extends some 2500 miles from the western frontiers of Egypt to the Atlantic. Despite the region's enormous size, visitors throughout Muslim history have been struck by the cultural features shared by its constituent societies. Islamic institutions spread rapidly among the mixed Berber and Arab populations, and the Arabic language became the lingua franca. The economy was based on small-scale grain, fruit, and olive gardening; animal herding by pastoral peoples; a small textile manufacturing sector; and a thriving long-distance trade that linked the Mediterranean with sub-Saharan societies. In contrast to these culturally unifying elements, the Maghrib has been politically unified only a few times throughout history, and even then, the actual area under centralized control was usually confined to the narrow coastal plain. Despite the overall pattern of uniformity, the Maghrib also exhibited distinctive regional traits.

The eastern Maghrib is known today as Libya, but historically, its three major regions were considered quite distinct. Cyrenaica, in the east, relied on a traditional economy of nomadic and seminomadic pastoralism. Tripolitania, in the west,

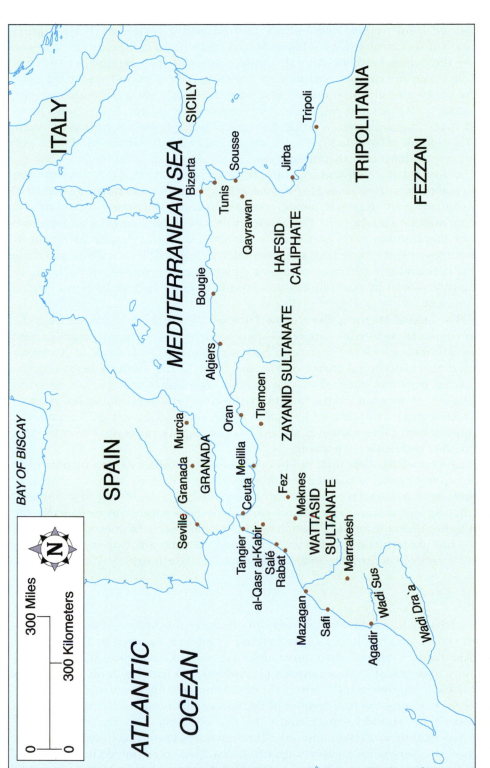

MAP 13.2 The Maghrib in the Early Sixteenth Century.

benefitted from irrigated agriculture and boasted a region of dense juniper forests. The spectacular ruins of Leptis Magna testify to the prosperity of the region during the Roman Republic. After the Arab conquest, Tripoli became its chief port. The city lay on an extremely narrow plain, almost in the desert, and was the terminus of the shortest of all the trans-Saharan trade routes. It was a cosmopolitan city, attracting merchants and craftsmen from many ethnic groups. Fezzan was Libya's third major region. It was a constellation of oasis villages in the desert, some 400 miles south of Tripoli. It grew cereals necessary for the survival of Tripoli and was a rest stop for trans-Saharan caravans.

Before the sixteenth century, Tripolitania was often regarded as the easternmost extension of the region known to Muslims as Ifriqiya, which extended northward to Tunis and westward to Bougie (modern Bejaia, Algeria). The central core of Ifriqiya became modern Tunisia. Olive gardens and wheat fields have covered the northern half of the Tunisian plain ever since Roman times. Tunis, despite its northerly location, enjoyed the benefits of the trans-Saharan trade. The agriculture and trade of this region allowed Ifriqiya to enjoy a generally prosperous—and occasionally spectacular—level of material life. As a result, it often had an effective central government.

The central Maghrib, the area we know as Algeria today, extended from the region around Bougie to the vicinity of Tlemcen. Algeria's topography is characterized by an alternating series of mountain ranges and plains. As a result, it has never enjoyed the agricultural riches of Tunisia. Prior to the modern period, it was populated largely by shepherds, goat herders, and camel drovers. Compared to Tunisia and Morocco, it was less wealthy and boasted far fewer examples of great art and architecture. The splendid exception to the rule was the city of Tlemcen, but the government there was never able to establish significant control over its large and mobile population of nomads.

The far western Maghrib, or Morocco, is divided into an eastern section and a western, or Atlantic, section of roughly equal sizes. Eastern Morocco's physical features bear a strong resemblance to those of Algeria, with rugged mountains alternating with plains. The Middle and High Atlas mountain ranges are the dominant physical features of the region. Atlantic Morocco, by contrast, comprises plains and plateaus and is where the majority of the cities are. Governments always found it easier to control the western half than the eastern half.

The Berber States

Almost the whole of the Maghrib was united under the Berber Almohad Empire (1147–1269), which at its peak stretched from southern Morocco to Tripoli. When the Almohad regime collapsed, three major Berber successor states arose to fill the vacuum. In the east, the Hafsid dynasty (1229–1569) was based in Tunis. The Hafsids had been loyal governors in Tunis for the Almohads and had ruled with little supervision during the first decades of the thirteenth century. After the fall of the Almohads, the Hafsid sultans claimed the title of caliph. The dynasty continued the long-standing maritime tradition of Tunisian states, importing timber from as far away as Scandinavia for its busy shipyards. It established commercial treaties with Italian city-states and would have done so with Aragon had it not been for the public outrage that followed Aragon's conquest of Valencia in 1236. Both Aragon and Tunis nevertheless maintained commercial contacts.

The Hafsid sultans were cultivated and civilized men who oversaw a sumptuous court. They commissioned the construction of many of the fine architectural monuments to be seen in Tunis today. Despite their claim to the caliphate, their actual concerns were decidedly secular and cosmopolitan. During the third quarter of the thirteenth century, in the immediate aftermath of the fall of most of the city-states of Andalus to the Reconquista, the caliphs permitted Dominican and Franciscan friars to preach Christianity to Muslims. They also employed Christian mercenary troops (largely from Aragon) in their army and palace guard.

The chief threat to the Hafsids was not Aragon or Castile, but rather the Marinid dynasty (1268–1465) based at Fez. Originally, the Marinids were a Berber pastoral tribe in southern Morocco. Later they became the chief factor in the collapse of Almohad power. In 1216, they began challenging Almohad authority and, despite a few setbacks, they seized one major city in Morocco after another until they captured the capital, Marrakesh, in 1269. The Marinids established their capital at Fez, but they did not attempt to centralize their administration in the Hafsid manner. True to their tribal orientation, they depended on allies to maintain stability in the provinces. Like the Hafsids, they employed Aragonese Christian mercenary troops, most of whom served in the cavalry.

Unlike the Almohads, the Marinids did not seize power in the cause of a particular religious doctrine. They were eager to establish their own legitimacy, however, and attempted to do so in a variety of ways. One was to exploit the sense of cultural and ethnic superiority that Arabs had traditionally expressed toward the Berbers. The Marinids, although ethnically Berber, made their court culture as "Arab" as possible, made a point of marrying daughters of prominent Arab leaders, and even contrived a family tree to establish their "descent" from a North Arabian tribe.

The Marinids also attempted to win popular support by their patronage of Sunni urban Islam. The violence and uncertainties of the thirteenth and fourteenth centuries spawned a myriad of popular religious movements in the Maghrib. Throughout the Maghrib, several individuals claimed to be the Mahdi, whom many Muslims expected to bring an end to history; others claimed to be the Shi'ite Twelfth Imam. Numerous revolts exploded in support of many of these pretenders. To combat these religious challenges, the Marinids invested huge sums and a public relations campaign in support of religious institutions. They built many madrasas, and—in contrast to the rest of the Muslim world—decreed that no madrasas could be supported by private religious endowments. They were contemptuous of the Hafsid claim to be at the head of a caliphate. In a gesture meant to insult the Hafsids, the Marinids recognized the figurehead Abbasid caliph of distant Mamluk Cairo, precisely because doing so entailed no obligations.

The buffer state between the Hafsids and the Marinids was the realm of the Zayanid dynasty (1236–1555) at Tlemcen. The Zayanid state was the weakest of the three. Its vulnerability and central location made it a constant target of Marinid and Hafsid ambitions. Algeria had few resources to covet, but Tlemcen was a glittering prize. It was situated inland on a fertile agricultural plain and was the terminus of trans-Saharan trade routes. It competed favorably with Tunis and Fez for the goods of sub-Saharan Africa and developed a large and prosperous mercantile class. Its proud citizens constructed elegant buildings, many of which still stand. Both the Marinids and the Hafsids captured Tlemcen at least once but could not retain control of it. The Zayanid state would have fallen permanently to one of its neighbors had it not been for the constant challenge of the other.

All three of the Maghribi states were affected by the tragic drama unfolding across the Strait of Gibraltar. Tens of thousands of refugees from Andalus poured into the Maghrib in the thirteenth century, triggered by the success of the Reconquista between 1236 and 1248. Andalusians in North Africa gained a reputation over the next several centuries for their architectural and administrative skills. The artistic influence of the Andalusian legacy is still visible today in the monumental buildings of Fez, Tlemcen, and Tunis that were constructed during this period. Andalusians introduced features of court etiquette and honed the diplomatic skills of Maghribi officials. They served as secretaries, financial advisers, and sometimes even as wazirs. Ibn Khaldun, the third-generation Andalusian historian born in Tunis, was typical in going from the service of one prince to another. The Andalusians' influence was felt with particular force in Tlemcen, which did not have the long ruling tradition of Tunisia or Morocco. Wherever Andalusians served, however, they remained outsiders and were vulnerable to the plotting of local families.

The power of all three dynasties relied on balancing the public support and revenues from the urban commercial populations with the military power of tribal allies in the countryside. These alliances constantly shifted as the fortunes and interests of the tribes fluctuated. As a result, the frontiers marking the three dynasties' areas of control were always in flux as well. By the middle of the fourteenth century, the dynamism of all three dynasties had declined relative to that of the tribes for reasons that are not clear. The plague may have played a role, but we do not have detailed information on its impact in the Maghrib other than evidence that it struck the port cities. Whatever the reason, the nomads became a growing threat to the security of the trans-Saharan trade and to agriculture alike. The power of the dynasties was increasingly confined to the towns. In the areas where the state ceased to provide security, Sufi organizations became increasingly important as a source of defense, spiritual solace, and material aid.

Sufism in the Maghrib was more provincial in some ways than in the eastern areas of the Muslim world. As a rule, the new orders that were spreading rapidly in the Dar al-Islam did not start making inroads into the Maghrib until the sixteenth century. Prior to that time, Maghribi Sufi organizations were based on the teachings of local Sufi teachers. They were more focused on ethical and ritual concerns than many in the east, and they were less likely to indulge in esoteric speculation. Precisely because of the emphasis that the shaykhs placed on personal integrity, the Sufi masters gained much stature among the local populations. As in other rural areas of the Muslim world, shaykhs became mediators among tribes, and some even became the leaders of tribal coalitions, often in opposition to state regimes.

Even as Sufi leaders were becoming an alternative to the dynasties as local power brokers, another development was taking place in Morocco that would have powerful repercussions later: the reemergence of sharifian prestige. Throughout the Muslim world a descendant of the Prophet through his daughter Fatima and her husband 'Ali is known as a *sharif*. Among Sunnis and Shi'ites alike, sharifs have always been accorded great respect. Within Sunni communities they were frequently the local teachers, their counsel was always respected, and if they fell on hard times, the community made provision for them out of honor for the Prophet. In Morocco, one sharifian family, the Idrisid clan, was honored for having come to Morocco in the late eighth century, founding Fez, and creating a short-lived state. The Idrisids subsequently lost power, but their descendants remained members of a respected family in northern Morocco.

In the fourteenth and fifteenth centuries—simultaneously with the rise to prominence of rural Sufi shaykhs—sharifianism once again became a source of political capital. The Idrisids rose to prominence again, and other sharifian families arriving from Arabia during this period quickly became established within the social fabric of the Arab tribes because of their status as mediators. The reason for this phenomenon seems to be that the Marinid and Zayanid states continued to decline in effectiveness throughout the period. Nomads disrupted the trade routes of the western Sahara, damaging the economies of the Marinid and Zayanid states while inadvertently diverting the trade to Tunis and benefitting the Hafsid regime for a few decades after 1390. Sharifian and Sufi leaders alike gained status while dynastic rulers were increasingly unable to defend their subjects. Ominously, the weakening of central rule in North Africa was taking place during the period when the Iberian states of the Christian West and the Ottoman state of the Muslim East were in the early stages of becoming the dominant powers in the world.

Crusaders, Corsairs, and Janissaries

In the fifteenth century, Portugal became one of the most dynamic societies in Europe. It had long been a land of hardscrabble farms and cattle herders, of little consequence to Andalus and Castile. In the early fifteenth century, it was still tiny—it contained fewer than one million people, hardly more than sixteenth-century Istanbul—but it embarked on an ambitious campaign of commercial and territorial expansion. Under King John, the country began its conquests in 1415 with an attack on the Moroccan port of Ceuta, sandwiched between the southern twin Pillars of Hercules. After capturing the city, the king appointed a governor to rule over it as a Portuguese possession.

Ceuta was only the first objective in a grandiose, two-pronged plan to gain control of trade routes to the Spice Islands and to link up with Prester John (whom Europeans now believed to be the monarch of Ethiopia) for a crusade against Islam. The impracticality of establishing trade routes across North Africa to the Indian Ocean soon became apparent, and the Portuguese began seeking a sea route to the Indies instead. Stories of a possible route around Africa encouraged them to begin sailing down the continent's western coast. Under the inspiration of Prince Henry the Navigator, Portuguese mariners began to improve their maps, charts, shipbuilding techniques, and navigational technology. Several of the advances (including the lateen sail, magnetic compass, and astrolabe) were direct borrowings from the Muslims. They enabled the Portuguese to venture out of the sight of land onto the fearsome Atlantic. By 1487, Bartolomeu Dias had rounded the southern tip of Africa, and in 1498, Vasco da Gama arrived in India using the sea route. From the Indian Ocean and the Red Sea, the naval commander Afonso de Albuquerque continued the quest to find Prester John during the early sixteenth century.

During their exploration of the Atlantic coast of Africa, the Portuguese wanted to acquire the gold of West Africa and establish bases in Morocco that would supply their fleet. They failed to capture Tangier on their first attempt in 1437, but over the next several decades, they learned the vulnerabilities of the Moroccan port cities. Between 1458 and 1514, all of them with the exception of Salé fell into Portuguese hands. Portuguese merchants established trading networks in the interior of the central and southern plains and gained a near-monopoly over the maritime trade. Exchanging clothing and metal products for slaves, gold, and ivory, Portugal siphoned the West African trade away from the Muslim markets of the Maghrib. By the end of the century, Lisbon's economy was booming, due in part to the fact that it was receiving West African goods without having to pay the middlemen and tax collectors of Maghribi ports on the Mediterranean. Once Albuquerque had secured most of the major ports of the Indian Ocean by 1515, the spice route to the Indies began to yield its riches. With these two developments in North Africa and the Indian Ocean, Portugal entered the ranks of the world's great commercial economies.

The early incursions of the Portuguese demonstrated the impotence of the Marinid government, causing many Moroccans to question the legitimacy of the dynasty's rule. A brutal revolt in Fez in 1465 ended the Marinid regime, but the Portuguese commercial domination of Morocco only intensified. The new Berber rulers of Morocco, the Wattasids, were more concerned about rival Arab tribes than about the Portuguese: They actually established a twenty-year truce with the Portuguese in order to be able to concentrate on fighting ambitious Arab chieftains. The truce required that they lift restrictions on trade with Europe. As a result, Christian merchants flooded into coastal and interior markets.

During the last several decades of Marinid rule, regional leaders had begun resisting the foreigners who were devastating Morocco. Sufi and sharifian leaders, in particular, began to fill the void of leadership. The bloodshed at Ceuta in 1415 caused by the Portuguese provoked such outrage that tens of thousands of volunteers followed Sufi leaders in an unsuccessful attempt to retake the city. Sharifian nobles led the successful defense of Tangier in 1437. Wattasid inactivity against foreign intervention led to mounting frustration among many Moroccans. Eventually, a sharifian family in southern Morocco known as the Sa'dis began an alliance with Sufi leaders to unify Morocco against the Portuguese. Between 1510 and 1549, they slowly brought Morocco under their control as they gradually mastered the art of using the arquebus and artillery. Their capture of the Portuguese fort at Agadir in 1541 forced the Portuguese crown to begin evacuating most of its other forts as well. By 1551, Portugal retained only Ceuta, Tangier, and Mazagan (Al Jadida). The Sa'dis ruled Morocco for more than fifty years, and they demonstrated military and administrative acumen. Their success created a long-lasting expectation among most Moroccans that the ruler of the country should be from a sharifian family.

The fifteenth-century capture by outsiders of Moroccan port cities on the Atlantic was a harbinger of a similar fate for many Maghribi port cities on the Mediterranean in the sixteenth century. To the east of Morocco, Spain and the Ottoman Empire vied for control of North Africa's port cities. After Spain conquered Granada in 1492, it joined Portugal as a Moroccan power when it occupied the port of Melilla in 1497. The period between 1497 and 1505 witnessed serious attacks on the Spanish coast by North African Muslim raiders and the 1499 revolt by Granadan Muslims who protested the forcible conversions ordered by Bishop Cisneros. In response to those threats, Spain decided on a systematic occupation of the main ports of the Maghrib. The next six years revealed that a startling shift in the balance of power had taken place in the western Mediterranean from the days when the Marinids and the Hafsids could reasonably regard themselves as the equals of Castile and Aragon: Between 1505 and 1511, Spain easily occupied Oran, Bougie, Algiers, and Tripoli, as well as several smaller ports.

Unlike Portugal, which had an economic interest in North Africa, Spain's interest in capturing North African ports was only to reduce attacks on its shipping. Spain was much more interested in exploiting the New World and in establishing its supremacy in Italy. The effort it had to expend in North Africa was an annoying diversion. As a result, the Spaniards did not bother to secure the hinterland of the Maghribi ports that they captured, forcing the coastal garrisons to be dependent on supplies from Spain, even for food. The territorial gap in the Spanish conquests—the Hafsid domain—now proved fateful. Spanish ships supplying Bougie and Tripoli had to run a gauntlet of Hafsid-sponsored corsairs in the Mediterranean.

Corsairs were at the center of a violent period of Mediterranean history. They shared characteristics with pirates and privateers. The term *pirate* is always a decidedly negative term and designates a robber in search of plunder who attacks from ships. The term *privateer* designates someone (or his ship) who, to all appearances, was a pirate, but who had an official commission (a *letter of marque*) from a government to attack ships belonging to an enemy nation. A government might find it useful to commission a privately owned and armed ship to take reprisals against another nation or, especially, to augment its navy during time of war. Although the crew members of privateers were not paid by the commissioning government, they were allowed to share in the plunder from captured vessels and were immune from prosecution by the commissioning government for their actions. The nations whose ships were attacked, of course, treated privateers as pirates. Moreover, privateers often found it difficult to give up their way of life after the termination of the letter of marque. They found it easy to segue into the life of a pirate and to become outlaws even among their own people.

Technically, a *corsair* was a privateer commissioned by a Muslim government. The Zayanids and Hafsids were among many North African and European ruling houses that commissioned privateers to enhance their naval capability. Some of the corsairs remained cooperative with their government, but others resisted attempts to control them. In the early sixteenth century, one group of corsairs established an independent base near Bougie and began making alliances with Berber tribes of the interior. The corsairs became so powerful that they threatened the security of both the Zayanids and the Hafsids. The two Muslim governments felt so vulnerable that they made alliances with Spain, their ostensible foe. In 1516, corsairs captured Algiers from Spain with the support of the town's Andalusian population, which understandably supported a vigorous war against Spain. Refugees from Andalus in Tlemcen and Tunis also led factions that opposed their own regimes due to their governments' alliances with Spain.

The unrest in the central Maghrib occurred simultaneously with the Ottoman annexation of the Mamluk Empire, 1516–1517. The Ottomans, who were concerned about the recent Spanish activity in North Africa, established contact with the corsairs of Algiers. In 1525, they placed several thousand Janissaries, numerous ships, and large amounts of cash at the disposal of the corsairs in order to harass the Spanish. The corsairs, now working as privateers of the Ottomans, turned Algiers into a de facto Ottoman naval base. The city rapidly rose from obscurity to rank with the most powerful port cities on the Mediterranean.

For some five decades, the Ottomans and their corsair allies engaged in a major confrontation with Spain for possession of North African ports. Tunis changed hands five times between 1534 and 1574. In 1541, the Spanish demonstrated how threatened they felt by Algiers by launching a massive expedition against it that was composed of 500 ships and 34,000 troops. Hernan Cortes, the recent hero in the war with the Aztecs, was an officer in the campaign. The huge force was destroyed by a storm before it reached Algiers, and the city remained the center of combined Ottoman and corsair activities against the Spanish.

Spanish-controlled Tripoli finally fell to corsairs in 1551 and became a major base for raids into Sicily and Italy. The Knights Hospitaller, however, defended Malta against a major Ottoman expedition in 1565, denying Suleyman possession of a strategic harbor and a daunting array of fortresses. Six years later, a European naval alliance destroyed the Ottoman fleet at Lepanto, in the Gulf of Corinth. Although the battle showed that the Ottomans were not invincible, the outcome settled nothing: The Ottomans replaced their fleet within two years. Perhaps the most disappointed group throughout this period was the community of Moriscos and especially those of Granada. For two years, the Granadan revolt of 1568–1570 held off the vaunted Spanish army without outside help. An Ottoman intervention during that time would have posed a lethal threat to the Spanish crown.

The far western Maghrib witnessed a contest between the Ottomans and the Sa'di dynasty of Morocco. The Sa'dis, concerned about Ottoman expansion, sent an army of 30,000 soldiers to seize Tlemcen in 1551. Tlemcen's inhabitants threw the city gates open to the Moroccans: They hated the Spanish, were disgusted with their wavering Zayanid rulers, and distrusted the Ottomans. The Ottomans, however, captured the city within a few months and chased the Sa'dis back to Fez. They repeatedly threatened to invade Morocco, and the Sa'dis were so concerned about attacks from both the Portuguese and the Ottomans that they moved their capital from Fez to the more remote Marrakesh.

After 1578, the Sa'dis could breathe more easily. In that year, the young king of Portugal resolved to destroy Islam in Morocco. He led an army across the strait, where he was joined by Muhammad, a former Sa'di ruler who had been overthrown by his uncle two years earlier. The uncle, 'Abd al-Malik, met the combined foes at al-Qasr al-Kabir, where the invaders were utterly annihilated by the skilled Sa'di musketry corps. The Portuguese king and both Sa'di rivals were killed in the fighting (as a result, the conflict is popularly known as the "Battle of the Three Kings" as well as the "Battle of Alcazar"). A brother of 'Abd al-Malik, Ahmad al-Mansur, succeeded to the throne in Marrakesh.

The Sa'di victory convinced the Ottomans and the Portuguese that the costs of further campaigns in Morocco outweighed any possible gains. The Sa'dis, having intimidated Europeans and Ottomans alike, were given free rein to build up their power. They asserted their sharifian status as an alternative to the caliphal authority of the Ottomans and carved out a realm in northwestern Africa independent of

Istanbul, Lisbon, and Madrid. With the hostile Ottomans in control of the rest of the North African coast, Ahmad al-Mansur realized that he had to base the Moroccan economy on trade between West Africa and Europe. In 1591, his army toppled the West African empire of Songhay and occupied the venerable city of Timbuktu. Gaining direct access to the gold of West Africa, the Sa'dis seemed ready to consolidate their power at the dawn of the seventeenth century.

The Regencies

The Ottomans and Spaniards finally agreed that their contest to keep each other out of North Africa was more expensive than it was worth. In 1580, they signed a truce that maintained the status quo in the Maghrib. Three years later, Spain annexed Portugal, including its remaining Moroccan ports of Ceuta, Tangier, and Mazagan. Over the next three centuries, Spain gradually relinquished all the port cities except Melilla and Ceuta, which it still rules.

Thus, during the last quarter of the sixteenth century, the bulk of the Maghrib was converted into a series of Ottoman provinces and an independent Morocco. Although local political disturbances continued to plague each region, the map of the area has remained remarkably stable for more than four centuries since then. Tripoli became the capital of a new dominion comprising Tripolitania and Fezzan. It eventually incorporated Cyrenaica, paving the way for modern Libya. The Ottomans created a new and powerful state in the central Maghrib, with its capital at the hitherto modest port of Algiers. As Algiers mushroomed in growth, Tlemcen declined to the status of a provincial town. The rise of Tripoli and Algiers left Tunis, in the middle, with a truncated version of the venerable old province of Ifriqiya.

The three Ottoman provinces of Algiers, Tunis, and Tripoli came to be known to Europeans as the Regencies. Throughout most of their history, they were confined to their coastal regions, for they faced formidable opposition among the Berber and Arab tribes of the interior. Within their coastal communities they had to balance the power of their seafaring elite of corsairs with that of their Ottoman soldiers.

The Regencies were the bases of the Barbary corsairs. Their notoriety spread throughout Europe for the next two and one-half centuries. Their violence eventually drew even the Marines of the infant United States into action on "the shores of Tripoli" during the presidency of Thomas Jefferson. The threat they posed was real enough: Between the early sixteenth century and late eighteenth century, hundreds of thousands of Europeans were captured and enslaved for service in harems or in the galleys of the corsair ships; hundreds of thousands of others were held for ransom; and huge quantities of plunder were seized from merchant ships and coastal villages.[1]

Shipping in the Mediterranean was vulnerable to both corsairs and pirates. Most of the Muslim pirates were based in the Adriatic Sea, where they competed with Christian pirates. They would sometimes attack even the Ottoman fleet. The Muslim corsairs, by contrast, were funded by the ruling elites of the Regencies. The Regencies received a portion of the plunder that the corsairs seized. Corsairs usually sailed in squadrons, some of which were as large as fifteen to twenty ships. Tunis was the least active in the corsairing enterprise, whereas Algiers was the most active. Algiers, unlike Tunis and Tripoli, had little contact with overland trade routes, and so it relied on maritime trade and corsairing for its accumulation of wealth.

The corsairs were a menace to Europeans, and the suffering they caused was immense. It is important, however, to place in historical perspective the accounts of corsairs that we find in European chronicles and literature, for the Europeans were not innocent of privateering. Three factors are worth noting. First, during the period of greatest activity by the corsairs (the late sixteenth and early seventeenth centuries), English monarchs commissioned Francis Drake and other sea captains to serve as privateers against Spanish shipping. The Dutch, French, and Spanish courts also commissioned privateers for activity against their rivals. Even the Hospitallers on the island of Malta served the same function for Christian powers as did the corsairs for the Ottomans. (Western privateering lasted into the nineteenth century. Article I, Section 8 of the United States Constitution authorizes Congress to issue letters of marque, and the Confederate States of America was the last government in the world known to do so.)

Second, the taking of captives for slavery was as common a practice among Europeans as among corsairs. Catholics and Protestants sold each other into slavery after the battles of the Reformation, and Christian-manned ships frequently captured Muslims and sold them into slavery. Third, the "Barbary" corsairs—who are usually referred to as Berbers, Arabs, or Turks (Europeans often used *Turk* as a synonym for *Muslim* during the sixteenth and seventeenth centuries)—were often renegade Christians (European Christian adventurers who made a nominal conversion to Islam in order to serve in the corsair fleets). European visitors to Algiers regularly expressed their surprise to discover that Christian renegades, primarily from Sicily and Corsica, were the most numerous group living in the town until the mid-seventeenth century. They were the "entrepreneurs" who rapidly transformed the sleepy fishing village into a thriving city whose vibrant market, luxurious suburbs, and numerous public baths made an immediate impact on all visitors.

The salient role of the renegades in the corsair fleets and among the political and economic elite of the Regencies provides an insight into conditions in the societies bordering the Mediterranean during the sixteenth century. Many among the poor of Christian Europe realized that Muslim societies offered more opportunities for social mobility than their own rigidly stratified societies provided. The great Ottoman admiral Khayr al-Din (Hayrettin)—known as Barbarossa to the Europeans—was an inspiration to many: Born to an Albanian sipahi and his Greek Orthodox wife, Barbarossa began his naval career as a corsair, but he earned a position as one of the most powerful men in the empire. Thousands of Europeans became corsairs, embarking upon careers that entailed raiding the ships and villages of their homelands. It was not unusual for them to raid their home village in order to settle personal scores with enemies. Some eventually returned home and "reconverted" to Christianity, but most did not.

Istanbul did not monitor the Regencies closely. Soon after the Ottomans acquired North Africa, the Jelali revolts provided evidence that the central government no longer had the capacity to control its provinces directly. The central authorities were compelled to focus their attention on the regions that possessed the greatest economic and strategic importance for the empire. Those areas lay around the eastern Mediterranean. By the second half of the seventeenth century, the three Regencies had all established only a very tenuous relationship with Istanbul, which suited the local elites. By 1689, the militia of Algiers was electing the leader of the Regency, and Algiers became, in effect, a military oligarchy. When, at the beginning of the eighteenth century, the political autonomy of Tunis was threatened by a military intervention from Algiers, the militia and notables of Tunis turned to one Husayn bin Ali, who reluctantly agreed to lead the resistance. His grudging involvement led to the creation of the Husaynid dynasty, which ruled Tunisia from 1705 until 1956 (although it was under French hegemony from 1881). Tripoli saw the installation of the Qaramanli dynasty, which ruled from 1711 until 1835.

Alawite Morocco

In Morocco, the Sa'dis proved to be more vulnerable than most contemporary observers had anticipated. The great Ahmad al-Mansur (1578–1603), who came to power as a result of the Battle of the Three Kings, appeared to have created a major power after he conquered Timbuktu and gained access to West African gold. With his new wealth, he constructed a palace in Marrakesh that rivaled any in the world. His government was organized on a bureaucratic basis and seemed to have overcome much of the area's endemic tribal divisiveness by possessing sharifian credentials. At his death in 1603, however, all three of his sons claimed the sharifian right to rule and contested the throne. For the next six decades, Morocco was engulfed in chaos. In addition to the civil war among Ahmad's sons, clashes took place among other sharifian leaders and Sufis, all of whom claimed the throne.

It was during this period of anarchy that the final expulsion of Moriscos from Spain took place, 1609–1614. Refugees settled all across the Maghrib and in Ottoman

FIGURE 13.2 The city walls of Rabat, Morocco, as seen from its sister city, Salé. The mouth of the Wadi Bou Regreg, which separates the two cities, became a busy staging area for corsairs after the fall of Granada. The most famous were those known as the Salé Rovers.

Fadel Senna / AFP / Getty Images.

territories, especially in Syria. Several thousand settled in Salé, next door to Rabat, on the Atlantic coast of Morocco. There they created a self-governing community of corsairs that threatened any ship that sailed the Atlantic waters in an area bounded by Gibraltar, the Madeira Islands, and the Canary Islands. They even ventured as far north as Iceland and Ireland to attack European villages and ships. Known to the British as the Salé Rovers, they recruited several notable Christian renegades.

At midcentury, a sharifian family from the region around Sijilmasa rose to prominence. Claiming descent from both the Prophet and his cousin and son-in-law 'Ali, it is known as the Alawite family. (The name signifies the family's descent from 'Ali; there is no connection with the Alawi religious groups of Syria, Turkey, and Iran.) In 1666, an Alawite named Moulay ("My Master") Rashid took control of Fez. Using that city as a base, he conquered much of northern Morocco before his death in 1672. His brother Moulay Isma'il (ruled 1672–1727) established his capital at Meknes and continued the process of unifying Morocco. Realizing the instability of an army based on tribal alliances, he relied on a slave army that was replenished by raids into West Africa. It eventually attained a strength of 150,000 men and proved capable of conquering the rest of the country. Isma'il developed a well-deserved reputation for cruelty, but his reign brought unaccustomed prosperity to Morocco.

Rashid and Isma'il were the first two rulers of the Alawite dynasty of Morocco, whose rule has lasted into the twenty-first century. Like the Sa'dis before them, they claimed legitimacy on the basis of their sharifian status and regarded themselves as caliphs with equal status to the sultan of Istanbul. Unlike the Sa'dis, they did not pursue the development of a bureaucratic apparatus to bring stability to the government. The weakness inherent in the sharifian claim was revealed at Isma'il's death, when all of his numerous sons could claim sharifian status. (Apparently, he divided his time equally between his harem and the battlefield, for he is reputed to have sired more than 1000 children.) Until the end of the nineteenth century, ambitious sons of sultans had to contest with their brothers to become the successor to their father. Having won the throne, the new sultan found that the loyalties given to his father had evaporated and that he would have to reconquer the country before he could rule it. Even then, the effective rule of the government extended only to the plains, due to fierce resistance on the part of the Berbers of the massive Atlas Mountains. Later sultans placed more and more emphasis on their function as religious leader and granted the tribes a large degree of local autonomy. They contented themselves with investing local chiefs who were chosen or supported by local notables.

The Sudan

The geographical term for the vast region lying between the Sahara and the rain forests of central Africa is the Sudan. It extends from the Red Sea and Indian Ocean in the east to the Atlantic in the west. It is not to be confused with the modern country of Sudan, which forms only a part of the eastern section of the geographical Sudan. The Sudan is divided into two major zones, the *sahel* and the *savanna*. The sahel, which in Arabic means "shore" or "coast," is the transition zone from the desert into the plains farther south. Beginning at roughly sixteen degrees latitude north of

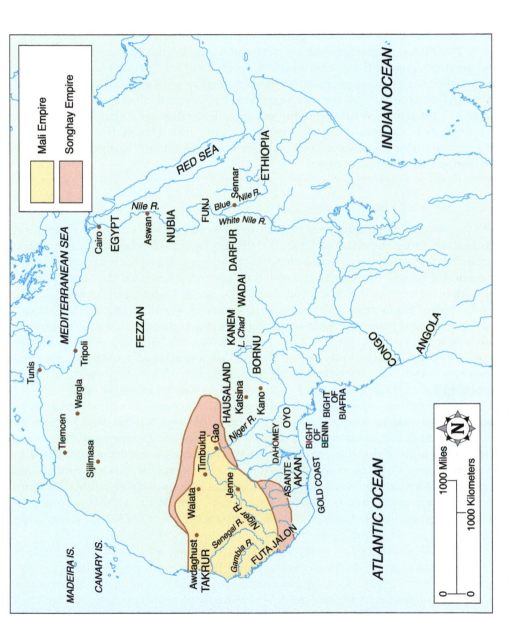

MAP 13.3 The Sudan, Fourteenth to Early Eighteenth Centuries.

the equator (on a line extending roughly from the mouth of the Senegal River on the Atlantic to where the modern boundary between the countries of Ethiopia and Sudan meets the Red Sea), the sahel is a region of scrub grass and thorny acacias. Still further south, and receiving more rainfall, is the savanna. It, in turn, comprises two major regions: The northerly one is characterized by tall grass among the acacias, whereas in the south the acacias give way to broad-leaved trees.

The Sudan ends where the tropical rain forest begins. On the Atlantic coast, the northerly edge of the rain forest is in Guinea. The forested zone sweeps eastward from there for an average width of one hundred miles, except for the region of modern Ghana, where the savanna interrupts it and extends all the way to the ocean. Islam's influence was restricted to the towns in the Sudan before the year 1400, but it eventually became the dominant religion in the area. During the period under review, two major themes dominate the history of the Sudan: Islamization and the intensification of the slave trade.

Trans-Saharan Trade

The Sahara is the largest and most extreme desert on earth. More than three thousand miles long and a thousand miles wide, it is larger than the United States. It has recorded the hottest temperature on earth (134 degrees), and some areas receive no measurable rainfall for years at a time. It is no surprise, then, that the desert posed a formidable barrier to the Arab conquests of the seventh and eighth centuries. The early Muslim zones of occupation in Africa were confined to the Mediterranean coastal plain and to the one pathway through the desert that could sustain an army— the Nile River. Even on the Nile, however, the Arabs were blocked in the vicinity of Aswan by the Christian kingdom of Nubia. Nubia remained a barrier for several centuries, with the surprising result that Islam's introduction into sub-Saharan Africa occurred through the western and central Sahara rather than up the Nile.

In Africa, the expansion of Islam was usually a result of commercial activity. Such was the case in West Africa, where commerce drew Muslim merchants from North Africa across the Sahara into the sahel and savanna. Entering the Sahara was the last act of bravado by amateurs, but savvy merchants knew when and where to cross the desert. Over the centuries, the survivors of desert crossings had contributed to a stock of life-saving knowledge regarding the location of water holes and routes that were not obliterated by shifting sand dunes. Merchants who were willing to hazard the potentially lethal heat and moon-dry landscape of the Sahara could make enormous returns on their investment.

West Africa offered a variety of products to North Africans willing to endure the hardships of a trans-Sahara crossing. From Roman times through the sixteenth century, it provided ivory, indigo, beeswax, and other commodities, but its most valuable products were salt and gold. Today, many of us monitor the inventory of sriracha and cumin in our pantry more closely than we do our salt, but as late as the nineteenth century, salt was one of the most valuable and sought-after commodities in the world. It is an essential nutrient, and a shortage of it causes an intense craving in both humans and animals. Although salt was probably never literally worth its weight in gold, it was not at all uncommon for people to rob and kill for it. It was scarce in the savanna and forest regions of Africa, but large deposits lay in the Sahara in ancient lake beds. During the late medieval period, West African entrepreneurs ran salt harvesting operations at Taghaza, halfway across the desert. The heat, wind-blown sand, and shortage of water made for brutal working conditions. No traditional building supplies were locally available, and so the buildings were made out of slabs of salt. The work was performed by slaves that were purchased from areas farther south; they had to be replaced frequently due to their high mortality rate.

The Umayyad and Abbasid dynasties of Cordoba, Damascus, and Baghdad did not have gold deposits of their own, and so they went to great lengths to obtain access to a reliable supply of the precious mineral. As a result, all three dynasties are famous among numismatists for the fine quality of their gold coins. West Africa was one of several regions that supplied gold to all three dynasties. When the European economy revived in the eleventh century, it too became dependent on West African gold. It is estimated that two-thirds of all the gold circulating in the Mediterranean area in the Middle Ages originated south of the Sahara. Prior to the eleventh century, the chief source of West African gold was the highland area between the upper tributaries of the Senegal and Niger rivers; thereafter, the main supplies came from the area now known as Ghana, but which Europeans once called the Gold Coast.

The two major routes across the Sahara were the "western," leading from Sijilmasa to Awdaghust, and the "central," leading from Tunis to the bend in the Niger River. A third route connected Tripoli, via Fezzan, to Kanem, east of Lake Chad. Still other routes connected West Africa with Egypt, but they were ephemeral due to the distance and insecurity of the various regions through which they had to pass.

The desert passage normally required about two months of travel. Resourceful merchants regarded the desert much as a sailor views the ocean: It was, indeed, a vast, empty region, but it was punctuated by a few islands (oases) where one could acquire provisions and recuperate after the rigors of travel. Given a trusty vessel (the camel) and a skilled navigator, one could make a comfortable living by transporting goods across it. Caravans from the north set out in winter because the horses that they brought to trade would not survive the summer heat. In addition to horses, Maghribi merchants also brought cargoes of dates, wheat, dried grapes, nuts, textiles, and manufactured goods of copper and silver. The camels and horses could go no farther than the Berber cities of Awdaghust, Walata, or Gao due to the danger of the tsetse fly. The cargo that was destined for southern markets was transferred to donkeys for the next leg of the trip.

The Islamization of the Western and Central Sudan

The trans-Saharan trade introduced Islam into West Africa. Its first carriers were Berber merchants from Sijilmasa and Wargla. Muslim merchants rarely acted as missionaries. Rather, their status as international merchants made them influential, and Islam acquired a certain cachet as a result. Rulers valued the merchants' literacy and often employed them as scribes at court. The merchants' contacts with agents in far-off, powerful countries made their services even more desirable. Local merchants who desired to participate in long-distance trade found that conversion to Islam facilitated their efforts, for it enabled them to socialize more freely with Muslim merchants in a wide variety of settings. Being Muslim also gave them access to Shari'a courts, where they enjoyed the benefits of numerous legal services, including the enforcement of contracts.

In towns, Muslims of all ethnic groups tended to live together so as to be near the mosque, the Qur'an school, and the legal services of the qadi. They formed the cosmopolitan, outward-looking element in the trading societies. They tended to acquire prestige and power due to their travel and correspondence, which provided them with knowledge of what was happening elsewhere. By the eleventh century, Muslim merchants played an important role in towns in the kingdom of Takrur on the lower Senegal River, the kingdom of Ghana in the sahel, Gao on the Niger River, and Kanem, east of Lake Chad. The ruler of Takrur became Muslim in the eleventh century, and the rulers of Gao and Kanem became Muslim by the twelfth century.

In the West African countryside, educated ulama were exceedingly rare, but Muslim holy men became a feature of social life by the late eleventh century. Some of the most famous were from Takrur. These men combined preaching with the teaching of rudimentary mystical practices, the making of amulets, and the treatment of disease with magico-medical procedures and applications. They proved to be as effective in their medical practice as the traditional healers, and their status in some cases was higher due to their ability to read and write. Although rural non-Muslims eagerly sought their healing and spiritual services, few converted to Islam, because traditional religious practices served their agricultural and hunting needs well.

The best-known phase of early West African Muslim history was the kingdom of Mali. In the thirteenth century, Mali's sphere of influence extended from the Atlantic in the west to Gao in the east, and from Awdaghust in the north to the gold fields of the Asante (Akan) peoples in the rain forest. More powerful than any West African dynasty that had preceded it, Mali prospered due to its agricultural resources on the Niger and its control of the gold fields. The city of Jenne (Djenne) became famous as a center of Islamic learning. Situated in the fertile "inland delta" region of the Niger River, where the Niger splits into several branches before resuming its single channel, Jenne was a prosperous and cosmopolitan city. The rulers of Mali were nominally Muslim, and they encouraged Muslim preachers who took their message eastward into Hausaland, where they introduced the rulers of Kano to Islam. As early as the second half of the thirteenth century, a ruler of Mali made the pilgrimage to Mecca, but the most famous instance of a Malian king making the hajj was that of Mansa Musa (ca. 1307–ca. 1336). When he passed through Cairo in 1324 en route to Mecca, he spent and otherwise distributed so much gold that his visit was discussed for generations afterward. Mansa Musa and his brother Mansa Sulayman (ca. 1341–1358) gained fame and respect among the Muslims of many lands for their construction of mosques and schools.

Despite its famous Muslim rulers, neither Mali nor any of the other West African states at this time was a "Muslim society," much less an "Islamic state." Mali's rulers were internationally recognized as professed Muslims and had warm relations with Muslim merchants and ulama, but visitors from North Africa or Egypt (including Ibn Battuta, who visited during the period of Mansa Sulayman's reign) were often shocked at what they considered to be the un-Islamic nature of Malian society. Even taking into consideration the visitors' ethnocentrism, it is clear that Islamic food prohibitions were ignored and that standards of modesty, especially for females, were strikingly different. Court ceremonials contained many pagan elements. In none of

FIGURE 13.3   The Jenne Mosque of Mali. The structure is made of mud brick. The primary function of the palm trunks that project from the sides is to support the workers who replaster the exterior each spring.

oversnap / iStock.

the West African societies was the Muslim population sufficiently large for Islamic law to take precedence over local custom.

Because traditional values and institutions were still dominant, Muslim rulers had to play a double role in order to maintain their power. In their dealings with other Muslim rulers and with Muslim traders, they acted as pious Muslims. When they interacted with most of their subjects, however, they carefully fulfilled their duties as divine kings. They patronized Muslim religious experts and their institutions, but they also used the services of traditional priests, even at court. Polytheistic ritual and custom were too deeply embedded in Sudanic culture to ignore or flout.

Nevertheless, Islam granted an international legitimacy that rulers coveted. Caravans brought merchants and scholars, books, commercial credit, and other tangible benefits. By 1400, it probably would have been difficult for societies in the Sudan to conduct trade with the Maghrib without employing the commercial practice of the Shari‘a. Thus, the typical Muslim ruler of West Africa from the thirteenth to the early eighteenth centuries attempted a compromise between the new culture and belief system of Islam and the ancient, persistent animism of the western Sudan.

In the 1450s, Portuguese efforts to reach the source of the gold trade began to bear fruit. When agents from Lisbon sailed up the Gambia and Senegal rivers and made direct contact with the Mali Empire, considerable commerce was redirected away from the Maghrib and toward the more accessible Atlantic coast. This diversion of commerce was among the final straws for the Marinid regime of Morocco, which fell in 1465. Meanwhile, Mali itself was coming under pressure. The city-state of Gao had broken free from Mali in the late fourteenth century, and by the mid-fifteenth century it was a growing challenge to Mali's hegemony in the area. Gao became the center of a kingdom dominated by the Songhay people. The Songhay Empire burst into prominence in the 1460s by conquering Timbuktu, which had eclipsed Jenne as the preeminent city of Islamic learning in the region. Timbuktu soon became better known outside the empire than the kingdom's political center at Gao.

The Songhay Empire destroyed Mali and became even larger than its illustrious predecessor. Under Askiya Muhammad (1493–1528) it continued to grow. Eventually, it extended from the basin of the Gambia River to Kano in Hausaland. Askiya Muhammad went beyond previous West African rulers in his patronage of Islam. Although he allowed traditional customs and practices in his court, his laws and policies were increasingly in accord with the Shari'a. His imperial venture was the most powerful and wide-ranging in sub-Saharan history before the colonial era.

Songhay, despite its dynamism, was one of the victims of the Portuguese diversion of trade to the Atlantic. Its preeminent cities, Timbuktu and Gao, were east of the new trade routes, and their markets began to dry up. Then, in 1591, Ahmad al-Mansur, the Sa'di ruler of Morocco, attacked. Morocco's own caravan cities were suffering from the rerouting of the West African trade and had lost access to the gold fields. Al-Mansur daringly sent his army across the vast desert to attack Songhay, hoping to gain control of the trade routes himself. The Songhay army outnumbered the Moroccan force by perhaps nine to one, but it was armed only with traditional weapons. Al-Mansur's musketeers, by contrast, had already demonstrated their effectiveness thirteen years earlier at the Battle of the Three Kings. The Moroccans defeated Songhay easily and captured Timbuktu. The victory gave al-Mansur access to the gold fields, enabling him to begin his monumental construction projects in Marrakesh and elsewhere.

Leo Africanus Describes Timbuktu

Al-Hasan ibn Muhammad al-Wazzan was born in Granada a few years before the principality fell to Spain. His family moved to Fez, where he became an emissary for the Wattasid ruler. In 1518, he was captured by a Spanish pirate, who presented him to Pope Leo X as a gift. Two years later, he was baptized and christened with a new, Latin, name: Leo Africanus. In 1527, Leo disappeared from the historical record. Some speculate that he remained in Europe; others think that he returned to the Maghrib.

Leo Africanus is best known for his Description of Africa, *which he wrote at the request of the Vatican. It apparently reflects his own experiences when he traveled as a diplomat for the ruler of Fez.*

The following extract is a description of Timbuktu at the time that the city was part of the Songhay Empire. The ruler whom Leo mentions was Askiya Muhammad (1493–1528), whose aversion to Jews is corroborated by other sources.

The name of this kingdom is a modern version of the name of a city that was built by a king named Mansa Sulayman in the year 610 A.H. (1213/1214 C.E.) about two miles from a branch of the Niger River. The city consists entirely of huts made of poles and mud and covered with thatched roofs. In the midst of the city stands a mosque constructed of stone and mortar by a master builder from Almeria, in Andalus. The same builder also constructed a large stone palace, which is where the king lives.

The city has numerous shops of artisans and merchants. Weavers of cotton cloth are particularly well-represented. Slave girls sell all the foodstuffs and fresh bread. The men wear fine black or blue cotton fabrics, some of which are imported from Europe by merchants from Berber territory. All the women here, except for the slaves, veil their faces.

The inhabitants of the city are quite wealthy, especially the foreigners among them. This explains why the present king has even given two of his daughters to two particularly wealthy brothers who are merchants. There are many wells with fresh, pure water. When the Niger floods, canals deliver water to the city. There is a great abundance of grain and livestock. The inhabitants consume much milk and butter, and there is much fruit. On the other hand, salt is in very short supply. It has to be brought in from Taghaza, 500 miles away. . . .

The king of Timbuktu is a mortal enemy of the Jews, which is why you will not find a single one anywhere in the kingdom. That is not all, however: If the king finds out that a Berber merchant has done business with Jews, participates with them in a trading company, or finances his business with Jewish credit, he arbitrarily confiscates all the merchant's goods. . . . He allows the victim as much gold as is required to return home.

The king provides patronage for many scholars, prayer leaders, and judges, for he esteems learned men. Many hand-written books from Barbary are sold, and sellers of books earn more from that source than from all their other goods combined. The people of Timbuktu use unrefined gold nuggets and gold coins as their standard currency, although for small purchases, they use cowries from Iran. . . .

SOURCE: The author's English translation of Dietrich Rauchenberger, *Johannes Leo der Afrikaner: Seine Beschreibung des Raumes zwischen Nil und Niger nach dem Urtext* (Wiesbaden, Germany: Harrassowitz, 1999), 275–283.

Far to the east of Mali, another early region of penetration for Islam was Kanem, on the eastern shores of Lake Chad. Its ruler was Muslim as early as the twelfth century. By 1250, several students from Kanem were studying in Cairo at al-Azhar mosque–university. In the fourteenth century, a military threat from a neighboring people forced a sizable proportion of the population of Kanem to migrate to the region southwest of Lake Chad. From then on, it was referred to as the kingdom of Bornu (Borno). Bornu reached its height of power and prestige during the period 1550–1700, when it cooperated with Tripoli to safeguard the caravan route between them. After the fall of Songhay to Morocco in 1591, Bornu was probably the most powerful state in black Africa. Culturally, its court was famous for the high standard of its legal and theological education. Militarily, it boasted a highly disciplined infantry armed with muskets and cavalry mounted on Barbary horses. The kingdom obtained the firearms and horses by trading slaves, which its raiders captured along its frontiers with the rain forests to the south.

Between Bornu and the eastern reaches of the Niger River lay Hausaland, a large region united only by a common language, Hausa. It was more isolated from the Maghrib than either Mali or Bornu, and it did not engage in regular caravan trade until the mid-fifteenth century. Hausaland was not politically unified before the nineteenth century, when it became a major regional power. Until then, it was characterized by a number of city-states that exercised influence over a radius of thirty to thirty-five miles from their city walls. The largest were Katsina and Kano. The evidence suggests that Islam first began to appear in Hausaland in the late fourteenth century. Whereas Islam entered the western Sudan by the mechanism of trade, it was introduced into Hausaland by preachers from Mali in the west and Bornu in the east. Both Katsina and Kano soon boasted rulers who, at different times, attempted to enforce the Shari'a. In each case, however, the strength of the traditional religions always doomed such efforts.

The Islamization of the Eastern Sudan

The upper (southern) Nile became progressively Arabized from the tenth century on. Nomads migrating up the river from Egypt sought additional grazing areas on the river's west bank, while miners and adventurers sought opportunities in the Eastern Desert between the river and the Red Sea. As early as the fourteenth century, Arabs arrived in the savanna region of the modern country of Sudan, at which point they began to migrate westward toward Kanem. In the fifteenth century, Christian Nubia began fragmenting from internal stresses. An age of anarchy ensued, characterized by conflicts among local warlords. Taking advantage of the vacuum of power, a people known as the Funj (Fung) moved into the general vicinity of modern Khartoum at the beginning of the sixteenth century. We know little about the origins of the Funj, but the names of their rulers make it clear that they were already at least nominally Arabized and Islamized. They quickly seized control of the Nile valley for about 300 miles in each direction from their capital at Sannar, which is about 150 miles up the Blue Nile from Khartoum. The kingdom of the Funj exercised power on the upper Nile until the mid-eighteenth century.

Farther west, nomadic groups that claimed Arab descent—but appear to have been neither Arab nor Nubian in origin—set up powerful states in Dar Fur and Wadai in the mid-seventeenth century. Funj, Dar Fur, and Wadai all boasted rulers who professed to be Muslim, and Islam gained a major foothold in the eastern Sudan by the mid-seventeenth century due to their rule. Each of the leaders adopted the honorific traditionally used for a caliph: *amir al-mu'minin*. They also held religious scholars in high esteem and honored them with grants of land. Islam in this region, however, was quite underdeveloped compared with its West African counterpart. The paucity of cities, the difficulty of communication with the greater Muslim world, and the nomadic ethos of the region created conditions similar to those of Turkic western Asia. The people of the eastern Sudan adopted certain attractive features of Islam for use within a framework of traditional religions. The essence of Islam tended to be understood as obedience to the ruler rather than doctrinal or ritual correctness. Muslims from Arab lands were usually scandalized by discovering the central role of pork and beer in the eastern Sudanese diet.

The peoples of Funj, Dar Fur, and Wadai enjoyed enhanced security due to the rise of these states, but the economic systems of all three kingdoms were based on supplying slaves to Ottoman Egypt. In return for shipping the slaves, they obtained guns, horses, and armor, which made them even more efficient in acquiring slaves. Thus, the prosperity and security of each were bought at the cost of unending misery for their neighbors to the south. The areas that we know today as northern Cameroon, southern Chad, and the Central African Republic were targets of continual slave raids during the sixteenth, seventeenth, and eighteenth centuries.

The Intensification of the Slave Trade

Prior to the sixteenth century, the slave trade in West Africa was only one element of a thriving export trade that included gold, salt, and other goods. Slavery, nevertheless, was common. The typical slave had lost his or her status as a free person due to having become a war captive. Slavery was also a common punishment meted out by judicial tribunals. The continuous wars waged by such kingdoms as Mali and Songhay produced tens of thousands of slaves who were sold in local markets. The treatment of slaves in West Africa varied. In many places, they became members of the households that acquired them, were given fictive family relationships, could marry nonslave members of the community, and might even inherit some of the family's assets. On the other hand, they might work in gold mines or on royal estates, where they endured brutal treatment; those who worked in the salt fields experienced the agonies of hell on earth.

Many West African war captives were sold to merchants for transport to the sahel or North Africa. In the sahel, and even in the desert, thousands of slaves were used to till the oases, mine salt, herd animals, and smelt copper. An even larger demand for slaves existed in the Mediterranean basin. As a result, slaves were among the "commodities" exchanged in the trans-Saharan trade. Most of the slaves who made the painful (and frequently fatal) two-month crossing of the Sahara were women and children. They were destined to become domestic servants or concubines. Reliable statistics related to the slave trade are impossible to obtain for any historical period, but no one disputes the assumption that thousands of slaves made the annual journey across the Sahara.

The dynamics of the slave trade began to change in the mid-fifteenth century with the arrival of the Portuguese off the Atlantic coast of Africa. As the Portuguese explored in the vicinity of the Gambia River, they realized that they were nearing the sources of the famed West African gold mines. As in Morocco, they attempted to gain what they wanted by force, but they had to change tactics due to the high death rate they suffered from malaria and yellow fever. They soon abandoned trying to penetrate the interior. Instead, they began to establish trading posts along the Atlantic coast. Eventually, these trading posts and forts dotted the coast for hundreds of miles. Their primary focus was the Gold Coast (modern Ghana). The Portuguese traded European manufactured goods for gold, but they also became middlemen for trade among the various river deltas. The regional trade in slaves proved to be so lucrative that some traders who had gone in search of gold switched to full-time slave trading. In the sixteenth century, Dutch, English, Danish, and French traders arrived at the coastal slave markets. Many of them entered the regional slave trade, raising the demand for slaves.

Until the sixteenth century, coastal societies in West Africa had lagged a century or two behind the interior kingdoms of the western Sudan in the acquisition of technology and commodities from the Mediterranean. Now, however, maritime commerce conferred new wealth upon them, enabling them to purchase modern weapons and other European goods. The increasing demand for slaves made slave raiding an irresistible temptation for them. With the new gunpowder weapons, the coastal towns were able to overwhelm the peoples of the rain forests and southern savanna. Their large-scale raiding coincided with the emergence of Songhay and the Hausaland city-states, the period of Bornu's greatest strength, and the rise of Wadai, Dar Fur, and the Funj kingdom. All of these Muslim states engaged in slave raiding and the sale of war captives. Like the coastal towns, the interior Muslim states were becoming increasingly militarized. Their contacts with Ottoman merchants in Tunis, Tripoli, and Egypt provided them with Barbary horses, padded armor, and modern weapons. Their primary target populations for slave raids were precisely the same as those of raiders from the coastal cities. They attacked from the north while the coastal raiders attacked from the south. Thus, most victims of the slave trade came from the southern savanna and rain forests.

The demand for slaves increased even more at the beginning of the seventeenth century when plantation colonies were established in the western hemisphere. Soon, the volume of the trans-Atlantic slave trade drew even with its trans-Saharan counterpart, which by that time exported an annual average of 10,000 slaves. By the end of the seventeenth century, some 30,000–50,000 slaves were making the infamous "Middle Passage" across the Atlantic each year. By 1750, the annual volume was 70,000. In stark contrast to the trans-Saharan trade, the trans-Atlantic trade was primarily composed of adult or adolescent males, destined to work in the difficult conditions of the sugar cane, indigo, or rice plantations.

Slave markets appeared in ports all the way from Senegal to Angola. Four areas supplied the bulk of slaves. The busiest region extended from Gabon to Angola. Its ports supplied at least one-third of the slaves for the trans-Atlantic trade. Because Portugal dominated this stretch of the coast, most slaves from here were shipped to Brazil. The Bight of Benin—off the coast of modern Togo, Benin, and western Nigeria—was second only to the Congo as a source of slaves. It became known as the Slave Coast. The Bight of Biafra—off the coast of modern Cameroon and eastern Nigeria—was already a well-developed trading area before the arrival of the Europeans. It was not a major slave zone until after 1650, but in the eighteenth century it matched Benin, shipping more than one million slaves across the Atlantic. The Gold Coast, too, was late entering the slave trade. As late as 1700, its gold exports were greater in value than the entire Atlantic slave trade; by 1730, however, it was importing gold and paying for it by exporting slaves.

Estimates of the number of Africans who suffered the brutal experience range widely, but most historians in recent years agree that some twelve million enslaved Africans crossed the Atlantic during the period 1525–1866. About ninety-five percent of them were bound for South America and the Caribbean; some five percent went to North America. Some two-thirds of the slaves were West Africans. Of these, the vast majority were from the rain forest and southern savanna. Some of the regions in these two areas suffered extensive depopulation, intense poverty, and misery. The coastal communities, by contrast, were almost immune from losses to the slave trade. They enjoyed considerable population increase and political development as a result of the Atlantic slave trade.

The Muslim states of the northern savanna engaged in slave raiding, but they also lost some of their population to the slave trade, a fact that accounts for the phenomenon of Muslim slaves in the English colonies of North America. During the seventeenth and eighteenth centuries, many of the Muslim states were in an almost constant state of warfare. The Hausa city-states quarreled, Muslim rulers of Senegambia (the region embracing the basins of the Senegal and Gambia rivers) contested for supremacy, and non-Muslim states such as the Asante kingdom, Oyo, and Dahomey began to expand at the expense of their neighbors. These wars produced large numbers of captives—Muslim and non-Muslim—and led to a spectacular increase in the number of slaves available for domestic and export markets.

Islam in the Sudan

Before the eighteenth century, the Islamization of the Sudan made slow progress. Islam was more deeply rooted in the western Sudan than in the eastern section. In West Africa, it was characteristically an urban religion, associated with towns on long-distance trade routes. Commerce and artisanry provided the economic basis for urban Muslim communities that were able to support a body of scholars dedicated to the study and implementation of the Shari'a. Jenne on the Niger became the primary center of Islamic learning in the fourteenth and fifteenth centuries, but by the fifteenth century Timbuktu began to surpass it. Its Sankore Mosque, founded in the late fourteenth century, became the foremost institution of Islamic learning in the Sudan. During the second half of the sixteenth century, it reached the height of its influence when it offered the teaching of both Shafi'i and Maliki law. The quality of its scholarship combined with the diversity of opinions offered granted it a higher level of prestige than any of the madrasas in the Maghrib, which taught only Maliki law.

The fall of Songhay to Morocco in 1591 was a setback in some ways to West African urban Islam. The era of great indigenous empires was over. Never again would West Africa experience a mighty ruler who could patronize Islamic scholarship and architecture on the scale that Mansa Musa or Askiya Muhammad had. Small states replaced the empires. Although they still engaged in the trans-Saharan trade, their markets were smaller. As the states became more insular and provincial, their rulers were less concerned than before to conform to Islamic values. In general, the ulama found it expedient to overlook the corruption and elements of un-Islamic practice that were characteristic of the regimes. They depended on the patronage of the rulers, and they did not risk offending them.

Even though the urban Muslim community was losing its vitality, Islam and literacy began to spread among the rural population in the seventeenth century. A major reason for that development was the appearance in the region from Senegambia to Hausaland of rural enclaves in which religious scholars studied the Qur'an, Hadith, and law. They served as nodes of literacy, which began to spread throughout rural West Africa for the first time. The communities in Hausaland were the most notable. They were founded by the Fulbe (Fulani) ethnic group, which had

FIGURE 13.4 The Sankore Mosque in Timbuktu, a major seat of Islamic learning by the sixteenth century.

oversnap / iStock.

migrated into the region from the upper tributaries of the Senegal during the fifteenth century. They became respected for their agricultural success, excellent horsemanship, martial prowess, and Islamic scholarship. The increasing numbers of slaves being marketed in West Africa caused prices to fall, enabling the Fulbe to buy them cheaply and have them work the farms while they studied. Several of these rural settlements developed into respected seats of learning. They often maintained a chilly relationship with nearby cities or towns, precisely because they regarded the urban areas (and their ulama) to be centers of vice.

By the dawn of the eighteenth century, the penetration of the rural areas of West Africa by religious communities such as these was beginning to have a noticeable impact on social relations. Peasants and pastoralists alike began interpreting their exploitation at the hands of rural landlords and urban-based rulers in terms of a violation of God's norms of justice. They considered the practice of Islam in the cities to be a debased form of the religion. The dynamic expression of Islam had shifted from the cities to rural strongholds.

In 1700, a protest movement began in what is now modern Guinea that foreshadowed fateful events in West Africa decades later. In Futa Jalon, a mountainous area in eastern Guinea that serves as sources for the Gambia, Senegal, and Niger rivers, prosperous Fulbe cattle herders sought relief from taxation and the threat of confiscation of their property by the Mandinka-speaking landowners of the region. They also demanded the freedom to establish mosques and schools. They expressed their grievances in Islamic and ethnic terms. For many years, their dissatisfaction was expressed primarily in sermons, but in 1725, they took military action and declared a jihad against their masters. By 1750, the Fulbe had overcome their rivals and they dominated the state. Their successful jihad would serve as a model for later reformers who would utterly transform West Africa in the nineteenth century.

Conclusion

As late as the thirteenth century, the Strait of Gibraltar served as a bridge between Europe and Africa and fostered cross-cultural exchanges. By the early seventeenth century, it had become instead a cultural barrier between Christian and Muslim societies. The stunning success of the Reconquista during 1236–1248 reduced Andalus to a single principality, the fall of Granada in 1492 ended the last independent Muslim state in the Iberian Peninsula, and the ethnic cleansing of Spain's Muslims between 1609 and 1614 destroyed the last remnants of Muslim society there.

Muslim culture on both sides of the Strait had been among the most creative in the world during the eleventh and twelfth centuries, but in the thirteenth century, it suffered a precipitous decline. Mudejars in the Iberian Peninsula struggled even to keep a tradition of learning alive until they were forcibly ejected. In the Maghrib, work in the sciences practically disappeared. Even the fields of jurisprudence and Sufi thought evolved separately from the currents in the rest of the Muslim world. The Maghrib had become isolated from its previous sources of inspiration. The threat of corsairs limited the number of European ships that entered Maghribi ports, and Maghribi merchants limited their own business activities to routes close to home. The rulers of the Regencies, who might have provided patronage for cultural production, were often from the same social background as their corsairs or Janissaries. They did not share the education and refinement characteristic of the Maghribi ruling elites of previous generations.

While Muslim societies in the Iberian Peninsula and the Maghrib were struggling or even disappearing, their counterparts in the Sudan were experiencing a period of dynamic growth. By the fifteenth century, several West African cities had become centers of Islamic learning. Timbuktu, in fact, developed into one of the greatest centers of scholarship in the Muslim world. In the seventeenth century, Islam ceased to be an exclusively urban phenomenon in West Africa and began to penetrate large areas of rural West Africa between Senegambia and Hausaland. It also expanded all along the sub-Saharan savanna. By that time, Muslim-ruled states formed a continuous line from the Atlantic to the Red Sea.

Islam entered the savanna peacefully as the faith of merchants. For several centuries, it was primarily the religion of a merchant class that valued stability. By the middle of the eighteenth century, however, the religion's themes of justice and righteousness had been appropriated by rural groups in West Africa that sought to effect a major transformation of the existing social, political, and moral order. The region was about to witness a series of wars that combined religious fervor and a zeal for plunder in a manner that had not been seen in the Muslim world for centuries.

NOTES

1 Recent research suggests that "between 1530 and 1780 there were almost certainly a million and quite possibly as many as a million and a quarter white, European Christians enslaved by the Muslims of the Barbary Coast." See Robert C. Davis, *Christian Slaves, Muslim Masters: White Slavery in the Mediterranean, the Barbary Coast, and Italy, 1500–1800* (Basingstoke, U.K., and New York: Palgrave Macmillan, 2003), 23.

FURTHER READING

The Iberian Peninsula

Barcia, J.R., ed. *Américo Castro and the Meaning of Spanish Civilization*. Berkeley: University of California Press, 1976.

Boswell, John. *The Royal Treasure: Muslim Communities Under the Crown of Aragon in the Fourteenth Century*. New Haven, Connecticut: Yale University Press, 1977.

Burns, Robert J. *Medieval Colonialism: Postcrusade Exploitation of Islamic Valencia*. Princeton, New Jersey: Princeton University Press, 1975.

Chejne, Anwar. *Islam and the West: The Moriscos*. Albany: State University of New York Press, 1983.

Elliott, J.H. *Imperial Spain: 1469–1716*. New York: The New American Library, 1963.

Harvey, L.P. *Islamic Spain, 1250–1500*. Chicago: University of Chicago Press, 1990.

———. *Muslims in Spain, 1500–1614*. Chicago and London: University of Chicago Press, 2005.

Perry, Mary Elizabeth. *The Handless Maiden: Moriscos and the Politics of Religion in Early Modern Spain*. Princeton, New Jersey, and Oxford, U.K.: Princeton University Press, 2005.

The Maghrib

Abun-Nasr. *A History of the Maghrib*, 3d ed. Cambridge, U.K.: Cambridge University Press, 1987.

Brett, Michael and Elizabeth Fentress. *The Berbers*. Oxford, U.K., and Cambridge, Massachusetts: Blackwell, 1996.

Cook, Weston F. *The Hundred Years War for Morocco: Gunpowder and the Military Revolution in the Early Modern Muslim World*. Boulder, Colorado: Westview Press, 1994.

Cornell, Vincent J. *Realm of the Saint: Power and Authority in Moroccan Sufism*. Austin: University of Texas Press, 1998.

Davis, Natalie Zemon. *Trickster Travels: A Sixteenth-Century Muslim Between Worlds*. New York: Hill and Wang, 2006.

Davis, Robert C. *Christian Slaves, Muslims Masters: White Slavery in the Mediterranean, the Barbary Coast, and Italy, 1500–1800*. Houndmills, U.K., and New York: Palgrave Macmillan, 2003.

Hess, Andrew. *The Forgotten Frontier: A History of the Sixteenth-Century Ibero-African Frontier*. Chicago: University of Chicago Press, 1978.

Julien, Charles-Andre. *History of North Africa*. Translated by John Petrie. New York: Praeger, 1970.

Laroui, Abdallah. *The History of the Maghrib: An Interpretive Essay*. Translated by Ralph Manheim. Princeton, New Jersey: Princeton University Press, 1977.

Oliver, Roland, and Anthony Atmore, eds. *The African Middle Ages, 1400–1800*. Cambridge, U.K., and New York: Cambridge University Press, 1981.

The Sudan

Ajaye, J.F.A., and Michael Crowder, eds. *History of West Africa*, 2d ed. Vol. 1. New York: Columbia University Press, 1976.

Diouf, Sylviane A. *Servants of Allah: African Muslims Enslaved in the Americas.* New York and London: New York University Press, 1998.

Hunwick, John, and Eve Troutt Powell, eds. *The African Diaspora in the Mediterranean Lands of Islam.* Princeton, New Jersey: Marcus Wiener Publishers, 2002.

Inikori, J.E., ed. *Forced Migration: The Impact of the Export Slave Trade on African Societies.* New York: Africana Publishing Company, 1982.

Insoll, Timothy. *The Archaeology of Sub-Saharan Africa.* Cambridge, U.K., and New York: Cambridge University Press, 2003.

July, Robert W. *Precolonial Africa.* New York: Charles Scribner's Sons, 1975.

Klein, Herbert S. *The Atlantic Slave Trade.* Cambridge, U.K.: Cambridge University Press, 1999.

Levtzion, Nehemiah, and Ronald Lee Pouwels, eds. *The History of Islam in Africa.* Athens, Ohio: Ohio University Press; Oxford, U.K.: James Currey; Cape Town, South Africa: David Philip, 2000.

Manning, Patrick. *Slavery and African Life: Occidental, Oriental, and African Slave Trades.* Cambridge, U.K., and New York: Cambridge University Press, 1990.

Oliver, Roland, and Anthony Atmore, eds. *The African Middle Ages, 1400–1800.* Cambridge, U.K., and New York: Cambridge University Press, 1981.

CHAPTER 14

Central Asia and Iran

Central Asia and Iran formed the core region of Timur's empire. Long-distance trade routes linked them together as far back as history can record. They also shared elements of the Persian cultural tradition from at least as early as the Achaemenid Empire of the sixth century B.C.E. Within three centuries of the introduction of Islam, Central Asia and Iran became the most creative and productive region in the Muslim world for philosophy, mathematics, theology, Qur'anic exegesis, Sufi theory, linguistic studies, and art. As neighbors, they suffered equally during the numerous invasions and wars of the period that extended from the eleventh to the fourteenth centuries.

For three centuries after Timur, Central Asia and Iran once again played major roles in the economic and cultural life of the Muslim world. The ethnic and religious transformations in this region are among the most important developments in Muslim history during the period we are considering. After a spectacular revival of their fortunes, however, both areas began to experience a decline in wealth and security by the late seventeenth century. By the end of the eighteenth century, the economy, political structure, and cultural life of Central Asia and Iran had suffered catastrophic collapse.

Central Asia

The term *Central Asia* refers to a region surrounded by Iran, Russia, South Asia, and the populous regions of China. For the purposes of this book, *Central Asia* denotes the areas now occupied by Kazakhstan, Uzbekistan, Turkmenistan, Kyrgyzstan, Tajikistan, China's Xinjiang province, and the portion of Afghanistan that lies north of the Hindu Kush mountain range. Although the climate is similar throughout Central Asia—hot in summer, cold in winter, and little rainfall—nothing about its topographical features would lead a geographer to define it as a natural region. It has an identity for a negative reason rather than a positive one: For much of history it lay outside the effective control of the empires in Iran, India, China, and Russia that bordered it. Throughout

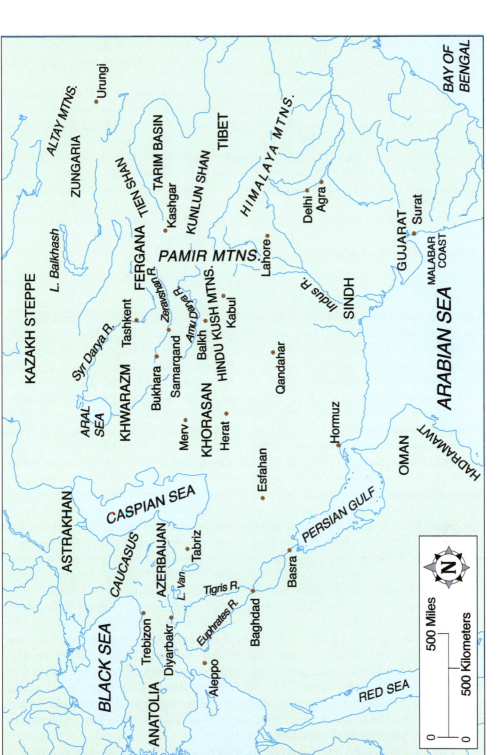

MAP 14.1 Central Asia and Southwest Asia.

the centuries, the bulk of Central Asia's population was concentrated in the valleys of the Syr Darya, Amu Darya, and Zeravshan rivers. Agriculture was highly productive and commerce thrived. Away from the river valleys, pastoralists grazed their animals on such vegetation as they could find.

Central Asia's climate, topography, and remoteness from more famous empires in the past might suggest that Central Asia has always been a peripheral region. In fact, its location at the interstices of several large empires meant that it was at the crossroads of them all. Fed by oasis agriculture and situated on major long-distance trade routes that connected China with the Mediterranean and India with Russia, Central Asia attracted people from various cultures who became familiar with religions, languages, technologies, and arts different from their own. It became the locus for the diffusion of many elements of the various civilizations along its caravan roads, and it reaped the benefits of being an entrepôt for Eurasian trade. Under the Timurids and Uzbeks, its major cities were among the most beautiful and cosmopolitan in the world.

The Timurids

When Timur died in 1405, his four sons followed the Turkic custom of fighting each other to determine his successor. In 1407, the youngest, Shah Rukh (1407–1447), seized power in Herat. During the next two years, he secured Khorasan, Transoxiana, Khwarazm, and Fergana (on the upper Syr Darya River). Shah Rukh fought furiously to gain control of his father's empire, but his attempts to restore Timurid rule to Azerbaijan, western Iran, and Iraq were frustrated by the Turkic group known as the Black Sheep (Qara-Quyunlu). The Black Sheep had established themselves in Azerbaijan in the middle of the fourteenth century, but Timur's invasion had scattered them. In 1406, only a year after Timur's death, they regained Tabriz and proved too powerful for Shah Rukh to subdue. As a result, Shah Rukh relied upon an old ally of his father—the Turks of the White Sheep (Aq-Quyunlu) clans, who had long been established at Diyarbakr in eastern Anatolia—to harass the Black Sheep and keep them from posing a threat to Timurid positions in central Iran.

Shah Rukh and his descendants consciously cultivated their links to Timur and the Mongol legacy. The Mongol mystique conferred great legitimacy among populations that had experienced its power during the previous two centuries. Even most of Shah Rukh's military commanders were descendants of Timur's Chaghatid amirs. Shah Rukh himself was a skilled warrior, but he had no intention of emulating Timur's career of ceaseless military campaigns. He developed a reputation as a pious Muslim and a ruler who was concerned to improve the quality of urban life. He established his capital at Herat and granted to his seventeen-year-old son Ulugh Bey the city of Samarqand to rule. For almost four decades, Shah Rukh ruled over Khorasan and left Transoxiana practically autonomous under Ulugh Bey's direction. He also exercised power in Delhi, which his father Timur had almost destroyed in 1398. A new dynasty, the Sayyids, replaced the Tughluqs of Delhi in 1413, but its members were careful to defer to Timur's successor. They sent tribute to Herat and obeyed all orders that Shah Rukh issued to them.

Jointly, Shah Rukh and Ulugh Bey became as famous for their patronage of the arts and sciences as Timur is for his brutal conquests. In the fifteenth century,

Herat, Samarqand, Bukhara, and Balkh (near modern Mazar-i Sharif) were among the most sophisticated cities in the world. Only a handful of Chinese cities could compete with them in sheer cultural brilliance: No European city could yet compare with them, and Cairo and Damascus had declined in creativity by the fifteenth century. The major Central Asian cities benefitted from their location at the juncture of important long-distance trade routes and were centers for the production of high-quality goods in the silk, cotton, leather, rug, jewelry, woodcarving, metal, and paper industries. The most prominent during the fifteenth century was Herat. Its scholars made significant contributions in mathematics and medicine, and its calligraphers, painters, and manuscript illuminators won a reputation as the finest in the Muslim world. The city's school of Persian miniaturists became the standard for all subsequent work in the genre. The greatest of all the Timurid miniaturists was the fifteenth- and sixteenth-century painter Bihzad. Herat was also the home of two of the most famous poets of the age. Jami (1414–1492) wrote in Persian, and Nava'i (1441–1501) was the greatest figure in the emergence of Turki, or Chaghatay, as a literary language.

Under Ulugh Beg (1411–1449), the major cities of Transoxiana competed with Herat for cultural preeminence. Bukhara and Samarqand became more noted for architecture than for painting and for science and mathematics than for literature. In contrast to his dour father, Ulugh Beg took pleasure in the talents of his court musicians and singers. He dabbled in philosophy and was a competent astronomer and mathematician. He ordered the construction of a large observatory in Samarqand and invited the most prominent astronomers and mathematicians to it. Because Maragha had been abandoned upon the collapse of the Il-khanate, Timurid Samarqand was the site of the most advanced astronomical and mathematical research in the world. Ulugh and his scientific team developed the famous *Zij-i Gurgani*, which contained a catalog of visible stars together with tables of the planets and calendar calculations. It was translated into Latin in the mid-seventeenth century and was used as far away as England.

Upon Shah Rukh's death in 1447, Ulugh Beg consolidated the rule of Herat and Balkh with that of Transoxiana, but his own son murdered him two years later. This act of patricide provoked a war among the Timurid princes. By 1451, Abu Sa'id, a nephew of Ulugh Beg, consolidated power over the cities that Ulugh Beg had united just before his death. Meanwhile, the Black Sheep and White Sheep began an intense competition with each other to control Azerbaijan, eastern Anatolia, Iraq, and western Iran. The White Sheep, under the leadership of Uzun Hasan (r. 1453–1478), won the contest of the two Turkmen groups in 1467. They then began expanding eastward at the expense of their former allies, the Timurids. In 1469, Abu Sa'id led an army to Azerbaijan to suppress the White Sheep, but the latter killed him and utterly routed his army.

Uzun Hasan now controlled the entire region from eastern Anatolia to Khorasan. He actively sought alliances with the Venetians as well as with the Christian rulers of Trebizon, who were descendants of the dynasty that ruled the Byzantine Empire during the First Crusade. Uzun's marriage in 1458 to Theodora Komnena (better known as Despina), the daughter of the emperor of Trebizon, committed him to defend Trebizon against the Ottomans. As we saw in the discussion of the career of Sultan Mehmet II, Uzun challenged Mehmet for supremacy in Anatolia in

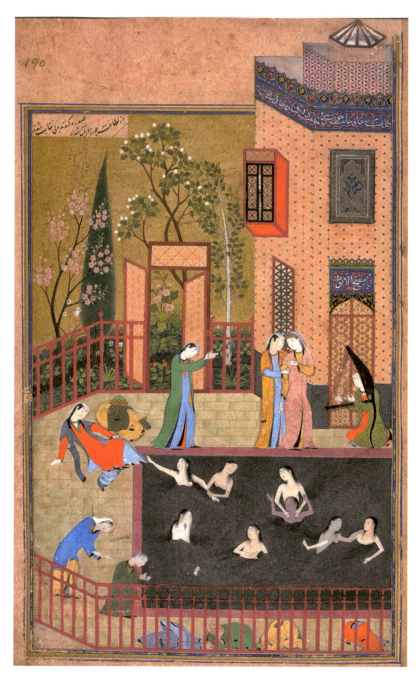

FIGURE 14.1 *Bahram Gur Observing Frolicking Women*, by Bihzad (ca. 1460–1525). Bihzad, one of the most outstanding of the Timurid painters, produced this illustration for an edition of the *Khamse* by Nizami, a great twelfth-century Persian poet. It reveals vividly that painters were not limited to religious themes. Note Bahram Gur's eye, just visible between the shutters on the second floor, sneaking a peek at the women who are bathing.

1473 but lost decisively. The White Sheep remained a regional power for three more decades, but they never again challenged the Ottomans.

Abu Sa'id's death in 1469 brought an end to the unity of Timurid rule. From that point on, the Timurid princes who governed the major cities of Central Asia jealously guarded their independence. The former empire became divided into tiny, weak principalities. The major Timurid cities were mutually hostile, held by relatives who feuded with each other. A century after Timur died, his descendants had become so divided and militarily weak that no one was surprised when an outside force saw an opportunity to pick them off one by one. During the first decade of the sixteenth century, Uzbeks began moving into Transoxiana and discovered that no Timurid could stand up to them without outside help. They began a new era in Central Asian history.

The Uzbek Khanate

The origin of the Uzbeks is unclear. Until recently, most scholars thought that they were the result of a schism within the Golden Horde; the dominant strain in the historiography of the subject now interprets their arrival on the Syr Darya as a southward migration of Mongols from their homeland in Siberia. Soon after settling

FIGURE 14.2 The Registan Square, in Samarqand. The central space is framed by three madrasas. The Ulugh Bey Madrasa, whose courtyard is visible in the foreground, was built by its namesake, the Timurid ruler, during 1417–1420. The Sher-Dor (1618–1636) and Tilya-Kori (1646–1660) madrasas, at the left and top right, respectively, were built during the Uzbek period.

© Aga Khan Trust for Culture-Aga Khan Award for Architecture / Ram Rahman (photographer).

on the Syr Darya, they seem to have suffered a secession movement, and the breakaway group came to be known as the Kazakhs. The origin of the Kazakhs, however, is as uncertain as that of the Uzbeks. What most scholars agree on is that both groups traced their lineage back to Chinggis Khan, both were Turkicized Mongols, and that, whereas the Uzbeks settled along the lower Syr Darya, the Kazakhs moved eastward into northern Moghulistan, a region that came to be known as Zungaria.

Soon after their arrival on the frontier with Transoxiana, the Uzbeks inflicted a major defeat on Ulugh Bey. They might well have conquered his domains had they not quarreled among themselves and become disorganized for several decades. Finally, in 1501, the Uzbek leader Muhammad Shaybani took advantage of a favorable conjunction of events: He had unified most of the Uzbek clans, and Ulugh Bey's successors were quarreling among themselves. Shaybani crossed the Syr Darya and attacked. He quickly seized Samarqand, and, over the next several years, he systematically conquered all of Transoxiana. He also took over much of Khorasan, including Herat.

Despite the ease with which Shaybani dispatched the various Timurid rulers, his ambitions were foiled by a twist of fate. His own conquests took place simultaneously with the meteoric career of Shah Isma'il of Iran, who created the Safavid Empire. Isma'il began conquering western Iran in 1501, the same year that Shaybani began his conquest of Transoxiana. Isma'il arrived in Khorasan in 1510 with the intention of annexing it. At Merv, the Safavid army defeated the Uzbeks, and Shaybani was killed in the fighting. Isma'il went on to capture Herat. Then, hoping to drive the Uzbeks out of Transoxiana while they were still in shock over Shaybani's death, he offered an alliance with the sole surviving Timurid ruler, Babur of Fergana. Isma'il made the offer contingent upon Babur's conversion to Shi'ism. Babur was a Sunni who was deeply devoted to the Naqshbandi Sufi order, but he accepted the terms as a matter of political expediency. A joint Timurid–Safavid campaign defeated the demoralized Uzbeks at Samarqand.

Babur ruled Transoxiana for two years, but his alliance with Isma'il turned out to be a Faustian bargain. He fulfilled his agreement with Isma'il by minting coins inscribed with the names of the Shi'ite Imams and ordering that sermons in the mosques be given in the name of Isma'il. The Sunnis of Transoxiana, however, suspected that worse was yet to come. They knew that Isma'il had forced Sunnis in Iran to convert to Shi'ism, and they feared that they would soon be compelled to do so as well. They protested violently against the policies. Important factions in Bukhara and Samarqand allied themselves with the Sunni Uzbeks, who attacked and forced Babur to flee to Kabul. The last of the Timurid rulers was now in exile south of the Hindu Kush.

The Uzbeks had regained Transoxiana from the Timurids, but they had lost Khorasan to the Safavids. They also lost the chance for a unified leadership when the charismatic Shaybani was killed. For the next seven decades, Uzbek clan leaders were content to remain in a loose confederation rather than see one of their peers become more powerful than the others. They were usually organized on the basis of confederations of nomadic clans, and the four or five most powerful clans established bases in cities. This was different from the tradition of the Horde, which ruled its tributary cities from rural encampments. The clans occasionally united in military expeditions to try to recover Herat and Merv from the Safavids, but they succeeded only in sacking Herat twice before retreating; their actual accomplishment was only to devastate the regions around those cities.

In 1582, a descendant of Muhammad Shaybani named 'Abd Allah Khan united the Uzbeks again by forcing fellow clan leaders to submit to him. As a result, he was able to field an army with a more unified command structure than any other Uzbek force since the time of Shaybani himself. With it, he took advantage of turmoil within the Safavid empire and seized Khorasan in 1588. The Shaybanid period (1582–1598) also witnessed the extension of Uzbek power into the Tarim Basin and the central Kazakh steppe. Soon after 'Abd Allah's death in 1598, a rival clan of the Shaybanids, known as the Astrakhanids, seized power. For several decades, they were organized into a confederation of two sub-khanates, one based at Bukhara and the other at Balkh. During the second half of the seventeenth century, the khanate was unified under a single Astrakhanid ruler who lived in Bukhara, but the clans still maintained a large degree of autonomy.

Despite the pastoral basis of the Uzbeks, the elites made great efforts to encourage the agricultural and commercial sectors of the economy. In order to promote wealth, they invested great sums in irrigation projects along the major rivers. They also facilitated long-distance trade by building new caravanserais and bridges. The Uzbeks' single greatest source of foreign earnings was the sale of horses. Central Asian horses were highly valued as far away as China and Russia, but their biggest market was India. Because of India's relative lack of good grazing pastures, it could not breed enough horses to keep the huge cavalry forces of its various rulers supplied. As a result, the trade in horses between South Asia and Central Asia was a major theme in Asian economic history until the late nineteenth century.

The cities of Transoxiana continued to flourish for more than a century and a half under the Uzbek khanates. Like the Timurids, the Uzbeks patronized the arts, although there was a perceptible change in the nature of the patronage. Due to the growing influence of the Naqshbandi Sufi order on Uzbek rulers, the scientific and mathematical legacy inherited from the Timurid era was neglected at the expense of religious endowments. Because the Naqshbandiya were centered at Bukhara, that city soon gained preeminence over the others. Its libraries and artisans' shops were widely known, attracting scholars and potential buyers of fine art. Samarqand, Balkh, and Tashkent also thrived, enjoying the prestige and benefits of monumental mosques and madrasas. The most famous architectural legacy of this period is the Registan of Samarqand, a triad of madrasas facing a large square. The oldest of the three monuments was commissioned by the Timurid Ulugh Bey, whereas the other two were built under the Astrakhanid dynasty between 1618 and 1660.

The flourishing life of the arts in the cities of Transoxiana stood in stark contrast to the fate of the cities of Khorasan. The numerous Uzbek campaigns of the sixteenth century against Herat, Merv, and other cities in Khorasan progressively impoverished the region. Herat suffered the greatest decline. The most splendid of the Timurid cities, it fell first to the Uzbeks and then to the Safavids in 1510. In 1522, the greatest of the city's painters moved to the Safavid capital of Tabriz. Due to Herat's location in the extreme eastern part of the Safavid Empire, it was vulnerable to continuing Uzbek attacks, and it gradually declined in importance during the sixteenth century.

During the second half of the seventeenth century, the wealth of Transoxiana began to shrink. The most tangible evidence of this development lay in the fields of architecture, painting, ceramics, and manuscript illumination, which experienced a dramatic decline in the production of noteworthy objects. More ominously for the ruling clans, independent Uzbek warlords began emerging in the horse-breeding centers of what is now northern Afghanistan, a symptom of the weakening of the power of the khan to control them. Much is obscure about the history of seventeenth- and eighteenth-century Central Asia, but it appears that the beginning of this economic decline was due in part to the global seventeenth-century economic crisis, which caused a slump in the trade in luxury goods. The economic slowdown did not persist, but when it ended, the volume of luxury goods traded through Central Asia had declined. By the late seventeenth century, the newly developed maritime routes dominated by Europeans had begun carrying more and more of the valuable luxury trade from Asia to Europe.

Market activity in Central Asian cities did not die. The east–west trade did not dry up completely, and the north–south trade through Transoxiana may even have increased. The Russians, who had long coveted the eastern goods that ended up in Astrakhan and Kazan, took over those cities of the old Golden Horde in the 1550s and established direct trading links with the Uzbeks and with commercial centers in India. The subsequent increase in the north–south trade, however, did not compensate the cities of Transoxiana for the decline in the profits of the east–west trade, for the north–south trade was in basic commodities rather than luxury goods and therefore was not as profitable as the old trade pattern had been. Thus, during the second half of the seventeenth century, Central Asia still appeared to be a bustling trading center, but its wealth was slowly declining due to the changed nature of the goods that passed through its markets.[1]

By the early eighteenth century, the Uzbek khans of Bukhara and Balkh ruled in name only. Warlords competed with each other over declining resources, and old alliances fragmented. Violence became chronic, damaging both trade and agriculture. In 1740, the ruler of Iran, Nadir Shah, ended the Astrakhanid period. Having already replaced the Safavids as the ruler of Iran, he now subjugated Transoxiana. He ruled both Iran and Transoxiana until he was assassinated in 1747.

The Uzbek khanate was a new stage in the Turkicization of Transoxiana. Historically a region in which Persian culture had predominated, Transoxiana became increasingly populated by Turkic groups after the tenth century. Under the Turks, the Persian language continued to be widely used in belles-lettres and as a chancery language for centuries, but its position was increasingly vulnerable due to the repeated waves of Turkic migrants into the area. By the late seventeenth century, the region was predominantly Turkic as far south as the northern arc of Khorasan (modern Turkmenistan). Although Persian speakers could still be found in Transoxiana and northern Khorasan, the "Persian frontier" had been pushed hundreds of miles south of the Amu Darya to roughly the northern borders of modern Iran, Afghanistan, and Tajikistan.

The Islamization of Central Asia

The period of Timurid and Uzbek rule marked an intensification and extension of the influence of Islam in Central Asia. The settled population of Transoxiana had been exposed to Islam for centuries, but pastoral populations were always less influenced by the formal doctrines and rituals of Islam than sedentary groups were. The Mongol invasions of the thirteenth century inaugurated an era of increased immigration by pastoral populations into Transoxiana. These new immigrants were overwhelmingly Turkic in language and culture. Most were also non-Muslim; as such, they were potential recruits to Islam. The Yasavi and Kubraviya Sufi orders had engaged in active missionary work in Central Asia even before the invasion of Chinggis Khan, and the Kubraviya had been the instrument through which both Berke of the Golden Horde and Ghazan of the Il-khanate had converted to Islam. By the late fourteenth century, however, the most dynamic and ultimately the dominant tariqa in Central Asia was the Naqshbandi order.

Baha' al-Din Naqshband (d. 1389) of Bukhara came of age during the period when the Il-khanate collapsed and the Chaghatay Khanate split. His importance lay not in the originality of his teaching—most of which he learned from his own pirs—but in his charisma and piety. He was able to unite a formerly disparate group of Sufis around a set of practices that included strict adherence to the Shari'a, rejection of music and dance, and the practice of a silent <u>dh</u>ikr. Although some branches of the order continued to practice a vocal <u>dh</u>ikr, the silent <u>dh</u>ikr became a major distinguishing characteristic of the Naqshbandiya. It reinforced the order's stress on the importance of continuous devotion, for it enabled the devotee to repeat the name of God silently and perpetually, even when engaged in other activities.

As early as the reign of Timur, the Naqshbandiya gained a following among the merchants and artisans in Bukhara and Samarqand. Soon, the Naqshbandis were active among the rural population as well. Preachers and traders fanned out among the nomads of Timurid-ruled Transoxiana and among the Uzbeks north of the Syr Darya River. Naqshbandi traders were already in Kashgar and other cities of the Tarim Basin by the early sixteenth century. During the sixteenth and seventeenth centuries, Naqshbandi *khwaja*s (pirs) extended their influence among the Uighurs, a Turkic people who had been settling in western China ever since the thirteenth century. By 1700, several khwajas had established thriving communities of Uighur disciples as far east as Gansu province (in the vicinity of the western terminus of the Great Wall, some 1500 miles from Kashgar). They also had followers among the Hui, the name applied to Muslims of central and eastern China, whose origins lay in the Muslim merchant communities that had existed for centuries along the Silk Road and the Chinese coast. As a result of Naqshbandi activity, the Uighurs along the trade routes of the Tarim Basin became predominantly Muslim. The basin became a Muslim preserve between Tibet to the south and northern Moghulistan to the north, both of which were Buddhist and shamanistic.

Naqshbandi leaders were famous for their political activism as well as for their missionary work. The order's insistence on a strict interpretation of the Shari'a brought it into conflict with the worldly ways of the Timurid ruling house during the fifteenth century. Naqshbandi leaders organized occasional mass protests in the streets, and Ulugh Bey attempted to pacify them by endowing madrasas and mosques in the larger cities. By the second half of the fifteenth century, Naqshbandi leaders were becoming prominent as spiritual advisors for several Timurid and Uzbek rulers who sought to enhance their standing among their subjects.

The acquisition of political influence on the part of Naqshbandi pirs happened at the time that Sufi and sharifian leaders from Morocco to China were gaining enhanced stature in the eyes of their followers. Their disciples often regarded them as more than mere teachers. They considered them to be spiritual intermediaries

FIGURE 14.3   The Great Mosque of Xi'an, China. The eastern terminus of the Silk Road, Xi'an hosted numerous Muslim merchants throughout the centuries. The original mosque was constructed in the early eighth century and has been renovated several times. It has no domes or minarets.

gionnixxx / iStock.

between their disciples and God and to have some degree of temporal authority, as well. In some orders, the actual mystic discipline was often submerged beneath the veneration of the pir. Because of their high prestige and perceived influence with God and with rulers, pirs were the recipients of gifts and bequests. Just as some ascetic monastic orders in medieval Europe eventually became wealthy due to the gifts and bequests that their admirers gave them, the Naqshbandiya of Central Asia became wealthy due to the awe and reverence that its leadership evoked. The order received religious endowments that included vast estates, artisanal workshops, and madrasas.

Despite the Naqshbandiya's growing wealth, its adherence to the Shari'a allowed it to escape some of the excesses characteristic of some of the other Sufi orders of the period. On the other hand, some of its khwajas became very powerful figures. The major Naqshbandi figure in the fifteenth century was Khwaja 'Ubayd Allah Ahrar (1404–1490). Khwaja Ahrar was already a wealthy landowner when he became a pir, and his combination of economic wealth, spiritual charisma, and political ties with the Timurid elite enabled him to wield great power. His diplomatic efforts secured an agreement among Uzbek leaders not to intervene in Transoxiana during the Timurid civil war of 1449–1451, allowing Abu Sa'id to secure leadership of Transoxiana and Khorasan. Based in Samarqand, Khwaja Ahrar mediated numerous conflicts among warlords, served as an advocate for ordinary people who sought justice or tax relief at Timurid courts, continued the trend toward a uniform system of Naqshbandi doctrine and practice, and managed a far-flung and diversified set of economic interests that yielded a continuous stream of revenue into the order. His career created a model for subsequent Naqshbandi khwajas who sought to exercise political influence, either by advising dynastic rulers or by exercising political power themselves.

The Naqshbandiya thrived under the Uzbeks as well as under the Timurids. Uzbek rulers enjoyed the prestige of lineal descent from Chinggis Khan, but so many of the Uzbek nobility shared in that status that no clan had an advantage in legitimacy. The successful leaders were the ones who worked out a symbiotic relationship with the Naqshbandi khwajas that allowed both to benefit. The warlords protected the khwajas, and the khwajas gave their blessing to the warlords. By the end of the sixteenth century, Naqshbandi khwajas served on the council that ratified the accession of a new khan.

Several Naqshbandi khwajas acquired sufficient political power to rule in their own right. During the 1520s, two sons of Khwaja Ahrar moved to Kashgar, in the Tarim Basin, which was under the control of the Chaghatay dynasty of Moghulistan. Over the next several generations, the influence of the Kashgari khwajas' descendants (who also became khwajas, due to the widespread assumption that spiritual authority was inherited) increased until they became governors in the region. During the seventeenth century, Naqshbandi khwajas went on missions to the east, to the region included in the modern provinces of Gansu, Ningxia, and Shaanxi. This was (and still is) the region in China with the largest concentration of the Hui people, or the Muslims of China whose first language was Chinese rather than a Central Asian language. It was the region where the major trade route between Mongolia and Tibet intersected with the legendary Silk Road, whose terminus was Chang'an (modern Xi'an, in Shaanxi province). Muslim traders from Central Asia had settled in this region over the centuries and had married Chinese women. Their children learned the Chinese language and culture of their mothers and the Islam of their fathers.

The introduction of Naqshbandi ideas and organizational structures into the Hui population produced a schism within the community. Prior to the Naqshbandi arrival, the Hui had not possessed an organizational structure beyond their local mosque and had few contacts with the larger Muslim world. They spoke Chinese, and only the itinerant imams and teachers knew Arabic or Persian. Despite their remoteness from the centers of Islamic learning, they worked hard to stay faithful to the norms of the Hanafi law school, and they prided themselves on their attention to ritual detail. The Hui who joined the Naqshbandiya, by contrast, were suddenly thrust into an international organization that looked to a leadership centered far to the west, in Kashgar and Bukhara. They performed rituals that were puzzling to their friends and family who did not become Sufis, and they sought a mystical experience to complement the ritual activity performed at the mosque. They quickly learned that they were expected to read and learn texts that were written in Arabic and Persian, and that nothing of value could be written in Chinese. The Hui became polarized into two groups: the Gedimu (from *qadim*, meaning "old" in Arabic), who adhered to traditional Hui customs, and the Khufiya (meaning "secret" or "concealed"), who belonged to the Naqshbandiya.

In 1678, the Chaghatays, who gradually had become Islamized over the centuries, were overwhelmed by an invasion of a non-Muslim Mongol people known as the Oirats. The Oirats were the western wing of the Mongols who had been expelled from China in 1368 by the Ming uprising. They had become established in Zungaria, or northern Moghulistan, the region north of the Tien Shan Mountains

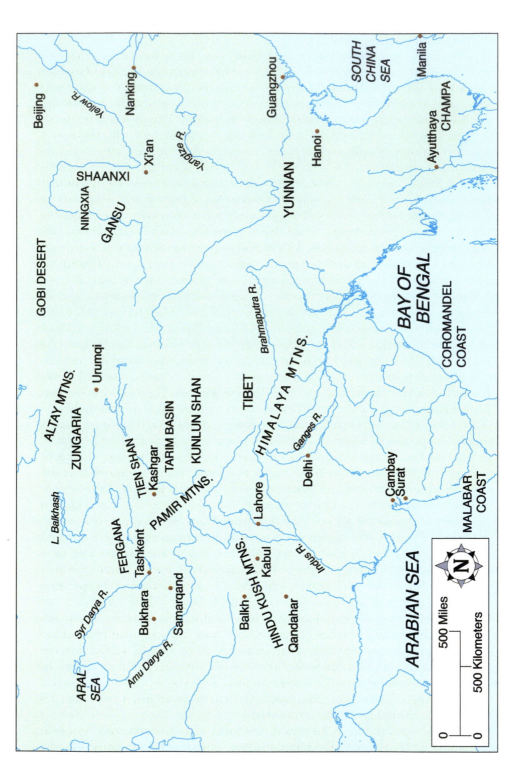

MAP 14.2 Central Asia and China.

and south of the Altay Mountains. The khwajas of the Tarim Basin adapted immediately to their new masters and remained governors of their provinces.

The Ch'ing (Qing) dynasty that ruled China from Beijing after overthrowing the Ming dynasty in 1644, however, viewed the Oirats suspiciously, for good reason. Several times after the 1670s, the Oirats attempted to expand eastward at the expense of the Ch'ing. Finally, after yet another Oirat attack in the early 1750s, the Ch'ing emperor decided that it was time to settle the issue with the Mongols. The Chinese army pursued them in a series of battles throughout the decade. They finally destroyed the Oirat army and began a campaign of extermination that almost totally obliterated the population of one million. In 1759, China annexed the Tarim Basin and Zungaria, which today compose the province of Xinjiang. When the government sent agents into the Tarim Basin to collect taxes, the Naqshbandi khwajas of Kashgar refused to pay. The Chinese sent a military unit into Kashgar, forcing the khwajas to flee westward into Transoxiana. The Chinese conquest, combined with a smallpox epidemic, depopulated much of the Tarim. China annexed the basin in 1759, and although the government allowed the remaining Muslims to follow their religious practices, it developed a long-lasting suspicion of Naqshbandi khwajas.

Iran

The potential for a Sufi order to become a powerful political force was realized in the fourteenth and fifteenth centuries in many regions. The most fertile region for Sufi activity that combined explicit spiritual content with implicit political content was Iran. There, during the fourteenth and fifteenth centuries, several messianic movements arose that combined Sufi doctrines and practices with the expectation that the leader of the movement was the *mahdi.*

The concept of the Mahdi arose during the second half of the first century of Islamic history, but the term was used in a variety of ways. Sunni Islamic history has witnessed the careers of several religiopolitical leaders who claimed to be the Mahdi, and it is clear that they did not share a common conception of what the role should entail. Some Sunnis expected the Mahdi to be a divinely appointed leader who would defeat the mundane forces of corruption and injustice in his generation, bringing a new order of purity and justice to subsequent history. Other Sunnis expected a divinely-appointed figure (Jesus was often mentioned) who would engage in a cataclysmic battle with the forces led by al-Dajjal, the Evil One, bringing history as we know it to an end.[2]

Among Shi'ites, the concept of the Mahdi fused with the doctrine of the Imam. Devout Twelver Shi'ites expected the "hidden" Twelfth Imam to return from where God had kept him in "concealment" since the year 874. His role was to redeem history from its corruption and oppression and to institute an era characterized by goodness and justice. Isma'ili, or Sevener, Shi'ites—the Nizaris and Tayyibis—had confidence that their respective Imams would one day be recognized by the masses as the legitimate spiritual and temporal leader.

In the violent and chaotic decades after the collapse of the Il-khanid regime in 1335, several movements arose in Iran that offered security to their followers as well as a secret knowledge that explained the chaos that was whirling around them. They featured charismatic spiritual leaders who provided a vision of social justice and a new moral order that would replace the oppression and chaos of the present. Some of the movements were examples of what most Muslims called the *ghulat* ("exaggerators" or "extremists"), which usually entailed the belief in reincarnation and in the divinity of 'Ali. Most of them lasted only during the lifetime of their founder or for a few generations. The Nizaris and Twelvers, on the other hand, had been in existence for six centuries or longer and have survived to the present day.

The Nizaris Regroup

After Hulagu's conquest of Alamut in 1256, the Nizaris scattered throughout Syria, Iran, Central Asia, and Sind.[3] According to Nizari tradition, a minor son of the last Lord of Alamut survived the Mongol catastrophe and became the new Imam. Out of fear of the Mongols and the petty rulers who came after them, he and his successors remained in hiding and were inaccessible to their followers for the next 200 years. Communication among the various clusters of Nizari followers was difficult. As a result, local traditions developed independently of each other. The Syrian community was forced to acknowledge the political suzerainty of the Mamluks, but in return it was allowed to retain its religious identity openly. Despite the continuing mistrust between the Mamluks and Syrian Nizaris, their shared hatred of the Mongols enabled the two groups to cooperate several times to fight the Il-khans. In Mongol-dominated Iran and Central Asia, however, it was dangerous to be known as a Nizari. As a result, the Nizari communities there practiced *taqiya*—the religiously sanctioned concealment of one's true beliefs—usually in the guise of Sufis. Local spiritual leaders functioned as Sufi murshids and their followers appeared to be their Sufi *murid*s, or disciples. The Nizaris appeared to be but one of many Sufi groups during the pre-Safavid period that revered 'Ali, practiced contemplation and mystical exercises, and avidly read Rumi, Ibn al-'Arabi, Hafez, and numerous other Sufi poets and theorists.

The Nizaris found it easy to assume the guise of Sufis due to their mystical inclination, hierarchical religious organization, and genuine appreciation for the great figures in Sufi history. Moreover, after the split with the Fatimids in 1094, the Nizaris lost the earlier, distinctive Isma'ili obsession with cosmology and cyclical history. They could easily have been mistaken for a Sufi group of the fourteenth century because they focused on attaining a spiritual experience with their Imam and sought the inner, mystical meaning of the Qur'an and Shari'a rather than remaining content with their literal meaning.

The Safavids: A Militant Sufi Order

While the Nizaris were still an underground movement, a Sufi tariqa emerged that ultimately claimed the leadership of Twelver Shi'ism and created a powerful empire. Shaykh Safi al-Din (1252–1334) gained a widespread reputation as a spiritual leader during his lifetime, which closely paralleled the Il-khanid era (1260–1335). Safi al-Din was based in Ardabil, a town about 100 miles east of Tabriz, the capital of the Il-khanate. His proximity to the seat of power paid off in influence. Several important Il-khanid family members considered themselves Safi al-Din's disciples, and intellectuals at the cosmopolitan Il-khanid court admired him. Within a year of his death, the Il-khanid regime collapsed, and Iran soon became divided into several petty kingdoms that constantly warred with each other. During this turbulent period, members of Safi al-Din's family not only maintained his organization, which is known as the Safavid order, but also engaged in active proselytism. Ardabil came under outside political control several times during the fourteenth and fifteenth centuries, but the Safavid organization remained intact due to its high quality of leadership.

During the Il-khanid period, the Safavid movement seems to have been a typical Sufi organization of the era, providing spiritual exercises and physical protection. Like many other Sufis, the Safavids did not attach much importance to labels such as *Sunni* and *Shi'ite*. We have seen that many Sufis regarded 'Ali as a great hero and that many Sufi orders traced their spiritual lineage back to him; they did not necessarily assume that his descendants had special spiritual knowledge. Many non-Shi'ite Sufis also admired and revered the Shi'ite Imams as great saints of God. A person could admire and emulate 'Ali and the Imams without becoming a Shi'ite.

Our knowledge of early Safavid history is sketchy, hampered by scarce and conflicting evidence, but what can be affirmed is that, during the fifteenth century, the Safavid order became transformed into a militant messianic movement. The degree to which it incorporated elements normally associated with the ghulat is not clear due to the paucity of trustworthy evidence and to the inherent ambiguity of Sufi discourse itself, which, as we have seen, revels in the enigmatic and the ambiguous. It appears that the order made the transition to militant messianism about 1447. In that year, two descendants of Safi al-Din—Junayd and his uncle Ja'far—each claimed to be the sole, legitimate leader of the order. They clashed, and Ja'far gained control of the headquarters at Ardabil under the protection of the Black Sheep Turkic confederation, which dominated northern Iran and Azerbaijan at that time.

We do not know what Ja'far's teachings were because it is with Junayd that the future of the movement lay. He fled westward and recruited followers from among pastoralists of eastern Anatolia and northern Syria. This area was not only a frontier where Ottoman and Mamluk interests were beginning to collide, but also the region where Uzun Hasan was building up his power. Uzun Hasan was the leader of the White Sheep confederation whom we have met before in his challenges to the Ottomans and the Timurids. Uzun was careful to patronize a wide variety of religious causes—Sunni, Twelver Shi'ite, and a variety of messianic ones—in his quest to build support. Junayd was fortunate to be looking for a patron at the moment when Uzun was looking for protégés. Uzun Hasan even arranged for his sister to marry Junayd as a sign of their alliance. The young couple soon had a son named Haydar.

Bolstered by the protection of the White Sheep, Junayd became an effective charismatic leader. His religious claims were combined with a call for jihad against Christian areas in the Caucasus and on the eastern shore of the Black Sea. (It is safe to assume that he did not attack Trebizon, the home of Uzun's wife Despina.) His victories reinforced his charismatic claims, and he was able to deliver large amounts of plunder to his soldiers. As a result, he developed a large and enthusiastic following. In 1460, however, Junayd was killed when he attacked the Muslim ruler of Shirvan, a regional power some 200 miles north of Ardabil.

At the time of Junayd's death, his son Haydar was too young to succeed him as the leader of his faction of the Safavids. Our knowledge of the era is so incomplete that we do not know who took Junayd's place during the next twenty years, but we do know that Uzun Hasan defeated his Black Sheep rivals in 1467 and took Ardabil from them. He thereby became the patron of the base of the order as well as of the group that Junayd had led. Just as he had made a marriage alliance with Junayd in order to maintain some leverage over a potentially disruptive religiopolitical movement, he also took care to make Haydar indebted to him. Haydar obtained a fine education at Uzun's court and then married Uzun's daughter, whose mother was Despina. He became the leader of the Safavids by 1480 at the latest, and he may have attained that position before Uzun died in 1478.

Haydar carried the Safavids to a higher degree of power than they had enjoyed before. He resumed the Caucasus campaigns that Junayd had begun, and he is credited with having devised a distinctive red headgear for his fighters. As a result, the Safavid fighters were soon known as the Qizilbash, or "Redheads." The Qizilbash regarded Haydar to be a special emissary from God, just as they had viewed his father. Haydar's success caused the White Sheep leaders who succeeded Uzun to become increasingly uneasy about the potential threat posed by the military successes of the Safavids. In 1488 the White Sheep joined a coalition of forces to defend Shirvan against the Safavids, and, like Junayd, Haydar was killed fighting the ruler of Shirvan.

The First Twelver Shi'ite Empire

The White Sheep leadership imprisoned Haydar's three sons for several years in order to deprive the Qizilbash of a leader around whom to rally. Only the youngest, Isma'il, survived to maturity. He was one year old when his father was killed in 1488. After his imprisonment at the hands of the White Sheep, his family's supporters spirited him away to hide him from the White Sheep. At first, he was taken to Fars, near the Persian Gulf, and then to Gilan, on the southwestern coast of the Caspian Sea. By 1494, both of his older brothers were dead. As a result, the community at Ardabil recognized Isma'il as its leader. In 1499, Isma'il left Gilan and returned to Ardabil with the goal of assuming his leadership position. The next year he raised an army, which he used to defeat the ruler of Shirvan, gaining some measure of revenge for the deaths of his father and paternal grandfather. He then attacked the White Sheep for their betrayal of his father and captured Tabriz from them in 1501. It became his capital city, and it was there that he proclaimed himself shah, the title last used by the rulers of the Sasanian Empire (226–651 C.E.). He then began the conquest of the rest of Azerbaijan, eastern Anatolia, western Iran, and northern Iraq.

For several years, it appeared that Isma'il was content to rule over the former empire of Uzun Hasan, but in 1510 he abruptly turned to the east. In a series of ferocious battles, he conquered Khorasan. He overpowered the Uzbeks at Merv and killed Muhammad Shaybani. He then aided the Timurid ruler Babur in his attempt to reconquer Transoxiana from the Uzbeks. Shortly after Isma'il returned to Tabriz, a quarrel broke out between the Turkic and Iranian officers in the Safavid army that he had left in Transoxiana. The Uzbeks seized the opportunity of the quarrel to drive the Safavids south across the Amu Darya River and to send Babur fleeing to Kabul. Thereafter, the Safavids regarded the Amu Darya as their northeastern frontier.

Isma'il impressed everyone who met him. His pedigree was impressive: He was a lineal descendant of Safi al-Din on his father's side and the grandson of Uzun and the Byzantine Christian princess Despina through his mother. Other military and political leaders throughout history have accomplished great deeds at a young age, but even in that elite company Isma'il stands out. Our sources—Safavid and Ottoman chronicles, as well as reports from European visitors to the Safavid court—are in agreement that Isma'il was twelve when he began his military campaign and fourteen when he captured Tabriz and named himself shah. He was a teenager when he conquered the heart of his eventual empire, and by the age of twenty-three he was the ruler of a region that roughly corresponded to the Il-khanid realm. Like his father and grandfather, he was revered by his followers and regarded as greater than a mere mortal. His soldiers fought for him with zeal and fearlessness that amazed friend and foe alike. Unlike his father and grandfather, he left behind a corpus of writings, in the form of poetry. He wrote more than 200 poems in which he identifies himself with 'Ali, Alexander the Great, various Iranian epic heroes, Adam, and the long-awaited Hidden Imam. In several poems, he claims to be God and demands the prostrations and absolute obedience due his divine status. Most of the poems appear to date from the first decade of Isma'il's rule—during the period of his conquests, when he was still a youth. As we have seen, Sufi poetry is replete with symbolism that is susceptible to multiple interpretations, but the claims that Isma'il repeatedly makes for himself are grander than most Sufi pirs made for themselves. Moreover, numerous inscriptions throughout his empire reiterate the claims that he had a divine nature.

European visitors who met Isma'il while he was still a teenager were impressed by his bearing, native intelligence, wisdom, and skill at wrestling and archery. Isma'il was unquestionably a well-rounded prodigy. On the other hand, due to his incarceration as a child and his military life during his youth, Isma'il did not receive the quality of education that either his father or his son Tahmasp enjoyed. Moreover, the chronicles make oblique references to a group of seven advisors—or spiritual guides—who protected Isma'il in Gilan, returned him to Ardabil, and accompanied him during the first several years of his reign as shah. What role this shadowy group played in his military successes, poetic production, and administrative policy has yet to be clarified.

Shah Isma'il Describes Himself to His Followers

Hundreds of poems are credited to Isma'il under the pen name of Khata'i. Like other examples of mystical poetry, they are full of metaphors and symbols. Some of the symbols would be recognized by Muslims belonging to any number of mystical paths, whereas others would be specific to the Safavid group. In this one, Isma'il makes particularly strong claims for possessing a divine nature.

The sixth verse refers to Mim. Mim is one of the letters in the Arabic alphabet but here the allusion is almost certainly to its appearance as one of a handful of such letters that appear in the heading of several of the chapters in the Qur'an. The function of the letters is unknown, but their

(Continued)

use has given rise to numerous theories. They are fruitful for mystics, for whom they have served as the start for meditations on the nature of God.

> I am God's eye (or God Himself); come now, O blind man gone astray, to behold Truth (God).
>
> I am that Absolute Doer of whom they speak. Sun and Moon are in my power.
>
> My being is God's House, know it for certain. Prostration before me is incumbent on thee, in the morn and even.
>
> Know for certain, that with the People of Recognition Heaven and Earth are all Truth. Do not stray!
>
> The Garden of Sanctity has produced a fruit. How can it be plucked by a shorthanded one?
>
> If you wish to join Truth to Truth, (here is) God who has reached the stage of Mim. The one of pure connections considers his own person. Suddenly Khata'i has come by a treasure.

SOURCE: V. Minorsky, "The Poetry of Shah Isma'il I," *Bulletin of the School of Oriental and African Studies,* 10 (1942): 1047a (poem 195). Reprinted with permission of Cambridge University Press.

One of the most important policy decisions that Isma'il ever made coincided with his assumption of the title of shah in 1501. Soon after capturing Tabriz, he announced that Twelver Shi'ism would be the official religion of his growing empire and that his subjects were required to profess it. All of our sources agree that Isma'il issued this edict and that his army forced Sunnis to curse the memory of the first three caliphs.[4] Many Iranians resisted the implementation of the policy, resulting in numerous casualties and much suffering. On the face of it, the account of the edict is astonishing and implausible. After all, it was during the decade following the proclamation that Isma'il wrote most of the poetry in which he makes claims for himself that would have been unacceptable to Twelver Shi'ites. He was actively trying to inspire his Qizilbash followers to believe that he had superhuman qualities, a claim that would have been blasphemous to Twelvers unless he were in fact the Hidden Imam. A second problem with the account is that it is hard to imagine the Qizilbash, whom Twelver Shi'ites regarded as heretics because they were ghulat, forcibly imposing Twelver Shi'ism upon Sunnis. The Qizilbash would have regarded doctrinal Twelver Shi'ism as bland, boring, and just plain wrong.

In all likelihood, the resolution to the paradoxes inherent in this account lies in the report that the Qizilbash forced Sunnis to curse the first three caliphs. It is certain that the unlettered Qizilbash did not require the conquered peoples to recite a formal catechism of Twelver Shi'ite beliefs. By forcing people to curse the first three caliphs, however, the soldiers would have made them imply that 'Ali should have been the first caliph, a conviction held by both the Qizilbash and the Twelver Shi'ites. Allegiance to 'Ali would have been the first step in the development of a national ideology that united the Iranians.

Isma'il's espousal of Twelver Shi'ism ran contrary to the claims that he made for himself in his poetry, but he wrote the poems in the Chaghatay Turkic dialect that Nava'i of Herat had pioneered, not in Persian. They were intended to motivate only the Turkic-speaking Qizilbash. Most of his followers would have been unaware of the differences between their beliefs and Twelver Shi'ism. Isma'il also needed the services of the talented Iranian administrative elites, however, who were repelled by the extreme doctrines of the Qizilbash. Twelver Shi'ism was much more acceptable to this educated, urban stratum, and for that reason Isma'il made claims (occasionally contradictory ones) regarding his place in the lineage of the Twelve Imams. An official religion of Twelver Shi'ism—deliberately left undefined at first so as not to confuse the Qizilbash—would have served to distinguish Isma'il's empire from that of his Ottoman enemies to the west and that of his Uzbek enemies to the east, facilitating his attempts to create a national identity and mobilize his subjects to fight "heretics," or Sunnis.

Despite the forcible "conversion" of Iranians to Shi'ism, the Safavid Empire did not become a Twelver society in any meaningful sense for more than a century. A major reason for the time lag was the powerful influence that the Qizilbash wielded due to their overwhelming dominance of the armed forces. They were comfortable with the doctrine of reincarnation, the view of the ruler as superhuman, and a relaxed approach to the Shari'a. The Twelver Shi'ism of the urban ulama did not appeal to them.

A second major reason for the slowness of the transformation of Iran into a Shi'ite society was the dearth of Twelver scholars in the country. The chroniclers report that not a single Twelver Shi'ite authority could be found in the capital city at the time of the proclamation of the faith as the national religion. The new government had to recruit scholars and teachers from the traditionally Shi'ite city of Qum, and later, when southern Iraq was conquered, others were brought in from the Shi'ite holy cities of Najaf and Karbala. In later decades, Twelver ulama were recruited from Lebanon and Bahrain.

For many pastoralists in Anatolia, Syria, Iraq, and western Iran, Isma'il's meteoric rise to power was the fulfillment of the messianic claims that his followers had been making for him. Moreover, much in the Safavid movement's ideology was familiar to them, for it had much in common with the teachings of the well-known Bektashi and Alevi groups of the region. Isma'il's spiritual gifts and his generosity in distributing the plunder of conquests were particularly attractive to pastoralists living in eastern Anatolia (under Ottoman rule) or Syria (under Mamluk rule), who were subject to imperial taxes and restrictions on their movements. After Isma'il's capture of Tabriz, fresh recruits flocked to his army from all over the region, fired with a zeal to reverse the effects of Ottoman and Mamluk policies. Isma'il welcomed some of them into his conquering army and sent others back into his opponents' empires in order to raid.

In this context, Isma'il's loss at Chaldiran in 1514 at the hands of Sultan Selim I was a major setback for the Safavid movement. Isma'il's ambitions to extend his influence into Anatolia were crushed, and the battle confirmed Ottoman hegemony there. The present border between Turkey and Iran is a legacy of Chaldiran: Despite subsequent gains and losses by both sides, the region around Lake Van consistently marked the frontier between the Ottomans and Safavids and between their successor states as well. As a result, the Safavid Empire was not fated to control the heartland of Uzun Hasan's Turkmen state (the upper Tigris and Euphrates rivers) after all. Its capital, Tabriz, was suddenly transformed into a border city after the loss at Chaldiran, precariously close to the Ottoman frontier. The subsequent course of events would shift the center of gravity of the empire eastward, transforming the state's Turkic character into a Persian one.

The Apocalypse Postponed

The major geopolitical consequence of the battle of Chaldiran—the establishment of a frontier zone between the Safavids and their Ottoman neighbors—is fairly easy to identify. More difficult, and more intriguing, is ascertaining the impact of the battle on Isma'il and on the faith and beliefs of most of the Qizilbash. Isma'il's army had lost once before—against the Uzbeks—but only when Isma'il was a thousand miles from the battlefield. At Chaldiran he was leading his army, yet the enemy won. What does it mean when God's emissary suffers a military defeat? Some chroniclers assert that, in the aftermath of the battle, Isma'il became despondent and remained so for the remaining decade of his life. A year or two after the battle, however, European ambassadors to Tabriz reported that his spirits seemed high. Moreover, we know that, during the next decade, Isma'il arranged alliances with numerous powerful chieftains, regardless of their religious affiliation, in an effort to secure stability in his realm. He also engaged in frequent correspondence with European rulers in an attempt to construct an anti-Ottoman alliance. The former efforts were more successful than the latter. Isma'il also introduced musket and artillery units into his army, although they never achieved the scale of their Ottoman counterparts.

The fact remains, however, that Isma'il never again took the field to lead an army in person, either against the Ottomans or the Uzbeks, his only two rivals. It is understandable why he would not have wanted to face Ottoman artillery again, but it is less clear why he did not challenge the Uzbeks: Their use of gunpowder weapons was rudimentary, and they controlled a wealthy region that historically had been within the zone of Persian cultural influence. We do not have sources that reveal the efforts by Isma'il or his Qizilbash followers to rationalize the catastrophe. The defeat at Chaldiran would not necessarily have disillusioned Isma'il's followers. Both his father and grandfather had been defeated and killed in battle without any apparent damage to their charisma or to the attraction of the Safavid cause. On the other hand, those two leaders had died as martyrs in the cause of ending "ordinary" history and ushering in an era that would embody God's will. Many thought that Isma'il had inaugurated the new age with his rapid conquests, but the decade between Chaldiran and Isma'il's death witnessed no tangible evidence of a transformation of history that would justify the passionate devotion of the Qizilbash to the Safavid cause. The nature of Qizilbash devotion, which combined elements of religious faith and the expectation of material gain, has yet to be fully understood.

In 1524, Isma'il died at the age of thirty-seven. This messianic figure who identified himself with God and the Hidden Imam was a heavy drinker, and the cause of his death was alcohol poisoning. Following in the tradition of Alexander the Great's devoted biographer, however, Isma'il's biographer carefully recorded the cause of death as a fever. The heir to the throne was Isma'il's ten-year-old son Tahmasp, who was not much younger than his father had been when he had created an empire. Tahmasp, however, inherited a powerful complex of Qizilbash military officers who were the ambitious leaders of seven powerful tribes. Several of them hoped to use the opportunity of the regency of the young boy to advance their interests; the others were equally determined to prevent that from happening. Iran quickly succumbed to a decade of civil war among Qizilbash chieftains and, to a lesser extent, Persian-speaking notables. Tahmasp was officially the shah, but he was subject to the influence of a regent who had little power in the empire as a whole. Several times, Tahmasp was targeted for assassination by supporters of rival aspirants to the throne, but he survived to assume control in his own right in 1533.

Although Tahmasp did not possess the charisma of his father, he reigned successfully for more than four decades (to 1576). He survived constant challenges from his own Turkic elites and from repeated invasions of his empire by both the Ottomans and the Uzbeks of Transoxiana. In retrospect, his achievement was nothing less than exceptional. He managed to dominate his Turkic opponents once he gained the throne. Between 1524 and 1538 he or his regent repelled five Uzbek invasions, and between 1533 and 1553 he survived four Ottoman invasions sent by Sultan Suleyman the Magnificent. These achievements were all the more impressive in view of the fact that Safavid armies were always inferior in numbers to both the Ottomans and the Uzbeks. The Uzbeks could not stand up to the firepower of the new Safavid gunpowder units, but the Ottoman threat was acute. Suleyman temporarily captured Tabriz in 1534 and again in 1548. The Ottomans also captured Iraq during the 1534 campaign and held it permanently except for a short period in the seventeenth century. The Treaty of Amasya in 1555 brought a needed respite in the long conflict between the Ottomans and Safavids. The Safavids conceded the loss of Baghdad and certain areas of eastern Anatolia to the Ottomans, and Suleyman officially recognized Safavid sovereignty. Tahmasp and Suleyman even began to exchange courteous diplomatic notes.

The Ottoman wars had major consequences for the Safavids. One was the loss of Iraq, which was particularly disturbing because it meant that Iranian pilgrims would find it difficult to travel to the holy cities of Najaf (the burial place of 'Ali) and Karbala (the burial place of Husayn, 'Ali's younger son and the Prophet's grandson). Another was that Tabriz had been demonstrated to be hopelessly vulnerable to Ottoman armies. Bowing to the inevitable, Tahmasp moved his capital at midcentury to Qazvin, almost 300 miles to the east. Transplanting the capital to the Iranian plateau meant that Persian influences would thereafter intensify at the Safavid court at the expense of Turkic influences.

In addition to warding off invasions, Tahmasp also engaged in campaigns of territorial expansion in the Caucasus. During the period 1540–1553, he waged four campaigns in that region and captured tens of thousands of Georgian, Circassian, and Armenian prisoners, most of whom were Christians. He placed many of the women in harems, including that of the royal court, whereas many of the male prisoners were incorporated into his army. Some were assigned to cavalry units; others were placed in infantry units and equipped with muskets and arquebuses.

After Tahmasp's death in 1576, a period of chaos set in that came close to destroying the dynasty. Like other Turkic groups before them, the Safavids believed that the right to rule was transmitted to all collateral members of the ruling family. As a result, rival Qizilbash groups had the opportunity to support different members of the Safavid family in order to achieve their political goals. During the resulting civil war, Qizilbash chieftains took advantage of the weakness at court to gain advantages over their rivals. Amid the confusion, both the Uzbeks and the Ottomans seized Safavid territory with impunity. A decade after the death of Tahmasp, almost half of the empire's territory had been lost, and the civil war was making the survival of the empire highly unlikely.

In 1587, Tahmasp's grandson 'Abbas (1587–1629) ascended the throne at the age of sixteen. The empire was at the nadir of its history, but 'Abbas proved to be one of his era's most gifted rulers. This multitalented teenager was primarily interested in recovering power for the royal court. He needed a counterweight to the destructive ambitions of the Qizilbash, and he found it among the descendants of the Georgians, Armenians, and Circassians whom Tahmasp had captured, as well as among others from those groups whom 'Abbas captured in his own campaigns. He reorganized the slave forces that he inherited and made them into a permanent army, answerable to the shah alone. He quickly developed a slave cavalry of 10,000 men, and he eventually commanded 12,000 artillerymen and 12,000 musketeers. Using his new slave units (usually referred to as *ghulam*) as auxiliaries to the Qizilbash who had remained loyal to the crown, he quickly subdued the refractory elements of the Qizilbash, who were still fighting each other.

The structure of 'Abbas's new army resembled that of the Ottoman army, with its large cavalry unit largely composed of Turks and its nucleus of musket- and artillery-equipped infantry of slave soldiers from Christian areas. The ghulam infantry, however, never developed into as formidable a force as the Janissaries. The musket units were not as well trained, and artillery was never valued highly. Field artillery was not as useful to the Safavids as it was to other armies. To the west and north, the Zagros and Elburz mountain ranges and the rugged valleys of Azerbaijan provided a natural barrier to Ottoman penetration, but they also made the transport of artillery difficult for either army. To the northeast, the Uzbeks were in possession of inferior guns and thus did not provoke an arms race in gunpowder weapons. To the east, the Mughal threat was only to Safavid control of Qandahar, which lay on the Safavid-Mughal frontier.

Once 'Abbas had united the Qizilbash with his slave army, he began recovering lands from the Uzbeks, Mughals, and Ottomans. He quickly regained Khorasan from the Uzbeks all the way to Herat. By 1603, he felt strong enough to challenge the Ottomans, who were severely limited in their capacity to respond due to the Jelali revolts. He recaptured Azerbaijan and campaigned strenuously in Georgia, although he could never control the region sufficiently to annex it. In 1622, he launched a lightning campaign against Qandahar, which had been surrendered to the Mughals in 1595 by a commander who was in disgrace with 'Abbas. The city fell quickly to the Safavid army. After two decades of fighting the Ottomans, 'Abbas even captured much of Iraq in 1623, although his successor lost those gains in 1638. Iran's border with Iraq has remained almost unaltered since then.

Society

Safavid Iran was one of the world's great powers during the sixteenth and seventeenth centuries. It was located between two much larger Muslim powers: the Ottoman and Mughal empires. The Safavid realm contained a population of some six to ten

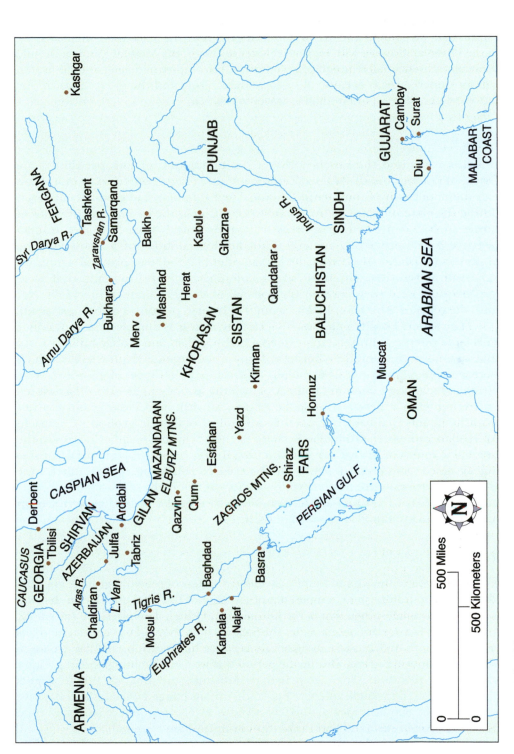

MAP 14.3 Safavid Iran.

million people, depending on the territories it controlled at a given time. Its population was comparable to contemporary England's, but less than one-third that of the Ottoman Empire and less than one-tenth that of the Mughal Empire. Despite its comparatively small demographic resources, the empire managed to hold its own against imperial rivals because of its formidable army and the great distance that Ottoman and Mughal armies had to travel to reach it.

Peasants and Herders

Peasants composed the vast majority of the population of Europe, China, the Ottoman Empire, and the Mughal Empire, but they formed only slightly more than half the population of the Safavid Empire. Their numbers had gradually declined during the eleventh through the sixteenth centuries as the calamitous invasions of northern Iran converted large areas from agricultural to pastoral use. Iranian peasants were perpetually vulnerable to the depredations of nomads and the oppression of landlords. Ghazan, the Il-khan ruler (1295–1304), planned significant agricultural reforms, but little was accomplished; improvements that were implemented were swept away by the collapse of the Il-khanate in the 1350s. Not until the reign of 'Abbas would the fortunes of Iranian peasants begin to rise again.

The Safavid Empire's pastoral subjects were almost as numerous as its peasants. This large reserve of horsemen provided a highly skilled and mobile military force that defended the empire's borders. Many were organized into tribes, which were groupings based at least nominally on kinship. Other types of groupings were possible, including temporary military or security arrangements. Isma'il's devoted followers included people who spoke Arabic, Kurdish, and Persian, but the vast majority of the Qizilbash belonged to a handful of Turkic groupings based in Azerbaijan and eastern Anatolia. Because of their "charter member" status as the original followers of Junayd, Haydar, and Isma'il, they possessed high social status as well as military and political power. During the sixteenth century, their chiefs were granted control of entire provinces in return for providing the shah with troops. The most powerful of the Qizilbash leaders held office in the central government in order to be in proximity to the shah himself.

Religious Minorities

The population of the Safavid Empire included a variety of religious groups, but non-Muslim religious minorities composed a percentage of the total population that was incomparably smaller than that of the Ottoman and Mughal empires. On the whole, non-Muslims fared more poorly under the Safavids than they did under the Ottomans and Mughals. To understand Safavid religious policy, however, it is essential to place it within its historical context. During the period that we are examining, the Inquisition was in full operation, Spain expelled its Muslims, the English Bill of Rights disenfranchised non-Anglicans, New England Puritans hanged Quakers and Baptists, and Christian communities almost everywhere in Central and Western Europe persecuted Anabaptists and Jews in the most brutal fashion imaginable.

The two non-Muslim groups that suffered the most in Iran were the Zoroastrians and the Jews. Zoroastrians had incurred the stigma of polytheism during the Arab conquests of the seventh century, and they were subject to periodic persecution thereafter. By the end of the Safavid period, almost no Zoroastrians were left in Iran. Most of the world's remaining Zoroastrians were by then known as Parsis (singular *Parsi*, a variant of *Farsi*, or *Persian*) and lived in the Indian regions of Gujarat or the Malabar Coast.

Jews had resided in Iran ever since the period of the Achaemenid Empire. Although that empire's rulers allowed Jews to return to Jerusalem after the Babylonian Captivity of the sixth century B.C.E., most remained. Much later, several thousand Sephardic Jews emigrated to Iran after their expulsion from Spain in 1492. On the whole, Iranian Jews were not as prosperous as those of the Ottoman Empire, but they fared well until the early seventeenth century. 'Abbas was the first ruler of Iran in four centuries to force Jews to wear distinctive clothing. During the 1620s, he was persuaded by a Jewish convert to Islam that Jews were writing dangerous talismans against him. In retaliation, he forced the Jews of Esfahan to convert to Islam. Although 'Abbas's successor allowed these Jews to return to Judaism, by midcentury the persecution of Jews became more intense and widespread throughout the empire. During the early eighteenth century, torture, starvation, and seizure of property became routine for Iranian Jews, who might well have disappeared as a community if the empire had not fallen in 1722.

Under 'Abbas, Christians generally fared better than any religious community in Iran other than the Twelver Shi'ites themselves. Most of the empire's Christians lived in the northwest, in Armenia. They suffered considerably during the various wars between the Safavids and Ottomans because Armenia was the primary battleground of those wars, and both sides employed a scorched earth policy there to deprive the opponent of food and forage. 'Abbas's campaigns during 1603–1605 were particularly horrifying in this regard, but the Armenians of Julfa won the sympathy of 'Abbas. In part, 'Abbas was motivated by the Armenians' having welcomed him into their city. Equally important, however, he hoped to exploit the commercial skills and contacts of the Armenian merchant community: Armenians had long been engaged in long-distance trade between Iran and its neighbors, and Armenians were well established on India's Malabar Coast and in the Mughal court.

'Abbas decided to give the Armenian international merchants the responsibility for carrying out his plan to rejuvenate the Iranian economy on the strength of the export of silk. He transported Julfans en masse to Esfahan, where he built a suburb for them called New Julfa. There the Armenians built a spectacular cathedral whose bells rang out across the city (a practice rarely allowed in Muslim lands). Even though they were a pampered community by the norms of the day, 'Abbas twice (in 1613 and 1621) extorted money from them and even demanded conversion to Islam, although the latter demand was not enforced.

Georgian Christians also fared relatively well under 'Abbas. They were well regarded, perhaps enjoying a halo effect produced by the fact that thousands of Georgian converts to Islam served in the shah's standing army and held important civilian positions in the government. Not least in the popular imagination was the fact that Georgian women had an unrivaled reputation in Iran for beauty (thousands lived in harems throughout Iran, obtained by force, purchase, or consensual marriage). Like the Armenians, Georgian Christians for several decades enjoyed generous government loans and religious toleration. After the death of 'Abbas in

1629, however, the position of both Armenians and Georgians became more vulnerable, and brutal persecution of both communities broke out several times during the remaining century of Safavid history.

It is useful to keep in mind that, despite recurrent Safavid persecution, the Armenians and the Georgians were each other's most consistent enemy. The Georgian Church was in close alliance with the Orthodox Church, whereas the Armenian Church was a Monophysite organization (like the Coptic Church of Egypt), which made it heretical in Orthodox eyes. Thus, hostility between the two groups raged unabated even when the Safavid court began persecuting them. Moreover, rivalry among factions within each church had a devastating impact on the cohesiveness and effectiveness of the major Christian groups in the country.

The Nizaris suffered severe persecution under Tahmasp, but in their inimitable way, they managed to find a way to adapt and survive. The group had reached a crisis point by the early fifteenth century, when it became clear that the long-term practice of taqiya and the lack of a central Nizari authority had caused the community to decline in size. Numerous individual Nizaris had lost their religious identity and became Sunnis, Twelver Shi'ites, or even—in Sind—Hindus. About the year 1460 (which was approximately the same time that Isma'il's grandfather Junayd was killed), the Nizari Imam took the initiative to try to reverse this trend. He established his headquarters in the village of Anjudan, south of Qum in modern Iran, and he became accessible again to his followers. He also began a concerted effort to bring the widely scattered Nizari communities under his control. His agents visited the numerous towns and villages across Syria, Iran, Sind, and the remote mountain valleys of Central Asia where Nizaris lived. They sought to reestablish the lines of communication between the Imam and his followers that had characterized the Alamut period. Due to the power and autonomy that local Nizari pirs had built up during the 200 years of the Imam's seclusion, the agents initially met with only mixed success. By the beginning of the sixteenth century, however, their persistence had created a widespread network of communities that looked to Anjudan for guidance.

This growth in the centralization of the Imam's authority took place during the chaotic period of Haydar's career, the creation of the Safavid Empire by Isma'il, and Tahmasp's early, vulnerable years as a ruler. Developments in Andujan did not become a major concern to the royal court until the second half of the sixteenth century, when Tahmasp could cut back on his military responsibilities and devote attention to affairs within his realm. Although the Nizaris appeared to be simply a Sufi order, the increasing number of pilgrims to Anjudan from places as remote as Sind must have made it obvious to state authorities that the Imam was more than a Sufi pir. The Safavid regime began harassing the order, and by 1574 Tahmasp became so suspicious of Nizari activity that he executed the Imam.

In response to the persecution, the Nizari community began to practice taqiya not merely as Sufis but also as Twelver Shi'ites. The transition was successful, and the Nizaris achieved an excellent relationship with 'Abbas. During his reign, the Nizari Imam even married a Safavid princess. Throughout the rest of Safavid history, the Nizari Imams continued to practice taqiya and simultaneously to work secretly to win over the allegiance of the Nizaris of the world who had not yet accepted their authority. By the end of the seventeenth century, the seat of the imamate had moved a few miles to the northeast of Anjudan, to Kahak. Almost all the Nizaris of Iran, Sind, and Gujarat recognized Kahak as the center of their faith

The capriciousness of Safavid religious policies is most clearly revealed in the regime's relations with its Hindu subjects, several thousand of whom made a comfortable living as moneylenders, money changers, and merchants. According to the tenets of the Qur'an and the Shari'a, most Hindus would qualify as idolaters and polytheists whom Muslims should have fought until they became Muslims. Just as the Mughals did not follow that policy with their huge Hindu majority, neither did the early Safavids, with their tiny (and economically useful) Hindu minority. By the second half of the seventeenth century, Hindus, like other religious minorities, were beginning to experience harassment and persecution, although no more severely than Sunnis.

Like the Ottomans, European Christians, Georgians, and Armenians, the Safavids were most likely to exhibit consistent religious intolerance in their dealings with co-religionists whose beliefs and practices were perceived to be a threat to their own spiritual or physical well-being. Whereas the Ottomans frequently persecuted Shi'ites, Safavids frequently persecuted Sunnis. To be a Sunni implied a rejection of the central tenet of Shi'ism: the necessity of following a lineal descendant of the Prophet Muhammad (through the line of 'Ali) as the true spiritual and temporal leader of all Muslims. Thus, Sunnis implicitly rejected the legitimacy of the Safavid dynasty, which justified its seizure of power and its right to rule on its reputed lineal descent from Muhammad.

Women

In some ways, the roles of Safavid women resembled those of their Ottoman and Mughal counterparts. Most women from the elite social strata, for example, cultivated the arts of reading, calligraphy, and composing letters. Tahmasp's daughters were considered by their contemporaries to have been especially well educated. Several royal women were active in patronizing monumental works of architecture, especially during the reign of 'Abbas I. Generosity in the funding of great works of architecture and charitable foundations, a high level of literacy, and a powerful influence on the ruler if he were one's husband or son are recurring features of women in the royal families of Muslim dynasties throughout history.

In other ways, however, Safavid women's behavior in the sixteenth century struck visitors as quite different from that of their counterparts in the Ottoman and Mughal empires. Ottoman and Mughal women—and urban, Persian-speaking Muslim women in Iran—had been acculturated for centuries into the norms of the Shari'a. These guidelines granted women property rights that had no equal in contemporary Europe but restricted their wardrobe options and tended to keep them secluded in the privacy of their homes (if their families could afford not to have them working). On the other hand, because the Turkic-speaking Qizilbash were pastoralists, they were accustomed to a high degree of interaction among males and females during both work and leisure activities. Their women commonly dressed in colorful garments, did not cover their faces, and enjoyed socializing in mixed female and male gatherings. Because the Qizilbash were the dominant political and social group in Iran during the sixteenth century, women in the early Safavid Empire were much more visible, both literally and metaphorically, than in other Muslim imperial courts.

Women played important political roles during the late sixteenth-century political crisis. Tahmasp's daughter Pari-Khan Khanum was one of his closest advisors and claimed the throne after his death. She contested for power with her brother Isma'il II (1576–1578) and was apparently involved in the plot that resulted in his murder two years later. She ruled for several weeks until her elder brother Muhammad Khudabanda (1578–1587) arrived in Esfahan and became shah. Muhammad's wife was responsible for Pari-Khan Khanum's assassination, and she herself reigned for some seventeen months when Muhammad was disabled by eye problems. During that time, she took personal command of the army in a war against the Ottomans.

The growth of power for the court at Esfahan came at the expense of both the power of the Qizilbash and social opportunities for women. Shah 'Abbas instituted the seclusion of royal women, and the growing influence of Twelver ulama throughout the seventeenth century brought greater pressure for all women to adhere to the norms of the Shari'a. The climax of this process came during 1694–1695 in a series of royal edicts. These new rulings forbade women to linger in the streets and bazaars or to stroll in gardens or the streets with anyone other than their husbands. They were also forbidden to participate in public gatherings or to visit coffeehouses. Women were ordered to cover their hair and bodies with an article of clothing that resembled today's chador, which covers everything but the face, hands, and feet. Officially, at least, conditions for Safavid women had changed profoundly since the sixteenth century. At the dawn of the eighteenth century, some European observers thought that the seclusion of women was even stricter in Iran than in the Arab regions of the Ottoman Empire, where women's movements were more restricted than in Anatolia or Rumelia.

The State

The Safavid shahs aspired to rule over a huge region that contained a large number of pastoral peoples. Their task can be contrasted with the opposite extreme: the ancient Egyptian pharaohs, who claimed the right to rule over the peasants of the Nile valley. The pharaohs needed only a small army to enforce their writ among farmers of the narrow Nile valley, whose fields and mud-brick villages were vulnerable to the demands of government tax collectors. Pastoralists, on the other hand, were highly mobile. Moreover, by virtue of their horse-riding skills and their need to protect their herds, their normal upbringing turned them into some of the most effective warriors in the world. Each grouping (tribe) of pastoralists competed for scarce resources with other such groupings and with urban populations. Scattered across almost a million square miles of territory, the tribes of the Safavid realm were a formidable force for any central power to control. Anyone who aspired to rule them would have to balance concessions on the part of the tribes with incentives from the central government. Thus, Qizilbash leaders were not only military officers but the equivalent of governors as well. They were highly autonomous, and their provinces were considered to be their private property. The central government intervened only if it was not receiving its expected revenue.

As a result of the considerable autonomy that tribal leaders had in Safavid Iran, historians usually regard the Safavid government to have been less centralized than its Ottoman or Mughal counterparts. Some historians cannot even bring themselves to speak of a Safavid state. That is an extreme position, because the Safavid government boasted a complex bureaucracy, and it obtained enough revenue to build some of the greatest architectural monuments in history. It is true that the

FIGURE 14.4 The Maydan-e Shah, Esfahan. Now known as Maydan-e Imam, it was the cen-
terpiece of the redesign of Esfahan by Shah 'Abbas. The Masjid-e Shah (now
Masjid-e Imam) is the mosque in the foreground; at top right is the dome of the
Masjid-e Shaykh Lotfollah, and at the upper left is the pavilion of the 'Ali Qapu.

Roger Wood / Corbis / VCG via Getty Images.

Safavid government did not evolve quickly. Isma'il had begun the process by staffing
his military with the Qizilbash Turks and his fledgling administration with Persian-
speakers, usually called Tajiks. Tahmasp was preoccupied throughout his half-century
reign with finding ways to keep independent-minded chieftains in line. He took a
tentative step toward diluting the military monopoly of the Qizilbash when he began
incorporating the Circassian, Armenian, and—especially—Georgian prisoners of war
into his army. 'Abbas built upon that base, creating a regular standing army composed
largely of Georgians. The new cavalry and gunpowder units were able to crush the
rebellious Qizilbash, and the Georgian units became the pillar of 'Abbas's power.

As a result of 'Abbas's skill and ruthlessness, the Safavid state attained an unprecedented degree of stability during the early seventeenth century. 'Abbas developed a powerful permanent standing army, gained leverage over the Qizilbash, and had the loyalty of a mature Twelver Shi'ite religious establishment. At the time of his ascension to the throne in 1587, the Safavid entity still retained many features of its origins as a tribal confederation under the leadership of a Safavid pir; by the end of 'Abbas's reign in 1629, the government had been transformed into a powerful, sophisticated, and wealthy enterprise.

The Decline of Tariqa Sufism in Iran

Tahmasp and 'Abbas were wary of the Qizilbash for reasons other than their tribal fractiousness. The same religious zeal that had brought the Safavids to power could also bring them down. Periodically, the rulers had to engage in suppressing messianic movements that challenged the legitimacy of the shah. The fear of competing religious movements led the shahs to extend their suspicion of the Qizilbash to Sufi groups because of the potential of their leaders to claim spiritual and political legitimacy and the potential of the Sufi membership to constitute a formidable army. This suspicion dovetailed with a deep-seated antagonism on the part of the Twelver ulama toward Sufi movements, and the result was a concerted effort by the shah and the ulama against Sufism that almost eliminated it from Iran.

Both Isma'il and Tahmasp had occasionally persecuted Sufis because of their loyalty to their own pir rather than to the shah. The Nizari "Sufis," as we have seen, managed to survive. For many Sufis, however, the threat was so great under those two rulers that they emigrated from Iran to South Asia during this period, seeking a less oppressive regime. Four years after 'Abbas took the throne, he became convinced that his father and grandfather had been justified in their actions. The year 1591 was the turn of the millennium because it marked 1000 years since the Hijra on the lunar Islamic calendar (it was 969 years on the Gregorian calendar). Many people all across the Muslim world expected that God would demonstrate His control of history by intervening in a dramatic manner. Some expected the arrival of the Mahdi, while others hoped at least for a radical improvement in social conditions and the implementation of justice. These expectations were at the heart of a plot within one of the popular Sufi orders in Iran—the Nuqtavi—to overthrow 'Abbas and place the pir of the order on the throne. The Nuqtavi order was a classic example of ghulat: It taught reincarnation, and it made little distinction between God and Muhammad. Its doctrines were popular among many of the Qizilbash, who, like the members of many mystical orders of the day, frequently belonged to more than one such organization.

'Abbas learned of the planned uprising just before it was scheduled to take place and ordered its leaders arrested and executed. The incident awoke 'Abbas to the implicit political threat that Sufi pirs posed to the authority of the state. He began a campaign to break the potential political threat of Sufism in his empire. The persecution of Sufism extended to the ranks of the Qizilbash, where spiritual guides were purged. 'Abbas no longer allowed the Qizilbash to be in attendance at the royal court or to serve in his personal bodyguard. Court chroniclers continued to refer to the shah as *murshid-i kamil* ("Ultimate Mystical Guide") and to the Qizilbash as Sufis, but the usage was perfunctory and sentimental, not descriptive of any actual relationship. Qizilbash leaders continued to serve as important military and administrative leaders, but the special relationship was over. 'Abbas and subsequent shahs maintained vigilance against Sufi orders, Sufi rituals, and individual Sufis.

Meanwhile, the Twelver Shi'ite ulama who were recruited into Safavid service from other countries had chafed for decades at the influence of groups that they considered to be ghulat, including the Qizilbash. They were determined to enforce the observance of the Shari'a and to ban doctrines such as the divinity of the shah and the transmigration of the soul. Thus, when 'Abbas I began his persecution of messianic groups, many of the ulama joined forces with him. 'Abbas distrusted Sufi orders because of their potential as breeding grounds for religious enthusiasm that might threaten the stability of the dynasty. The actual religious practices of apolitical Sufis had not been the target of his campaign—he had a lifelong interest in mystical practices himself, and he frequently consulted ulama who found Sufi meditative practices and interpretive techniques to be useful in their own devotional lives. He had even sought spiritual guidance from the Nuqtavi pir who subsequently tried to overthrow him in 1591. The militant, Shari'a-minded ulama, however, equated all mystical thought and practice with the ghulat. In their quest to purify Safavid society and to establish acceptable norms for Twelver rituals and doctrines, they were determined to eliminate religious practices that they considered heretical.

The seventeenth-century campaign in Iran against Sufism was one more stage in the centuries-long struggle between Shari'a-minded ulama and mystically oriented personalities. The opponents of Sufism resented the claims of mystics to be spiritual authorities. Members of the ulama, who had undergone many years of rigorous academic work, were contemptuous of the self-taught Sufis who claimed to be able to lead novices into the presence of God. Many were also resentful of those among their fellow ulama who asserted that the life of the Shari'a was incomplete without a mystical experience. Moreover, many Shi'ite ulama sensed that the master–novice relationship characteristic of Sufism was essentially incompatible with the relationship between the Hidden Imam and the believer. If a Sufi looked to his master for spiritual guidance, did that not challenge the spiritual authority of the Imam? In an effort to restore the doctrine of the centrality of the Hidden Imam, it was necessary to extirpate Sufism, root and branch. The fact that a victory in that effort would benefit the Shari'a-minded ulama in both status and wealth was an added bonus.

The campaign against Sufi orders was brutal. With the power of the royal court and army allied with the antimystical ulama, Sufi orders did not stand a chance. As had been the case in the sixteenth century, many Sufis fled to neighboring regions, especially India. Some orders went underground in an attempt to survive. The campaign against mysticism caused a conflict even within the community of the mujtahids, or highest-ranking ulama. Some of the ulama found both mysticism and Sufi philosophy attractive, and they fought a rear-guard action against the reformers. The most prominent was the brilliant and politically well-connected Mulla Sadra (d. 1640), who was associated with the so-called School of Esfahan. The School of Esfahan continued the tradition of the Illuminationist school founded by al-Suhrawardi al-Maqtul (d. 1191). Al-Suhrawardi was a philosopher who had mastered the spectrum of Greek philosophy. Rejecting the rationalist and empirically grounded Aristotelian tradition, he favored the idealism and mystical orientation of Pythagoras and Plato. He acknowledged the value of the rational mind, but he argued that mystical knowledge (*'irfan*) was even more important. In order to obtain wisdom, it was necessary to develop both the rational and intuitive aspects of the mind.

Mulla Sadra acknowledged the need to acquire a deep knowledge of the Shari'a and to follow it scrupulously and wholeheartedly, but he also insisted on the reciprocal relationship of formal knowledge and experience. The complete religious life requires the mystical vision or illumination that comes only after fasting, self-denial, and mystical practices. Mulla Sadra's corpus of writings was a brilliant synthesis of the Illuminationist tradition and Twelver Shi'ism. It provided the philosophical underpinnings for Shi'ite 'irfan. The legalistic mujtahids continued to rail against 'irfan, but it survived even within the halls of the madrasas. Students who wished to take private tutorials in the theory and practice of mysticism were usually allowed to do so, as long as it was not part of the official curriculum of the madrasas and as long as the instruction remained on an individual basis. 'Irfan continues to be viewed with suspicion by the majority of the highest spiritual authorities in Shi'ism. On the other hand, equally influential authorities, such as the Ayatollah Khomeini (d. 1989), have been ardent practitioners of it.

Mystical thought in Iran thus continued within circles of the elite classes, but organized Sufism among the lower classes declined dramatically under the combined assault of the throne and the Shari'a-minded ulama. The near-demise of the tariqas was an ignoble fate for these organizations, which had been a vehicle for the survival of Shi'ism in Iran during the period of the Mongols and their chaotic aftermath. The changed conditions of the seventeenth century put organized, institutional Sufism under suspicion of being potentially heretical as well as treasonous. The development reflected a major change in Safavid religious life: Whereas mystical experiences were the characteristic religious expression of the first century of the Safavid state, the ulama of the second century increasingly linked religious expression to the exposition of texts.

The Economy

Under 'Abbas, Iran's economy reached a level of prosperity that it had not known for many centuries. The chief factor in that rebound was the enhancement of Iranian commerce that was a major policy objective of 'Abbas. Iran's physical location made it the crossroads of overland trade routes that had linked Asia, Africa, and Europe for two millennia. As a result, the long-distance carrying trade in luxury goods had traditionally been a staple of the Iranian economy. In addition to the overland routes, Iran also benefitted from maritime trade. Hormuz, in the Gulf, became Iran's major port in the fourteenth century. Despite its location in a desolate salt waste, it became a wealthy city that served as an entrepôt for the Indian Ocean basin, a staging area for goods bound for Tabriz, and a supply station for the trade that flowed from the Indian Ocean to the Mediterranean through Iraq.

During the sixteenth century, Iran's natural geographical advantage for overland trade ceased to serve it as well as before. The Portuguese discovery of a sea route around Africa meant that a small, but steadily increasing, percentage of the long-distance luxury trade shifted to the sea, and Iran's only access to it was in the Persian Gulf. In 1515, even that outlet was lost when Afonso de Albuquerque captured Hormuz for the Portuguese, and the customs duties that Hormuz received from trade subsequently went to Lisbon rather than the Safavid capital. Meanwhile, the Safavids were involved in an almost constant state of war with both the Uzbeks, to the northeast, and the Ottomans, to the west. During the frequent outbreaks of war, caravan travel was difficult, and the Ottoman government was so hostile toward the Safavids that Istanbul occasionally declared trade with Iran to be illegal, even though Ottoman merchants made huge profits from trading in Iranian silk.

In addition to serving as a conduit for commodities from abroad, Iran was also an important producer of silk. From the thirteenth to the seventeenth centuries, Iranian raw silk and finished silk products were highly desired in the West. Silk products were almost as important for Iran's export revenue at that time as petroleum is today. Prior to the thirteenth century, Iranian silk production was based in Khorasan, but in the aftermath of the Mongol invasions, production shifted to Gilan and Mazandaran, on the southern coast of the Caspian Sea. It was then that it became noticed by Europeans. Under the Il-khanids, Italian merchants flocked to Tabriz in order to purchase the precious commodity. European demand continued to increase, but the development of Ottoman–Safavid hostility meant that the most direct routes to Europe were occasionally closed.

European demand for Iranian silk mushroomed during the 1590s, the first decade of 'Abbas's rule. One of the new shah's major objectives was to secure trade routes to Europe that would not be vulnerable to the Ottomans. One new trading partner was Russia, which served the dual role of market and transit route to Europe. Russia had gained a strategic foothold near the Caspian Sea when it captured Astrakhan in 1556, and it was eager to trade with the Safavids. The Russians, like the Safavids, were motivated both by the desire to gain profits and to hurt the Ottomans economically.

'Abbas also negotiated directly with Western Europeans, realizing that if he could sell to them without going through middlemen, he could make a higher profit. He sought commercial and diplomatic relations with European countries and even promised the pope to allow Christian missionaries into his empire as an inducement to cement diplomatic ties. European merchants flocked to Iran by the thousands, cash in hand, buying silk on 'Abbas's terms. When the Dutch and English began challenging Portuguese dominance in the Indian Ocean and the Gulf, 'Abbas began negotiations with them. With the help of the English East India Company, he managed to recapture Hormuz from the Portuguese in 1622, thereby gaining access to trade in the Gulf. 'Abbas's policies enabled Iranian industry and trade to revive, and the standard of living rose dramatically.

'Abbas was not content merely to negotiate trade treaties. He also implemented policies that encouraged the development and marketing of silk in a manner that foreshadowed the mercantilism that emerged in Europe several decades later. He built royal factories to produce silks as well as velvets, satins, damasks, taffetas, brocades, and carpets. When he reconquered the areas south of the Caucasus from the Ottomans, he not only resettled Armenian merchants in New Julfa, but he also forced many Armenian Christians to move into the traditional silk-producing area south of the Caspian Sea in order to revive that industry. 'Abbas built numerous caravanserais, bridges, and bazaars in order to stimulate commerce, and he increased security along the roads. By end of his reign, security for travelers was greater than in the Mughal and Ottoman empires and most of Europe.

Iranian agriculture also improved under 'Abbas. The agricultural economy of the northern part of the country had suffered repeated hardships from the time of the Saljuq invasions in the eleventh century through the invasions of the Mongols, Timur, and the Safavids themselves. The destruction of irrigation systems and the conversion of cultivated areas into grazing lands had not been corrected under the early Safavid shahs. 'Abbas brought about important changes, although they were byproducts of self-serving policies. As part of his program of consolidating power in his own hands, 'Abbas placed large tracts of state agricultural land under his personal ownership. In the past, pastoral groups had ranged freely over such land because peasants had been unable to stop them from foraging. 'Abbas, however, prohibited grazing on his personal domains, knowing that the practice would damage his property. The peasants who worked the land were beneficiaries of the new policy and were much less likely to have their crops destroyed or their other possessions seized by herders. The changed conditions also gave them an incentive to rebuild the irrigation works that had been damaged in the invasions, because they had confidence that the investment would result in increased production. As a result, 'Abbas increased his revenue and the peasants enjoyed a rise in their security and standard of living. Throughout the seventeenth century, several rulers intervened on behalf of peasants against exploitation by local elites, and peasants enjoyed the cessation of wars and raids that had long disrupted the agriculture of northern Iran. Europeans visiting the Safavid Empire during this period reported the peasants to be well-nourished and decently clothed, and they compared their condition favorably with that of the peasants in the most fertile regions of Europe.

Culture

Like the ruling elites of most Muslim empires, members of the Safavid dynasty created a cosmopolitan atmosphere at court. Safi al-Din himself may have been Kurdish, although his family rapidly assumed a Turkic identity in a largely Turkic region. In keeping with the predominance of Turkic culture in the area of Ardabil, Isma'il spoke and wrote poetry in Chaghatay. It remained the language spoken at court throughout Safavid history. As Isma'il and Tahmasp employed more and more Persian-speaking bureaucrats in their administrations, however, the Persian language and culture became increasingly influential, particularly since the Persian language was already the predominant language of diplomacy in the eastern Muslim world. Persian was the language of poets and the educated middle class. It became the vehicle of diplomatic correspondence, belles-lettres, and history.

Tahmasp's transfer of the capital from majority-Turkic Azerbaijan to Qazvin signified a growing identification of the Safavid court with its Iranian territory. In 1590, 'Abbas made this identification complete when he moved the capital from Qazvin to Esfahan.[5] Esfahan had served as the administrative center for the Saljuqs more than 500 years earlier and already boasted one of the most impressive mosques in the world: the Masjid-e Jami'. 'Abbas was determined to build upon that legacy and turn the city into an imperial capital. His project became the greatest example of urban design and planning in the Muslim world since the creation of Baghdad in the eighth century. Esfahan became a large and impressive capital city that supported 20,000 court functionaries of all levels. It was so beautiful and offered so many opportunities for wealth, culture, power, and entertainment that it became common for Iranians to say *Esfahan nesf-e jahan*: "Esfahan is half the world."

At the center of the city, 'Abbas laid out the Maydan-e Shah, a large square (today known as the Maydan-e Imam). The open space measures 1600 by 540 feet, or about the size of twenty football fields. It was intended to serve as a market, polo ground, and general entertainment venue for jugglers, magicians, and games. At its southern end is the royal mosque, the Masjid-e Shah, decorated with brilliant enameled tiles. At the eastern end is the Masjid-e Shaykh Lotfollah, the mosque that 'Abbas used for his private devotions. On the west is the 'Ali Qapu, which served as an audience hall and from whose balcony the shah could watch polo games or other entertainment taking place in the square. On the north is a monumental arched gateway that leads to the mile-long, enclosed royal bazaar. During the Safavid period, a person could leave the Maydan-e Shah and follow the Chahar Bagh, an avenue that led to the summer palace. Over two miles long, it was lined with gardens and lavish residences and was decorated with basins, fountains, and rows of trees. 'Abbas obviously meant for the new additions to the city not only to impress subjects and foreigners alike, but also to provide for his own enjoyment. As it turned out, military campaigns kept him far from his capital for all but three years of the last three decades of his reign.

Safavid cultural excellence was not limited to monumental architecture. The art of bookmaking achieved its zenith there, and Europeans valued Safavid ceramics as highly as they did the products of China. Perhaps most famous, however, was the art of painting. In 1522, the great Timurid painter of Herat, Bihzad, relocated to Tabriz when his pupil, Tahmasp, was recalled home by his father the shah. Bihzad became the head of the royal workshop. Unlike the Arabs, for whom painting always posed at least a potential violation of the prohibition of idolatry, the Iranians prized paintings. They took particular delight in miniatures and also excelled in manuscript illumination. The Tabriz school produced an illustrated edition of the eleventh-century epic poem the *Shah-nameh* that is considered one of the world's greatest masterpieces of illuminated manuscript art. 'Abbas encouraged the paintings of such nonreligious themes as battles, hunts, and life at the royal court.

Whereas the Safavids continued the Timurid tradition in the arts, we do not have evidence that they followed its lead in the sciences. They produced some excellent maps and astrolabes, but they are not known for important work in such fields as astronomy, mathematics, optics, or medicine. The reasons for those lacunae are unknown. On the other hand, some of their intellectuals produced impressive work of lasting value in philosophical theology.

The End of an Empire

The achievement of Shah 'Abbas can be appreciated by comparing the stability of the regime before and after his reign. In contrast to the two long civil wars that occurred between Isma'il's death in 1524 and the accession of 'Abbas in 1587, the transfer of power from shah to shah occurred peacefully all four times between the death of 'Abbas in 1629 and the end of the empire in 1722. 'Abbas had devised a formula that allowed the ghulam, Qizilbash, ulama, and wealthy merchants to have a stake in the perpetuation of the Safavid monarchy. This was particularly significant in light of the fact that the theory of the shah as Mahdi had fallen into disuse. Iranians had come to look upon their ruler in much the same way that Ottomans did.

Another difference in Safavid history between the sixteenth and seventeenth centuries was that, in contrast to the repeated invasions by Uzbeks and Ottomans that Tahmasp had to face, the empire was subject to no external threat for several decades after 1639. In that year, the Safavids and Ottomans signed the Treaty of Zuhab after the Ottomans invaded and captured Baghdad the previous year. By the terms of the treaty, the two parties agreed to a frontier that closely reflects today's Iran–Iraq border. The two countries never fought again, and the Ottomans encouraged the transshipment of Iranian silk across Iraq and Syria to the Mediterranean. In fact, for the remainder of the century after the death of 'Abbas in 1629, the history of Safavid Iran was undisturbed by cataclysms. The country's lack of outside threats did not mean that life was secure: Every nation in the world during that era had to experience occasional famines and plagues. Compared to most other large societies in the world, however, Iran seems to have been fortunate.

The avoidance of major catastrophes did not mean that all was serene within the empire. Economic hardships occurred, particularly in conjunction with the periodic famines. As a way of distracting the people's attention from their hardships, the administration embarked upon its occasional persecutions of religious minorities, much as imperial Russia did two centuries later when it encouraged pogroms against Jews. The campaign against Sufism continued and may have reached its peak in the 1690s. Then, in the eighteenth century, the Safavid government lost its ability to protect itself. In 1709, the Afghan Ghilzai tribe revolted and seized Qandahar, a city that had been under Safavid control for several decades after alternating between Safavid and Mughal occupation. In 1716, another Afghan tribe, the Abdali, captured Herat from the Safavids. Four years later, in 1720, revolts flared all over the empire: the northwest, southwest, and northeast.

Historians do not yet know enough about Safavid history to say with confidence why the breakdown in security occurred in the early eighteenth century, transforming Iran from one of the safest places to travel into one of the most dangerous. The definitive episode was also the most curious. It occurred during 1721–1722, when a member of the new ruling family in Qandahar, Mahmud Ghilzai, led an army westward in search of plunder. He failed in his attempts to capture Kirman and Yazd, but that did not deter him from advancing to Esfahan. The massive capital city, seat of the empire and headquarters of the army, should have been invulnerable to him. Yet, in the spring of 1722, his undisciplined tribal levies of some 18,000 troops crushed the Safavid army of at least 40,000 troops. Ghilzai then laid siege to the city from April to October, causing incalculable suffering. Starvation drove victims to cannibalism and the consumption of human excrement. Typhus and cholera ran rampant. Some 80,000–100,000 people died from hunger and disease. When the Afghan army finally took the city, it burned major buildings, including libraries and the royal archives.

The Safavid shah became a puppet of the Afghan regime. The Ottomans and Russians took advantage of the confusion in the empire to partition the region between the Black Sea and the Caspian Sea. By 1724, Iran was divided at least four ways by Afghans, Ottomans, Russians, and forces still loyal to the Safavids. The loyalists were centered on Mashhad in northeastern Iran, where Nadir Afshar, a member of one of the great Qizilbash tribes, maintained his base. Nadir gradually built up his power, and in 1730 he captured Esfahan from the Afghans. He installed a Safavid prince on the throne but made all the important decisions himself. In 1736, having grown impatient in the role of protector of a titular shah, he deposed the last Safavid ruler and declared himself Nadir Shah.

Nadir Shah proved to be a talented but flawed military leader. He reconquered western and northern Iran as far as Tabriz. Then he moved east and captured Qandahar, Ghazna, Kabul, and Lahore. In 1739, he plundered the Mughal capital of Delhi. He also annexed Uzbek lands on the Amu Darya River and occupied Oman between 1736 and 1744. Nadir's leadership abilities began slipping in the 1740s, when he began showing signs of mental instability. He treated his troops in an increasingly brutal fashion until 1747, when his own Afshar tribesmen murdered him out of fear for their lives.

The period between the fall of the Safavids in 1722 and Nadir's assassination in 1747 was important for Twelver Shi'ites and Nizaris alike. Two and a half centuries after Isma'il began the transformation of Iran into a Twelver Shi'ite society, Nadir attempted to unravel that history overnight. Not interested in the finer points of religious doctrine, he was quite interested in two consequences of the integral relationship of Shi'ism to the Iranian monarchy. First, since he could not claim Safavid lineage, his position as ruler would always be challenged by supporters of Safavid family members. Second, the Shi'ite identity of Iran had made the country a pariah state in the eyes of the Ottomans and Uzbeks, with whom it would be useful to have good diplomatic relations. Nadir announced that he wanted Shi'ism to lose its separate identity and be recognized simply as a fifth school (_madhhab_) of Sunni law. When the Shi'ite ulama resisted, he persecuted them and seized much of the property that they administered.

Due to Nadir's relentless attacks on Twelver ulama, many of them moved to Iraq. The most prominent of them taught at Karbala and Najaf, the preeminent centers of learning in the Shi'ite world. Living and teaching in Ottoman territory, these scholars were careful not to antagonize their Sunni rulers, but they continued to provide their followers in Iran with spiritual leadership. The eighteenth century would prove to be a notable one for Twelver organizational history.

By the early eighteenth century, the Nizaris again discovered that their long period of practicing taqiya had taken a heavy toll on their community. Many Iranian Nizaris had assimilated into the Twelver society to which their parents had only pretended to belong. By the end of the Safavid regime in 1722, the Nizaris in Iran were outnumbered by those in Sind and Gujarat. Kahak's remoteness from Sind and Gujarat became a major problem due to the chaos that engulfed Iran after the fall of Esfahan to the Afghans. Nizari pilgrims from South Asia who set out for Kahak were frequently robbed and killed. Many were dissuaded from making the trip, and the financial condition of the Imamate deteriorated as a result. In the 1740s, the Imam moved 500 miles to the southeast, to Kerman province, so that his South Asian followers would not have so far to travel in order to meet with him. In post-Safavid Kerman, the circumstances of the Nizari leadership vastly improved. The Imam now felt safe enough to allow his followers to abandon taqiya. In addition, the number of pilgrims arriving from South Asia increased dramatically, restoring the financial stability of the Nizari organization.

Nadir's death in 1747 marks a turning point in Iran's history. With his heavy hand gone, Iran collapsed into another paroxysm of civil war that lasted sixteen years. His death also led directly to a division of the historic Iranian cultural area that has endured to the present. One of Nadir's most trusted followers, a young Afghan named Ahmad Abdali, returned to western Afghanistan with his troops when Nadir died. There he was named paramount chief of the Afghan warlords, and he adopted the name Ahmad Durrani (from a phrase meaning "Pearl of Pearls"). Durrani (ruled 1747–1772) began the process of creating Afghanistan, which had never been united before. Herat, Qandahar, Kabul, and Balkh all came under his control. He and his son even controlled Khorasan until the 1790s. Iran regained western Khorasan but would never again count Herat or Qandahar among its possessions.

Conclusion

Of the new Islamic groups that emerged in Iran during the fourteenth and fifteenth centuries, one of the most influential was the Safavid movement. Its importance lay not in its doctrines and practices—which in any case did not last long in their original form—but in the fact that the order was responsible for creating an empire. The consequences of this development were immense: The creation of the Safavid Empire entailed the forcible conversion of Sunni Muslims to Shi'ism, and the transformation of Iran into a Shi'ite society exacerbated natural rivalries between it and its Sunni neighbors to the east and west. Ironically, the government of the Safavid Empire eventually became implacably hostile to Sufi orders, and by the late seventeenth century, the empire created by Sufis was the region in the Muslim world where a visitor would have to look the hardest to find a Sufi.

The period from Timur to Nadir Shah witnessed profound developments in Central Asia and Iran. Historically, Central Asia was a Persian cultural area, but most of it became Turkicized during this time. Numerous Turkic confederations entered the region, and a few were so influential that, in the early twentieth century, they became immortalized in the names of the countries where they predominated. The massive immigration of pagan Turks posed a potential threat to the Islamic heritage of Central Asia, but active missionary work by the Yasavi, Kubravi, and Naqshbandi Sufi orders resulted in widespread Islamization among the new arrivals. Some of the urban ulama criticized the syncretistic admixture of shamanism and Islam practiced by many of the Turks, but others were confident that the Islamic elements would eventually triumph. The spread of Islam among the Turks was good news to Central Asian Muslims, but developments in the economic and cultural history of the era were not. The region's wealth slowly ebbed, and its cultural production faded accordingly. Central Asian cities that had once been the envy of contemporaries had faded into obscurity by the close of the eighteenth century.

During the period that Persian Central Asia became Turkicized, the Turkic religious movement that led Iran became Persianized. The Safavid leadership of Iran increasingly adopted Timurid cultural elements, culminating in the striking grandeur of reborn Esfahan. Under the Safavids, Iran assumed roughly the geographic shape that we identify with it today. Under their leadership, also, Iran became an almost exclusively Shi'ite state for the first time in its history. The Safavids declared Twelver

Shi'ism to be Iran's state religion during the process of carving out an empire. As a result, Sunni and Shi'ite identities became embroiled in the imperial rivalries and competing ambitions of Safavid Iran, the Ottoman Empire, and the Uzbek Khanate. The hostilities and mutual suspicion that developed between Sunnis and Shi'ites of that era have not dissipated to this day.

NOTES

1 For an introduction to the historiography of the controversy regarding the Central Asian economy during the seventeenth and eighteen centuries, see Jos J. L. Gommans, *The Rise of the Indo-Afghan Empire c. 1710–1780* (Leiden, Netherlands; New York; and Köln, Germany: E. J. Brill, 1995), 1–6. For a more detailed treatment, see S. A. M. Adshead, *Central Asia in World History* (New York: St. Martin's Press, 1993), 178–186 and 198–201.

2 An excellent treatment of Muslim views of the end of times is David Cook, *Studies in Muslim Apocalyptic* (Princeton, New Jersey: Darwin Press, Inc., 2002).

3 This survey of Nizari history relies exclusively on Farhad Daftary, *The Ismailis: Their History and Doctrines* (Cambridge, U.K.: Cambridge University Press, 1990), 435–500, *passim.*

4 Shi'ites believe that 'Ali should have been the successor, or caliph, to the Prophet as the leader of the Muslims, but he did not become caliph until after three other men had served in that position. As a result, Shi'ites have traditionally held the first three caliphs in contempt for having usurped the rightful place of 'Ali.

5 The traditional date for the development of Esfahan as the Safavid capital is 1598, but Stephen Blake makes a convincing case for the earlier date. See his "Shah 'Abbas and the Transfer of the Safavid Capital from Qazvin to Isfahan," in Andrew J. Newman, ed., *Society and Culture in the Early Modern Middle East: Studies on Iran in the Safavid Period* (Leiden, Netherlands, and Boston: E. J. Brill, 2003), 145–164.

FURTHER READING

Central Asia

Adshead, S.A.M. *Central Asia in World History.* New York: St. Martin's Press, 1993.

Allworth, Edward A. *The Modern Uzbeks: From the Fourteenth Century to the Present: A Cultural History.* Stanford, California: Hoover Institution Press, Stanford University, 1990.

DeWeese, Devin. *Islamization and Native Religion in the Golden Horde: Baba Tukles and Conversion to Islam in Historical and Epic Tradition.* University Park, Pennsylvania: Pennsylvania State University Press, 1994.

Fletcher, Joseph. *Studies on Chinese and Islamic Inner Asia.* Edited by Beatrice Forbes Manz. Brookfield, Vermont: Variorum, 1995.

Levi, Scott C. *The Indian Diaspora in Central Asia and Its Trade, 1550–1900.* Leiden, Netherlands, and Boston: Brill Academic Publishers, 2002.

Lipman, Jonathan N. *Familiar Strangers: A History of Muslims in Northwest China.* Seattle and London: University of Washington Press, 1997.

McChesney, R.D. *Waqf in Cental Asia: Four Hundred Years in the History of a Muslim Shrine, 1480–1889.* Princeton, New Jersey: Princeton University Press, 1991.

Mainz, Beatrice Forbes. *Power, Politics, and Religion in Timurid Iran.* Cambridge, U.K.: Cambridge University Press, 2007.

Sengupta, Anita. *The Formation of the Uzbek Nation-State: A Study in Transition.* Lanham, Maryland: Lexington Books, 2003.

Soucek, Svat. *A History of Inner Asia.* Cambridge, U.K.: Cambridge University Press, 2000.

Starr, S. Frederick, ed. *Xinjiang: China's Muslim Borderland.* Armonk, New York: M. E. Sharpe, 2004.

Iran

Arjomand, Said Amir. *The Shadow of God on Earth and the Hidden Imam.* Chicago: University of Chicago Press, 1984.

Babaie, Sussan, Kathryn Babayan, Ina Baghdiantz-McCabe, and Massumeh Farhad. *Slaves of the Shah: New Elites of Safavid Iran.* London and New York: I. B. Tauris, 2004.

Babayan, Kathryn. *Mystics, Monarchs, and Messiahs: Cultural Landscapes of Early Modern Iran.* Cambridge, Massachusetts, and London: Distributed for the Center for Middle Eastern Studies of Harvard University by Harvard University Press, 2002.

Bashir, Shahzad. *Messianic Hopes and Mystical Visions: The Nurbakhshiya Between Medieval and Modern Islam.* Columbia, S.C.: University of South Carolina Press, 2003.

Blake, Stephen P. *Half the World: The Social Architecture of Safavid Isfahan, 1590–1722.* Costa Mesa, California: Mazda Publishers, 1999.

Floor, Willem. *Safavid Government Institutions.* Costa Mesa, California: Mazda Publishers, Inc., 2001.

Foran, John. *Fragile Resistance: Social Transformation in Iran from 1500 to the Revolution.* Boulder, Colorado: Westview Press, 1993.

Garthwaite, Gene R. *The Persians.* Malden, Massachusetts: Blackwell, 2005.

Ghougassian, Vazken S. *The Emergence of the Armenian Diocese of New Julfa in the Seventeenth Century.* Atlanta, Georgia: Scholars' Press, 1998.

Matthee, Rudi. *Persia in Crisis: Safavid Decline and the Fall of Isfahan.* International Library of Iranian Studies. London: I. B. Tauris, 2012.

———. *The Politics of Trade in Safavid Iran: Silk for Silver, 1600–1730.* Cambridge, U.K., and New York: Cambridge University Press, 1999.

Mazzaoui, Michel M., ed. *Safavid Iran and Her Neighbors.* Salt Lake City: University of Utah Press, 2003.

Melville, Charles, ed. *Safavid Persia: The History and Politics of an Islamic Society.* London and New York: I. B. Taurs & Co., Ltd, 1996.

Newman, Andrew. *Safavid Iran: Rebirth of a Persian Empire.* London and New York: I. B. Tauris, 2006.

Petrushevskii, I.P. *Islam in Iran.* Translated by Hubert Evans. Albany: State University of New York Press, 1985.

Stierlin, Henri. *Islamic Art and Architecture from Isfahan to the Taj Mahal.* London: Thames & Hudson, 2002.

Turner, Colin. *Islam without Allah? The Rise of Religious Externalism in Safavid Iran.* Richmond, U.K.: Curzon, 2000.

Woods, John E. *The Aqquyunlu: Clan, Confederation, Empire.* Rev. and expanded ed. Salt Lake City: University of Utah Press, 1999.

CHAPTER 15

South Asia

The subcontinent of South Asia was an alluring wonderland in the imagination of the peoples of Southwest Asia. *Al-Hind* was a land of fabulous wealth and strange customs that seamen, scientists, adventurers, and merchants longed to visit. For the first few centuries of Muslim history, the sheer distance that one would have to travel from the major centers of Islamic culture to reach South Asia contributed to the sense that the region was exotic and alien. Until the thirteenth century, few Muslims inhabited South Asia other than in the Indus River valley and along the Malabar Coast, the regions closest to the Muslim heartlands. These two areas were isolated from the rest of South Asia by a large, harsh desert and a steep escarpment, respectively.

Newcomers to South Asia from the Arabic-speaking world or Iran sometimes found it difficult to interact with Hindus. Hinduism—a catch-all term for a wide variety of religious expressions indigenous to South Asia—was at odds in many ways with the doctrines and practices that the ulama of Arab and Iranian societies had come to accept as the essentials of Islam. Equally problematic were modes of social interaction prescribed by the caste system of South Asia. Members of each caste and sub-caste were taught that they had specific duties to perform and certain activities to avoid in order to earn a higher existence when reincarnated. The prescribed behavior included detailed regulations regarding how to relate to people not belonging to one's caste. It was easy for a newcomer to offend—and be offended by—Hindus without knowing what behavior or words had triggered the misunderstanding.

Despite the difficulties, Muslims and Hindus learned to coexist. The social elites among both groups discovered that they shared many important values, and it was not uncommon for wealthy Muslim merchants to socialize with high-caste Brahmins, who found ways not to be ritually defiled by contact with them. At the other end of the social scale, Muslim and Hindu peasants visited each other's shrines and celebrated each other's religious festivals. The nature of the political leadership played a great role in shaping the patterns of Muslim–Hindu interaction.

South Asia after the Delhi Sultanate

Because of the initial physical and cultural obstacles to the spread of Islam in South Asia, it would have been no surprise if Islam had failed to leave a trace there. In fact, however, the Delhi Sultanate was only the first of numerous Muslim-ruled states that proliferated across the subcontinent after the thirteenth century. The royal courts of these states attracted soldiers, scholars, artists, and holy men from all parts of the Muslim world. These immigrants left a permanent imprint on South Asian society.

Southern and Central South Asia

The Deccan Plateau is a major topographical feature of South Asia, constituting most of the peninsular section. The Narmada River is the traditional boundary between the plateau and the central plains. The Satpura mountain range immediately south of the river marks the beginning of the plateau, which is bounded on the west and east by the Western and Eastern Ghats, two mountain ranges that separate the plateau from the coastal regions of the peninsula. For 700 miles, the Western Ghats loom as the backdrop to the peninsula's narrow Malabar Coast. The mountain peaks there rise sharply above the coastal plain to heights of 3000 to 8000 feet. The Deccan slopes gently eastward from the Western Ghats to the Eastern Ghats, which range in height from 2000 to 4000 feet. Whereas the Western Ghats give the appearance of a uniform line of cliffs and peaks, the Eastern Ghats are composed of disconnected masses of hills. They descend to the Coromandel Coast on the eastern side of the peninsula.

The Deccan was the site of the most vibrant Muslim presence in South Asia between Timur's sack of Delhi in 1398 and the rise of the Mughal Empire. In the 1330s, during the widespread revolt against Muhammad ibn Tughluq, sections of the Deccan began breaking away from Delhi's rule. Soon most of the plateau was consolidated into two kingdoms. The northern one was the Muslim Bahmani kingdom, named after its founder, 'Ala al-Din Bahman Shah. The southern kingdom was Vijayanagar, ruled by Hindus.

The Bahmani kingdom was founded in 1347. This was during the period that the Mongol polities in Iran, Russia, and Central Asia were breaking up into chaos and the plague was sweeping across Eurasia. As a Muslim-ruled state, the Bahmani kingdom offered Turks and Iranians fleeing the violence of the post-Il-khanate period a new chance for a career. The kingdom needed the services of skilled military officers, civilian bureaucrats, and religious specialists. The Iranians became dominant. Soon, their culture created a Persianate cast to the Bahmani court, which used the Persian language as its vehicle of literature and diplomacy. The kingdom's capital was in Gulbarga until 1424, when it was moved to Bidar.

The Bahmani kingdom developed a high level of cosmopolitan culture. When it exchanged ambassadors with Sultan Mehmet II (1451–1481) of Istanbul, it became the first state in the subcontinent to exchange ambassadors with the Ottomans. Governing a Muslim-ruled state with a majority Hindu population, its rulers worked hard to achieve a modus vivendi with their subjects. The kingdom engaged in bloody wars with its major rival, the Hindu kingdom of Vijayanagar, but the two states were not enemies for religious reasons. Both tolerated adherents of other faiths and they shared a remarkably similar culture. The Bahmanis did not interfere with the religious practice of their Hindu majority population, and the capital city of Vijayanagar contained a mosque for the Muslim soldiers who served in its army. The real problem was the desire of the two kingdoms to dominate the rich agricultural region of Raicha that lay between them south of the Krishna River. The Bahmani kingdom also had to struggle against several new Muslim-ruled states—especially Malwa and Gujarat—over territorial issues.

Internally, the Bahmani court suffered from tension between the "Foreigners" and the "Deccanis." The Foreigners were the Turkic and Iranian immigrants, whereas the Deccanis included several groups. Among their number were descendants of early Arab traders in the area, Turks (the majority of whom were soldiers) who had immigrated during the period of Delhi's rule, descendants of Abyssinian (Ethiopian) slaves, local converts to Islam, and Hindus. The Deccanis were jealous of the success of the newly arrived Muslims from the west. They were also perturbed that active recruitment of Iranians continued: The court even dispatched ships to bring them to the kingdom. Ominously, the military ranks were dominated by Deccanis of Turkic descent, whose loyalty became increasingly problematic. Between 1484 and 1525, Deccanis led secession movements in four provinces—Ahmadnagar, Bijapur, Golkonda, and Berar—leaving the capital city of Bidar only a fragment of its former territory to rule (see Map 15.1). From 1525, this remnant of the Bahmani kingdom was known as Bidar.

During the sixteenth century, the most powerful of the five successor states of the Bahmani kingdom were Bijapur, Golkonda, and Ahmadnagar. All three were much more powerful than Berar and Bidar, which were landlocked. The three larger states had Shi'ite rulers for most of their history. Because they were rivals, they formed shifting patterns of alliances with—and against—each other and Vijayanagar. The two smaller Muslim states survived by siding with the dominant alliance at any given time. All five cultivated a Persianate court culture and, as a result, suffered from continuing Foreigner–Deccani tensions and occasional violence.

Bijapur was situated on a flat and barren plain, but it possessed great natural resources. It controlled a prosperous section of the Arabian Sea coastline. It also secured Raicha, the rich agricultural area over which the Bahmani kingdom and Vijayanagar had fought. Its founder was a Turk from Anatolia who, in his youth, became a follower of the Safavid leader Junayd, the grandfather of Shah Isma'il. Migrating to the Deccan, he became governor of Bijapur under the Bahmanis but declared his independence in 1489. When Isma'il declared Twelver Shi'ism to be the religion of his Safavid Empire, the ruler of Bijapur did so as well.

During the first century of its existence, Bijapur's official religion alternated between Shi'ism and Sunnism with each generation. By the 1580s, its rulers were consistently Shi'ite, although one of them was so heterodox in his rituals that many of his contemporaries thought he was a Hindu. Close maritime links continued between Bijapur and Persian Gulf ports despite aggressive attempts by the Portuguese after 1498 to control the entire commerce of the Indian Ocean. In 1510, the Portuguese seized Bijapur's major port of Goa and turned it into their headquarters in Asia. Bijapur, however, was able to use smaller ports farther north to evade Portuguese efforts to blockade the coastal trade. Relations with the Gulf continued uninterrupted. By the seventeenth century, Bijapur had developed into a city of several hundred thousand inhabitants that was adorned with impressive works of monumental architecture.

Golkonda was founded by a descendant of the founder of the Black Sheep Turkmen clan of western Iran. Unlike Bijapur, which maintained ports on the

Arabian Sea, Golkonda had ports on the Bay of Bengal. The inland city of Golkonda (modern Hyderabad) was famous as a source of diamonds. It was perhaps the wealthiest city in the subcontinent during the fifteenth and sixteenth centuries. Because of its wealth and its Shi'ite court, it attracted numerous Iranian immigrants.

Ahmadnagar, the third of the great Muslim Deccan states, was founded by the son of a converted Hindu Brahmin (the highest caste) in 1490. The dynasty became Shi'ite in 1538. The sultanate was distinctive in that its "Foreigner" and "Deccani" factions exhausted each other by the end of the sixteenth century through constant fighting, and they were replaced by Marathas and Ethiopians. The Marathas were Hindus who spoke the Marathi language. We will hear more about them later. The Ethiopians, or *Habshis*, were brought in as slaves, but, like military slaves in some regions, many had gained their freedom and attained high office. One notable example of a freed Habshi was Malik Ambar, who became the power behind the

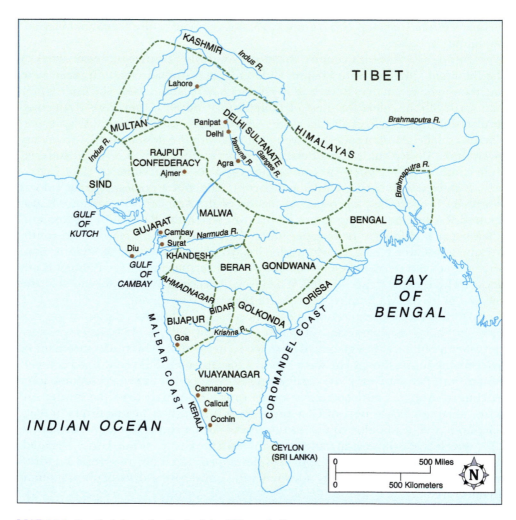

MAP 15.1 South Asia at the End of the Fifteenth Century.

throne in Ahmadnagar from about 1600 until his death in 1626. He served as regent for the young sultan, even when the latter attained his majority, and was the undisputed authority in both civil and military affairs. He led the successful military defense of the sultanate against repeated Mughal aggression. Of his 50,000 troops, some 10,000 were Habshis.

To the north of the successor states of the Bahmani kingdom lay still more Muslim-ruled kingdoms. Khandesh, the northernmost of the Deccan states, emerged in the 1380s. North of the Deccan, Gujarat gradually became independent of Delhi during the latter's civil war, between 1390 and 1401. Gujarat's cities were important centers for textile production, and its ports were important entrepôts for commodities from South Asia and Southeast Asia that were destined for East Africa and the Mediterranean. The textile-manufacturing center of Ahmadabad and the port of Cambay (Khambat) became world-famous in the fifteenth and sixteenth centuries. Cambay ranked with Aden, Hormuz, and Melaka as one of the chief ports of the Indian Ocean in the early sixteenth century.

To the east of Gujarat lay Malwa, which threw off Delhi's control in 1401. Founded by an Afghan noble, it lay in a barren region but thrived on the taxes it imposed on the transit trade connecting Gujarat with the interior. Its rulers also launched raids into surrounding regions in pursuit of plunder to supplement the kingdom's meager natural resources.

Hundreds of miles to the east of Malwa, in the delta of the Ganges (Ganga) River, lay Bengal, which seceded from the Delhi Sultanate in the 1350s. Turks dominated it for most of the next two centuries. Due to the shifting course of the Ganges, the rulers had to move the capital several times, with the result that no single city became identified as the seat of government. As in the other Muslim states, Persian language and culture dominated the Bengal court despite the Turkic background of most of the rulers. Bengal's ample supply of water produced an environment strikingly different from those of most of the other Muslim-ruled states. It exported rice and sugar but was even more famous for its cotton textiles. The region had exported cotton products at least as early as the tenth century. By the sixteenth century, it was attracting Portuguese, Dutch, and English merchants, who exchanged silver for fine-quality cloth.

The Indo-Gangetic Plain

The power base of the Delhi Sultanate had been the 1500-mile-long arc of the Indus and Ganges river valleys that is known as the Indo-Gangetic plain. Its relatively flat terrain facilitated the movement of armies, and its productive, irrigation-based agricultural economy generated lucrative tax revenues. Timur's destruction of Delhi was so thorough, however, that for three years after he left, the city was almost uninhabited. A member of the Tughluq dynasty attempted a revival of power in 1401, but the weak effort lasted only to 1413, when a Turk overthrew the regime. The new government was dominated by the Sayyid dynasty, which was also short-lived. As we saw in the previous chapter, it was in effect a vassal state of Shah Rukh (1407–1447) of Herat. In 1451, the Sayyids were overthrown by an Afghan who had served in the Sayyid army and administration. The new ruler founded the Lodi dynasty, which ruled Delhi until 1526. During this period, thousands of Afghan peasant–herdsmen and adventurer–soldiers migrated into the Indo-Gangetic plain. Afghans gradually supplanted Turks and Iranians to become the most powerful and widely dispersed foreign Muslim group in the region. Many settled on the land as local lords who controlled the majority Hindu peasantry. Afghan warlords dominated the Punjab and conquered existing states on the Ganges, including Bengal. The Lodi government was able to co-opt some of them and expanded Delhi's control once again. By the early sixteenth century, the dynasty ruled the area from the Punjab to Bihar in the east.

The Lodis reinvigorated Delhi, but they faced formidable challenges. Fellow Afghans in Bengal refused to cooperate with them, and the Rajputs—a Hindu warrior class in Rajasthan—began to challenge their authority. The last of the Lodis, Ibrahim (1517–1526), was unable to command the allegiance of the warlords who had served his father, and he soon found himself confronted with unrest both in Bihar and Lahore. As we shall see later in this chapter, this unrest left him vulnerable when the Mughal army appeared before his gates in 1526.

Islam in South Asia

South Asia was on the periphery of the Muslim world until the middle of the thirteenth century, when Delhi emerged as a major metropolis and political power. For several centuries thereafter, the subcontinent attracted tens of thousands of Muslim migrants, but Islam became the majority religion in only a few regions. Overall, South Asia did not become as Islamized as Iran or Andalus. Like the Balkans, it bore the distinct impress of Muslim rule, but most of its inhabitants retained their earlier religious identity. Although Islam has never become the religion of the majority of the population of South Asia, the region's huge overall population has meant that the absolute number of Muslims there became very large indeed—today South Asia contains more Muslims than any comparable land area in the world.

Patterns of Muslim Influence

Muslim traders began appearing along the Malabar Coast of western India soon after the Prophet's death in 632. The coast—especially its southern extension, known as Kerala—had long been a staging area for Arab and Iranian traders because of its location in the Indian Ocean. The cyclical movements of the monsoon winds dictated that any commerce across the width of the ocean include a layover on the Malabar Coast or the Coromandel Coast; the former offered far more port cities for the purpose than did the latter. After the rise of Islam, most of the merchants and sailors from the Persian Gulf region were Muslims. Their frequent business dealings along the Malabar Coast resulted in the creation of a Muslim community in Kerala that was an extension of the societies ringing the Persian Gulf. The community maintained close contacts with the Gulf thanks to the sea route, whereas its contacts with the interior of the Deccan were limited due to the difficulty of crossing the formidable Western Ghats. The Muslims of the coast were usually under the political dominance of Hindu princes. Members of the Hindu and Muslim communities developed a symbiotic relationship in which the merchants relied upon the security provided by

FIGURE 15.1 The Charminar in Hyderabad. The ruler of Golkonda constructed this mosque (the prayer area is on the top floor) in 1591 when he moved his capital to the new city of Hyderabad.

Stuart Forster / Alamy Stock Photo.

the rulers, and the rulers benefitted from the wealth and overseas contacts provided by the merchants.

In contrast to the peaceful growth of Muslim settlement of the Malabar Coast, most of the rest of South Asia experienced the first arrival of Muslims in the form of violent conquests. By 715, Arab armies had conquered Sind and Multan, in the lower and middle Indus River valley, respectively. These areas were situated on overland trade routes linking South Asia with Iran. The Muslim community of this area began to lose its Arabic character in the early eleventh century when Mahmud of Ghazna led plundering expeditions into the Punjab and Gujarat. Mahmud was of Turkic background, but he admired and cultivated Persian language and culture. Eventually, Mahmud took possession of most of the Punjab and the Indus valley. His dynasty, the Ghaznavids, established Lahore as a major city.

During the late twelfth century, the Muslim Ghurid clan from Afghanistan seized power from the Ghaznavids. The Ghurids expanded their rule down the Ganges as far as Bihar. The Delhi Sultanate replaced the Ghurids in the early thirteenth century and extended Muslim influence into the Deccan and Bengal. As we have seen, the Delhi Sultanate did not retain its dominance over the subcontinent for long, but its many successor states maintained Muslim rule over a vast area. From the fourteenth century until the waning of the Mughal Empire in the eighteenth century, the dominant political and military figures of the Indo-Gangetic plain and of the Deccan were of Turkic or Afghan origin, but they patronized Persian culture at court.

These conquests were only the latest in a long series of destructive invasions of South Asia. The Muslim invasions, however, are better documented and more recent. As a result, they are seared into the historical memory of Muslims and Hindus alike. To the former, the invasions were heroic episodes of military glory and religious duty in which the true faith was extended to pagans. To the latter, they were brutal assaults that resulted in cultural humiliation, physical destruction, and mass suffering. Centuries later, they still touch a raw nerve and are occasionally exploited by Hindu politicians.

Recent research demonstrates that both perspectives require modification. The early raids of Mahmud of Ghazna into Gujarat were, indeed, vicious and rapacious. Mahmud conducted a public relations campaign with the Muslim world, portraying the incursions as expressions of jihad, but they are hard to explain as other than murderous looting. Mahmud's conquest of the Punjab was a more complicated process in which the inevitable violence of invasion was mitigated by policies to stabilize the economy and work out a modus vivendi with the local population. Subsequent Muslim invasions into most of South Asia followed a similar pattern. The period of conquest was characterized by murder, rape, kidnapping, and looting. Some Hindu temples were not only razed but replaced by mosques. Subsequently, however, Hindus resumed a routine of life similar to what they had experienced prior to invasion.

This pattern of violent destruction, followed by a return to normalcy, was characteristic not only of Muslim invasions, but also of wars among regional Hindu rulers. Triumphant Hindu generals destroyed temples that were devoted to the particular gods or goddesses associated with the previous ruler's regime. The practice was a way of delegitimizing the former regime. A similar policy was followed by most Muslim conquerors. Temples not associated with the royal cult were not molested. Moreover,

Muslim rulers often repaired Hindu temples and sometimes even financed the construction of new ones.[1]

Muslim conquerors rarely attempted forcible conversion to Islam except when a ruler felt that the profession of Islam by a local leader would result in the pacification of a troubled area. Muhammad ibn Tughluq, the Sultan of Delhi who is known for his toleration of all religions, nevertheless forcibly "converted" several rulers in the Deccan in an effort to consolidate his rule there. Numerous reports survive of forcible conversions of tribal leaders in what is now the border area between Afghanistan and Pakistan. Once a hostile territory became a revenue-paying province, however, the overwhelming majority of Muslim rulers in South Asia followed a laissez-faire religious policy. Only rarely did any of them even impose the head tax and land tax on non-Muslims that were stipulated in the Shari'a. Although the tax records of these regimes refer to such taxes, they are almost always instances of using the terminology of the Shari'a for a tax that both Muslims and Hindus paid.

Because the subject of this book is the worldwide Muslim community, discussions focus on religious affiliation more than on ethnic identity. It is important, however, to be aware that the Indian chroniclers who wrote at the time of the Muslim invasions referred to the invaders as Turks or Afghans, not Muslims. The invaders were not viewed by the victims as representatives of a religion, but as yet more instances of the martial Turk or Afghan at war. Thus, in the context of world history, the Muslim invasions of India were Turkic and Afghan invasions, just as history books describe the Catholic soldiers and missionaries under Cortes and Pizarro as having participated in a Spanish conquest of Mexico and Peru, and the Puritans who violently dispossessed the Indians of New England as being English settlers.

The degree of Islamization varied widely in the areas under Muslim rule. Muslims ruled the middle and lower Indus River valley continuously after the early eighth century, and so the indigenous population had many centuries to respond to inducements to convert. Perhaps an even more important factor was that Hinduism had never been well established there, and Buddhism had been weakened by Hindu persecution in the seventh century. In the basins of the upper and middle Yamuna and Ganges rivers, however, Islam made little impact, even though Muslim regimes were based in this north-central area of the subcontinent almost continuously from the early thirteenth century into the nineteenth century. In this densely populated region, Hinduism and its patterns of social organization were deeply entrenched. Strong social ties, patterned behavior, and peer pressure reinforced traditional rituals and doctrines.

South Asian Sufism

Sufism became the majority expression of Islam in South Asia as it did in most areas of the Muslim world after the fifteenth century. Numerous orders made their appearance. By the seventeenth century, the Qadiriya, Naqshbandiya, and Shattariya had large followings, but the two most popular were the Suhrawardiya and the Chishtiya. Both entered South Asia at the end of the twelfth century. The founder of the Chishtiya, Mu'in al-Din Chishti, was born in Chisht, near Herat, but in 1193 he moved to Ajmer, where he died. As a result, the Chishti order is usually considered to be the most "Indian" of the major orders of the subcontinent. The tomb (*dargah*) of Mu'in al-Din Chishti at Ajmer and that of his successor, Nizam al-Din Awliya, in Delhi became major pilgrimage sites for both Hindus and Muslims.

The Chishtiya scandalized members of the Qadiriya and Naqshbandiya because of their practice of *sama'* (musical session) and *raqs* (dancing) during their dhikr. They were enthusiastic advocates of Ibn al-'Arabi's concept of the Unity of Being, the doctrine that all Reality is an expression of the Being of God. Many other Sufis were influenced by the Unity of Being, but the Chishtiya were the most consistently identified with it. The early Chishtis developed a reputation for asceticism and avoided royal courts and courtly affairs. By the mid-fourteenth century, however, Chishti saints in the Deccan were siding with the court of the Bahmani kingdom because of a shared hostility toward Muhammad ibn Tughluq, the ruler of Delhi. Within a short time, Chishti devotees in that region, at least, were in agreement with many other Sufis that pirs had an important political role. They were the true sovereigns of this world who had delegated political sovereignty to kings in order to free themselves for purely spiritual concerns. The Bahmani king built a dargah in Bidar for the Chishti saint who had brought him to power, and it became a major object of pilgrimage in the Deccan.

Sufism in South Asia received a boost in the sixteenth and seventeenth centuries as a result of the repeated waves of persecution that the Safavid regime directed against Iranian Sufis. Leading pirs and lowly disciples alike fled from Iran to the subcontinent, where the Muslim courts were Persian-speaking. Several major pirs migrated to the Deccan, where the Twelver Shi'ite courts usually welcomed them in order to enhance their own spiritual legitimacy.

It was once thought that Sufis played an active role in the conversion of South Asians to Islam by means of preaching and teaching. That idea has been modified in recent years. Research has shown that some Sufis did engage in active proselytizing in the subcontinent, just as they did in Central Asia. Far more Sufis, however, regarded Hindus to be beyond hope of salvation and had no interest in trying to convert them. It now seems more accurate to say that Sufis played an important, but indirect, role in the spread of Islam in South Asia. Many Hindus were attracted to Sufi pirs due to their reputation as healers, miracle-workers, and exorcists. They did not go to the pir in order to learn the highly demanding spiritual exercises that he taught his inner circle of disciples. Rather, they went in the hope of gaining a spiritual benefit, just as they would seek help from a *saddhu*, or Hindu holy man. They took some token gift, and the pir or his assistants blessed the supplicants or provided an amulet in the form of a piece of paper etched with the names of God or a verse from the Qur'an.

As in other parts of the Muslim world, the spiritual power of the lodge did not fade away with the death of the pir. His dargah became the object of pilgrimage and the site of festivals and prayers. One of his direct descendants would typically become the administrator of the shrine. He was known in South Asia as a *pirzada*. As the saint's proxy, he possessed the *baraka* (blessings, or presence of God) of the saint. The tomb-shrines became the primary means by which many peasants came to experience Islam. For illiterate peasants who lacked convenient access to a mosque and who certainly could not read the Qur'an, dargahs provided the space where they could encounter the mystery and mercy of God as mediated by the pirzada.

Most of the supplicants who sought favors from a pir or pirzada were women. While visiting a shrine they would hear the songs of worship that the murshids sang, which drew upon local religious vocabulary and local styles of verse and music. Back home they would hum a few of the verses while doing household chores or sing them as lullabies to their children. The amulets, poetry, and general veneration in which the pirs were held provided the children with impressions of Islam. As they grew up, they assimilated these ideas into their own families' patterns of worship. It was common for people of any faith to visit both the dargah and the Hindu temple, as well as to participate in both Muslim and Hindu festivals. Few peasants thought of Islam or Hinduism as exclusive religious systems; rather, they viewed them as spiritual traditions that contained techniques for drawing upon supernatural assistance in solving problems or enhancing one's position in the world.[2]

An Isma'ili Revival

In the aftermath of Hulagu's destruction of the Nizari organization centered on Alamut, some Nizaris stayed in Iran and struggled to survive in a hostile environment. Others migrated hundreds or even thousands of miles to escape persecution. Many settled in the towns and villages of Sind and Gujarat. Their experience in those regions laid the foundation for today's community of Khoja Muslims. Meanwhile, members of a rival branch of Isma'ilism known as Tayyibi Islam were also seeking a haven from persecution. Based in Yemen, large numbers of the group migrated to Gujarat, where a branch of their organization had existed since the late eleventh century. The Tayyibis of Gujarat evolved into today's community of Bohra Muslims. Thus, as Isma'ilis found life increasingly unsustainable in the region from Yemen to Iran, many sought refuge on the western fringes of South Asia, where most of them are found today.

Nizaris (Khojas)

Of the Nizaris who fled their villages when Hulagu destroyed Alamut in 1256, a considerable number migrated to Sind. The area was under the rule of an independent dynasty and was inhabited by both Muslims and followers of Indic (Hindu) religious practices. Very little is known about the history of the Nizaris in Sind for the next several centuries. All that is certain is that several outstanding spiritual teachers kept the community intact. Whether they engaged in active proselytization is unclear, but by the fourteenth century, the community had begun to gain adherents from the local population. The Nizaris were especially successful in winning followers among the Lohanas, a lineage group known for its trading activities. The Lohanas of Sind used the word *khwaja* as a respectful form of address for each other, and the practice carried over into the Nizari community. Over time, this title became a distinctive characteristic of the Nizaris of the area. Thus, the Nizaris of Sind came to be known as Khojas. By at least the mid-sixteenth century, the Khojas outnumbered the Nizaris of Iran.

Like Nizari groups everywhere between the fall of Alamut (1258) and the establishment of Nizari headquarters at Anjudan (1460), the Khojas developed doctrines and practices independently of the Imam in Iran. In fact, the Khojas splintered into several groups. Some became closely identified with Sunnism, others were attracted to Twelver Shi'ism, and still others adopted local Indic concepts into their religious practice. The Khoja group that is most widely known today (the followers of the Aga Khan) developed a doctrine called the *Satpanth,* or "true path." The Satpanth bore the stamp of Nizari assimilation into Indic religious traditions. Achieving the true path enabled converts to be liberated from the cycle of rebirth and attain salvation in Paradise. Khojas consider the Qur'an to be the last of the Vedas (the sacred scriptures of Hinduism), which abrogated the older ones. 'Ali, the first Imam, was the anticipated tenth avatar (incarnation) of Krishna. His essence continued in his successor Imams. Whereas Sunnis and Twelver Shi'ites supplement the Qur'an with a collection of accounts regarding the Prophet's sayings and model behavior called the Hadith, the primary devotional literature for the Khojas is a body of literature called the Ginans. Apparently composed by early Khoja pirs, the Ginans are hymnlike poems that began as oral traditions and were only later recorded in writing. Other Khoja practices that set the early community apart from Sunnis and Twelver Shi'ites were a prohibition on widow remarriage, a limitation of inheritance to males, and a substitution of three daily ritual prayers recited in the Gujarati language for the five Arabic-language prayers of the salat.

During the second half of the sixteenth century, the Khojas of Sind began suffering from Sunni persecution, causing many to flee to Gujarat. This was the period during which the Imam in Anjudan was seeking to establish his authority over all the scattered Nizari communities as persecution intensified in Iran under Tahmasp. The Khoja community responded favorably to the Imam's outreach, and they submitted to his authority. As it turned out, the Mughals conquered Gujarat in 1574, and the emperor Akbar practiced a policy of religious toleration. Relieved of the fears of persecution and linked to the Imam, the Khojas of Gujarat thrived. By the seventeenth century, the Khoja community no longer had its own pir. Instead, the Imam appointed a special representative for the community who relayed communication between the Imam and his followers. Ties between the Khojas and the Imam became even stronger after the latter's transfer to Kerman in the eighteenth century.

Tayyibis (Bohras)

Tayyibi Isma'ilis were rivals of the Nizaris. Whereas the Nizaris had broken from the Fatimids of Egypt in 1094, the Tayyibis seceded from the Fatimids in 1130, soon after the murder of al-Amir, the Fatimid caliph-Imam. They acquired their name due to their insistence that al-Amir's toddler son, Tayyib, should have succeeded to the throne after his father's murder. Al-Amir's cousin al-Hafiz seized it instead, and his descendants ruled Egypt until the end of the Fatimid line four decades later. Fearing for Tayyib's life, the boy's supporters spirited him away to Yemen.

The Isma'ili leaders of Yemen formally adopted Tayyib's cause and rejected the authority of Cairo. Moreover, the Isma'ili community in Gujarat, which had been established by Fatimid missionaries from Yemen in the 1060s, also accepted Tayyib as their Imam at this time. Tayyib lived incognito in Yemen. His followers gained their spiritual guidance from the Imam's *da'i mutlaq,* or "chief missionary." Tayyibis believe that Tayyib's son inherited the Imamate from him and that the line has continued to the present day. None of the Imams has ever made himself known, and yet his followers have been convinced that the Imam's physical presence is necessary to sustain the very existence of the world. Technically, he is not in seclusion but rather lives among his people in the world, perhaps as a successful corporate executive or as a fishmonger in some poverty-stricken village. The public face of the Imam continues to be the da'i mutlaq, who commands the absolute obedience of the faithful. Unlike Nizaris, Tayyibis retained a large corpus of Fatimid writings on cosmology, the nature of history, and spiritual discipline, and have thus remained closer in doctrine and practice to the Fatimid tradition.

In Yemen, the Tayyibis struggled almost continuously with the Zaydis, who slowly gained the upper hand in a contest for territory. The Tayyibi community in the region lost its dynamism and began to shrink. Meanwhile, their co-religionists in Gujarat made numerous conversions among a Hindu merchant caste. As a result, they gradually became known as Bohras, from a Gujarati term for "merchant." They prospered in the international maritime trade until 1298, when Gujarat was conquered by the Delhi Sultanate. Because of persecution by Delhi's rulers, most Tayyibis began to practice taqiya in the form of Sunnism. Later, under the Sultanate of Gujarat, they suffered even more intense persecution. Well over half the community converted definitively to Sunnism in the first half of the fifteenth century.

By the mid-sixteenth century, the Tayyibis of Yemen were trapped between a newly aggressive Zaydi campaign in the highlands and the Ottoman occupation of the Yemeni lowlands that had begun in 1538. The situation became desperate, because moving to Gujarat was not a viable option given the need to practice taqiya there. Fortunately for the movement, the Mughal conquest of Gujarat (1574) occurred before disaster struck in Yemen. The da'i mutlaq moved the Tayyibi headquarters to Gujarat at the very time that Khojas from Sind were coming into the province to escape persecution. Under the Mughal policy of religious toleration, the Bohras resumed practicing their religion openly.

In Gujarat, the Bohras thrived economically and their community began to grow again. The cessation of persecution, however, allowed differences within the community to burst into the open. As early as 1589, the Bohras experienced a major controversy over the issue of succession to the office of da'i mutlaq. A minority seceded from the main group and became known as the Sulaymani Bohras. Their new da'i mutlaq soon relocated their base of operations to the region around Najran, in the Arabian Peninsula. The larger, original group has been known as the Da'udi Bohras since the secession. Another succession dispute within the Da'udi Bohras resulted in the creation of the 'Aliya Bohras in 1624. The Da'udi and 'Aliya groups have remained based in Gujarat. Even after four centuries, doctrinal and ritual differences among the three groups are trifling. The original schisms were triggered only by disagreements over which person should inherit the mantle of the da'i mutlaq.

The Timurids in South Asia: The Mughals

The descendants of Timur cultivated a dazzling cultural life in Central Asia during the fifteenth century. Unfortunately for their dynasty, their political exploits at that time did not match their cultural achievements. They were ousted from their thrones one by one, and the last Timurid—Babur—was not able to retain Transoxiana even with the help of Shah Isma'il's army. Among Babur's many exemplary traits, however, were persistence and creativity. He soon turned his ambitions and energy toward South Asia. His exploits there laid the foundation for the Timurids' greatest achievement: the Mughal Empire.

The Mughals (Moghuls) referred to themselves as the *Gurkani*, a word that derives from *gurkan*, a Persianized form of the Mongolian word *kuragan*, meaning "son-in-law." Timur appropriated the term as an honorific title. His greatest regret was that he could not claim descent from Chinggis Khan. He made up for his deficiency by marrying not merely one, but two, Chinggisid princesses. He was thus a "son-in-law" of the great conqueror twice over (albeit several generations removed). Babur and his descendants, always proud of their Timurid lineage, continued to use the title. Many Arabic- and Persian-speaking contemporaries, however, referred to them as "Mongols" (*al-mughul*), and the name has stuck.

The Formation of the Mughal Empire

Babur was born in 1483 in Fergana (Farghana), a large valley in the eastern extremity of what is now Uzbekistan. Fergana is effectively enclosed by the precipitous mountain ranges that tower over it on the east, north, and south. It contains the headwaters of the Syr Darya River, and its fertile soil has supported a large population for centuries. Babur's father was the Timurid ruler of Fergana, and his mother could trace her ancestry to Chinggis Khan. Babur thus had a notable pedigree as a fifth-generation descendant of Timur and a thirteenth-generation descendant of Chinggis Khan. Like his contemporary Shah Isma'il of the Safavid Empire, he was an unusually gifted individual. Best known for his military and administrative achievements, he was also a writer of considerable ability. His autobiography—the *Babur-nameh*—reveals him to have been cultured, witty, gregarious, insatiably curious, and possessed of a keen eye for the beauty of nature.

In Timurid fashion, Babur's father had regarded himself eligible to rule any part of Timur's domain, and he spent his life trying to gain control of Transoxiana. Babur followed in his footsteps, fighting fellow Timurids for their holdings. He managed to capture Samarqand from one of them, but then the Uzbeks invaded Transoxiana and his forces were overwhelmed. In subsequent battles with them, he lost both Samarqand and Fergana. In desperation, he retreated 500 miles south to Kabul, which he captured in 1504. Kabul became his new base, and from there he watched as the Uzbeks captured Herat, the last remaining Timurid realm, in 1507.

In 1510, Shah Isma'il appeared in Khorasan with his army, having conquered the rest of Iran. Isma'il respected the Timurid lineage but distrusted the Uzbeks. He offered Babur an alliance to reconquer Transoxiana if he would rule the region as a Shi'ite. The stipulation ran counter to Babur's convictions: He was a devoted follower of the Naqshbandi order, which was hostile to Shi'ism. On the other hand, he saw the alliance as his last chance to claim the patrimony of his ancestors. The moment must have been similar to the one faced by the French king Henry II a few decades later, when he had to choose between remaining a Huguenot or converting to Catholicism and being accepted as king by the majority of the French population. Just as Henry II is said to have concluded that "Paris is well worth a mass," Babur donned the red headgear of the Qizilbash and joined Isma'il in a war to recover what he considered his patrimony. After the Timurid and Safavid armies conquered

Transoxiana, Babur honored his agreement with Isma'il. His implementation of Shi'ite practices, however, alienated his Sunni subjects. When they revolted in 1512, the Uzbeks reestablished their control over the region.

Defeated for a second time by the Uzbeks, Babur had to return to Kabul. He now realized that what he considered his natural destiny—ruling over Timur's empire—was out of the question for the foreseeable future. Transoxiana to the north and Khorasan to the west were divided between the Uzbeks and Safavids, each of which was too powerful for him to challenge. Kabul was inadequate for his ambitions, however, and so he began exploring other possibilities for imperial rule. To the east lay only towering, ice-covered mountain peaks and remote canyons, but to the south the way was open to wealthy agricultural and commercial regions. He soon began raiding the environs of Qandahar and then ranged across the Khyber Pass into the Punjab. He reorganized his army, developing an effective corps of musketry and artillery that supplemented the cavalry corps.

In 1522, Babur felt strong enough to attack Qandahar itself, and he captured it. In 1526, he organized a military expedition whose target was the Lodi dynasty of Delhi. Over the next three years, far from home and surrounded by formidable enemies, he won a series of military victories that made him famous. At Panipat, fifty miles north of Delhi, his small army of some 12,000 met Ibrahim Lodi's much larger army that included one hundred war elephants. Babur's use of artillery unnerved the elephants and Afghan soldiers alike, and his cavalry's wheeling tactics routed the enemy. After his victory at Panipat, Babur was challenged by the charismatic leader of the large Hindu Rajput confederacy. Again facing overwhelming odds, Babur defeated the Rajputs in 1527. He followed that victory with a crushing defeat of the huge army of one of Ibrahim Lodi's brothers near Lucknow in 1529. Babur, whose reputation had been in tatters in 1512, was now master of the Indo-Gangetic plain as well as southern Afghanistan.

Babur, Horticulturist

Babur was the quintessential Timurid ruler: He was a brilliant military commander, polished writer, skilled translator, Sufi adept, and connoisseur possessed of an insatiable curiosity. His autobiography is fascinating for its revelations of its author's interests. This selection is drawn from his account of his expedition of conquest into northern India, or Hindustan. He confesses that he did not like many features of Hindustan—its climate, people, and architecture—but he did find much about the flora and fauna that captivated him. It is easy to imagine that the military commander of an invading army would be single-mindedly focused on the pressing issues of keeping his army fed and prepared for battle. Babur, as we know, took care of business with regard to his military aims, but, as this selection reveals, he was also a man upon whom nothing was lost.

There are some marvelous flowers in Hindustan. One is the hibiscus, which some Hindustanis call *gudhal*. It is not a shrub but a tree with stems. It is somewhat taller than the

(Continued)

red rose, and its color is deeper than the pomegranate flower. It is as large as a red rose. The red rose blossoms all at once after budding, but when the hibiscus blossoms, from the middle of the petals yet another slender stalk is formed, as long as a finger, from which still more hibiscus petals open. The result is a double, fairly amazing flower. The flowers look beautiful in color on the tree but do not last long. They blossom and fade within a day. They bloom well and plentifully during the four months of monsoon and often throughout most of the year. Despite their profusion they have no odor.

Another flower is the oleander, which occurs in both white and red. It has five petals like the peach blossom. The red oleander bears a resemblance to the peach blossom, but the oleander blooms with fourteen or fifteen flowers in one place, so that from a distance it looks like one big flower. The bush is larger than the red rose. The red oleander has a faint but agreeable smell. It too blooms beautifully and abundantly during the monsoon and can be found throughout most of the year.

The screw pine is another. It has a delicate scent. Whereas musk has the disadvantage of being dry, this could be called "wet musk." In addition to the plant's having a strange appearance, the flowers can be from one-and-a-half to two spans long. The long leaves are like those of the reed and have spines. When compressed like a bud, the outer leaves are spiny and greenish and the inner leaves soft and white. Nestled among the inner leaves are things like in the middle of a flower, and the good scent comes from there. When it first comes up, before it develops a stalk, it resembles the male reed bush. The leaves are flattish and spiny. The stalk is extremely unharmonious. The roots are always exposed.

Then there is the jasmine. The white variety is called champa. It is larger and has a more pronounced fragrance than the jasmine in our country.

SOURCE: *The Baburnama: Memoirs of Babur, Prince and Emperor,* translated, edited, and annotated by Wheeler M. Thackston (Washington, D.C.: Freer Gallery of Art and Arthur M. Sackler Gallery, Smithsonian Institution; New York: Oxford University Press, 1996), 347–348.

A few months after Babur secured his new realm, his son Humayun fell critically ill. In a formal ceremony, Babur asked God to take his own life in exchange for Humayun's. Humayun recovered, whereupon Babur fell ill, dying in 1530 at the age of forty-seven. It soon became evident that Babur's bargain with God had been a poor one. Humayun lacked many of the qualities of leadership that his father possessed. His apparent weaknesses elicited challenges from within his own military as well as from the Afghans who had retreated down the Ganges valley after their defeat at the hands of Babur. Humayun missed several opportunities to consolidate his power, primarily due to his indulgence in wine and opium, which he took simultaneously.

In 1539, an Afghan noble who was based in the Ganges valley, Sher Khan Sur, led an army made up of Afghan expatriates and defeated Humayun. The Mughal prince fled to the Punjab. There he found that even his own brothers in Lahore and Qandahar were plotting against him. He wandered aimlessly in Sind for several years, his career apparently at an end. Then, in 1544, he sought refuge in Herat, in Safavid territory. During his stay there, he received an invitation from Tahmasp to come to his court at Qazvin.

Tahmasp made Humayun an offer similar to the one their fathers had agreed upon thirty years earlier: Safavid military aid would be at the Timurid prince's disposal on condition of his acceptance of Shi'ism. Contradictory accounts leave us in the dark regarding what actually happened at the meeting, but it seems that, after a tense confrontation that threatened the lives of all in the Timurid party, Humayun conceded just enough to win Tahmasp's help without making him subservient to the Safavid emperor. Humayun returned to Qandahar with several thousand Safavid troops to begin winning back his kingdom. He captured Qandahar without difficulty, but he had to capture Kabul three times from his brother before it was secure. He could then turn his attention to the regions that his father had conquered two decades earlier.

Sher Khan Sur, who adopted the title Sher Shah Sur after defeating Humayun, had quickly taken control of the Punjab, Kashmir, and the entire Ganges valley. In addition to his military achievements, he instituted innovative and constructive reforms in taxation and administration. He also began negotiations with the Ottoman sultan Suleyman I to create an alliance to crush the Safavids between them. Sher Shah Sur's considerable accomplishments over a short period of time suggest that he was well on his way to creating an impressive state in South Asia. In 1545, however, he was killed in battle. Eight years later, a treaty among his successors divided the Indo-Gangetic plain into four Afghan-dominated mini-states. The creation of the four small states was a godsend to Humayun. He attacked immediately, before any of their rulers could begin to recombine them. By the summer of 1555, both Lahore and Delhi were once again under his control. Just as Humayun could begin to feel satisfaction that he had proven his detractors wrong about his abilities, however, he fell down a stone staircase after smoking opium, suffering a fatal concussion. He was succeeded by his twelve-year-old son, Akbar.

Akbar (1556–1605) was a charismatic leader of the stature of Isma'il, Babur, and Sher Shah Sur. Due to his age, regents made the important decisions in his name for the first five years of his reign. During this period, the army scored quick victories in the Punjab, Rajasthan, Malwa, and the central Ganges valley. Akbar himself took the throne in 1561 and continued the series of Mughal conquests. During the 1560s, he completed the subjugation of Rajasthan; in the 1570s, he secured control of Gujarat, Bihar, and much of Bengal; and during the 1580s, he annexed Kashmir and Sind. During the 1590s, he subdued the Indus delta, Khandesh, part of Ahmadnagar, and Berar. Of all his campaigning, Akbar's experience in Bengal was the most frustrating. The region's Afghan warlords fought ferociously, and the rain forests and delta terrain caused great logistical problems for the huge Mughal army. Akbar fought off and on in Bengal until he died in 1605.

The empire's frontiers remained relatively stable during the half-century after Akbar's death. Akbar's son Jahangir (1605–1627) stated that his goal was to conquer the Timurid homeland of Transoxiana, but nothing came of that plan. His armies did subjugate the parts of Bengal that were still not under Mughal control, and in 1616, he captured much of Ahmadnagar. However, that sultanate's Habshi regent, Malik Ambar, initiated a brilliant guerilla war against the Mughal army, inflicting severe damage on it. The heavy-handed Mughal military presence also provoked Maratha resistance. Marathas had served with Habshis in Ahmadnagar's military, and one, Shahji Bhosle, came from a particularly distinguished family, his father having served as Malik Ambar's most trusted assistant. After Malik Ambar's death in 1626,

Shahji assumed the role that the Habshi regents had served for more than three decades. Shahji led the Maratha resistance to the Mughals until Ahmadnagar was finally divided by the Mughals and Bijapur in 1636. His legacy of anti-Mughal guerilla activity remained alive, however. As we shall see, his son would play a role in undermining Mughal power by the end of the century.

It was Jahangir's son Shah Jahan (1627–1658) who finally defeated and formally annexed Ahmadnagar in 1636 after killing the last member of the ruling dynasty. Guerilla warfare by the Marathas continued, but the stationing of the Mughal army in the kingdom did force Bijapur and Golkonda—cities that were more vulnerable to the Mughal armies than elusive guerilla fighters were—to pay tribute. In 1646, Shah Jahan attempted to fulfill the long-time Mughal ambition to conquer Transoxiana. As his army encountered the Uzbeks in the frontier area beyond Kabul, however, the campaign bogged down. The Mughals had an overwhelming advantage in firepower, but their opponents had learned from their confrontations with the Safavids not to charge into the face of artillery and musket fire. The Uzbek light cavalry avoided the gunpowder units and harassed the heavy cavalry of the Mughals. The campaign could not advance beyond Balkh in northern Afghanistan, where the army's tens of thousands of horses ran out of grazing area as winter closed in. Shah Jahan's army was forced to retreat, and it suffered heavy casualties on the way back to Kabul. At enormous expense in treasure and lives, the Mughals had managed to extend their frontier about forty miles.

Shah Jahan's son Aurangzeb (1658–1707) devoted the bulk of his career to military campaigns. His primary focus was the Deccan, where he conquered Bijapur and Golkonda during the period 1685–1687. Both kingdoms suffered massive damage as a result of particularly brutal campaigns. The large and beautiful city of Bijapur was practically destroyed. Aurangzeb extended the Mughal frontier almost to the tip of the peninsula, but his progress ended in 1687. For the remaining two decades of his life, he was embroiled in suppressing revolts, most of which were led by Marathas. He was in the field, living in a tent, for almost the entire period, neglecting events that were causing his nobles to become restive.

The Mughals ruled the most powerful state to have emerged in South Asia for a millennium and a half. They never related to another South Asian kingdom as an equal. Rather, they regarded all other states in the region merely as potential future provinces of the Mughal Empire. The Mughals commanded a formidable military machine, and their conquests appear to have vindicated their self-confidence and arrogance. What is often overlooked about the Mughal military victories, however, is that many of them were achieved only with the utmost determination. Babur's victories were achieved against dramatic odds in manpower, they were hard fought, and each victory could easily have been a loss. From Akbar's reign through that of Aurangzeb, the Mughals commanded large armies that boasted tens of thousands of cavalrymen in addition to archery units, artillery, and musketry. Nevertheless, the Mughals' opponents also had large armies, fought fiercely, and provided no easy victories. Even Akbar could not subdue his opponents in the rain forests and marshes of Bengal. Jahangir, Shah Jahan, and Aurangzeb all encountered military frustrations. As long as the Mughals fought in the Indo-Gangetic plain, they had the advantage over their opponents, but in the Deccan, Bengal, and Afghanistan, they reached the limits of their expansion.

Along the frontiers of South Asia, the Uzbeks and Safavids were the Mughals' only rivals. Relations with the Uzbeks were hostile due to the long-standing dream of the Mughals to reclaim their homeland from the Uzbek usurpers. Commercial relations, however, remained open, and trade flowed freely. Relations between the Safavids and Mughals were usually proper and, occasionally, even cordial. "Ambivalent" might be the best description of their attitude toward each other. Until the late seventeenth century, the only bone of contention between them was control of Qandahar, a major agricultural and commercial center. Possession of it was important to the Mughals for protecting communications with Kabul and for keeping open the route to Central Asia. Nevertheless, the Mughals had to contest the Safavids for it and were not as successful as their rivals. The Safavids, who had less than one-tenth the population of the Mughals, occupied the city for most of the period from 1558 to 1709. Until the 1630s, nevertheless, native Persian-speakers formed a large contingent within the Mughal nobility and administration, and they maintained close ties with their families in Iran. Both the Mughal and Safavid courts were Persianate in language and culture.

Although Jahangir (1605–1627) and Shah 'Abbas (1587–1629) never met, they established a cordial diplomatic relationship and frequently exchanged letters, embassies, and gifts. Jahangir esteemed the Persian aesthetic and was married to an Iranian woman, Nur Jahan. She and several of her relatives were powerful forces at the Mughal court. Because of the close relationship that Jahangir had developed with 'Abbas, he was shocked by 'Abbas's recapture of Qandahar in 1622 (Akbar had seized it in 1595 while 'Abbas was preoccupied with trying to control his Qizilbash). 'Abbas dismissed the event as a mere affair of state that should not affect their personal relationship. During the reign of Shah Jahan, relations with the Safavids became more distant, not least because Shah Jahan made it clear that he wanted to recapture Qandahar, extend his rule over Central Asia, and annex the Shi'ite states in the Deccan.

Society

The Mughal Empire had the largest population in the world after China. Scholars estimate that in 1600, the empire contained sixty to one hundred million people, and that by 1700, following Aurangzeb's conquests, it may have contained 150 million inhabitants. The Ottoman Empire (twenty-five to thirty million) and the Safavid Empire (six to eight million) paled in comparison, while the combined population of all the countries of Europe west of Poland amounted to approximately seventy million in 1600 and eighty-five million in 1700.

The empire was a study in diversity. It encompassed a wide variety of climatic zones—from the deserts of Sind to the rain forests of Bengal—and of topographical features—from the Himalayas to rice paddies—while its people spoke a thousand languages and dialects. The vast majority of the population adhered to what we call Hinduism, a term that encompasses a staggering variety of religious doctrines and practices. The caste system that is so intimately bound with Hinduism produced a much more rigidly stratified social structure than was found in the lands to the west, where Islam had developed. Research into the mutual interaction of the caste system and Islam is in its infancy, but the evidence suggests that Islam's insistence on spiritual equality did little if anything to break down social inequalities. Low-caste

FIGURE 15.2 The Red Fort, Agra. Akbar constructed this large fortress on the site of earlier forts, and Shah Jahan created a lavish palace in the interior. The two periods reveal a transition from Hindu-inspired architecture to Persianate styles.

Robert Harding Picture Library.

Hindus who converted to Islam were embraced neither by the ruling Muslim elite nor by high-caste Hindus who converted to Islam. Formal caste distinctions did not continue to identify a person who converted to Islam, but social distinctions continued to be sharply defined.

Slavery was a common feature in South Asia before and after the arrival of Muslims. Until the late sixteenth century, slaves were most commonly obtained as part of the plunder of conquest: The wives and children of defeated soldiers could expect to become slaves for the rest of their lives. Akbar ended this practice, and from his reign on, most slaves—the vast majority of whom were of South Asian origin—were purchased. Although the Delhi Sultanate and some of its successor states used slave soldiers, the Mughals did not. We also have little evidence that slaves were used for agricultural purposes. Mughal slavery in South Asia was overwhelmingly found in the home or palace. Slaves performed a wide variety of functions, from the most menial and degrading to the most sophisticated. They served as maids, servants, guards, business agents, advisors, and tutors. A powerful nobleman might have hundreds of domestic slaves; an emperor would have thousands. Many of the female slaves were concubines who lived in the *zanana* (women's quarters) of the palace. Some of the numbers are amazing: Akbar's zanana was home to 5000 women and Aurangzeb's contained 2000. Although many female relatives lived in the zanana, these numbers clearly suggest the presence of many slave concubines.

Women's roles in the Mughal Empire were similar to those of contemporary Ottoman society and the last few decades of Safavid society. Women in elite families were ordinarily secluded, both in the sense of wearing a veil and of being confined

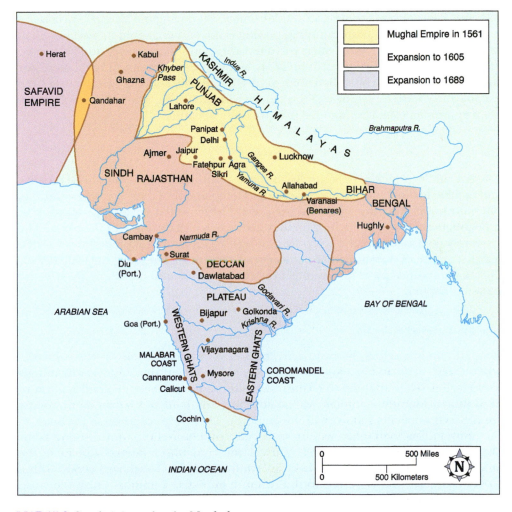

MAP 15.2 South Asia under the Mughals.

within the women's quarters of the home. In South Asia, the seclusion of women is known as *purdah*. As in other Muslim societies, lower-income women were much less likely to practice purdah. Many of them worked outside the home in artisanal occupations or in the fields as peasants.

Women in the royal household were typically highly educated and sophisticated as well as wealthy. Many of them were patrons of the arts. Women in Shah Jahan's family commissioned some of the most impressive construction projects of the new capital city that he built: The city's two enormous bazaars and six congregational mosques were the result of the beneficence of women in the royal court. Whereas in most of the Muslim world women were a tiny minority of mosque attendees, in India they were usually prohibited from entering a mosque at all. We do not know if the ladies who built the congregational mosques were welcome to pray in them.

Indian society has always been complex and riven with paradoxes. The Mughal period was no different in that regard. The same culture that practiced purdah and prohibited women from entering mosques also featured women who served as warriors. Paintings by both Hindu and Muslim artists during the Mughal era contain scenes in which women are hunting, playing polo, and engaging in warfare. Shah Jahan and other South Asian rulers recruited armed women warriors, and by the end of the eighteenth century, the Nizam of Hyderabad (the ruler of a Mughal successor state in the Deccan) controlled a corps of 2000 female soldiers who guarded the zanana and escorted members of the zanana when traveling. During the eighteenth century, women even commanded military units in battle.[3]

The State

The size and complexity of South Asian society required the Mughals to be creative and flexible in their approach to governing. The splendor of their court was dazzling, but their power was more apparent than real. They found it necessary constantly to renegotiate the terms of the bargain they had struck with the elites of the realm. The system worked as long as the rulers were at least tacitly aware that their power rested on the consent of the elites. When the central government began acting unilaterally during the second half of the seventeenth century, the central government's effective power collapsed.

The Mansabdari System

Mughal administrators, like those in the Delhi Sultanate, had to deal with the complexities of operating a Muslim government in a society that was overwhelmingly non-Muslim. They adapted the Timurid model of government (a combination of Persian and Mongol elements) to the complex South Asian environment. At the center, four ministers reported to the emperor. They were responsible for finance, the army, judicial and religious issues, and the royal household. A division of labor also existed at the provincial level, where a governor who reported directly to the emperor was responsible for security and military affairs. He shared power with a revenue official who reported to the revenue minister, a military paymaster who reported to the military minister, and a religious official who reported to the minister for religious affairs.

Superimposed over this framework was yet another flow chart of responsibility known as the *mansabdari* system. Royal princes, provincial governors, and powerful warlords were assigned a graded position (*mansab*) that designated how many troops they were responsible for providing to the emperor when he demanded them. During Akbar's later years, there were almost two thousand of these *mansabdars* who were responsible for over 140,000 heavy cavalrymen in addition to war horses, war elephants, and both mounted and foot musketeers. Many of them were responsible for providing only a few troops, but a few were obligated to command and outfit as many as 7000 soldiers each.

A mansabdar was granted a *jagir* to finance his military obligation. A jagir was the right to collect the taxes of a specified region, which could be as small as a few fields or as large as a whole governate. Jagirs were assigned by the imperial revenue minister, and each mansabdar received a new jagir every few years so that he would not be able to establish a power base in a given area. Seven-eighths of the empire's taxable land was assigned as jagirs; one-eighth was reserved for the emperor.

At first glance, the jagir appears similar to the Ottoman timar, but it was quite different. The Ottoman government awarded timars to the tens of thousands of cavalrymen in the sultan's army. Jagirs were handed out to only a few hundred great nobles, with the result that the Mughal government's reach did not extend as deeply into its society as the Ottoman government's did into its own. On the other hand, the degree of centralization in the Mughal Empire was considerably more advanced than that of the Safavid Empire until the period of 'Abbas, when the Safavid ruler consolidated considerable power.

Unlike the Ottomans and the later Safavids, the Mughals did not have a corps of military slaves to balance the power of free soldiers. Thus, the emperors had to satisfy the political and economic ambitions of mansabdars by granting them an honorable degree of autonomy as well as an income that was commensurate with their status. The vast majority of the subcontinent's warlords discovered that participation in the mansabdari system provided them with as many rewards as they had enjoyed prior to having been conquered by the Mughals. The system was open to Hindus as well as Muslims, and to native Muslims as well as immigrant Turks, Iranians, Uzbeks, and Afghans.

Despite the apparently uniform administrative system of the empire, the central government actually maintained a variety of relationships with its constituent parts. Akbar and his immediate successors did not try to be consistent in every instance. For example, they granted some of the Hindu Rajput nobles and warlords more autonomy than other notables enjoyed because of an unusual premium that Rajput culture placed on status and dignity. On the other hand, emperors had to be able to assert their authority over all nobles in order to maintain stability. Much of the system's equilibrium actually depended on the personality of the emperor himself and the degree to which he won both the respect and the loyalty of the great nobles of the realm.

Even this sophisticated and powerful imperial system faced many problems, however. A drought in one region might render the jagirs of a large number of mansabdars worthless. A period of rapid conquest might bring many new mansabdars into the system, but the conditions in the newly conquered area might become dangerous and unproductive due to continuing warfare. As a result, there would be more mansabdars than viable jagirs. The practice of periodically transferring jagirs was to the advantage of the emperor, but it was a nuisance for nobles, who resisted its enforcement. The terms of the relationship between a mansabdar and the emperor were constantly being renegotiated—and occasionally resisted—by the empire's elites.

Even more problematic for the empire's stability was the fact that, at the local level, traditional notables known as *zamindars* wielded considerable power. A zamindar was typically a large landowner and was the head of the dominant family in a large village or cluster of smaller villages. His wealth and kin connections, combined with his position at the apex of traditional lines of authority in a hierarchical society, endowed him with a great deal of influence. His actual power derived from his command of local military forces. In the Indo-Gangetic plain, peasants had a tradition of being heavily armed and of honing their martial skills. Many of them, like their Swiss, Scot, and Irish contemporaries, left their villages to become mercenaries. Whether they left or stayed at home, they frequently found short-term or long-term employment as soldiers in local or regional private armies. Zamindars thus had a large pool of soldiers from which they could draw. Constant skirmishing took place as mansabdars attempted to collect more revenue than zamindars wanted them to or as provincial governors attempted to fulfill their duty of providing security by disarming zamindars.

Establishing Imperial Legitimacy

No single city embodied the notion of the "imperial center" for the Mughals the way that London did for Akbar's contemporary Elizabeth of England (1558–1603) or the Paris–Versailles axis did for Aurangzeb's contemporary Louis XIV (1643–1715). The Mughals moved their capital even more frequently than the Safavids did, enabling several cities in the Indo-Gangetic plain to enjoy the huge imperial investment in monumental architecture. Upon becoming emperor in 1561, Akbar established his headquarters at Agra. The city remained his capital until 1571 when he built Fatehpur Sikri, a vast imperial center twenty-five miles west of Agra.

In 1585, Akbar transferred his headquarters once again. This time he moved to Lahore in order to be closer to Afghanistan, where the leader of the Uzbek khanate, 'Abdullah Khan Uzbek, had been successful in provoking Afghan tribes to challenge the Mughal regime at Kabul. By 1598 (when 'Abdullah Khan died), Akbar felt that he had secured his Afghan frontier, and so he moved his capital back to Agra. His son Jahangir (1605–1627) retained Agra as his capital, but Jahangir's son Shah Jahan (1627–1658) built a new imperial city in the 1640s in an open space near the ruined city of Delhi. This fabulous new city of palaces, mosques, and gardens became known as Shahjahanabad ("Shah Jahan's City"). Today it is known as Old Delhi. (New Delhi was begun by the British in the early twentieth century.)

Mughal rulers could not establish their political legitimacy in the same manner as Ottoman, Safavid, and Uzbek rulers. By the mid-sixteenth century, the Safavids and Uzbeks ruled populations that were largely Muslim, and Muslims within the Ottoman Empire were at least a large minority of the sultan's subjects. Because Muslim religious leaders could influence public opinion toward the government, rulers carefully cultivated relations with them (or destroyed them, as the Safavids did with many Sufi leaders). Rulers had to adjust their claims as conditions changed, but they knew that appeals to religious legitimacy were effective. European rulers of the seventeenth century such as James I of England and Louis XIV of France attempted a similar course in their almost exclusively Christian societies by claiming a "divine right" to rule. Likewise, Chinese emperors claimed the "Mandate of Heaven."

The Mughal Empire, however, had a huge non-Muslim majority that probably exceeded ninety percent. Non-Muslims were not impressed by a ruler's title of caliph, his boast of a lineage that derived from the Prophet or his Companions, or claims that he possessed special insight into the meaning of the Qur'an. As a result, the early Mughal court made few appeals to religion, and its rulers faced the constant challenge of how to persuade their subjects to be loyal to them. They knew that many of their subjects were asking themselves, "By what right do the Mughals rule other than through the exercise of sheer force?"

Muslim regimes in South Asia prior to the Mughals made little or no formal distinction between Muslims and non-Muslims. Although the Shari'a required that non-Muslims pay a head tax, Muslim rulers in South Asia had rarely imposed it. Babur (1526–1530) and Humayun (1530–1539, 1555–1556) were both devout Muslims and followed the teaching of Sufi pirs (Babur identified with the Naqshbandiya, and Humayun followed the Shattariya). Both rulers, however, spent their entire careers leading military campaigns and never had to develop an ideology for the regime. Akbar (1556–1605) began his career as a devout Muslim, but he quickly made it clear that his government would not support the Islam of the ulama. Subsequent Mughal rulers had to decide whether they would accept, modify, or reject Akbar's policy.

Akbar began his reign as a pious follower of a Chishti saint. When the saint's prophecy of the birth of Jahangir was fulfilled, Akbar dedicated an enormous palace–mosque complex as a memorial to the pir near his dargah at Fatehpur Sikri. During his early years in Fatehpur Sikri, Akbar demonstrated his devotion by sweeping the floor of the great mosque and serving as its prayer leader. During the 1570s, however, Akbar's natural inquisitiveness and impatience with dogma led to a dramatic change in his religious orientation. The first signs of his disaffection with Shari'a-based Islam appeared several years after he began inviting Muslim scholars to the palace to discuss theological topics. Akbar was the only Mughal ruler who was illiterate (some scholars suspect that he had dyslexia), but all who met him were struck by his intelligence and his learning, which he picked up from having books read to him and from engaging in discussions. He enjoyed—and actively participated in—philosophical and theological discussions.

To Akbar's disappointment, the palace seminars often degenerated into bitter arguments and charges of heresy being hurled by one scholar at another. He was disillusioned by these scenes. He was searching for Truth, both to satisfy his own quest for meaning and to find a universal religion that all his subjects could share. He began inviting scholars of other religions to the discussions, including representatives of Hinduism, Jainism, Zoroastrianism, and Judaism. In 1579, he invited Jesuits from the Portuguese enclave at Goa to come to his palace, and they became prominent members of the seminar.

As a result of the court discussions, Akbar became increasingly convinced that all the religions possessed only a partial understanding of the spiritual realm. He concluded that to patronize any one of them would be unjustifiable, since to do so would inevitably splinter his subjects into factions. With the help of Abu al-Fazl (a

Shi'ite Iranian émigré and Akbar's closest advisor and confidante), Akbar began developing a new religious path. Inspired in part by al-Suhrawardi's theory of Illuminationism, the religion was called the *din-i ilahi*, or Divine Religion.

The new faith taught that the emperor was divinely illumined to be the leader of his people. Akbar now claimed to be the Perfect Man, a venerable Sufi concept that suggested that he had attained spiritual fulfillment in his quest for the presence of God. He also declared that, when disagreements arose over a point of interpretation within any religion, religious authorities should bring the issue to him for resolution. Akbar himself worshiped the sun four times a day and made a sacred fire the center of further devotions. He began each day by appearing at a window of his palace as the sun rose, and the crowd that had gathered outside would greet him by prostrating before him.

Akbar never promulgated the Divine Religion widely, and he certainly did not attempt to impose it on his subjects. Outsiders viewed it as an ersatz Sufi order or even an attempt to capture the aura of Twelver Shi'ism. It echoed Sufi concepts in its portrayal of Akbar as pir and Perfect Man, and it suggested Shi'ite influences by its exaltation of Akbar as the enlightened Imam. The new "path" was intended for the elite of society. A large number of the Mughal nobility—perhaps even a majority of them—applied to be Akbar's disciples, and in their initiation ceremonies they vowed their willingness to sacrifice their lives, wealth, and honor for him.

Despite the self-promoting aspects of his new faith, Akbar seems to have made a genuine effort to formulate an official ideology that conveyed the message that the emperor was a spiritual leader whose wise guidance promoted the well-being of the entire realm. He asserted that reason, rather than faith, should be the basis for determining religious truth, and he sought to instill the idea that ethics, rather than doctrine or ritual, should be at the heart of religious concerns. He made it known that he had begun to abstain from meat consumption, sexual intercourse, and—perhaps even more surprising in a Mughal ruler—the drinking of alcohol.

Akbar openly demonstrated his break with Islam not only by his worship of the sun, but also by terminating government sponsorship of caravans and flotillas for the hajj, a practice that had begun with the capture of Gujarat in 1574. He formally abolished the head tax on non-Muslims and the taxes on Hindu pilgrims. He also banned child marriage and forbade Hindu girls from converting to Islam as a condition of marriage to Muslim men. Rather than enforcing the Shari'a's ban on the construction and repair of temples, he contributed financially to the construction of Hindu temples as well as to hospitals and caravanserais.

Pious Muslims were bitterly opposed to Akbar for these policies. Some of the initiatives were clearly heretical, but the ulama had the additional grievance that the new policies deprived them of authority. Akbar had asserted his sole sovereignty—both temporal and spiritual—and had made it clear that he would be the arbiter of the meaning of the Shari'a. Some Muslims were also upset that non-Muslims continued to be treated as the equals of Muslims. They felt that, with the establishment of a major Muslim-ruled state, the secondary status of non-Muslims should be enforced.

The Economy

For centuries, outsiders viewed South Asia as a source of fabulous wealth. The subcontinent was almost economically self-sufficient: It needed to import only precious metals, war horses, and certain spices. For the rest of the world, it was a major source of such valuable commodities as pepper, saffron, sugar, indigo (a word that derives from the Greek word that signified *Indian dye*), and silk and cotton textiles.

Prior to the sixteenth century, commerce in South Asia took place across vast distances despite a large number of independent states and frequent wars. Merchants, however, knew that business could be even better if their caravan agents did not have to pay numerous tariffs and bribes as they crossed frontiers, suffer exposure to raids by highwaymen, change currency frequently, and encounter a wide variety of road conditions. The reign of Sher Shah Sur (1539–1545), who chased Humayun out of Delhi in 1539, marked a major step forward in the economic history of the subcontinent. The Afghan brought about several reforms that had a lasting impact. He introduced the *rupiya* (rupee) coin, which gained wide distribution throughout the subcontinent; improved the system of crop taxes by making them regular rather than arbitrary; and began construction of a network of roads. The Grand Trunk Road lay at the center of this transportation system, extending from the Khyber Pass to Bengal.

The Mughal conquests that began in the second half of the sixteenth century resulted in unprecedented internal commercial ties within South Asia and allowed Sher Shah Sur's reforms to have an impact over a wide area. The annexations linked Bengal, Gujarat, Delhi, the Punjab, and Kabul. The Mughals' trade policy was to encourage overland trade with the Safavids and even with their old nemesis the Uzbeks. They placed no frontier restrictions on the trade that connected the subcontinent with Iran and Central Asia. The Mughals allowed merchants from all nations to trade in their ports and to travel and live freely within the empire. This freedom of movement stood in stark contrast to the situation in China, where foreigners were tightly controlled by imperial officers, and in Japan, where foreigners were excluded after 1639.

The Mughals also recognized the importance of the maritime trade on their coasts. If the Mughals had come to power earlier in the sixteenth century, they might have clashed with the Portuguese. The Portuguese conquered Goa on the Malabar Coast and established Hughly in Bengal, intending to control all commerce on both sides of the subcontinent. By the time the Mughals arrived on both coasts, however, Portuguese power had declined dramatically. The Sa'dis of Morocco defeated the Portuguese army during the same decade that Akbar conquered Gujarat, and shortly thereafter, Spain annexed Portugal. In 1633, the Mughal army expelled the last Portuguese soldiers from Hughly.

As Portuguese power waned in the central Indian Ocean, English, Dutch, and French activity increased. These Europeans found that Cambay was no longer the major port of the subcontinent, as it had been during the previous three centuries. The channel into Cambay's harbor had been gradually silting up throughout the sixteenth century, and it finally became impossible for larger ships to berth at the city's wharves. Surat, located closer to the open sea, displaced Cambay as the major port in the subcontinent by the last quarter of the sixteenth century.

The vast overland trade network that the Mughals controlled now linked up with the maritime networks of the Dutch, English, and French companies to bring unprecedented economic prosperity to most of the subcontinent. The volume of South Asian exports bound directly for Europe increased dramatically during the seventeenth century, especially the cotton textiles that the English East India Company bought.

Although the volume of Mughal trade with Europe was growing, the subcontinent's most important markets remained Iran, Central Asia, and the lands that bordered the Indian Ocean. Many of the commodities that were traded in the seventeenth century were familiar to long-time customers. Saffron, sugar, and indigo continued to be important, and cotton textiles grew in importance during the Mughal period. Gujarat had a reputation for making cheap, coarse textiles, and the Coromandel Coast and Bengal were noted for their high-quality fabrics.

Because of new developments taking place in the global trading networks, the pattern of exports from South Asia experienced some significant changes in the seventeenth century. One was the introduction of tobacco cultivation. Only a few years after Captain John Smith helped to establish tobacco as a cash crop in Virginia, the "weed" became an important export from the Mughal Empire. Another was a precipitous decline in the export of black pepper. For centuries, this spice had been grown almost exclusively on the Malabar Coast, but by the seventeenth century, Sumatra had displaced the Malabar Coast as the major producing region. A third change was that the Coromandel Coast became a major source of slaves. The Dutch East India Company began acquiring Indian slaves there after 1635 and exported tens of thousands of them to other regions in the Indian Ocean basin.

The Mughals themselves were particularly interested in the importation of war horses. The subcontinent's climate and relative dearth of good grazing grounds meant that thousands of horses had to be imported every year to supply the huge Mughal cavalry. Some came from the Arabian Peninsula, but most came from Safavid and Uzbek territories. The Mughal palace kitchens also stimulated a rise in the imports of spices from Southeast Asia, and Mughal nostalgia for Central Asia caused the ruling elites to import large quantities of melons, dried apricots, almonds, and carpets from there.

The largest economic project undertaken by the Mughals was the transformation of eastern Bengal into a major rice-growing region. Western Bengal had been settled for centuries and was predominantly Hindu. Eastern Bengal was a heavily forested region that lay beyond the influence of Sanskritic civilization. Shah Jahan initiated a policy that encouraged the clearing of jungles in eastern Bengal, but the major effort had to wait until the 1660s, after piracy had been eliminated from the major estuaries. Aurangzeb's administration awarded tax-free grants of land to individuals who brought forested areas into rice cultivation. These grantees, in turn, recruited peasants to clear-cut the forest and cultivate rice.

The grantees were also obligated to build a temple or mosque for the cultivators. Since most of the agents were Muslims, they tended to build mosques for their workers and appointed Chishti pirs to be the supervisors of the mosques. The cultivators, most of whom followed local, animistic religions, were drawn to the spiritual gifts of the pirs. Despite a Mughal ban on proselytizing the non-Muslims in the region, eastern Bengal became heavily Islamized. The Islamization of eastern Bengal is one of the most impressive testimonials that history offers to illustrate the spiritual charisma of Sufi pirs.

The development of eastern Bengal dates from this Mughal initiative. The region's population grew enormously, and Islam became the primary religion.

FIGURE 15.3 The Taj Mahal, Agra. Built by Shah Jahan for his late wife, the tomb complex reflects the Persianate influence that was at its height at the Mughal court in the first half of the seventeenth century.

Rawpixel.

The region's economy boomed, for rice and sugar cane were produced on a commercial scale, and large quantities of both were exported. The profit made on these crops supplemented the wealth that was generated from the export of the world-famous Bengali silk and fine cotton textiles.

Merchants from around the world came to the subcontinent during the Mughal period, and South Asian merchants fanned out across the continent and the Indian Ocean to facilitate the marketing of South Asian agricultural and manufactured goods. South Asian merchants and financiers were to be found in ports of any size all around the Indian Ocean. Thousands of them—Muslim and Hindu—lived and worked in Iran and Central Asia during the seventeenth century. They provided services as money changers, lenders, and financiers. Others were in the retail or wholesale trade. Many other South Asian businessmen made their way as far north as Astrakhan and Moscow during the early seventeenth century. These businessmen enjoyed the same competitive advantages and edge in expertise as their Venetian counterparts had when their services had been in demand throughout Europe during the fourteenth and fifteenth centuries.

Culture

South Asia contains a large number of distinctive regional cultures, but the notable aspect of Mughal elite society was the prominent role that Persian cultural elements played in it. For several hundred years, Persian culture streamed into South Asia by way of the Delhi Sultanate, the Deccan kingdoms, Gujarat, and Bengal. Under the Mughals, the Persian language, literary themes, and motifs in the visual arts became even more influential. This development coincided with the dominance of Persian culture among the Uzbeks and Safavids and the high regard that Persian culture enjoyed in the Ottoman Empire. The result was that the ruling elites from Bengal to the Balkans shared similar tastes in manners and customs, styles of dress, literature, and the visual arts. During the seventeenth century, educated individuals in Dhaka, Delhi, and Lahore could value the same art, enjoy the same poetry, and adhere to the same values as their peers in Bukhara, Esfahan, and Istanbul.

As an educated Timurid, Babur was fluent in both Persian and Chaghatay. His grandson Akbar designated Persian to be the official language of the Mughal court, and Persian became not only the language of imperial recordkeeping and correspondence but also of belles-lettres. Akbar encouraged the immigration of Persian-speaking intellectuals, who came largely from the Safavid and Uzbek realms. Many of them were attracted by the greater wealth of the Mughal Empire. Others were Sunnis, Sufis, or Zoroastrians threatened by the unsettled political conditions of the Safavid Empire during the second half of the sixteenth century or the increasing restrictions on cultural creativity in Central Asia under the rule of Abdullah Khan Uzbek.

In 1590, Akbar commissioned the *Babur-nameh* to be translated from Chaghatay into Persian and the *Mahabharata,* the great Hindu epic, to be translated from Sanskrit into Persian. Under Akbar and Jahangir, Iranian philosophy, especially the works of al-Suhrawardi, became a major focus of study. South Asian Sufism, already more strongly influenced by the Iranian schools of thought than by the Arab world, now became even more heavily Persianized than before. Numerous commentaries were written on the work of the great Sufi masters who wrote in Persian. Persian culture was at its height during the reign of Jahangir (1605–1627) when the emperor's wife, the Iranian Nur Jahan, exercised enormous power, both directly and through members of her family who were prominent at court.

Shah Jahan, Jahangir's son (but not Nur Jahan's son), resented the influence of the Iranians and began recruiting Central Asians in their place. During the reign of Shah Jahan's son Aurangzeb (1658–1707), Central Asians came to dominate the court. Persian culture continued to have a powerful influence, however. After Aurangzeb's conquest of the Deccan in the 1680s, many of the cultured elites of the Deccan were absorbed into the court culture at Delhi. They brought with them their Dakani language, which had developed over the previous two centuries as a hybrid of Persian and local Deccan languages. Its intelligibility to speakers of Indo-European languages in the Indo-Gangetic plain, combined with its grammatical simplicity, facilitated its rapid transformation into the lingua franca of Muslims of the region. During the eighteenth century, the language was increasingly called Urdu, and it became the vehicle for a remarkable literary flowering. In the twentieth century, it became the official language of modern Pakistan.

The use of the Persian language was, on the whole, restricted to the elites of South Asia. It must be noted, however, that the language had a much greater impact than that bald fact might indicate, for two major reasons. First, Hindus as well as Muslims used the language. Especially in the north, many upper-caste Hindus read Persian, just as some Muslims read Hindi. The use of Persian as the official language of government no doubt spurred many Hindus to learn the language, but many cultured Hindus learned it simply because they and their Muslim counterparts often shared the same arts and learning. Many Hindus in business and finance used Persian because it was the language of commerce in the region that extended from the Punjab to the Syr Darya River in the north and to the Zagros Mountains in the west.

The second reason for the influence of Persian is that, like many other languages of the Indo-Gangetic plain, it is an Indo-European language. Since it shares features of grammar and vocabulary with many dialects spoken in northern India, it is easy to learn for anyone who speaks those languages. It appears that the use of Persian among Muslims in the Deccan kingdoms and among Muslims and Hindus of the Mughal Empire made South Asia the center of Persian culture in the early seventeenth century. Assuming similar literacy rates in Iran and South Asia, the huge population of the latter would have ensured that far more people used Persian in South Asia than in Iran.[4]

Among tourists to South Asia, the Mughals are even more famous for their patronage of monumental building and miniature painting than for their literature. It is worth noting that, whereas the most famous Ottoman and Safavid buildings are mosques, the Mughals are known for their forts, palaces, imperial cities, gardens, and tombs. The architectural works that Akbar commissioned, such as those of the complex at Fatehpur Sikri, tend to reflect traditional indigenous styles. Jahangir was less interested in architecture than in miniature paintings and imperial gardens. Like all the Mughal emperors, he loved the beautiful valleys of Kashmir, where he built some particularly noteworthy gardens.

Shah Jahan was the greatest of the Mughal patrons of architecture. He is famous for having commissioned the imperial city of Shahjahanabad, the Red Fort at Delhi, and the Peacock Throne. The Peacock Throne required seven years to design and build. It was inlaid with rubies, diamonds, pearls, and emeralds. Above its canopy stood the peacock that gave the throne its name. The bird's body was made of gold inlaid with precious stones and its tail was made largely of sapphires.

As remarkable as these commissions were, Shah Jahan is most famous for the Taj Mahal, a tomb he commissioned for his wife Arjumand Banu Begam, a niece of Nur Jahan. She is better known by her nickname, Mumtaz Mahal ("Beloved of the Palace"). Mumtaz Mahal died in childbirth in 1631, bearing the couple's fourteenth child in nineteen years of marriage (only seven lived past infancy). Like most royal marriages, it had been arranged purely for political reasons. Unlike most such marriages, it was characterized by deep and abiding affection: Shah Jahan and Mumtaz Mahal were inseparable companions after their marriage in 1612. Her death was a crushing blow to him, and he vowed to build a monument worthy of her. He brought in skilled artisans from all over the Persianate world to construct a forty-two-acre garden tomb in the Central Asian tradition. The mausoleum was placed in the middle, flanked by a guest house and a mosque. Shah Jahan expected pilgrims to visit the tomb, which would eventually house his body as well as that of his wife.

We have little information regarding advances made in the fields of the natural sciences and mathematics during the Mughal period. Little research has been done in these areas. It appears that, although Mughal emperors provided patronage for literature, art, and architecture, none after Babur was interested in the sciences. The astronomer of the Mughal period about whom we are best informed was Sawai Jai Singh (1688–1743), who inherited the rule of one of the most powerful mansabs in Rajasthan in 1700 at the age of twelve. After the death of Aurangzeb in 1707, he accumulated power so skillfully that, by the mid-1720s, he became autonomous without having clashed with Delhi. He was so powerful that it was commonly said that he owned all the land between Delhi and Surat.

Jai Singh, a Hindu, was intellectually precocious as a youth, and he continued his passionate curiosity about astronomy throughout his life. He was disturbed by discrepancies between the planetary and lunar tables that he possessed (from both the Sanskritic tradition and the Timurid tradition of Ulugh Bey), on the one hand, and the findings of continuing observations, on the other. He launched a massive project to improve astronomical knowledge: He built libraries, constructed observatories at five different cities in order to compare data, personally designed instruments to measure time and angles, and assembled teams of astronomers that included Hindus, Muslims, and Jesuit missionaries from Portugal. The observatory at Jaipur remains almost intact and is an impressive monument to Jai Singh's commitment to science. Also impressive was Jai Singh's determination to tap into the astronomical knowledge accumulated in Europe. Unfortunately, his European contacts were the Portuguese of Goa, with whom he made arrangements to send a delegation to Lisbon. The group remained in Portugal throughout the year 1729, but it remained unaware of the heliocentric theory that had become dominant in northern Europe. Because of the hostility of the Catholic Church of the period toward the heliocentric theory, members of the delegation never had access to the works of Copernicus, Galileo, Kepler, or Newton.

Islam gained numerous adherents in South Asia during the Mughal period. In addition, the large-scale immigration of Sufis from Iran and Central Asia expanded the offerings in what was already a wide spectrum of spiritual paths from which South Asian Muslims could choose. The most important order introduced during this time was the Naqshbandiya, brought to Delhi from Kabul in the 1590s by Khwaja Muhammad Baqi Billah. One of his disciples was Ahmad Sirhindi (1563–1624), who in turn became a famous khwaja. Sirhindi continued the Naqshbandi emphasis on balancing the mystical experience with the requirements of the Shari'a, cautioning Sufis against becoming "intoxicated" by their experiences. He also tried to reinterpret Ibn al-'Arabi's doctrine of the "Unity of Being"—which underlay almost all Sufi movements of the period—in a way that did not infringe on the traditional doctrine of God's unity.

Sirhindi was widely admired, but no one held him in higher esteem than himself. A considerable number of his followers believed that he was in the line of "renewers" whom Muslims believed were sent by God at the beginning of each Islamic century to reform Islam. Sirhindi himself believed that he was not merely the eleventh century's renewer, but the renewer of the entire second Islamic millennium, which began in 1591. Although he conceded that prophecy had come to an end with Muhammad, he claimed that certain individuals (including himself) had direct experience of divine inspiration and possessed prophetic qualities. His extravagant claims for himself provoked such a hostile reaction from other members of the ulama that Jahangir was compelled to imprison him during 1619–1620 to allow passions to cool.

The growing number of Sufi orders provided South Asian Muslims with increased opportunities to develop the inward, spiritual life. Those opportunities, however, came at the expense of the creation of new ideas regarding the broader role of Islam within the empire. When Akbar began devising his universal religion, he was, in effect, challenging the ulama to demonstrate how Islamic institutions should function in a largely Hindu empire ruled by a Muslim dynasty. Rather than confront the problem, Muslim religious leaders tended either to retreat from society into their mystical path or simply to charge Mughal rulers with heresy or apostasy. Despite Sirhindi's reputation today as an activist who sought to influence court policy in the tradition of Central Asian khwajas, he actually exerted few efforts in that direction and had no discernible political influence on Mughal emperors.[5]

Neither Sirhindi nor any other seventeenth-century religious leader devoted serious efforts to the problem of reconciling Islamic ideals to Mughal realities. As a result, emperors lurched from one religious policy to another. Jahangir maintained Akbar's policy of treating all religions alike. Like his contemporary Shah 'Abbas, who ignored the royal cult established by Isma'il, Jahangir gradually abandoned the royal cult established by Akbar. He also ruled without reference to Islam. Shah Jahan, by contrast, reactivated the ban on the construction or repair of churches and temples, and he ordered that recently built temples in the Hindu holy city of Benares be razed. Unlike Akbar and Jahangir, he publicly participated in Islamic festivals and stressed their importance.

The End of Imperial Rule

After a century of existence, the Mughal Empire in the 1650s was wealthy and powerful. Its achievements had been legion. Its conquests had unified such widely scattered territories as Bengal, Gujarat, and Kabul; brought them under a uniform revenue system; and granted them a relative degree of stability and peace. The integration of these regions generated a long period of economic growth. The pattern of South Asia's commercial relations with the outside world sheltered it from the seventeenth-century economic crisis that affected Europe, the Ottomans, and the Safavids. The new capital city of Shahjahanabad was an impressive symbol of imperial glory. Even pious critics of the regime grudgingly conceded that reforms were occurring that gave more centrality to Islamic themes. The imperial ruling class could justifiably expect the next century to be even better.

Rather than consolidating its rule, however, the Mughal dynasty entered upon a period in which its power unraveled. It is a saga that still intrigues historians—and must have confounded contemporaries—for by outward appearances, the empire seemed to prosper. The territorial and demographic size of the empire greatly increased by 1689 and the economy in most areas continued to grow. Ominously, though, the dynasty itself was not able to solve challenges to its authority that in the past it would have handled easily. Local and provincial leaders, accustomed to the give-and-take of challenge and compromise with the Mughals, now found that when they resisted the financial or military demands of the Mughals, they got away with their defiance.

The Reign of Aurangzeb

The empire's problems began with a civil war that erupted when Shah Jahan seemed to be dying in 1657. Years earlier, Shah Jahan had made it clear that his eldest and favorite son, Dara Shukoh, was his choice to be his successor. Now, however, the four surviving sons that Mumtaz Mahal had borne for him began to contest for the throne.

Two of the brothers dominated the struggle. Dara Shukoh was an intellectual. He was a master of languages, philosophy, and religions, and he appreciated fine music and art. He developed a high regard for Hinduism and translated the Upanishads into Persian. His chief challenger was his youngest brother, Aurangzeb. Aurangzeb's personality stood in sharp contrast to that of Dara Shukoh, for he was an ascetic and scrupulous observer of Islamic ritual. His intense piety and his contempt for music and art may have led Dara Shukoh to underestimate him, for he was no religious hermit: He combined great military and administrative abilities with high ambitions, and he seems to have considered the prospect of Dara Shukoh's accession to the throne to be a catastrophe for Islam.

The civil war among the brothers lasted from 1657 to 1661. Shah Jahan temporarily threw the ambitions of his sons into question by recovering from his "terminal" illness, but they had too much invested in the war to allow him to regain the throne. In 1658, Aurangzeb imprisoned him in a fortress near the Taj Mahal. For the remaining eight years of his life, he could see from his window, but was never allowed to visit, the shrine that he had commissioned for his beloved wife. By 1661, Aurangzeb had defeated and killed his brothers. He took the title *Alamgir*, which, like *Jahangir*, means "world-seizer."

Aurangzeb (1658–1707) felt a sense of responsibility to rule the empire in accordance with the will of God. His affiliation with the Naqshbandiya had reinforced his disdain for the universalist and inclusive nature of the Mughal regime's ideology. He was also hostile to both Sikhism[6] and Shi'ism, apparently viewing both as intolerable threats to Sunni Islam. Although previous Mughal rulers had coexisted with Sikhs, Aurangzeb began a systematic attack on them in the Punjab, where most of them lived. The ruthless wars created a long-lasting hatred of Muslims by Sikhs.

Aurangzeb's most famous conquests were in the Deccan. In the 1670s, his authority was challenged by a talented young Maratha named Shivaji, who was the son of Shahji Bhosle, the noble who had led the last formal resistance to the Mughal capture of Ahmadnagar in the 1630s. Shivaji inherited the charisma and ability of his father, and he led disaffected Marathas to throw off Mughal rule, creating an avowedly Hindu kingdom that extended from Surat to Goa. After it became clear that Shivaji could not be coaxed back into the Mughal Empire, Aurangzeb went to war. He had a dual purpose in doing so. The main objective of defeating Shivaji was complemented by a desire to annex Golkonda and Bijapur. The two kingdoms were still wealthy, but they had become militarily weak. All the Mughal leaders had coveted them, but Aurangzeb had additional motives: Both of these Shi'ite kingdoms had recently installed Brahmins (high-caste Hindus) as chief ministers, exacerbating Aurangzeb's loathing of them. In addition, Shivaji had sought an alliance with Golkonda against Delhi, and Aurangzeb used that as a pretext to attack both Golkonda and Bijapur.

In an effort to rally the Muslims of the empire behind him in what would undoubtedly be a long and expensive war, Aurangzeb announced changes in governmental religious policy. He enforced the Shari'a-mandated head tax on non-Muslims, and he taxed Hindus who went to their own religious festivals. Perhaps most shocking to other members of the ruling family, he prohibited the consumption of wine and opium. Aurangzeb could be utterly ruthless in the execution of his policies, but we should note that some of his attempts to implement Islamic principles actually benefited non-Muslims. Although he imposed the head tax on non-Muslims, he also abolished a number of taxes *not* authorized by the Shari'a that had fallen primarily on Hindus. Although he destroyed some Hindu temples, he authorized the construction of a few Hindu temples for political reasons and occasionally gave land grants to Brahmins. On the whole, however, there can be no doubt that many non-Muslims became disaffected from the regime because of his policies. The disaffection was noticed not so much among the elites as among the urban masses, who were harassed and abused by collectors of the head tax.

The Mughal army defeated Shivaji and took control of the major Maratha cities. Shivaji and his successors, however, continued to conduct guerilla warfare against the Mughal army. Aurangzeb could never be certain that he exercised control in the region, and he had to station large numbers of troops in it. Meanwhile, between 1685 and 1687, Aurangzeb conducted a scorched-earth policy against Golkonda and Bijapur. His army devastated the two kingdoms in an orgy of destruction, looting, and rape. No one—including his family members, leading ulama, and generals—could dissuade him from wreaking devastation. He also ignored protests and appeals from Esfahan. The Mughal–Safavid relationship, which had been correct and occasionally warm despite genuine competition, became unremittingly hostile due to Aurangzeb's anti-Shi'ite policies. There were no diplomatic missions between the Mughals and the last two Safavid emperors (1666–1722).

By 1689, Aurangzeb had annexed the ruins of Golkonda and Bijapur and had destroyed the Maratha state. The Mughal leader was at the peak of his career, and,

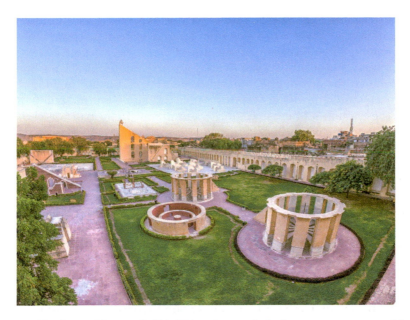

FIGURE 15.4 The Jantar Mantar, Delhi. This astronomical observatory was one of five that Jai Singh constructed at various sites across India in order to gain comparative readings. In the foreground is the Samrat Yantra, or sundial, and in the background is the circular Ram Yantra, which showed the altitude and azimuth of sun, stars, and planets.

Meinzahn / iStock.

at least on the map, he had re-created the boundaries of Muhammad ibn Tughluq of the Delhi Sultanate. Aurangzeb claimed to be master of the region from Kabul in the north to a line just above Calicut in the south. Like Ibn Tughluq, too, he had overreached himself by venturing deep into the Deccan. Although he campaigned there constantly after 1681, he could not return to Delhi in triumph. Numerous rebellions began breaking out all over the empire, but they were especially severe in the Maratha areas. An old man, Aurangzeb lived in military field camps without a break between 1689 and 1706, when he sought rest in the city of Ahmadnagar. He died there the following year at the age of 88.

Collapse

Upon Aurangzeb's death, a war of succession broke out. Before it was over, two of his sons and three of his grandsons were dead. His eldest son, sixty-four-year-old Bahadur Shah, succeeded to the throne in 1707. He faced unrest all over his empire, and his treasury was depleted because of the expenses of his father's unending wars. He tried to win over disaffected Hindus by repealing the discriminatory measures enacted by Aurangzeb, but that gesture hardly mattered: His chief rivals were fellow Muslims. After his death in 1712, two more wars of succession took place before 1720.

None of Aurangzeb's successors, once having achieved the throne, could quell the provincial revolts that had begun during Aurangzeb's reign. Provincial and local forces became more and more autonomous until they could act without referring to Delhi. Sikhs in the Punjab broke free from Mughal control in 1708. A Maratha state quickly reemerged, and other states south of Delhi were autonomous soon after 1710. The weakness of the Mughal dynasty was so evident that Nadir Shah of Iran, having deposed the last puppet Safavid ruler, attacked Delhi in 1739. His troops sacked the city and returned to Mashhad with a treasure trove, including the Peacock Throne, the symbol of Mughal authority and might. Delhi had not experienced a trauma on the scale of Nadir Shah's attack since Timur Lang's atrocities two and one-half centuries earlier. Judging from the written accounts from the period, the inhabitants of northern India viewed it as a cataclysm.

Encouraged by the ease and thoroughness of Nadir Shah's victory, the Marathas began expanding their influence from the Western Ghats northward until they controlled the region almost to the valley of the Ganges. From the western side of the Punjab, another in a long series of Afghan incursions into India began. This time was different, however: The leader of the military campaigns was not a mere military adventurer, but the first ruler of Afghanistan, Ahmad Shah Durrani. Durrani made major changes in the map of India. For many centuries, the Kabul valley had been under Indian influence, and it was a major outpost of Mughal power. When Durrani united it with Qandahar and Herat, it became part of Afghanistan, and it has remained so to this day. A much more temporary victory in India was Durrani's acquisition of the entire Indus valley in 1749, including the Punjab as far east as Lahore and the length of the river to the Arabian Sea. He attacked Delhi three times, in 1748, 1757, and 1760. After capturing the city in 1757, he forced a treaty from the hapless Mughal ruler. Although Mughal "emperors" remained in Delhi for another century, their writ barely extended beyond the walls of the city.

The fragmentation of the empire occurred with stunning rapidity. Whereas the contemporary Ottoman system survived even while suffering simultaneous blows from a severe economic crisis, internal revolts, and external attacks from international military alliances, the Mughal system collapsed from within, at the very height of its territorial expansion and economic health. It was moribund even before Delhi suffered the attack from Nadir Shah.

The rapid collapse of the empire's power was the outcome of a long-term shift in power from the center to the periphery of the empire. The Mughals had ruled by co-opting the empire's few hundred warlords into a system that offered wealth and the prestige of being affiliated with a dazzling imperial court. The governors and other mansabdars found it to their advantage to cooperate with the court in order to suppress ambitious and powerful zamindars, whose authority was limited to the local level. Zamindars could command surprising power due to the large numbers of armed peasants in many areas, but they were no match for concerted imperial power.

By the end of the seventeenth century, two developments converged to doom this system. One, ironically, was economic success. The Mughals had developed a well-integrated domestic economy at the very time that world demand was growing for South Asian products. Peasants, moneylenders, financiers, artisans, merchants, and zamindars all benefited. Vast amounts of wealth accumulated at the local level, and new alliances formed among social groups to try to expand and protect that wealth. The zamindars were at the center of such alliances, and they became wealthier, better organized, and more experienced than before. Their armed forces became formidable challenges to mansabdars.

The growing wealth and power of the zamindars coincided with the second development, which was Aurangzeb's opening of the Pandora's box of the Deccan. The Deccan wars caused a great financial drain on the mansabdars who had to supply the troops for more than two decades of continual warfare. When they tried to extort more tribute from zamindars, the latter had become able to resist effectively. The central government, which normally would have sided with the mansabdars, was too distracted by the Deccan campaigns to respond. Without assistance from Delhi, governors began to formulate their own policies for dealing with local challenges. Inevitably, the new policies entailed a smaller amount of revenue being sent to the imperial capital. When Delhi objected, governors and zamindars found common cause. One by one, the provinces became autonomous, until the Mughal emperor had no empire.

Despite the collapse of Mughal power, the imperial legacy lived on. The aura of power and legitimacy possessed by the Mughals was one that all of their successors wished to share. Few of the new states had a natural legitimacy of their own that allowed them to rule over their own people unchallenged, much less to exert hegemony over the other new states. Provincial rulers found that it was in their interest to continue the fiction of Mughal authority, despite the lack of actual power at Delhi. Even Sikhs and Marathas sought the Mughal imprimatur. Thus, throughout the eighteenth century, many South Asian provincial rulers went through the motions of obtaining an honorary "office" in the ceremonial court at Delhi in order to share in the aura of the "emperor." They offered only token financial tribute to Delhi, and their deference was merely perfunctory. Most of their own subjects, of course, never realized that their rulers were engaged in a shadow play.

By the middle of the eighteenth century, South Asia had fragmented into a number of autonomous and ambitious states. Among the most powerful were Durrani's Afghan empire, the Maratha confederacy, Bengal, Hyderabad (the new name for Golkonda), and Mysore. The Mughal court retained enormous prestige, but it exercised power only in the vicinity of Delhi. The new states were highly competitive, and the century witnessed a correspondingly high level of violence as a result.

A noteworthy feature of the political relationships in South Asia during the eighteenth century was their nonsectarian nature. Today it is easy to assume that Hindu states that broke free from Mughal control would have engaged in religious wars with Delhi and other Muslim states. There were, indeed, Muslim and Hindu religious leaders who urged their rulers to act in the name of their religion against people of other faiths. In fact, however, little violence took place that can be identified as having religious roots. Maratha rulers abandoned the ideal of a Hindu empire and were satisfied to rule the country in the name of the emperor, fully content to act and behave like other Mughal nobles. Nizam al-Mulk, the Muslim ruler of Hyderabad, did not intervene when Marathas encroached on Delhi's territory, and the Mughal emperor encouraged Maratha expansion in the Deccan that came at the expense of Nizam.

Despite the numerous wars of the eighteenth century, the cultural life of South Asia entered a vibrant period compared with the reign of Aurangzeb. The new states competed culturally as well as militarily as they strove to develop sophisticated capital cities. Numerous South Asian rulers—rather than a single emperor—offered patronage to intellectuals, poets, and artists. By the middle of the eighteenth century, religious leaders were becoming active in reform movements, poets were producing a huge body of literature in the new Urdu language, painters were experimenting with new themes, and architects were designing new palaces and mosques for the glory of South Asia's new rulers. The ominous feature of the fragmentation of political and military power that had made the cultural efflorescence possible was that South Asia had become vulnerable to the ambitions of outside powers. The greatest threat came from an unlikely source: a joint-stock English company whose ambition and avarice knew no bounds whatsoever.

Conclusion

Timur's destruction of Delhi in 1398 did not diminish the Muslim presence in South Asia. For more than three centuries after Timur's orgy of looting and murder, Muslim-ruled states became the norm in the region. From the western Punjab to eastern Bengal and from Kashmir to the Deccan, most of the population were subjects of Muslim sovereigns. During this period, large numbers of Muslim immigrants poured into South Asia. Many of them came from Iran and Central Asia. They brought with them the Persian language, Irano-Timurid administrative practices, and artistic styles. Long after the Mughal Empire had lost its effective power, the Timurid legacy was still evident in the arts, architecture, and languages of the region. The empire's grandeur and its vision of unitary rule for the subcontinent sparked the imagination of many of South Asia's inhabitants.

Islam spread widely throughout South Asia during the three and one-half centuries under examination in this section. Enormous numbers of people came into contact with pirs at their lodges or shrines and with qadis at their courts of law. They adopted features of the Islamic tradition that met their immediate needs and they integrated their new practices into their preexisting worldview. As a result, it was common in South Asia to witness "Hindus" attending Muslim shrines and festivals, and "Muslims" attending Hindu shrines and festivals.

The varieties of Islamic expression were more diverse in South Asia than in Iran or the Ottoman Empire. The Mughals, unlike the Safavids and Ottomans, did not attempt to impose state control of Islam and did not develop the elaborate bureaucracies that regulated religious life in the other two empires. One of the great ironies of South Asian history is that the regions where the most dramatic Islamization occurred—East Bengal and the western regions of modern Pakistan—lay on the fringes of Muslim rule in the subcontinent, where government rule was weak. The regions in the Delhi–Agra axis—the heart of Mughal power—were, by contrast, only lightly Islamized.

Mughal power collapsed simultaneously with the Safavid Empire and during the period that the Ottoman Empire was in a century-long diminution of central power. In each case the central government lost the advantage that it had enjoyed over regional elites within its respective empire. The contrast between the decline of central authority in these states and the increased power of central governments in contemporary Europe is striking. Each of the Muslim empires had its own unique set of circumstances, and yet the simultaneous weakening of all three governments raises provocative questions about the possibility of a general crisis affecting the huge area from Delhi to Istanbul. Answers to those questions are inconclusive at this point. All that is certain is that the decline in central government power rendered the areas vulnerable to future outside interference.

NOTES

1   See Richard M. Eaton, "Temple Desecration and Indo-Muslim States," in *Beyond Turk and Hindu: Rethinking Religious Identities in Islamicate South Asia*, eds. David Gilmartin and Bruce B. Lawrence (Gainesville: University Press of Florida, 2000), 246–281.

2   This section on the role of the dargah in the gradual spread of Islam in much of South Asia is based on Richard M. Eaton's study, "Sufi Folk Literature and the Expansion of Indian Islam," in his *Essays on Islam and Indian History* (New York: Oxford University Press, 2001), 189–199.

3   See Gavin R. G. Hambly's article, "Armed Women Retainers in the Zananas of Indo-Muslim Rulers: The Case of Bibi Fatima," in his *Women in the Medieval Islamic World* (New York: St. Martin's Press, 1998), 429–467.

4   Juan R. I. Cole, "Iranian Culture and South Asia, 1500–1900," in Nikki R. Keddie and Rudi Matthee, eds., *Iran and the Surrounding World: Interactions in Culture and Cultural Politics* (Seattle and London: University of Washington Press, 2002), 18.

5   See Yohanan Friedmann, *Shaykh Ahmad Sirhindi: An Outline of His Thought and a Study of His Image in the Eyes of Posterity* (New Delhi: Oxford University Press, 2000).

6   Sikhism is a religion that has been rooted in the Punjab since its founding in the fifteenth century by Nanak (ca. 1469–1538). It shares elements of its faith with both Islam and Hinduism: Sikhism is monotheistic, and the believer's highest aspiration is to be absorbed

into God. Salvation is not the achievement of paradise after death, but rather the loss of personal identity in a union with God. This can be achieved only by constant meditation on God; to be distracted by the things of this world only prolongs the round of rebirths that karma inflicts on humanity.

FURTHER READING

South Asia after the Delhi Sultanate

Alam, Muzaffar. *The Languages of Political Islam: India, 1200–1800*. Chicago and London: University of Chicago Press, 2004.

Eaton, Richard M. *A Social History of the Deccan, 1300–1761: Eight Indian Lives*. The New Cambridge History of India. I, 8. Cambridge, U.K., and New York: Cambridge University Press, 2005.

Lal, Kishori Saran. *Twilight of the Sultanate*. New York: Asia Publishing House, 1963.

Michell, George, and Mark Zebrowski. *Architecture and Art of the Deccan Sultanates*. The New Cambridge History of India. I, 7. Cambridge, U.K., and New York: Cambridge University Press, 1999.

Rizvi, Saiyid Athar Abbas. *A Socio-Intellectual History of the Isna 'Ashari Shi'is in India*. Canberra, Australia: Munshiram Manoharlal Publishers Pvt. Ltd., 1986.

Roy, Atul Chandra. *History of Bengal: Turko–Afghan Period*. New Delhi: Kalyani Publishers, 1986.

Islam in South Asia

Asani, Ali S. *Ecstasy and Enlightenment: The Ismaili Devotional Literature of South Asia*. London and New York: I. B. Tauris, 2002.

Bayly, Susan. *Saints, Goddesses and Kings: Muslims and Christians in South Indian Society 1700–1900*. Cambridge, U.K., and New York: Cambridge University Press, 1989.

Blank, Jonah. *Mullahs on the Mainframe: Islam and Modernity among the Daudi Bohras*. Chicago and London: University of Chicago Press, 2001.

Daftary, Farhad. *The Ismā'īlīs: Their History and Doctrines*. Cambridge, U.K., and New York: Cambridge University Press, 1990.

Eaton, Richard M. *Essays on Islam and Indian History*. New Delhi and Oxford, U.K.: Oxford University Press, 2001.

———. *The Rise of Islam and the Bengal Frontier, 1204–1760*. Berkeley, Los Angeles, London: University of California Press, 1993.

———. *The Sufis of Bijapur, 1300–1700: Social Roles of Sufis in Medieval India*. Princeton, New Jersey: Princeton University Press, 1978.

The Timurids in South Asia: The Mughals

Alam, Muzaffar. *The Crisis of Empire in Mughal North India: Awadh and the Punjab, 1707–48*. Delhi and New York: Oxford University Press, 1986.

Bayly, C.A. *Indian Society and the Making of the British Empire*. Cambridge, U.K., and New York: Cambridge University Press, 1988.

Dale, Stephen F. *The Garden of the Eight Paradises: Babur and the Culture of Empire in Central Asia, Afghanistan and India*. Leiden, Netherlands, and Boston: Brill Academic Publishers, 2004.

Dale, Stephen Frederic. *Indian Merchants and Eurasian Trade, 1600–1750*. Cambridge Studies in Islamic Civilization. Cambridge, U.K.: Cambridge University Press, 1994.

Gommans, Jos J. L. *The Rise of the Indo-Afghan Empire c. 1710–1780.* Leiden, Netherlands, and New York: E. J. Brill, 1995.

Gommans, Jos J. L., and Dirk H. A. Kolff, eds. *Warfare and Weaponry in South Asia, 1000–1800.* New Delhi and New York: Oxford University Press, 2001.

Hintze, Andrea. *The Mughal Empire and its Decline.* Aldershot, U.K., and Brookfield, Vermont: Ashgate, 1997.

Richards, John F. *The Mughal Empire.* Cambridge, U.K.: Cambridge University Press, 1993.

Streusand, Douglas E. *The Formation of the Mughal Empire.* Delhi and New York: Oxford University Press, 1989.

CHAPTER 16

The Indian Ocean Basin

Just as the Mediterranean Sea linked the fates of Southern Europe, North Africa, and Southwest Asia, the Indian Ocean facilitated commerce and cultural contacts among East Africa, Southwest Asia, South Asia, and Southeast Asia. Although a distant third in size behind the Pacific and Atlantic oceans, the Indian Ocean's shape enabled the people along a vast swath of the globe to interact on a regular basis with each other even before the emergence of modern transportation technology. A sailor today who sets out from the Cape of Good Hope at the southern tip of Africa to visit the major ports of the ocean would travel more than 18,000 miles by the time he arrived in Perth, on the western coast of Australia. A sailor who had the same goal 500 years ago would have concluded his voyage at Banten, on the western coast of the island Java, because the last leg of the trip to Australia was unknown. The significant fact is that he would have sailed 16,000 miles, or two-thirds of the circumference of the earth at the equator, without losing sight of land for more than a few hours.

From at least Roman times, the foodstuffs, incense, and luxury items produced in the Indian Ocean basin have been highly prized in Europe, the Muslim world, China, and Japan. By the Umayyad period, Muslim merchants and sailors—at first largely Arabic- or Persian-speaking—fanned out from Southwest Asia to the east coast of Africa and the Asian coasts all the way to China. Some were only transient visitors, while others settled into merchant communities. These scattered pockets of Muslim settlement contributed to the fact that, by 1400, most of the trade of the Indian Ocean was in the hands of Muslims. The communities also became centers for the diffusion of Islam throughout East Africa and Southeast Asia. As in West Africa, Islam was introduced into these areas not in the wake of military conquest, but by means of trade.

Muslims were not the only ones interested in exploiting the Indian Ocean trade. Europeans who had to purchase Indian Ocean products from middlemen were eager to gain direct access to the source of production. Europe was not the most technologically advanced region of the world at the beginning of the fifteenth century, and its eventual dominance of the Indian Ocean in the sixteenth century was not inevitable. During the first third of the fifteenth century, the Ming dynasty of China (1368–1644) made repeated demonstrations of its naval strength to the port cities all around the ocean. Had it maintained its presence there, it would easily have prevented any European nation from entering the region. During the 1430s, however, the dynasty pulled its navy back, closed its country to the rest of the world, and withdrew into isolationism. Meanwhile, Prince Henry of Portugal was planning expeditions to send his country's ships around Africa into the Indian Ocean. When they did arrive at the end of the century, they encountered no other warships at all. Their captains entered with a determination to dominate the trade of the region and the military means to accomplish that goal.

A Muslim Lake

One of the more memorable figures from *The Thousand and One Nights* is Sindbad the Sailor, who sailed the Indian Ocean. Sindbad recounts adventures from a career that spanned seven voyages. He tells of surviving shipwrecks, encountering whales, and being tortured by savages in his quest to obtain precious goods in distant ports. He informs us that among his cargo were precious stones, sandalwood (the oil from its roots and heartwood were used as an incense), camphor (often used as a liniment, it began as the resin from a tree), coconuts, cloves, cinnamon, pepper, ivory, and ambergris (a black, stinky, gooey substance excreted by the sperm whale that, upon being exposed to air and light, becomes grayish, waxy, and fragrant and is used in perfumes).

Sindbad's exploits and hardships are embellishments of the experiences of mariners who were based in Persian Gulf ports but whose careers sent them out onto the Indian Ocean. Along the coasts of that ocean's vast basin they encountered a wide variety of cultures and ecosystems. They also found a correspondingly wide variety of products for which they could trade. Sailors followed the seasonal winds, or monsoons (from *mawsim*, Arabic for "season"): From April to August, the monsoons blow from the south, whereas from December to March they blow from the north.

It was not uncommon for traders during the Roman period and early Muslim history to make the trip from the Gulf all the way to Southeast Asia and even up to China. The trip was longer than the miles would suggest. Because a ship had to catch the seasonal winds, it would have to lie in various harbors for months awaiting a propitious time to sail. A round trip would normally require three years. Eventually, mariners decided that it was far more efficient to develop a network of entrepôts across the Indian Ocean where traders could await the change of monsoon or the arrival of trading partners from distant lands.

Over the centuries, a number of cities functioned as the primary commercial ports in the region, but by the fifteenth century, Aden served as the entrepôt for traffic in the Red Sea and along the eastern coast of Africa; Hormuz served the Persian Gulf; Cambay was the major port in Gujarat; Cochin (Kochi), Cannanore (Kannur), Goa, and Calicut (Kozhikode) competed for business along the Malabar Coast; Ma'bar on the Coromandel Coast was a favorite of Chinese merchants; and Melaka (Malacca) was emerging as the hub of trade in Southeast Asia. Ships from China and the Spice Islands unloaded their cargoes at Melaka, where other ships would take the goods to the Coromandel or Malabar coasts. There they would be loaded on yet other ships to be transported to Hormuz or Aden for distribution to their ultimate market.

Because of this network, a large quantity and a wide variety of goods traveled halfway around the world without merchants having to visit either the point of origin or the ultimate destination of the goods they traded. In many cases, the ultimate participants in a transaction did not know each other and depended on middlemen to deal with trustworthy local merchants. Like their contemporaries in the Mediterranean basin who were also engaged in long-distance trade, these traders developed mechanisms of deferred payments, credit, and limited-liability investment in order to facilitate their risky business.

The network also facilitated the diffusion of the practice of Islam around the ocean basin. The process by which Islam became a major—or even the dominant—religion was determined by local conditions, and individuals had a wide variety of motives for assuming a Muslim identity. Nevertheless, it is reasonable to agree with scholars who suggest that at least some non-Muslims in port cities around the Indian Ocean concluded that visiting Muslim merchants had two advantages over them. One was the universality of their religion. Adherents of traditional religions typically worshiped spirits that were known locally but were not recognized in other regions. Once away from their homes, such people were beyond the range of familiar spirits and at the mercy of spirits that could be manipulated by their enemies. Islam offered universally recognized values and a deity who was always available. Regardless of where a Muslim went, he would remain in a predictable, moral world in which God would protect him from evil spirits. The other advantage that Muslim merchants possessed was that their trading partners thousands of miles away shared the same Islamic legal and moral system that they followed. Contracts and bills of credit were worth much more when moral and legal systems existed to reinforce mutual trust and respect. The universal qualities of Islam may well have played a major theme in the spread of the religion in commercial cities.

By the fifteenth century, the Indian Ocean was ringed with settlements whose economies were dominated by Muslims. These towns were linked by ties of economic interdependence, possessed sophisticated commercial and maritime techniques, and accepted Islamic religious and legal precepts. On the other hand, they were small and commanded practically no navy. Prior to the sixteenth century, they had no reason to develop a maritime military power because the commercial routes were threatened only by the occasional pirate. Maintenance of the economic network worked to the advantage of everyone in the region, and Indian Ocean commerce was not plagued by the frequent wars that characterized the Mediterranean.

The East Coast of Africa

Islam came into the Horn of Africa (Ethiopia, Eritrea, Djibouti, and Somalia) and East Africa (Kenya, Uganda, and Tanzania) by way of the sea. As in West Africa, traders—rather than soldiers—introduced Islam into the area. These Muslim traders or their descendants often joined the ranks of the leading social groups of many of the port cities that dotted this long coastline. Although the cities thrived on long-distance maritime commerce, none of them became large or developed into major states during the period that we are studying. Like the Greek city–states two millennia earlier, these city–states prospered for a time, but they proved to be highly vulnerable when a major foreign power sent its military forces into the area.

Berbera and the Land of the Zanj

Arab geographers referred to the coastline north of Mogadishu as Berbera, and they called the region south of that city the Land of the Zanj (*zanj* means "black"). Eastern Africa exhibits a variety of land forms and climate. The entire Horn of Africa and the coastline of southern Tanzania are largely arid, whereas the coastline that Kenya and northern Tanzania share is green and fertile. The coastal plain of Kenya and Tanzania is quite narrow and rises to the west in a series of plateaus. Where the rainfall is adequate, the coast and the highlands support woodlands, but the rain

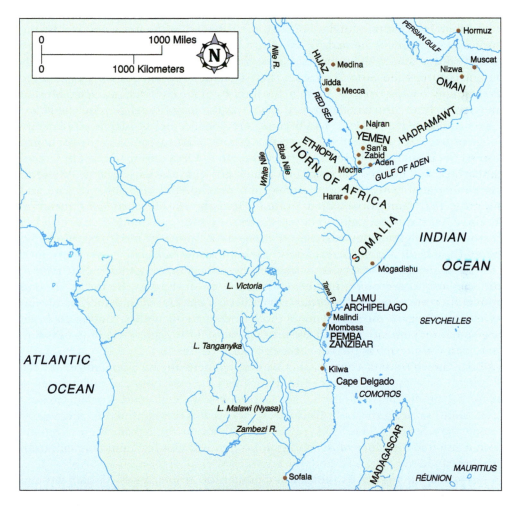

MAP 16.1 Western Indian Ocean and East Africa.

forests of West and Central Africa do not extend into East Africa. East Africa was not blessed with a wealth of natural resources. Its main products were ebony and mangrove timber, coconut oil, tortoise shell (used to make combs), ambergris that had washed up on shore, and, particularly, ivory. Trade in slaves was a minor segment of the economy south of Ethiopia until the eighteenth century.

Romans described well-established commercial links between eastern Africa and southern Arabia during the early Christian era, but no known documents record anything about the region south of Ethiopia during the first few centuries of the Islamic period. Only archaeological excavations testify that Muslim communities began to appear along the Ethiopian coast of the Red Sea in the eighth and ninth centuries and that a mosque was built as far south as the Lamu Archipelago off the coast of Kenya by the ninth century. As a result, historians assume that trade between Africa and southern Arabia continued during this period. Merchants from Muslim lands who wished to trade with the residents of eastern Africa could send vessels on winter's northerly monsoon as far south as Kilwa, in modern Tanzania, and the southeasterly monsoon could bring them back in summer.

Mogadishu, in present-day Somalia, was founded in the tenth century. By the twelfth century, many nomads in the Horn of Africa had become Muslim. Islam spread widely among the nomadic tribes of the interior of the Horn. The highly mobile nature of the pastoral societies there facilitated the faith's dispersal, and the trade routes that ran from the Horn to the interior of the continent attracted Muslim merchants. By the thirteenth century, Islam was the majority religion on the Harar plateau, and the city of Harar had become a regional center of Islamic scholarship.

Archaeological evidence suggests that groups of Bantu-speaking people began settling the coastal regions from Mogadishu south to Kilwa during the first or second century C.E. and became the dominant ethnic group by the early Islamic era. Over the next several centuries, these immigrants developed a distinctive culture and language that came to be called Swahili (from the Arabic word *sahel*, meaning "coast"). They spoke a patois that was based on Bantu grammatical structure but borrowed heavily from the vocabulary of indigenous languages and from traders who visited from lands across the sea. Many of them became Muslim.

After the tenth century, Arab travelers describe a thriving trade in the region, and they report a growing number of prominent Muslims in the towns. A large number of them were the descendants of earlier generations of Arab merchants who settled in the region and sought mates (both wives and concubines) among the local, largely Bantu, population. Their offspring possessed the high status of the Muslim merchant class as well as the kin network of local families.

By the thirteenth century, the Muslim element of the population was the dominant social group along the coast. It included the most powerful rulers as well as many of the prominent merchants, large landowners, and craftsmen. A striking feature of Muslim life along the East African coast was that it was confined to the narrow coastal plain. South of Somalia, every mosque and Muslim tomb that remains from the period prior to the nineteenth century is located within a few minutes' walk from the shoreline.

During the twelfth or thirteenth century, the city–states of Mogadishu and Kilwa emerged as the most powerful political units in eastern Africa. Both were ruled by Muslims. Kilwa thrived due to its control of the gold trade that had its origins on

FIGURE 16.1 The historic mosque at Kilwa. It was first constructed in the tenth century and had major additions in the twelfth and thirteenth centuries.

John Warburton-Lee Photography / Alamy Stock Photo.

the upper Zambezi River. In the fourteenth century, Ibn Battuta visited both Mogadishu and Kilwa. Kilwa was the more prosperous of the two cities, but Mogadishu had a Shari'a court. The court, like those in Egypt and the Sunni regions of Yemen, administered law according to the rules of the Shafi'i school. The law court was, in fact, worth noting for by all accounts the other Muslim cities along the coast had no ulama in them. Until the mid-sixteenth century, when a madrasa was established in Lamu, students as far south as Kilwa who wanted to study the Qur'an, Hadith, or the Shari'a had to travel to Mogadishu, Yemen, or Egypt to find qualified instructors.

By the end of the fifteenth century, some thirty Muslim cities dotted the East African coast from Mogadishu to Kilwa. Most were only nominally Muslim, for their inhabitants had little or no access to religious instruction. On the whole, they were geared more toward commerce than war, although quarrels did break out. To the north, in the Horn of Africa, a much different history was being played out. There, Muslim settlements were established well inland in both Somalia and Ethiopia. In the early fourteenth century, the Christian Ethiopian king and various Muslim chieftains were encroaching on territories that the others claimed, and almost constant fighting occurred in the region until the late sixteenth century.

The Impact of Imperialism

European merchants paid premium prices for the products of the Indian Ocean basin when they bought them in the Mamluk ports of Egypt and Syria. A new era opened in 1498, when Vasco da Gama rounded the Cape of Good Hope and entered the harbor of Calicut on India's Malabar Coast. Six years after Columbus mistakenly thought he had arrived in the Indies by sailing west, da Gama finally achieved the Portuguese dream of entering the Indian Ocean by sailing east. The event marked the beginning of an era of great opportunity for Europeans—first the Portuguese, and later the English and Dutch—who eagerly sought the spices and other commodities of the East.

The Indian Ocean was the theater in which European imperialism—as opposed to colonialism—conducted its dress rehearsal for the more famous nineteenth-century version. In the Indian Ocean of the sixteenth and seventeenth centuries, we see the attempts of novices. The Portuguese government could never dissociate its economic goals from that of a religious crusade, and the Dutch and English governments tried to obtain economic gains on the cheap by leaving the dirty work in the hands of chartered private companies. Both approaches had their distinct limitations, which gradually became apparent back home. By the second half of the nineteenth century, European governments regarded imperialism to be a matter of national security strategy. It was a secular affair of the state, and it was too important to the perceived national interest to be delegated to a business corporation without government supervision.

Da Gama visited many ports along the East African coast in April 1498. He was surprised and angered to find Muslims in so many commercial cities and to discover that Muslims were the leading merchants in the region. Despite the ethnic differences between these Muslims and the Muslims he had encountered in the Maghrib, he called them *Moros*, or Moors. At Malindi, da Gama hired a Muslim pilot who knew the way to Calicut. Da Gama's voyage to Calicut accomplished little other than offending the port's Hindu ruler.

A second Portuguese fleet, under the leadership of Pedro Cabral, made an even worse impression in Calicut. Its visit provoked a violent uprising in the city, with the result that da Gama returned in 1502 with twenty ships to exact revenge on the city. En route to India, he secured control of the sea lanes along the eastern coast of Africa. Since the region was dotted by small city–states, he found them easy to subjugate. He forced all the cities between the mouth of the Zambezi River and Kilwa to pay tribute. Throughout the rest of his voyage he employed indiscriminate violence against local shipping interests, particularly when Muslims appeared to be involved. This voyage began a period of more than a century of staggering violence that the Portuguese directed against Muslims of the Indian Ocean. In the course of the campaign, the Portuguese regularly bombarded cities without cause and massacred hapless fishermen. They captured every ship that they suspected of being owned or manned by Muslims. After plundering the ship, they either decapitated and mutilated the crew and passengers or burned the ships along with the passengers and crew.

The Portuguese practiced unrestrained violence because they were continuing the crusade against Islam that they had begun in the Maghrib. Since they had not found Prester John in North Africa, they hoped to discover him in the Indian Ocean. With his help and the wealth derived from control of the spice trade, they would be able to extirpate Islam root and branch. In the meantime, they occasionally looted coastal towns and periodically bombarded them in order to force them to pay tribute.

All ships not flying the Portuguese flag were liable to be destroyed. Trade along the East African coast diminished, and the wealth of the coastal cities declined precipitously. The one exception was Malindi, which allied itself with the Portuguese in order to compete with its more powerful rival, Mombasa. It served as an independent supply and repair port for the Portuguese fleet.

In 1517, the Portuguese attacked and burned cities along the Somali coast of the Gulf of Aden. In the same year, the Ottomans defeated the Mamluks and annexed their empire. From that point on, the Ottomans and Portuguese tried to contain each other without having to engage in a costly conflict. A major arena of conflict for them was the coast of Ethiopia. During the 1530s, Muslim sultanates in Somalia and in the southern and eastern regions of what is now Ethiopia (especially at Harar) began capturing Ethiopian territory. Portugal's entry into the region had made it a potential ally of Christian Ethiopia, and in 1543, the two powers formed an alliance that defeated a coalition of local Muslims and the Ottomans. Ethiopia thereupon recovered most of the territory it had lost. The Ottomans continued to patrol the area, with the result that Muslim influence increased along the coast of the Red Sea and Gulf of Aden, although it declined in the interior of Ethiopia.

During the first fifteen years of the sixteenth century, the Portuguese engaged in a frenetic campaign to establish military bases on the eastern and northern rims of the Indian Ocean basin in order to control the trade of the region. For many decades, they did not do so in East Africa, where they were satisfied to maintain access to the port at Malindi. The economy of the African coast did not interest them, and they did not want to sustain the expenses that maintaining a garrison in a port city would entail. By the 1580s, however, their violent policy toward local shipping had provoked a reaction in kind from local residents. The Portuguese began to suffer an increasing number of attacks on their own ships, which they condemned as piracy. The combination of local attacks and the growing threat from the Ottomans forced them to consider the establishment of a military presence along the coast. They attacked and captured Mombasa, at that time the largest of the cities along the coast. In 1593, they consolidated their presence in the city by completing the construction of Fort Jesus, the most imposing citadel in all of Africa.

Portugal's dominance of Indian Ocean trade was gradually reduced by the Dutch and the English, but it was Oman that delivered the coup de grâce. Throughout the second half of the seventeenth century, the Omanis developed a fleet that was able to compete with the finest of the Portuguese ships. Using it with skillful effect, they gradually pushed the Portuguese out of Oman and much of eastern Africa. At the invitation of the inhabitants of Mombasa, Oman laid siege to the city during 1696–1698 and finally captured Fort Jesus. When the fort fell, Portugal lost all the territory that it had possessed north of Cape Delgado, the northernmost part of modern Mozambique. The Omanis quickly revealed that they were liberating Mombasa from Portuguese control only for the purpose of incorporating it into their own nascent imperial project. Despite suffering a catastrophic civil war during the first half of the eighteenth century, the Omanis continued to expand their influence along the East African coast. In particular, they secured control of Pemba and Zanzibar, which became the jewels of their nineteenth-century mini-empire.

Kerala

The southwestern coast of India has been known by a variety of names. In modern history, the region from around the city of Mumbai (formerly Bombay) south to the city of Goa has been known as the Konkan Coast and the region south of Goa to the tip of the peninsula has been called Malabar. During the period that we are examining, the term *Malabar* was often used to refer to the entire coast up to the head of the Gulf of Khambat (formerly known as Cambay). The term *Kerala* was used to denote the section of Malabar that lay south of Goa. Even more confusing is the fact that after India became independent of British colonial rule, the new government created a state named Kerala that encompasses only the southern half of historic Kerala. In this chapter, we will use the older meaning of the terms: *Malabar* will denote the entire southwestern coast, whereas *Kerala* will denote the region of the coast lying south of Goa.

The Land of Pepper

The northern section of the Malabar Coast is semiarid, but Kerala is well watered by the monsoons. As a result of abundant rainfall, Kerala is covered with evergreen forests and boasts numerous rivers. Rice is the staple of its inhabitants' diet. The narrow coastal plain is bounded by the Western Ghats, the steep escarpment that extends parallel to the Arabian Sea for more than 700 miles, making communication with the interior of the subcontinent difficult. Because of this natural barrier, Kerala's contacts with the political and cultural developments of the interior were limited. By contrast, communication with Southeast Asia, Arabia, and East Africa was relatively easy. Even the Roman Empire had trading contacts with Kerala. The region became famous in Christian lore as the legendary destination of St. Thomas, one of the Twelve Apostles, who was said to have been martyred there.

Kerala became heavily involved in the Indian Ocean trade. Its forests yielded a variety of hardwoods, which were valued for lumber, and aromatic woods, which masked disagreeable odors and served a number of symbolic functions in religious rituals. Ginger, cardamom, and cinnamon also grew there, but Kerala was particularly renowned for its black pepper. As a result, it was known for centuries as "the land of pepper." In addition to supplying its own high-demand commodities, Kerala lay at the midpoint of the voyage between the Strait of Melaka and East Africa. It was a natural point for goods to be delivered from all around the Indian Ocean basin and then redistributed to specific markets. Cochin, Calicut (Kozhikode), Cannanore, and Goa became flourishing ports in Kerala that competed for trade with Cambay, located on the northern end of the Malabar Coast.

Jews, Nestorian Christians, and Arabs established settlements in Kerala in pre-Islamic times, but the region's history during the early Islamic period is as obscure as that of eastern Africa. The coast's Arab population may have become rapidly Islamized after the spread of Islam out of Arabia, but the first actual evidence of a Muslim presence there comes from the ninth century. As a consequence of Kerala's close contacts with the Arabic-speaking lands, its Muslim communities maintained a culture that was noticeably distinct from that of the Turkic–Persian sultanates of Lahore, Delhi, and the Deccan. Preserving Arabic as their primary language, they also preferred the Shafi'i school of law, in contrast to the Hanafi school used by the Turks.

In the fourteenth century, Ibn Battuta reported meeting Muslims in every port he visited along the Malabar Coast. They included Arabs from all around the Arabian Peninsula and from Baghdad, as well as Iranians from Qazvin. The largest settlement of foreign merchants, especially Arab Muslims, was at Calicut. Calicut became an important port through the sheer force of will of its Hindu ruler, whose title was *zamorin*. The city had no natural harbor, forcing sailors to cast anchor three miles offshore and unload their cargoes onto small boats. Despite the inconvenience—a dramatic contrast with the fine natural port at Goa—Ibn Battuta discovered that Calicut attracted a large number of merchants from all around the Indian Ocean and even from China.

Politically, most of Kerala was divided among a number of independent Hindu rulers. The wealth that poured through Calicut established the Zamorin as the most powerful of them. Goa's superb harbor made it irresistible to the landlocked kingdoms in the Deccan. From 1347 to 1489, the Muslim-ruled Bahmani kingdom and its great rival, Hindu-ruled Vijayanagar, contested for control of it. In 1489, Bijapur seceded from the Bahmani kingdom and took Goa with it.

Although Kerala and the part of the Deccan that lay south of the Bahmani kingdom were ruled by Hindus, many communities of foreign Muslim traders were scattered throughout the Hindu states. They exercised considerable political influence on their rulers due to their commercial contacts and diplomatic skills. By the end of the fifteenth century, tens of thousands of Kerala's inhabitants had adopted Muslim identities. They are known to history as Mappilas (Moplahs), a name that derives from an early term of respect in the region. Their society was to be transformed forever by the Portuguese invasion.

The Impact of Imperialism

Vasco da Gama's arrival at Calicut in 1498 was the culmination of more than sixty years of Portuguese efforts to establish a route to India and the Spice Islands by sailing around the southern tip of Africa. After all those decades of exploration, the Portuguese were strangely unprepared when they finally arrived in India. As had happened when they explored the East African coast, they were surprised and outraged to find "Moors" dominating commerce in general and the spice trade in particular. Da Gama's visit to Calicut was a harbinger of the future relations between the Portuguese and Indian Ocean settlements. Da Gama offended the Zamorin by presenting him with cheap trinkets instead of the luxury goods to which the ruler was accustomed. He also antagonized the local community by kidnapping several residents to take back as trophies to his king. Perhaps most surprisingly, this veteran seaman who was proud of his ability to take the measure of men came away from Calicut with the assumption that the Zamorin, a Hindu, was a Christian.

Subsequent Portuguese expeditions into the Indian Ocean had two primary purposes. One was to secure control of critical choke points around the Indian Ocean basin that would enable Portugal to control the spice trade. The other was to obliterate the Muslims both as a religious community and as commercial competition. Despite rivalries among Portuguese commanders and the hostility of most of the cities they entered, the overwhelming superiority of their vessels and firepower enabled them to seize all the cities that they targeted except Aden. On the Malabar Coast, Afonso de Albuquerque captured Cochin and Goa. Bijapur retook Goa from the Portuguese, but Albuquerque launched another attack in 1510 and captured it again. This time he systematically massacred 6000 Muslim men, women, and children over a period of four days. The Portuguese subsequently established forts at Cannanore and Calicut, although the one at Calicut was abandoned after two decades. Goa's harbor was so superior to the others along the coast that it became the headquarters for the Portuguese on the Malabar Coast.

The Portuguese seized Hormuz in 1515, but their failure to capture Aden meant that the goal of controlling all the choke points in the Indian Ocean would not be achieved. Trade between Southeast Asia and Egypt resumed by midcentury, to the satisfaction of the inhabitants of both regions. For the Mappilas, the failure of the Portuguese to obtain all of their goals was little consolation. Unlike East Africa, Kerala was dotted with Portuguese forts, and the Europeans closely monitored developments along the coast. Kerala attracted Portuguese attention because of its large population of Muslims and its role as a source of luxury goods. The Portuguese made a concerted effort to gain control of the coastal commerce and to exclude Muslim merchants. They began with a monopoly on pepper and ginger and then extended their control to all spices and rice. They systematically burned cities and mosques in the area, killed pilgrims performing the hajj to Mecca, and insulted Islam and the Prophet.

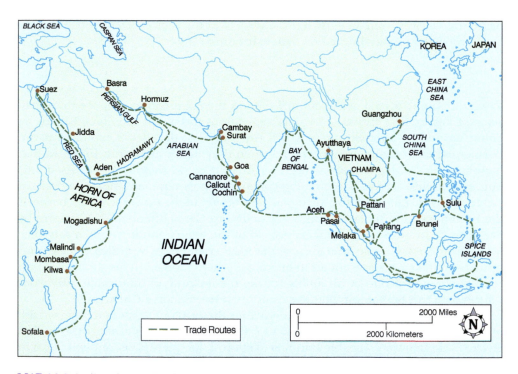

MAP 16.2 Indian Ocean Trade Routes.

As if these pressures were not enough, the global pepper industry experienced a major structural change. By the second half of the sixteenth century, Kerala's role as the source of black pepper for Southwest Asia and Europe was being challenged by Sumatra, where the plant could be grown more cheaply. By the middle of the seventeenth century, the advantages enjoyed by Southeast Asia resulted in a startling turn of events: Consumers in the land of pepper were importing black pepper from Sumatra.

The Portuguese crusade against Islam in the Maghrib ended during the late sixteenth century with the loss at the Battle of the Three Kings. The crusade in Kerala lasted much longer, even though the Portuguese had lost their sovereignty to Spain. Portuguese attacks in Kerala provoked a response in kind from the Muslims, who interpreted their fight against the Portuguese to be an expression of jihad. In the Shari'a, one of the two major functions of jihad is to defend Islam against hostile aggression. The Portuguese had made it clear that they intended to destroy Islam, and thus the Muslim defensive response was obligatory from the standpoint of Islamic law. The treatises on jihad, however, assumed that a Muslim ruler would be in charge to coordinate activities, and they assumed that the emergency situation would be only temporary. They did not prepare believers for the situation in Kerala: The Mappilas were a minority population, typically under the authority of Hindu rulers. Thus, their expression of jihad could not take the form of organized, state-led warfare. In addition, the Portuguese crusade was not a single expedition but a campaign that was waged for more than a century. Jihad in Kerala began as a form of guerilla warfare, but it eventually evolved into suicidal attacks. The tradition of jihad had always honored the martyr (*shahid*), but becoming a martyr had never been the object of jihad. The object was to survive in order to enjoy victory, glory, and plunder. What happened in Kerala was quite different, for a veritable cult of martyrdom arose. Much as in the early Roman Church, martyrdom became the ideal to which a believer could aspire, and the rewards and benefits of martyrdom became the object of poems and devotional literature. For Mappilas, however, it was not enough simply to sacrifice one's life; the true believer should die in the act of striking against the cruel oppressor.

The desperate reaction by the Mappilas against Portugal's attempt to exterminate them exacerbated relations with their Hindu neighbors. The Muslim community had become armed and defensive, and many Muslims increasingly interpreted any social slight or economic exploitation at the hands of Hindus to be a threat as serious as that of the Portuguese. In addition, some Hindu rulers cooperated with the Portuguese in order to protect their economies, provoking the Mappilas to greater hostility. By the end of the sixteenth century, the harmonious Muslim–Hindu relations characteristic of the fifteenth century had deteriorated into mutual suspicion and occasional violence.

In the middle of the seventeenth century, the Dutch began evicting the Portuguese from Kerala. By 1663, they had removed them from all their forts south of Goa. (Goa itself remained under Portuguese control until India annexed it in 1961.) The Hindus and Muslims of the area welcomed this development and initially viewed the Dutch as allies against the Portuguese. The Dutch soon disabused them of their illusions, as they tried to enforce their own monopoly over the spice trade in the area. Muslim resistance in Kerala simply changed its target from the Portuguese

FIGURE 16.2 The Western Ghats, with a tea plantation in the foreground.

Zzvet / iStock.

to the Dutch. By the middle of the eighteenth century, Muslim society in northern Kerala was widely known throughout the Indian Ocean basin for its militancy and religious zeal. Three centuries of struggle for religious and economic survival against the Portuguese and Dutch imperialists and Hindu landowners and merchants had conditioned many Muslims there to be xenophobic and to regard social conflict as having religious implications.

Southeast Asia

Southeast Asia encompasses the modern countries of Myanmar (Burma), Thailand, Laos, Cambodia, Vietnam, Malaysia, Singapore, Brunei, the Philippines, Indonesia, and Papua New Guinea. The region lies astride the sea routes linking the western Indian Ocean with China. Seafarers making the passage between the Indian Ocean and the South China Sea are forced to employ one of two narrow straits: the Strait of Melaka between present-day Malaysia and the island of Sumatra, or the Sunda Strait, between Sumatra and Java. Throughout history, it was more convenient for most mariners engaged in long-distance trade across the Indian Ocean to use the

Strait of Melaka. The Sunda Strait was used only when piracy or war rendered the more northerly passage too dangerous to enter. Southeast Asia also contains the famed Spice Islands, or Maluku (the Moluccas). For centuries, these islands were the world's preeminent source of nutmeg, cloves, and mace.

Because of Southeast Asia's strategic location and spices, Muslim merchants from Arabia, Iran, and South Asia visited the area and established residence in several locations. From these small bases, Islam then spread to other areas in the region. Although Islam was historically late in coming to Southeast Asia, it became one of the three dominant religions in the area. Today there are more Muslims in Indonesia than in any other country in the world. (*Indonesia* is a modern word, but for simplicity's sake this chapter will use it in the discussion of the premodern history of the area encompassed by the modern country.)

The Malayo–Polynesian Lands

Southeast Asia has a tropical climate. Before the modern exploitation of its timber, almost the entire region was covered in dense forests. On the mainland, human settlement is concentrated in the broad alluvial plains and fertile deltas of large rivers. These regions support intensive rice agriculture and large numbers of people. Southeast Asia also boasts the largest number of islands in the world. The Philippines has 7000 islands, strung along a north–south axis of 1000 miles. Most are very tiny, but about 500 are a square mile or more in area. Indonesia has 13,667 islands spread across some 3000 miles. The vast majority are too small to be inhabited, but the largest, Sumatra, is 1000 miles long. Most of the islands feature a mountainous interior and a swampy coast. The major exception is Java, whose interior plateau allowed the growth of inland cities. On the other islands, settlements were usually established in the coastal areas that were suitable for rice agriculture.

The Portuguese Sack of Mombasa, 1505

In 1505, Grand-Captain Francisco d'Almeida led a Portuguese fleet of fourteen large men-of-war and six caravels around the Cape of Good Hope. The expedition's objective was to subdue and loot the port cities of the Swahili coast. The fleet rounded the Cape of Good Hope on June 20 and entered the harbor of Kilwa on July 22. The Portuguese easily overwhelmed the city's resistance and plundered its wealth. The fleet then sailed to Mombasa, some sixty leagues (180 nautical miles) to the north. It arrived there on August 13, 1505. The following extract is from an account of the pillaging of Mombasa that is believed to have been written by Hans Mayr, a German sailor in the service of the Portuguese.

Mombasa is a very large town and lies on an island from one and a half to two leagues round. The town is built on rocks on the higher part of the island and has no walls on the side of the sea; but on the land side it is protected by a wall as high as the fortress. The houses

(Continued)

are of the same type as those of Kilwa: some of them are three storeyed and all are plastered with lime. The streets are very narrow, so that two people cannot walk abreast in them: all the houses have stone seats in front of them, which made the streets yet narrower.

The Grand-Captain met with the other captains and decided to burn the town that evening and to enter it the following morning. . . . Once the fire was started it raged all night long, and many houses collapsed and a large quantity of goods was destroyed. For from this town trade is carried on with Sofala and with Cambay by sea. There were three ships from Cambay and even these did not escape the fury of the attack. . . .

The Grand-Captain ordered that the town should be sacked and that each man should carry off to his ship whatever he found: so that at the end there would be a division of the spoil, each man to receive a twentieth of what he found. The same rule was made for gold, silver, and pearls. Then everyone started to plunder the town and to search the houses, forcing open the doors with axes and iron bars. . . . A large quantity of rich silk and gold embroidered clothes was seized, and carpets also. . . .

On the morning of the 16th they again plundered the town, but because the men were tired from fighting and from lack of sleep, much wealth was left behind apart from what each man took for himself. They also carried away provisions, rice, honey, butter, maize, countless camels and a large number of cattle, and even two elephants. . . . There were many prisoners, and white women among them and children, and also some merchants from Cambay. . . .

The King of Mombasa wrote the following letter to the King of Malindi: May God's blessing be upon you, Sayyid Ali! This is to inform you that a great lord has passed through the town, burning it and laying it waste. He came to the town in such strength and was of such cruelty, that he spared neither man nor woman, old nor young, nay not even the smallest child. Not even those who fled escaped from his fury. He not only killed and burnt men but even the birds of the heavens were shot down. The stench of the corpses is so great in the town that I dare not go there; nor can I ascertain nor estimate what wealth they have taken from the town. I give you this sad news for your own safety.

Source: G. S. P. Freeman-Grenville, *The East African Coast: Select Documents from the First to the Earlier Nineteenth Century*. Oxford, U.K.: The Clarendon Press, 1962, 108–111.

One of the most striking differences between the mainland of Southeast Asia, on the one hand, and the Indonesian and Philippine archipelagos, on the other, is that the latter are volcanically active, whereas the former is not. Most of the islands were formed from volcanic eruptions, and dozens of their volcanoes are still active. The view of the mountains from a distance is striking, for some of them rise to altitudes well above 12,000 feet, towering over their low-lying plains or plateaus. The periodic deposit of volcanic ash on the level areas of Java and a few other islands over a period of thousands of years has created some spectacularly productive agricultural areas.

In the areas that developed large Muslim populations—the Malay Peninsula, central and western Indonesia, and the southern Philippines—hundreds of languages are spoken, all deriving from the Malayo–Polynesian family of languages. The Malayo–Polynesian peoples have been great seafarers for thousands of years. Some of them made their way westward across the open sea to settle Madagascar

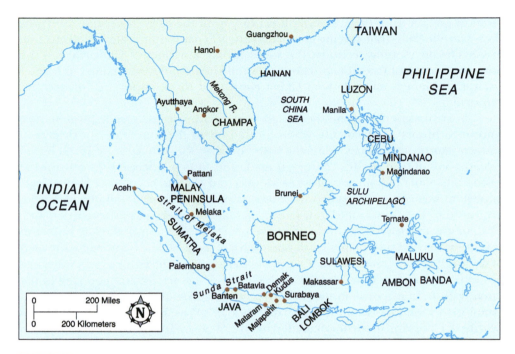

MAP 16.3 Southeast Asia.

(5000 miles away); others sailed to the east and settled South Pacific islands as far away as Easter Island. Malayo–Polynesian settlements extended across a swath of the globe that was 10,000 miles long.

At least as early as the beginning of the Christian era, commercial interests linked Southeast Asia with South Asia, China, and the Roman Empire. These commercial contacts opened Southeast Asia to foreign cultural influences. Its relations with South Asia proved most decisive in this regard. Between the first and eighth centuries, South Asian influences were particularly strong in the basin of the Irrawaddy River (in modern Myanmar), the Gulf of Thailand, Java, Bali, the lower Mekong River (in southern Vietnam), and the plains of central Vietnam. Buddhism became widely practiced on the mainland, but on the islands the impact of Hinduism and Buddhism was usually restricted to aristocratic and royal families. The royal courts adapted Indian elements for their calendar, coinage, myths, administrative and legal institutions, and art and architecture.

The most striking examples of Indian architectural influences on the islands are in central Java, where the ruler converted from Hinduism to Buddhism in the middle of the eighth century. Over the next century, the royal family commissioned the construction of huge Buddhist temple complexes. The largest, at Borobudur, compares favorably with Cambodia's Angkor Wat. Despite the clear evidence of Indian cultural influence on the islands, social relations were usually unaffected. The most notable exception to this rule was Bali, where the Hindu caste system and ritual life became firmly established.

One of the best known of the Indicized states was the Buddhist kingdom of Srivijaya. Located on Sumatra, Srivijaya dominated the maritime commerce of the

Strait of Melaka from the late seventh century until the early eleventh century. Its ships patrolled the strait, forcing merchant vessels to pay the equivalent of protection money. In the eleventh century, the south Indian kingdom of Chola sacked the Srivijayan capital of Palembang. Thereafter, the kingdom never regained its former strength, although its trade with China continued to be important for another century.

As Srivijaya declined, another kingdom in Southeast Asia rose to prominence. Known to history as Majapahit, it was located far to the southeast of Srivijaya in eastern Java. Its wealth was originally based on the rice cultivation of Java's fertile volcanic soil. By the twelfth century, it made the strategic decision to control the spice trade of the region. Southeast Asia's spice harvest had become an increasingly important segment of its exports. Its cloves, nutmeg, and mace—all of which were produced in the cluster of islands known as Maluku—were in particular demand. The clove is the dried flower bud of an evergreen tree that, until the late sixteenth century, was found only on five small islands in northern Maluku. Nutmeg is the seed of yet another evergreen tree that, until the late eighteenth century, grew only on a tiny cluster of islands in southern Maluku. Mace is the dried outer covering of the nutmeg fruit. In response to the increasing value of Maluku's products, Majapahit established a monopoly over the external trade of spices. By virtue of its increasing wealth, the kingdom gradually extended its control westward to Sumatra itself, filling the vacuum of power left by Srivijaya. Its golden age was the second half of the fourteenth century, when it sent embassies to China and the major states on the mainland of Southeast Asia. Its elite culture was a syncretistic mixture of Hinduism and Buddhism.

Muslims Establish a Presence in Southeast Asia

Although Muslims did not establish a significant presence in Southeast Asia until the fifteenth century, Muslim merchants and sailors from the Red Sea, Persian Gulf, and Indian coasts were frequent visitors to the region long before then. Many passed through Southeast Asia on their way to Guangzhou (Canton) in the eighth and ninth centuries. Many other Muslim merchants lived permanently in Guangzhou, part of a large community of foreign merchants there. They purchased goods that arrived in Guangzhou's markets from inland China and then shipped them to markets in the western Indian Ocean. This arrangement lasted until 879, when a xenophobic Chinese reaction resulted in the massacre or expulsion of almost all foreign merchants from the city. Many of the surviving Muslims resettled in Southeast Asia. Some settled in or around Srivijaya, where they continued to engage in international trade. In their new home, they served as middlemen for Chinese and Southeast Asian products. Others gained high posts in the Srivijayan court. Individual Muslims continued to play important roles in the strait after the collapse of Srivijaya due to their commercial contacts and practical skills. Marco Polo, visiting northern Sumatra in 1292, encountered Muslims who served as advisors to the ruler whose court he visited there. Muslims began returning to China under the Sung dynasty (960–1279). Many Muslims in eastern and central China intermarried with local Chinese women and adapted to the local culture. They were the genesis of the indigenous Chinese Muslim community that later came to be called the Hui.

Scattered evidence—usually in the form of tombstones—demonstrates that, as early as the eleventh century, indigenous Muslims lived in the predominantly Hindu kingdom of Champa in what is now southern Vietnam. Others lived in Brunei, the Malay Peninsula, and the Sulu Archipelago in the fourteenth century. The most tantalizing discoveries are tombstones from eastern Java that suggest that some members of the elite families in the Hindu–Buddhist state of Majapahit were Muslim when that state was at the pinnacle of its influence in the 1350s.

In the 1360s and 1370s, thousands of Muslim refugees once again arrived in Southeast Asia from China in an eerie replication of the ninth-century Muslim flight from Guangzhou. The stimulus for the exodus was the fall of the Mongol Yuan dynasty in 1368 and its replacement by the Ming dynasty. The cause of the exodus was that the Muslims of China had developed a good working relationship with the Mongols, who had subjugated China during the thirteenth century. The ethnic Chinese, by contrast, did not bother to conceal their contempt for their conquerors, whom they regarded as barbarians. As a result, the Mongols regarded the Chinese as security threats. When possible, they used ethnic groups other than the Chinese to staff their bureaucratic posts. Marco Polo is the most famous example of these civil servants for the Mongol regime who combined the possession of mercantile skills with a lack of local family ties. Numerous Muslims, as well, staffed customs posts, served as tax collectors, and filled other positions that kept the empire functioning. When the Ming dynasty overthrew the Mongols in 1368, many Muslims—both foreign and indigenous—were killed or expelled on the grounds that they had collaborated with the detested Mongols. Many of them resettled in Southeast Asia, on the trade routes that had led their ancestors to China in the first place.

The bulk of Maluku's spice harvest was exported to China prior to the late fifteenth century. This trade intensified in the early part of the fifteenth century, during a period highlighted by a series of voyages between 1405 and 1433 sponsored by the Chinese Ming emperor. The commander of the six maritime expeditions was Zheng He (Cheng Ho), a Central Asian Muslim. The ships and fleets were huge for their era. Some of the vessels were 300 feet long (the ships of da Gama and Columbus at the end of that century were 60–100 feet long). One of the fleets was an armada of sixty-two ships with 27,000 people on board. The voyages were extensive: Zheng He's ships visited Hormuz, Aden, and the eastern coast of Africa. In Southeast Asia, Zheng extended offers of protection to port cities in return for "gifts" (tribute) to the Ming emperor. He also destroyed several pirates' nests in the region of the Strait of Melaka.

The precise objectives of the expensive Chinese voyages across the Indian Ocean are obscure, but historians assume that they included intelligence-gathering about any potential threats to China in the region and securing trade relations with the rulers of the port cities. The expeditions were discontinued in 1433, when advisors persuaded the emperor that the voyages' benefits did not justify their costs. In a radical change of policy, the Ming dynasty soon entered upon a formal policy of isolationism, forbidding its Chinese subjects (even fishermen and merchants) from embarking upon private ventures abroad. Foreign visitors were prohibited from entering China's ports other than Guangzhou. Despite the edict, foreign trade continued on a large scale due to smuggling and lack of enforcement of the ban by local officials.

The quarter-century period of Zheng He's expeditions witnessed the growth of several port cities in Southeast Asia. This growth seems to be related to close ties that developed between the port cities and China. Brunei, Sulu, Manila, and cities in Thailand, Cambodia, Champa, and Java began to offer tribute to and exchanged envoys with China. Of particular note is Melaka, located on the Malay Peninsula side of the strait that shares its name. Melaka had been a sleepy fishing village until the volume of maritime traffic through the strait increased at the beginning of the fifteenth century. The port offered fair trading practices and reliable docking and warehousing facilities. In 1405, Zheng He blessed it with a declaration of protection. The Chinese admiral made good on his promise, docking there several times and destroying pirates that hindered trade in the strait.

Within a few years, Melaka became a major international port. It was strictly an entrepôt, for it had no goods of its own to export and had to import all of its food supplies. Sometime during the first third of the fifteenth century, the ruler of Melaka adopted Islam and even began missionary work on behalf of his faith. At midcentury, one of his successors began to conquer towns on both sides of the strait in order to gain control of their food products and gold. By the 1470s, the city controlled the main population centers along the strait and had grown into the largest city in Southeast Asia. Its population of 100,000–200,000 was comparable in size to contemporary Paris and London. Due to its location on the strait and its efficiency as a port, shippers from numerous countries chose to collect their cargoes there rather than going all the way to Java or Maluku. Melaka had joined Aden, Hormuz, and the cities of the Malabar Coast among the elite group of entrepôts in the Indian Ocean.

The northern coast of Java lay on the route between Melaka and Maluku. As traffic on the route increased, Muslims who were ethnically Chinese, Indian, Malay, or Arab began to settle in Javanese port cities. Little is known about the early history of these communities except that some of them were led by Muslims of foreign origin and others were led by indigenous Muslims. Still other Muslims made their way to Maluku itself, where rulers on several islands had become Muslim by the mid-fifteenth century. Within a few decades, the most powerful of these rulers was underwriting successful missionary campaigns in the southern Philippines, especially on the island of Mindanao.

Thus, by the beginning of the sixteenth century, Muslims could be found throughout the extent of the archipelago. Muslims ruled Sulu, much of Maluku, and most of the cities along the northern coast of Java and along the Strait of Melaka. These thriving port cities were beginning to challenge the dominance of the older, agrarian-based cities on the interior of the islands. The most dramatic example of the struggle was in Java, where the coastal cities were engaged in periodic warfare with Majapahit.

Still, Muslims might have remained a tiny minority in Southeast Asia had it not been for a growing demand for spices as Western Europeans during the early Renaissance began abandoning the religious ideal of the mortification of the flesh and turned increasingly to indulging it, instead. One of the ways to do this with the fewest qualms for one's conscience was by stimulating the taste buds with spices. Medieval Western Europeans had little knowledge of the wide variety of spices available to the peoples of the eastern Mediterranean until Crusaders began returning with a taste for more exotic dishes than the bland provisions back home offered. As more and more people in Western Europe discovered the sensuous delights of spices—and the satisfaction of being in the vanguard of the latest fad—the demand for the commodities rose sharply. Spices were a luxury that only the very wealthy could afford: A German price table of the fourteenth century set the value of a pound of nutmeg at seven fat oxen.

The Venetians became the primary middlemen for the spice trade to Europe. Merchants from Venice purchased spices in Muslim-controlled ports in the eastern Mediterranean and shipped them to Western Europe, sailing their galleys as far as the British Isles. Their customers became increasingly frustrated with what they perceived to be price-fixing by the Venetians, and they began searching for alternative sources. This was one motivation for Prince Henry the Navigator's sponsorship of expeditions down the Atlantic coast of Africa. Some Europeans evaded the Venetians by purchasing spices in Constantinople, which obtained them by an overland route that wound its way from the Persian Gulf across Iran to the Black Sea and then by ship to Constantinople. The Ottoman capture of Constantinople in 1453 closed that source, prompting merchants and princes to start looking for ways to bypass the Ottomans and Venetians and purchase the spices at their source. They spoke of finding a route to "the Indies" or even to "India": The name "India" was often applied to all the regions of South and Southeast Asia that were influenced by Hindu and Buddhist culture.

Just where in the Indies the spices were to be found growing was still unknown to Europeans. The Romans had imported many of the spices that we use today as early as the first century C.E., but they, too, did not know where most of them came from, since they were buying them from middlemen. The only source known with some certainty was Kerala, for its black pepper. Between the years 500 and 1000, Arab and Persian merchants sailed beyond India into Indonesia and all the way to China. In doing so, they discovered that Sri Lanka was the source of cinnamon, and they learned that cloves, nutmeg, and mace were grown only in what were called the "Spice Islands," whose location was a trade secret. Ferdinand and Isabella of Spain knew that Portugal was obsessed with finding a route to the reach the Indies by sailing around Africa, and they were concerned when, in 1487, Bartolomeu Dias announced that he had rounded the southern tip of that continent. As a result, Isabella did not require much evidence from Columbus in 1492 when he asserted that he could reach the Indies by sailing westward for two or three months. Despite making four voyages to the Western Hemisphere, Columbus could never accept that he had not arrived in "the Indies," which is why the islands of the Caribbean became known as the West Indies. Meanwhile, the Portuguese struck the mother lode.

The Impact of Imperialism

All of the "what ifs" in history are fruitless discussions, but some are irresistible. For example, what if the Ming dynasty had not abandoned its interest in the Indian Ocean in the 1430s? Its huge ships in its large armadas, its tens of thousands of troops, and its mastery of gunpowder weapons would seemingly have been invincible against any force that the Europeans could have sent to the region. But they were not there at the beginning of the sixteenth century, and tiny Portugal began making a concerted effort to monopolize the spice trade in the Indian Ocean. Eleven years after Dias's voyage around the Cape of Good Hope, Vasco da Gama landed in India. Then, in 1511, the Portuguese secured control of Melaka and were preparing to penetrate the inner islands. During the next 100 years, the Spanish, Dutch, and English entered the area as well, using techniques of overwhelming force and monopoly commerce to achieve their ends. By 1650, Europeans had gained control of the important ports and products of the region.

The Portuguese and Spanish

The distribution system that evolved over the centuries to transport goods from one end of the Indian Ocean to the other was a marvel of international cooperation. Merchants at both ends of the ocean could count on staying in business even though their goods were shipped across thousands of miles and through the hands of numerous middlemen, who used a bewildering array of languages, currencies, and systems of weights and measures. Prior to the coming of the Portuguese, no council governed the trade, and no navy patrolled the sea lanes to protect the commerce.

As the Portuguese attempted to bring the spice trade under their control, they found that these features of the commercial network worked to their advantage. Since goods were routed to a few entrepôts, the Portuguese could exploit their military technology to establish permanent bases at these crucial choke points. The most important one for their purposes was Melaka, since it lay beside the strait through which all the spice trade usually passed. The Portuguese made a reconnaissance voyage to Melaka as early as 1509, a year before they secured Goa. They discovered that the city–state was experiencing unrest and was vulnerable to attack. In part, the city's problems were due to corruption and instability within the government itself, and in part to resistance from the cities that it had subjugated along the coasts of the strait. The Portuguese resolved to attack.

As soon as Albuquerque retook Goa from Bijapur in 1510, he converted its harbor into the staging area for an expedition to Melaka. In 1511, Albuquerque set out for Melaka with nineteen ships. His fleet destroyed much of the city in a naval bombardment, and then his soldiers captured what was left. Then, using the memoirs of the Italian explorer Ludovico di Varthema, who had sailed among the clove- and nutmeg-producing islands in 1505, Albuquerque sailed to Maluku, where he established a base. Maluku subsequently became the focus of intense Portuguese efforts to control the spice trade and to spread Catholicism.

Soon after the capture of Melaka, Albuquerque turned his attention to the Red Sea and the Persian Gulf. He failed in his attempt to capture Aden in 1513, but he took control of Hormuz in 1515. Except for Aden, the Portuguese had obtained their objectives by 1515. They occupied Melaka, Goa, and Hormuz, and soon controlled the entire coast of Kerala. The plan that had looked so good on paper, however, did not work out in practice. The Portuguese quickly learned that Melaka was dependent on outside sources for food and that they would have to trade with, or fight, traditional suppliers to maintain the flow of provisions. Because the city was so far from Portugal and any Portuguese naval base, the city was chronically short of currency and manpower.

Portuguese expectations suffered another blow when it became clear that the conquest of Melaka disrupted the organization of the trading system. The biggest miscalculation of the Europeans turned out to be their assumption that Melaka was essential to the spice trade. When spice vendors discovered that the Portuguese demanded spices at lower-than-market prices, they simply developed other trade routes. Those who had traditionally sold to Chinese and Japanese merchants abandoned Melaka and took their products to Brunei and Sulu instead. Those who intended to ship goods to Aden transported their cargoes by caravan across the Malay Peninsula to ports for shipment across the ocean or through the Sunda Strait and up the southwestern coast of Sumatra. Melaka began to wither away.

Portuguese ambitions to destroy the Muslim-dominated trade from the Indian Ocean into the Mediterranean failed. Their naval dominance in the Indian Ocean did allow them to divert a third of the spice trade around the Cape of Good Hope over the next two decades, thus denying the Mamluk regime a significant amount of customs revenue, but demand for the products of the Indian Ocean basin (which included dyes and cotton and silk goods as well as spices) grew rapidly. Due to the new routes that avoided Portuguese control, the spice markets of Cairo and Aleppo (under Ottoman control after 1517) were once again bustling as early as the 1530s.

The Portuguese intended the conquest of Melaka to deliver a serious blow to Islam as well as to lead to control of Indian Ocean trade routes. One of the great ironies in history is that, in the immediate aftermath of the fall of Melaka, the Islamization of Southeast Asia accelerated. Muslim merchants and teachers who fled Melaka established bases along the new trade routes that rapidly developed. The dynamism of Brunei and Sulu, combined with the increasing volume of international trade along the southwestern coast of Sumatra, led to the introduction or intensification of Islam in those areas.

In the vicinity of the Strait of Melaka and Sunda Strait, anti-Portuguese sentiment led to the adoption of Islam as an ideological symbol of resistance. The rise of Aceh (Acheh, Atjeh) on Sumatra is the clearest example. The rulers of Aceh appear to have become Muslim in the mid-fourteenth century, but they were minor players in regional politics for the next 200 years. After the fall of Melaka, they became more important. As the Portuguese began intervening in the affairs of other ports on the strait, rulers in the area supported the sultan of Aceh in his drive to unite the northeastern Sumatran coast into a force that could resist the Portuguese. From the 1520s into the mid-seventeenth century, Aceh was a serious military threat to the Portuguese position at Melaka. In addition, merchants in Aceh demonstrated that they could send their cargo ships to the Red Sea directly across the Indian Ocean without having to stop over on the Portuguese-dominated Malabar Coast.

Major changes were also taking place in Java. The Muslim cities on the northern coast of Java were fighting Majapahit even before the Portuguese entered the region. In 1528, they defeated the Hindu city. Some five decades later, a new Muslim kingdom of Mataram arose in its place, with its capital near the present site of Yogyakarta. Mataram's economic base lay in the same rich rice-growing region that had supported the Buddhist shrine complex of Borobudur. Despite the profession of Islam by its rulers, the kingdom also patronized the arts and manners of the local Indicized culture.

Western Java had resisted the encroachments of the Muslim cities on the northern coast for years, but that changed in the 1520s. When the Portuguese attempted to establish an alliance with a Hindu kingdom in the Sunda Strait,

Sumatran and Javanese rulers cooperated to create the Muslim port city of Banten on Java's west coast. The new city soon extended its authority to the rich pepper-growing districts of southern Sumatra. Whereas Aceh sent its pepper westward, Banten supplied the China market.

Farther east, Brunei and Sulu became busier ports after the fall of Melaka as Chinese and Japanese merchants came to these ports to purchase spices. The ruler of Brunei soon converted to Islam. He acquired a reputation for sponsoring Islamic missionary activity in the Philippine Islands. The missionary work in the Philippines paid off with the rise of Muslim political power in the islands. By midcentury, Muslim rulers were ruling in cities as far apart as Magindanao (on the southern island of Mindanao) and Manila (on the northern island of Luzon).

By the middle of the sixteenth century, Portugal's investment in Indian Ocean enterprises had stalled. It was apparent that the Portuguese navy would never be able to achieve a monopoly over the region's trade and that it was more cost-effective simply to maintain a handful of bases to protect the nation's merchant marine. By this time, too, many Portuguese merchants and seamen had become aware of the potential wealth to be achieved in the trans-Atlantic slave trade. They were more interested in the potential profits to be made at the mouth of the Congo and in Brazil than in Southeast Asia. Portuguese influence in Maluku declined after 1550, and the government abandoned it in 1575. Thereafter, Catholic priests who remained in the area could not rely on the support and protection of the Portuguese government. A handful of Portuguese military and civilian personnel remained in Maluku, but Portuguese activity in the Indian Ocean focused on Kerala thereafter.

As Portugal was reducing its activity in Southeast Asia, Spain entered the region. Ferdinand Magellan was a Portuguese nobleman who had served for a decade in the Portuguese navy's Indian Ocean fleet, but a plot against him cost him the support of the king. Magellan then offered his services to Spain, instead. Familiar with the Indian Ocean, he proposed a circumnavigation of the globe. Setting sail with five ships in September 1519, he survived a storm-tossed voyage around the tip of South America, periods without wind for his sails in the Pacific, and bouts of scurvy and ravenous hunger, only to be killed in a skirmish with inhabitants of the southern Philippines in April 1521. One of his navigators led the sole surviving ship back to Seville in September 1522.

The Spanish sent three further expeditions to the Philippines, but they all met disaster. The fifth voyage to the islands, commissioned by Philip II, established the first permanent Spanish settlement in the archipelago in 1565, on the island of Cebu. Due to the settlement's success, the archipelago was christened the Philippines in honor of the king. The Spanish were astonished to find a large Muslim presence in the region, for they assumed that Islam was confined to North Africa and Southwest Asia. Like the Portuguese, they called the Muslims there *Moros*, or Moors.

The establishment of Spanish control over the Philippines took place during the height of the fierce clash between the Ottomans and Spanish for control of the Maghrib. As a result, Madrid's policy in the archipelago was driven by an obsession to convert the peoples of the region to Catholicism and to extirpate Islam. In 1571, an expedition destroyed the Muslim sultanate at Manila and replaced it with a Spanish settlement. In 1578, another expedition burned the mosque in Brunei. By the end of the century, the coastal areas of the northern and central Philippines were largely under Spanish control. The numerous Muslim societies of Sulu and Mindanao, on the other hand, succeeded in thwarting Spanish efforts to subdue them until the late nineteenth century.

The Dutch and English

In 1587, the Dutch gained their de facto independence from Spain after four decades of brutal fighting. More war would be required in the early seventeenth century to secure a peace treaty and full independence, but the Dutch wasted no time in establishing a global trade network. Their merchant marine was already the primary supplier of sea transport in the North Atlantic. Over the course of the next century, Dutch mariners became the dominant power in global maritime commerce. Every bit as courageous and brutal as the Portuguese, they possessed better guns and ships, organization, and financial backing.

After the Spanish annexation of Portugal in 1580, the Iberians jointly dominated Southeast Asia. The Dutch, however, were confident that their seafaring skills would enable them to displace their former masters in the islands. The first Dutch expedition to Southeast Asia set sail in 1595 and made port at Banten the following year. The commercial success of that voyage triggered intense competition among Dutch merchants, and many companies sent ships to the Indies. Spice prices quickly plummeted. In an effort to reduce the risks of open competition, several Dutch companies merged in 1602 as the United East India Company (Verenigde Oost-Indische Compagnie, or VOC). The government granted it a legal monopoly over the spice trade in return for helping to fight the enemies of the Netherlands. The VOC possessed quasi-sovereign power to conclude treaties, build fortresses, and wage war in the vast area east of the Cape of Good Hope and west of the Strait of Magellan.

The VOC's strategy was different from that of the Portuguese. Rather than attempting to capture the entrepôts of the Indian Ocean trade, it was interested solely in controlling the source of the spice trade. In 1605, the VOC took control of Maluku. The company normally did not sponsor missionary activity, but its antipathy toward the Portuguese caused it to make an exception in this case. It expelled the Portuguese Catholic priests and began applying pressure to encourage local Catholics to convert to Calvinism. Although Maluku was the focus of Dutch interest, it was not the ideal location for a company headquarters. In 1619, the company chose Jakarta, which had the best harbor on Java and was conveniently located for access to the Strait of Melaka. The VOC overthrew the ruling Muslim prince and renamed the city Batavia. Batavia became the VOC headquarters in the east, outfitted with offices, warehouses, and ship repair facilities.

The Dutch attempt to monopolize the spice trade was quickly challenged by yet another European power. The original goal of the English East India Company (EIC), founded in 1600, had been to reap profits from the Spice Islands. Its fleet arrived at Banten only a few months after the company was created. For the next twenty years, its merchants and armed sailors competed with the Dutch for control of the spice trade. They obtained monopolistic treaties with rulers of various islands—sometimes through negotiations and sometimes through force—and attacked spice-bearing ships in the region that were not under their flag. As a result of the combined activity of the VOC and the EIC, a milestone in global trade had been reached by the 1620s:

Istanbul had to import its pepper and other spices from Western European merchants. The Dutch, however, fiercely maintained their position in the islands, finally forcing the English to concede defeat after two decades of struggle. Control of the Spice Islands trade had been the explicit rationale for the founding of the English East India Company, and the company's directors were pessimistic about finding an adequate substitute for it. Fate was with them, however. They set up trading posts on the coasts of the Mughal Empire, and a century later, when the empire was collapsing, their company was in a position to take advantage of the chaos. Using mercenary armies, it eventually became the ruling power of India.

Achieving the Dutch goal of monopolizing the spice trade in the islands was facilitated by the fragmented nature of local political and military power. Since all the numerous local rulers were weak and jealous of their rivals, even the rise of a relatively powerful local ruler did not necessarily jeopardize the Dutch position. For example, the port of Makassar, on the southwest tip of the island of Sulawesi, became prosperous due to its export of rice, rather than spices, and its ruler was ambitious. Using a combination of military campaigns and diplomacy, he and his successors gained the submission of most areas on Sulawesi by 1640. During this period, Makassar's rulers were so defiant of Dutch monopolistic intentions that they allowed Portuguese merchants and mercenaries—men who had previously been personae non gratae in the region—to reside in Sulawesi. Despite Makassar's dynamism, the VOC was able to contain it by making alliances with local states whose rulers were more fearful of Makassar than of the Dutch.

The reaction of Makassar's neighbors was characteristic of local rulers. Despite frequent demands for a combined war against the Dutch, individual rulers were unwilling to allow a rival to become the leader of an anti-VOC coalition for fear of his gaining an advantage over them and perhaps even annexing their realms. The Dutch, after all, simply wanted a monopoly over trade; they signed a contract to purchase a ruler's stock of spices and paid him a negotiated price in silver. The drawback was that the ruler was not permitted to negotiate a better deal with a competitor to the Dutch. Rivalries among the islands allowed the VOC to consolidate its power in the islands relatively easily. Even when the Dutch used genocidal measures to enforce their monopolies, neighboring states did not band together to stop them. The first major instance of massive blood-letting was during the period 1620–1623, when the VOC declared a monopoly over the nutmeg and mace trade in southern Maluku. When the islanders resisted, the Dutch utterly exterminated them.

The only two regional powers that could pose a significant challenge to the VOC in the seventeenth century were Mataram and Aceh. The Dutch did not try to subdue Aceh until the late nineteenth century, but Mataram was an early threat because of its proximity to Batavia. During the fifty years after its founding in the 1570s, Mataram had expanded to control all of central and eastern Java. In 1628 and 1629, Mataram attacked Batavia, but it had to withdraw both times without capturing the city. From then on, the two rival powers worked out a modus vivendi. Batavia needed to buy rice and timber from Mataram, and Mataram occasionally sought Batavia's assistance against rebels and local rivals. The price for Mataram of such assistance was the cession of land to the Dutch, which was a factor in the progressive weakening of the Muslim kingdom.

FIGURE 16.3 The minaret of the mosque at Kudus, Java. Dating from the early sixteenth century, it takes its inspiration from watchtowers of fortified Hindu temples.

B.O'Kane / Alamy Stock Photo.

The Appeal of a Universal Faith

The period of commercial intensification and European intervention coincided with a religious transformation in Southeast Asia. Several of the great world religions made major gains during this time. On the mainland, Buddhism and Confucianism achieved their final geographical consolidation. Islam spread rapidly in the Malay Peninsula and Indonesia after the Portuguese captured Melaka. Catholic Christianity made rapid gains in the Philippines and in central Indonesia as a result of intensive missionary work by Spanish and Portuguese priests. Of the great religions in the region, only Hinduism declined, perhaps because its influence had rarely extended far beyond the royal palaces. Only in Bali and nearby small islands did local variants of Hinduism continue to flourish.

During the period that Islam spread among the islands of the various archipelagoes, it also made gains on the mainland of Southeast Asia. Small communities of Muslims had existed in several of the mainland ports since at least the ninth century, but they began to grow in the late fifteenth century. During the seventeenth century, the Muslim presence became particularly noticeable in Cambodia, Thailand, and the kingdom of Champa, in what is now southern Vietnam. Just as the population of Champa's Muslims reached a critical mass, the kingdom of Vietnam, which lay to the north, annexed Champa. The Confucian-dominated court of Vietnam began a major persecution of the Muslims, most of whom fled to Cambodia. From there they became dispersed throughout the region.

Factors in the Spread of Islam

Prior to the sixteenth century, most Muslims in Southeast Asia were concentrated in a handful of cities. After 1511, many port cities throughout the region received the thousands of Muslim merchants, teachers, and artisans who fled the Portuguese conquest of Melaka. Their diffusion served to create bases from which Islam could penetrate the hinterland of their new homes. The growth of the Muslim community coincided with intensive Christian missionary activities. From the mid-sixteenth to the mid-seventeenth centuries, both Islam and Christianity became solidly entrenched in the region. Historians estimate that, by 1700, half the population of the islands and of the Malay peninsula adhered to one or the other of the two religions.

Another way that Islam spread was through war. Islam's introduction into the islands was peaceful, but the traditional, chronic warfare among the states in the region made it almost inevitable that religion would become a factor in the conflicts. The most striking example of this phenomenon involved Makassar on Sulawesi. Makassar's ruler, who converted to Islam in 1605, forced his defeated rivals on Sulawesi to declare a formal conversion to Islam. Soon, most of Sulawesi had become nominally Muslim.

A third factor in the spread of Islam was its use as a symbol of resistance to subjugation. The Portuguese and Spanish came into the area with the explicit intention of waging holy war against the region's Muslims. The Portuguese were particularly brutal against Muslims in Melaka and Maluku. As Portuguese momentum slowed, the Spanish took their place. During the period 1580–1660, Spanish Catholic missionary work extended south from Luzon to Mindanao, northern Sulawesi, and Maluku in an explicit attempt to defeat Islam in the cause of Christianity. In the regions of the most intense conflict, local inhabitants were under intense pressure to choose between the two faiths. Missionaries preached the need for salvation, merchants favored fellow believers, and armed men made implicit or explicit threats. The Europeans made it clear that the conflict was between two international religious alliances, one of Christians and one of Muslims. In the face of such pressure, many Indonesians felt it advisable to convert to one or the other faith.

Muslim resistance to Christian aggression led to notable instances of pan-Islamic cooperation during the second half of the sixteenth century. From as early as 1538, when the Ottoman Empire tried to capture Diu from the Portuguese, Muslims around the Indian Ocean basin slowly gained an awareness of the potential for the Ottoman Empire to thwart the Portuguese attempt to gain a monopoly over the shipping of the region. In 1566, the sultan of Aceh sent a petition to Istanbul, requesting military aid against the Portuguese. Two years later, Sultan Selim II dispatched two ships with a cargo of artillery as well as several dozen gunners and military engineers. The two rulers also opened diplomatic relations with each other.

Interregional Muslim cooperation against Portuguese aggression also involved Muslim states in the Deccan. An alliance of Bijapur, Golkonda, and Ahmadnagar attacked Portuguese Goa in 1570 but failed. Golkonda then formed an anti-Portuguese alliance with Aceh, supplying arms and men for its assaults on Portuguese-held Melaka. The involvement of the Ottomans and Indian Muslims in conflict against the Portuguese stimulated a spirit of pan-Islamic solidarity in the Indian Ocean that generated a spirit of confidence and a sense of momentum for several decades.

Variations on a Theme

Despite the wave of conversions to Islam and the heightened self-consciousness of Muslim identity in the region, visitors to the islands—Muslims and Christians alike—observed that the practice of Islam in the islands was different from what they had seen in the cities of North Africa and Southwest Asia. In itself, that is not surprising, for, as we have repeatedly seen, the practice of Islam varies from society to society, just as the practice of any major religion does. Nonetheless, several features of Indonesia would frustrate any Muslim missionary, Sunni or Twelver Shi'ite, who might move there and work as a missionary. In the islands, the bulk of the population was attuned to a mystically inclined polytheism, and the elites in many of the islands were heavily Indicized.

Many new converts did, in fact, make important changes in their lives that enabled them to call themselves Muslim. They began using Islamic forms of salutation, and some modified their wardrobe. The practice of circumcision was already common on many of the islands, and thus its adoption as a Muslim identity marker was not the major cultural shift that it was in many other societies. On some of the islands, in fact, both males and females had traditionally undergone circumcision, a feature that is usually associated with the Nile River valley and the Horn of Africa, where the Shafi'i school of the Shari'a prevails. The Shafi'i school was the only one of the four major legal traditions in which many jurists argued that both male and female circumcision are obligatory. The earliest Muslims to the region were Shafi'is, and they were gratified to discover that, on some of the islands, both men and women were already following a practice converts in many other cultures were reluctant to accept. Thus, a local customary rite was given new prominence and an Islamic interpretation.

Judging by the anecdotal evidence of recorded observations by visitors to the islands, it may be said that most new Muslims renounced pork but that fewer gave up alcohol. Much more powerful emotions attended the adoption of Islamic funerary rites and dietary practices. The cremation of corpses was a widespread practice in the archipelago prior to the advent of Islam. The Shari'a, however, requires that Muslims be buried in the ground, facing Mecca. For islanders who believed that the funeral pyre's flames had a purifying effect on the corpse, the switch to burial—which entailed the decomposition of the body—was a major concession to their new religion.

The spread of both Islam and Christianity in the archipelago had an impact on the social roles of women. Information about women during the period under review is scarce, but it is clear that, traditionally, women had served the important function of spirit medium and ritual healer. Islam and Christianity not only limited acceptable worship to a single deity who was referred to as male, but religious leadership was also dominated by males. Catholicism's priesthood was an exclusively male preserve, and women could achieve leadership positions only within the cloistered world of the convent. Within Islam the roles were not as rigidly delineated: Males might seek guidance from highly respected female Sufis and Hadith scholars, and women could be Qur'an reciters and spiritual advisers to other women. On the other hand, all public leadership positions at mosques were restricted to males. Ulama who were educated in Islam's heartland expected women to dress more modestly than before and to play a less public role.

The introduction of the two monotheistic religions sparked a backlash among some women. Women led resistance to the introduction of Christianity in the Philippines and against Islam in Lombok and Sulawesi. Despite the resistance, the new gender norms became dominant. Women's clothing became more modest (by the 1650s, some women in Makassar were entirely covered from head to foot, but that was an isolated case in Southeast Asia). Women's opportunities for religious leadership declined as male Catholic priests monopolized Christian leadership positions in the Philippines and as the growing number of ulama in Southeast Asia allowed no women into their ranks.

Opportunities for women in roles other than religious ones also disappeared. On both the mainland and in the islands, numerous females had ruled in the pre-Islamic and early Islamic periods, either as regents or in their own right. In early seventeenth-century Mataram, women armed with pikes and muskets guarded the royal household and protected the Muslim king. Such occasions became increasingly rare during the seventeenth century, when ulama agitated against the presence of female political rulers. In Aceh, four women ruled in succession during the period 1641–1700, but they were the last to do so. By the eighteenth century, no women were allowed to hold political power in the region.

Despite these concessions to Islamic identity, most new converts to Islam from traditional religions only slowly gave up many of their previous customs, rituals, or even deities. Many self-proclaimed Muslims continued to eat the meat of dogs (the Shari'a regards the dog to be as religiously unclean as the pig), drank wine, allowed their daughters to marry pagans, and made offerings to trees, stones, and spirits. Despite their willingness to bury their dead, they continued to fear that they must placate the spirits of the departed in order to avoid retribution from them. As a result, Muslims in Southeast Asia continued to pray as much to the dead as for the dead. They adapted the observance of Ramadan to that end. In addition to the practice of praying in a cemetery for several days after a funeral, they held feasts at the grave site during the week before and the week after Ramadan, asking the forgiveness of elders—both dead and living—for sins they may have committed.

It was too much to expect that a uniform tradition of Islamic belief and practice could take root in the archipelago. Indonesian Islam took a variety of forms, primarily because of the large number of different cultures and independent principalities in the area. Another factor may have been the lack of a well-defined urban space in the port cities. It is useful to recall that, in Southwest Asia and North Africa, Shari'a-based Islam was more likely to be found in the cities than in the countryside (although some rural Sufi lodges, especially in Morocco, were important centers of legal studies). It was in the cities, after all, that mosques, lodges, law courts, and a variety of other institutions mediated the teachings of the learned scholars of Islam to the general public. The cities were typically demarcated from their arid or semiarid countryside by a wall. Urban space was sharply distinguished from rural space, and the clear lines of separation made it easy to regulate behavior and the patterns of interaction within the walls.

The distinction between urban and rural was not as clearly drawn in Indonesia as it was in the Arab world. Visitors to the islands from the Arab world expressed their wonder at how the region's cities appeared in profile—most buildings were constructed of wood rather than stone or mud—and in physical layout. Before the aggressive intrusion of European navies, city walls were practically unknown (except for the formidable walls of the interior citadel/palace complex), and thereafter they were usually built only on the side facing the sea. Rather than a sharply defined urban space, cities resembled the suburban sprawl that characterizes our metropolitan areas today. They were composed of a number of irregular hamlets and settlements clustered around markets, rivers, and the fortified compounds of wealthy notables. The constituent settlements were separated from each other by forested areas, and notables exercised independent power over the area around their compound by hiring armed retainers. The ill-defined borders of these urban agglomerations, coupled with the competing jurisdictions of ambitious men, made it difficult for any political or religious leader to impose his will on a metropolitan area. Without a strong urban base of Shari'a observance, widespread application of the Shari'a throughout the region would take centuries.

The slow process of Islamization was frustrating for local Muslim scholars. They had traveled widely, studying and discussing their faith with other educated men. Many had visited Mecca. As a result, they were aware of universal beliefs and practices associated with Islam. In an effort to bring this understanding to the new Muslims of Southeast Asia, several outstanding individuals translated Islamic concepts into vernacular texts. It is not clear when the first ones were written, but no known Islamic text written in Malay or Javanese can be dated earlier than 1590.

The momentum of Islamization continued well into the seventeenth century. Local Muslim traders maintained their extensive international connections during this period and joined ulama who pushed for greater implementation of the Shari'a. Muslim rulers of the region found that it was to their advantage to make changes in the legal system and to make symbolic gestures such as constructing mosques. In doing so, they not only gained the support of their mercantile community, but also facilitated contacts with the wider Muslim world.

Aceh and Java

Aceh and Java are the classic illustrations of how Islam was adapted to particular conditions in the Malay Archipelago. The two not only had very different cultural backgrounds, but also maintained relations with the outside Muslim world in different ways. Aceh had no important legacy of Indic influence prior to the arrival of Islam, for it had been outside the effective sphere of influence of Srivijaya. Islam spread rather quickly throughout the society after the mid-fifteenth century, and the sultanate became a rival of Melaka. Despite the rivalry, Aceh could take no satisfaction in Albuquerque's subjugation of Melaka in 1511. The Portuguese were a much more lethal threat than Melaka had been, for they made it clear that they were attempting both to monopolize the trade of the strait and to destroy Islam. Because of this dual threat, Aceh engaged in a desperate, life-and-death struggle with the Portuguese. The explicit religious aspect of the struggle caused the Aceh version of Islam to assume a militant and defensive cast.

Of all the Southeast Asian societies, Aceh had the best communication with the Arab world and the Muslims of South Asia. After the Portuguese began their campaign to capture the ports along the Malabar Coast, Aceh sent its spice ships directly to the Red Sea to avoid Portuguese harassment. As a result, the sultanate established direct contacts with the Hijaz, Yemen, Hadramawt, and Egypt. Commercial contacts led to religious exchanges, for the Acehnese were determined to counter the Portuguese offensive of the sixteenth century with a vibrant Islam. A number of Arab scholars made Aceh their temporary or permanent home, preaching and disputing with one another there. Most of them were from Hadramawt, on the southern Arabian coast. The most famous was Nur al-Din al-Raniri (d. 1658). He grew up in Gujarat, the son of a Hadramawti father and a mother who was either Gujarati or Malay. He moved to Aceh, where he served as chief judge from 1636 to 1643.

Al-Raniri was remarkably erudite and possessed native-level fluency in Arabic, Persian, Urdu, Malay, and Acehnese. He had a profound effect on Aceh, for he combined a prolific output of books and treatises with an active life at the court, where he tried to gain royal support for the enforcement of his doctrines. His legacy is mixed: On the one hand, he wrote the region's first handbooks on the correct performance of rituals, he wrote the region's first universal history and first book on comparative religions, and he made useful criticisms of local Sufi interpretations of Ibn al-'Arabi's doctrine of the "Oneness of Being," providing as a corrective the standard inter-pretations of that doctrine that were prevalent in the Arab world. On the other hand, al-Raniri did not just criticize local Sufis for their version of Ibn al-'Arabi's theory; he persuaded the sultan to kill them as apostates and to burn their books.

The exchange of scholars between Aceh and the Arab world was not merely in a west-to-east direction. Several scholars from Sumatra went to Arabia to study. A few stayed and were numbered among the outstanding teachers in the Holy Cities at whose feet students from all over the world studied. Others returned to Southeast Asia. One of the most famous who returned was 'Abd al-Ra'uf al-Sinkili (ca. 1615–ca. 1693). After studying for nineteen years in Arabia, al-Sinkili returned to Aceh about 1661. Like al-Raniri, he was a prolific scholar and was concerned with correcting what he considered to be errors in doctrine and practice. He was particularly concerned about insisting that the practice of the Sufi path required fulfillment of the obligations of the Shari'a. His main difference from al-Raniri was that his reform efforts were implemented by reason and personal example rather than coercion.

By contrast with Aceh, Java possessed the most developed Indicized court culture of any of the Southeast Asian societies that accepted Islam. Prior to the advent of Islam, Indic culture was most closely identified with the courts of the interior of the island. The Muslim-ruled states of the northern coast that sprang up in the late fifteenth century were on the periphery of that culture and were considered less developed. That status began to change after the coastal cities defeated Majapahit in 1528. Thereafter, they began attracting many of the island's most talented artists and crafts-men, and the rulers of the coastal cities and the new Muslim kingdom of Mataram in central Java commissioned works in the Indic tradition. Mosques and shrines incorporated the great wooden pillars that support the traditional Javanese pavilion as well as the brickwork and ornamentation characteristic of the architecture of Majapahit.

Java's differences with Aceh extend to that of ethos. Whereas dramatic performances were repugnant to the Arab-influenced Muslims of Aceh, the *wayang,*

FIGURE 16.4 A *rumah gadang,* or "big house," of the Minangkabau people on Sumatra. The horned, or spired, roof is characteristic of this area. The big house was constructed for the extended family and, consistent with the region's matriarchal ethos, was owned by the women who lived there.

Tjetjep Rustandi / Alamy Stock Photo.

or shadow play, continued as popular as before in Muslim Java. Worship of the Goddess of the Southern Ocean continued to be the most important spiritual force in the lives of many Javanese in the central section of the island. Eastern and central Java are also famous for the ongoing strength of *kejawan,* or "Javanism," even today, after five centuries of diffusion of Islam on the island. Kejawan connotes a specific spiritual discipline that stresses the control of passions, a refusal to become beguiled by wealth, and the quest for enlightenment. It stresses living in harmony with nature and with people, and suggests a general lack of concern for the legalistic issues associated with a strict interpretation of the Shari'a. The persistence of kejawan is not due to some innate character trait among the Javanese of the eastern half of the island. It derives in some part, at least, from policies of the rulers of Mataram. Although they were nominally Muslim, they did not brook criticism from ulama. Dutch accounts of the seventeenth century report that the kings of Mataram killed numerous members of the ulama who insisted on the implementation of the Shari'a.

A Loss of Dynamism

One of the great ironies of Southeast Asian history is that, whereas a major objective of Portuguese activity in the region had been to eradicate Islam, the actual effect of Portuguese policies was to stimulate the spread of Islam throughout the Malay Archipelago. Conversely, although the Dutch VOC followed a secular policy and was unconcerned about religious issues unless they affected profits, its policies were instrumental in dealing a devastating blow to the vitality of Islamic life in the archipelago.

The dispersal of Muslims throughout the islands occurred during the early part of the sixteenth century. The period of the most rapid growth of Islam was from the mid-sixteenth century to the mid-seventeenth century. This was also the period of the greatest demand by the world market for the products of the region. Muslim merchants and rulers became wealthy, and their contacts with the outside Muslim world thousands of miles away were evidence of their dynamism. Many residents of the islands found compelling reasons to adopt a Muslim identity. Motives were different—and mixed—in each case, but the new religion offered a superior spiritual experience to some, an ideological challenge to the Portuguese to others, and a way to participate in the material benefits of a global commercial community to still others.

The economic boom disappeared by the middle of the seventeenth century. Between 1635 and 1641, the Tokugawa shogunate closed off Japan from the world, forcing Japanese merchants residing in Southeast Asia to return home. In the 1640s, Chinese demand for Southeast Asian commodities began to wane due to the growing economic crisis of the period. In the same period, Europeans discovered other products in the Indian Ocean—notably Indian fabrics and indigo—that interested them as much as spices had. Whereas in 1640 spices and pepper constituted the vast bulk of European cargoes shipped from the Indian Ocean, by 1700 they were a small fraction of such cargoes.

In order to cope with the declining demand for Southeast Asian products, the Dutch took decisive action. Having already gained absolute control over the nutmeg and mace trade, the VOC progressively monopolized the trade in cloves between

1640 and 1653. In 1641, the VOC captured Melaka—the last major presence of the Portuguese in the region—and settled Cape Town in 1652 in order to control the shipping lanes around Africa. By 1658, the VOC controlled most of Sri Lanka, the source of most of the world's cinnamon. In 1683, the Dutch began planting groves of clove trees on one of the islands in Maluku in order to have direct control of production. When the trees were mature and began producing, the VOC destroyed all the clove trees on the other islands. The islanders, outraged by the destruction of their trees, fought back, and the Dutch massacred them in large numbers. The VOC also subjugated previously independent cities, such as Makassar and Banten, when they continued to resist signing contracts for monopolies.

The Dutch developed an effective monopolistic system. The VOC set an arbitrary minimum price that it paid to growers, and all Asian intermediary traders and ports were eliminated from a share in the profits. By the second half of the seventeenth century, the company was able to sell spices in Europe at about seventeen times the price for which it had bought them in Maluku, with none of the profit passing into Asian hands. In their single-minded fixation on making profits, the Dutch effected several important changes in the patterns of trade in the Indian Ocean. They introduced the cultivation of coffee into Sri Lanka and took Sri Lanka's traditional product of cinnamon to plantations in Southeast Asia. They also introduced the cultivation of coffee, sugar, and tobacco into Southeast Asia. For the previous three centuries, most coffee had been grown in Yemen and Ethiopia, but the Dutch introduced coffee into Java in 1696. The first harvest was delivered in 1718. Dutch techniques to market their "Java" were so successful that Yemen's share of the world's coffee production declined rapidly in the eighteenth century.

The impact of Dutch policy on Muslim-ruled states was profound. As late as 1600, merchants and rulers of most port cities in Southeast Asia interacted as equals with Europeans, but by 1700 the situation had been dramatically transformed. The wealthy merchant class of the region was shrinking rapidly. In many regions, local farmers switched from cash crops to staples due to the low prices that the Dutch were paying for spices. Visitors to the region commented on the impoverishment of formerly wealthy cities such as Banten, where the inhabitants had begun to weave their own coarse cloth because they could no longer afford fine Indian fabrics. The immense cities of Southeast Asia lost population and wealth after the mid-seventeenth century: Melaka, Makassar, and Banten lost three-fourths of their inhabitants. Banten and Makassar, which had been among the most cosmopolitan and dynamic cities in the region, stagnated and exhibited little interest in the ideas and technology of the outside world.

Under the new Dutch mercantile system, local rulers could be autonomous only if they were inland, out of the reach of Dutch gunboats. The disadvantage of being inland was that it left local culture at least somewhat closed off from developments in the world at large. The establishment of VOC headquarters at Batavia had the long-term effect of closing off Javanese society from the larger Muslim world. As Mataram gradually lost control of its port cities to the Dutch in the second half of the seventeenth century, its communication with developments in the larger Muslim world became intermittent and indirect. Javanese of the interior remained Muslim, but during the eighteenth century they were only vaguely aware of the major developments taking place in the Muslim world as a whole.

As Southeast Asia's contacts with the outside world declined, its religious dynamism subsided. Because the crusading Portuguese were no longer a threat to local Muslims, Islam no longer served the ideological function of providing a unifying and oppositional identity to a hostile enemy. The decline in wealth of the regional economy provided fewer opportunities for religious scholars from the larger Muslim world to find patronage in the islands. There were no more reformers with the stature of al-Sinkili to persuade local communities that the old spirit cults were a threat to the welfare of the Muslim community. Thus, it was easy for many Muslims to assume that abstention from pork and the presence of a mosque made a community Islamic even though—as numerous observers bear witness—mosque attendance throughout the region was sporadic at best. The evidence we have suggests that, at the beginning of the eighteenth century, only Aceh and Banten had Shari'a courts. The presence or absence of Shari'a courts usually serves as a barometer of Islamic practice: In a society without qadis to rule on matters of Islamic law, the provisions regarding criminal law, real estate issues, contracts, marriage, inheritance, and divorce are unenforceable. If many urban Muslims had only a marginal grasp of the basics of their faith, villagers could hardly begin to understand Islam's strict monotheism and its accompanying ethic and rituals. For most of the people, Islam assumed a variety of meanings that enabled them to cope with their world of demons and spirits, nights of impenetrable darkness, and diseases without cures.

The economic stagnation of the seventeenth century eventually led to the disintegration of Mataram, the largest Muslim state in the region. Between 1740 and 1755, Java experienced almost unremitting violence. At Batavia, the slowing economy left thousands of Chinese immigrants unemployed, and some of them created criminal gangs in order to survive. In response, the Dutch announced that they were going to deport immigrants who did not have permits. Rumors swept the Chinese community that the Europeans were going to arrest them and dump them at sea. Desperate, angry, and feeling trapped, thousands of Chinese formed an armed band that attacked Batavia. Inside the city walls, the Europeans panicked. Suspecting that the Chinese who lived in the city would help the attackers, the Europeans massacred them; contemporary Dutch chroniclers estimated that 10,000 Chinese were murdered.

Many of the city's surviving Chinese and remnants of the attacking mob fled to the east, where they encountered other Chinese in coastal cities and Javanese peasants from the interior who had lost their land due to high taxes and low prices for their crops. The Chinese and Javanese joined forces and, in a manner that echoes the Jelali Revolts in the Ottoman Empire a century earlier, they began attacking estates, towns, and VOC-held forts. Javanese property owners and the Dutch cooperated in fighting the rebels and finally put down the revolt by 1743. Rather than trying to stabilize the kingdom, the nobility of Mataram soon embarked upon a bitter civil war over the scarce resources that survived the rebellion. This war raged until 1755, when a treaty arranged a division of the kingdom. One branch of the royal family maintained its royal court at Surakarta, and the other built its palace complex at Yogyakarta, some thirty-five miles away. As had happened so many times before in the islands, the local rulers had played into the hands of the Dutch: The Europeans were pleased to see Mataram split into two small kingdoms that could not challenge the power of the VOC.

Conclusion

Prior to the fifteenth century, the process of the introduction of Islam into the Indian Ocean littoral bore striking similarities to the spread of Islam in West Africa. In both cases, the Muslims who introduced their monotheistic faith to their communities lived in societies dominated by polytheistic and animistic religions. These Muslims were not warriors but merchants and holy men. Unlike the West African case, Muslim merchants in many of the small states of East Africa and the Malay Archipelago became political rulers. They usually intermarried with local families, became members of the elite social stratum, and established new cultural syntheses. Islam spread as more and more merchants in the region realized the universal features of the new religion.

The fifteenth and sixteenth centuries witnessed a commercial revolution in the Indian Ocean. The intensification of the spice trade monetized many local economies for the first time, capital accumulated, and cities grew rapidly. The economic growth of the period would have been sufficient to induce major social, political, and cultural changes, but whatever indigenous developments were underway in that regard were quickly preempted by the violent intrusion of the Portuguese and Spaniards. These two European powers were obsessively focused on the dual goals of controlling commerce in the region and destroying Islam. The Portuguese did not expend much effort to extirpate Islam in East Africa, but they made a concerted effort to do so in Kerala and Southeast Asia. Likewise, the Spaniards massacred or evicted all Muslims that they found in the Philippines, Sulu, and Brunei.

The Portuguese crusade in Indonesia had the opposite effect from what was intended. Islam spread rapidly throughout the islands as a result of the flight of Muslim refugees from the Strait of Melaka and Maluku. Moreover, many inhabitants of the region adopted a nominal Muslim identity as they saw their Muslim neighbors justifying their defensive war against the outsiders with the concepts of justice and divinely sanctioned war by God's people against the enemies of God. Outside Indonesia, the Iberian crusaders accomplished some of their objectives. Some historians believe that the brutal Portuguese and Spanish military campaigns were all that prevented Kerala and the Philippines from eventually joining Indonesia in the rank of Muslim-majority societies.

As destructive as the sixteenth-century Portuguese and Spanish campaigns had been on the Muslims of the Indian Ocean, they paled in comparison with the effects of developments in the second half of the seventeenth century. The seventeenth-century global commercial crisis, combined with the slowing of demand from Japan, the Ottoman Empire, post-Safavid Iran, and the Mughal court, would have forced some readjustments in the region's economy. Dutch policy preempted any such readjustments. The VOC had no quarrel with Islam. Its monopolistic economic policies, nevertheless, had devastating effects on the economies of the Indian Ocean. It used violent methods to compel compliance with enforced contracts, paid artificially low prices to producers, and excluded indigenous merchants from participating in international commerce. As a result, local economies withered, the cosmopolitan cities of the region became provincial and culturally isolated, and the knowledge and practice of Islam remained in a state of arrested development for more than a century. No contemporary observer could have guessed that the archipelago would become the world's most populous Muslim nation by the twentieth century.

FURTHER READING

A Muslim Lake

Boxer, C.R. *The Portuguese Seaborne Empire 1415–1825*. London: Hutchinson & Company, 1969.

Chaudhuri, K.N. *Asia Before Europe: Economy and Civilisation of the Indian Ocean from the Rise of Islam to 1750*. Cambridge, U.K.: Cambridge University Press, 1990.

————. *Trade and Civilisation in the Indian Ocean: An Economic History from the Rise of Islam to 1750*. Cambridge, U.K.: Cambridge University Press, 1985.

Das Gupta, Ashin and M.N. Pearson, eds. *India and the Indian Ocean, 1500–1800*. New York and Calcutta: Oxford University Press, 1987.

Kearney, Milo. *The Indian Ocean in World History*. New York: Routledge, 2004.

The East Coast of Africa

Beachey, R.W. *A History of East Africa, 1592–1902*. London: I. B. Tauris & Co., 1995.

Hiskett, Mervyn. *The Course of Islam in Africa*. Edinburgh, Scotland: Edinburgh University Press, 1994.

Horton, Mark and John Middleton. *The Swahili: The Social Landscape of a Mercantile Society*. Oxford, U.K., and Malden, Massachusetts: Blackwell Publishers, 2000.

Insoll, Timothy. *The Archaeology of Sub-Saharan Africa*. Cambridge, U.K., and New York: Cambridge University Press, 2003.

Levtzion, Nehemiah and Randall L. Pouwells, eds. *The History of Islam in Africa*. Athens: Ohio University Press; Oxford, U.K.: James Currey; Cape Town, South Africa: David Philip, 2000.

Maxon, Robert M. *East Africa: An Introductory History*. Morgantown: West Virginia University Press, 1994.

Nurse, Derek and Thomas Spear. *The Swahili: Reconstructing the History and Language of an African Society*. Philadelphia: University of Pennsylvania Press, 1985.

Pearson, Michael N. *Port Cities and Intruders. The Swahili Coast, India, and Portugal in the Early Modern Era*. Baltimore and London: The Johns Hopkins University Press, 1998.

Kerala

Bayly, Susan. *Saints, Goddesses and Kings: Muslims and Christians in South Indian Society 1700–1900*. Cambridge, U.K., and New York: Cambridge University Press, 1989.

Dale, Stephen Frederic. *Islamic Society on the South Asian Frontier: The Mappilas of Malabar, 1498–1922*. Oxford, U.K.: Clarendon Press; New York: Oxford University Press, 1980.

Miller, Roland E. *Mappila Muslims of Kerala: A Study in Islamic Trends*. Madras, India: Orient Longman, 1976.

Southeast Asia

Azra, Azyumardi. *The Origins of Islamic Reformism in Southeast Asia: Networks of Malay–Indonesian and Middle Eastern 'Ulamā' in the Seventeenth and Eighteenth Centuries*. Crows Nest, New South Wales, Australia: Asian Studies Association of Australia in association with Allen & Unwin; Honolulu: University of Hawai'i Press, 2004.

Chaudhuri, K.N. *Asia Before Europe: Economy and Civilisation of the Indian Ocean from the Rise of Islam to 1750*. Cambridge, U.K.: Cambridge University Press, 1990.

————. *Trade and Civilisation in the Indian Ocean: An Economic History from the Rise of Islam to 1750*. Cambridge, U.K: Cambridge University Press, 1985.

Gordon, Alijah, ed. *The Propagation of Islam in the Indonesian–Malay Archipelago*. Kuala Lumpur: Malaysian Sociological Research Institute, 2001.

Hadi, Amirul. *Islam and State in Sumatra: A Study of Seventeenth-Century Aceh*. Leiden, Netherlands, and Boston: Brill, 2004.

Hooker, M.B. *Islam in South-East Asia*. Leiden, Netherlands: Brill, 1983.

Keay, John. *The Spice Route: A History*. Berkeley and Los Angeles: University of California Press, 2006.

Reid, Anthony. *Southeast Asia in the Age of Commerce, 1450–1680*. 2 vols. New Haven, Connecticut: Yale University Press, 1988, 1993.

———. "Islamization and Christianization in Southeast Asia: The Critical Phase, 1550–1650." In *Southeast Asia in the Early Modern Era: Trade, Power, and Belief*, ed. Anthony Reid, 151–179. Ithaca, New York, and London: Cornell University Press, 1993.

Ricklefs, M.C. *A History of Modern Indonesia Since c. 1300*, 3d ed. Stanford, California: Stanford University Press, 2001.

Riddell, Peter G. *Islam and the Malay-Indonesian World: Transmission and Responses*. Honolulu: University of Hawai'i Press, 2001.

Shaffer, Lynda Norene. *Maritime Southeast Asia to 1500*. Armonk, New York, and London: M. E. Sharpe, 1996.

Tarling, Nicholas, ed. *The Cambridge History of Southeast Asia*. Vol. 2, *1500–1800*. Cambridge, U.K.: Cambridge University Press, 1992.

Glossary

For additional pronunciation tips, please consult the Note on Transliteration and Dating in the front matter.

'abd: An Arabic word meaning "slave" or "servant." In conjunction with the name of God or one of His attributes, the word is a component of many Muslim names: 'Abd Allah ("servant of God;" also rendered *'Abdullah*), 'Abd al-Rahman ("servant of the Merciful"), 'Abd al-Karim ("servant of the Eminent"), and so forth. It is worth noting that *Abdul ('Abd al-)* is not a name by itself, despite popular representations of it in English. It must be followed by the name of God or one of His attributes; otherwise, it simply means "servant of the."

abu: An Arabic word meaning "father." Many Arab men consider it a point of pride to be called the father of their firstborn son. Hence, Abu Hasan is a nickname for someone who was born with a name such as Mahmud until his son Hasan was born, at which time he became known as Abu Hasan.

A.H.: An abbreviation of the Latin phrase *anno Hegirae*, referring to the dating system based on the Islamic calendar. Muslims decided to use the year of the Hijra (622 C.E.) to begin their calendar and to use a lunar, rather than a solar, calculation, resulting in a calendar of 354 days rather than 365/6 days. As a result, the Islamic calendar gains a year on the Gregorian calendar approximately every thirty-three years. Thus, the year A.H. 100 did not correspond, as one might think, with 722 C.E., but extended instead from August 718 through July 719.

ahl: An Arabic word meaning "family," "household," or "people." *Ahl al-kitab* means "People of the Book," referring to the Jews and Christians; *ahl al-sunna* are "those who follow the Prophet's example."

Alid: A lineal descendant of 'Ali.

amir (ă-MEER): An Arabic term connoting "military commander" or "ruler." The caliph's title was frequently *amir al-mu'minin*, or "commander of the faithful."

Ashura (ă-SHŪ-ră): An Islamic holy day observed on the tenth day of Muharram, the first month of the Islamic calendar. Muhammad had designated Ashura to be a day of voluntary fasting, but it became most celebrated when Husayn, the younger son of 'Ali by Fatima, was killed at Karbala. Because of this tragedy, Ashura became the major religious day of the year among Shi'ites. Many of them dedicate the first ten days of the month to fasting, reading from the Qur'an, prayers, and reenactments of the martyrdom. Many Sunnis also observe Ashura, but on a more subdued note, and normally only on the tenth day.

baraka (BĀ-rä-kä): An Arabic word for the spiritual power of a holy man. It can be "tapped" by a supplicant whether the holy man is living or dead.

baqa' (bă-QĀ'): An Arabic word used by Sufis to suggest the "survival" of personal identity in the material world during the mystical experience; it is paired and contrasted with *fana'*.

batin (BĀ-tĭn): An Arabic term for the inner, hidden, or esoteric meaning of a text. It is paired and contrasted with *zahir*.

bayt: The Arabic word for "house." It is often used metaphorically, as in Bayt al-Hikma ("House of Wisdom"), the institute created by the Abbasid caliph al-Ma'mun (813–833) to translate scientific and philosophical texts into Arabic.

bid'a: An Arabic word for "innovation." In religious usage, the term came to imply "heresy," since nothing should be added to Islam that is not found in the Qur'an or hadith.

dar: An Arabic word meaning "abode" or "dwelling." It is often used metaphorically, as in Dar al-Hikma ("Abode of Wisdom"), the institute of higher learning in the Fatimid caliphate; Dar al-Islam, the term used for the lands under Muslim rule; and Dar al-Kufr ("Realm of Unbelief") and Dar al-Harb ("Realm of War"), terms used for the lands not yet under Muslim rule.

dargah: The word used in South Asia to denote the shrine of a holy man.

dervish: The Turkish variant of the Persian word *darvish*, literally meaning "poor." Sometimes it is used as a synonym for *Sufi* in general, but more often it is used to designate a wandering, mendicant spiritualist who is regarded as being beyond the bounds of respectability.

devshirme (DĔV-shĭr-mŭ): The Turkish term for the levy of young Christian boys that was begun in the late fourteenth century to staff the infantry and higher civil administration in the Ottoman realm.

dhikr (thĭkr; zĭkr): An Arabic term for "recollection" or memory. The term is used for Sufi devotional practices intended to accentuate the awareness of the presence of God. In later Sufi history, the various *tariqas* were differentiated in part by their distinctive dhikrs.

dhimmi (THĬM-mee; ZĬM-mee): A free non-Muslim subject living in a Muslim country who, in return for paying a head tax, was granted protection and safety.

fana' (fă-NĂ'): An Arabic word used by Sufis to express the "passing away" or "annihilation" of personal identity during the mystical experience; it is paired and contrasted with *baqa'*.

fatwa: A ruling on a point of Islamic law made by a *mufti*, who is a very high government-appointed member of the ulama.

fiqh: Islamic jurisprudence, or the method of determining the Shari'a. The jurist who follows the method is called a *faqih* (fă-QĔH).

gazi: A Turkicised form of the Arabic word *ghazi*, meaning "raider." Arabs had referred to bedouin raiders as *ghazi*s. Later, after the frontiers between the Dar al-Islam and Byzantine territory became relatively stabilized, Turks who migrated into Anatolia after the eleventh century found Byzantine settlements attractive targets to plunder. The raiders became known as gazis, since their actions were so similar to the bedouin. But because they were Muslims attacking Christian targets, they acquired the status of *mujahid*s (participants in jihad) even though their goals and tactics did not resemble the classic definition of jihad. This confusion between *gazi* and *mujahid* marks a significant step in the corruption and growing irrelevance of jihad in Islamic doctrine.

Ghadir Khumm (ghă-DĒR khŭm): A Shi'ite festival instituted by the Buyids in the tenth century. It derives its name from the Pool (*ghadir*) of Khumm, located between Mecca and Medina, where Shi'ites believe that Muhammad formally designated 'Ali to be his successor as spiritual and political leader of the Umma.

ghulam (ghŭ-LĀM): Literally, "boy" or "servant," but in the Safavid Empire the term was applied to the slave soldiers from Georgia, Armenia, and Circassia that became the standing army for 'Abbas I and subsequent shahs.

ghulat (ghŭ-LĀT): "Exaggerators," or "those who go beyond the proper bounds." The term is usually applied to certain Shi'ites who have claimed a divine status for 'Ali, believed in metempsychosis, and engaged in rituals that seem to other Muslims to violate Islamic norms.

hadith (hă-DĒTH): A "report" of something that takes place. In religious usage, it means reports (sometimes called "traditions") of what the Prophet said or did. These accounts were passed down through the generations, documented by chains of transmissions in the form, "So-and-So told So-and-So that the Prophet said such-and-such." The hadith were compiled into collections and became a source of religious authority second only to the Qur'an itself.

hajj: The annual pilgrimage to Mecca. One of the Five Pillars of Islam, it is to be performed at least once in a lifetime if possible, during the month of Dhu al-Hijja. It is distinguished from '*umra*, which is a pilgrimage to Mecca at any other time of the year.

Hanafi (HĂN-ă-fē): Referring to the *madhhab* attributed to Abu Hanifa (699–767).

Hanbali (HĂN-băl-ē): Referring to the *madhhab* attributed to Ahmad ibn Hanbal (780–855).

hijra: An Arabic word meaning "departure," "exodus," or "emigration." The most famous hijra was Muhammad's trek from Mecca to Medina in 622 after it became clear that Meccans were not going to accept his message. That marked the beginning of the Muslim calendar. Throughout history, Muslims have spoken of "performing hijra" in emulation of the Prophet when circumstances make it impossible to live an authentically Islamic life. It entails leaving one's home and moving to a land where the Shari'a is followed.

Hui (whey): The Muslims of central and eastern China who speak Chinese as their native language and do not identify with a non-Sinitic ethnic group.

Ibadi (ĭ-BĂD-ē): A follower of an Islamic sect that had its origins in the schismatic Kharijite group of the seventh century. Whereas Kharijites were notorious for their tendency to kill Muslims who did not agree with them, Ibadis abandoned that tactic in favor of withdrawing from sinful society. Their major settlements were primarily in Oman and the deserts of North Africa.

ibn: The Arabic word for "son." Just as Arab men are often known to their friends as the "Father of So-and-So," their sons are often known as the "Son of So-and-So" rather than by their personal name: Ibn Sina, Ibn Khaldun, Ibn Battuta, and so on. *Ibn* is often abbreviated, as in Ahmad b. Hanbal, and it is sometimes rendered *bin,* as in Usama bin Laden.

ijaza (ĭ-JĂ-ză): An authorization or license to teach a certain book on the grounds that the recipient of the ijaza has shown that he or she fully understands it. The ijaza that a student receives is one in a long chain of such licenses that extends from teacher to teacher, all the way back to the original author of the text, guaranteeing that the chain of authorities who have taught the material have conveyed the intent of the author.

ijtihad (ĭj-tĭ-HĂD): The independent judgment that is exercised when ruling on a given point in the field of Islamic jurisprudence. One who exercises ijtihad is a *mujtahid.* Practicing ijtihad is the opposite of practicing *taqlid.*

imam (ĭ-MĂM): A cognate of the Arabic preposition meaning "before" or "in front of." Among Sunni Muslims, the term has been applied to (1) the prayer leader at a mosque, since he stands in front of the congregation, (2) the caliph, and (3) an outstanding religious scholar, especially the founder of a *madhhab.* Among Shi'ite Muslims, the imam (rendered in this book as Imam) is the legitimate leader of the Muslim world. Shi'ite sects have defined the characteristics of their Imams in different ways over the centuries, but generally the Imam is understood not to have prophetic status. He does, however, provide indispensable religious guidance, and he is the rightful head of the entire Muslim community. Some Shi'ite groups consider their Imam to be "hidden" or "invisible" because they do not know where he is, whereas other groups have a "visible" Imam who lives among them and from whom they can obtain direct guidance.

iqta' (ĭq-TĂ'): A grant of land or of its revenues by a government to a military officer or civil official in lieu of direct cash payment for services.

'irfan ('ĭr-FĂN): A Persian borrowing of an Arabic word suggesting gnosis, a type of knowledge accessible only to spiritual adepts. Thus, it is the type of mystical knowledge that Sufis and other mystics can acquire only through rigorous training and special techniques, and is comparable to the concept of "enlightenment" that is found in many mystical traditions.

isnad (ĭs-NĂD): The chain of names of the transmitters of a hadith, cited to guarantee its validity.

jami' (jă-mĭ'): A cognate of the Arabic word connoting "to gather, unite, combine." It is the term used for the large, officially designated congregational mosque in a large city that usually combines the functions of worship, education, and information.

jihad (jĭ-HĂD): An Arabic term meaning "struggle" or "exertion." The Qur'an urges believers to "struggle" to implement God's will, and the text makes it clear that in extreme cases the means of doing so may require the use of violence. The schools of Islamic law drew up detailed regulations concerning the execution of jihad. Jihad could be aggressive, for the expansion of the Dar al-Islam, or defensive, for the protection of the Dar al-Islam.

kalam (kă-LĂM): An Arabic word literally meaning "speech," "discussion," or "discourse." As '*ilm al-kalam,* or "the science of discourse," it refers approximately to what is called theology in Christianity.

khan: A Turkish term for "ruler." It can also mean a "hostel" for merchants or students or a "marketplace," as in Cairo's famous Khan al-Khalili.

khanaqa: A Persian word for a lodge that Sufis visit or live in when pursuing the mystical way.

Kharijite (KHĂ-rĭ-jīt): A name given to seventh-century Muslims with a perfectionist ethic who did not tolerate leaders who engaged in acts that they considered unworthy. The first Kharijites killed the caliph 'Ali when he agreed to negotiate with a rival: 'Ali preferred to negotiate rather than shed the blood of fellow Muslims, but the Kharijites said that his willingness to negotiate proved that he was not God's chosen leader after all but an impostor. The early Kharijites advocated the position that any Muslim who sinned should be killed, and as a result they themselves were killed or driven out by the majority.

khutba (khŭt-bă): The sermon that is delivered at the noon Friday worship service in the mosque. It contains prayers for the ruler as a declaration of his sovereignty.

Kurds: Members of an ethnic group located primarily in the mountains and highlands of western Iran, northeastern Iraq, and eastern Turkey who speak languages belonging to the Indo–European linguistic family. Their languages are closely related to Farsi (Persian).

kuttab (kŭt-TĂB): A cognate of the Arabic root word for "book" and "read," the word connotes a primary school whose most important function is to teach the memorization of the Qur'an. It is often rendered *maktab.*

madhhab (mă<u>th</u>-hăb; măz-hăb): An Arabic term indicating a formalized system or method of determining *fiqh.* It is often translated as "school of (Islamic) law." Hundreds of such schools arose during the early history of Islam, but only a handful remained by the thirteenth century.

madrasa (mă-DRĂ-să): A cognate of the Arabic word to "study," it connotes a school for the study of Islamic jurisprudence, Qur'an interpretation, hadith, biographies of great Muslims, and dialectic. In North Africa, it is usually rendered *medersa.*

Maghrib (MĂ-ghrĭb): Literally, "West." In general, it denotes North Africa west of central Libya (the Gulf of Sidra), but some commentators denote by it all of North Africa west of Egypt; still others use it to identify the area comprising Tunisia, Algeria, Morocco, and even Andalus.

mahdi (MĂH-dē): An Arabic term meaning "guided one," an eschatological figure who is first mentioned in the literature of Islam's first century. He is usually considered to be a Muslim leader who will be sent by God at the end of history to bring an end to the corruption and injustice of a wicked world and to implement God's will. Within Shi'ism the use of the term is usually understood to mean the Hidden Imam.

Maliki (MĂ-lĭ-kē): Referring to the *ma<u>dh</u>hab* attributed to Malik ibn Anas (715–797).

mamluk (măm-LŪK): Arabic term meaning "owned," usually connoting a slave soldier, most often of Turkish origin.

Mamluk: When capitalized, the term refers to the regime that ruled Egypt from 1260 to 1517 that was composed of mamluks.

masjid (măs-jĭd): An Arabic term meaning "place of prostration." It is the word from which "mosque" is derived, connoting an edifice designed for the performance of the *salat.*

mihrab (mīh-RĂB): The niche or recess in a wall of a mosque that designates the *qibla.*

*Mudejar (*MŪ-dĕ-har): A Spanish term that denoted a Muslim who was a subject of a Christian ruler in the aftermath of the Reconquista.

mujahid (mŭ-JĂ-hĭd): A person who engages in jihad.

mujtahid (mŭj-TĂ-hĭd): A legal scholar who engages in *ijtihad.*

murabit (mŭ-RĂ-bĭt): An Arabic word meaning "one who lives in a *ribat.*" In some locales at certain periods of time, the term meant "a soldier who defended the frontier." At other times and places, it could connote a pious individual who spread the message of Islam among rural people. The word *Almoravid* is a derivation of *al-murabit.*

murid (mŭ-RĒD): A Sufi aspirant or disciple who follows a *murshid/shaykh/pir.*

murshid (MŬR-shĭd): A Sufi guide; the equivalent of a *shaykh* or *pir.*

nabi (nă-bē): An Arabic word meaning "prophet." Muslims use it to refer to the Hebrew prophets and Jesus as well as to Muhammad.

Oghuz (also "Ghuzz"): A Turkish confederation that, during the tenth century, roamed the area north of the Aral Sea and Syr Darya River. The Saljuq family was the most famous group from this confederation.

pir (pēr): The Persian word for a Sufi master who leads disciples on the mystical way.

pirzada (pēr-ZĂ-dă): The administrator of a *dargah.*

Punjab (also *Panjab*): A geographical region deriving its name from the words *punj* meaning "five" and *aab* meaning "waters," referring to five rivers that are tributaries of the Indus River: the Sutlej, Beas, Ravi, Chenab, and Jhelum rivers. Today, the Punjab is divided between Pakistan and India.

pro-Alid: A Muslim who believed that only an Alid could be the legitimate caliph.

qadi (qă-dē): The Arabic term for a member of the ulama who sits in a Shari'a court and rules on cases, using as his reference the body of jurisprudence (*fiqh*) worked up by scholars over the centuries.

qanun (qă-NŪN): An Arabic word that refers to secular government statutes and laws that dealt with issues not covered in the Shari'a. The word was derived from the Latin *canon* (itself borrowed from the Greeks), which refers to the codification of imperial Roman law.

Qara-khanid (qă-ră-khănĭd): A dynasty from the Qarluq group of Turks who invaded Transoxiana during the last decade of the tenth century. Although the members of the dynasty were not able to maintain control over the entire region for long, they ruled in many of the individual oases for the next three centuries.

Qara-khitai (qă-ră-khĭ-tī): A Mongol group that dominated the area north and east of the Syr Darya River in the twelfth and early thirteenth centuries before Chinggis Khan defeated them.

Qarluq (qar-lūq): A Turkish confederation which, in the tenth century, roamed north of the Syr Darya River. Its leading dynasty, the Qara-khanid, invaded Transoxiana on the eve of the eleventh century.

qibla (qĭb-lă): The direction in which to perform the *salat* while facing the Ka'ba from a given point on earth.

Qipchaq (qĭp-chăq): A Turkish confederation that dominated the so-called Qipchaq Steppe north of the Black Sea. They were the primary source for the recruitment of the soldiers and ruling elite of the Mamluk Empire from 1260 to 1382 and became the dominant cultural and demographic element within the Golden Horde.

rasul (ră-SŪL): The Arabic term for "messenger" or "apostle." It is the most common title for Muhammad, as a channel for revelation from God.

ribat (rĭ-BĀT): Originally, a fort that guarded frontier areas in North Africa and al-Andalus. It served as a garrison for what was often a volunteer force serving at least in part out of religious commitment, and thus became associated with religious devotionals as well as with the idea of a garrison. When conditions changed and a ribat was no longer needed for defensive purposes, it might become a Sufi lodge. In North Africa, Sufi lodges, whether they had originally been used as forts or built new for specifically devotional purposes, were typically called ribats.

Rum (rūm): The name given by Arabs to the Byzantine Empire, which viewed itself as the successor to Rome. Since Anatolia was the part of the empire that most Muslims encountered, it was known as Rum for several centuries even after the Byzantines lost it at the Battle of Manzikert (1071). One faction of Saljuq Turks established the Sultanate of Rum in western Anatolia.

salat (sŭ-LĂ): The Arabic term for the worship service of congregational prayer, performed five times daily. It is one of the Five Pillars of Islam. The final "t" in the word is not pronounced unless there is a word following it that specifies which of the five prayers during the day is being specified, as in *salat al-fajr* ("the dawn prayer").

Saljuq: The dynasty from the Oghuz Turkish confederation that conquered huge areas of the Muslim world in the eleventh century.

sawm: The Arabic word for "abstinence" or "fasting." Fasting from dawn until sundown during the month of Ramadan is one of the Five Pillars of Islam.

Shafi'i (SHĂ-fi'ē): Referring to the *madhhab* attributed to al-Shafi'i (767–820).

shahada (shă-HĂ-dă): The declaration that there is no god but God and Muhammad is his messenger. It is one of the Five Pillars of Islam.

shari'a (shă-RĒ-'ă): An Arabic word originally connoting "the approach to a watering hole" in the desert. It was later identified with Islamic law and was derived from the Qur'an, hadith, analogy, and consensus.

sharif (shă-RĒF): An Arabic word literally meaning "illustrious" or "distinguished." It is used to denote descendants of the Prophet, who continue to maintain a high social status.

shaykh: An Arabic term connoting "elderly man" or "venerable gentleman." It is also used to denote a chieftain or a Sufi leader.

silsila (sĭl-sĭl-ă): An Arabic term for "chain," it is used for the "spiritual family tree" that linked the teachings of the founder of a Sufi order to the teachings of the Prophet himself.

sipahi (sĭ-PĀ-hē): An Ottoman cavalryman.

Sufism: The most common expression of the mystical life in Islam, organized into *tariqa*s and focused on meetings in *khanaqa*s.

sultan (sŭl-TĀN): A title for a ruler that was derived from the Arabic word *sulta*, meaning "power" or "authority." Buyid and Saljuq military rulers assumed the title to distinguish their actual power from the nominal authority of the Abbasid caliph; in later centuries, the Mamluks and Ottomans used it to refer to their sovereigns.

sunna: An Arabic term meaning "customary practice." It came to mean the ritual and ethical practice of (1) the Companions of the Prophet or (2) the Prophet himself.

sura: A chapter in the Qur'an. Individual verses are called *ayat*.

taqiya (tă-QĒ-ya): A doctrine within the Shi'ite community that allows a believer who is being persecuted to dissimulate or deny his or her beliefs.

taqlid (tăq-LĒD): "Uncritical, unquestioning acceptance." It was used as a contrast to *ijtihad* in the debate over how much latitude a Muslim jurist had in exercising his own judgment.

tariqa (tă-RĒ-qă): An Arabic word literally meaning "path" or "route," it was used metaphorically to indicate the particular method of spiritual growth that a Sufi master taught. Over time, it came to apply to the group of Sufis who followed his teachings. In English, it is often translated as "brotherhood" or "order."

tekke: A Turkish term for a lodge that Sufis visit or live in as they pursue the mystical way.

timar (tĭ-MĀR): The grant of land given to an Ottoman sipahi for his sustenance.

ulama (ū-lă-MĂ): An Arabic word literally meaning "scholars," it usually denotes the specialists in Qur'an, hadith, and religious law.

umma: An Arabic word for "nation" or "people," it came to be applied to the Muslim community as a whole.

vizier (vĭ-ZĒR): The English transliteration of the Turkish variant of *wazir*.

wali (wă-LĒ): An Arabic word that, in everyday use, implies a person who can be trusted. It is used to mean "sponsor," "guardian," "protector," and so forth. In Sufism, it is used to refer to a man whose spirituality is so revered by others that he is regarded as "a friend of God." In English, this Sufi usage is often translated as "saint."

waqf: An Arabic word meaning "religious endowment." The Shari'a allowed a person to allocate part or all of his or her estate to an endowment that would provide funds to build and maintain mosques, schools, fountains, orphanages, hospitals, and so on.

wazir (wă-ZĒR): An Arabic word denoting the chief administrative officer to the head of state (caliph or sultan) in a premodern Muslim government. In the modern era, the term usually denotes the head of a ministry or department within the national government.

zahir (ZÄ-hĭr): An Arabic term for the apparent, external, surface meaning of a text. It contrasts with *batin*.

zakat (ză-KĂ): An Arabic word denoting the contribution that Muslims are expected to make as a tax to support charity and governmental services. It is one of the Five Pillars of Islam. As is the case with *salat*, the final "t" is not pronounced unless there is a qualifying noun following it.

zawiya (ZĂ-wĭ-yă): An Arabic term for a lodge that Sufis visit or live in as they pursue the mystical way.

Index